REVELATION
OF JESUS CHRIST

Commentary on the Book of Revelation

REVELATION
OF JESUS CHRIST

Commentary on the Book of Revelation

Second Edition

Ranko Stefanovic

Andrews
University Press

Berrien Springs, Michigan

Andrews University Press
Sutherland House
8360 W. Campus Circle Dr.
Berrien Springs, MI 49104-1700
Telephone: 269-471-6134
Fax: 269-471-6224
Email: aupo@andrews.edu
Website: http://universitypress.andrews.edu

ISBN 978-1-883925-67-3

Printed in the United States of America
23   22   21   20   19   6   7   8   9   10

The author's own translation of the text for the book of Revelation appears in bold italic type. Unless otherwise stated, scripture quotations from books other than the book of Revelation are taken from the New American Standard Bible®, Copyright © 1960, 1962, 1963, 1968, 1971, 1972, 1973, 1975, 1977, 1995 by The Lockman Foundation. Used by permission.

Library of Congress Cataloging-in-Publication Data

Stefanovic, Ranko.
  Revelation of Jesus Christ : commentary on the book of Revelation / Ranko Stefanovic.
    p. cm.
  Includes bibliographical references (p.   ) and indexes.
  ISBN 978-1-883925-67-3 (hard cover)
  1. Bible. N.T. Revelation--Commentaries. I. Title.
  BS2825.53.S74 2009
  228'.077--dc22

2009030470

Project Director	Ronald Alan Knott
Project Editor	Deborah L. Everhart
Copy Editor	Deborah L. Everhart
Cover Designers	Tiago Baltazar, Robert N. Mason
Text Designers	Tiago Baltazar, Edrey Santos
Typesetter	Tiago Baltazar

Typeset: 10.5/16 Constantia

This commentary is dedicated to
Jon Paulien
Teacher
Colleague
and Friend
whose love for the last book of the Bible
has been a great inspiration to me.

TABLE OF CONTENTS

THE CONTENTS OF THE SEVEN-SEALED SCROLL

FOREWORD

Ranko Stefanovic is one of the finest Bible teachers in North America. His classes are stimulating and well-received. His student-oriented warmth (greatly aided by his effervescent wife) makes a big difference in the lives of so many youth. His writings have come to the attention of scholars both inside and outside of the Seventh-day Adventist community. With the combined weight of his study and teaching to support him, it is not surprising that he would produce a commentary of such significance as this one.

Why another commentary on the book of Revelation? Literally hundreds of commentaries on this book have been produced in just the last century. But it has been said that if you find twelve students of Revelation they will hold thirteen different opinions about the book. And a careful examination of the many commentaries already in print leads one to the conclusion that very few commentators have engaged in serious interaction with the text in its whole literary context and with careful attention to the original language. This lack is even more striking when you limit yourself to Adventist studies on the book. These tend to be primarily concerned either with historical application (Uriah Smith, C. Mervyn Maxwell) or with improving and clarifying Adventist understandings of the book of Revelation (Roy C. Naden, Hans LaRondelle). A serious, textual analysis of the book had been greatly needed in its own right—not primarily in defense of Adventist teachings, but in search of its inner meaning and the genius of God's intention for the passage. That analysis was provided in the first edition of this book and is now further improved upon in this second edition.

This commentary is an excellent starting point for such an approach to the book of Revelation. It is the fruit of years of careful textual observation. It does not claim to contain a final answer for every issue of interpretation, nor do I believe that Stefanovic has captured every nuance of the text. But it would be unrealistic to expect that of any commentator on Revelation. The quality of Stefanovic's work will speak for itself. No reader of the book can come away without a fresh perspective on the text—a perspective that may well completely transform the way one looks at the Apocalypse. I invite you to follow Ranko Stefanovic on his journey through the book of Revelation. Drink in his insights, puzzle with him, and argue with him over the text of this marvelous book. You will not be sorry you did!

Jon Paulien
Dean, School of Religion
Professor of Religion and Theological Studies
Loma Linda University
Loma Linda, California

PREFACE

The idea of writing a commentary on the book of Revelation was prompted primarily by repeated requests from my students, as well as from audiences at campmeeting and workers' meetings, to put my lectures on Revelation into writing. I did not anticipate that my original plan to write a brief book would turn into a large and comprehensive commentary on the last book of the Bible.

This book is a verse-by-verse commentary based on an exegesis of the text. The organization of the commentary follows the major thematic sections of Revelation in order to determine the unified message of the whole book. Before providing a detailed analysis of each section, an overview deals with questions of a general matter that seem important for a meaningful interpretation of the text. The analysis of each major section begins with my own translation followed by notes on key words and phrases from the text. The notes include scholarly discussion providing insights regarding the text. A verse-by-verse exposition of the text follows. Finally, each chapter concludes with a "Retrospect" which summarizes the findings and attempts to make sense of the text and shows how it relates to the subsequent text.

Although a distinctive work, the commentary draws the best from both Adventist and non-Adventist scholarship. In particular, it builds on the foundation laid by the pioneering contributions of Kenneth A. Strand and Hans K. LaRondelle to the Seventh-day Adventist understanding and interpretation of Revelation. It also reflects in many points Jon Paulien's significant contribution to the Seventh-day Adventist church in the field of eschatological studies during the last quarter century. Paulien's presence in scholarly circles on Revelation has contributed in significant measure to the fact that today New Testament scholars are considering the Adventist interpretation of Revelation more seriously. Paulien's scholarly profile, however, has not prevented him from serving the church in a capacity of a loyal Adventist preacher in many local churches, as well as at campmeeting and workers' meetings in many parts of the world, as he shows his support for the church and its mission.

This commentary fills the gap for an Adventist text-focused and Christ-centered approach to the book of Revelation. The volume is written with the general reading audience in mind. It is intended for use in both college and seminary courses, yet it will appeal to the informed layperson. It is an expression of my strong desire to present academics, students, pastors, and laypeople with a fresh approach to Revelation so as to assist them in exploring the meaning of the book from the text through the procedure of biblical exegesis, rather than through allegorical imagination. I hope that this commentary will make a contribution to the understanding of this often misinterpreted and misused New Testament book. In writing, I have paid special attention to the appeal of Ellen G. White to Seventh-day Adventist ministers and preachers:

> There is a need of much closer study of the word of God; especially should Daniel and the Revelation have attention as never before in the history of our work. We may have less to say in some lines, in regard to the Roman power and the papacy; but we should call attention to what the prophets and apostles have written under the inspiration of the Holy Spirit of God. The Holy Spirit has so shaped matters, both in the giving of the prophecy and in the events portrayed, as to teach that the human agent is to be kept out of sight, hid in Christ, and that the Lord God of heaven and His law are to be exalted....When we as a people understand what this book means to us, there will be seen among us a great revival. We do not understand fully the lessons that it teaches, notwithstanding the injunction given us to search and study it....One thing will certainly be understood from the study of Revelation—that the connection between God and His people is close and decided. (*Testimonies to Ministers and Gospel Workers,* 112–114)

The ultimate objective of this work is to apply Revelation's message to the contemporary life situation of the church as it endeavors to present the gospel message to the lost, suffering world.

It is difficult to express adequately my thanks to all those who have graciously helped in the realization of this project. First, Jon Paulien from the School of Religion, Loma Linda University, for his generous encouragement after I timidly mentioned my decision to him. He has used every opportunity to encourage me to persist in bringing this project to its completion. Then, Larry Herr from Canadian University College for his continual support and broadening many ideas expressed in this commentary during the two-year Revelation seminar that we held together for the faculty and students of Canadian University College. My students Gerald Smith, Paul Soper, Campbell Page, and Zeljka Stefanovic (my daughter) for proofreading the manuscript. Lynn Newman McDowell for proofreading the first part of the book. My deep gratitude also goes to the administration of Canadian University College for providing a one-time financial assistance for my research. I am especially grateful to Woodrow Whidden II from the Adventist International Institute of Advanced Studies for generously devoting his time to reading and polishing the manuscript and making valuable suggestions; my friend John Markovic from Andrews University for assisting in the clarification of some historical application expressed on pertinent texts; my colleagues from the Department of Religion for giving me continual support and encouragement; and reviewers Hans LaRondelle and Beatrice Neall who made helpful suggestions. Special thanks go to the Andrews University Press personnel for preparing the manuscript for publication and publishing this commentary—in particular, Ronald Knott, who showed special interest in the quality of the work, and Deborah Everhart, for the final editing of the manuscript and patient proofreading and polishing of the text. I am also deeply indebted to all the unnamed others who are a part of this work and whose encouragement made it possible to complete the project.

My deepest gratitude is especially reserved for those who are closest to me, particularly my wife Estera; without her loving support and persistent encouragement, this commentary would never have been attempted. She and my children Vladimir and Zeljka deserve much more than a word of thanks.

But above all, all glory and thanks for the completion of this project goes to my God for giving me good health and sober mind during these years of writing and textual consideration. To him belongs "blessing and honor and glory and might for ever and ever."

A NOTE ON THE SECOND EDITION

The reception of the first edition of *Revelation of Jesus Christ* since its publication has been gratifying, and I praise God for the ways in which he has used this work for his glory rather than my own. An ever-increasing interest in the prophecies of the book of Revelation has resulted in new evidence which has been introduced here, and questions raised by readers across the globe have led me to explore some aspects of this biblical book further since the publication of the original volume.

This edition makes no major changes in structure. But a number of updates have been included, and several items have been clarified here. Some of the various areas further elaborated upon in this edition are methods of interpretation, historical applications and fulfillments, literary techniques, scriptural comparisons, and discussion of symbolism.

During the preparation of this revised and updated volume, scholars have again looked at my work and offered helpful suggestions and feedback. The staff members at Andrews University Press who guided the original edition to publication were again available to prepare this new volume, which aided the editing process and eased the transition to the new design.

I am glad to present an updated commentary on the book of Revelation. I pray that this new edition will first and foremost be used to reveal Jesus Christ, "the One who loves us and released us from our sins by his blood." To him "be glory and might forever and ever. Amen."

Ranko Stefanovic
Professor of New Testament
Seventh-day Adventist Theological Seminary
Andrews University
Berrien Springs, Michigan

INTRODUCTION

The book of Revelation belongs to the genre of apocalyptic writings, and it is the only one of this kind in the New Testament. It is replete with strange symbols and scenes which the contemporary reader finds difficult to understand. Numerous commentaries and other studies have tried to interpret and explain the book's symbols and scenes. They range from scholarly exposition of the text to popular works offering interpretations derived mainly from current events written in newspaper articles and from one's imagination based on allegorical speculation. It is no wonder that the interpretations are as numerous and diverse as the commentaries on the book. As a result, many have pronounced Revelation a sealed book. One despairing expositor even went so far as to say that "the study of the *Revelation* either finds or leaves a man mad."[1]

On the other hand, in spite of the negative attitudes expressed by many, and the book's peculiar language and difficult style, Revelation has been a source of comfort, courage, and hope to each generation of Christians throughout history who, in the midst of the suffering and hardship of life, might question whether God is still active and in control. This strange book has provided inspiring resources in their time of critical need as they were experiencing rejection and persecution by a world hostile to the gospel. The book has given them a glimpse of Christ and heavenly realities and issues in the cosmic conflict that can be found nowhere else. When readers understand the book's central message, they are moved to live virtuous lives. Ellen G. White stated clearly that a better understanding of Revelation leads inevitably to an entirely different religious experience.[2]

This commentary represents a modest contribution to the understanding of this often misinterpreted and misused New Testament book. In offering a fresh approach to the book of Revelation, this commentary helps the reader to explore the text and reach a meaningful interpretation that was intended by the inspired author. The reader will come to realize that this difficult book contains the gospel message, and that it is indeed worth studying.

It is customary, before studying the text in detail, to discuss questions of a general matter with regard to the book of Revelation as a whole. The present commentary is no exception. The first half of this introductory section deals with the basic questions of authorship and time period, the purpose for writing the book and its main theme, and the correct method for studying Revelation. The second half of this introduction describes the objectives of the commentary and provides the structural organization and plan for the entire book of Revelation.

THE AUTHOR OF REVELATION

The author of the book of Revelation identifies himself simply as John (Rev. 1:1, 4, 9; 22:8). He is writing to the Christians in the Roman province of Asia (Rev. 1:4, 11), providing practical counsel for the problems they faced. John speaks of himself as their "brother and fellow partaker in the affliction and kingdom and endurance in Jesus" (1:9). This suggests that he knows well the churches of Asia and that he is well known by them. Thus, his name is sufficient to provide the credentials for his book. Evidence indicates that the early Christian authors—including Justin Martyr, Irenaeus, the Muratorian Canon, Tertulian, and Clement of Alexandria[3]—viewed the author of Revelation as the apostle John, the son of Zebedee, the writer of the Fourth Gospel and three epistles.

Many scholars today question whether Revelation was indeed written by John the disciple. Revelation and the Fourth Gospel, they argue, could not have been written by the same person. One argument against the traditional understanding is the obvious difference in the language of the two books. The grammar in the gospel of John is simple yet accurate, while the Greek of Revelation is infected with many grammatical irregularities. The author of Revelation obviously was not well versed in Greek. In addition, the writing style and theological content are different.

The difference in style and theological content of the two books is due to the fact that Revelation is an apocalyptic work. It is filled with strange images and symbols. The gospel of John, however, tells the story of Jesus. It is a straightforward record of Jesus' life. One explanation for the irregularities in grammar is that John was a Palestinian Jew, and Greek was not his native language. It is possible that he wrote his gospel in Ephesus with the assistance of a secretary and an editor who revised and polished the language. We know that Paul (cf. Rom. 16:22; 1 Cor. 1:1; 16:21; Col. 4:18) and Peter (1 Pet. 5:12) used secretarial and editorial assistance. John wrote the book of Revelation by himself as a prisoner on the island of Patmos, where he was obviously deprived of such assistance. This could also explain the many differences in style between Revelation and the Fourth Gospel.

Other scholars note that, despite the obvious differences, striking similarities appear in the books of Revelation and the Fourth Gospel. For instance, of all the New Testament books, only the Fourth Gospel and Revelation call Jesus "the Word of God" (cf. John 1:1–14; Rev. 19:13) and refer to him as the Lamb (although different words are used in the Greek; cf. John 1:29, 36; Rev. 5:6–8); both quote "those who pierced him" from Zechariah 12:10 (cf. John 19:37; Rev. 1:7).[4] These are the only two books of the New Testament in which the verb "tabernacle" is found (John 1:14; Rev. 7:15). And both books are founded on the word of testimony or witness (cf. John 21:24; Rev. 1:2). In addition, the father/son relationship much emphasized in John's gospel also appears in Revelation (2:27; 3:5, 21).[5] While Revelation invites: "Let the one who thirsts come" (22:17), the gospel declares: "If any man is thirsty, let him come" (John 7:37). All of this evidence suggests that, despite the apparent difficulties, there is enough support for the traditional view that John the apostle is the author of the last book of the New Testament.

THE PLACE AND DATE OF THE WRITING OF REVELATION

John wrote Revelation while on Patmos, a small rocky island in the Aegean Sea some fifty miles off the southwest coast of Asia Minor (modern Turkey). The traditional view has been that the island served as a kind of labor camp to which the Roman authorities sent offenders (like an ancient Alcatraz). That view, however, has been contested by some modern scholars who argue that there is little record that Patmos was used as a penal colony. The fact that is not contested, however, is that John was on this island in exile for some time. John himself states that he was on Patmos "because of the word of God and the testimony of Jesus" (Rev. 1:9). It is not clear from this statement whether he was exiled to Patmos as a result of persecution or had gone there voluntarily as a missionary.[6] However, early Christian tradition affirms that John's effective witnessing for the gospel led the governing authorities to exile him to Patmos during the reign of the Roman emperor Domitian (A.D. 81–96) where he was forced to work in the quarries.[7] He was later released by Nerva and permitted to return to Ephesus. While on Patmos, John received the visions of Revelation which he was instructed to write on a scroll and send as a pastoral letter to the churches in Asia (Rev. 1:11). The letter was sent because the Christians in Asia were troubled by an increasing number of problems coming from outside and inside the church.

The book of Revelation was written in a time of Roman hostility toward Christianity that eventually turned into direct persecution. Generally two different views exist among scholars on the exact date of the writing of the book. Some argue that it was written during the persecution of Christians under Nero (A.D. 54–68). This view is based on the assumption that the numerical value of the Hebrew letters for Nero Caesar is 666, which is the very number of the beast of Revelation 13:18.[8] There was also a legend that Nero would reappear in the East after his death (see *Notes on Rev.* 17:9). These types of arguments, however, are based on sheer conjecture. Also, Nero's persecution of Christians was of a personal nature and based mainly on insanity of some kind. Therefore, general scholarly consensus holds that Revelation was written during the time of Domitian (A.D. 81–96). It is equally held that the Fourth Gospel was written after Revelation. This date for the writing of Revelation is preferable for the reasons which follow.

First, John stayed in Jerusalem for a number of years, eventually leaving Palestine shortly before the destruction of Jerusalem in A.D. 70. He subsequently settled in Ephesus in Asia Minor. The churches which he refers to in his book had been in existence for a considerable number of years. At the time of the writing of Revelation, they were in a condition of spiritual decline and apostasy, one that was rapid for some of the churches. The early date does not fit into such a historical situation, because the churches in Asia Minor were not founded until the early sixties. They were still prospering during the reign of Nero.

Second, early Christian writers, including Irenaeus, the disciple of Polycarp (A.D. 60–150), who was John's disciple, held that the book of Revelation was written during the time of Domitian.[9]

Third, the book of Revelation was written in a time when Christians were experiencing hardship and pressure because of their refusal to comply with popular demands for emperor worship. While worship of the living emperor had been fostered by Romans since Augustus Octavian (27 B.C.–A.D. 14), Gaius Caligula (A.D. 37–41) was the first emperor to demand worship for himself. The next emperor to demand worship for himself was Domitian (A.D. 81–96). "It was under this emperor, that the question of emperor worship became, for the first time, a crucial issue for Christians."[10] Although widely spread, the worship of Caesar was especially practiced in Asia where Christians came into conflict with the authorities because of their opposition to such worship. Though the persecution of Christians initiated under Domitian was not on a wide scale, it precursored many violent persecutions to come. The book of Revelation was suited and designed to provide hope and encouragement to oppressed Christians of John's day in their frightening circumstances and to prepare them to meet future crises. All of these historical facts suggest that the book of Revelation reflects the situation taking place toward the end of the first century.

PURPOSE OF THE BOOK OF REVELATION

The book of Revelation was originally written as a letter. The fundamentals for understanding any letter involve finding by whom and to whom it was written, and also the reason(s) why it was written and sent. "The more we can discover about the first readers, the ones to whom the letter was originally addressed, the better we can understand the reason for and the significance of that message."[11]

The book of Revelation was no doubt intended primarily for the seven Christian communities in the Roman province of Asia: "John to the seven churches that are in Asia" (Rev. 1:4). The glorified Christ commissioned John: "Write down what you see in a scroll and send it to the seven churches" (Rev. 1:11). These churches are further identified as the ones in Ephesus, Smyrna, Pergamum, Thyatira, Sardis, Philadelphia, and Laodicea. They had been in existence for a considerable period of time. John resided in Ephesus and was apparently overseeing those local communities. It is likely that he visited the churches from time to time to help them with their needs. Toward the end of the first century, the situation in those churches was characterized by spiritual decline and apostasy. The churches were facing an increasing number of problems, both external and internal.

EXTERNAL PROBLEMS OF THE CHURCHES IN ASIA

A number of problems coming from outside disturbed and troubled the Christians in Asia of John's day.

First, the Christians in Asia faced pagan opposition and accusations because they did not participate in social activities. They avoided celebrations that were characterized by immoral practices and the eating of food dedicated to pagan gods. Christians were accused of atheism for worshiping only their God (whoever did not worship the emperor was considered an atheist by the Romans). They were also charged with cannibalism in relation to the Lord's Supper where they were thought to be eating human flesh and drinking their blood. Stories were circulated that they were sacrificing children at their services. As a result, the Christians were gradually losing their legal status in society.

A second problem that the churches faced was persecution. A serious threat to the church was the development of the imperial cult of worship to the emperor. Revelation 2:13 reports the death of a person in Pergamum named Antipas who suffered martyrdom by Roman authorities for his faith. The persecution also threatened the churches in Smyrna (2:10) and Philadelphia (3:10). The book of Revelation indicates that John expected an intensification of persecution, "with the prospect that a number of the weaker and less devoted among the church's members would fall away."[12] All of these factors created an insecure situation in the churches; the believers were filled with fear about what the future might bring.

Finally, the churches were suffering due to conflicts with the Jews. Christianity began as an offshoot of Judaism. The book of Acts depicts a shift in the early church from continuity in the relationship toward separation between the two religions. The separation was hastened by the destruction of Jerusalem by the Romans in A.D. 70. After the war in A.D. 70, Christians were not welcome in the synagogue because of their refusal to join the Jews in the war with the Romans. Right after the destruction of Jerusalem, the Jews added an eighteenth benediction to the seventeen which were recited in closing the synagogue services. It really was not a benediction, but rather a curse against Christ and Christians. The Christians evidently were refusing to recite the eighteenth benediction, and thus were eventually expelled from the synagogue.

Toward the end of the first century, the relationship between the Christians and Jews was characterized by antagonism and hostility. The Christians were banished from the synagogue and lost their legal status. The Jews enjoyed a legal status, were recognized by Roman authorities as *religio licita* (a legal religion) with the privileges of worshiping on the Sabbath, and were exempted from emperor worship. Revelation itself refers two times to the hostility of Jews toward the Christians in the Roman province of Asia (Rev. 2:9; 3:9). Their opposition to the gospel and their persecution of the Christians made them the servants of Satan.

INTERNAL PROBLEMS OF THE CHURCHES IN ASIA

Problems of an internal nature also troubled the churches in Asia. As the seven messages indicate, the Christians in those churches were seriously divided on certain issues. For some of the churches, while the majority of members were faithful, some individuals, including church leaders, were not faithful and opposed John. In other churches—such as Thyatira, Sardis, and Philadelphia—the majority of believers were in apostasy. In Sardis, just "a few names" had "not defiled their garments" (Rev. 3:4); the church in Philadelphia was left with but "little strength" (Rev. 3:8). The whole church in Laodicea appeared to be in apostasy, and nothing good was found in it. John obviously was not much appreciated in many of those churches.

The basic issues that the Christians in Asia were wrestling with involved the food offered to idols and sexual immorality (cf. Rev. 2:14–15, 20). These were the very two things which the Council of Jerusalem instructed all the Christians to spurn (Acts 15:20). These two issues threatened the unity of the churches in Asia because they were related to the popular demands of the society in Asia. Christians in the Roman Empire were a part of the society in which they lived and, as such, were expected to participate in all civic obligations. All citizens were expected, first of all, to participate in the religious festivals in pagan temples. Those who refused to participate suffered ridicule and the hardships of social isolation and economic sanctions.

The Christians in Asia faced at least two problems with regard to their involvement in the pagan religious festivals. The first problem was related to that of eating food offered to idols. Participants at the pagan festivals would usually feast on food that consisted mainly of meat that had been offered to the local patron god. The festivals often ended with drunkenness and immoral activities. The second problem with regard to the pagan religious festivals was cultic prostitution. Temple prostitution was a part of many ancient, pagan religions. Sexual intercourse with the temple prostitutes was for the fertility of the land and the prosperity of society. Anyone who wanted economic, political, or social status in society had to meet these religious demands. Involvement in the pagan religious festivals called for a compromise to Christian belief and values.

The churches in Asia were divided on the issue of participation. Some Christians responded to the demand with a decisive "no." Some groups, for the sake of influence on the society and in the interest of business and commercial prosperity, advocated a compromise. These opponents of John are referred to by different names (see *Notes* on Rev. 2:6 and 20). In Ephesus they were known as Nicolaitans (Rev. 2:6), in Pergamum as Baalamites (Rev. 2:14), and in Thyatira as the followers of a prominent and influential woman in the church named Jezebel (Rev. 2:20). All three groups opposed John and advocated a compromise, thus causing many in the churches in Asia to commit fornication and eat the things sacrificed to idols (Rev. 2:14, 20). They most likely "recognized that pagan social life was an open field for the operations of Satan, and that those who entered it did so at their peril"; however, they believed that "it was their Christian duty to participate as fully as possible in the pagan society around them, to identify themselves with the common life of their city."[13] They could find theological justification for their reasoning in the writings of Paul, who required subjection to the governing authorities (cf. Rom. 13:1–8; 1 Tim. 2:1–4). Paul also made clear that feasting at the pagan festivals was not to be an issue for Christians; idols were nothing (cf. 1 Cor. 8; Rom. 14).

John had to take a stand on the issue of food offered to idols. In seeming contrast to Paul, he argued against any compromise. Idols might be nothing, but to participate in the pagan religious festivals meant to compromise the Christian faith and honor Satan himself. In light of the soon coming of Christ, Christians ought to be on the right side. For the sake of being faithful to Christ and the gospel, they must, if necessary, withdraw themselves from the world and sacrifice their social or business prosperity.

The primary purpose of John's writing Revelation, therefore, was to help the first-century Christians in the Roman province of Asia with their condition and problems. Confronted with the growing hostility of Rome, as well as the invading heresy and increasing apostasy within the church, the Christians in Asia were concerned about their own identity and existence. What would the future bring to the church? The book of Revelation was intended to provide the answer. It declares that although the situation in the world seems threatening and hostile to God's people, and the future might appear gloomy, God in Christ is indeed still "the master of history." He is and always will be with his people. He will "fully vindicate them at a grand and glorious eschatological climax."[14]

INTERPRETING THE BOOK OF REVELATION

Biblical scholars have long debated whether Revelation is an apocalyptic work or a prophecy. The book itself claims to be a prophecy (1:3; 22:7, 18–19), the messages of which are presented in the apocalyptic style. The book was originally sent as a letter in prophetic-apocalyptic style to real people in real places, namely, to the seven churches which were in the Roman province of Asia (cf. 1:11). As a letter, the book of Revelation is as subject to time, places, and circumstances as any Old Testament prophecy or New Testament epistle. The question arises: How can the prophecies of Revelation be relevant to us today when the book was originally written for those in another place and time, with a different culture and life setting, and in a different language? The following section presents the basic principles for approaching the Bible with these considerations in mind.

BASIC STEPS OF BIBLICAL EXEGESIS

The science and art of the study of biblical text is called "hermeneutics." The word simply means "interpretation." Biblical hermeneutics is an interpretive process of discovering how the ancient biblical text has relevance for us today. When hermeneutics is applied to the analysis of biblical text, we call it "exegesis" (a loan word from the Greek, meaning "to draw out"). Exegesis is the process of deriving meaning from biblical text by bridging the gap between the world of the Bible at the time of the inspired author and the reader of today. Its purpose is to let "the biblical text speak for itself, rather than imposing on the passage a meaning that originates with the reader."[15] Exegesis involves the study of units and passages, not isolated verses. It gives attention to the meaning of words, the relation of words to each other in the sentences, the structural organization of a passage, and the immediate context of the passage. After the units are studied, they are brought together to form a unified and coherent body of biblical themes. When various biblical themes are compiled, we refer to it as biblical theology.

Biblical exegesis involves two basic steps. The first involves determining **what the text meant** for the time when it was written. Before we try to discover the relevance of the biblical text for us today, we must understand what its author intended to convey to the readers of his time. This phase of exegesis seeks to determine both *what* the inspired author tried to say to the original readers, and *why* he said it. What reasons prompted him to write the text? In searching for meaningful answers to these questions, the interpreter must first learn what can be known about the original readers, namely, their social setting and their concerns that prompted the inspired author to write. Second, the interpreter must explore the linguistic, literary, historical, geographical, religious, philosophical, and cultural contexts of the time when the biblical text was written. Such an approach to the text assumes serious involvement and willingness to make an effort with all the rigor and tools of scholarship.

The same principle applies to the prophetic word. Every biblical prophecy deals primarily with the time of its author. Unless the conditions during the time of the inspired author are understood, the meaning of the prophecy for any future period will remain veiled. As stated earlier, the book of Revelation was originally written for the churches in Asia during John's time (Rev. 1:4; cf. 1:11). As such, the messages of the book might be understood against the background of the situation of the church in Asia during the first century. The observations of Douglas Ezell are helpful:

> Lest the reader begin to worry that the Christian hope will be denied, let me declare a strong positive statement in support of the true prophetic character of John's message. *He is a prophet.* His message is a prophecy in apocalyptic form. But what is prophecy? At its heart, it is essentially "forth-telling." The prophet had a message from God for his day. Foretelling arose out of such messages to the people of God in a particular time and place. Because God will act in this manner in the present, He will also act in the same manner in the future. The controlling and decisive message the prophets wanted to share was not the future, but the *God who holds the future.* This is authentic prophecy.
>
> John spoke an authentic word of God to His troubled people. From his understanding of the revelation of God for his day concerning the end time, he painted some broad strokes upon the canvas of the future. John saw his day as if it were backed up against the end, and it could well have been, but for the patience and long-suffering of God (2 Pet. 3:8–10). As God acts in our immediate crisis, John states, so He will act in the end, for He is the same yesterday, today, and tomorrow.
>
> The prophets had a single hope which related to their hearer's immediate situation and to the final future. In light of God's revealed character, they proclaimed God's will for the ultimate future, and applied that will to the people in their present

historical crisis. Because of the way God displayed His will in the immediate present, they were able to picture and describe the inevitable Day of the Lord. As God had come in judgment and salvation in the present, so He would inevitably come in judgment and salvation at the end.

If we keep this in mind, the understanding of John's message as directed to the immediate, historical circumstances does not conflict with understanding this crisis as a symbolic representation of the ultimate consummation. The historical situation, from which and to which John spoke, formed the springboard for John's description of Christ's victory at the end of time (Rev. 19:11ff.). As God surely would overthrow Rome, so He would overthrow the "Babylon" of the end.[16]

The second step of exegetical analysis is to ask **what the text means** for the reader today. Although the books of the Bible were originally sent to the people of the time of their authors, the significance of the biblical text extends beyond the time of those readers. A timely message recorded by the prophets becomes God's timeless message applicable to any place (cf. 2 Pet. 1:19–21). The book of Revelation is no exception.

TRADITIONAL METHODS OF INTERPRETATION

The message of the book of Revelation has often been obscured by biased and subjective approaches. Traditionally, four distinct approaches to Revelation have been used. While expositors usually follow one of those four approaches, some contemporary scholars combine the strongest elements of two or more of the traditional approaches in their exposition of the book.

Preterism. The preterist method holds that the book of Revelation addresses primarily the situation of the Christian church in the Roman province of Asia in the first century A.D. Preterists hold that John the revelator could foresee the things to happen in the immediate future. However, the book does not contain any predictive prophecy. Its purpose was rather to provide hope and encouragement for the church facing impending persecution by imperial Rome in John's day. No matter how terrible imminent persecution was, God would intervene and deliver his people from the oppression of Rome and establish his kingdom. The basic assumption of the preterist method is that Revelation describes the universal persecution of the church by Rome in the first century. John allegedly wrote his book with the purpose of encouraging the Christians of his time to persevere because the Lord was about to come to overthrow Rome and rescue his people. The problem with this approach is that no valid extra-biblical evidence exists to support the view of an empire-wide, systematic persecution of the first-century church.[17] Revelation itself refers to local persecutions of Christians in Asia (cf. Rev. 2:10, 13; 3:10) under which John himself experienced exile to Patmos (Rev. 1:9).

Idealism. The idealist method argues against any historical purpose of the symbols in Revelation. Rather, the book contains a symbolic description of the ongoing struggle between good and evil which cannot be applied to any historical time period or place. The symbols of the book do not refer to any specific events in history. The stress is on timeless ethical truth and principles that apply to believers at any time in history, rather than historical occurrences. The idealist method is based on the preterist ideas. It does not see any literal or historical significance of John's vision.

Futurism. In contrast to preterism, futurism places the entire significance of the book in the future. The futurist method maintains that Revelation (particularly chapters 4–22) is a prophecy of future events—even from today's perspective—to take place just prior to and after the Second Coming. The book is relevant exclusively for the last generation of Christians living in the time of the end.

Historicism. The historical method holds that the book of Revelation provides a symbolic presentation of the prophetic outline of the future course of history from the apostolic times until the time of the end. This method argues that Revelation is rooted in the book of Daniel which deals with sequential periods of history. The symbols of the book portray "various historical movements and events in the western world and the Christian church."[18] And those predictive prophecies are in the process of fulfillment.

All of these approaches have some elements of truth. As Robert H. Mounce notes, "each approach has some important contribution to a full understanding of Revelation...no single approach is sufficient in itself."[19] As he further observes, John the Revelator "wrote out of his own immediate situation, his prophecies would have a historical fulfillment, he anticipated a future consummation, and he revealed principles which operated beneath the course of history."[20]

Each method, however, is vulnerable to criticism. First, the stress of preterism on the historical background of Revelation deserves serious attention. Certainly the book did speak powerfully to the Christians in Asia at the end of the first century.

They found contemporary significance in the symbols of Revelation.[21] However, the messages of the book were not limited solely to the first century. No matter what applications the Christians of John's time or later might have seen in Revelation, the fulfillment of the book's prophecies were reserved for the future from John's perspective. The problem with preterism is that it deprives Revelation of its predictive character. Although it was originally sent to the Christians of John's day to provide them with encouragement and hope in the face of impending persecution, Revelation also contains predictive prophecies with regard to the events in history that were still future from John's perspective (Rev. 4:1). The messages of the book were intended to benefit the church of every generation throughout history—at any time and place—from John's day until the Second Coming.

The same criticism might be directed to the idealist approach. Revelation contains themes and principles that are valid for each generation of Christians in every time and place. As William G. Johnsson observes, because of the universality of the great controversy, the messages of Revelation find "repeated applications for God's people throughout history."[22] Different calls throughout the book usually begin with words such as "whoever" or "anyone." The major problem with idealism is that it, like preterism, denies the prophetic character of the book. John claimed that he received the messages of Revelation directly from God. What he saw in the visions he simply recorded in the book and sent to the churches. While the book indeed contains principles that apply to believers at any time in history, its purpose is to show to God's people the things that will take place in the future (Rev. 1:1). The preterist and idealist approaches to the book of Revelation have some validity only if the prophetic elements are taken into consideration and applied to the time that extends beyond John's day.

The prophetic elements of the book are significantly applied in the two remaining approaches—namely, futurism and historicism. The contribution of the futurist interpretation is noteworthy. While the messages of Revelation were meaningful for the Christians of John's time, the book also points to the future beyond that period. Many events are still in the future even from our point in time. Much of what is portrayed in Revelation will take place at the time preceding the Second Coming, and even beyond that. Futurists, however, overlook the fact that Revelation deals with the situation of the church in the world throughout the entire Christian era, not just at the time of the end.

One might thus observe many difficulties with preterism and futurism. These two interpretative approaches imply that Revelation has nothing to say to the generations between the time of John and the time of the end. The historicist approach is corrective at this point. Despite the fact that historicism has generally been denied and marginalized by modern scholarship, this commentary shows it to be the most appropriate approach to the book of Revelation. Historicism allows for the events predicted in Revelation as taking place both in the past and in the future as well as in the centuries that lie between. Although the focus of the book is on the return of Christ, its contents cover the period from the ascension of Christ to heaven until his return to earth. Strong evidence, however, must demonstrate that the scenes and symbols in the text point to events throughout all of history, rather than to those primarily in John's time or the time of the end.

The historicist approach, however, has often been misused by various attempts to fit every detail of the text into a historical fulfillment. The exposition of the text for many historicists has been based primarily on the allegorical method, rather than on adequate Old Testament background. Also, the explanation of symbols employed in the book has often been derived from newspaper articles and history books, rather than from the Bible.

A good commentary on Revelation should not impose any particular approach on the text. The method of interpretation an author chooses normally governs the way he or she reads and interprets the text. It usually results in forcing an interpretation into the framework of a predetermined idea, regardless of whether or not it fits the context. Such interpretation is often used to prove a point rather than to find the meaning of the text. The exposition of the text and the approach applied must be controlled by the intent of its author, who should tell us what we are supposed to find in it and whether to apply it to the past, present, or future. It is imperative that every expositor let the text govern its interpretation instead of imposing one's idea on the book.

HOW TO INTERPRET THE BOOK OF REVELATION

John the revelator himself seems to provide a clue about how to interpret his book's content. He states in Revelation 1:19 that what he saw in the visions while on Patmos was basically made up of two things: "the things which are" and "the things which are about to take place after these things." In Revelation 4:1, John is invited in vision to see the things which would "take place after these things," namely, after the seven messages to the churches (1:9–3:22; see *Notes* on Rev. 1:19). Many scholars recognize that the phrase "the things which are" in 1:19 refers to the messages sent to the seven local churches in Asia (1:9–3:22), and that "the things which are about to take place after these things" refers to chapters 4–22:5.[23] It should be noted, however, that 1:9–3:22 contains a number of promises that look for future fulfillment just as some visions in 4–22:5 refer to the past from John's perspective (including chapters 4–5 and 12).

We have seen that the Christians in the seven early congregations faced an increasing number of problems and challenges. The seven messages of Christ sent through John were intended to help those congregations in their immediate situations. Thus, Revelation 1:9–3:22 must be understood as essentially forth-telling, although some texts there contain predictive prophecies. The first step in understanding the first three chapters of Revelation is to determine what they *meant* to the Christians in Asia of John's day, and, then, in the final analysis, what it means to us today (see "Overview: Revelation 1:9–3:22").

The situation, however, seems to be quite different with regard to Revelation 4–22:5. This section largely concerns events that were to take place in the future, immediate and distant, from John's perspective (Rev. 4:1), although some visions (e.g., chapters 4–5 and 12) deal with the past. We have seen earlier that John's fellow Christians in Asia, oppressed and downtrodden, were concerned about their own identity and existence. Their dire circumstances may have led them to question whether God was still active and in control, and what the future would bring to the church. While the entire book (Rev. 1:9–3:22 in particular) addressed their concerns, Revelation 4–22:5 was particularly suited to instruct them about what the future would bring to the church. Thus it appears that the visions of Revelation 4–22:5 were intended to be understood as the prophecies of the church and the world throughout the Christian dispensation until the eschatological consummation. (The historicist approach is very instructive at this point.) These prophecies are thus primarily foretelling in their intention and design.[24]

The Christians of the time of John and the succeeding 200 years no doubt would have found contemporary relevance in the material of Revelation 4–22:5.[25] They strongly believed in the soon return of Christ. They would have seen the signs of the end as having been fulfilled in their own time. Presumably, in the description of the prostitute Babylon sitting on the beast in Revelation 17, they saw the symbol of imperial Rome. The combination of religion and state could echo their current experience. In the image of the dragon of Revelation 12 and the mortal wound of the sea beast of chapter 13 and its healing, they perceived "satanic forces and designs behind the might of imperial Rome, raised against them by Nero and Domitian and to fall ever more heavily in the succeeding 200 years. We notice a strong movement from Romans 13 to Revelation 13. In the former the state is ordained of God, but in the latter it has become an agent of Satan."[26] In addition, these Christians perhaps also saw "elements of the imperial cult behind the land beast whose efforts were directed toward the exaltation of the sea beast."[27] Then, in John's vision of chapters 18–19, they most likely saw the prophecies of the demise of imperial Rome. As surely as God overthrew ancient Babylon, so he would eventually overthrow the Babylon of the end, namely imperial Rome itself.

This assertion can hardly be contested. However, no matter what applications and relevance Christians of John's day and the succeeding century might have seen in the symbols of Revelation 4–22:5, it is essential that we discover John's intention and purpose in recording the visions he saw, for he states clearly that they looked beyond the first century (cf. 4:1). It is essential for a responsible interpretation of Revelation 4–22:5, particularly in view of the fact that the language of the book is often highly figurative, that we discover, first of all, *what John meant* in the text, and, then, what meaning the book might have conveyed to the readers to whom it was originally addressed. The latter is of great importance for unlocking the symbolic language of the book because, as is shown later, it was a language with which the first-century Christians were obviously very familiar. But to focus only and exclusively on how the first-century Christians might have interpreted and applied the messages of Revelation 4–22:5 to their immediate situation would be clearly contrary to the intention and purpose of the inspired author.

One might thus see that Revelation itself points to historicism as the most appropriate approach to a fair interpretation of the book's contents. Written from the perspective of faith and applying the principles of biblical hermeneutics spelled out here, this commentary explores the book of Revelation passage by passage. Then the individual units are brought together and grouped into unified and coherent themes, creating a unified message for the whole book of Revelation. The ultimate goal of this commentary is to assist contemporary Christians in discerning what the messages of Revelation are saying to us today in these timeless words and in applying their meaning to contemporary and immediate life situations and needs.

SYMBOLIC NATURE OF REVELATION

In a style typical to apocalyptic writing, a very distinguishing feature of the book of Revelation is its peculiar and symbolic language. John states at the very outset (Rev. 1:1) that the contents of his book were revealed to him in symbolic or figurative language (Gr. *smain* means "to make known by signs"). Thus, Revelation does not contain photographic presentations of heavenly realities or coming events that are intended to be understood in a literal way. Its messages are rather conveyed through symbolic or figurative presentations. John makes clear that the visions he saw were from God (cf. Rev. 1:1–2). However, the language in which those visions were communicated through the inspired author was human, and, as such, appropriate to the time, place, and circumstances of John's time. It is of decisive importance for a meaningful interpretation of the book, therefore, to take seriously its symbolic nature and to be on guard against inadequate literalism in exploring and interpreting the book's prophecies.

Revelation 1:3 indicates that the symbolic language of Revelation was intended to be heard with understanding by the Christians of John's day. It thus appears that the first-century Christians had relatively little difficulty understanding the symbols of the book for it was the language of their time.[28] In order to derive a meaningful interpretation from the book, it is necessary to determine, as much as we can, how the original recipients would have understood those symbols and images. As a safeguard, Revelation should be approached with a presupposition that the scenes and actions portrayed there are symbolic or figurative in nature, unless the context clearly indicates that a literal meaning is intended. There is no question that such persons and things as John on Patmos, the seven churches, Christ, tribulation, war, and death are intended to be taken literally.

To interpret the symbolic language of Revelation, it is necessary, first of all, to explain the meaning of "symbolic." To say that Revelation is a symbolic book does not mean that its language is abstract but rather pictorial.[29] The symbolic language of Revelation was not born in a vacuum, but was grounded firmly in reality. Jon Paulien stresses: "The words that people use and the meanings that those words carry are the product of a people's past experience. Language is limited in expression to that which is familiar to people in a given time and place. Even the future can only be described in the language of a people's past and present experience."[30]

It is important to keep in mind that, while the prophecies of Revelation often refer to our future, the language in which the prophecies were communicated was the language of the time and place of the inspired author rather than our own. "It is all too easy to impose upon the text meanings more appropriate to our time and place than to the situation within which God originally spoke. Discovering the original meaning of the language of the text safeguards us against our natural tendency to remake the biblical text into our own image."[31]

Therefore, an understanding of Revelation's prophecies involves learning what can be known about the sources from which John, under the inspiration of the Holy Spirit, gleaned the symbols and images he used in describing the visions he saw. It has been generally recognized that the symbolic language of Revelation can be traced to at least four sources: the Old Testament, Jewish apocalyptic writings, the first-century Asia Minor setting, and the New Testament writings.

THE OLD TESTAMENT SOURCES

In recording the visions he saw, John drew symbols almost entirely from the Old Testament while responding to first-century religious, social, and cultural milieu.[32] Although he never quotes the Old Testament directly in writing the prophecy—only alluding to it "with a word here, a concept there, a phrase in another place"—he draws heavily on its imagery.[33] It has been demonstrated by many scholars that out of 404 verses in Revelation, 278 contain references or allusions, direct or indirect, to the Old Testament.[34] The book thus appears to be "a perfect mosaic of passages from the Old Testament."[35] William Milligan argues that the book of Revelation is "absolutely steeped in the memories, the incidents, the thoughts, and the language of the Church's past. To such an extent is this the case that it may be doubted whether it contains a single figure not drawn from the Old Testament, or a single complete sentence not more or less built up of materials brought from the same source."[36] This suggests that the Christians of John's time would have perceived the similarities between Revelation and the Old Testament and eventually would have understood "the book's symbols in the light of the Old Testament background."[37]

In order to unlock the symbols of Revelation, the reader today must search for the most appropriate Old Testament background. Jon Paulien notes that "whoever tries to understand Revelation without a thorough knowledge of the Old Testament will find it virtually impossible to understand the book."[38] He also observes that the all-pervasiveness of the Old Testament in Revelation "indicates that it is the major key to unlock the meaning of the book's symbols."[39] This commentary demonstrates how, for instance, the vision of chapters 4–5 is built on the coronation of Israelite kings (cf. Deut. 17:18–20; 2 Kings 11:12); that the Old Testament covenant curses (cf. Lev. 26:21–26) lie in the background of the vision of the seven seals; that the 144,000 standing victoriously on the sea of glass and singing the song of Moses and of the Lamb is a clear allusion to Exodus 15; and that the scene of Revelation 16:12–18:24 is built on the capture of historical Babylon by Cyrus the Persian and his armies (cf. Isa. 44:26–45:7; Jer. 50–51). Trumpets, locusts from the abyss, Sodom and Egypt, Mount Zion, Babylon, Euphrates, and the battle of Armageddon are all taken from the history of Israel.

In communicating his present will as well as his plans for the future to his people, God uses the language of the past. The prophecies of Revelation are especially built on the greatest and key events from sacred history: the creation, the flood, the exodus, God's covenant with King David, and the exile to Babylon.[40] These events are intended to build the reader's faith on the grounds that God's acts of salvation in the future will be very much like God's acts of salvation in the past. The same powerful and faithful God who did marvelous acts for his people in the past, and who is doing the same things in the present, is the God who gives his people the certainty of keeping his promises pertaining to their future.

The Seventh-day Adventist Bible Commentary points out that

> ...a clear understanding of these [Old Testament] citations and allusions in their historical setting is the first step toward understanding the passages where they occur in the Revelation. Study may then be given to the context in which John uses them, to ascertain their adapted meaning. In particular this applies to the names of persons and places, and to things, incidents, and events.[41]

It seems impossible to have a right understanding of the book's prophecies if the Old Testament background is not taken seriously. "Without such an understanding," Paulien stresses, "the meaning of the book remains hidden to a large extent."[42]

SETTING IN ASIA MINOR

The book of Revelation also reflects the real first-century world in Asia Minor. John recorded the vision he saw in the common language of the time. Although drawn almost entirely from the Old Testament, the material he used to describe the visions he saw is transformed into the time, place, and setting of the original readers. The language is often colored with contemporary Greco-Roman practices and motifs. In order to communicate his revelation effectively to those living in the pagan environment and culture, the inspired prophet used the language and terms that made sense to them. Also, in dialoging with the pagan world, namely, contesting pagan ideas that threatened the purity of the Christian faith and offering a critique of pagan religions, John used language and concepts known by the people in Asia. The symbols and concepts "came to him as living expressions that would be familiar to anyone who lived in Asia Minor at the time."[43]

A number of commentaries and other studies provide much information on ancient parallels to various scenes in Revelation. When handled responsibly, these parallels can help the reader to understand better the Greco-Roman setting of the visions of Revelation. For instance, David Aune, an expert in both the book of Revelation and the ancient Greco-Roman world,[44] draws parallels between the description of the glorified Christ, the keybearer of Revelation 1:13–18, and Hekate, a Hellenistic goddess, who was thought to possess the keys to the gates of heaven and Hades (see *Notes* on Rev. 1:18).[45]

Also, while the description of the scene of Revelation 4–5 is built on the Old Testament coronation ceremony of Israelite kings, some studies show how the scene could equally evoke the Roman imperial court and cult ceremonies in the minds of the original readers.[46] In the same way, the description of the new Jerusalem in Revelation 21:10–22:5 echoes the ancient idea of an ideal and safe city.

APOCALYPTIC LANGUAGE

The symbolic language of Revelation is of the Jewish apocalypticism. Some of the Jewish apocalyptic works, like 1 Enoch (the Ethiopic Enoch), 2 Enoch (the Slavonic Enoch), 4 Ezra, and 2 Baruch, were widely popular and read in the first century A.D. As such, they shaped, in significant measure, popular Jewish feelings, theology, and expectations. Common to apocalyptic writing is the claim that its content was based on visionary experience while the author was "in the Spirit" (cf. Rev. 1:10) conversing with angels. The writer is frequently carried away in vision to distant places and allowed to observe grandeur and majestic supernatural scenes. Thus the first-century author of 2 Enoch claims that he saw in his vision of heaven "standing in front of the face of the Lord, and carrying out his will cherubim and seraphim standing all around his throne, six-winged and many eyed; and they cover his entire throne, singing with gentle voice in front of the face of the Lord: 'Holy, Holy, Holy, Lord Sabaoth, Heaven and earth are full of his glory.'"[47] One can easily detect several parallels between this text and Revelation 4:8. Also, the following text from 4 Ezra (first century) reminds one of Revelation 6:9–11: "Did not the souls of the righteous in their chambers ask about these matters, saying, 'How long are we to remain here? And when will come the harvest of our reward?' And Jeremiel the archangel answered them and said, 'When the number of those like yourselves is completed.'"[48]

The apocalyptic writer finds literal language inadequate to portray supernatural things and subtle heavenly realities. In describing them he uses highly symbolic language. Thus many symbols and concepts of Revelation—for instance, a seven-headed dragon, vicious beasts, horns, stars, four winds of the earth, and the end-time battle—were already known in the widely circulated and read Jewish apocalyptic literature. This suggests that the apocalyptic symbols and concepts were much a part of the people's vocabulary in the time when Revelation was written.[49] Most likely the first-century Christian readers had relatively little difficulty understanding the main symbols of the book. The figurative presentations of Revelation communicated very effectively to them.

The interpreter of Revelation today will consult the apocalyptic literature in order to understand how apocalyptic language was perceived by the people of John's day. This will help to clarify many symbols of the book.

THE NEW TESTAMENT PARALLELS

Placed at the end of the New Testament, Revelation, as Donatien Mollat states, functions as a summary statement for the theological themes of the whole Bible.[50] The Old Testament points to Christ (John 5:39), and the New Testament shows the fulfillment of the Old Testament prophecies. The book of Revelation is here in line with the teaching of the New Testament that the promises to Israel are fulfilled in Christ and his faithful people of old.[51] As has been observed by Robert Jamieson, A. R. Fausset, and David Brown, "in this book all the other books of the Bible end and meet."[52] The material of Revelation is permeated with Old Testament imagery interpreted through the person of Jesus Christ and his life and ministry. In recording his visions, John had primarily in mind the first-century Christians whose every belief and proclamation were motivated by the understanding that their Lord died, was resurrected, ascended to heaven, and subsequently has been enthroned in heaven at the right side of the Father (cf. Acts 2:33–36; Rom. 8:34; Eph. 1:20; Phil. 2:5–11; Heb. 12:2).

Although different in style, vocabulary, and subject matter, the book of Revelation is replete with numerous parallels and allusions to other books of the New Testament which were written previously. It appears that the messages of Revelation are built upon theological ideas from the rest of the New Testament. Many passages reflect, in particular, the sayings of Jesus and occasionally statements of Paul.[53] For instance, some scholars see Revelation as "the enlargement of the discourse" by Jesus on the Mount of Olives.[54] Fully grasping the meaning of Revelation's message involves paying careful attention to New Testament parallels to the various passages of the book.

OBJECTIVES OF THE COMMENTARY

What follows are the objectives and guidelines that governed the writing of this commentary. They explain the author's own philosophy of a responsible commentary on the book of Revelation.

The biblical book is a divine revelation. The opening verses of Revelation point to the divine origin of the book (cf. Rev. 1:1–3). Paulien states: "Regardless of the position one takes with respect to the origin of the visions, John himself appears to understand his book to be more of a divine construct than his own composition."[55] The messages of Revelation are not a product of John's fertile imagination, but were shown to him in vision by God. John stresses repeatedly that his work is "the words of the prophecy" (Rev. 1:3; 22:7, 10, 18–19). While it is true that Revelation was written by a human person in the first-century setting in Asia Minor, the presence of the divine element in the book indicates that its ultimate meaning often goes beyond what the human author might have understood. As Peter stated, "no prophecy was ever made by an act of human will, but men moved by the Holy Spirit spoke from God" (2 Pet. 1:21). The content of Revelation reflects John's visionary experience which he penned under the control of the Holy Spirit. As such, Revelation is equal in authority to any Old Testament prophecy or apostolic writing. It is, therefore, of extreme importance in handling the text to take seriously into account the divine element of Revelation.

Along this line a note of clarification is necessary. When the text is dealt with in this commentary in terms of, for instance, "John's purpose/intent" or "what John endeavored to communicate to the reader," it is not to be understood that the book of Revelation is approached as merely a human product. A statement by Ellen White is very instructive at this point:

> The Bible is written by inspired men, but it is not God's mode of thought and expression. It is not the words of the Bible that are inspired, but the men that were inspired. Inspiration acts not on the man's words or his expressions but on the man himself, who, under the influence of the Holy Ghost, is imbued with thoughts. But the words receive the impress of the individual mind. The divine mind is diffused. The divine mind and will is combined with the human mind and will; thus the utterances of the man are the word of God.[56]

The references to John's intent or purpose in this commentary are rather a convenient way to explore the text in accordance with the intention of the inspired author as the last one in the chain of transmission of Revelation (cf. Rev. 1:1–2).

Revelation was originally a circular letter (like the letters of Paul or Peter) written in the prophetic-apocalyptic style. Thus the contents of Revelation should be dealt with in a manner similar to the letters of Paul. As we observed earlier, the book was originally sent to the Christian communities in Asia Minor, addressing their immediate needs and life situations. Revelation, however, makes clear that its contents are not limited to the first-century Christians and the Roman Empire. As a book of prophecy, its messages were "given for the guidance and comfort of the church throughout the Christian dispensation."[57] The book covers the history of the church and the world between the cross and the Second Coming with a strong focus on the time of the end. As such, Revelation still speaks to us today as it spoke to the Christians of John's day. It reminds us that God controls the future which he has revealed to us through his servants the prophets.

Revelation is a book for the church. The book of Revelation was intended by its author to be read in a church setting (Rev. 1:3). Therefore, the objective set for this commentary is to provide an exposition of Revelation that will benefit the church as a whole and serve as a help for the present experience of Christians. Biblical prophecy is not given to satisfy a sheer curiosity about the future. The church in Revelation has its definite place and task in the world. The study of the prophecies of Revelation should stimulate God's people to reach others for Christ. There are clearly some things in Revelation with regard to the future which we may never fully understand before their fulfillment. Studying the book of Revelation should help the church to find its place in prophecy as an agent of God's witness to the world. Detailed prophetic charts could better be replaced by geographical charts with sincere questions about how to reach those who are still unreached for Christ.

Focus should be on the text. A good commentary on Revelation must be faithful to the Word in allowing the text to speak, rather than imposing a theology or agenda upon the text. It endeavors to discover what the text is saying rather than what the expositor wants it to say. This commentary concentrates primarily on the text, rather than on history. As Jon Paulien observes, it is possible "to pay so much attention to history that we miss the literary dynamics of the biblical text on which the historical applications must be based." Some interpreters often jump from details of the text straight to history and then seek to fit the various historical applications together into a coherent whole. In the process, the inner coherence of the text itself is often lost. The purpose of this commentary is "to stay with the text as long as it takes to expose its inner dynamics. Only when the text has been thoroughly understood can sound historical applications be drawn. It is the biblical text that sets the framework for the Bible's interpretation of history."[58]

The Bible is the best interpreter of Revelation. We have seen that the Old and New Testaments offer good building material for Revelation's prophecies. The symbolic presentations of Revelation must be explained and clarified primarily from the Bible, according to the "intent and purpose of the inspired writer, and the meaning the book conveyed to the readers to whom it was originally addressed." Otherwise, the interpretation of the book's prophecies conveyed in symbolic language usually reflects nothing but personal opinion derived from allegorical imagination or current events.[59] The interpretive key for the book's symbols should not be allegory but rather typology.

Christ is the center of all prophecy. The opening words of Revelation make clear that the book is primarily "the revelation of Jesus Christ" (Rev. 1:1). This indicates that the book was written from the perspective of Christ. Its symbols and images should have their focus on Christ. Nothing else should dominate one's exposition and interpretation of the book's prophecies, neither history nor sheer curiosity about the future. "Unless the significance of Jesus Christ and His cross is allowed to permeate the symbols of Revelation, the resulting interpretation will not be a Christian one, no matter how often Christ may be named in its explication."[60] It is only in and through Christ that the symbols and images of the book of Revelation receive their ultimate meaning and significance.

LITERARY ARRANGEMENT OF REVELATION

It appears that the structural design of Revelation is not without significance for the understanding of the sweeping thematic progression of the book. It warns against any study and interpretation of a passage or section in isolation from the rest of the book. The interpretation of the text must agree with the general purpose of the whole book.

The literary arrangement of Revelation is very complex. Although it has been generally recognized that the structural composition of the book is essential to the understanding of its messages, no general scholarly consensus has been reached with regard to its basic structure. Commentators and expositors have offered a variety of proposals as to what the structural organization of Revelation was intended to mean by the inspired author, but hardly two expositors share exactly the same view.

The following sections explore some of the most representative proposals with regard to the structural organization of the last book of the Bible. These proposals should not be viewed as mutually exclusive and determinative. Although some offer more promising insights into the structural arrangement of Revelation than others, the proposals express a broad spectrum of interpretations about the book's design and composition, as well as its overall theme. Considered together, they unpack the intention of the writer much more than otherwise possible.

SIGNIFICANCE OF SPRINGBOARD PASSAGES

The book of Revelation is characterized by particular literary features. It has been observed that the key to the larger significance of major sections of the book is often located in the concluding statement of the preceding section. Such a statement functions as the springboard passage concluding what precedes and introducing what follows. For instance, the section of the seven messages to the churches (chapters 2–3) is preceded by the statement of Revelation 1:20 which concludes the vision of the glorified Christ (1:9–20). This concluding statement functions at the same time as an introduction to Revelation 2–3. The vision of the sealed 144,000 (chapter 7) elaborates and explains the concluding statement of Revelation 6:16–17 in the form of a question regarding who will stand before the great wrath of the Lamb. The concluding statement of Revelation 12:17, referring to the war against "the remaining ones of her offspring," is developed in chapters 13–14. Revelation 15:2–4 serves both as the conclusion of Revelation 12–14 and the introduction to the seven last plagues.

Several springboard passages seem to provide foresight for larger portions of the book. As discussed later, Revelation 3:21 seems to provide the interpretive outline for chapters 4–7, and 11:18 for the entire second half of the book (Rev. 12–22:5). Likewise, Revelation 6:9–10 (which finds its fullest confirmation in 8:2–6 and 13) gives a clue for understanding the nature and purpose of both the seven seals and the seven trumpet plagues.

The springboard principle enables the interpreter to find information that is imbedded in various passages of Revelation. It suggests that the inspired author has clearly defined his intention regarding the understanding of the text, a fact that rules out one's search outside the book for creative interpretation. To ignore this principle would limit the understanding of the author's own intention for the book.[61]

IDENTIFICATION–DESCRIPTION PATTERN

Another important literary strategy of Revelation can aid the interpreter in more clearly understanding some difficult texts of the book. Whenever a new key player in the book is introduced, he or she is first identified in terms of personal description or historical role and activities. Once the player is identified, John moves into the description of the player's function and activities that are especially important to the vision. This literary strategy is first evident with reference to Revelation 1:9–3:22. The identification of the resurrected Christ is provided in Revelation 1:9–20 with a list of his various characteristics. The messages to the seven churches follow in Revelation 2–3. Various characteristics of Christ portray different aspects of his ministry to the churches.

The same technique can be seen with reference to the vision of the seven seals. Before describing Christ's opening of the seals (Rev. 6–8:1), John describes in chapter

5 Christ's unique qualifications for the task of unsealing the seals of the sealed scroll. In Revelation 11, the identification of the two witnesses (11:3–6) is followed by their activities and experiences that are important to the vision (11:7–13). Also, before referring to Satan's anger and his determination to engage in the final conflict (Rev. 12:17), John provides his identification and the reason for his anger and fury (Rev. 12:3–16).

This literary strategy seems to be especially helpful for the clear understanding of Revelation 13 and 17. Although the focus of Revelation 13 is on the final battle of this world's history, not all things pertaining to the sea beast in this chapter relate to the end time. Before describing the very role and activities of the sea beast during "the forty-two months" of the Christian age (13:5–7), John in 13:1–4 first identifies the beast in general terms. Then, with 13:8, he moves on to describe the role and function of the beast in the final crisis. The same might be applied to Revelation 17. Before describing the role and function of end-time Babylon and the resurrected beast in the final crisis (17:14–18), John describes their historical role and function. The principle of the identification/description literary strategy enables the interpreter to find the sound information that the inspired author imbedded in the text.

"I HEARD" AND "I SAW" PATTERN

The revelator sometimes uses another literary technique that is expressed with the phrases "I heard" and "I saw" or "I looked." In this avenue of explaining the things he witnessed in vision, John sometimes first *hears* something in the vision and what he subsequently *sees* is essentially the same thing, yet in some way different. What he sees is actually a different facet of the things he heard before. The following is a list of things that were communicated by this literary technique:

- Chapter 1: John first hears "a loud voice as of a trumpet" behind him (1:10); when he turns around, he instead sees Jesus walking in the midst of the seven lampstands (1:12–13).
- Chapter 5: John first hears that the Lion from the tribe of Judah has overcome; when he turns to see the Lion, he sees the Lamb as having been slain (5:5–6). Both are the images of Christ: the Lion shows what Christ did and the Lamb how he did it.
- Chapter 7: John first hears the number 144,000 as being God's embattled, sealed people (7:4); when he sees the same group, they appear to him as a

great multitude that nobody could count (7:9). The groups are thus the same saints in different roles and circumstances.

- Chapter 17: John hears of "the great prostitute sitting on *many waters*" (17:1); what he later sees is "a woman sitting on *a scarlet beast*" whose name is Babylon (17:3). This shows that the beast and the waters refer to the same political, secular entity specified in 17:15.
- Chapter 21: John first hears of "the bride, the wife of the Lamb" (21:9), but he actually sees "the holy city Jerusalem" in its glory (21:10–11).

This literary technique is the clue for understanding some important visions in the book, especially the two groups of saved saints in chapter 7. Understanding this will help the interpreter to find the meaning of the text as intended by the inspired author.

APPROACHES TO THE STRUCTURE OF REVELATION

In looking at Revelation, one will discover something beyond the basic structure of the book. This section provides a glimpse into several peculiar structural features of Revelation pointed out by some contemporary scholars.

Recapitulative or repetitive structure. A number of repetitive structures in Revelation fall into groups of seven: the seven churches, the seven seals, the seven trumpets, and the seven bowl plagues. A critical problem for the interpreters of Revelation is whether these septenaries should be understood as parallel or recapitulatory accounts of the same events, or as a continuous or progressive chronological sequence of end-time events in which the trumpets follow the seals and the bowl plagues follow the trumpets. It was Victorinus of Pettau (d. ca. 304) who introduced the principle of recapitulation in Revelation that has been followed with some modification by subsequent interpreters.[62]

The recapitulative parallels between the seals and trumpets series appear to be evident. A comparison between the two series as given in the "Overview: Revelation 8–9" shows their parallel structures. First of all, both the trumpets and the seals are arranged in groups of four and three. Then, both series are interrupted by interludes between the sixth and the seventh trumpet and seal, respectively. It also becomes evident that both begin with the first century and conclude with the time of the end, something not noticeable in the seven-bowl-plagues series. In addition, as the "Introductory Sanctuary Scenes" structure below indicates, the seals and the trumpets presumably cover the entire Christian age. On the other hand, the seven last plagues are evidently set at the conclusion of this earth's history.

The application of the recapitulative principle can be very helpful to the interpreter of Revelation. Information and insight obtained from clear passages may unlock the theological meaning of parallel difficult ones. For instance, Revelation 7 may be the clue for understanding chapters 10–11, particularly with regard to the identity of the two witnesses. Also, one can notice that the seven trumpets and the seven-bowl-plagues series are deliberately parallel in terms of their language and content. Although the two series are evidently not the same (see "Overview: Revelation 15–18"), the examination of their structural parallels can help the reader gain the deeper theological meaning that the inspired author intended in writing the book of Revelation.

Various theories of the structure of Revelation. A number of scholars assume that the number "seven" plays an important part in the structure of the book of Revelation. The proposals, however, range from a fourfold to eightfold structure, each of which is based on the number seven. In order to acquaint the reader with the complexity of the questions related to the structure of Revelation, care will be taken to present the full spectrum of views on the subject. Since many commentators offer criticism on these views, they will be explored here without such detailed criticism.

Eugenio Corsini, for instance, argues that Revelation falls into four groups of seven events (the seven letters, the seven seals, the seven trumpets, and the seven bowls) which "determine the whole structure and message of the book."[63] Jacques Ellul finds five septenaries—the churches, the seals, the trumpets, the bowls, and a group of visions introduced with the formula: "Then I saw."[64] Some scholars divide the book into six sections, each of which is based on the number seven. For Merrill C. Tenney, the six divisions are the churches, the seals, the trumpets, the bowls, seven personages (woman, dragon, child, Michael, Lamb, the beast from the sea, and the beast from the earth), and seven new things (new heaven, new earth, new peoples, new Jerusalem, new temple, new light, new paradise).[65] Austin M. Farrer also sees Revelation as being divided into six sections, each consisting of seven subdivisions.[66]

Farrer's scheme was adopted with some minor modifications by A. Yarbro Collins who suggests an eightfold structure: prologue (1:1–8); seven messages (1:9–3:22); seven seals (4–8:1); seven trumpets (8:2–11:19); seven unnumbered visions (12–15:4); seven bowls (15–16:21) with Babylon appendix (17–19:10); seven unnumbered visions (19:11–21:8) with Jerusalem appendix (21:9–22:5); and epilogue (22:6–21).[67] This structure with the "unnumbered" sections and two appendices appears to be very arbitrary and problematic. In addition, more than a few scholars argue for the sevenfold structure and see septets with all of their seven main visions.[68] At this point the comment of Gerhard Krodel is very instructive: "We should not construct cycles of sevens where John did not number his visions."[69]

No doubt some element of truth exists in many of these various proposals. The very proliferation of all such theories and the "lack of consensus about the structure of Revelation should caution the reader about accepting any one approach as definitive."[70] David Aune argues persuasively on the basis of Revelation 1:19 for the twofold structure: (1) 1:9–3:22, which centers on the theophany of the exalted Christ, and (2) 4–22:9, a series of episodic vision narratives introduced with a heavenly journey.[71] Aune's simple structure is very persuasive, and it is clearly suggested by John (cf. Rev. 1:19; 4:1). However, despite its attractiveness, this avenue of interpretation overlooks the fact that Revelation 12 begins a new (eschatological) division of the book; it clearly splits the book into three distinctive divisions.

INTRODUCTORY SANCTUARY SCENES

Kenneth A. Strand divided the book of Revelation into eight basic visions, with a prologue and an epilogue. He found each of the visions to be preceded by a "victorious-introduction scene with temple setting."[72] Building on Strand's research, Richard M. Davidson and Jon Paulien argue for a sevenfold structure of Revelation, with the prologue and epilogue, based on the temple setting.[73] They have convincingly shown that each of the seven major divisions is introduced with a sanctuary scene. It appears that the entire book is set up on the sanctuary system typology:

Prologue (1:1–8)

1. Introductory sanctuary scene (1:9–20)

   The messages to the seven churches (chapters 2–3)

2. Introductory sanctuary scene (chapters 4–5)

   The opening of the seven seals (6–8:1)

3. Introductory sanctuary scene (8:2–5)

   The blowing of the seven trumpets (8:6–11:18)

4. Introductory sanctuary scene (11:19)

The wrath of the nations (12–15:4)

5. Introductory sanctuary scene (15:5–8)

The seven last plagues (chapters 16–18)

6. Introductory sanctuary scene (19:1–10)

The eschatological consummation (19:11–21:1)

7. Introductory sanctuary scene (21:2–8)

The New Jerusalem (21:9–22:5)

Epilogue (22:6–21)

These seven introductory sanctuary scenes seem to form the skeleton of the book of Revelation. They indicate that the heavenly temple in Revelation is seen as the center of all divine activities. In fact, the entire Revelation vision (4–22:5) is "apparently perceived from the vantage point" of the heavenly temple.[74] In addition to the constant references made either to the temple or to features found there, all divine actions that take place upon the earth are described as being preceded by scenes of divine activities in the heavenly temple.

The structure of these introductory sanctuary scenes indicates two definite lines of progression.[75] First, there is a complete circle moving from earth to heaven and then back to earth again. Then, there is a definite progression from the inauguration of the heavenly sanctuary to intercession, to judgment, to the cessation of the sanctuary function, and finally to its absence. The following table reflects a chiastic structure of the book:

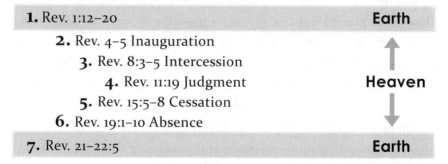

1. Rev. 1:12–20	**Earth**
2. Rev. 4–5 Inauguration	↑
3. Rev. 8:3–5 Intercession	
4. Rev. 11:19 Judgment	**Heaven**
5. Rev. 15:5–8 Cessation	
6. Rev. 19:1–10 Absence	↓
7. Rev. 21–22:5	**Earth**

It can be observed that the first and seventh paralleled segments are set on the earth while the second through the sixth are set in heaven. The second and the sixth describe a sanctuary worship scene; they refer to the throne, worship, the Lamb, the twenty-four elders, and praise to God Almighty. While the second has the largest quantity of sanctuary allusions, however, in the sixth sanctuary scene no explicit reference to the sanctuary is found. Also, while the third scene portrays the continual services of intercession in the temple, involving the burning of incense, the fifth scene points to the cessation of intercession in the temple. It is filled with smoke from the glory of God, and no one can approach the throne of grace to receive mercy and forgiveness. The fourth sanctuary scene is set in the center. This literary arrangement indicates that chapters 12–14 form the central portion of the book, and that the church standing on the threshold of the great end-time conflict is the focal point of the entire book of Revelation.

A definite progression also moves from the continual daily (*tamid*) services to the yearly services of the Old Testament sanctuary. The structure of Revelation appears to be based on the daily and yearly sanctuary services pattern. Recent studies have drawn striking parallels between the first half of the book and the order of the daily service (*tamid*) in the temple from the first century when John wrote.[76]

A basic description of the daily order of the *tamid* service was prescribed by the tractate *Tamid* in the Mishnah, a second-century A.D. collection of Jewish laws, traditions, and practices based on earlier tradition.[77] The *tamid* service began when a selected priest entered the first department of the temple, where he trimmed the lampstands and refilled them with a fresh supply of oil (*Tamid* 3.7, 9; cf. Rev. 1:12–20). The great door of the Temple remained open (*Tamid* 3.7; cf. Rev. 4:1; the Greek text indicates that the door had been opened before John saw it in vision). Both the Mishnah and Revelation refer to the slaying of a lamb (*Tamid* 4.1–3; cf. Rev. 5:6). The lamb's blood was poured out at the base of the altar of burnt offering in the outer court of the Temple (*Tamid* 4.1; cf. Rev. 6:9). After pouring out the blood, the priest offered incense at the golden altar in the Holy Place (*Tamid* 5.4; Luke 1:8–11; cf. Rev. 8:3–4). While the priest ministered the incense on the golden altar, the audience kept silence for a short period of time (*Tamid* 7.3; cf. Rev. 8:1). Then trumpets were blown announcing the conclusion of the service (*Tamid* 7.3; cf. Rev. 8:2, 6).

This would show that the progression of the events of the first half of Revelation follows the same order as did the daily service of the sanctuary. At this point, Paulien remarks: "Not only does this portion of the Apocalypse contain potential allusions to all the major details of the *tamid* liturgy, it alludes to them in essentially the same order. Thus, the material making up the septets of the churches, seals, and trumpets would be subtly associated with the activities in the temple related to the continual or *tamid* service."[78] The first part of Revelation is clearly modeled directly on the daily sanctuary service.

The second half of Revelation is evidently set on the annual service of Yom Kippur. As Kenneth A. Strand demonstrates, Revelation 11:1–2 contains explicit allusions to the Day of Atonement (see *Notes* on Rev. 11:1).[79] Yom Kippur was the day of judgment; the central activities of this festival took place in the most holy place. Revelation 11:19 makes reference to the *naos* (the inner sanctuary of the temple; see *Notes* on Rev. 11:19). From these points in Revelation there is repeated focus on the *naos* where the central activities of Yom Kippur took place (Rev. 11:19; 14:15; 15:5–8; 16:1, 17). "Judgment language and activity, a central theme of Yom Kippur, is also a major concern of the second half of the Apocalypse"[80] (cf. Rev. 14:7; 16:5, 7; 17:1; 18:8, 10, 20; 19:2, 11; 20:4, 12–13).

This structure of sanctuary scenes renders a number of implications for the literary understanding of the book of Revelation. It shows that Revelation 11:18 must be taken as the dividing line between the historical and eschatological parts of Revelation (see "Overview: Revelation 12–22:5"), rather than Revelation 14:20 as suggested by Strand. Revelation 1–11 (the seven churches, seals, and trumpets) focus on the entire Christian age, and Revelation 12–22:5 on the final events of this earth's history. The structure affirms, for instance, the view that the vision of Revelation 4–5 does not refer to the investigative judgment scene, but rather to the enthronement of Christ that occurred at Pentecost (see "Overview: Revelation 4–11"). It also indicates that the seals and the trumpets must be understood as covering the broad sweep of Christian history, while the seven last plagues are set in the time of the end.

ANNUAL CYCLE OF FESTIVALS

Some scholars have suggested that the structure of the book of Revelation is also modeled on the annual feasts of the Hebrew cultic calendar established by Moses on Mount Sinai: Passover, Pentecost, the Feast of Trumpets, the Day of Atonement, and the Feast of Tabernacles (cf. Lev. 23).[81] Life for ancient Israel revolved around these festivals. No wonder one would discover their eschatological implication in the book of Revelation, since, as we have seen, the book draws heavily on Old

Testament imagery. While such assertions are easily overdrawn, the evidence seems to support the view that the general outline of Revelation follows in sequence the Jewish annual feasts.

Passover. The introductory vision with the messages to the seven churches appears to reflect the paschal concept and theme (Rev. 1:5, 17–18). Nowhere else in the book is there such a strong emphasis on Christ's death and resurrection. Christ is referred to as "the faithful witness, the first-born from the dead," the One "who loves us and released us from our sins by his blood" (Rev. 1:5). "I am the first and the last, and the living One, and I was dead and behold, I am alive for ever and ever, and I have the keys of Death and Hades" (Rev. 1:17–18). Jon Paulien suggests that "Christ's intense scrutiny of the churches reminds us of each Jewish household's search for leaven to remove it just before Passover" (cf. Exod. 12:19; 13:7).[82] Also, M. D. Goulder sees strong parallels "to an ancient tradition for each church to have a Paschal candle burning in worship from Easter to Pentecost."[83] The call for a meal of mutual fellowship (Rev. 3:20) is reminiscent of the paschal meal. Since Passover was the only festival that the first-century Christians considered as having been fulfilled in the earthly Christ (cf. John 19:35–37; 1 Cor. 5:7), "it is fitting that it would be associated with that portion of the book where He is portrayed in His ministry to the churches on earth."[84]

Pentecost. Revelation 4–5 is fittingly associated with Pentecost. The inauguration/enthronement ceremony of Christ in the heavenly temple "took place during the ten days following Christ's ascension, reaching its climax on the day of Pentecost."[85] It was then that the Holy Spirit was poured out on the earth (cf. Rev. 5:6). In Revelation 5:9–10, the song of the twenty-four elders (representatives of redeemed humanity) recalls Exodus 19:5–6; the "flashes of lightening and sounds and peals of thunder" proceeding from the throne (Rev. 4:5; cf. Exod. 19:16), the sound of the trumpet (Rev. 4:1; cf. Exod. 19:16–19), and the summons to "come up" (Rev. 4:1; cf. Exod. 19:20, 24) also recall the Mount Sinai event.[86] The giving of the law to Moses parallels the taking of the book of the covenant by Christ in Revelation 5. It should be noted that Exodus 19–20:23 and Ezekiel 1 (another major literary background to the throne vision of Revelation 4) were the traditional Jewish lectionary readings for the Feast of Pentecost.

Feast of Trumpets. The series of the blowing of the seven trumpets of Revelation 8–9 echoes the seven monthly new-moon festivals that covered the span between the spring and fall festivals (cf. Num. 10:10). The Feast of Trumpets was the climax which summoned the people of Israel to prepare for the coming day of judgment, known as the Day of Atonement or Yom Kippur. The seven trumpets in Revelation, therefore, "represent the ongoing sequence of seven months with the seventh trumpet representing the Feast of Trumpets itself. It is, interestingly, within the seventh trumpet (Rev. 11:18) that we find the first explicit use of judgment terminology in Revelation. In Jewish thought the seventh-month Feast of Trumpets ushered in the time of judgment that led up to the Day of Atonement (cf. Rev. 11:18–19). Correspondingly, from Rev 11:19 to near the end of the book there is an increasing focus on judgment."[87]

Day of Atonement. While the first half of Revelation appears to be modeled on the *tamid* or daily service of the Hebrew cultic system, Revelation 12–22:5 reflects the annual service of Yom Kippur. We have seen that, starting with Revelation 11:1–2, the elements of Yom Kippur are alluded to throughout the second half of the book.

Feast of Tabernacles. The last in the sequence of the five main Jewish festivals was the Feast of Tabernacles or Sukkoth that followed Yom Kippur. This feast, known also as the Feast of Ingathering, came after the gathering of the harvest into the granary. Its purpose was to keep afresh, in the minds of the people, Israel's wilderness wandering to the promised land. It was a special time of celebration and rejoicing before the Lord (Lev. 23:40) filled with the waving of palm branches, singing and music, and a great feast.[88] The final section of the book of Revelation contains many allusions to the Feast of Tabernacles. The harvest is over and the wilderness wandering of God's people is finished (Rev. 14–20). God's people are gathered into the new Jerusalem where God is "tabernacling" with them (Rev. 21:3). There is much celebration accompanied by singing (Rev. 7:9–10; 14:3; 15:2–4; 19:1–10), the playing of harps (14:2), and the waving of palm branches (Rev. 7:9). In addition, the primary features of the Feast of Tabernacles—water and light commemorating the water from the rock and the pillar of fire during the wilderness wandering—have their ultimate fulfillment in Revelation 22:1–5.

CHIASTIC STRUCTURE

An increasing number of contemporary scholars observe a chiastic structure in the book of Revelation. The word "chiasm" (derived from the Greek cross-shaped letter X) refers to a typical form of organization for the Hebrew people. While literary outlines today are based on the A-B-C pattern, the chiastic outline is based on an A-B-A' principle. Chiasm is best defined as an inverted parallelism. For instance, the statement:

> **God** is *good*
> the **Lord** is *merciful*

is a synonymous parallelism in which the second line repeats in different wording what the first line says. However, when the same statement is expressed in the form of inverted parallelism:

> **God** is *good*
> *merciful* is the **Lord**

it is referred to as chiasm. In the chiastic outline the climax of the text is set in the center with the corresponding sections moving up to and away from it. Section A parallels section A' at the end, B to B', C to C' until we come to the center. When one knows how chiasm works, it is much easier to discern the theological emphasis of the content of the book as intended by the inspired author.

Some studies argue for the sevenfold chiastic structure. Such a structure has been proposed by E. Schüssler Fiorenza:[89]

> **A.** 1:1–8
>   **B.** 1:9–3:22
>   **C.** 4:1–9:21; 11:15–19
>   **D.** 10–15:4
>   **C'.** 15:5–19:10
>   **B'.** 19:11–22:9
> **A'.** 22:10–21

Despite the attractiveness of this structure, the parallels between the corresponding parts are not easy to demonstrate.

Kenneth A. Strand argued that the book falls naturally into two parts, historical and eschatological, with a dividing line in chapter 14.[90] While Strand's twofold division into the historical and eschatological is undeniably evident in Revelation, the context does not support the dividing line as he suggested it to be in chapter 14. The context suggests the line between the historical and eschatological divisions to be rather in

Revelation 11:18. A careful study indicates that the first half of Revelation focuses on the realities of the whole Christian era, while the focus of the entire second half of the book—rather than just chapters 15–22—is set into the eschatological framework focusing on the events surrounding the Second Coming.[91]

This commentary suggests the following outline of Revelation that synchronizes more precisely the chiastic parallel segments:

A. Prologue (1:1–8)

    B. Promises to the overcomer (1:9–3:22)

        C. God's work for humanity's salvation (4–8:1)

            D. God's wrath mixed with mercy (8:2–9:21)

                E. Commissioning John to prophesy (10–11:18)

                    F. Great controversy between Christ and Satan (11:19–13:18)

                E'. Church proclaims the end–time gospel (14:1–20)

            D'. God's final wrath unmixed with mercy (15–18:24)

        C'. God's work for humanity's salvation completed (19–21:4)

    B'. Fulfillment of the promises to the overcomer (21:5–22:5)

A'. Epilogue (22:6–21)

It must be noted that the first half in this chiasm focuses on the entire history of the Christian age, while its chiastic counterparts focus exclusively on the time of the end. The segment at the center points to the central theological theme of the book. In comparing the prologue and the epilogue, the parallels become self-evident:

PROLOGUE	PARALLELS	EPILOGUE
1:1	"to show to his servants"	22:6
1:1	"the things which must soon take place"	22:6
1:1	Jesus sends his angel	22:6, 16
1:3	"blessed is the one who keeps…"	22:7
1:3	"the words of the prophecy"	22:7
1:3	"the time is near"	22:10
1:4	"the seven churches"	22:16
1:8	"the Alpha and the Omega"	22:10

The parallels clearly indicate that the themes and concepts which begin the book are drawn to their conclusion. Their purpose appears to be that of taking readers back to the beginning, to prevent them from resting in a kind of self-sufficient utopian dream, and motivating them to endure oppression and persecution until the very time of the end.

Likewise, the contents of the messages to the seven churches parallel the material regarding the new Jerusalem. The last two chapters of the book might rightly be titled "The overcomer will inherit these things" (Rev. 21:7), because many promises given to the overcomers in chapters 2–3 (having access to the tree of life, escaping from the second death, receiving a new name, having authority over the nations, being dressed in white, not having their names blotted out of the book of life, being acknowledged before the Father, being pillars in the temple and never having to leave it, having the name of God written on them, and sitting with Jesus on his throne) find their fulfillment in 21:6–22:5.

Segment C shows Revelation 4–8:1 to be parallel to 19–21:4. Both passages begin with heavenly worship scenes. Chapters 4–5 and 19 contain the throne, the twenty-four elders, the four living beings, and worship with exclamations of praise.[92] All of these elements are found as a group only in these two chapters. While Revelation 4–8:1 focuses on the realities of the entire Christian age, however, its chiastic counterpart is clearly an end-time passage. While in chapters 4–5 God is praised as the Creator and Christ as the Redeemer, the praise in chapter 19 is for the destruction of Babylon. Further parallels are found between 19:11–21 and the seven seals, including the white horse and the rider with the crown(s). The statement: "And behold a white horse, and the one sitting upon it" (6:2) is repeated verbatim in Revelation 19:11. However, while in 6:2 the rider on the white horse wears a garland, the victory crown, in 19:12 the rider wears a diadem, the royal crown. It is not until the eschatological conclusion that Jesus wears the royal crown and reigns among his people on earth.

There are many other parallels. For instance, chapter 6 also raises the question: "How long, O Lord, holy and true, will you not judge and avenge our blood upon those who dwell on the earth?" Revelation 19:2 states that God has judged and "avenged the blood of his servants." As another example, the scene of the breaking of the sixth seal refers to kings, magistrates, military commanders, the rich, the strong, slaves, and free men running in terror and trying to hide themselves at the coming of Christ. On the other hand, Revelation 19:18 refers to kings, military commanders, the strong, slaves, and free men found among the slain at the coming of Christ. Parallels are also found between Revelation 7:9, 13–14 and the invitation for the wedding supper of the Lamb in 19:7–10; both texts portray God's redeemed people dressed in white robes. Also, both 7:15–17 and 21:3–4 speak of God's tabernacle with his people, and that God "will wipe away every tear from their eyes." Finally, the silence "for about half an hour" of the seventh seal (8:1) might correspond to the "silence" of the millennium in Revelation 20.

The parallels in segment D are also self-evident. Both passages have visions introduced with sanctuary scenes. However, while in 8:2–6 there are the continual services of intercession in the heavenly temple, 15:8 points to the cessation of intercession in the temple. This suggests that the seven trumpets are God's judgments mixed with mercy, while the pouring of the seven bowl plagues are the execution of God's final wrath unmixed with mercy. Further comparison shows evident parallels between the two series:

	THE SEVEN TRUMPETS	THE SEVEN BOWLS
1st	Earth (8:7)	Earth (16:2)
2nd	Sea turns into blood (8:8–9)	Sea turns into blood (16:3)
3rd	Rivers and fountains (8:10–11)	Rivers and fountains (16:4)
4th	Sun, moon, and stars (8:12)	Sun (16:8–9)
5th	Darkness from the abyss, locusts (9:1–11)	Darkness over the throne of the beast (16:10–11)
6th	River Euphrates (9:14–21)	River Euphrates (16:12–16)
7th	Loud voices: the kingdom has come and Christ reigns (11:15–16)	A loud voice: It is done (16:17–21)

This chiastic outline sets the seven trumpet plagues in the historical section, while the execution of the bowl plagues comes at the time of the end. This structure suggests that the trumpet and bowl plagues are deliberately parallel in terms of language and content; the trumpet plagues are intended to be the foretaste and forewarning of the future execution of God's judgments shown in their fullness in the seven final plagues.

Finally, segment E parallels Revelation 10–11:18 with 14:1–20. John is commissioned to "prophesy again concerning many peoples and nations and tongues and kings" (10:11); then two witnesses prophesy to "those who dwell on the earth" (11:1–14).

Chapter 14 describes first God's faithful people (14:1–5) and then the proclamation of the everlasting gospel "to those who dwell on the earth, and every nation and tribe and tongue and people" (14:6–13). Both sections refer to the giving of glory to God (11:13; 14:7) and fearing him (11:18; 14:7). Revelation 11:18 states that the time has come to give the reward to God's servants and to "destroy the destroyers of the earth." Revelation 14 first describes the gathering of God's faithful people in terms of the wheat harvest (14:14–16), and, then, the judgment of the wicked in terms of the trampling of the winepress (14:17–20).

This brings us to the central segment of the structure (Rev. 12–13). The great controversy between Christ and the counterfeit trinity—Satan and his two associates, the sea and earth beasts—is the focal point of the entire book. This section defines the framework of the material in the book from the perspective of the great controversy with a special emphasis on the final conflict at the conclusion of the history of this world.

THREEFOLD STRUCTURE OF REVELATION

While recognizing the potential of the various options with regard to the structural organization of the book, this commentary argues for the threefold structure of the book of Revelation, with a prologue (1:1–8) and an epilogue (22:6–21). Such a structure is self-evident on the basis of Revelation 1:19, and 11:19 introduces a completely new division, which, as is shown later, describes the content of the little scroll of Revelation 10. The first main division comprises the messages to the seven churches of John's day (1:9–3:22); the second major division focuses on the opening of the seven-sealed scroll that covers the sweep of history from John's day until the time of the end (chaps. 4–11); and the third division deals with the eschatological consummation of this earth's history and the ultimate establishment of God's kingdom (12–22:5).

Each of these three major divisions opens with an introductory vision of Christ. Revelation 1:9–20 presents the messages of the seven churches (chapters 2–3), chapters 4–5 begin the section on the opening of the seven-sealed scroll, and Revelation 12:1–17 introduces the eschatological division of the book. Each introductory vision portrays Christ in a unique role. The portrayal of Christ in the introductory sections seems to be the key to understanding the remaining part of each division, and it defines its respective theme and content.

1. MESSAGES TO THE SEVEN CHURCHES (REV. 1:9–3:22) WITH THE OPENING VISION OF CHRIST AS THE HIGH PRIEST (1:9–20)

The first major division of Revelation opens with the vision of the glorified Christ walking among the seven lampstands as High Priest (Rev. 1:9–20). He is here pictured as fulfilling the covenant promise given to ancient Israel: "I will also walk among you and be your God, and you will be My people" (Lev. 26:12). In walking among the churches, Christ is serving them individually. He knows everything about each one of them. Much more than that, he has the solution to their problems and needs. This is the reason why he commissions John to write the things revealed to him and pass them on to the churches (Rev. 1:11). Each of the messages to the churches begins by introducing Christ and concludes with an appeal to listen to the Spirit. In between is Christ's special message suited to the actual situation, condition, and needs of the respective church to which it is addressed, together with the particular historical situation of the city in which the church was located. Christ makes visits to help each church prepare to meet the coming crisis. If the churches want to make a decisive "turnaround," they need only to listen to the messages of the One who knows them.

The first three chapters of Revelation, together with the special introduction of Christ, provide the foundation upon which the prophetic portion of the book (chapters 4–22:5) builds. These chapters define the nature and purpose of the entire book of Revelation—to reassure the church throughout history of Christ's perennial promise: "Lo, I am with you always, even to the end of the age" (Matt. 28:20).

2. OPENING OF THE SEALED SCROLL (REV. 4–11) WITH THE OPENING VISION OF CHRIST AS THE ESCHATOLOGICAL RULER (CHAPS. 4–5)

The second major division of Revelation is introduced with the vision of Christ as the promised king of Davidic lineage (chapters 4–5). This introductory scene depicts in figurative language the inauguration of the resurrected Christ into his universal dominion and lordship over the world. In taking the seven-sealed scroll—representing the transference of all authority and sovereignty to him—Christ was seated upon the throne of the universe at the right hand of the Father. Now the preordained eschatological ruler of Davidic lineage (cf. Rev. 5:5), "who, on the basis of the saving work completed by him, is called to discharge with authority God's plan for the end of history."[93]

Revelation 4–5 is thus the starting point for interpreting what chapters 6–11 describe. These chapters provide the panoramic survey of history in the scene of the opening of the seven seals and the blowing of the seven trumpets from Christ's ascension to heaven until his return to earth. The section describes "events and conditions within historical time which are preparatory to the opening" of the sealed scroll in the eschatological consummation.[94] It provides God's people with the assurance that, though they may experience oppression and hardship in a hostile world, they can have the certainty that their Lord and King who rules on the throne of the universe is in ultimate control. He will bring the history of this world to an ultimate end and deal permanently with the problem of evil.

3. CONTENTS OF THE SEALED SCROLL (REV. 12–22:5) WITH THE OPENING VISION OF CHRIST AS THE APOCALYPTIC MICHAEL (CHAP. 12)

The last of the three major divisions of the book of Revelation (12–22:5) appears to be the disclosure of a part of the sealed scroll of Revelation 5 (see "Overview: Revelation 12–22:5"). This section introduces the great conflict between Christ and Satan in 12:1–17 in which Christ is portrayed in his role as the apocalyptic warrior Michael. As the commander of the heavenly armies, Christ is a constant victor. He defeated Satan through his banishment from heaven and to earth, by his death on the cross and his ensuing ascension to the Father, and during the entire period of the Christian era. Satan is frustrated by constant defeat, and becomes furious with the "remaining ones of her [the woman's] offspring" (Rev. 12:17). With a firm determination to win the final battle, he associates himself with two allies—the sea beast and the earth beast. By forming the counterfeit trinity, he uses every available means to prevent the accomplishment of God's plans for the world. What follows in the rest of the book (chapters 13–22) is a description of the events leading to the conclusion of the cosmic drama and the ultimate establishment of God's eternal kingdom.

Revelation 12 is intended to provide God's people with assurance in the closing period of this world's history. The saints are clearly in the front line of the final battle described in Revelation 12. But just as Christ defeated Satan and fought the battle on behalf of his people during the history of Satan's attempt to destroy them, so he will be with his end-time people in the final crisis. The future may at times look gloomy, and the eschatological events threatening and frightening, yet the believers must remember that Satan has already lost the battle. Christ the Victor will wage war until the forces of darkness are finally defeated. The satanic triumvirate and the oppressors of God's people will find their end in the lake of fire (Rev. 19:20–20:15), while God's people will triumphantly find their rest in New Jerusalem (Rev. 21–22:5).

The foregoing brief analysis of the three introductory visions to the major divisions of the book of Revelation defines the main theme of the book as intended by the inspired author and explains the theological perspective of this commentary. It demonstrates that the purpose of the last book of the Bible is not just to warn about events in the world (whether historical or eschatological), but to help the faithful understand God's plan for them. It is not so much to reveal the future as to acquaint readers with the God of Revelation who holds the future. It provides them with the certainty of Christ's presence with his faithful people throughout history and, particularly, during the time of the end (cf. Matt. 28:20).

On the basis of the aforementioned threefold structure, we can observe the following outline of the book of Revelation:

1. *Prologue (1:1–8)*
   Introduction (1:1–3)
   Greetings and Doxology (1:4–6)
   The Theme of the Book (1:7–8)
2. *The Messages to the Seven Churches (1:9–3:22)*
   A. The Introductory Vision: Christ as Priest and Judge (1:9–20)
      John on Patmos (1:9–11)
      The Vision of the Glorified Christ (1:12–20)
   B. Christ's Messages to the Churches (2–3:22)
      The Message to the Church in Ephesus (2:1–7)
      The Message to the Church in Smyrna (2:8–11)
      The Message to the Church in Pergamum (2:12–17)
      The Message to the Church in Thyatira (2:18–29)
      The Message to the Church in Sardis (3:1–6)
      The Message to the Church in Philadelphia (3:7–13)
      The Message to the Church in Laodicea (3:14–22)
3. *The Opening of the Sealed Scroll (4–11:19)*
   A. The Introductory Vision: Christ as King (4–5:14)

The Heavenly Throne Vision (4:1–11)

The Seven–Sealed Scroll (5:1–14)

B. The Opening of the Seven Seals (6–8:1)

The Opening of the First Seal (6:1–2)

The Opening of the Second Seal (6:3–4)

The Opening of the Third Seal (6:5–6)

The Opening of the Fourth Seal (6:7–8)

The Opening of the Fifth Seal (6:9–11)

The Opening of the Sixth Seal (6:12–17)

The Interlude:

The Sealed Saints and the Great Multitude (7:1–17)

The Sealed Saints (7:1–8)

The Great Multitude (7:9–17)

The Opening of the Seventh Seal (8:1)

C. The Seven Trumpet Plagues (8:2–11:18)

The Introductory Scene: The Prayers of the Saints (8:2–6)

The First Trumpet (8:7)

The Second Trumpet (8:8–9)

The Third Trumpet (8:10–11)

The Fourth Trumpet (8:12–13)

The Fifth Trumpet (9:1–12)

The Sixth Trumpet (9:13–21)

The Interlude (10–11:14)

The Open Little Scroll (10:1–11)

The Two Witnesses and the Measuring of the Temple (11:1–14)

The Seventh Trumpet (11:15–18)

D. The Appearance of the Ark of God's Covenant in the Temple (11:19)

4. *The Contents of the Seven-Sealed Scroll (12–22:5)*

A. The Introductory Vision: Christ as Warrior (12:1–17)

The Woman, the Child, and the Dragon (12:1–6)

The War in Heaven (12:7–12)

Satan and the Seed of the Woman (12:13–17)

B. The Two Beasts (13:1–18)

The New Heaven and Earth (21:1–8)

The New Jerusalem (21:9–22:5)

5. *The Epilogue (22:6–21)*

ENDNOTES

1. William Barclay, *The Revelation of John*, 2d ed., The Daily Study Bible Series (Philadelphia, PA: Westminster Press, 1960), 1:2.

2. Ellen G. White, *Testimonies to Ministers and Gospel Workers* (Boise, ID: Pacific Press, 1962), 114.

3. Justin Martyr *Dialogue with Trypho* 81.15 (*The Ante-Nicene Fathers*, 1:240); Irenaeus *Against Heresies* 4.14.2; 4.20.11 (*The Ante-Nicene Fathers*, 1:479, 491); Tertulian *Against Marcion* 3.25 (*The Ante-Nicene Fathers*, 3:342); Clement of Alexandria *Stromata* 6.13 (*The Ante-Nicene Fathers*, 2:504); Hippolytus *Treatise on Christ and Antichrist* 36–42 (*The Ante-Nicene Fathers*, 5:211–212); Origen *Commentary on John* 2.45 (Fathers of the Church 80, 106).

4. See Elisabeth Schüssler Fiorenza, *Revelation: Vision of a Just World*, Proclamation Commentaries (Minneapolis, MN: Fortress Press, 1991), 44.

5. Donald Guthrie, *The Relevance of John's Apocalypse* (Grand Rapids, MI: Eerdmans, 1987), 56.

6. Merrill Tenney, *Interpreting Revelation* (Grand Rapids, MI: Eerdmans, 1957), 15.

7. Irenaeus *Against Heresies* 5.30.3 (*The Ante-Nicene Fathers*, 1:559–560).

8. For the objections to such a view, see Richard Bauckham, *The Climax of Prophecy* (Edinburgh: T&T Clark, 1993), 387–389.

9. Irenaeus *Against Heresies* 5.30.3 (*The Ante-Nicene Fathers*, 1:559–560); Victorinus *In Apocalupsi* 1.11; Eusebius *Historia Ecclesiae* 3.18.1 (*The Nicene and Post-Nicene Fathers*, 2d ser., 1:148); Jerome *Lives of Illustrious Men* 9 (*The Nicene and Post-Nicene Fathers*, 2d ser., 3:9).

10. *The Seventh-day Adventist Bible Commentary*, ed. F. D. Nichol, 2d ed. (Washington, DC: Review and Herald, 1980), 7:721.

11. Douglas Ezell, *Revelations on Revelation* (Waco, TX: Word Books, 1977), 26.

12. Martin Rist, "The Revelation of St. John the Divine," *The Interpreter's Bible* (Nashville, TN: Abingdon Press, 1957), 12:354.

13. G. B. Caird, *The Revelation of St. John the Divine*, Harper's New Testament Commentaries (New York: Harper and Row, 1966), 44. (Caird places the word "Satan" in bold, identifying it as coming directly from the scriptural passage which he is discussing.)

14. Kenneth A. Strand, "Foundational Principles of Interpretation," in *Symposium on Revelation—Book 1*, Daniel and Revelation Committee Series 6 (Silver Spring, MD: Biblical Research Institute, 1992), 13.

15. Jon Paulien, "Interpreting Revelation's Symbolism," in *Symposium on Revelation—Book 1*, Daniel and Revelation Committee Series 6 (Silver Spring, MD: Biblical Research Institute, 1992), 82.

16. Ezell, 18–19.

17. See George E. Ladd, *A Commentary on the Revelation of John* (Grand Rapids, MI: Eerdmans, 1972), 8.

18. In Ladd's words; ibid., 11.

19. Robert H. Mounce, *The Book of Revelation*, The New International Commentary on the New Testament (Grand Rapids, MI: Eerdmans, 1977), 43.

20. Ibid., 44.

21. William G. Johnsson, "The Saints' End-Time Victory Over the Forces of Evil," in *Symposium on Revelation—Book 2*, Daniel and Revelation Committee Series 7 (Silver Spring, MD: Biblical Research Institute, 1992), 9.

22. Ibid., 22.

23. See David E. Aune, *Revelation 1–5*, Word Biblical Commentary 52a (Waco, TX: Thomas Nelson Publishers, 1997), 105–106; see Gregory K. Beale, *The Book of Revelation*, The New International Greek Testament Commentary (Grand Rapids, MI: Eerdmans, 1998), 152–169, for possible objections to such a view.

24. Strand's distinction between "apocalyptic prophecy" and "classical prophecy" is problematic in many ways ("Foundational Principles of Interpretation," 11–26); Revelation proves to be rather a book of prophecy written in the apocalyptic style. Aune (*Revelation 1–5*, lxxxix) maintains that Revelation 1–3 has a more prophetic character, while he sees 4–22:9 to be an apocalypse.

25. Johnsson, 22.

26. Ibid.

27. Ibid.

28. See further Philip Mauro, *The Patmos Visions* (Boston, MA: Hamilton Brothers, 1925), 22–24.

29. Beale, 51.

30. Paulien, "Interpreting Revelation's Symbolism," 74.

31. Ibid., 75.

32. Elisabeth Schüssler Fiorenza, *The Apocalypse* (Chicago, IL: Franciscan Herald Press, 1976), 12; this reflects the important contribution made by Jon Paulien, *Decoding Revelation's Trumpets*, Andrews University Seminary Doctoral Dissertation Series 11 (Berrien Springs, MI: Andrews University Press, 1987), 10–121.

33. Paulien, "Interpreting Revelation's Symbolism," 80; Paulien argues that one must distinguish between Old Testament "direct allusions" and "echoes" in Revelation (see ibid., 83–92).

34. Henry B. Swete, *The Apocalypse of St. John* (New York: Macmillan Company, 1906; reprint, Grand Rapids, MI: Eerdmans, 1951), cxl–clviii.

35. William Milligan, *Lectures on the Apocalypse* (London: Macmillan, 1892), 76.

36. Ibid., 72.

37. Paulien, *Decoding Revelation's Trumpets*, 6.

38. Jon Paulien, *What the Bible Says About the End-Time* (Hagerstown, MD: Review and Herald, 1994), 135.

39. Paulien, "Interpreting Revelation's Symbolism," 80.

40. See Paulien, *What the Bible Says About the End-Time*, 41–71.

41. *The Seventh-day Adventist Bible Commentary*, 7:725.

42. Paulien, "Interpreting Revelation's Symbolism," 80.

43. Ibid., 78.

44. David Aune, *Revelation 1–5* (1997), *Revelation 6–16* (1998), and *Revelation 17–22* (1998), Word Biblical

Commentary, vols. 52abc (Waco, TX: Thomas Nelson Publishers). Other helpful sources are Barclay's two-volume *The Revelation of John*; Fiorenza, *Revelation: Vision of a Just World*; John P. M. Sweet, *Revelation*, TPI New Testament Commentaries (Philadelphia, PA: Trinity Press International, 1990).

45. Aune, *Revelation 1–5*, 104–105.

46. Fiorenza, *Revelation*, 59; Aune, "The Influence of Roman Imperial Court Ceremonial on the Apocalypse of John," *Biblical Research* 28 (1983): 5–9, 22–23; idem, *Revelation 1–5*, 275–374; Aune suggests the influence of the royal or imperial edict on the form of the seven messages to the churches of Revelation 2–3 ("The Form and Function of the Proclamations to the Seven Churches [Revelation 2–3]," *New Testament Studies* 36 [1990]: 182–204; *Revelation 1–5*, 126–129).

47. 2 Enoch 21:1 (James H. Charlesworth, *The Old Testament Pseudepigrapha* [Garden City, NY: Doubleday & Company, 1983], 1:134).

48. 4 Ezra 4:35–36 (Charlesworth, 1:531); see also 2 Baruch 21:19 (Charlesworth, 1:629).

49. See Bauckham, *The Climax of Prophecy*, 38–91.

50. Donatien Mollat, *Une Lecture pour aujourd'hui: L'Apocalypse*, 2d ed. (Paris: Les Editions du Cerf, 1984), 30.

51. Ezell, 29.

52. Robert Jamieson, A. R. Fausset, and David Brown, *A Commentary, Critical, Experimental, and Practical, on the Old and New Testaments*, rev. ed. (Grand Rapids, MI: Eerdmans, 1961), 1526.

53. See a list of parallels to the New Testament theological ideas and themes in Rudolf Halver, *Der Mythos im Letzten Buch der Bibel*, Theologische Forschung 32 (Hamburg-Bergstedt: Herbert Reich Evangelischer Verlag, 1964), 58–70; Swete, clvi–clviii.

54. Milligan, *Lectures on the Apocalypse*, 58.

55. Paulien, *Decoding Revelation's Trumpets*, 44 n. 2.

56. Ellen G. White, *Selected Messages* (Hagerstown, MD: Review and Herald, 1958), 1:21.

57. Ellen G. White, *The Acts of the Apostles* (Nampa, ID: Pacific Press, 1911), 581, 583.

58. Paulien, *What the Bible Says About the End-Time*, 111. (Original quotation was italicized.)

59. *The Seventh-day Adventist Bible Commentary*, 7:724.

60. Paulien, "Interpreting Revelation's Symbolism," 94.

61. Ibid., 83.

62. Aune, *Revelation 1–5*, xci–xcii.

63. Eugenio Corsini, *The Apocalypse: The Perennial Revelation of Jesus Christ*, Good News Studies 5 (Wilmington, DE: Michael Glazier, 1983), 62–63.

64. Jacques Ellul, *Apocalypse* (New York: Seabury Press, 1977), 36–45.

65. Tenney, 38.

66. Austin M. Farrer, *A Rebirth of Images* (Glasgow: University Press, 1949; reprint, Albany, NY: State University of New York Press, 1986), 45.

67. A. Yarbro Collins, *The Combat Myth in the Book of Revelation*, Harvard Dissertations in Religion 9 (Missoula, MT: Scholars Press, 1976), 13–39; idem, *The Apocalypse*, New Testament Message 22 (Wilmington, DE: Michael Glazier, 1979), xii–xiv; see also Alan Johnson, "Revelation," *The Expositor's Bible Commentary* 12

(Grand Rapids, MI: Zondervan, 1982), 411; on the criticism of this structure, see Bauckham, *The Climax of Prophecy*, 17, and Aune, *Revelation 1–5*, xciv.

68. See, e.g., Ernst Lohmeyer, *Die Offenbarung des Johannes*, Handbuch zum Neuem Testament 16 (Tübingen: J. C. B. Mohr, 1926), 181–185; J. W. Bowman, "Revelation, Book of," *The Interpreter's Dictionary of the Bible* (Nashville, TN: Abingdon Press, 1962), 4:64–70. For other representative sevenfold outlines, see Bowman, 66–67.

69. Gerhard A. Krodel, *Revelation*, Augsburg Commentary on the New Testament (Minneapolis, MN: Augsburg Fortress, 1989), 60.

70. Mounce, 46; for an extensive appraisal on the various approaches to the structure of Revelation, see Beale, 108–151.

71. Aune, *Revelation 1–5*, c–cv.

72. Revelation 1:10b–20; 4–5:14; 8:2–6; 11:19; 15–16:17; 16:18–17:3a; 19:1–10; 21:5–11a; see Kenneth A. Strand, "The Eight Basic Visions in the Book of Revelation" (107–121), and "The 'Victorious-Introduction Scenes' in the Visions in the Book of Revelation" (267–288), in *Andrews University Seminary Studies* 25 (1987). Both were reprinted with some modifications in *Symposium on Revelation—Book 1*, Daniel and Revelation Committee Series 6 (Silver Spring, MD: Biblical Research Institute, 1992), 35–72.

73. Richard M. Davidson, "Sanctuary Typology" (112–115), and Jon Paulien, "Seals and Trumpets: Some Current Discussions" (187–188) in *Symposium on Revelation—Book 1*, Daniel and Revelation Committee Series 6 (Silver Spring, MD: Biblical Research Institute, 1992); Jon Paulien, "The Role of the Hebrew Cultus, Sanctuary, and Temple in the Plot and Structure of the Book of Revelation," in *Andrews University Seminary Studies*, 33.2 (1995): 247–255; Aune also notes these introductory temple scenes (see *Revelation 1–5*, xcvii–xcviii). The point of departure between Davidson and Paulien and Strand is Revelation 16:18–17:3a which Strand treats as an introductory vision with temple setting that sets chaps. 17–18 as a separate vision. Paulien sees chaps. 17–18 as an elaboration of the seven-bowls vision of chaps. 15–16.

74. Aune, "The Influence of Roman Imperial Court," 7.

75. Paulien, "Seals and Trumpets," 188. The following section of the chapter (including the table) is taken from Paulien's "Seals and Trumpets," 187–189.

76. Paulien summarizes the parallels in "The Role of the Hebrew Cultus," 225–256; Daniel T. Niles (*As Seeing the Invisible* [New York: Harper & Brothers, 1961], 112–114) was the first who noted the connection between Revelation 1–8 and the Mishnah, but, as Paulien notes, he unsuccessfully attempts to pursue the parallels throughout the book. See Alberto R. Treiyer's criticism of the comparison (*The Day of Atonement and the Heavenly Judgment* [Siloam Springs, AR: Creation Enterprises International, 1992], 669–672).

77. The following parallels reflect Paulien's study (see the Mishnah *Tamid* 1–7, trans. Herbert Danby [London: Oxford University Press, 1974], 582–589).

78. Paulien, "The Role of the Hebrew Cultus," 256.

79. Kenneth A. Strand, "An Overlooked Old-Testament Background to Revelation 11:1," *Andrews University Seminary Studies* 22 (1984): 322–325.

80. Paulien, "The Role of the Hebrew Cultus," 256–257.

81. Including Farrer; M. D. Goulder, "The Apocalypse as an Annual Cycle of Prophecies," *New Testament Studies* 27 (1981): 342–367; Niles; Davidson, "Sanctuary Typology," 119–125; Paulien, "Seals and Trumpets," 190–192; idem, "The Role of the Hebrew Cultus," 257–261. This entire section reflects Davidson's and Paulien's research.

82. Paulien, "The Seals and Trumpets," 258.

83. Goulder, 355.

84. Paulien, "The Seals and Trumpets," 190.

85. Davidson, 122.

86. Ibid., 123.

87. Paulien, "The Role of the Hebrew Cultus," 259–260.

88. For the second-temple practice of the Feast of Tabernacles, see Mishnah *Sukkah* 1–5 (Danby, 172–181).

89. See E. Schüssler Fiorenza, "Composition and Structure of the Apocalypse," *The Catholic Biblical Quarterly* 30 (1968): 344–356; idem, *Revelation*, 35–36; Beale (*The Book of Revelation*, 131) proposes a ninefold structure.

90. Kenneth A. Strand, *Interpreting the Book of Revelation* (Worthington, OH: Ann Arbor Publishers, 1976), 43–59; C. Mervyn Maxwell follows the same division (*The Message of Revelation*, God Cares 2 [Boise, ID: Pacific Press, 1985], 60–61).

91. David Marshall, *Apocalypse* (Alma Park: Autumn House, 2000), 57; a constructive criticism of Strand's view is offered by Norman R. Gulley, "Revelation 4–5: Judgment or Inauguration?" *Journal of the Adventist Theological Society* 8.1–2 (1997), 64–65; see also Paulien, "The Seals and Trumpets," 192.

92. For structural parallels between the two texts, see William H. Shea, "Revelation 5 and 19 as Literary Reciprocals," *Andrews University Seminary Studies* 22 (1984), 251–257.

93. Jürgen Roloff, *The Revelation of John*, The Continental Commentary (Minneapolis, MN: Fortress, 1993), 76.

94. Strand, *Interpreting the Book of Revelation*, 57.

PROLOGUE

*"Blessed is the one who reads and the ones listening
to the words of the prophecy and keeping the things
that are written in it, for the time is near."*

PROLOGUE
REVELATION 1:1–8

The opening eight verses of Revelation form the prologue which provides a general summary and vital information about the contents of the entire book. The Prologue explains how and for what purpose the book was written, introduces the book's author, and describes the nature and main themes of Revelation, thus setting the tone for the rest of the book. It consists of three parts: the introductory section (1:1–3), the greetings and doxology (1:4–6), and the statement of the book's main theme (1:7-8).

INTRODUCTION (1:1–3)

The first part of the prologue is a typical ancient-letter introduction. The author first gives the title of the book; then he provides some basic information about the book's author, how the revelation was received, the nature and purpose of the book, and how the book should be read.

> **¹The revelation of Jesus Christ, which God gave him to show to his servants the things which must soon take place, and he signified it by sending it through his angel to his servant John, ²who testified to all that he saw, that is, the word of God and the testimony of Jesus Christ. ³Blessed is the one who reads and the ones listening to the words of the prophecy and keeping the things that are written in it, for the time is near.**

NOTES

1:1 *Revelation of Jesus Christ.* The word "revelation" comes from the Greek word *apokalupsis* (the Apocalypse) which is a compound word consisting of *apo* ("away from") and *kalupsis* ("a veiling" or "a covering"). Thus, "apocalypse" means "an unveiling" or "an uncovering." The term denotes a disclosure of something that was previously concealed, hidden, or secret.[1] In the New Testament, it is used exclusively with reference to divine revelation (cf. Luke 2:32; Rom. 16:25; Eph. 3:5).

The phrase "of Jesus Christ" can be interpreted as either a subjective or an objective genitive. It may refer to Christ as the One who reveals ("revelation from Jesus Christ"), or as the One who is revealed ("revelation about Jesus Christ"). Grammatically, either is possible. The context favors the former as the primary meaning, because Jesus receives the revelation and conveys it to John. "I, Jesus, have sent my angel to testify to you these things for the churches" (22:16). The text, however, identifies God the Father as the author of the Apocalypse (1:1; 22:6) rather than Jesus Christ, who is in the book as a mediator of the revelation. Yet Christ in his post-resurrection activities on behalf of his people is the dominant character from the very outset of the book (cf. 1:12–20). He is clearly the content of the Apocalypse, which suggests strongly that the second meaning is equally implied here. While the book is the "revelation from Jesus Christ," it is at the same time also the "revelation about Jesus Christ" and his salvific activities on behalf of his faithful people.

The things which must soon take place. The phrase "the things which must take place" (Gr. *ha dei genesthai*; repeated in 22:6) echoes in particular Daniel 2:28 of the Greek Old Testament in the story of Daniel relating to Nebuchadnezzar's dream and its interpretation. The phrase also reflects Jesus' discourse on the Mount of Olives (Matt. 24:6; Mark 13:7; Luke 21:9). In the light of these background texts, the word "must" should be understood to denote not the necessity of blind chance but "the sure fulfillment of the purpose of God revealed by the prophets."[2]

Signified. The Greek word *sēmainō* ("to signify," "to show by a sign or symbol," "to explain," "to convey in a sign or symbol," "to make known") means specifically to convey or make known by some sort of sign.[3] In other places in the New Testament, the word is used consistently for a figurative presentation that pointed to a future event. Jesus signified "the kind of death by which he was to die" (John 12:33; 18:32; cf. 21:19). The prophet Agabus signified under the inspiration of the Spirit a great famine during the reign of Claudius (Acts 11:28). The word *sēmainō* ("*sign*-i-fy") in Revelation 1:1 indicates that the visions of Revelation were communicated to John in figurative or symbolic presentation.

1:2 Who testified to all that he saw. The verb "testify" or "to witness" (*martureō*) is the past tense, the so-called epistolary aorist, which suggests that John was writing his book with his readers in mind; for when they read Revelation from their point in time, his testimony would be in the past. The verb *martureō* occurs only here and in 22:16, 18, 20 and refers to communicating the divine revelation.

The word of God and the testimony of Jesus Christ. Three times the phrases "the word of God" and "the testimony of Jesus" are conjoined in the book of Revelation (1:2, 9; 20:4). "The word of God" in the Old Testament functions as a technical expression for the message ("the word of the Lord") that the prophets received from God (Jer. 1:2; Hos. 1:1; Joel 1:1; Jon. 1:1; Zeph. 1:1; Zech. 1:1). Sometimes the expression "the word of God" is supplemented with the phrase "which he saw" (Isa. 2:1; Mic. 1:1; Zech. 1:7). This suggests that "the word of God" in Revelation must be understood in the same way that "the word of the Lord" is in the Old Testament. That John refers to "all that he saw" as "the word of God" suggests that he considers himself to be in the line of the Old Testament prophets, and that the book of Revelation has all the authority of Old Testament prophecy.[4] The context indicates that the expression "the testimony of Jesus Christ" in Greek here is the subjective genitive. The phrase refers to "the word of God" that Jesus communicated to John in visionary presentation ("that John saw").[5] "The word of God and the testimony of Jesus" are thus the things that John saw. When John writes down "all that he saw," the book is called "the words of the prophecy [of this book]" (Rev. 1:3; 22:7, 10, 18), that is, the book of Revelation, "to show to his servants the things which must soon take place" (Rev. 1:1). Revelation 19:10 further defines "the testimony of Jesus" as "the spirit of prophecy," that is, "the Spirit who speaks through the prophets."[6]

1:3 *Blessed is the one who reads and the ones listening.* This reference denotes the public reading of the book in a church setting. The word for "blessed" in Greek is *makarios* ("happy"), from which the word "macarism" ("happiness") is derived. It is the same word used by Jesus in the Beatitudes of the Sermon on the Mount (Matt. 5:3–12). In the New Testament, the word means more than just happiness in the mundane sense; it refers to "the deep inner joy of those who have long awaited the salvation promised by God and who now begin to experience its fulfillment. The *makarioi* are the deeply or supremely happy."[7]

This is the first of seven beatitudes in the book of Revelation:

- "Blessed is the one who reads and the ones listening to the words of the prophecy" (1:3)
- "Blessed are the dead who die in the Lord from now on" (14:13)
- "Blessed is the one who watches and keeps his garments" (16:15)
- "Blessed are those who are invited to the wedding supper of the Lamb" (19:9)
- "Blessed and holy is the one who has a part in the first resurrection" (20:6)
- "Blessed is the one who keeps the words of the prophecy of this book" (22:7)
- "Blessed are those who wash their robes" (22:14)

The following outline demonstrates the careful chiastic structure of these seven beatitudes:

A 1:3 – reading the book
  B 14:13 – death
    C 16:15 – keeping the garment
    C' 19:9 – the wedding supper
  B' 20:6 – death
A' 22:7 – reading the book
D 22:14 – to wash the robes

A correlation can be observed between the first, second, and third beatitudes and the sixth, fifth, and fourth beatitudes, respectively. The first and the sixth open and close the book of Revelation, while the second beatitude parallels the fifth, and the third matches the fourth. The seventh one appears to be the climax of the beatitudes, stating that the genuine happiness of Christ's followers is found in the washing of their robes of character. This sevenfold blessing of the book is balanced by the sevenfold occurrence of the words "woe" and "alas" (8:13; 9:12; 11:14; 12:12; 18:10, 16, 19).[8]

EXPOSITION

The introductory part of the prologue stresses points which are important for understanding the difficult parts of the book which come later. It first of all identifies God as the source of the revelation who speaks through his Son and shows his people the things that must take place.

1:1 John opens his book with the phrase *the revelation of Jesus Christ* which functions as the title of the book. It names the book the "Revelation [apocalypse] of Jesus Christ." This can be understood in two ways: either that the visions given to John were from Jesus Christ or that he, Jesus Christ, is the person revealed. It is most likely that both concepts are intended. The book of Revelation is the unveiling of Jesus Christ—his revelation—in which he reveals his post-Calvary ministry on behalf of the church. Revelation, just as the Scriptures of the Old Testament (John 5:39), testifies about Christ.

As such, the last book of the Bible begins where the four gospels end. In the gospels, Jesus Christ is described as a man from Nazareth like all other human beings. The book of Revelation explains that at his ascension Christ was seated on the throne of the universe at the right hand of the Father. There, he is no longer a man of sorrows, but the King and Lord over the entire universe.

Readers of the book of Revelation must understand from the start that the last book of the Bible is not just "the revelation" (as it is commonly referred to) of horrible events to come (such as the battle of Armageddon, famines, persecution, or judgments of God). Rather, the book clearly states that it is the revelation *of Jesus Christ*. It was intended to create a portrayal of Christ that can be found nowhere else. The book points to Christ as the One who is the A to Z (of history), "the beginning and the end" (21:6; 22:13), and "the first and the last" (1:17; 2:8; 22:13). He is the very content of Revelation. Take Christ out of the book, and it would become a "Hollywood apocalypse" of horrible things and bizarre events—a book presenting a frightening future without any hope.

The last book of the Bible contains the gospel of Jesus Christ in the full meaning of the word "gospel"—"the good news." Kenneth A. Strand puts it in the following way:

In Scripture there is assurance that God has always cared for His people: that in history itself He is ever present to sustain them, and that in the great eschatological denouement He will give the full vindication and an incomprehensibly generous reward in life everlasting. The book of Revelation picks up and expands beautifully this same theme, and thus Revelation is not by any means some sort of offbeat apocalypse that is out of tune with biblical literature in general; it conveys the very heart and substance of the biblical message. Indeed, as Revelation emphatically points out, the "Living One"—the One who conquered death and the grave (1:18)—will never forsake His faithful followers and that even when they suffer martyrdom they are victorious (12:11), with the "crown of life" awaiting them (see 2:10; 21:1–4; and 22:4).[9]

John next spells out the purpose of Revelation. It was intended to show God's people *the things which must soon take place.* This phrase points, first of all, to Daniel 2:28 where Daniel declares to Nebuchadnezzar that there is a "God in heaven who reveals mysteries," and he makes known to the king "the things which must take place in the last days." John was evidently employing this phrase with Daniel 2 in mind. Furthermore, on the Mount of Olives Jesus pointed to the things that "must happen" before the Second Coming (Matt. 24:6; Mark 13:7; Luke 21:9). John is telling his readers that the purpose of Revelation is to ensure that God will bring to fulfillment the things which were predicted by Daniel, and which were further pointed out and outlined by Jesus in the discourse on the Mount of Olives.

The fact that some events *must* take place before the end comes indicates that history is not accidental in Revelation. As Jürgen Roloff states, "events in the world are shaped neither by blind chance nor by human initiative but rather unfold according to a plan decided by God before all eternity."[10] It is with the cross that earth's history has entered its final phase. Between the cross and the Second Coming are certain things that *must* happen so that God's plan, revealed through John, might be fulfilled here on the earth. The purpose of the book is to explain from God's perspective why and how those events are going to happen. Its purpose is not to satisfy our obsessive curiosity about the future, but to assure us that God holds that future.

It is also important to note that the prophecies of Revelation tell us what will happen at the time of end to move us to readiness. The things that are important and profitable for our salvation and entry into the kingdom are revealed to us in the prophetic word. What Revelation does not show us is exactly when and how the events will take place. It seems that these things are not intended to be revealed to us.

"The secret things belong to the Lord our God, but the things revealed belong to us" (Deut. 29:29). Humans are unable to know divine secrets; the timing and manner of the unfolding of the final events are secrets that God has reserved for himself (Matt. 24:36; Acts 1:7). Exactly when and how the final events will take place will be clear at the time of their fulfillment, not before.

It appears, however, that the portrayal of future events, especially those to unfold at the time of the end, have a deeper intention. These events, as bizarre and frightening as they might be, are recorded to impress upon our minds Christ's promise to be with his people "always, until the very end of the age" (Matt. 28:20). Christ in his wisdom knew that the full impact of his promise to be with us during the final events would not be very effective without unpacking them in the prophetic word. Their graphic portrayal has the goal of impressing upon us a seriousness about the final crisis and our dependency on God. Their unfolding to God's people will be a reminder of Christ's promise to be present with them and sustain them during those difficult times. "These things I have spoken to you," Jesus said, "so that when their hour comes, you may remember that I told you of them" (John 16:4). "When these things begin to take place, lift up your heads, because your redemption is drawing near" (Luke 21:28).

The book of Revelation is in line with the heart and substance of the biblical message. The book nowhere promises that God will take the faithful out of the trials of life. It rather provides an assurance that Christ will walk with his faithful people through the trials of life. He will be with them *always*, until the very end of the age.

Next, the text states that the events in Revelation must take place *soon* (1:1, 3; 22:6). Even in John's day, the Second Coming is portrayed as "soon" (cf. Rev. 2:16; 3:11; 22:7, 12, 20). How should we understand this imminence of the end in light of the fact that almost two thousand years have passed since the promise was given through John? It seems clear that John focuses not on the final fulfillment of the prophecies with regard to the end but on the beginning of the fulfillment. This "soon" must, first of all, be understood from God's perspective. With him a thousand years is like one day (2 Pet. 3:8). The realization of his plans regarding the earth has entered the final phase.[11] Thus, from his perspective, "the time is near" (Rev. 1:3). For Satan, then, his time is short (Rev. 12:10–12). The cross has made him a defeated enemy. The realization that his time is short makes him determined to prevent the accomplishment of God's purpose in the world more than ever before. This "soon" has a special application with reference to the people of the earth. We do not know when Jesus will come, whether today or tomorrow. The time and opportunity to be ready for his coming is always now, rather than in the future. The readers of the Apocalypse are urged to realize the imminence of the Second Coming in their own time.[12] Jesus' coming was "soon" even in John's time; since then, it has been potentially near for every generation.

John explains further that the revelation given to him is **signified** by Jesus Christ. The contents of Revelation are not photographic descriptions of the heavenly realities or coming events to be understood in a literal way; they are rather expressed in figurative or symbolic language. Revelation speaks in the pictorial manner. While the scenes and events predicted are themselves literal and real, they were shown to John in vision through symbolic presentations.

The text seems to indicate that it is not John but God who chose the symbols of Revelation. God meets people where they are. When he communicated his message to John, he did it in the language that the aged prophet could understand. What John saw in vision he now records, under the inspiration of the Holy Spirit, in his own words. In writing it down, however, he often found the human language inadequate to describe the heavenly realities. Therefore, he often added his own symbols, using the words "like" and "as" to explain and clarify the things he had seen in vision.

It is important, therefore, for modern readers of Revelation to remember its symbolic nature. Messages come not through a literal understanding of its contents but through the interpretation of symbols. Keeping this in mind will safeguard us against a literal understanding of many symbols in the book. Reading the rest of the Bible presupposes a literal understanding of what is found in the text unless it is clear that a symbolic understanding is intended. However, studying Revelation calls for a symbolic understanding of the scenes and events recorded, unless the text indicates clearly that a literal meaning is intended.

Determining what should be understood symbolically and what should be taken literally is not always an easy task for the interpreter of Revelation. While some symbols are defined in the book (cf. 1:20; 12:9; 17:9–11, 15), most are not explained. In trying to understand the symbols, we must be careful not to impose on the text a meaning that comes out of allegorical imagination or from the current meaning of those symbols. The interpretive key of the book's symbols is not allegory but typology. The meaning of the symbols must be controlled by the intention of the inspired author as well as by the meaning the symbols conveyed to those to whom Revelation was originally addressed.

It is important to keep in mind that the prophecies of Revelation were communicated in the language of the time and place of the inspired author rather than our own. That language was of the apocalyptic symbolism commonly known in the ancient world. Revelation 1:3 clearly indicates that John, guided by the Holy Spirit, described his visions in symbols and images that would have been generally understood by the first-century Christians in Asia Minor. The language reflected the daily realities of their historical, social, cultural, and religious milieu. As such, the symbols of Revelation appealed, and still do, "not only to the intellect but also to the emotions of the reader or hearer."[13] The first task in determining the meaning of the figurative language, therefore, is to discover how the original recipients, namely, the Christians of John's day, would have understood it.

Careful study indicates that most of the book's symbolism is drawn from the Old Testament. Revelation is replete with scenes and images from sacred history. Names in the book—such as Jezebel, Moses, David, Sodom, Egypt, Babylon, Jerusalem, and the Euphrates River—as well as motifs expressed in terms of the lamb, trumpets, locusts from the abyss, Mount Zion, the song of Moses, the drying up of the river Euphrates, the temple and its articles, and hundreds of others are all taken from the Old Testament. In portraying the events to take place in the future, inspiration employs the language of the past.

The prophecies of Revelation are especially built on key Old Testament events such as creation, the flood, the exodus, God's covenant with King David, and the Exile. The allusions to these events were intended to impress on the minds of God's people the truth that God's acts of salvation in the future will be very much like his acts of salvation in the past. The hope of God's people with reference to the future is firmly grounded on what God did for his people in the past. The same almighty God who was ever present with his people in the past will be also with his people in the future.

However, while most symbolic language in Revelation is drawn from the Old Testament, the portrayal of many scenes that John witnessed in the visions is colored with contemporary Greco-Roman motifs and practices. Also, the language of Revelation reflects significantly the symbolism of Jewish apocalyptic writings (e.g., vicious beasts, heads, horns, stars, four winds of the earth, woman, and seven-headed dragon). These apocalyptic symbols and concepts were much a part of the people's vocabulary in the first century and the people understood them. Finally, numerous passages in the book have direct parallels with New Testament theological concepts and themes. Many concepts in Revelation reflect in particular on the sayings of Jesus and some statements of Paul. Paying careful attention to New Testament parallels to the various passages of Revelation opens up the potential for a broader understanding of the book's message.

Thus, a meaningful understanding of Revelation's messages must start with paying careful attention to the Old Testament as the primary source from which John gleaned the symbols and images in his book. Once the Old Testament background to a symbol is determined, efforts should be made to understand how the Old Testament images under consideration were transformed by the gospel. Then, a study should be given to the context in which the inspired author used that symbol to ascertain its adapted meaning.[14] This will help the reader to clarify many symbols of Revelation and understand the message the inspired author tried to convey in the text where each symbol occurs.

1:2 John **testified to all that he saw.** Revelation is authored by God.[15] Its messages are not a product of John's fertile imagination, but were shown to him by God in vision. As a faithful witness, the inspired prophet communicates all that he saw in vision. What John saw was **the word of God and the testimony of Jesus Christ.** The revelation of Jesus Christ is "the word of God" because God is its author. When Christ communicates the word of God to the prophet in a symbolic visionary presentation, it becomes "the testimony of Jesus Christ." According to Revelation 19:10, the testimony of Jesus is "the spirit of prophecy." John wrote out the testimony of Jesus and passed it on to God's people as the words of prophecy. John makes it very clear that the contents of the book of Revelation are not his ideas. He is just the bearer of divine revelation. The Apocalypse is, therefore, as much a book of prophecy (1:3; 22:7) as any Old Testament prophecy, and it should be approached and interpreted as a prophetic book.

1:3 The introduction to the prologue concludes with a promise: **Blessed is the one who reads and the ones listening.** This is the first of seven beatitudes in Revelation (1:3; 14:13; 16:15; 19:9; 20:6; 22:7, 14). The word "blessed" in the Bible means the supreme happiness of the recipients of the gospel. Therefore, the text may read: "Happy is the one who reads and those listening and observing the book of prophecy." In light of the fact that the number "seven" plays a crucial role in Revelation, denoting divine fullness and totality, it is probably not a coincidence that there are seven beatitudes in the last book of the Bible. They suggest that the fullness of blessing is promised to every Christian.[16]

In that the text promises special blessings of happiness to the reader and the listeners of the book of Revelation, no doubt reading in church is meant here. The reader is the person who reads publicly the book of prophecy—that is to say, the preacher—while the listeners are the assembled congregation listening to the reading. While the reading and the hearing of the prophecies are very important, the fullness of the blessing is pronounced particularly upon those **keeping** its messages. This blessing is repeated in the conclusion of the book: "Behold, I am coming soon. Blessed is the one who keeps the words of the prophecy of this book" (Rev. 22:7). Philip E. Hughes explains: "Reading or hearing is of course a preliminary necessity, but to heed the warnings and obey the precepts the prophecy contains is the essential response, apart from which all reading and hearing is worthless."[17]

The Apocalypse, accordingly, is not an ordinary book, but the word of prophecy—namely, the word of God and testimony of Jesus (1:2). It was sent to God's people to be read in the church setting and heard and observed by the whole community of believers. The person who reads its messages must make it understandable to the congregation. When listeners understand this book of prophecy as the revelation of Jesus Christ, they respond by accepting and observing its message as the word of God. Jesus recommended this when he said: "Blessed are those who hear the word of God and observe it" (Luke 11:28).

Happy indeed is the church which takes the word of God and the testimony of Jesus seriously, **_for the time is near._** The description of the time of the end and the final events in the book of Revelation is indeed very frightening. But the last book of the Bible is a constant reminder to God's people that Jesus Christ is and always will be with them, even to the end of the age (Matt. 28:20).

GREETINGS AND DOXOLOGY (1:4–6)

After providing the very basic information about the purpose and contents of his work, John addresses the original recipients of the book. The text contains the Trinitarian greetings that merge into a climatic song of praise to the glorified Christ for his great acts of salvation on behalf of his people.

⁴*John to the seven churches that are in Asia: Grace to you and peace from the One who is and who was and who is coming, and from the seven Spirits who are before his throne, ⁵and from Jesus Christ, the faithful witness, the first-born from the dead, and the ruler of the kings of the earth. To the One who loves us and released us from our sins by his blood, ⁶and made us a kingdom, priests to his God and Father, to him be glory and might forever and ever. Amen.*

NOTES

1:4 *Grace to you and peace.* This greeting formula is used by Paul and Peter at the beginning of their letters (cf. Rom. 1:7; 1 Cor. 1:3; 2 Cor. 1:2; Gal. 1:3; 1 Pet. 1:2; 2 Pet. 1:2), and might well have been a common greeting in the early church. It actually combines the customary Greek greeting word *charis* ("grace") with the Hebrew greeting word *shalom* ("peace"; Gr. *eirēnē*), which became a greeting widely used among the early Christians. The association of these two customary words here "goes beyond the level of human greetings and wishes: the writer tells his readers of the certainty of the end-time life of salvation (*shalom*) that has already begun in the gift of God's grace in Jesus Christ."[18]

The One who is and who was and who is coming. This tripartite title refers most likely to the great Old Testament covenant name *Yahweh* (cf. Exod. 3:14), expressing the eternal existence of God in the past, present, and future.[19] That the phrase undoubtedly refers to God the Father is seen in 1:8 and 4:8 where it is associated with another divine title, the Almighty. The title "the One who is and who was and who is coming" refers to "the eschatological 'visitation' of God."[20] The phrase here indicates at the very beginning that the end-time presence of God in the book of Revelation must be understood in light of both his past and future actions.

The seven Spirits. The plurality of the Holy Spirit occurs also in Revelation 22:6. "The seven Spirits before the throne of God" are identical to "the seven Spirits of God" in 3:1. Elsewhere in the book, "the seven Spirits of God" are portrayed as "seven torches of fire" burning before the throne (4:5) and "seven eyes...sent out into all the earth" (5:6). The Old Testament background of this imagery is found first in the Greek translation (Septuagint) of Isaiah 11:2 where seven designations of the Spirit of the Lord are mentioned: the spirit of wisdom and understanding, the spirit of counsel and might, the spirit of knowledge and godliness, and the spirit of the fear of God. Another reference is in Zechariah 4 where the prophet saw the seven lamps (4:2) which were to denote "the eyes of the Lord which range throughout the earth" (4:10). These refer to the activity of the Holy Spirit in the world (Zech. 4:6). John uses Zechariah's images in portraying the Holy Spirit in his sevenfold fullness.[21] The fact that "the seven Spirits" are here (Rev. 1:4–6) associated with the Father and Christ as the equal source of grace and peace strongly suggests that in 1:4 we have a reference to the sevenfold activity of the Holy Spirit on behalf of the churches. The number "seven" must, of course, be taken symbolically as divine fullness and perfection (see *Notes* on Rev. 5:1).

The seven "Spirits" parallel the seven churches in which the Spirit operates.[22] Each of the letters to the seven churches concludes with this exhortation: "He who has an ear, let him hear what the Spirit says to the churches." If the churches are a symbolic representation of the universality of the Christian church, then the meaning is clear: "the seven Spirits" seem to refer to the fullness and universality of the activity of the Holy Spirit on behalf of God's faithful people.

1:5 *The faithful witness, the first-born from the dead, and the ruler of the kings of the earth.* These three titles are evidently an allusion to Psalm 89 of the Greek Old Testament which is entirely about the Davidic covenant of 2 Samuel 7:8–16. In Psalm 89:27 and 37, the descendant of David is referred to as the first-born of Yahweh and "the highest of the kings of the earth." It is promised that he will be established on the throne as "the faithful witness in heaven."

Witness. The Greek word *martus* normally means "witness." Around the time the book of Revelation was written, many faithful witnesses in the early church had been killed for their faith. The word *martus* also came to mean "martyr," namely, "one who witnessed unto death" (cf. Rev. 2:13), whereas "the death of Jesus was regarded as the first martyrdom."[23]

The first-born from the dead. The Greek *prōtotokos* means literally "first-born" and is taken from Psalm 89:27 for David's descendant: "I also shall make him My first-born, the highest of the kings of the earth." This text was interpreted by Jewish scholars as a reference to the coming of the Messiah. The title "the first-born from the dead" is used by Paul in Colossians 1:18 where, as in Revelation 1:5, Jesus is declared the sovereign occupant of the first place of honor and glory (cf. Phil. 2:5–11). The phrase "the first-born from the dead" suggests that by virtue of his resurrection, Jesus occupies the first place of honor and supremacy and has highest authority over the earth as "the ruler of the kings of the earth" (1:5).

The One who loves us (lit. "the one loving us"). The present participle suggests a present and ongoing action: he loves us now and goes on loving us.

Released us from our sins is an aorist (past tense) participle pointing to an action completed at a point in time. Unlike the love of Jesus which is continuous and present, the release from sin is a past, completed action.

1:6 *Made us a kingdom, priests* is in the aorist indicative, denoting "what has been ideally or potentially accomplished in the purpose of God."[24]

EXPOSITION

1:4 *John to the seven churches that are in Asia.* The book of Revelation is introduced here as a letter. "John to the seven churches that are in Asia" reminds us of the letters of Paul: "Paul to the church of God that is in _____" (cf. 1 Cor. 1:1–2; 2 Cor. 1:1; Gal. 1:1–2; Phil. 1:1; 1 Thess. 1:1; 2 Thess. 1:1). Revelation claims further to be a prophecy (1:3; 22:7, 18–19), the messages of which are presented in the apocalyptic style (cf. 1:1). Therefore, it is a letter in prophetic-apocalyptic style originally sent to the seven historical churches situated in the Roman province of Asia (cf. 1:11), addressing their particular and immediate situations and needs.

These seven churches were obviously the real churches of Asia Minor. The fact that "seven" is a symbolic number in the book of Revelation, standing for fullness and totality, suggests that in writing to the seven churches in Asia, John was writing to the whole church throughout history.[25] The oldest list of the New Testament books, known as the Muratorian Canon (2nd cent.), says regarding the book of Revelation: "For John also in the Revelation writes indeed to seven churches, yet speaks to all."[26] This might well be true when we recall how John repeats over and over again: "He who has an ear, let him hear what the Spirit says to the churches" (2:7, 11, 17, 29; 3:6, 13, 22; cf. 13:9).

Grace and peace to you. This phrase is used as a common epistolary greeting in most of the New Testament letters. It is further evidence of the epistolary form of the book of Revelation. Widely used among the early Christians, it is more than a casual greeting. "Grace is the divine favor showed to man, and peace is that state of spiritual well-being which follows as a result."[27] As Bruce M. Metzger observes, the words "grace and peace" always stand in this order; it is never "peace and grace." Both words come from God, and remind us of "the favor and acceptance that God has extended to believers. And it is because of God's grace that his people can enjoy peace—peace with God as well as the peace of God, resulting in inner poise and tranquility, even amid the hardest experiences of life."[28]

This grace and peace comes from the three divine persons: ***from the One who is and who was and who is coming, from the seven Spirits who are before his throne, and from Jesus Christ, the faithful witness***. Although the word "trinity" does not appear in the book of Revelation (nor in the rest of the Bible), the very beginning of the book introduces the three persons of the Godhead working on behalf of God's end-time people. They are together the source of grace and peace to the church. This becomes especially significant in light of the fact that the second half of the book introduces the satanic trinity counterfeiting the true God and his salvific activity for his people (see "Overview: Revelation 12–22:5").

The first in the trinity of the persons is referred to as ***the One who is and who was and who is coming.*** This is a reference to the God of the Old Testament. In Exodus 3:14, God identified himself to Moses as "I am who I am." From here on, Yahweh is the name of the Old Testament covenant God. This shows that "the One who is and who was and who is coming" is nobody else but God the Father as the first person of the Godhead. The God who did marvelous things for his people in the past, and who is doing the things of salvation in the present, is the God who gives us the certainty and assurance that he keeps his promises with regard to our future. The same powerful and faithful God will stand and act on behalf of his people in the time of the end.

The second in the trinity of the persons is referred to as *the seven Spirits who are before his throne.* Here is a reference to the Holy Spirit. The number "seven" is symbolic and denotes the fullness and universality of the work of the Holy Spirit. "The seven Spirits" parallel the seven churches in which the Spirit operates. In the New Testament, there is an idea of the distribution of the Holy Spirit (Heb. 2:4) or its different manifestations in the church (1 Cor. 12:7; 14:32; Rev. 22:6). "So the idea here would be that the seven Spirits stand for the share of the Spirit which God gave to each one of the seven Churches."[29] Each church is urged to "hear what the Spirit says to the churches."

1:5 Jesus Christ completes the trinity of persons. *From Jesus Christ, the faithful witness, the first-born from the dead, and the ruler of the kings of the earth.* With these three titles, John describes who Jesus really is. First, he is the faithful witness (cf. 3:14). His entire life in the gospel of John is described as witnessing to the truth of God (John 3:11, 32–33; 8:13–14). Jesus said to Pilate: "For this I have come into the world, to bear witness to the truth" (John 18:37). He sealed his faithful witness by his death on the cross; his death thus has become the first martyrdom. However, Jesus is the first-born from the dead, or the firstfruits of the resurrection (1 Cor. 15:23). By virtue of his resurrection, he, the risen and glorified Christ, has become the ruler of the kings of the earth.

In the temptation story, Jesus was taken up by the Devil upon a high mountain and shown all the kingdoms of the earth and their glory. The Devil told Jesus that the kingdoms of the earth had been delivered to him (Luke 4:6) and offered him a bargain: "All these things I will give You, if You fall down and worship me" (Matt. 4:8–9; Luke 4:6–7). Jesus refused this compromise. The lordship over "the kingdoms of the earth," which the Devil offered him in return for worship, Jesus won for himself through his death on the cross and the resurrection. Now he reigns on the heavenly throne as the Lord over the universe (Rev. 3:21). It was after his resurrection that he made a claim: "All authority has been given to Me in heaven and on the earth" (Matt.

28:18). The manifestation of that authority was initiated when the Father "seated Him at His right hand in the heavenly places, far above all rule and authority and power and dominion, and every name that is named, not only in this age, but also in the one to come" (Eph. 1:20–21; cf. Rom. 1:4).

The Old Testament background for these three titles—the faithful witness, the first-born from the dead, and the ruler of the kings of the earth—is evidently in Psalm 89:27 and 37 of the Greek Old Testament, where the descendant of David is referred to as the first-born of Yahweh and "the highest of the kings of the earth" reigning on the throne as "the faithful witness" in heaven. These three titles identify Christ as the fulfillment of all the Old Testament promises and hopes. By virtue of faithful witnessing in his life on earth, the resurrection, and his powerful reign in heavenly places, Jesus Christ is everything that God's people need, especially as history is coming to its end.

1:5b–6 Having thus identified Jesus, John proceeds with a description of what Jesus does. What follows here is actually a doxology or an ancient song of praise for the mighty acts of God (cf. Rom. 11:36; Jude 24–25; Rev. 5:13). The doxology is about what Christ has done on behalf of his people: "To the One who loves us and released us from our sins by his blood, and made us a kingdom, priests to his God and Father, to him be glory and might forever and ever. Amen."

Christ's three activities correspond to his three titles, all of which are on behalf of his people. **To the One who loves us** means, as the Greek text indicates, that Jesus Christ loves us continually. Next, John presents two-fold evidence of Christ's ongoing love for his people. First of all, the One loving us has **released us from our sins by his blood.** A change of tense occurs here. The Greek speaks of one act completed in the past when, through his death on the cross, Christ loosed us once and for all from our sins by his blood. But, he loves us always. In other words, "what happened on the Cross was one availing act in time which was an expression of Christ's continuous love for us."[30]

Another evidence of Christ's perpetual love for his people is that **he made us a kingdom, priests to his God and Father** (cf. Rev. 5:9b–10; 20:6). This is the status that the redeemed have in Christ as a result of their redemption from sin. "They not only have been made part of his kingdom and his subjects, but they have also been constituted kings together with him and share his priestly office by virtue of their identification with his death and resurrection."[31] In the ancient world, kings and priests held the most powerful status with reference to the political and religious realms. The designation of a kingdom of priests is drawn from the Old Testament and built on the experience of the Exodus. Because God continually loved Israel (Deut. 7:6–8), he delivered them from the oppression of Egypt and promised through Moses that they would be his own possession and chosen people among the nations. Israel was to be God's kingdom of priests in the world (Exod. 19:5–6). Failing to keep the covenant with God, Israel did not fulfill the role of priest. In the New Testament, the titles and privileges offered to ancient Israel are now the possession of Christians as the true Israel (cf. 1 Pet. 2:9–10). As with Israel in the Exodus, so the New Testament people of God are always loved by Christ and released from the bondage of sin and made kings and priests to God.

A basic difference exists between the message to ancient Israel and what is said to the church, however. The future promise to Israel ("You shall be to me a kingdom of priests") is given to the Christians as something that has already taken place in the past. The followers of Christ have been already made a kingdom and priests (cf. also Rev. 5:10). The same idea is expressed in 1 Peter 2:9: "You are a chosen race, a royal priesthood, a holy nation." It is because of Christ's perpetual love and the great deliverance from the bondage of sin that his followers are already elevated to the glorious status of "a kingdom and priests." According to Paul, Christians are raised with Christ and made to sit with him in the heavenly places in Jesus Christ (Eph. 2:6). "So then you are no longer strangers and aliens but you are fellow citizens with the saints, and are of God's household" (Eph. 2:19). God's saved people are already elevated in the heavenly places, participating with Jesus in his glory, although presently they must live in this world. In contrast, those outside the divine grace are consistently referred to as "the ones who dwell on the earth" (cf. Rev. 6:10; 8:13; 11:10; 13:8, 14; 14:6).

The fact that a Christian is a citizen of heaven creates a constant awareness that this world is not home (cf. Phil. 3:20). The *Seventh-day Adventist Bible Commentary* explains: "Attachment to one's country leads him to be loyal to it. Wherever he may be living he will conduct himself in a way that will honor the good name of his country. Keeping in mind the kind of life we expect to live in heaven, serves to guide us in our life on earth. The purity, humility, gentleness, and love we anticipate experiencing in the life to come may be demonstrated here below. Our actions should disclose that we are citizens of heaven."[32]

Though the redeemed are still on the earth, this amazing love makes them feel and live like kings and priests dwelling in heavenly places. Corporately, they are a "kingdom" of God—people united in Christ as the church of God in this world. Individually, they are priests. Like the priests in the Old Testament, they have immediate access to God. His presence gives the followers of Christ hope for the future. As the history of this world is quickly drawing to its end, they may always come "with confidence to the throne of grace," that they may "receive mercy and may find grace to help in time of need" (Heb. 4:16).

Because of Christ's continual love, his gift of freedom from the bondage of sin, and the new glorious status as kingdom and priests to which he has elevated his people, Christ is worthy to receive *glory and might forever and ever. Amen.* This is what praise to God is all about in the New Testament. When the people realize and understand what Christ has done for them, they spontaneously respond with a song of praise (cf. 2 Tim. 4:18; Heb. 13:21; 1 Pet. 4:11; 2 Pet. 3:14; Rev. 7:10). Here in Revelation, the praise is a response of the redeemed for Christ's perpetual love for his people, through which they have been given freedom from sin and raised to a glorious status in him. According to Revelation 14:7, this is exactly what end-time people are urged to do: "fear God and give him glory." To glorify and praise God is a reason to exist.

What a great beginning for the book of Revelation! One will certainly agree with Jon Paulien:

> The book of Revelation is not only a revelation of who Jesus Christ is, but it's a revelation of what we become when we unite with him. As glorious as Jesus is, we can participate in that glory if we but choose to unite our lives with him. The book of Revelation, above all, is a great appeal to God's people not to be constantly looking into the things of the world, not to be stuck in the sorrow and the troubles of this world, but to lift our eyes up, to see Jesus in heavenly places, to see that we have been elevated in these heavenly places with him. When we see this fresh status that we have in Jesus, then we can really get excited about praising him, and really get excited about serving him.[33]

John now will direct all attention to the central theme of his book—the soon return of Jesus Christ in glory and majesty.

THE THEME OF THE BOOK (1:7–8)

The conclusion of the prologue announces the theme of the book of Revelation with regard to the triumphant and glorious return of Jesus Christ to the earth.

> **⁷Behold, he is coming with the clouds**
> **and every eye will see him,**
> **even those who pierced him,**
> **and every tribe of the earth will mourn over him. Yes, amen.**
> **⁸ "I am the Alpha and the Omega," says the Lord God, "the One**
> **who is and who was and who is coming, the Almighty."**

NOTES

1:7 *He is coming* (Gr. *erchetai*). The futuristic present tense suggests an action to take place in the future as it is already occurring. The use of the futuristic present tense in this case stresses the certainty as well as the imminence of the Second Coming.

1:8 *The Alpha and the Omega.* Alpha is the first and Omega the last letter of the Greek alphabet. Later in Revelation, this phrase is interpreted as "the beginning and the end" (21:6) and "the first and the last" (22:13), namely, "from A to Z." Isaiah points to the eternal existence of God: "I am he, before me there was no God formed, and there will be none after me" (Is. 43:10b; cf. Isa. 41:4; 44:6; 48:12). The phrase "the Alpha and the Omega" is seen to express "not eternity only, but infinitude, the boundless life which embraces all while it transcends all."[34] The phrase "the first and the last" is used in Revelation 1:17 and 2:8 with reference to Christ.

The Almighty. The Greek word *pantokratōr* (the Almighty) is used in the Greek Old Testament for "The Lord of Sabaoth" ("The Lord of hosts"; cf. Hos. 12:5; Amos 9:5). Nine times in the book of Revelation (1:8; 4:8; 11:17; 15:3; 16:7, 14; 19:6, 15; 21:22) it refers to God's supremacy; it is best defined in the acclamation: "Our Lord God Almighty began to reign" (19:6).

EXPOSITION

1:7 Having described who Jesus is and what he has done, John directs his readers' attention to what Jesus will do: **Behold, he is coming with the clouds, and every eye will see him, even those who pierced him.** This solemn statement announces the theme of the book of Revelation. The literal and personal return of Christ to this earth is the event toward which all else moves in the book. His coming will mark the end of this world's history and the beginning of the eternal kingdom. In creating an impressive picture of the Second Coming, John links the portrayal of the "One like a son of man" coming on the clouds of Daniel 7:13 with the prophetic portrayal of the end time from Zechariah 12:10–14, where the inhabitants of Jerusalem look on the One they pierced and mourn for him. Then he links these two passages to Jesus' prophetic discourse on the Mount of Olives: "Then the sign of the Son of Man will appear in the sky, and then all the tribes of the earth will mourn, and they will see the Son of Man coming on the clouds of the sky with power and great glory" (Matt. 24:30).

The phrase "he is coming" refers to the future event as a present reality. Elsewhere in the book of Revelation, the Second Coming is mentioned in the present tense—"I am coming" (cf. Rev. 2:16; 3:11; 22:7, 12, 20)—as it is already occurring, rather than in the predictive future, "I will come." This denotes both the certainty of the Second Coming and its imminence. The certainty of Jesus' return is confirmed with the words "Yes, amen." In Greek it is *nai* and *amēn*. (*Nai* is the Greek word of affirmation, and *amēn* is the Hebrew.) When combined, the two words express an emphatic affirmation: "Yes, indeed." A similar thought appears at the end of the book: "'Yes, I am coming soon.' Amen. Come, Lord Jesus" (22:20).

The closing passage of the prologue is a reaffirmation of the eternally existent God, Yahweh. **I am the Alpha and the Omega, says the Lord God.** He is, as we would say, from A to Z. He is the one **who is and who was and who is coming, the Almighty.** This world history from the biblical perspective has both a meaningful beginning and conclusion because of Christ. The Second Coming is in reality the coming of the God who acts. He acted in the past, he is present now, and he always will be. A promise is as strong and trustworthy as the one giving the promise. Here it is given by the eternal and omnipresent God. The conclusion of this world's history will come not through "a gradual process" of either degradation or development, but through the coming of Christ in glory and majesty.[35] And the fulfillment of that promise is to come in accordance with his eternal nature and plans. The purpose of the book of Revelation is not primarily to inform us about the future, but to present the eternal and mighty God who holds the future. It assures Christians throughout history that no matter what the future brings, the eternally existent Almighty God is in control. He knows what the future brings and ultimately directs the course of history. And he is the originator of the revelation of Jesus Christ.

A RETROSPECT ON REVELATION 1:1–8

In working through these few verses, we have observed several things which seem to be of vital importance for interpreting the messages of Revelation. First of all, John makes clear from the very beginning that the book of Revelation revolves around two dominating themes. The first is Jesus Christ—who he is and what he does for his people. Christ is evidently the book's primary focus. He is the Alpha and the Omega, the first and the last of the book's messages. The second dominating theme is "the things which must soon take place," namely, the coming of Christ alongside the final events of this world's history. The Second Coming is the event toward which everything in the book moves.

Any interpretation making the Apocalypse only a revelation of the end misses the primary purpose of the book. John tells us clearly that his book is intended to be a revelation of Jesus Christ. The end-time theme has significance only in the light of what has already taken place on the cross. As we continue to work through the book and try to understand its strange images and scenes, we must remember that the book begins with the One who died on the cross and who is now the resurrected Lord on the throne of the universe in heavenly places. The Christ of Revelation is in control. The description of the end-time events in the book of Revelation may be quite daunting. Yet the same Christ who died on the cross has given to his people the promise which still stands firm: "Do not be afraid. Indeed, I am coming soon."

Ellen White warns against any preoccupation with the future: "Many will look away from the present duties, present comfort and blessings, and be borrowing trouble in regard to the future crisis. This will be making a time of trouble beforehand, and we will receive no grace for any such anticipated troubles."[36] She also adds: "There is a time of trouble coming to the people of God, but we are not to keep that constantly before the people....There is to be a shaking among God's people, but this is not the present truth to carry to the churches."[37]

The prologue also indicates that the book of Revelation is a letter in the prophetic-apocalyptic style. At least two vital points must be stressed here. Like the letters of Paul, the Apocalypse was sent originally to the Christian communities in Asia Minor. It addressed real-life situations and problems. Though presented in figurative language, its messages were generally understood by those first-century Christians. In order to discern the meaning of those terms and images, we must first endeavor to determine how the readers of those Christian communities in Asia Minor understood the figurative presentations.

Beyond being a letter, the book of Revelation is also a book of prophecy. Although it was sent originally to the churches of the first century, its messages were intended for Christians throughout time. As such, the book of Revelation still speaks to us today as it spoke to Christians of John's day. The book traces the history of this world from the cross to the Second Coming with a clear focus on the time of the end. Its message is that God holds the future which he has revealed to us through his servants the prophets. The prophetic word is not given to satisfy somebody's obsessive curiosity about the future, but to stimulate God's people to right living today.[38] There are some things in the book with regard to the future which we may never be able to understand completely before they occur. Before his departure, Jesus cautioned his disciples: "Now I have told you before it happens, so that when it happens, you may believe" (John 14:29; cf. 13:19). Ellen White makes this statement: "We are not now able to describe with accuracy the scenes to be enacted in our world in the future, but this we do know, that this is a time when we must watch unto prayer, for the great day of the Lord is at hand."[39] The purpose of Revelation is to prepare us to understand God's plan for us as the earth approaches its end. Rather than being a revelation about the time of the end, the book is the revelation of Christ with his people in the time of the end.

Finally, the prologue provides us with the basic structure of the book of Revelation. The introduction of the prologue (1:1–3) informs us that the contents of Revelation were passed down to the church through a chain of transmission from God to Jesus Christ who communicates the revelation through his angel to John. John records the word of God and the testimony of Jesus and then passes it on to the church in the form of a book of prophecy. What we see here is a three-part process:

a. Jesus receives the revelation from God,
b. Jesus sends his angel who communicates the
   revelation to John, and
c. John communicates to the churches the things which
   he saw in vision as the word of prophecy.

This transmission of the revelation will be found later in the book. First, in chapter 5, we see Jesus receiving the revelation from God the Father in the form of a sealed book. Then, in chapter 10, a mighty angel gives John a book which is now open.

After receiving the book, John is ordered to communicate its message to the people as a word of prophecy (10:11). Since Revelation 12:1 is a completely new section, it appears that Revelation 12–22:5 describes the content of the sealed book.

This chain of transmission shows significantly that the messages of the book of Revelation are not something that originated with John. Peter warned his readers: "But know this first of all, that no prophecy of Scripture is a matter of one's own interpretation...but men moved by the Holy Spirit spoke from God" (2 Pet. 1:20–21). The messages of Revelation originated in the heavenly places with Jesus. They were communicated to John by means of visions in figurative presentations. John wrote out what he saw and sent it to God's people as a word of prophecy. It is the duty of God's people to pay attention to the prophetic word "as to a lamp shining in a dark place, until the day dawns and the morning star arises in your hearts" (2 Pet. 1:19). This is precisely what Jesus stated: "I am coming soon. Blessed is the one who keeps the words of the prophecy of this book" (Rev. 22:7).

ENDNOTES

1. Tenney, 28.

2. Swete, 2.

3. F. J. A. Hort, *The Apocalypse of St. John* (London: Macmillan, 1908), 6; Aune, *Revelation 1–5*, 15.

4. Aune, *Revelation 1–5*, 19.

5. Strand attempts, unsuccessfully in my view, to show that "the word of God and the testimony of Jesus" are the Old and New Testaments ("The Two Witnesses of Rev 11:3–12," *Andrews University Seminary Studies* 19.2 [1981]: 127–135).

6. Bauckham, *The Climax of Prophecy*, 160.

7. Donald A. Hagner, *Matthew 1–13*, Word Biblical Commentary 33a (Dallas, TX: Word Books, 1993), 91.

8. William H. Shea, "The Covenantal Form of the Letters to the Seven Churches," *Andrews University Seminary Studies* 21 (1983): 74.

9. Kenneth A. Strand, "The Seven Heads: Do They Represent Roman Emperors?" in *Symposium on Revelation—Book 2*, Daniel and Revelation Committee Series 7 (Silver Spring, MD: Biblical Research Institute, 1992), 206.

10. Roloff, 19.

11. Ibid.

12. Jon Paulien, The Bible Explorer, Audiocassette Series (Harrisburg, PA: TAG, 1996), 2:1.

13. Fiorenza, *Revelation*, 40.

14. *The Seventh-day Adventist Bible Commentary*, 7:725.

15. Fiorenza, *Revelation*, 40.

16. See Barclay, *The Revelation of John*, 1:26–27.

17. Philip E. Hughes, *The Book of Revelation* (Grand Rapids, MI: Eerdmans, 1990), 17.

18. Roloff, 23.

19. See Martin McNamara, *The New Testament and the Palestinian Targum to the Pentateuch* (Rome: Pontifical Biblical Institute, 1966), 101–105; more recently Aune argues that the tripartite divine name was borrowed from Hellenistic sources (*Revelation 1–5*, 30–32), the view refuted by McNamara in the aforementioned work (see Aune's objections to the view: *Revelation 1–5*, 32–33).

20. Aune, *Revelation 17–22*, 939–940.

21. See Bauckham, *The Climax of Prophecy*, 162–166.

22. Swete, 6.

23. Walter Bauer, *A Greek-English Lexicon of the New Testament and Other Early Christian Literature,* 3d ed. (Chicago: University of Chicago Press, 2000), 620.

24. Robert L. Thomas, *Revelation 1–7: An Exegetical Commentary* (Chicago: Moody Press, 1992), 71.

25. Barclay, *The Revelation of John*, 1:29.

26. *The Canon Muratory* 57–59 (Wilhelm Schneemelcher, ed., *New Testament Apocrypha*, 2d ed. [Louisville, KY: Westminster, 1991], 1:36). I am indebted to Barclay (ibid., 1:29) for this reference.

27. Mounce, 68.

28. Metzger, *Breaking the Code: Understanding the Book of Revelation* (Nashville, TN: Abingdon, 1993), 23.

29. Barclay, *The Revelation of John*, 1:40.

30. Ibid., 34.

31. Beale, 192.

32. *The Seventh-day Adventist Bible Commentary*, 7:172.

33. Jon Paulien, The Bible Explorer, 2:1.

34. Swete, 11.

35. Herman Hoeksema, *Behold, He Cometh* (Grand Rapids, MI: Reformed Free Publishing Association, 1969), 27.

36. Ellen G. White, *Last Day Events* (Nampa, ID: Pacific Press, 1992), 17.

37. Ibid.

38. Paulien, The Bible Explorer, 2:1.

39. Ellen G. White, *Last Day Events,* 17.

THE MESSAGES TO THE SEVEN CHURCHES

JESUS AMONG THE LAMPSTANDS (1:9–20)
> John on Patmos (1:9–11)
> The Vision of the Glorified Christ (1:12–20)

CHRIST'S MESSAGES TO THE CHURCHES (2–3:22)
> Christ's Message to the Church in Ephesus (2:1–7)
> Christ's Message to the Church in Smyrna (2:8–11)
> Christ's Message to the Church in Pergamum (2:12–17)
> Christ's Message to the Church in Thyatira (2:18–29)
> Christ's Message to the Church in Sardis (3:1–6)
> Christ's Message to the Church in Philadelphia (3:7–13)
> Christ's Message to the Church in Laodicea (3:14–22)

"The one who has an ear, let him hear what
the Spirit says to the churches."

With Revelation 1:9 the first main section of the book begins, namely, the messages to the seven churches. This section clearly falls into two distinctive parts: the vision of the glorified Christ (1:9–20) and the seven messages to the churches (2–3:22).

After his reassuring words—"Stop being afraid! I am the first and the last, and the living One, and I was dead and behold, I am living for ever and ever, and I have the keys of Death and Hades" (1:17–18)—the exalted Christ commissioned John to write out the things revealed to him and pass it on to the churches (1:19–20; cf. 1:11). It appears that the seven messages were not intended to be sent "separately" to the churches.[1] They were composed as one letter and, as such, were sent with the rest of the book of Revelation to all seven churches together (cf. 1:11). A message directed to "an individual church was apparently also intended for the other six churches" (see especially 2:23).[2] Therefore, before analyzing the contents of each message in detail, it is necessary to discuss the letter as a whole.

THE ORDER OF THE SEVEN MESSAGES

To begin with, the churches to which the seven messages were addressed are listed in a certain geographical order. The cities in which these seven churches were established (cf. 1:11) were located on main interconnecting Roman roads at intervals of about thirty to forty miles, thus forming a circuit.[3] A person visiting these cities would travel in a semicircle beginning with Ephesus, closest to Patmos, and move in a clockwise direction north to Smyrna and Pergamum, and then southeast to Thyatira, Sardis, Philadelphia, and, finally, Laodicea. It is possible that the messages to the churches were carried along this route. "Letters delivered to these seven cities would easily circulate in the surrounding areas; and since every letter had to be hand-written, each letter would need to be sent where it would reach most easily the greatest number of people."[4]

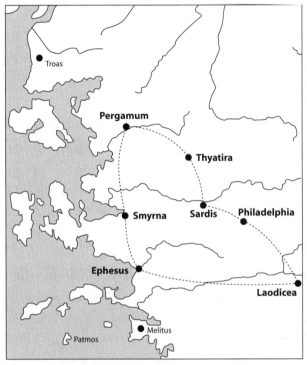

Location of the seven churches in relation to each other

It appears that the order of the seven churches also reflects the position of lamps of a seven-branched lampstand. Each lamp on one side of the lampstand corresponds to its parallel on the opposite side. It seems that the seven messages function exactly in such a way. The first and last messages, to Ephesus and Laodicea, are clearly parallel; both churches are in great danger of lovelessness and legalism. The second and sixth, to Smyrna and Philadelphia, commend the churches for faithfulness; they do not receive a rebuke, and both are opposed by those "who call themselves Jews" (2:9; 3:9). The third and fifth messages, to Pergamum and Sardis, are parallel in apostasy; there is little good to be said about them. The fourth message, to the middle church of the series, Thyatira, is clearly different. It is a divided church; and this message is the longest of all. In parallel structures such as this one, an understanding of one side of the parallel helps us to understand the other side.

THE FORMAT OF THE SEVEN MESSAGES

"The Harmony of the Messages to the Seven Churches," a chart which appears at the end of this chapter in the commentary (see page 90), sheds more light on the structure of the seven messages. Each message has a common sixfold format with only minor differences from the other messages. By comparing the similar elements in all of the messages, one may gain fuller insight into the meaning of their contents.

First, each of the messages opens with the **address**: "To the messenger of the church in _____ write." Every church is known by its name. Christ addresses the churches individually.

Second, the message to each of the churches begins with the phrase **"thus says"** which parallels "thus says the Lord" in Old Testament prophetic oracles. Here, Christ is clearly the speaker. When he speaks, the church is to listen and obey. While the messages introduce Jesus as the one speaking, the conclusion refers to the Holy Spirit as the one speaking (2:7, 11, 17, 29; 3:6, 13, 22). This means that Jesus talks to the churches through the Holy Spirit. In such a way Jesus is fulfilling the promise to the disciples in the upper room that he will communicate to them through another Paraclete (John 14:26; 15:26; 16:13). It is through the Holy Spirit that the reality of Jesus' presence is manifested among God's people, and through his speaking the voice of the risen Savior is heard among God's people.

"Thus says" is followed by a brief **description of Jesus Christ** as the sender of the message. Christ identifies himself in terms of some of his characteristics from the great vision of the "One like a son of man" (1:12–20) walking "in the midst of the seven lampstands" (cf. 2:1) in Revelation 1:9–20. The characteristics used were relevant and particularly suited to the situation of each of the local churches and specific problem(s) each faced:

> *Ephesus* (2:1–7): This church is threatened by false teachers and has lost its first love. Jesus comes to that church as the one holding "the seven stars in his right hand, who walks in the midst of the seven golden lampstands" (2:1). He is the one who has full control over the church which is in danger of losing her place as a lampstand (2:5).
> *Smyrna* (2:8–11): To the suffering Christians in Smyrna going through dire persecution, Jesus presents himself suitably as the one who himself was once dead

and came back to life (2:8). He assures them that he himself has experienced what they are presently going through. He gives them a promise of resurrection (2:10–11).

Pergamum (2:12–17): The church in Pergamum faces external as well as internal problems—persecution outside and false teachers inside the church. Jesus comes to this church with a "sharp two-edged sword." He will wage war, first, against their persecutors (2:13). Then, with the sword of his mouth he will judge the false teachers in their midst (2:16).

Thyatira (2:18–29): Thyatira is a divided church. Some of the believers there are still faithful, while others are led into apostasy by seductive and corruptive influences in the church. Jesus comes to this church with penetrating eyes—searching minds and hearts (cf. 2:23)—and feet of burnished bronze of uncompromising stability.

Sardis (3:1–6): This is a spiritually dead church; even a small number of those who have remained faithful are about to die (3:2). Jesus comes to this church with "the seven Spirits of God." The only hope of this lifeless church is in the awakening Holy Spirit who can revitalize them and bring them back to life.

Philadelphia (3:7–13): The church in Philadelphia has little strength (3:8). Jesus comes to her to open the door which no one will be able to shut.

Laodicea (3:14–22): Laodicea is in such an extremely bad condition that Jesus has nothing good to say to her. To this lukewarm and self-sufficient church, Jesus comes as the faithful and true witness and the beginning of God's creation. His discerning testimony exposes the true condition of this church. Yet this halfhearted and lukewarm church is still loved by Christ, and his creative power to bring something from nothing is their only hope.

Third, the description is followed by **Jesus' appraisal of the church.** This section begins with the formula: "I know." Five of the seven churches Jesus addresses with the words "I know your works," while the messages to Smyrna and Pergamum have "I know your affliction" and "I know where you dwell," respectively. This difference is due to the peculiar circumstances of these two churches.

Christ first analyzes the spiritual condition of each of the churches. He claims an intimate and full knowledge of them. His "penetrating eyes" reveal "the true situation of each church, sometimes reversing the church's own estimation of itself."[5] He knows each church individually, because he walks in the midst of them. If the churches want to know how to live and change, they need to listen to what Christ says to them. First, Christ commends a church with words of praise for its good qualities, with the exception of Sardis and Laodicea where there is little to be praised. Following are words of criticism concerned with the deficiency of the church. Smyrna and Philadelphia are exempted here; they have nothing to be blamed for. They are not even asked to repent.

Fourth, the appraisal is followed by words of **counsel**. After analyzing the spiritual condition of each church, Christ advises it to change its condition. The church is either called to repent and to change its ways, or it is encouraged to remain firm in faithfulness and obedience.

Fifth, then, each church is urged **to hear what the Spirit says to the churches**. "The one who has an ear, let him hear" echoes the words with which Christ concludes his sayings in the gospels (e.g., Matt. 11:15; 13:9, 43; Mark 4:9, 23; Luke 8:8; 14:35). The phrase suggests a wider audience than a single church. Christ speaks through the Holy Spirit (cf. John 16:13). What Christ says to those seven local congregations in the first century is what the Holy Spirit says to the universal church and individual Christians everywhere and in every time.

Sixth, each message concludes with **a word of promise to the overcomer**. (The fifth and sixth elements are given in a reverse order in the last four messages.) Christians are called to a life of victory and loyalty to Christ. It may be observed that though each church has declined further when compared with the preceding one, each receives more promises than the one before it did:

- Ephesus: the tree of life (2:7);
- Smyrna: a crown of life and escape from the second death (2:10–11);
- Pergamum: the hidden manna, a white stone, and a new name (2:17);
- Thyatira: authority over the nations, rulership over the nations with an iron scepter to dash the nations into pieces, and the morning star (2:26–28);
- Sardis: to walk with Jesus, to be dressed in white garments, to have their names not blotted out of the book of life, to be acknowledged before the Father, and to be acknowledged before the angels (3:4–5);
- Philadelphia: to be kept from the hour of trial; to be the pillars in the temple which they would never leave; and to have written on them the name of God, the name of the city of God, and God's new name (3:10–12);
- Laodicea: to sit with Jesus on his throne (3:21). In reality, this promise incorporates all other promises given to the churches. To sit with Jesus on his throne means to have everything.

Each church is in decline when compared with the preceding one, yet each receives more promises than the one before it did. This increase in promises, along with the spiritual decline in the churches, relates to Paul's statement that where sin increases, grace abounds all the more (Rom 5:20). Alan Johnson observes that the promises given to the overcomers echo Genesis 2–3; that is to say, what was lost originally by Adam in Eden is regained in Christ.[6] The fulfillment of these promises is described in the last two chapters of the book (Rev. 21–22).

THE STRUCTURAL PATTERN OF THE SEVEN MESSAGES

Two different proposals are suggested for the structural pattern of the seven messages of Revelation 2–3. On one hand, William H. Shea proposes that the form of the messages follows the covenant formulary. The ancient covenant treaty consisted of five standard elements: (1) preamble, (2) prologue, (3) stipulations or demands, (4) blessings and curses, and (5) witnesses. In applying these elements to the contents of each of the seven messages to the churches, Shea observes their presence in each case: (1) the preamble introduces Christ with the phrase "Thus says the One who..." and a subsequent title; (2) the prologue speaks of past relations in such terms as "I know your works"; (3) the stipulations are introduced with the imperative of "repent" followed by other instructions; (4) the blessing consists of a statement of reward such as "To the One who overcomes," while threats of curses occur irregularly; and (5) the Spirit functions as the witness to whom the churches are to listen. Shea thus concludes that the seven messages function as the covenant renewal statements to each of the seven churches.[7]

On the other hand, David Aune reflects some other authors by suggesting the influence of the royal and imperial edicts on the format of the seven messages: (1) the *praescriptio* (introduction); (2) the central section; and (3) the conclusion.[8] Aune holds that the seven messages follow this threefold structure: (1) an introduction; (2) a central section introduced by "I know"; and (3) a double conclusion containing a call for vigilance and a victory saying. He further argues that the "thus says" formula, which was the primary feature of royal and imperial decrees promulgated by Roman magistrates and emperors after Persian kings, classifies the seven messages as edicts (which were formal and public) rather than letters (which were informal and private). In using the royal/imperial edict form, John presents the exalted Christ as a king addressing his subjects, in contrast to "the Roman emperor, who is but a pale and diabolical imitation of God. In his role as the eternal sovereign and king of kings, Jesus is presented as issuing solemn and authoritative edicts befitting his status."[9]

These two proposals should not be regarded as mutually exclusive but rather correlative and complementary. They serve as an example for how the book of Revelation as a whole reflects a wide spectrum of background motifs. While the covenant formulary idea points to the covenant aspect and character of the first main division of Revelation, the royal/imperial edict view shows how the form of the seven messages of Revelation 2–3 communicated effectively to the first-century Christians in the Asia Minor setting.

THE INTERPRETATION OF THE SEVEN MESSAGES

The question of how the seven messages to the churches should be understood and interpreted is one of enormous importance and deserves serious consideration. The book of Revelation itself clearly indicates that the contents of the seven messages reflect and relate to a particular time and place. Yet, according to 1:19, the contents of Revelation have to do with "the things which are and the things which shall take place after these." In 4:1, John was told that the visions he would see are "the things which must take place after these" (in the Greek it is the same wording). "These [things]" clearly equate to "the things which are" of Revelation 1:19—namely, the messages to the seven churches (Rev. 2–3).

This shows that the seven messages were originally addressed to the actual churches in the Roman province of Asia (1:11); each message names the city in which a particular church was located. A message reflects the current situation and condition of the church to which it was written, together with the particular historical situation of the city in which the respective church was located.[10] Christ visits each church to prepare it to meet the coming crisis. He addresses particular and real problems, needs, and circumstances. Therefore, in order to understand these messages and interpret them correctly and meaningfully, we must read them primarily in the context of their original historical setting.

As mentioned before, the seven messages were not sent separately to the churches, but were sent to all seven churches together with the entire book of Revelation (cf. 1:11). The concluding section of the messages "to the churches" indicates that "the message to each church is at the same time a message to all churches."[11]

The seven churches of Revelation were most likely selected to represent a larger number of churches in the province of Asia at that time, including Colossae (Col. 1:2), Hierapolis (Col. 4:13), Troas (Acts 20:5; 2 Cor. 2:12), and Miletus (Acts 20:17). The number "seven" here must be taken as symbolic of fullness and completeness. While the messages were written originally to seven churches, they were also intended for all churches of the province of Asia, and probably for the whole Christian church throughout history as well.[12] As Merrill C. Tenney points out, the location of the churches in the circuit suggests that "they may represent the entire cycle of Christian faith and of Christian progress as exemplified by the visible church of all time."[13]

However, although the seven messages were initially intended for the churches in Asia of John's day, they transcend time and place limitations. They are "in a sense, descriptive of the whole church at any time during its history."[14] They speak to all Christians in every generation, and their contents hold implications for everyone who reads them. The fact that each message concludes with an explicit appeal to anyone who will listen to "hear what the Spirit says to the churches" suggests that they were intended for a wider audience beyond the local congregations. Through the Holy Spirit's continual presence, these messages are relevant to God's people at all times and in all places. They address different people and their different life situations and needs: those persecuted like the church in Smyrna, faithful witnesses like those in Philadelphia, spiritually dead Christians like those in Sardis, or lukewarm Christians like those in Laodicea. While the seven messages must be read with the purpose of understanding what they meant to these seven Christian communities in Asia in their own time and places, their contents can apply to various conditions of different churches and each individual Christian everywhere and at any time in history who is willing to listen. However, the book of Revelation claims to be a prophecy (1:3; 22:7, 10, 18–19) and, as such, must be approached as prophecy. Since prophecy is both foretelling and forth telling, a prophet's message to the people of his day also extends beyond his own time. The seven messages to the churches of Revelation 2–3, although primarily intended for the first-century audience, could be seen as also having a special significance for the future from John's perspective. "The seven churches provide examples of the kinds of things that can go wrong in any church."[15]

Some expositors understand the seven messages of Revelation 2–3 to be the predictive prophecies of the seven successive periods of Christian history running from John's day to the Second Coming. In this avenue of interpretation, Ephesus represents the church of the first century of the Christian era, Smyrna the period of persecution of the second and third centuries, Pergamum the church of compromise of the fourth and fifth centuries, Thyatira the church of the Middle Ages, Sardis the Reformation and post-Reformation era from the fifteenth through the eighteenth centuries, Philadelphia the church of missionary movements of the late eighteenth and nineteenth centuries, and Laodicea the church at the time of the end.

One thing seems certain, however: the context does not indicate that the seven messages were intended to be the prophetic outline of the history of the Christian church (as is Dan. 2, for example). Yet several things suggest that the messages to the seven churches of Revelation 2–3 have had much broader significance for Christians throughout history.

It is particularly interesting to note the given order of the churches. Some of the great church historians, such as Philip Schaff, outline the history of the Christian church into seven main periods: (1) the apostolic period; (2) the period of trouble and persecution of the church; (3) the period of compromise and the union of church and state; (4) the medieval period; (5) the period of Reformation; (6) the period of the Protestant orthodoxy, when doctrine became more important than practice; and (7) the period of infidelity and world-wide mission.[16] It is especially interesting that the seven messages of Revelation might apply to the character of the seven periods of the church as outlined by Schaff, although not all of the seven messages apply equally in every period of church history.[17] Yet it appears that the seven churches somehow typify Christian church history, and it is quite possible to see a progression from Ephesus to Laodicea covering the major periods of the Christian church. The seven messages of Revelation 2–3 could very well be those of God to his people at different points in history, addressing their particular circumstances and needs.

Jon Paulien has observed some verbal parallels between the message to the church in Laodicea (Rev. 3:17–18) and the final warning to God's people during the battle of Armageddon: "Blessed is the one who watches and keeps his garments so that he does not walk naked and they see his shame" (Rev. 16:15). The key words in both texts are "clothing," "nakedness," and "shame." John uses the language of the message to the church in Laodicea to give the final warning to God's people at the end of time. This suggests that Laodicea, the last in the sequential order of the seven churches, is related to the church of the last period of this world's history. Paulien believes that this additional piece of evidence supports the view that the messages sent to the seven local congregations in the province of Asia had a deeper intention.[18]

In summary, John the Revelator never indicates that the seven messages to the churches were intended to be the sequential prophecies of the history of the Christian church. However, the foregoing evidence suggests that the seven messages are not confined only to a historical point in time, but may stand for the whole church at any time and place. Thus, it would be quite appropriate to read the seven messages of Revelation 2–3 in the final stage of interpretation as Christ's evaluation of the Christian church throughout history.

At this point, the *Seventh-day Adventist Bible Commentary*[19] calls for caution with regard to applying the seven messages to the successive periods of church history. First of all, the messages to the seven churches are not to be taken as a time prophecy because no specific chronological data accompany them. They must be taken as descriptive of successive experiences of the church and are not to be treated as the classical time prophecies (such as, e.g., Dan. 2 and 7). Second, the respective historical periods typified by the seven messages can hardly be marked off by exact dates. "So used, dates are at best convenient landmarks of a rather general sort, not exact boundary markers. Actual transition from one period to another is a gradual process." Thus, all dates for marking off those various historical periods should be regarded as suggestive and approximate. For one thing, all "these variations in dates do not materially affect the over-all message found in the letters to the seven churches." Along the same line, Herman Hoeksema states:

> Maintaining, therefore, that these seven churches are representative of the whole church as she is in the world at any period of history, and rejecting the view that each of them represents a limited period in the history of the church of the new dispensation, we nevertheless believe that in a general way there is in the order in which these seven churches are addressed an indication of the trend of development the church in the world will follow.[20]

The messages sent to the seven local congregations in Asia continue to be the message of Christ to his people of all time. They have significance for both the local and universal church as well as for individual Christians everywhere and in every time in the history of the church. They are intended for everyone "who has an ear," who is ready and willing to listen.

ENDNOTES

1. W. M. Ramsay, *The Letters to the Seven Churches*, 2d ed. (Peabody, MA: Hendrickson, 1994), 143.

2. Johnson, 431.

3. Ramsay, 134.

4. Barclay, *The Revelation of John*, 1:28.

5. M. Eugene Boring, *Revelation*, Interpretation: A Bible Commentary for Teaching and Preaching (Louisville, KY: John Knox Press, 1989), 89.

6. Johnson, 432.

7. Shea, "The Covenantal Form of the Letters to the Seven Churches," 71–84.

8. Aune, "The Form and Function of the Proclamations to the Seven Churches," 182–204; idem, *Revelation 1–5*, 126–129.

9. Aune, *Revelation 1–5*, 129.

10. Boring, *Revelation*, 85.

11. Metzger, *Breaking the Code*, 46.

12. Leon Morris, *The Book of Revelation*, 2d ed., Tyndale New Testament Commentaries (Grand Rapids, MI: Eerdmans, 1987), 58.

13. Tenney, 50.

14. *The Seventh-day Adventist Bible Commentary*, 7:735.

15. Tenney, 50.

16. Philip Schaff, *History of the Christian Church*, 3d ed. (Grand Rapids, MI: Eerdmans, 1910), 13–20.

17. Hoeksema, 49.

18. Paulien, The Bible Explorer, 2.3.

19. *The Seventh-day Adventist Bible Commentary*, 7:752–753.

20. Hoeksema, 49.

THE HARMONY OF THE MESSAGES TO THE SEVEN CHURCHES

	Ephesus (2:1–17)	Smyrna (2:8–11)
Address	To the angel of the church in Ephesus write:	To the angel of the church in Smyrna write:
Description of Christ	Thus says the One who holds the seven stars in his right hand, who walks in the midst of the seven golden lampstands:	Thus says the first and the last, the One who was dead and came to life:
Christ's appraisal of the church: "I know"	I know your works, namely, your labor and endurance, and that you cannot bear evil ones, and that you have tested those who call themselves apostles—and they are not—and you have found them to be liars; and you have perseverance and you have born up because of my name, and you have not grown weary. But I have against you that you have left your first love.	I know your affliction and poverty—but you are rich—and the slander of those who say that they are Jews, and they are not, but are the synagogue of Satan.
Exhortation	Keep remembering, therefore, from where you have fallen, and repent and do the first works; but if not, I am coming to you and I will remove your lampstand from its place, unless you repent. But this you have, that you hate the works of the Nicolaitans which I myself also hate.	Stop fearing the things which you are about to suffer! Behold, the devil is about to cast some of you into prison that you may be tested, and you will have tribulation for ten days. Remain faithful to the point of death, and I will give you the crown of life.
Call to hear the Spirit	The one who has an ear, let him hear what the Spirit says to the churches.	The one who has an ear, let him hear what the Spirit says to the churches.
Promise to the overcomer	To the one who overcomes, I will give him to eat from the tree of life which is in the paradise of God.	The one who overcomes shall not be harmed by the second death.

Pergamum (2:12–17)	Thyatira (2:18–29)	Sardis (3:1–6)
To the angel of the church in Pergamum write:	To the angel of the church in Thyatira write:	To the angel of the church in Sardis write:
Thus says the One who has the sharp two-edged sword:	Thus says the Son of God, the One whose eyes are as a flame of fire, and his feet like burnished bronze:	Thus says the One who has the seven Spirits of God and seven stars.
I know where you dwell, where the throne of Satan is, and you are holding fast my name, and you did not deny my faith even in the days of Antipas, my faithful witness, who was killed among you, where Satan dwells. But I have a few things against you, because you have there those who hold the teaching of Balaam, who taught Balak to cast a stumbling block before the sons of Israel to eat the things sacrificed to idols and to commit fornication. Thus you also have those who hold the teaching of the Nicolaitans likewise.	I know your works, namely, your love and faith, that is your service and perseverance, and that your last works are greater than the former. But I have against you that you tolerate the woman Jezebel who calls herself a prophetess and teaches and leads astray my servants to commit fornication and eat things sacrificed to idols. And I gave her time that she might repent, and she does not want to repent of her fornication. Behold, I am casting her into bed, and those who commit adultery with her into great affliction, unless they repent of her works, and I will kill her children, and all the churches will know that I am the One who searches kidneys and hearts, and I will give to each of you according to your works.	I know your works, that you have a name that you live, and you are dead. Keep watching and strengthen the remaining ones that are about to die, for I have not found your works fulfilled before my God.
Repent, therefore; but if not, I am coming to you quickly and I will make war against them with the sword of my mouth.	Now, I say to you, those remaining ones in Thyatira, all those who do not have this teaching, who have not known the deep things of Satan, as they say; I do not lay on you another burden, except, hold what you have until I come.	Keep remembering, therefore, how you have received and heard, and keep it and repent. If therefore you do not watch, I will come as a thief; you will in no way know at what hour I will come upon you. But you have a few names in Sardis who have not defiled their garments, and they will walk with me in white, because they are worthy.
The one who has an ear, let him hear what the Spirit says to the churches.	The one who has an ear, let him hear what the Spirit says to the churches.	The one who has an ear, let him hear what the Spirit says to the churches.
To the one who overcomes I will give of the hidden manna, and I will give him a white stone, and on the stone a new name written which nobody knows except the one who receives it.	To the one who overcomes and who keeps my works until the end, I shall give to him authority over the nations and he will shepherd them with a rod of iron, as the vessels of a potter are smashed together, as I also have received it from my Father, and I will give him the morning star.	The one who overcomes thus will be clothed in white garments, and I will not erase his name from the book of life, and I will confess his name before my Father and before his angels.

THE HARMONY OF THE MESSAGES TO THE SEVEN CHURCHES (CONT.)

	Philadelphia (3:7–13)	Laodicea (3:14–22)
Address	To the angel of the church in Philadelphia write:	To the angel of the church in Laodicea write:
Description of Christ	Thus says the holy One, the true One, the One who has the key of David, who opens and no one shuts, and shuts and no one opens:	Thus says the Amen, the faithful and true witness, the beginning of God's creation:
Christ's appraisal of the church: "I know"	I know your works; behold, I have given before you an open door which no one is able to shut, because you have little strength, and you kept my word and did not deny my name. Behold, I am giving some of the synagogue of Satan who say that they are Jews, and they are not, but they lie—behold, I will make them come and bow before your feet, and to know that I have loved you. Because you have kept the word of my endurance, I will also keep you from the hour of trial that is about to come on those who dwell on the earth.	I know your works, that you are neither cold nor hot. I would that you were cold or hot. Thus, because you are lukewarm and neither cold nor hot, I am about to vomit you out of my mouth. Because you say, "I am rich and have become wealthy, and have need of nothing," and you do not know that you are wretched and miserable and poor and blind and naked,
Exhortation	I am coming soon; hold what you have, that no one take your crown.	I counsel you to buy from me gold refined in fire that you may be rich, and white garments that you may clothe yourself, so that the shame of your nakedness may not be exposed, and eyesalve to anoint your eyes so that you may see. As many as I love, I discipline and reprove; therefore, be zealous and repent. Behold, I am standing at the door and knocking; if anyone hears my voice and opens the door, I will come in to him and eat supper with him and he with me.
Call to hear the Spirit	The one who has an ear, let him hear what the Spirit says to the churches.	The one who has an ear, let him hear what the Spirit says to the churches.
Promise to the overcomer	The one who overcomes I will make a pillar in the temple of my God, and he will never go out of it, and I will write upon him the name of my God and the name of the city of my God, the new Jerusalem which descends out of heaven from my God, and my new name.	To the one who overcomes I will grant to sit with me on my throne, as I also overcame and sat with my Father on his throne.

The introductory section of the messages to the seven churches describes John's encounter with the resurrected and glorified Christ on the island of Patmos (1:9–20) and how Christ commissioned him to write in a book the things he saw in vision and pass it on to the churches (1:11). As noted below, the introductory section of the seven messages to the churches apparently applies to the entire book of Revelation.

JOHN ON PATMOS (1:9–11)

This section describes the circumstances under which John received the visions of Revelation together with the commission to write the things that he saw and to convey them to the churches.

> **⁹I, John, your brother and fellow partaker in the affliction and kingdom and endurance in Jesus, was on the island called Patmos because of the word of God and the testimony of Jesus Christ. ¹⁰I was in the Spirit on the Lord's day, and I heard behind me a loud voice as of a trumpet, ¹¹saying: "Write down what you see in a scroll and send it to the seven churches, to Ephesus and to Smyrna and to Pergamum and to Thyatira and to Sardis and to Philadelphia and to Laodicea."**

NOTES

1:9 *Patmos*. This small, rocky, and desolated island in the Aegean Sea (today called Patino) belongs to the Sporades Islands, some fifty miles southwest off the coast of Asia Minor (modern Turkey). The island is about sixteen miles square. It has been traditionally understood that the island was a penal settlement, a kind of labor camp, to which the Roman authorities sent offenders (like an ancient Alcatraz). However, this view has been contested by some modern scholars who argue that there is little record that Patmos was used as a penal colony. Whatever position one takes, however, one thing seems clear: John was on Patmos in exile for some time. Because of his effective witnessing about Christ, John was, according to tradition, banished to Patmos during the reign of the Roman emperor Domitian (A.D. 81–96) and forced to work in the quarries. Later he was released by Nerva and permitted to return to Ephesus.

The word of God and the testimony of Jesus Christ. See *Notes* on Revelation 1:2.

1:10. *The Lord's day.* The phrase "the Lord's day" (Gr. *hē kuriakē hēmera*) appears only here in the entire Bible. Five main proposals suggest the probable meaning of the phrase.

First, most commentators have taken the phrase to mean Sunday, the first day of the week.[1] The proponents of this view argue that the phrase "the Lord's day" was used in the Christian writings from the early second century with reference to Sunday, because of Jesus' resurrection on that day. However, the original Greek for these sources does not support this view. The two early second-century Christian works, *Didache*[2] and the letter of Ignatius of Antioch to the Magnesians,[3] which are regarded as the strongest evidence for the view, actually use not *kuriakē hēmera* ("the Lord's day") but *kata kuriakēn* ("according to the Lord's"). The internal evidence does not indicate that the Lord's day is intended; the phrase means rather "the Lord's teaching" or "the Lord's commandments."[4]

The first conclusive evidence of the usage of *kuriakē hēmera* ("the Lord's day") with reference to Sunday comes from the latter part of the second century in the apocryphal work *The Gospel of Peter*.[5] The first church father who used the term "the Lord's day" with reference to Sunday was Clement of Alexandria (ca. A.D. 190).[6] Since documents such as these appear almost a century after Revelation was written, they are not admissible as evidence for the understanding of the phrase "the Lord's day" as Sunday in Revelation. On the contrary, it could be that these authors took the phrase from the book of Revelation and applied it to Sunday as the first day of the week. The New Testament consistently refers to Sunday as the "first day of the week" (Matt. 28:1; Mark 16:2; Luke 24:1; John 20:1, 19; Acts 20:7; 1 Cor. 16:2), rather than "the Lord's day."

Second, a few scholars think that "the Lord's day" refers to Easter Sunday, as an annual event, rather than the weekly Sunday.[7] It is argued that it was on that day of the annual celebration of the resurrection that John was in the Spirit to meet the resurrected Christ. Evidence from the writings of the church fathers confirms that "the Lord's day" was used to designate Easter Sunday, particularly in Asia Minor where Christians celebrated Easter in memory of Jesus' resurrection.[8] However, this evidence is also of a much later date (ca. 2nd century A.D.); as such, it cannot be used as proof for a much earlier usage of the phrase from the book of Revelation.[9]

Third, some authors think that the reference is to the Emperor's day.[10] Adolf Deissman shows that the word *kuriakos* was current in the first century, denoting what belonged to the Roman emperor who claimed the title *kurios* ("lord").[11] Although inscriptions confirm that Egypt and Asia Minor had a day known as Sebaste which was devoted to the Roman emperor,[12] it is difficult to see a connection between the "Lord's day" and "Sebaste day." First of all, the two phrases are completely different; no conclusive evidence has been discovered indicating that the phrase *kuriakē hēmera* was used for an imperial day honoring the emperor. Also, it is unlikely that John referred to the Emperor's day in Revelation 1:10 at the time when the Christians in Asia were persecuted for refusing to call the emperor *kurios* and to worship the emperor.[13]

Fourth, another view holds that "the Lord's day" means Sabbath, the seventh day of the week. Such an understanding reflects the strong tradition of Seventh-day Adventist interpretation;[14] Ellen White also held this view.[15] The phrase "the Lord's day" is never used elsewhere in the Bible; yet the seventh-day Sabbath is called "my holy day" and "the holy day of the Lord" (Isa. 58:13). All three Synoptics quote Jesus as saying, "The Son of Man is Lord of the Sabbath" (Matt. 12:8; Mark 2:27–28; Luke 6:5). The phrase "the Lord's day" may, therefore, indicate that John received his vision on the Sabbath, the seventh day of the week, rather than on Sunday. Even J. Massynberde Ford, who struggles with the meaning of the expression, admits: "Most probably the Christian would still be keeping the Sabbath, the seventh day."[16]

Fifth, a number of scholars hold that John may have used the phrase "the Lord's day" with reference to the eschatological day of the Lord (Gr. *hēmera tou kuriou or hēmera kuriou*).[17] John was taken in vision to that day to witness the events leading toward the eschatological day of the Lord being unfolded before him. The phrase "the day of the Lord" is often used by prophets in the Greek translation of the Old Testament (LXX Joel 2:11, 31; Amos 5:18–20; Zeph. 1:14; Mal. 4:5) as well as by New Testament writers (Acts 2:20; 1 Thess. 5:2; 2 Pet. 3:10) with reference to the time of the end. Yet John uses not the Old Testament phrase "the day of the Lord" but "the Lord's day." This problem vanishes in light of the fact that John could have taken the familiar Old Testament term and rephrased it. John's use of the adjective (as in "the Lord's day") rather than the noun in the genitive case ("the day of the Lord") does not make a substantive change in meaning but rather in emphasis between the two words.[18] It is thus plausible that the phrase "the Lord's day" is simply one of the many different designations—e.g., "the day of the Lord" (1 Thess. 5:2; 2 Pet. 3:10), "the day of our Lord Jesus Christ" (1 Cor. 1:8; 2 Cor. 1:14), "the great day" (Jude 6), "the great day of his wrath" (Rev. 6:17), "the great day of God" (Rev. 16:14)—for the day of Christ's coming.[19]

An objection to this view is that since John gives the specific place ("the island called Patmos") and circumstances ("because of the word of God and the testimony of Jesus") under which he received the vision, it would be logical to conclude that the phrase "the Lord's day" refers to the specific time when John saw the vision.[20] However, the text does not state that John was on Patmos on the Lord's day when he received the vision, but rather that *while* he was on Patmos he came to be *in the Spirit on the Lord's day*. And in this John is consistent throughout the book; whenever he is "in the Spirit" (cf. 4:2; 17:3; 21:10), that which follows in the text always refers to a symbolic rather than a literal time/place. If in Revelation 1:10 a specific, literal time is intended, it would be very inconsistent with the rest of the book.

So when did John receive the vision? Sunday as the Lord's day is very unlikely because it cannot be supported either by biblical or extra-biblical evidence. Stronger evidence favors the seventh-day

Sabbath as the Lord's day. On the other hand, the eschatological character of the book as a whole is also in favor of the eschatological day of the Lord (cf. 1:7). Although written "for the guidance and comfort of the church throughout the Christian dispensation,"[21] the book of Revelation was composed with the perspective of the eschatological day of the Lord and the events leading up to it. However, considering the central role that the Sabbath, the seventh day of the week, itself would play in those eschatological events ("the things that must soon take place," 1:1), as will be seen, it is not unreasonable to see a double meaning in John's enigmatic phrase. In other words, John may have wanted his readers to know that the vision came to him on "the Lord's day" (the Sabbath) because the vision was about "the day of the Lord" (end-time judgment), in which the Sabbath would be an important focus.

EXPOSITION

1:9 The revelator introduces himself as *I, John, your brother.* The self-designation, "I, John" reminds one of "I, Daniel," which occurs often in the second half of the book of Daniel (cf. 8:15, 27; 9:2; 10:2, 7). The two books, Daniel and Revelation, are related in a special way. A comparison of the last vision of Daniel (Dan. 10–12) with John's first vision (1:12–20) clearly reveals that the book of Revelation begins where the book of Daniel concludes. The final prophetic vision that Daniel had was of a divine figure, a scene which is almost identical to the vision of the resurrected Christ in Revelation 1:12–20. Further on, the book of Daniel provides an outline of history from Daniel's perspective of the four world empires. The last vision in Daniel (11–12:4) seems to extend beyond the fourth world empire. It is exactly there that the prophecies of Revelation begin. The book of Revelation covers the history of the Christian era from John's day until the Second Coming. This suggests that Revelation builds on Daniel; the two books thus function like a two-volume set.

John identifies himself with those to whom he writes the "revelation of Jesus Christ." He is the brother of the Asian Christians; he knows them very well and speaks their language. He is a co-participant with them in *the affliction and kingdom and endurance in Jesus.* Only a person who speaks the language of the people and participates in their experience can be used effectively by God to communicate the revelation of Jesus Christ. The tribulation that John experienced foreshadowed the tribulation that all Christians throughout history were to go through. George E. Ladd states:

> The church is the people of God to whom the Kingdom has come and who will inherit the Kingdom when it comes; but as such, it is the object of satanic hatred

and is destined to suffer tribulation. Tribulation here includes all the evil which will befall the church, but especially the great tribulation at the end, which will be only the intensification of what the church has suffered throughout all history.[22]

John informs readers that he was *on the island called Patmos* when he received the visions and messages that are recorded in his book. This brief statement sets the tone for the main message of the book. Patmos, a small rocky island, served in the first century as a Roman penal settlement. John was exiled there because of his faithful testimony to *the word of God and the testimony of Jesus Christ*. On this barren island, he suffered tribulation while surrounded by the sea. It is especially interesting that the word "sea" plays a significant role in the book, occurring twenty-five times. William Barclay refers to Strahan who states that the revelation John wrote is full of "the sights and the sounds of the infinite sea." He further states: "Nowhere is 'the voice of many waters' more musical than in Patmos; nowhere does the rising and setting sun make a more splendid 'sea of glass mingled with fire'; yet nowhere is the longing more natural that the separating sea should be no more."[23] The sea becomes for John a symbol of separation and suffering. His persecution and the rejection of his faithful testimony becomes the symbol of the experience of God's end-time people because of their faithfulness to the gospel. No wonder that in describing the new heaven and earth in his last vision, the revelator first observes that "the sea is no longer" (21:1). There is no longer that "sea" which caused him to suffer so much on this earth, for "the first things have passed away" (Rev. 21:4).

1:10a *I was in the Spirit on the Lord's day.* Within the climate of the Patmos experience described above, John is carried away in the Spirit into the sphere of the eschatological day of the Lord to observe the events in history "that must soon take place" (1:1), leading toward the Second Coming and the time of the end. It appears, however, that John might have used the phrase "the Lord's day" in a twofold meaning. He may have wanted to inform his readers that he was taken by the Spirit into vision to witness the events from the perspective of the eschatological day of the Lord, and that the vision actually took place during the seventh-day Sabbath. The association of the two days by John would fit the eschatological connotation of the Sabbath in the Bible (Isa. 58:13–14; 66:23) as the sign of the day of deliverance (Deut. 5:15; Ezek. 20:10–12). This also fits the portrayal of the final events in Revelation within which the Sabbath will play a central role in the end-time scenario. And this would also explain why John coined the phrase "the Lord's day" in order to incorporate the two biblical concepts into a single one.

John's experience "in the Spirit" may have been similar to Paul's, who was "caught up to the third heaven and heard inexpressible words" (2 Cor. 12:2–4). John is about to be shown a representation of events and forces affecting God's people throughout history, leading toward the time of the end.

These forces had begun to work even in John's day. William Milligan observes: "From the beginning to the end of the book the Seer is continually in the presence of the great day, with all in it that is at once so majestic and terrible."[24] John's own situation on the island of Patmos, however, as well as the situation of the churches he is addressing (cf. Rev. 2–3), is a foretaste of the future reality of the day of the Lord. When John was carried away by the Spirit in vision to observe the events to take place throughout the Christian Age, he was already experiencing the nearness of the end time. This is why he could speak of the day of the Lord as being at hand. The nearness of the Second Coming added urgency to the message John communicated to his fellow Christians (cf. Rev. 1:3; 22:7, 12, 20). He, together with the churches he was addressing, experienced the eschatological "day of the Lord" as a present reality.

1:10b–11 While in vision, John hears behind him *a loud voice as of a trumpet.* This phrase designates the Old Testament divine epiphany, the coming-in appearance of God. The trumpet-like voice uttered the Ten Commandments from Sinai (Exod. 19:16). In the New Testament, the sound of the trumpet announces the appearance of Christ on the clouds (Matt. 24:31; 1 Cor. 15:52; 1 Thess. 4:16). In other words, the trumpet-like sound denotes the presence of God who speaks. The same trumpet-like voice which was heard from Sinai now commissions John to write out the divine message and send it to the churches with the purpose of being read and heard by them. The messages of the book of Revelation are as important to God's people as the Ten Commandments themselves, since they are coming from Christ.

The trumpet-like voice commissions John to *write down* in a scroll the vision he sees and send it to the Christian communities located in the Roman province of Asia: *to Ephesus and to Smyrna and to Pergamum and to Thyatira and to Sardis and to Philadelphia and to Laodicea.* Christ knows the churches by the names of the cities in which they are located. He knows the churches individually and intimately, and he knows all about them (note the repetition of "I know" in each of the letters—2:2, 9, 13, 19; 3:1, 8, 15). The messages that he is sending to them through John are an expression of his love for them. Their purpose is to help the believers in their present dire circumstances and to prepare them for the coming crisis.

THE VISION OF THE GLORIFIED CHRIST (1:12–20)

This section describes the first vision of the book of Revelation. After hearing the trumpet-like voice, John encounters the resurrected Christ, glorified and triumphant, whose appearance is given in a symbolic presentation.

12And I turned to see the voice that was speaking with me, and having turned I saw seven golden lampstands, 13and in the midst of the lampstands I saw one like a son of man clothed in a robe reaching down to the feet and girded with a golden girdle. 14His head and hair were white as white wool, as snow, and his eyes as a flame of fire, 15and his feet were like burnished bronze as refined in a furnace, and his voice was like the sound of many waters, 16and he had in his right hand seven stars, and out of his mouth proceeded a sharp two-edged sword, and his countenance was as the sun shining in its power.

17And when I saw him, I fell at his feet as a dead person, and he placed his right hand on me, saying: "Stop being afraid! I am the first and the last, 18and the living One, and I was dead and behold, I am alive for ever and ever, and I have the keys of Death and Hades. 19Write, therefore, the things which you saw, namely, the things which are and the things which are about to take place after these things. 20With regard to the mystery of the seven stars that you saw in my right hand, and the seven golden lampstands, the seven stars are the angels of the seven churches, and the seven lampstands are the seven churches."

NOTES

1:12 *Seven golden lampstands.* The lampstands (Gr. *luchnia*, "lampstand," "candlestick") are modeled after the seven-branched, golden lampstand of the earthly Tabernacle (Exod. 25:31–37) or the golden lampstand with seven lamps from Zechariah 4:2. Revelation 1:12–13 says that John saw seven separate golden lampstands and Christ walking among them. John later explained that the lampstands represent the seven churches to whom the seven messages were addressed (1:20). In

Jewish tradition, the image of the lampstand symbolized Israel's obedience to God.[25] In the Old Testament, Israel was appointed to be God's light-bearing witnesses (Isa. 42:6–7; 49:6; 60:1–3). In the New Testament, this role is transferred to the church. According to Matthew 5:14–16, the church is like a lamp that gives light to the world (cf. Phil. 2:15). The lamp is to be put on a "lampstand" to shine (Mark 4:21; Luke 8:16). In Revelation 11:4, God's two witnesses in their prophetic role are identified as the "the two lampstands standing before the Lord of the earth" (cf. Zech. 4:2–6, 14). The foregoing references suggest that the lampstand emblem defines the essential role of the church as God's witness in the world.

1:13 *Like a son of man.* This title is taken from Daniel 7:13–14 where the Ancient of Days gave the kingdom and the power and the dominion to "one like a son of man." The title "the Son of Man" became associated with the Messiah in the New Testament. In Mark 13:26, Jesus applied the passage from Daniel 7:13 to himself. "The Son of Man" was his favorite title in the gospels. He used it frequently with reference to himself (e.g., Matt. 24:30, 37, 39, 44; 26:46; Mark 13:26; 14:62; Luke 19:10). The Son of Man in Revelation 1 is evidently Jesus Christ himself and is almost identical to the description of the divine figure of Daniel 10:5–12.

DANIEL 10:5-12	REVELATION 1:12-18
A certain man	One like a son of man
Clothed in linen	Clothed in a robe reaching to the feet
Girded with a belt of pure gold	Girded with a golden girdle
His eyes like torches of fire	His eyes like a flame of fire
His feet like polished bronze	His feet like burnished bronze
Voice like a roaring multitude	His voice like the sound of many waters
No strength, face to ground	John falls at his feet as dead
Hand touches Daniel	Hand laid on John
"Fear not!"	"Fear not!"

A robe reaching down to the feet. The Greek word describing this robe is *podērēs*, which literally means "reaching down to the feet." This same word is used in the Greek Old Testament (LXX) for the priestly attire (Exod. 28:4, 31; 29:5; Zech. 3:5). Jewish historian Josephus states that the High Priest wore *podērēs* ("a long robe reaching to the feet") with a girdle around his chest.[26] The portrayal of the risen Christ dressed in *podērēs* walking among the lampstands conveys the temple setting of Revelation 1:9–20. Christ is seen here primarily in his priestly role. However, "a long robe" must not be limited solely to the priestly garments, for those in high offices could also wear long robes with girdles around their chests (cf. Isa. 22:21).[27] It is also significant that the portrayal of Christ in Revelation 1 picks up on Daniel 10:5–12. There, the divine person Daniel saw dressed in a robe and girded with gold (10:5) was evidently not in a priestly role. Furthermore, the heavenly person in the role of judge in Ezekiel's vision marking the faithful in Jerusalem was clothed in the *podērēs* robe (LXX Ezek. 9:2–3, 11). This suggests that John saw the risen Christ in vision wearing the regal priestly attire functioning in his priestly as well as royal dignity roles.

1:14 *His head and hair were white as white wool, as snow.* The head and hair "white as white wool, as snow" of Christ is taken from the description of the Ancient of Days of Daniel 7:9a, whose "vesture was like white snow, and the hair of His head like pure wool." This shows that the resurrected Jesus has the same characteristics as the eternal God.

His eyes as a flame of fire. This description of Christ also appears in the message to the church in Thyatira (2:18) and in the vision of the victorious return of the conquering Christ coming to judge his enemies (19:12). In Zechariah's vision, the seven lamps on the lampstand symbolized "the eyes of the Lord which range to and fro throughout the whole earth" (Zech. 4:10). John explains later that the seven eyes of the Lamb who was worthy to take the sealed book symbolized "the seven spirits of God sent out into all the earth" (5:6). This most likely signifies his ability and right to both rule and judge.

1:15 *His feet were like burnished bronze, as refined in a furnace.* Drawn from Daniel 10:6, this phrase also reminds one of the feet of the four living beings in Ezekiel 1:7 which "gleamed like burnished bronze." This description of Christ's feet is most likely "to add to the magnificence and strength of the portrayal."[28]

His voice was like the sound of many waters. This description is evidently drawn from Ezekiel 43:2 where the prophet describes the voice of God as "the sound of many waters."

1:16 *He had in his right hand seven stars.* In Daniel 12:3, God's faithful people are associated with stars. In Malachi, the priests and messengers of God's people are referred to as angels (Mal. 2:7; 3:1), an idea that also appears in the New Testament (cf. Matt. 11:10). The context here suggests that the angels stand for the leaders of the churches.[29] As Isbon T. Beckwith notes, "they represent the churches in such a way that they are practically identified with them, and are responsible for the conditions of the churches."[30]

Out of his mouth proceeded a sharp two-edged sword. This description of Christ is repeated often in the book (2:12, 16; 19:15, 21). The imagery is drawn from Isaiah 49:2, where God makes his servant's mouth like a sharp sword. In Psalm 149:6, the two-edged sword is used to execute judgment upon the wicked. It reminds one also of Hebrews 4:12, where "the word of God is living and active and sharper than any two-edged sword." Paul refers to "the sword of the Spirit, which is the word of God" (Eph. 6:17). In Revelation 19, Jesus' name is "Word of God" as he goes to battle the enemies of God.

1:17 *Stop being afraid!* The grammatical construction of the present imperative indicates the stopping of an action already in progress. John is told to stop being afraid.

1:18 *The keys of Death and Hades.* In the Greek text both "death" and "hades" come with the definite article "the." "Death" here must be understood in relation to Hades. The Greek word *hadēs* here refers to the power of death. In Hellenistic Greek, according to David Aune, "Hades can be referred to either as a person or as a place"[31]—the realm of the underworld and the kingdom of the dead (Heb. *she'ol*). In Revelation, while Hades is a place where the dead go (cf. 6:8; 20:14), it also refers to the demonic powers of death. Jürgen Roloff explains: "It governs the world of the dead and, as is evident in the Greek depictions of the god Hades, possesses the key as an attribute of its strength. But now Christ has overcome Death and Hades, that demonic pair; he has seized from them the key to that place where they guarded the dead (cf. 1 Cor. 15:26; Acts 2:27, 31). His followers participate in this victory and need not fear death anymore."[32] According to Revelation 20:14, the second death is the end of Death and Hades.

Aune observes that the portrayal of the glorified Christ in Revelation 1:17–18 as "the first and the last" who holds "the keys of Death and Hades" bears striking resemblance to the description of a Hellenistic goddess Hekate, who was very popular in Asia Minor at the time of the writing of Revelation. Hekate was ascribed universal sovereignty; she was considered both the source and ruler of heaven, earth, and Hades, and the agent by which they would come to their end. She was called the mistress of the cosmos and the "keybearer" (Greek *kleidouchos*) because she was popularly thought to possess the keys to the gates of heaven and Hades. She could travel back and forth between heaven and earth and report on earth what was going on in heaven and in heaven what was happening on earth. In addition, she used angels to mediate her messages. She was frequently addressed in this way: "Beginning and end [*arshē kai telos*] are you, and you alone rule all. For all things are from you, and in you do all things. Eternal One, come to their end."[33] It appears that Revelation 1:13–18 was intended to evoke parallels to the popular concept in the minds of the original reader, portraying Christ as "usurping the authority of Hekate as well as that of every other natural or supernatural authority."[34]

1:19 *The things which you saw, namely, the things which are and the things which are about to take place after these things.* The word "namely" is expressed in Greek with *kai* ("and"), which functions here in the text epexegetically. Some commentators hold that the clause simply refers to what John had just seen in vision (1:12–16), and what he was to see afterwards as still in the future.[35] However, "the things which are" refers clearly to the seven messages sent to the churches (chapters 2–3). In 4:1, John is told that he will be shown "the things which must take place after these things," namely, the things recorded in chapters 2–3. "The things which must take place after these things" in 4:1 is the same wording found in Revelation 1:19b, suggesting that "the things which will take place after these things" refer to chapters 4–22.[36]

1:20 *The seven stars are the angels of the seven churches.* See *Notes* on Revelation 1:16.

EXPOSITION

1:12–13 After turning around, John sees ***seven golden lampstands.*** He explains later that the golden lampstands represent the seven churches to whom Jesus addresses his messages (1:20). The church is supposed to bear the light of the gospel to the darkened world (Matt. 5:14–16; Phil. 2:15). If the church fails to do this, it loses its reason for existence (cf. Rev. 2:5). The churches represented by the seven lampstands correspond to the sevenfold activity of the Holy Spirit on behalf of the churches (cf. Rev. 1:4), suggesting the fullness and universality of the activity of the Holy Spirit on behalf of God's people. Each of the churches has the full support of the Holy Spirit and a task to perform in the world.

In the midst of the lampstands, John sees *one like a son of man.* This expression is taken from Daniel 7:13, where the kingdom and the power and the dominion were given by the Ancient of Days to One like a son of man. "The Son of Man" was Jesus' favorite title in the gospels. The description of Jesus in Revelation 1:12–18 corresponds to the description of the messenger from Daniel 10:5–12 who was sent to Daniel with a special message regarding the things to happen at the end of time. Jesus is here portrayed as a messenger from God. We saw earlier that the revelation of Jesus Christ is something that God gave to Jesus to show his servants the things that must take place (Rev. 1:1).

In the light of this Old Testament background, Jesus appears in the book of Revelation as the final messenger from heaven with a special message for the church about things to come. The divine messenger in Daniel 10 is a man-like figure. The fact that Jesus is referred to as the "One like a son of man" (both in Rev. 1:13 and 14:14) and that he is described in terms of the man-like figure of Daniel 10 was especially significant to those seven churches in the province of Asia. Jesus lived on this earth like a man and suffered. He is to the churches the One who understands human problems and suffering, because he himself experienced all of these.

According to Revelation 2:1, the glorified Christ is walking among the seven lampstands. This scene evokes, first of all, God's promise given to ancient Israel: "Moreover, I will make My dwelling among you, and My soul will not reject you. I will walk among you and be your God and you will be My people" (Lev. 26:11–12). Now, we see Christ fulfilling that promise in a symbolic walk among the lampstands. The same God who walked with Old Testament Israel now walks in Christ with his New Testament people.

The scene also evokes the priests officiating services in the Old Testament tabernacle. The priests would trim and refill the lamps that were still burning, and also remove the wick and old oil from the lamps which had gone out, supplying them with fresh oil and relighting them.[37] Here in Revelation 1, Christ is portrayed as ministering to the churches in the role of the Old Testament priests. He ministers to them wearing *a robe reaching to the feet and girded with a golden girdle.* These robes were worn by the priests as well as the kings in the Old Testament. This portrayal emphasizes the priestly as well as the royal character of the glorified Christ. He is no longer a man of Nazareth, but the exalted Christ "who was dead and now is alive" (1:18). In his prophecy of the messianic shoot from the stem of Jesse, Isaiah explains that "righteousness will be the belt about His loins, and faithfulness the belt about His waist" (Isa. 11:5).

The man-like glorified Lord walks among the churches in the full priestly capacity ministering to his people, and in the full capacity of King, ruling over the kingdom which is his church. As the seven messages reveal, the churches are not perfect; they are rather weak and far from ideal. Yet, Jesus assures them of his presence. It is very important in our Christian experience to know that Christ is able to sympathize with our weaknesses, because he was tempted "in all things as we are, yet without sin" (Heb. 4:15). He is faithful to his promise, and he walks among his people despite, rather than because of, their weaknesses. And he will be with them always until the close of the age (Matt. 28:20).

1:14–16 John now takes some Old Testament descriptions of God and applies them to the resurrected Christ. First, Christ's *hair was white as white wool.* This description appears in Daniel 7:9 for the Ancient of Days, which is the title of God in Daniel. In the ancient world, white and gray hair symbolized wisdom and aged experience (Job 15:10; Prov. 20:29) as well as dignity (Prov. 16:31). In ancient Jewish tradition, God goes out to war as a young man with black hair (Song of Sol. 5:11); however, when he sits at court as an old man, his hair is white.[38] Then, *his voice was like the sound of many waters* reminds one of the description of God in his glory in Ezekiel 43:2. Drawing on imagery from Ezekiel, John declares that the glory of God which visited Israel in the Old Testament now comes in Jesus Christ, giving the message of repentance to the churches.

We read further that Christ's eyes were *as a flame of fire.* Nothing remains hidden from the penetrating eyes of Christ.[39] *And his feet were like burnished bronze as refined in a furnace.* This description adds to the "magnificence and strength of the portrayal."[40] The burnished or gleaming bronze affirms the majesty of the glorified Christ. *He had in his right hand seven stars.* The stars are the angels or leaders of the churches (Rev. 1:20). This signifies that Christ has the leaders of the churches in his care. Situations seem very bad in the churches, but Christ is in control.

From Christ's **mouth proceeded a sharp two-edged sword.** The two-edged sword in the Old Testament is associated with the execution of judgment upon the wicked (Ps. 149:6). Revelation 19 pictures the returning Christ from whose mouth proceeds a sharp sword to execute judgment on the wicked (19:15, 21). In Revelation 2–3, Christ wages war with the churches. To the church of Pergamum he sends this message: "I will make war against them with the sword of my mouth" (2:16; cf. 2:12). The fact that the two-edged sword comes from Christ's mouth rather than from his hand shows that this battle is verbal in nature rather than physical. "For the word of God is living and active and sharper than any two-edged sword, and piercing as far as the division of soul and spirit, of both joints and marrow, and able to judge the thoughts and intentions of the heart" (Heb. 4:12). **His countenance was as the sun shining in its power.** John witnessed earlier, together with two other disciples, the glory of Christ on the Mount of Transfiguration, when Jesus was "transfigured before them; and His face shone like the sun" (Matt. 17:2). Now, more than a half a century later, John sees the face of Christ again, now exalted in glory and majesty.

1:17–18 Jesus Christ appears to John as a human being; yet, he is the glorified Lord. His white hair and his voice like the sound of many waters remind one of the presence of God. He is dressed in a robe of power, dignity, and authority. His eyes are like a flame of fire, his feet like burnished bronze, and his face shining like the sun; these are metaphoric descriptions of the glory and majesty of the exalted Christ. He is the victorious Messiah equipped with the two-edged sword coming from his mouth. No wonder that John, overwhelmed by his glory, falls at his feet like a dead person, as he did earlier on the Mount of Transfiguration (Matt. 17:6). This is the common reaction of a man who is in the presence of God's glory (Josh. 5:14; Ezek. 1:28; 3:23; 43:3; Dan. 8:17; 10:9, 11; Matt. 28:9). This reminds us also of the event in Galilee (Luke 5:1–11), when, after the great catch of fish, Peter glimpses who Jesus is and falls down at his knees, conscious only that he himself is a sinful man.

As on the Mount of Transfiguration (Matt. 17:7), John again experiences the calming hand of Jesus who places his right hand on him with the words **Stop being afraid!** John had often heard this phrase from the lips of Jesus when together with the other disciples (Matt. 14:27; 28:10; Mark 6:50; John 6:20).

"Stop being afraid" for *I am the first and the last.* The statement "I am the first and the last" is very significant. It mirrors the statement in Isaiah's account of the God of the covenant: "I am the first and the last, and there is no God apart from Me" (44:6; cf. 41:4; 48:12). In using this Old Testament description of God, Jesus is identifying himself as none other than the Old Testament Yahweh of the covenant. At the outset of this vision, the resurrected Christ is "one like a son of man" fulfilling God's covenant promise to ancient Israel: "I will also walk among you and be your God and you will be My people" (Lev. 26:12). Through the symbolic walk among the lampstands, Christ signifies his presence and ministry to the churches. This concluding portion makes clear that in the resurrected and exalted Jesus Christ, the very God of the covenant has come down, and he is with his New Testament people. He is their only hope as the end draws near, for "there is no God apart from him." God spoke through Isaiah:

> "You are My witnesses," declares the LORD,
> "And My servant whom I have chosen,
> So that you may know and believe Me
> And understand that I am He.
> Before Me there was no God formed,
> And there will be none after Me.
> I, even I, am the LORD,
> And there is no savior besides Me.
> It is I who have declared and saved and proclaimed,
> And there was no strange god among you;
> So you are My witnesses," declares the LORD,
> "And I am God.
> Even from eternity I am He,
> And there is none who can deliver out of My hand;
> I act and who can reverse it?" (Isa. 43:10–13)

The resurrected and exalted Christ is none other than the God of the covenant. In him, the covenant promises given to ancient Israel have found their fulfillment.

To the churches facing persecution and tribulation, Jesus introduces himself by reminding them of his own suffering, death, and resurrection. He is *the living One, and I was dead and behold, I am alive for ever and ever, and I have the keys of Death and Hades.* This statement would have reminded the Christians of John's day of the goddess Hekate, popularly called "the beginning and end" and "the key-bearer" holding the keys to the gates of heaven and Hades. Here Christ's authority surpasses "the authority of Hekate as well as that of every other natural or supernatural authority,"[41] as Paul stated, "of those who are in heaven, and on earth, and under the earth" (Phil. 2:10). He experienced death in the course of his ministry. He broke the power of death, however, and he lives forever with his people and sustains them. His victory over death has empowered him to possess "the keys of Death and Hades." According to Paul, "the last enemy that will be abolished is the death" (1 Cor. 15:26, lit. trans). In Revelation, Hades symbolizes the demonic power (cf. 6:8; 20:14). But now Christ has overcome that demonic power (cf. 1 Cor. 15:26). His followers have a share in this victory and need not fear death any longer because they are already with Christ in heavenly places. They stop being afraid because the One who is "the first and the last" is with them, and he is in control.

1:19–20 Next, the glorified Christ commissions John: ***Write, therefore, the things which you saw.*** The word "therefore" means "in light of the foregoing." Thus the text would read this way: "In the light of the fact that I am the first and the last, the living One, the One who conquered death and have power over the demonic powers that are threatening your lives, write the things which you saw." The book of Revelation is the unveiling of Jesus Christ and his activities on behalf of his people as history comes to its close. Its purpose is to show to God's people "the things which must take place soon" in the light of the cross, and what Christ means to his people. Because of what Jesus Christ is and what he does, these things are written for the purpose of telling God's people to "stop being afraid! I am in control. I will be with you always, even to the end of the age."

John plainly states that the things that he is about to write fall into two parts: ***the things which are and the things which are about to take place after these things.*** "The things which are" refer to the situation and needs of the seven local churches of his own time. "The things which are about to take place after these things" refer to the visions described in chapters 4 through 22. This section describes the ongoing great controversy between the forces of good and evil that is moving toward the end when God will definitely and for ever deal with the problem of evil and establish his eternal kingdom.

A RETROSPECT ON REVELATION 1:9–20

On the barren island of Patmos, surrounded by "the many waters," John encounters the resurrected Christ and receives a word of assurance. John is the elder of the seven churches of Asia Minor (cf. 2 John 1; 3 John 1). He needs encouragement. Jesus comes to him with these words: "Stop being afraid! I am in control. I have conquered the demonic powers; and, I have the keys of death. I will be with you always, even to the end of age." This is what the revelation of Jesus Christ is all about. As Kenneth A. Strand reminds us, "it is important for us to bear in mind that the very purpose of the book of Revelation was to give spiritual knowledge and strength to persecuted followers of the Lamb."[42] The book is to be a constant reminder, both to the churches and their leaders experiencing the pain and hardship of a "Patmos," that a "Patmos" of tribulation for faithfulness to the gospel always results in a Patmos experience, namely, the revelation of Jesus Christ. Whenever God's servants feel discouraged and rejected, surrounded by "many waters," they can feel the presence of the glorified Christ and his words of assurance: "Do not be afraid! I conquered the demonic powers. I am with you always." The demonic powers can threaten to harm their lives and make them suffer, but Jesus has the keys. The day is coming when Death and Hades, already conquered enemies, will experience their ultimate destruction in the lake of fire (Rev. 20:14).

Not only did Jesus meet the situation and needs of John as leader, but he met also the situation and needs of each individual church to whom the messages of the book of Revelation are addressed. Revelation 1:12–18 lists various characteristics of Jesus Christ. It is particularly interesting to note that all of these characteristics are mentioned again in the messages to the seven churches. Each message begins with a brief description of Christ from the composite picture:

> To the angel of the church in Ephesus: *Thus says the one who holds the seven stars in his right hand and walks among the seven lampstands* (2:1; cf. 1:13, 16).
> To the angel of the church in Smyrna: *Thus says the first and the last, who was dead and has come to life* (2:8; cf. 1:17–18).
> To the angel of the church in Pergamum: *Thus says the One who has the sharp two-edged sword* (2:12; cf. 1:16).
> To the angel of the church in Thyatira: *Thus says the Son of God who has eyes like a flame of fire, and his feet are like burnished bronze* (2:18; cf. 1:14–15).
> To the angel of the church in Sardis: *Thus says the One who has the seven Spirits of God, and the seven stars* (3:1; cf. 1:4, 16).
> To the angel of the church in Philadelphia: *Thus says the holy One, the true One, who has the key of David, who opens and no one will shut, and who shuts and no one*

opens (3:7; cf. 1:18; the holy and true is found in 6:10).

To the angel of the church in Laodicea: *Thus says the Amen, the faithful and true witness, the ruler of God's creation* (3:14; cf. 1:5a).

Almost all of the various characteristics of the resurrected Christ mentioned in Revelation 1 are used to introduce the messages to the seven churches. The seven descriptions of Christ portray different aspects of his ministry to the churches. The particular aspect of Christ used in each message relates to the specific situation and need of each church.[43] In the same way, the four gospels give different portraits of Jesus. Each gospel presents a unique picture of Jesus meeting the problems and needs of the people to whom it was sent.

To each individual church Jesus presents himself in a unique way. No church gets the whole Jesus, and no two of them share the same aspect of Jesus. We saw earlier how the sevenfold manifestation of the Holy Spirit corresponds to the situations of the seven churches in which he operates (Rev. 1:4). Each church experiences different manifestations of the Holy Spirit, because each church has different situations and needs. Jesus walks among them, serving each of the churches individually and meeting them where they are. The Holy Spirit is manifesting the reality of Jesus' presence among the churches. The churches must pay heed to the message and recognize the authority of the One speaking to them.

As Merrill C. Tenney observes, this portrait of Christ in Revelation 1 is "the key to the section. As the various churches are weighed and discussed one can see the living Christ in action among His own people. He does not appear to them as the terrible sovereign on the throne nor as the conqueror riding to battle. He walks among them as a Lord who seeks to commend their virtues even more than to expose and punish their faults. These letters are His particular warning and counsel to the church of all time as its various aspects appear under the guise of their seven historic places."[44] The glorified Lord still walks in the midst of his church. He speaks to his end-time church today through the Revelation of Jesus Christ. He presents himself to his people in various ways, addressing problems in their different life situations and needs. He meets them where they are now, as he met the Christians of those seven congregations in the province of Asia in John's day.

The strong appeal of the book of Revelation to Christians today is to follow the Lord's way in proclaiming the gospel message to the world. It is, therefore, the sacred duty of the church to present Jesus Christ—his character and ministry—in a way that meets the people where they are. The symbolic representation of the church as the seven-branched lampstand denotes that the church has the full support of the Holy Spirit and a full task to perform. The first duty is to be the light to the world—to proclaim Jesus in words and action. Through the church today, Christ meets people with aspects of himself which correspond to their own life circumstances and relate to their individual needs. The church is the only light that Jesus shines through. For the church to fail in her role is to lose her reason for existence; her lampstand will be removed (Rev. 2:5; cf. Matt. 5:16).

ENDNOTES

1. E.g., Swete, 13; Wilfrid J. Harrington, *Understanding the Apocalypse* (Washington, DC: Corpus Books, 1969), 78; Mounce, 76; Morris, 52; Ladd, 31; Fiorenza, *Revelation*, 50; Thomas, *Revelation 1–7*, 90–92; Aune, *Revelation 1–5*, 83–84; Beale, 203.

2. *Didache* 14.1 (Holmes, *The Apostolic Fathers*, 266–267).

3. Ignatius of Antioch *To the Magnesians* 9.1 (Holmes, *The Apostolic Fathers*, 154–155).

4. See Kenneth A. Strand, "The 'Lord's Day' in the Second Century," in *The Sabbath in Scripture and History* (Washington, DC: Review and Herald, 1982), 346–351.

5. *The Gospel of Peter* 9.35 (Schneemelcher, *New Testament Apocrypha*, 1:224).

6. Clement of Alexandria *Miscellanies* 14 (*The Ante-Nicene Fathers*, 2:459).

7. E.g., J. Massynberde Ford, *Revelation*, The Anchor Bible 38 (New York: Doubleday, 1975), 384; Sweet, *Revelation*, 67; Johnson, "Revelation," 425.

8. "Fragments from the Lost Writings of Irenaeus," 7 (*The Ante-Nicene Fathers*, 1:569–570).

9. For arguments against this view, see Richard Bauckham, "The Lord's Day," in *From Sabbath to Lord's Day*, ed. D. A. Carson (Grand Rapids, MI: Zondervan, 1982), 230–231; see also Samuele Bacchiocchi, *From Sabbath to Sunday* (Rome: The Pontifical Gregorian University Press, 1977), 118–123.

10. E.g., Adolf Deissman, *Light from the Ancient East* (reprint of 1927; Peabody, MA: Hendricksen, 1995), 357–361; James Moffatt, "The Revelation of St. John the Divine," *The Expositor's Greek Testament* (reprint of 1942; Grand Rapids, MI: Eerdmans, 1961), 5:342; Robert H. Charles, *A Critical and Exegetical Commentary on the Revelation of St. John*, The International Critical Commentary (Edinburgh: T. & T. Clark, 1920), 1:23; Lohmeyer, 15; Barclay, *The Revelation of John*, 1:43; George R. Beasley-Murray, *The Book of Revelation*, 2d ed., The New Century Bible Commentary (Grand Rapids, MI: Eerdmans, 1981), 65.

11. See Deissman, 357–358.

12. See further ibid., 358–361.

13. *The Seventh-day Adventist Bible Commentary*, 7:736.

14. See *The Seventh-day Adventist Bible Commentary*, 7:735–736; Strand, "Another Look at 'Lord's Day' in the

Early Church and in Rev. 1:10," *New Testament Studies* 13 (1966/1967): 180; Walter F. Specht, "Sunday in the New Testament," in *The Sabbath in Scripture and History* (Washington, DC: Review and Herald, 1982), 127; Desmond Ford, *Crisis! A Commentary on the Book of Revelation* (Newcastle, CA: Desmond Ford Publications, 1982), 2:250–251; Maxwell, 82–85.

15. White, *The Acts of the Apostles*, 581.

16. J. M. Ford, *Revelation*, 384.

17. E.g., William Milligan, *The Book of Revelation*, The Expositor's Bible (Cincinnati: Jennings & Graham, 1889), 13; J. A. Seiss, *The Apocalypse* (New York: Charles C. Cook, 1909), 1:20, 22; Phillip Carrington, *The Meaning of the Revelation* (London: Society for Promoting Christian Knowledge, 1931), 77–78; E. W. Bullinger, *The Apocalypse* (London: Eyre and Spottiswoode, 1935), 9–14; Walter Scott, *Exposition of the Revelation of Jesus Christ* (London: Pickering and Inglis, 1948), 36; Bacchiocchi, *From Sabbath to Sunday*, 123–131.

18. See Bullinger, *The Apocalypse*, 12; Werner Foerster, "*kurios*, et al.," in *Theological Dictionary of the New Testament*, ed. G. Kittel and G. W. Bromiley (Grand Rapids, MI: Eerdmans, 1964–1976), 1096.

19. Bacchiocchi, 127–128.

20. See *The Seventh-day Adventist Bible Commentary*, 7:735.

21. White, *The Acts of the Apostles*, 583.

22. Ladd, 30.

23. Strahan in Barclay, *The Revelation of John*, 1:51.

24. Milligan, *Lectures on the Apocalypse*, 136.

25. Roloff, 34.

26. Josephus, *The Jewish Antiquities* 3.7.2–4 (Whiston, *The Works of Josephus*, 88–89).

27. See Aune, *Revelation 1–5*, 93–94.

28. Ladd, 33.

29. Tenney, 55; for a fuller treatment of various views regarding "the angels of the seven churches," see Aune, *Revelation 1–5*, 108–112.

30. Isbon T. Beckwith, *The Apocalypse of John* (Grand Rapids, MI: Baker, 1919; reprint 1967), 440.

31. See further in Aune, *Revelation 6–16*, 401–402.

32. Roloff, 37–38.

33. Aune, *Revelation 1–5*, 104–105.

34. Ibid., 117.

35. Johnson, 429; the most recent arguments for this view have been expressed by Beale, 152–169.

36. The view has been recently defended by Aune, *Revelation 1–5*, 105–106.

37. See the Mishnah *Tamid* 3.9; Alfred Edersheim, *The Temple: Its Ministry and Services*, updated ed. (Peabody, MA: Hendrickson, 1994), 125.

38. The Babylonian Talmud, *Hagigah* 14a.

39. Roloff, 36.

40. Ladd, 33.

41. Aune, *Revelation 1–5*, 117.

42. Strand, "The Seven Heads," 205.

43. Ezell, 35.

44. Tenney, 55.

We now analyze the seven messages to the churches. Each analysis begins with the historical and contemporary background of the city in which the church was located. Then we analyze each message in detail. We should keep in mind that these seven messages are not letters, as it is generally assumed. They were all sent together with the rest of the book of Revelation to be read by all of the seven churches. Information about the city in which a respective church was located enables us to understand the import of the message given to that church.

CHRIST'S MESSAGE TO THE CHURCH IN EPHESUS (2:1–7)

[1]*To the angel of the church in Ephesus write:*
Thus says the One who holds the seven stars in his right hand, who walks in the midst of the seven golden lampstands: [2]*I know your works, namely, your labor and endurance, and that you cannot bear evil ones, and that you have tested those who call themselves apostles—and they are not—and you have found them to be liars;* [3]*and you have perseverance and you have born up because of my name, and you have not grown weary.* [4]*But I have against you that you have left your first love.* [5]*Keep remembering, therefore, from where you have fallen, and repent and do the first works; but if not, I am coming to you and I will remove your lampstand from its place, unless you repent.* [6]*But this you have, that you hate the works of the Nicolaitans which I myself also hate.* [7]*The one who has an ear, let him hear what the Spirit says to the churches. To the one who overcomes, I will give him to eat from the tree of life which is in the paradise of God.*

113

NOTES

2:1 *Ephesus.* The city was located about sixty miles from Patmos. At the time of the writing of the book of Revelation, Ephesus was the largest and principal city of the Roman province of Asia.[1] As a metropolis, it was a famous and important political, commercial, and pagan religious center. It had the status of a free city, with self-government within its own limits. It was also the center of the Panionian Games when the whole population of the province gathered together at Ephesus.[2] In addition, in the city there were two temples devoted to the worship of the emperor.

The city was the home of the many-breasted goddess of fertility Artemis or Diana, "whom all of Asia and the world" fanatically worshiped (Acts 19:27). Her image was believed to have fallen down from heaven (Acts 19:35). The magnificent temple devoted to the goddess was the pride of the citizens of Ephesus (cf. Acts 19:35); it was reckoned among the wonders of the ancient world. The inner shrine of the temple of Diana was a safe deposit for an enormous number of valuables from all over the Levant; this made the temple "one of the most important financial centers in the ancient world."[3] William Barclay says: "The temple possessed the right of asylum. That is to say, if any man committed a crime, if he could reach the precincts of the temple before he was arrested, he was safe. That immunity extended to an area of one bowshot, or two hundred yards, all around the temple." Thus, the temple housed the "choicest collection of criminals in the ancient world."[4]

Ephesus was also famous for superstitious practices and magical arts (Acts 19:19). As Barclay points out, "so into Ephesus there poured a stream of criminals of every kind, fugitives from the law, escapers and avoiders of justice, and into Ephesus there flowed a torrent of credulous, superstitious people, for in a superstitious world Ephesus was well-nigh the most superstitious city in the world."[5] He further explains that the reputation of the citizens of the city was "notoriously bad," and the people were regarded as "fickle, superstitious, and immoral." In Ephesus lived the famous philosopher Heraclitus known as "the weeping philosopher," who, it was said, never smiled. According to an ancient writing, he never laughed or smiled because he lived amidst terrible uncleanness of the inhabitants of Ephesus who "were fit only to be drowned."[6]

In Ephesus was located probably the most influential Christian church in the province at the time of the writing of the book of Revelation. It was the church founded by Aquila and Priscilla (Acts 18:18–19) and the young preacher Apollos (Acts 18:23–26). Paul worked in Ephesus for about three years (Acts 20:31), and to this church he addressed his letter which we know today as Ephesians. It was in this city that some of the greatest victories of the gospel were won. In spite of the city's notorious reputation, the church in Ephesus grew rapidly. Later, Timothy and John the apostle spent a great deal of time in ministry there. G. R. Beasley-Murray notes: "It is comprehensible that teachers of many kinds and of every shade of doctrine were drawn to Ephesus, to seek the patronage of the church and to influence its ways."[7] Barclay makes an interesting observation: "Sometimes we say that it is hard to be a Christian in a modern, industrial, competitive civilization. Let us remember Ephesus, and let us remember that there were Christians there."[8]

Holds. The Greek *krateō* is a very strong word meaning "to hold fast" or "to grasp." See 1:16 where Jesus has the seven stars in his right hand.

2:2 *I know your works, namely, your labor and endurance.* In Greek, the word *kai* ("and") functions here epexegetically and is usually translated as "namely" or "that is." It means that what follows will explain what has gone before in the text. So both "labor" and "endurance" are parallel to the previously mentioned "works."

Labor. The Greek *kopos* means "hard work," or "labor to the point of weariness and exhaustion"[9] (cf. Rom. 16:12; 1 Cor. 15:10; Gal. 4:11; 1 Thess. 2:9). The special characteristic of this word is that it describes "the kind of toil which takes everything of mind and sinew that a man can put into it."[10]

Evil ones...who call themselves apostles. This is a reference to the heretical groups called the Nicolaitans (see *Notes* on Rev. 2:6).

2:5 *Keep remembering.* In Greek, the present imperative suggests a continuous and ongoing attitude or action, "keep remembering." In the Greek concept, remembering is not simply recalling but "bearing in mind."

Repent. The aorist imperative suggests a decisive "turning around." Barclay pictures this concept as "a man facing in one direction—away from God—and in repentance he changes his direction—towards God. Repentance means a turning round and a facing in the opposite direction."[11]

Do the first works. The aorist imperative here means, "Start doing the first works."

I will remove your lampstand from its place. In the Bible, the lampstand emblem defines the role of the church as God's witnessing people in the world (see *Notes* on Rev. 1:12). The warning to the church in Ephesus that Christ will remove their lampstand from its place parallels the saying of Jesus in Mark 4:21–25 and Luke 8:16–18 where those who fail to shine their light will have their light-bearing role taken from them.[12]

2:6 Nicolaitans. The identity of this group is unknown to us. According to early Christian writers such as Irenaeus[13] and Hippolytus,[14] the Nicolaitans were the heretical followers of Nicolas (Gr. Nicolaos) of Antioch, one of the seven deacons of the early church (Acts 6:5) who ended up in heresy. Their presence in the church "threatened to destroy the integrity and purity of Christian faith and conduct."[15] They gained adherents among some members of the church in Pergamum; in the message to the church of Pergamum, the Nicolaitans are clearly related to the heretical group which is referred to as those "who hold the teaching of Balaam" (2:14–15). It could be that the Nicolaitans were the same people as those in Pergamum. Nicolas and Balaam seem to be parallel terms; Nicolaos is a compound Greek word (*nikaō* and *laos*) and means "the one who conquers the people." Balaam can be derived from two Hebrew words—*am* ("people") and *baal* (from *balaᶜ*, "to destroy" or "to swallow"), meaning "destruction of people." Thus *Nicolaos* could be the Greek version of the Hebrew *Balaam*, meaning exactly the same thing. So it could be that these two heretical groups were propagating the same error.

According to Numbers 31:16, Balaam was the instigator of idolatry and fornication among the Israelites (Num. 25:1–6). When Balak, the king of Moab, realized that he could not fight against

115

Israel militarily, he hired Balaam, a prophet of God, to curse Israel, hoping that God would forsake Israel and that Balak could conquer them. Instead of cursing Israel, however, from Balaam's mouth came only blessings. When Balaam saw that he could not curse Israel, he advised Balak to use sexual immorality and the glamor of pagan feasts—involving the eating of food sacrificed to the Moabite gods—in order to tempt many Israelites into sin. Thus, Balaam in the New Testament is regarded as a predecessor of the corrupt teachers in the church. Similarly, the false teachers in Pergamum, the ones "who held the doctrine of Balaam," enticed some of their fellow Christians "to eat the things sacrificed to idols and to commit fornication" (Rev. 2:14).

As a part of the civic obligations of the society in which they lived, the Christians in Asia were expected to participate in religious festivals in the pagan temples. A refusal to participate brought ridicule and the hardships of social isolation and economic sanctions. The Christians in Asia faced at least two problems with regard to their involvement in the pagan religious festivals. The first problem was related to the eating of food offered to idols.[16] The participants at the pagan festivals would usually feast on food that consisted primarily of meat that was offered to the local patron god. The festivals often ended with drunkenness and immoral activities. The second problem with regard to the pagan religious festivals was cultic prostitution, the practice that was a part of many ancient pagan religions. Anyone who wanted economic, political, or social status in the society had to participate in these religious demands.

The Christians in Asia were evidently divided on the issues. Involvement in the pagan religious festivals in Asia called for a compromise of Christian faith and beliefs. On one side were those who obediently followed the decision of the Council of Jerusalem to abstain from the food offered to idols and the practice of cultic prostitution obligatory for all citizens (Acts 15:20). On the other side were those who advocated compromise. Such permissive teachings and misconduct were typical characteristics of the Balaamites in Pergamum and the wicked woman "Jezebel" in the church in Thyatira, who caused Christians to practice immorality and to eat things sacrificed to idols (Rev. 2:14, 20). It could be that "the Nicolaitans" and "those who hold the teaching of Balaam" and "Jezebel" refer to three groups of false teachers with the same permissive teaching of compromise, who were thus doing much harm to the local congregations in Asia.[17] All of this indicates, as Barclay suggests, that the Nicolaitans likely taught that Christians are freed from all law and can live as they wish. "They perverted the teaching of Paul [cf. 1 Cor. 8] and turned Christian liberty into Christian license."[18]

2:7 Overcomes. The Greek word *nikaō* means "to be the victor," "to be victorious," "to overcome." The present participle implies continuous victory, "keeps on overcoming" or "continues to be victorious." Overcoming is a recurring theme in the book of Revelation (2:7, 11, 17, 26; 3:5, 12, 21; 5:5; 12:11; 15:2; 17:14; 21:7). Kenneth A. Strand sees it as one of the key motifs of the book.[19] Robert H. Charles explains that the word "implies that the Christian life is a warfare from which there is no discharge, but it is a warfare, our author [John] teaches, in which even the feeblest saint can prove victorious."[20]

Paradise. A Persian loan word, this means "a park" or "a garden"; in the Septuagint (LXX), the word "paradise" is used with reference to the garden of Eden (Gen. 2:8–10). The paradise of God in Revelation symbolizes the restored garden of Eden in which the redeemed will share the gift of eternal life which Adam enjoyed before the entrance of sin into the world.

EXPOSITION

John begins the route of the seven churches with Ephesus, the nearest to Patmos of all the seven cities. Jesus introduces himself to this church as the One who holds fast *the seven stars in his right hand* (cf. Rev. 1:16) and *who walks in the midst of the seven golden lampstands* (cf. Rev. 1:12). The seven stars and the seven lampstands both stand for the seven churches (Rev. 1:20). Christ has complete control over the whole church. His presence is in the church and he has full knowledge of the church's situation and needs.

Jesus' appraisal of the church (2:2–4, 6). Jesus' appraisal of the church in Ephesus is very positive. The church is praised for great qualities: exhausting hard work and patience. The members there *have not grown weary*. They bear up under all kinds of pressure for the sake of Christ's name. That is to say, they have "persevered for the sake of the purity of the message they preach."[21] The church is doctrinally sound; it does not tolerate evil men and tests *those who call themselves apostles—and they are not*. It hates the practices of *the Nicolaitans* (2:6), the heretical group that advocates Christian compromise and promotes the view to their fellow Christians that there is "nothing wrong with a prudent conformity" to the pagan practices (cf. 2:14–15).[22]

The presence of the heretical group of Nicolaitans in the church in Ephesus "threatened to destroy the integrity and purity of Christian faith and conduct."[23] Some fifty years earlier in his farewell speech, Paul warned the Ephesian elders: "I know that after my departure savage wolves will come in among you, not sparing the flock; and from among your own selves men will arise, speaking perverse things, to draw away the disciples after them" (Acts 20:29–30). Fifty years later, the prediction had come true. According to William Barclay, Nicolaitans "were the most dangerous of all heretics from a practical point of view, for, if their teaching had been successful, the result would have been that the world would have changed Christianity, and not Christianity the world."[24] As an energetic church, the Ephesians had tested these false teachers and had found them liars, and they were very determined to preserve sound doctrine and conduct.

Something went wrong with this energetic, patient, and doctrinally sound church, however. It was backsliding in love. Christ gently rebukes the members of the church: *But I have against you that you have left your first love* (2:4). This could mean that their "first love" for Christ and the gospel had been disappearing. This reminds one of the situation of Israel before the Exile, as described by Jeremiah (2:2). Despite devotion to God in the early days, "the devotion of your youth, the love of your betrothals" was now past. The church in Ephesus was in a very similar situation. The initial members of the church in Ephesus were known for their "faith in the Lord Jesus" and their ardent "love for all the saints" (Eph. 1:15; Acts 20:37–38). But what characterized the religion of this church in the beginning was now lacking. The enthusiasm was gone and the members were starting to lose touch with God and love for one another.

Religion in the church of Ephesus became legalistic and loveless. The vertical relationship with God normally defines the horizontal relationship with humanity. It was stated that the Ephesians could not tolerate false teaching. In dealing with heresy and disciplining those who were not doctrinally sound, they evidently tended to be severe, censorious, critical, and fault-finding. It was clear that in emphasizing the soundness of doctrine and checking the orthodoxy of their fellow members, the church was abandoning the loving characteristic of the gospel and becoming legalistic. Sound doctrine, hard work, and church order are undeniably important. However, no good qualities have value without love (1 Cor. 13). The Ephesians put the whole emphasis on the side of sound doctrine and hard work. It was a good decision, but they were backsliding from true, ardent love for Christ and their fellow believers that characterized them in their early days. They had forgotten that only the gospel can balance religious duty with loving affection for fellow Christians.

Jesus' counsel to the church (2:5–6). Though hardworking with high standards, the church in Ephesus was backsliding from its first love. Christ makes a strong appeal with three great imperatives: *Keep remembering...repent...do the first works.* First, they had to keep remembering. As the Greek text indicates, the Ephesians had not forgotten; they were not ignorant of their former condition. Remembering means more than simply recalling the past; it means bearing in mind and keeping afresh the past and applying it in the present. That is why Jesus calls for a decisive turning around and admonishes us to repent. The entire church is called upon to repent, implying that the entire church has declined in love. Repentance denotes a radical change of the whole direction of life. It is a decisive break with the present situation. Remembering and repentance moves one to do the first works. The "first works" are the outcome of the "first love." Philip E. Hughes comments:

> Departure from first love is a falling; it is symptomatic of a decline in practice as well as in devotion, for first love and *first works* belong together: the latter spring naturally from the former. Consequently, the disappearance of the first love entails the disappearance also of the first works, which are works distinguished by selfless zeal and joyful dedication. To recapture the first love is to return to the first works, and this is what the church in Ephesus needs to do if it is to recover its well-being before God.[25]

A return to the first-love Christian experience always results in the first-works experience.

The proof of repentance is a return to devotion characterized by ardent love for God and fellow believers. Jesus' counsel to the Ephesians reflects the experience of the prodigal son who in the far country suddenly remembered his home and the previous status he enjoyed, and then made a decisive turnaround (Luke 15:17–19). Likewise, the Ephesians are called to remember their former devotion and to make a decisive break from their present situation; then they should start doing those works which characterized their devotion at the earliest stage of their existence.[26]

If the Ephesians fail to repent and do their first works, Christ warns that he is coming in judgment to them: *I will remove your lampstand from its place*. In Revelation, God's witnessing people are referred to as lampstands (11:4). As ancient Israel was called to be God's light-bearing witness to the world (cf. Isa. 42:6–7; 49:6; 60:1–3), so is the church in Ephesus. When the Israelites "renounced their calling to be a light to the nations, God removed them as his light-bearing people and transferred the emblem of that call to the church."[27] The church is called to be the light for Christ in the world (Matt. 5:14–16; Phil. 2:15). If it does not exercise its call to shine, it loses the very essence of its existence; consequently, it will have its witnessing lampstand removed from its place, just as Israel in the Old Testament.

The promise to the overcomer (2:7). The overcomer in the church of Ephesus is given the promise that he or she will *eat from the tree of life which is in the paradise of God* (cf. also 22:14). This reference reminds one of the garden of Eden with "the tree of life in the midst of the garden" (Gen. 2:9) in which man and woman were placed at creation. To eat from the tree of life was "to live forever" (Gen. 3:22). It was from that garden, after they had sinned, that Adam and Eve were expelled and forbidden to approach the tree of life and eat of it (Gen. 3:23–24). Through Christ, this situation has been changed. The faithful followers of Christ will, in the new earth (which in Revelation is described as the restored garden of Eden) have access to the "the tree of life producing twelve fruits, yielding its fruit every month, and the leaves of the tree were for the healing of the nations" (Rev. 22:2). The tree of life symbolizes the eternal life free of death and suffering. The overcomer in Ephesus is promised a permanent home in the restored Eden in which he or she will share the gift of eternal life which Adam and Eve enjoyed before the entrance of sin into the world.

Call to hear the Spirit. The message to the church in Ephesus is a strong appeal to all Christians who are backsliding in ardent love for the gospel. They are urged to examine their past lives and to bring to mind what it was like when they were in love with Christ, and how in those early days of their devotion to Christ they responded enthusiastically with "works" of love in their relation to other members of the believing community as well as those outside that community.

Christ's message to this church suggests that the best place to start renewing that relationship is to bear in mind the first-love experience. Like the prodigal son (Luke 15:11–24), we will never be satisfied until we return to the first-love experience with Christ, doing "the first works" that initially characterized that relationship. That is to say, we must make Christ our religion.

Throughout history, Christians have often found themselves strained between love on one side and obedience on the other. In emphasizing strongly the love aspect of the gospel, obedience to the requirements of the gospel can easily be disregarded. In focusing on duty and the preserving of sound doctrine (and often exposing heresy and fighting against it), Christians very often lose love for each other. Upholding doctrine and church order without focusing on Christ is useless, and religion not based on the gospel has no value; it is rather a lifeless, dead religion. Genuine religion is Christ-centered; it is based on both the vertical and horizontal relationships characterized by love for Christ and love for each other.

Historical application. In seeking to apply Jesus' message to the church in Ephesus to a particular period of the history of Christianity besides its local significance, one may observe that the situation and spiritual condition of that church characterized by faithfulness and good works coincided with the situation and spiritual condition of the Christian church of the apostolic period (and some time after). This period was a great start for the church characterized by love and faithfulness to the gospel. But by the time John wrote the book of Revelation, namely, the last decade of the first century, the church had begun losing the fire of its first love, thus departing from the simplicity and purity of the gospel. Thus the church in Ephesus could aptly represent the Christian church of the first century.

CHRIST'S MESSAGE TO THE CHURCH IN SMYRNA (2:8–11)

[8]To the angel of the church in Smyrna write:

Thus says the first and the last, the One who was dead and came to life: [9]I know your affliction and poverty—but you are rich—and the slander of those who say that they are Jews, and they are not, but are the synagogue of Satan. [10]Stop fearing the things which you are about to suffer! Behold, the devil is about to cast some of you into prison that you may be tested, and you will have tribulation for ten days. Remain faithful to the point of death, and I will give you the crown of life. [11]The one who has an ear, let him hear what the Spirit says to the churches. The one who overcomes shall not be harmed by the second death.

NOTES

2:8 *Smyrna.* Smyrna, modern Izmir, was a harbor trade city located on the eastern shore of the Aegean Sea and on the crossroad to Phrygia and Lydia. It was about thirty-five miles north of Ephesus. In the first century, it could have had about 200,000 residents. It had the status of a free city; it was a political, religious, and cultural center noted for the science and medicine that flourished there. It was proud of its famous stadium, library, and the largest public theater in the province, seating some twenty thousand people. It was a wealthy and exceptionally beautiful city, claiming to be "the glory of Asia." The city claimed to be the birthplace of the famous epic poet Homer. Smyrna had a special relationship with Rome, and claimed to be the first in the ancient world to build a temple in honor of *dea Roma* (goddess Roma).

The life of the Christian community in Smyrna was one of "affliction and poverty" (Rev. 2:9).

Two things contributed to the miserable and life-threatening situation of the church. First, the city was the center of emperor worship. At the time the book of Revelation was written, emperor worship became mandatory. Once a year, every Roman citizen was obliged to perform the religious duty of burning incense on the altar to the godhead of Caesar, and then was issued a certificate. To refuse brought about the threat of death. Smyrneans were openly very hostile toward the Christians in the city because of their refusal to participate in emperor worship.

The second thing that made life miserable for Christians in Smyrna was the presence of a large and strong Jewish population also very hostile toward Christians. In their bitterness, the Jews joined the pagans in hating and persecuting Christians. They slandered the Christians before the local government, making malicious accusations, thus stirring up the pagans against the Christians and inciting the authorities to persecute them. (Christians were charged with being cannibals, atheists, and disloyal to the government.)[28] John depicts these Jews as "the synagogue of Satan" (3:9). Although in dire danger, the Christians in Smyrna were found faithful; many of them experienced heroic suffering and death. Among those who suffered martyrdom was Polycarp, the famous bishop of the church in Smyrna in the first half of the second century, who in his youth was associated with John, the author of the book of Revelation.

The One who was dead and came to life. In the Greek, "came to life" is in the aorist tense describing an action completed in the past. It refers here to the death and resurrection of Jesus.

2:9 Affliction. The Greek *thlipsis* basically means "pressure," "the burden that crushes."[29]

Poverty. The Greek *ptōcheia* denotes extreme poverty and destitution—having nothing at all.

The slander of those who say that they are Jews. See *Notes* on Revelation 2:8 (see also "Introduction" of this commentary: "External Problems of the Churches in Asia").

2:10 Stop fearing. In Greek, the present imperative suggests a continuous and ongoing attitude or action. The present tense suggests that Smyrneans were worried and afraid at the time.

Ten days. Most scholars hold that "ten days" was the normal ancient expression for a relatively short period of time (cf. Gen. 24:55; 1 Sam. 25:38; Dan. 1:12–15; Acts 25:6).[30] David Aune maintains that it is probably related to the fact that the sum of all fingers is ten.[31] These "ten days" represent a period of testing the faithfulness and endurance of the community in Smyrna, like the ten days of testing for Daniel and his friends in Babylon (Dan. 1:12–15).[32]

The crown of life. "The crown of life" is also mentioned in James 1:12; elsewhere in the New Testament it is spoken of as the crown of righteousness (2 Tim. 4:8) and the crown of glory (1 Pet. 5:4). In Greek, two words are used for crown: *diadēma*, which is the royal crown (from which the English word "diadem" comes), and *stephanos*, which is used here in the text. *Stephanos* is not the royal crown, but the crown of victory, a garland of leaves or flowers. It was given to the victorious athletes in the Olympic games held in Smyrna, signifying the joy that comes from victory. In the New Testament, the word refers to the eschatological gift of God to believers. *Stephanos* is the word which Paul uses in 1 Corinthians 9:25 for referring to "a perishable crown." In Revelation 12:1, the victorious church wears *stephanos* of twelve stars upon her head. The "of" in the phrase means "consists of"; the phrase should be thus understood to mean, "the crown consists of life." To receive the crown of life is to receive life.[33]

2:11 Overcome. See *Notes* on Revelation 2:7.

EXPOSITION

Smyrna was the next closest city to Ephesus, being about forty miles to the north. The message to the church in this city is the shortest of the seven. Jesus introduces himself as *the first and last, the One who was dead and came to life* (2:8; cf. 1:17). This introduction of Jesus is well suited to a suffering church passing through dire, constant persecution. These are the words which John heard earlier when he fell down at Jesus' feet: "Stop being afraid! I am the first and the last, and the living One, and I was dead and behold, I am living for ever and ever" (1:17). We observed earlier that "the first and the last" is a reference to the Old Testament Yahweh, the God of the covenant. Jesus begins his message to the Smyrneans by reminding them of his own suffering and death. He experienced the worst that life could bring; he died, but he was raised to life again. In identifying himself with the Smyrneans, Jesus is telling them that no matter what might happen, he, the resurrected and glorified Lord, can help because he has gone through it. He remains faithful to his promise to be always with his suffering people.

Jesus' appraisal of the church (2:9). Jesus knows the "affliction and poverty" of the church in Smyrna. The members of the church are in dire peril. In Greek, *affliction* means a serious tribulation, under the pressure of a burden that crushes. This pressure comes from outside, namely, from the demands for emperor worship and the malignant slander of the Jews. Second, the members are in extreme *poverty*. As the Greek text indicates, they possess nothing. Their poverty is undoubtedly the result of the persecution the church is going through. It certainly contrasts with the wealthy church of Laodicea which boasts of its material riches and is in need of nothing; but it possessed nothing of spiritual things (3:17). The Christians in Smyrna lived in one of the wealthiest cities, and yet they are extremely poor. Although poor in material things, however, they are rich in grace and faith.

Jesus' counsel to the church (2:10). The Smyrneans are under serious pressure from the outside. They are told that they will soon suffer even more in the days to come. They will experience trial and imprisonment for ten days—that is to say, for a very short period of time, just as Daniel and his friends were tested for ten days (Dan. 1:12–15). Although short, this time of testing will be very sharp. It is commonly believed that prison in the ancient world was a place where the accused awaited sentencing which resulted either in execution or banishment.

Stop fearing the things which you are about to suffer! This sounds rather like a gentle rebuke. The Smyrneans evidently worry. Jesus is telling them: "Stop being afraid! I am in control. I have personally experienced death and come back to life. I am the first and the last, and I am faithful to my promise." Jesus counsels Smyrna again: **Remain faithful to the point of death, and I will give you the crown of life.** This church has already been faithful, and Jesus urges continued faithfulness. The reward for faithfulness is "the crown of life," namely, the crown that consists of life. It is not a royal crown, but the crown of victory, the garland, given to the winner at the Olympic games, signifying the joy that comes from victory.

The Smyrneans must keep their eyes fixed on the reward. The pressure and distress will not last; those who stand faithful will be rewarded. "Blessed is the man who perseveres under trial; for once he has been approved, he will receive the crown of life, which the Lord has promised to those who love Him" (James 1:12). Paul could speak with confidence and great anticipation: "I have fought the good fight, I have finished the course, I have kept the faith; in the future there is laid up for me the crown of righteousness, which the Lord, the righteous Judge, will award to me on that day" (2 Tim. 4:7–8). Indeed, "the sufferings of this present time are not worthy to be compared with the glory that is to be revealed to us" (Rom. 8:18).

The promise to the overcomer (2:10b–11). Those who remain faithful will receive **the crown** consisting of **life**; that is to say, they will not experience the second death. In Revelation, the second death means the total extinction of the wicked (20:14); it stands in opposition to eternal life. The Smyrneans were in constant fear of physical death. To the faithful, however, physical death is temporary; it is like a sleep, and, as such, means nothing because of the hope of the resurrection. It is the second death that should be feared—eternal death from which there will be no resurrection. Jesus warned his followers: "Do not fear those who kill the body, but are unable to kill the soul; but rather fear Him who is able to destroy both soul and body in hell" (Matt. 10:28). By virtue of his death on the cross and resurrection, Jesus broke the power of death. He is the One having "the keys of Death and Hades" (Rev. 1:18). He lives forevermore on behalf of his people. The faithful will receive the crown of eternal life and, therefore, will not be harmed by *the second death* (cf. Rev. 20:6) which is reserved for the wicked (Rev. 20:14; 21:8).

Call to hear the Spirit. The message to the church in Smyrna still applies to Christians suffering under the pressure of life or the pressure of antagonism and injustice. It is for those who may be afraid because they fear the suffering to come. Jesus' counsel is for them: "Stop fearing! I am in control. There is nothing in life or in death, in time or eternity, nobody and nothing, that can separate you from my love" (cf. Rom. 8:38–39).

Historical application.   The experience of the church in Smyrna coincided with the severe persecution of the faithful Christian church throughout the Roman Empire during the second and third centuries. Historicist interpreters have generally applied the "ten days" (2:10) to the notorious intermittent imperial persecution (A.D. 303–313) initiated by Diocletian and taken over by his successor Gallerius. This period was also characterized by further departure from the simplicity of the gospel. In such a way, the church in Smyrna could represent the period in church history from the beginning of the second century until approximately A.D. 313 when Constantine the Great issued the famous Edict of Milan granting Christians religious freedom.

CHRIST'S MESSAGE TO THE CHURCH IN PERGAMUM (2:12–17)

12To the angel of the church in Pergamum write:
Thus says the One who has the sharp two-edged sword: 13I know where you dwell, where the throne of Satan is, and you are holding fast my name, and you did not deny my faith even in the days of Antipas, my faithful witness, who was killed among you, where Satan dwells. 14But I have a few things against you, because you have there those who hold the teaching of Balaam, who taught Balak to cast a stumbling block before the sons of Israel to eat the things sacrificed to idols and to commit fornication. 15Thus you also have those who hold the teaching of the Nicolaitans likewise. 16Repent, therefore; but if not, I am coming to you quickly and I

will make war against them with the sword of my mouth. ¹⁷ The one who has an ear, let him hear what the Spirit says to the churches. To the one who overcomes I will give of the hidden manna, and I will give him a white stone, and on the stone a new name written which nobody knows except the one who receives it.

NOTES

2:12 *Pergamum.* In John's day, Pergamum (or Pergamos) was the capital city of the Roman province of Asia, located some forty miles northeast of Smyrna. In addition to its political importance, Pergamum was celebrated as the center of intellectual life in the whole Hellenistic world. Its famous library of nearly 200,000 volumes was second only to the library of Alexandria. The city was the home of Galen, the famous physician in the ancient world, who studied at the medical school of Asclepios.

Pergamum was also a great and important religious center; it was famed for its magnificent temples erected to Zeus, Athena, Dionysus, and Asclepios. On the hill above the city stood the great altar of Zeus, the central portion of which is exhibited in the Pergamum Museum in Berlin. "Forty feet high, and it stood on a projecting ledge of rock. It looked exactly like a great seat or throne on the hillside; and all day every day it smoked with the smoke of sacrifices offered to Zeus."[34] Near the city stood the immense shrine of Asclepios, the serpent-god of healing. In John's time, the shrine experienced great popularity; people came from all over the world to be healed by the god Asclepios. Pergamum was really the "Lourdes of the Province of Asia."[35] Both Zeus and Asclepios were called "the Savior" and were represented by a serpent (an emblem retained by the modern medical profession). Pergamum was the first city in Asia to support the imperial cult and have a temple dedicated to the worship of the Roman emperor. This may explain the city's description as the place "where Satan's throne is."

2:13 *Where you dwell.* The Greek word *katoikeō*, "to settle down," means to reside permanently.

The throne of Satan. The Greek word *thronos* means "throne" and "seat of the authority" (cf. Matt. 19:28; Luke 1:32). The phrase possibly refers to the city as a stronghold of both pagan religious life and emperor worship. Pergamum was famous for the Zeus and Asclepios cults bringing people from far and near. A religion which had a serpent symbol—regarding the serpent as an incarnation of the god himself and associating him with the term "Savior"—could only fill Christians with horror, reminding them of Satan "the ancient serpent" (Rev. 12:9). It may be that which caused Christians to call Pergamum the place of Satan's throne.

Above all, the greatest danger to the Christian church came from the demands for emperor worship. The city was the center of the imperial cult of the province of Asia. In John's day, emperor worship was a sacred duty of all citizens. Every citizen of the province had to appear before the local magistrates in Pergamum once a year and offer a pinch of incense to a representation of the emperor, saying, "Caesar is Lord," and then be issued a certificate. The worship of the emperor was a test of loyalty to Rome, and a refusal to take part in the worship and receive the certificate meant persecution and death.[36] The Christians in Pergamum lived in the very place "where Satan dwelt." They were apparently asked to deny and give up their faith in Christ (cf. Rev. 2:13).

Antipas, my faithful witness. "Antipas," a common Greek name, refers most likely to a Christian in Pergamum who underwent martyrdom for his faith and remained loyal. We know nothing about him; it might be that his martyrdom was the price he paid for refusing to worship the emperor. According to later tradition, he was "burned to death in a brazen bull" during the reign of the emperor Domitian.[37] The Greek word *martus* normally means "witness." When later in the early church many faithful witnesses were killed for their faith, the word *martus* also came to mean martyr, namely, "one who witnessed unto death" (see *Notes* on Rev. 1:5).

2:14 *Those who hold the teaching of Balaam* are here clearly related to the Nicolaitans (cf. Rev. 2:15), which suggests that the followers of Balaam and the Nicolaitans were one and the same group. They symbolized the false teachers in the Pergamum church who were encouraging their fellow Christians into religious and moral compromise with regard to food sacrificed to idols and fornication (see *Notes* on Rev. 2:6).

2:16 *Repent.* The Greek aorist imperative suggests a decisive action of turning around (see *Notes* on Rev. 2:5).

2:17 *Overcomes.* See *Notes* on Revelation 2:7.

The hidden manna. According to Jewish tradition, the ark of the covenant—in which the pot of manna was placed for a memorial (Exod. 16:32–34; cf. Heb. 9:4)—was taken by Jeremiah at the destruction of Solomon's temple and hidden in a cleft in Mt. Sinai; it would stay there until the Messiah comes.[38] The manna will then be recovered as the food for the messianic kingdom: "And it will happen at that time that the treasury of manna will come down from on high, and they will eat of it in those years."[39] In the context of the situation of the church in Pergamum, the hidden manna symbolizes participation in the eating of the heavenly manna, "the bread of the angels" (Ps. 78:25), in contrast to eating the food sacrificed to pagan gods.

A white stone. Many suggestions have been made with regard to "a white stone," because in the ancient world white stones were given for many different reasons; no one view seems to be entirely satisfactory. In the context here, the white stone refers most likely to *tessera*, the reward for the victor at the games. It had his name inscribed on it, and it entitled him to special honor and privileges, including admission to public festivals. The white stone gives to the overcomer in the church in Pergamum admission to participate in the heavenly banquet (Rev. 19:7–9).

EXPOSITION

Jesus identifies himself to the church in Pergamum as **the One who has the sharp two-edged sword** (cf. Rev. 1:16). The Roman governor, with headquarters in Pergamum, had the right of the sword; that is to say, he claimed to have the power of life and death. At his command, a person could be put to death on the spot, and he could use it at any given moment against any Christian. But the very outset of the message to the church urges the Christians not to forget that the last word is still with the risen Christ, who has the sharp, two-edged sword. According to the epistle to the Hebrews, the word of God is sharper than any two-edged sword (4:12). The persecutors of God's people might be "satanically powerful," yet the power of the resurrected Christ is greater.[40] "In the world you have tribulation, but take courage; I have overcome the world" (John 16:33). He is indeed in control.

Jesus' appraisal of the church (2:13–15). Jesus has full knowledge of this church's situation: *I know where you dwell, where the throne of Satan is.* Jesus recognizes Pergamum as a very dangerous place. The Christians in Pergamum lived in a religious and moral climate hostile to their faith. The Greek text indicates that they resided there permanently. On one hand, they were surrounded by paganism and its magnificent and splendid temples; on the other, they were exposed to a pagan religious lifestyle and immoral practices. No wonder the lifestyle of the pagan religion was, in its own way, very appealing to some Christians in Pergamum. Above all, the emperor worship created a difficult environment for this church. At any time, the authorities could summon the Christians and order them to worship the emperor and denounce Christ on threat of persecution and death; those who complied were issued a certificate. This made the city the place *where Satan dwells* and where his rule was the strongest. The repeated references in verse 13 to the city as the ruling and dwelling place of Satan indicates how dangerous Pergamum could be for Christians living there.

Despite the circumstances, the Christians in Pergamum remained faithful. *And you are holding fast my name, and you did not deny my faith even in the days of Antipas, my faithful witness, who was killed among you.* In spite of the fact that Pergamum was a very dangerous place for Christian faith and existence, and that they had many reasons to escape and live elsewhere, the Christians decided to stay firm and live and bear witness for Christ where life had set them, namely, where Satan's rule was the strongest. They stayed and remained loyal, even in the face of the persecution and death as experienced by Antipas, who was probably one of the faithful in the church in Pergamum.

It is especially significant that Jesus calls Antipas "my faithful witness." This is

Jesus' own title in the book (Rev. 1:5; 3:14). In the early church, the Greek word *martus* meant both "witness" and "martyr." That is to say, to be a witness for the truth often meant to be a martyr. Jesus is the faithful witness/martyr, and all who bear witness for him have often to suffer with and for him. Even today, one who bears witness for Christ is often a martyr for Christ, not so much in the sense of having to give up his or her life for Christ, but in the sense of having to suffer for Christian principles. But one thing must be remembered: to those who are faithful as Antipas was, Jesus Christ gives "nothing less than his own title." To suffer for Christ is to go through what Christ has already gone through and, in the end, to share the glory with him.[41]

The second part of Jesus' appraisal of this church, however, is not pleasant at all. The Pergamenians are evidently a divided church. Some of them, like Antipas, held fast Christ's name and did not deny their faith; namely, they were opposed to any compromise with the world's conduct and lifestyle. Others in Pergamum held to the teachings of **Balaam** and **the Nicolaitans**. While the Ephesians perceived the destructive effects of the deceptive teachings of the Nicolaitans, the churches in Pergamum and Thyatira tolerated these false teachers and the compromises made to their religion. The fact that the Balaamites and Nicolaitans are mentioned together suggests that they are somehow related. We met them earlier in Ephesus and will meet them again in the message to the church in Thyatira. These false teachers advocated compromise and sought to persuade their fellow Christians that there was nothing wrong with a "prudent conformity to the world's standards" in order to escape persecution (cf. 2 Pet. 2:15; Jude 11).[42]

Christians are called to be holy, that is, separated and different from the world: "Come out from their midst and be separate" (2 Cor. 6:17). This separation, however, means neither a separation and isolation from the rest of the people in the world nor a hatred for them. Jesus prayed that his disciples not be taken from the world but be kept from "the evil one" (John 17:15–16). In order to save the world, followers of Christ will seek to be "all things to all men" (following Paul's example) so that they might save some (1 Cor. 9:22). Christians "compromise," so to speak, so that people may be saved and brought up to the level of Christian faith and life rather than bringing Christianity down to the level of the world. The problem with the Nicolaitans was that they followed a "policy of compromise" in their loyalty to Christ in order to avoid discomfort and trouble in the world.[43]

Jesus' counsel to the church (2:16). Jesus' counsel to the entire church in Pergamum is similar to that given to the Ephesians (cf. 2:5): *Repent, therefore.* If those advocating compromise do not repent, dreadful consequences will result. Christ says that he will come to them *quickly and will make war against them with the sword of his mouth.* This instrument evokes God's threat to Balaam of punishment with the sword (Num. 22:23, 31–32). In the war waged against the Midianites, Balaam was slain with the sword (Num. 31:8), along with those he induced to sin (Num. 25:5). Similar judgment is directed against the Balaamites and the Nicolaitans in Pergamum. According to the author of Hebrews, the word of God is sharper than any two-edged sword and judges "the thoughts and intentions of the heart" (Heb. 4:12). Paul also speaks of "the sword of the Spirit, which is the word of God" (Eph. 6:17). The sword, then, is the word of Christ. The Greek present tense indicates a real threat; Christ is already on his way to wage a war and perform judgment with "the sword of his mouth" (cf. Rev. 19:13–15). The only way to escape the impending judgment is to make a decisive turnaround and repent.

The promise to the overcomer (2:17). Those who repent are given a threefold promise: they will be given the hidden manna, a white stone, and a new name written on the stone. The false teachers in Pergamum advocated compromise in eating the pagan food sacrificed to idols in order to get a certificate and avoid discomfort. The day is coming when those who remain faithful and refuse to participate in pagan feasts will participate in a feast of heavenly food—*the hidden manna*—"bread of the angels" (Ps. 78:25), reserved only for the overcomers who reject compromise and hold fast Christ's name. Instead of the Roman certificate, they will receive *a white stone* with a *new name* inscribed on it as the award for remaining faithful and loyal to Christ.

A new name in the Bible stands for a person's new relationship with God (cf. Gen. 17:5; 32:27–28; Isa. 62:2; 65:15; Rev. 14:1). In the context of persecution and false accusations of the church in Pergamum, the "new name" signifies a restoration of dignity of a "good name." A white stone with a new name inscribed on it entitles the overcomer to the special privilege of participating in "the wedding supper of the Lamb" in the heavenly city at the Second Coming. "Blessed are those who are invited to the wedding supper of the Lamb" (Rev. 19:9).

Call to hear the Spirit. The situation of the Christians in Pergamum clearly shows that it is perfectly possible to be a follower of Christ under horrendous circumstances. Christians are invited to live lives of a "faithful witness" where life has set them. If they are in "Pergamum" where Satan's influences and power are the strongest, then there they must live and demonstrate that they are the followers of Christ who himself was "the faithful witness."[44]

Historical application. In applying the message to the church in Pergamum to Christian history, the situation of this church seems to aptly fit into the period after the conversion of Constantine to Christianity in A.D. 313. The church finally won its struggle with paganism, and Christianity became the state religion. The Christians did not have to fear persecution or outside pressure anymore. Tradition was gradually replacing the Bible as the source of teaching and belief. Although many Christians remained unwavering and faithful to the gospel during this period, the fourth and fifth centuries of the Christian era were characterized by spiritual decline and apostasy, during which the church wrestled with the temptation of compromise.

CHRIST'S MESSAGE TO THE CHURCH IN THYATIRA (2:18–29)

[18]To the angel of the church in Thyatira write:

Thus says the Son of God, the One whose eyes are as a flame of fire, and his feet like burnished bronze: [19]I know your works, namely, your love and faith, that is your service and perseverance, and that your last works are greater than the former. [20]But I have against you that you tolerate the woman Jezebel who calls herself a prophetess and teaches and leads astray my servants to commit fornication and eat things sacrificed to idols. [21]And I gave her time that she might repent, and she does not want to repent of her fornication. [22]Behold, I am casting her into bed, and those who commit adultery with her into great affliction, unless they repent of her works, [23]and I will kill her children, and all the churches will know that I am the One who searches kidneys and hearts, and I will give to each of you according to your works. [24]Now, I say to you, those the remaining ones in Thyatira, all those who do not have this teaching, who have not known the deep things of Satan,

as they say; I do not lay on you another burden, [25]except, hold what you have until I come.[26]To the one who overcomes and who keeps my works until the end, I shall give to him authority over the nations [27]and he will shepherd them with a rod of iron, as the vessels of a potter are smashed together, as I also have received it from my Father, [28]and I will give him the morning star. [29]The one who has an ear, let him hear what the Spirit says to the churches.

NOTES

2:18 *Thyatira*. Thyatira was located some forty miles southeast of Pergamum. It was the smallest and least important of the seven cities; it had no special religious or political significance. It was an important commercial city, however, especially known for its dyeing industry and its manufacturing of the royal purple and woolen goods. Lydia, the seller of purple in Philippi—the first Christian convert in Europe—was from Thyatira (Acts 16:14). The citizens of the city were mainly poor laborers, as opposed to those living in Pergamum.

The Christians in Thyatira evidently did not face the danger of splendid pagan religions or pagan lifestyle. Neither were they under the oppression of emperor worship or menaced by Jewish opponents. The threat to this church did not come from outside but from within. Thyatira was known for many trade guilds; it might be that the danger which threatened the church in this city came directly from these trade guilds. A merchant or trader could not have a job and make money unless he was a member of his trade guild. This created a real problem for the Christians in Thyatira, for they could not join a trade guild. Guild members were expected to attend the guild festivals in the pagan temples and to share a common meal which would largely consist of meat offered to the guild's patron god; the festival often ended with drunkenness and immoral activities. Those who refused to participate in the meals would suffer ridicule and the hardships of social isolation and economic sanctions.

2:19 *Your works, namely, your love and faith, that is your service and perseverance*. The Greek conjunction *kai* ("and") functions here epexegetically, meaning "namely" or "which is."

2:20 *The woman Jezebel*. "Jezebel" may be the symbolic name of a prominent woman in the church in Thyatira who claimed to have the prophetic gift and exercised great authority, which she claimed to have received from God. She is named Jezebel after the wife of the Old Testament king, Ahab, who corrupted the faith in Israel by introducing the idolatrous worship of Baal and Astarte (1 Kings 16:31–33). Whoever she might be, "Jezebel" in Thyatira had a persuasive influence in the church.

As mentioned before, the burning problem in the church in Thyatira was whether Christians could participate in the pagan feasts and festivals held by the trade guilds and the activities associated with them. Jezebel was the leader of a movement which was promoting compromise with the world's standards with pervasive influence. She encouraged her fellow Christians to participate in activities associated with the trade guilds that often involved food sacrificed to the pagan gods, drinking, and sexual immorality. This was all done "in the interest of business and commercial prosperity."[45] Her permissive teaching of compromise was the same as that of the Nicolaitans and the Balaamites in Ephesus and Pergamum, who did much harm to the local congregations in the province of Asia. She could have been a leader of the Nicolaitans in the church in Thyatira (see further *Notes* on Rev. 2:6). Most of those in the church were evidently seduced by the prophetess to compromise and "to commit fornication and eat things sacrificed to idols" (Rev. 2:20).

2:23 *I will kill her children.* This is evidently an allusion to king Ahab's seventy children who were slaughtered by Jehu (2 Kings 10:6–8). The saying in Revelation 2:23 should, of course, be taken symbolically.

The One who searches kidneys and hearts. This statement is drawn from Jeremiah 17:10 where to search kidneys (often translated as "minds") and hearts belongs only to God (cf. 1 Kings 8:39; Prov. 24:12). In the ancient world, kidneys were regarded as "the seat of emotions," and the heart as "the seat of intelligence or the will."[46]

2:24 *Who have not known the deep things of Satan.* Paul speaks of "the depths of God"— the knowledge of which Christians can experience through the Holy Spirit (1 Cor. 2:10; cf. Rom. 11:33–34). The phrase "the deep things of Satan, as they say" refers to the misleading teaching of the Nicolaitans, which can be briefly described like this: a Christian who has knowledge of "the deep things of Satan" (who has experienced sin in its fullness) is able to enjoy the full freedom in Christ and can have a real appreciation of grace. Those who remained at "the elementary instruction of the apostles, who feared to join in the activities of the trade guilds and kept themselves apart from the world" should be looked upon with pity.[47]

I do not lay on you another burden. The language here is related to the conclusion of the decree of the Council of Jerusalem: "For it seemed good to the Holy Spirit and to us to lay upon you no greater burden than these essentials: that you abstain from things sacrificed to idols, and from blood and from things strangled and from fornication" (Acts 15:28–29).

2:26 *Overcomes.* See *Notes* on Revelation 2:7.

EXPOSITION

The message to the church in Thyatira is the longest of the seven. To the Christians there Jesus comes as **the Son of God, the One whose eyes are as a flame of fire, and his feet like burnished bronze** (cf. Rev. 1:14–15). In the introductory vision Jesus appears as "a son of man" (1:13), but here he is the Son of God. His description reminds us of the divine messenger in Daniel: "His eyes were like flaming torches, his arms and feet like the gleam of polished bronze" (10:6). The flaming eyes symbolize Christ's penetrating ability to see the innermost part of human beings. The feet like burnished bronze signify his uncompromising stability. The church is evidently under intense and careful scrutiny by the penetrating discernment of *the one who searches kidneys and hearts* (Rev. 2:23).

Jesus' appraisal of the church (2:19–23). The church in Thyatira is clearly a divided church. On the surface, it is a very active church, full of love and faith manifested in service and perseverance. Love and faith go together in the New Testament (cf. Gal. 5:6; Eph. 1:15; 6:23; 1 Thess. 3:6; 2 Tim. 1:13; Philem. 5). Service is the outcome of love (1 Thess. 1:3; Heb. 6:10), and perseverance the product of faith (Col. 1:23; 2 Thess. 1:4; Heb. 6:12). In the book of Revelation, faith and perseverance are the main characteristics of God's faithful people (14:12; cf. 13:10). Moreover, Thyatira is an improving church, for her *last works are greater than the former.*

In the eyes of Christ, however, an active church does not always mean a faithful church. As Barclay notes, the threat to the church has not come from outside of the church—from persecution, appealing pagan worship, or worship of the emperor. The threat has come rather from the inside, from those who claim to have authority from God but have led the church astray with the most dangerous doctrines for the Christian church—"a doctrine of compromise."[48] This apostate group is referred to in terms of Jezebel, the Old Testament queen who led Israel into sin by supplanting the worship of the true God with the worship of Baal. Jezebel in Thyatira *calls herself a prophetess* (2:20). In the early church, women also received the gift of prophecy (Luke 2:36; Acts 21:9). The gift of prophecy was highly respected, because prophets were regarded as receiving direct revelation from God.

Jezebel in Thyatira claims to have that gift; she is portrayed as one who *teaches and deceives my servants to commit fornication and eat things sacrificed to idols.* This is what we met in the churches of Ephesus and Pergamum. While these two churches were beset by this same false teaching, the church in Thyatira, as the Greek text plainly indicates, allowed or tolerated its presence. The prophetess openly taught and promoted compromise with the world's standards, and she did it with great success, for most of the congregation followed her seductive teaching. Only a minority, who are referred to as the "remaining ones" (Rev. 2:24), had not succumbed to her persuasive influence and remained faithful to the gospel preached by John. While the church in Ephesus lacked ardent love and focused only on the obedience to God, thus becoming legalistic and severe in dealing with and checking those who were not doctrinally sound, the church in Thyatira went to another extreme. In emphasizing love and the gospel, this church tolerated the false teaching that perverted sound doctrine and conduct, doing much harm to the purity of the gospel teaching and church unity.

Christ was not pleased with the compromising attitude of this woman and her followers. So he took some decisive steps. First, he *gave her time that she might repent.* Because she persistently refused to do so, he threatened to bring great affliction upon her and *those who commit adultery with her* (that is to say, her followers). In the Bible, unfaithfulness to God is often expressed in terms of adultery (Exod. 34:15–16; Deut. 31:16; Hos. 9:1; Matt. 12:39; Mark 8:38). Here, Jezebel and her company, who tried to compromise and conform to the world, are described as committing spiritual infidelity. Therefore, as the final step, Jesus threatened to *kill her children* with the plague. This is a very serious threat, although the saying must be taken symbolically. The execution of judgment on this compromising group served as a warning, with redemptive purposes, to others: *And all the churches will know that I am the One who searches kidneys and hearts, and I will give to each of you according to your works* (2:23). To search kidneys (the seat of emotions) and hearts (the seat of intelligence or the will) belongs only to God (Jer. 17:10; cf. 1 Kings 8:39; Prov. 24:12). The Christians in Thyatira are under the scrutinizing eye of the only One who is able to penetrate the inmost thoughts, feelings, and governing motives. Nothing is hidden from Christ's penetrating gaze (Heb. 4:13).

Jesus' counsel to the church (2:24–25). Jesus called those who remained faithful in Thyatira "the remaining ones." This phrase is used in the book of Revelation in a special sense with reference to God's faithful end-time people (12:17). These remaining ones are those *who have not known the deep things of Satan.* The verb "to know" in the Bible means more than intellectual knowledge; it denotes the knowledge that comes through experience, including the sexual relationship (cf. Gen. 4:1; 19:5, 8). This remnant has not been involved in the spiritual adultery of experiencing in their lives the depth of Satan's deceptive teaching, but has remained loyal and unaffected by his deception. And Jesus promises that he will *not lay on you another burden, except, hold what you have until I come.* "Another burden" refers clearly to the instruction given by the apostles at the Council of Jerusalem (cf. Acts 15:28–29).

The promise to the overcomer (2:26–28). The overcomers in Thyatira, those who remain loyal to Christ, are given a twofold promise. First, they will be given *authority over the nations.* We recall the words of Psalm 2:8–9: "Ask of Me, and I will surely give the nations as Your inheritance, and the very ends of the earth as Your possession. You shall break them with a rod of iron, You shalt shatter them like earthware."

Jesus has been given the authority to rule over the nations (Rev. 12:5; 19:15; cf. Matt. 28:18; Rev. 12:10). To the church in Thyatira, he gave the promise that the day is coming when the faithful and loyal remnant will share in the authority of Jesus; they will rule with him (cf. Rev. 1:6; 3:21). The fulfillment of the promise given in Psalm 2 is realized in Revelation 20–22, when God's people are on the throne and rule with Jesus in the heavenly places.

A second promise is given: ***And I will give him the morning star.*** In Revelation 22:16, Jesus calls himself "the Bright Morning Star." All of this reminds us of Balaam's prophecy: "A star shall come forth from Jacob, and a scepter shall rise from Israel" (Num. 24:17). As Barclay points out, "the promise of the morning star is the promise of Christ himself."[49] Not only will the conquerors be with Christ and rule with him, but they will have a special and close relationship with him; they will never lose him and will be with him forever.

Call to hear the Spirit. The experience of a minority of the believers in the church of Thyatira proves that love and faith manifested in Christian service and perseverance can be experienced even in churches where the majority have chosen to follow a way of compromise to the world's standards and conform to a non-Christian lifestyle. Christian service and perseverance are the result of the working and transforming influence of the Holy Spirit upon the heart, and they are not conditioned by favorable circumstances.

Historical application. Applied historically, the Middle Ages, or so-called Dark Ages (the sixth up to the sixteenth century), fit well into the time of the church in Thyatira. It was a dark and difficult period in the history of the Christian church when church tradition replaced the Bible as the source of teaching and conduct.

Rather than teaching true biblical doctrine and conduct, the church was promoting sinful action and false teaching and things contrary to the Bible. Thus people were led astray from the simplicity of the gospel; works came to be regarded as a means of earning salvation. Those who resisted the apostasy and corrupting influences of the institutional church experienced rejection and persecution. Toward the end of this period, many voices of reform arose which led toward the movements of the Reformation and a revival of the simplicity and the purity of the gospel.

CHRIST'S MESSAGE TO THE CHURCH IN SARDIS (3:1–6)

[1]To the angel of the church in Sardis write:
Thus says the One who has the seven Spirits of God and seven stars: I know your works, that you have a name that you live, and you are dead. [2]Keep watching and strengthen the remaining ones that are about to die, for I have not found your works fulfilled before my God. [3]Keep remembering, therefore, how you have received and heard, and keep it and repent. If therefore you do not watch, I will come as a thief; you will in no way know at what hour I will come upon you. [4]But you have a few names in Sardis who have not defiled their garments, and they will walk with me in white, because they are worthy. [5]The one who overcomes thus will be clothed in white garments, and I will not erase his name from the book of life, and I will confess his name before my Father and before his angels. [6]The one who has an ear, let him hear what the Spirit says to the churches.

NOTES

3:1 *Sardis*. Sardis lay thirty miles southeast of Thyatira. The city had a splendid history. Some six centuries before the book of Revelation was written, Sardis had been one of the greatest cities in the ancient world. It had been the capital of the kingdom of Lydia, ruled by the wealthy Croesus. By the Roman period, Sardis had lost prestige in the ancient world. While continuing to enjoy its prosperity and wealth, in John's time its glory and pride was rooted in past history rather than in present reality. According to W. M. Ramsay, "No city of Asia at that time showed such a melancholy contrast between past splendor and present decay as Sardis."[50] In the first century, Sardis was the center of the wool and dyeing industries. The patron deity of the city was the goddess Cybele whose temple hosted eunuch priests. According to Robert H. Mounce, this goddess (equating to the Greek Artemis) "was believed to possess the special power of restoring the dead to life."[51]

3:2 *Keep watching.* This admonition of Christ to the church in Sardis is very appropriate in light of the historical background of the city. Sardis was built on a hill so steep that it was considered a natural citadel, and its defenses seemed secure. The location of the city made the citizens overconfident; as a result, the city walls were carelessly guarded. The city was captured twice by surprise, first by Cyrus the Persian (549 B.C.) and later by Antiochus (218 B.C.). On both occasions, enemy troops climbed the precipice by night and found that the Sardians had set no guard. The city was captured and destroyed because of the overconfidence of the citizens and the failure of the guards to watch. It seemed that this carelessness had crept into the church; hence the warning: "Keep watching."

The remaining ones (Gr. *ta loipa*). The grammatical problem here is that "the remaining ones" in Greek is neuter adjective plural. Some have argued that, as such, the word cannot refer to people but to things. That neuter adjectives can also refer to people is clear from other New Testament texts including 1 Corinthians 1:27–28 and Hebrews 7:7.

3:3 *Keep remembering.* This phrase is in the present imperative, which suggests a continuous and ongoing attitude and action. The Greek text does not suggest an idea of recalling but of "bearing in mind."

Repent. The aorist imperative suggests that a decisive turning around be made (see *Notes* on Rev. 2:5).

3:4 *Defiled their garments.* This phrase refers most likely to the compromise with the pagan environment, the problem that troubled all of the seven churches of the province of Asia.

3:5 *Overcomes.* See *Notes* on Revelation 2:7.

The book of life. This book refers to the concept of the heavenly record book or register in which the righteous are registered by name. Both the Old (Exod. 32:32–33; Ps. 69:28; Dan. 12:1) and New (Luke 10:20; Phil. 4:3; Heb. 12:23) Testaments mention a heavenly book—the book of life—in which the names of God's saved people are written. In Isaiah 4:3, the book of life contains the names of those who live in Jerusalem. In Daniel 12:1, it is the eschatological register of the saved. In the book of Revelation, the book of life is an eschatological register in heaven of those who have been saved by faith in the death of Christ on the cross of Calvary, and, therefore, is called the Lamb's book of life (13:8; 21:27). The blotting of someone's name from the book of life deprives him of eternal life. At the final judgment, only those whose names are found written "in the book" will enter the new earth (Rev. 20:12, 15; 21:27).

EXPOSITION

To the church in Sardis, Jesus introduces himself as ***the One who has the seven Spirits of God and seven stars.*** As in other messages to the churches, this description is drawn from the composite picture of the glorified Christ and is appropriate to the particular situation of the church (Rev. 1:16; cf. 1:4). The Sardians are a spiritually dying church. Jesus comes to them with the fullness of his awakening Spirit; only the Holy Spirit can revitalize a dying church (cf. Rom. 8:11). The seven stars symbolize "the angels" of the churches, namely, the leaders (Rev. 1:20). Christ has the destiny of the church in his hands; he knows everything about them, and they need to heed his warning.

Jesus' appraisal of the church (3:1b–2). From its outset, the tone of this message is alarming. The church in Sardis receives no commendation from Christ, but only a rebuke: *I know your works, that you have a name that you live, and you are dead.* The Christians in Sardis are not blamed for any specific sin or heresy, but for being lifeless. The church has a great reputation ("name") for being alive and active, but it is spiritually dead; no feeling of the working presence of the Holy Spirit is alive there.

The New Testament often refers to sin in terms of death. A person is dead through transgression and sin (Eph. 2:1), coming to life only through Christ (Rom. 6:13; Eph. 2:5). "She who gives herself to wanton pleasure is dead even while she lives" (1 Tim. 5:6). The prodigal son was dead and came to life again (Luke 15:24). Those who claim to be spiritually alive while in reality are dead are those who "hold to a form of godliness, although they have denied its power" (2 Tim. 3:5). Christians living in Sardis had absorbed the character of the city's conditions. No life or spirit was there.

The church in Sardis is evidently in serious trouble. Though having the reputation of being alive and active, Christ says that he has not found their *works fulfilled before my God*—"their works have not measured up to God's standard."[52] Most believers have evidently come to a compromise with their pagan environment. Their loyalty to Christ is in the past, and they are in a condition of spiritual lethargy and death, thus being Christians in name only. They live "in a such a way as to call into question whether or not they possess true, living faith in Christ."[53] However, there was still "the remnant," described in verse 4 as *a few names in Sardis,* who have remained faithful and firm. This small number of believers *have not defiled their garments* with the compromise of many in the church. Yet even this small number "that have not defiled their garments" have not shown further spiritual progress and are *about to die* and conform to the lethargic atmosphere in the church in Sardis.

The situation in this lifeless church, however, is not yet hopeless. The only way Christians can be rescued from their spiritual lethargy and avoid the approaching judgment (cf. 3:3) is to wake up and *keep watching*. This warning had a special meaning for the Christians living in Sardis. Their lethargic condition was a result of their failure to keep watching. The church evidently suffered from the same self-confidence and failure to keep watching as that which led the city of Sardis to be captured twice and destroyed by its enemies (see *Notes* on Rev. 3:2). Christ uses these past events to warn the church. The Christians in Sardis need to learn a lesson from the history of the city in which they live; they must realize the seriousness of their situation and awake from their lifeless condition and be on guard. To put it in the words of Paul: "Awake, sleeper, and arise from the dead, and Christ will shine on you" (Eph. 5:14). Otherwise, death without the hope of a resurrection will follow.

Jesus' counsel to the church (3:3–4). Like the Christians in Ephesus, the Sardians are urged, first of all, to bear in mind (*keep remembering*) what they received and heard. The Greek text suggests that they have not forgotten. In order to improve their condition they must keep on remembering and never allow themselves to forget their first love for Christ and their former devotion to him. To remember only, however, is not enough, for remembering means more than simply recalling the past. Remembering means keeping afresh the past and applying it to the present. The Sardians need to heed what they have received and heard and put it into practice.

Jesus next calls the Sardians to a decisive break from their present condition with an exhortation: *Repent*! Like the prodigal son in Jesus' parable (Luke 15:17–19), the Christians in Sardis must bring to mind their previous status and make a decisive turnaround from their present lethargic condition. As Barclay stated: "In the Christian life there must be a decisive moment, when a man decides to be done with the old way, and to begin on the new."[54]

Next, Christ gives the church a warning: *If therefore you do not watch, I will come as a thief; you will in no way know at what hour I will come upon you.* If the church does not watch, Jesus will visit them unexpectedly with judgment. Just as a thief comes when least expected, so Jesus will come to them. In his sermon on the Mount of Olives, Jesus said that his coming would be like a thief in the night (Matt. 24:42–44; Mark 13:35–37; cf. 1 Thess. 5:2; 2 Pet. 3:10). He further indicated that a lethargic condition of falling asleep will characterize most of those looking forward to the coming of Christ. This suggests that in warning the church in Sardis, Jesus was referring to the Second Coming. In their lethargic condition, the Sardians failed to watch and to keep their eyes fixed on Christ and his return. Here they are given a new chance. If they do not watch, the coming of Christ will take them by surprise.

The small remnant has remained faithful in Sardis; the text says that they **have not defiled their garments.** They are the ones who have remained undefiled by compromise. They are, therefore, given a promise that **they will walk with me in white, because they are worthy.** The fulfillment of this promise is described in Revelation 7:9–17 and 19:7–8 where John sees God's saved people before the throne in the kingdom dressed in white garments. These white garments symbolize the justified people of God (Rev. 19:8; cf. 3:18; 6:11). "These are those who are coming out from the great tribulation, and they have washed their robes and made them white in the blood of the Lamb" (Rev. 7:14). Those who remain faithful today will be found "worthy" when the judgment comes.

The promise to the overcomer (3:5). The overcomers in the church of Sardis are given a threefold promise. First, they **will be clothed in white garments.** This repeats the promise given previously to the remnant in Sardis (3:4). Those who have "washed their robes and made them white in the blood of the Lamb" (Rev. 7:14) will be found worthy to be clothed in those white garments (cf. Rev. 6:11). According to Barclay, on the day when the Romans celebrated a war victory, all the citizens of Rome clothed themselves in white. The white robe promised to the Christians in Sardis is the reward reserved for those who have won the victory and remained faithful (cf. Rev. 7:9).[55]

With the white garments comes a new name—a change from having "a name" of being spiritually alive (while in reality the Sardians are dead) to the name "overcomer" or "victor." Of the overcomer, it is promised that Christ **will not erase his name from the book of life.** In the Bible, the blotting out of somebody's name from the book of life means death (Exod. 32:32–33; Ps. 69:28). In the book of Revelation, only those whose names remain in the book of life shall live in God's kingdom on the new earth (21:27); those who are blotted out will be cast into the lake of fire (20:15).

The final promise to the overcomer is that Christ **will confess his name** before the **Father and before his angels.** In the gospels, Jesus promises that the person who acknowledges Christ before others will one day be acknowledged before the Father;

and the one who denies Jesus will be denied before the Father and his angels (Matt. 10:32–33; Luke 12:8–9). Those who keep their garments undefiled and acknowledge Jesus in this present life will be acknowledged by Jesus when he comes again.

Call to hear the Spirit. The message to the church in Sardis, like the message to the church in Ephesus, is a strong appeal to all who feel half-hearted and divided in their devotion to God. They may not feel the same enthusiasm which they had when they first received and heard the gospel, and they may find it difficult to continue serving God. Jesus' appeal to all who have **an ear,** to **let him hear what the Spirit says to the churches,** shows that what happened to the Christians in Sardis can happen to every Christian, regardless of place and time.

A church can have a great name and reputation and brilliant works, and yet be spiritually lifeless and lethargic. The fact that it was faithful to the Lord at some time in the past does not mean that it will remain faithful. The only way to reclaim the wholehearted and original enthusiasm and devotion to Christ is to bear in mind and keep afresh past experience and apply it to the present. Then follows the radical decision and action expressed by the exhortation which sounds like a command: "Repent!" In the life of every Christian who is backsliding from ardent love for Christ, there must be a decisive moment when a firm, radical decision allows for a new beginning.[56] Such a decision puts God in the place in life where he truly belongs.

Historical application. In addition to its primary local application in John's time, the message to the church in Sardis might also aptly apply to the condition of the Christian church of the sixteenth and seventeenth centuries—named by some as the period of Protestant scholasticism. During this period, the vibrant generation of the Reformers who had awakened the church passed away. Their successors became more and more involved in fervent doctrinal polemics and controversies, gradually degenerating into lifeless formalism and spiritual lethargy. Toward the end of this period, under the impact of the rising tide of philosophical rationalism and secularism, the saving grace of the gospel and commitment to Christ waned, giving place to rationalism and theological arguments. The church of this period, although appearing to be alive, was in reality spiritually lifeless.

CHRIST'S MESSAGE TO THE CHURCH IN PHILADELPHIA (3:7–13)

7To the angel of the church in Philadelphia write:

Thus says the holy One, the true One, the One who has the key of David, who opens and no one shuts, and shuts and no one opens: 8I know your works; behold, I have given before you an open door which no one is able to shut, because you have little strength, and you kept my word and did not deny my name. 9Behold, I am giving some of the synagogue of Satan who say that they are Jews, and they are not, but they lie—behold, I will make them come and bow before your feet, and to know that I have loved you. 10Because you have kept the word of my endurance, I will also keep you from the hour of trial that is about to come on those who dwell on the earth. 11I am coming soon; hold what you have, that no one take your crown. 12The one who overcomes I will make a pillar in the temple of my God, and he will never go out of it, and I will write upon him the name of my God and the name of the city of my God, the new Jerusalem which descends out of heaven from my God, and my new name. 13The one who has an ear, let him hear what the Spirit says to the churches.

NOTES

3:7 *Philadelphia.* Philadelphia (modern Alasehir) was the youngest of the seven cities, located some twenty-five miles southeast of Sardis. It was situated on a high volcanic plateau, making it a strong, fortress city. It was founded by the Pergamenian king Attalus II (159–138 B.C.), whose love for his brother Eumenes II gave him the epithet Philadelphus; it was after him that Philadelphia ("brotherly love") was named. This prosperous city lay on the imperial post road. From its inception, Philadelphia was intended to serve as a missionary city for the promotion of the Greek language and culture to the area of Lydia and Phrygia. Its geographical location, however, made it subject to occasional earthquakes; in particular, the severe earthquake of A.D. 17 devastated Philadelphia together with Sardis and other surrounding cities.

The true One. The Greek word used here is *alēthinos* meaning "genuine" or "real" as opposed to that which is unreal (it must be distinguished from *alēthēs* which means "true" as opposed to that which is false). In the Old Testament context, this word designates the faithfulness of God to his promises (cf. Ps. 146:6; Isa. 65:16).

The key of David. The immediate background for this imagery is Isaiah 22:20–22 where the key of David is the key of the king's storehouse. King Hezekiah had a faithful servant Eliakim, who

143

received the key of the chief steward of the royal household and had full control and access to the storehouse of the king, thus exercising the full authority of the king. To him God gave a promise: "Then I will set the key of the house of David on his shoulder; when he opens no one will shut, when he shuts no one will open" (Isa. 22:22). In the message to the church in Philadelphia, Jesus is the One who has received full authority and has access to the heavenly storehouse.

3:8 *An open door.* The city's strategic location made it the gateway to the East. From its very beginning, Philadelphia was deliberately built to be "the missionary city" for spreading the Greek culture and language among the barbarian tribes throughout the regions of Asia. Being on the imperial post road, Philadelphia was indeed given an open door for spreading Greek ideas throughout the region. That was what the risen Christ meant when he spoke of the open door that was set before Philadelphia. Just as the way became open for the Philadelphians to spread Greek ideas widely, the church in that city was given a "great missionary opportunity" to carry the gospel message of Jesus Christ to the world.[57] In the context of the message to the church in Philadelphia, therefore, the metaphor of "an open door" appears to denote a great opportunity for service and preaching of the gospel (cf. 1 Cor. 16:9; 2 Cor. 2:12; Col. 4:3).

3:9 *The synagogue of Satan.* As with the church in Smyrna, the main problem for the church in Philadelphia came from the Jews; see *Notes* on Revelation 2:8.

3:11 *Crown.* Greek *stephanos* (see *Notes* on Rev. 2:10).

3:12 *Overcomes.* See *Notes* on Revelation 2:7.

EXPOSITION

To the church in Philadelphia Jesus introduces himself with three great titles: ***the holy One, the true One, the One who has the key of David, who opens and no one shuts, and shuts and no one opens.*** In the Old Testament, the phrase "the holy One" refers to God, denoting his divine essence. Isaiah heard in his vision the song of the seraphs: "Holy, holy, holy is the Lord of hosts" (Isa. 6:3). "Thus says the high and exalted One, who lives forever, whose name is Holy" (Isa. 57:15). "I am the Lord, your Holy One, the Creator of Israel, your King" (Isa. 43:15; cf. Hab. 3:3). The phrase is also a designation of Jesus in the New Testament (Mark 1:24; John 6:69; 1 John 2:20). Here, the exalted Christ shares the essence of the divine nature. He is also "the true One" (cf. 3:14; 19:11). Jesus is real; he is the true God, faithful to all the promises given to his faithful people.

Finally, Jesus introduces himself as the One who has "the key of David," which symbolizes his full authority. What he opens, nobody shuts. Isaiah 22:22 presents a picture of Eliakim, the faithful chief steward of the king who was given authority over the royal palace and the royal storehouse. In the New Testament, Christ is given all authority (Matt. 28:18). He is appointed "as head over all things to the church" (Eph. 1:22), and he is "faithful as a Son over His [God's] house" (Heb. 3:6). Now, he presents himself to the Philadelphians as the One who has received full authority and has access to the heavenly storehouse and the riches of God. From there, he is able to give to the overcomers in the churches many different and wonderful promises.

Jesus' appraisal of the church (3:8–10). This church of "brotherly love" has a great opportunity. Jesus has set before her *an open door* of opportunities for service *which no one is able to shut.* "An open door" is a metaphor for the opportunity of preaching the gospel. Paul says that "a wide door for effective service has opened to me" (1 Cor. 16:9; 2 Cor. 2:12). He also prayed "that God may open up to us a door for the world, so that we may speak forth the mystery of Christ" (Col. 4:3). In his report to the church in Antioch, he spoke of how God "opened a door of faith to the Gentiles" (Acts 14:27). When God opens the door, no one is able to stop Christians in their service for God.

It is a church faithful to God's word and Christ. It *kept my word, and did not deny my name*; it has not fallen into compromise or apostasy. It is further a church of patience and endurance (3:10). Although faithful with an open door of opportunities set before them by Christ, however, this church has a significant weakness: it is not driven by a dynamic force for God, for it has but *little strength.*

When God opens the door of opportunities for the preaching of the gospel, the enemy's forces are always there to shut that door. While Paul rejoiced that God opened "a great and effective door" for service to him, he observed that "there are many adversaries" (1 Cor. 16:9). Jesus accused the scribes and Pharisees of shutting people out of the kingdom of heaven (Matt. 23:13; Luke 11:52). This is evidently what happened in Philadelphia. This church confronted the same problem as did the church in Smyrna with those *who say that they are Jews* but in reality are of *the synagogue of Satan* (3:9; cf. 2:9). But Jesus gives this church the assurance that he loves them despite their weakness, and that he is already dealing with their opponents. The day is coming when their enemies, who are doing Satan's work, will be humiliated and will admit that God loves the Philadelphian church. When God opens the door of opportunities for this weak church, all the power of the enemy will not be able to shut that door.

Because the Philadelphians **have kept the word of my endurance,** Jesus gives them the assurance that he will be with them and protect them in the eschatological hour of trial: **I will also keep you from the hour of trial that is about to come on those who dwell on the earth.** The phrase "those who dwell on the earth" consistently refers to the wicked (6:10; 8:13; 11:10; 13:8, 14; 14:6; 17:8). This "hour of trial" clearly refers to God's judgment against the enemies of God and his people, which will be poured out prior to the Second Coming as portrayed in Revelation 16.

The question is whether Christ promises to keep his faithful people *from* or *during* that time of trial. In his intercessory prayer Jesus prayed: "I do not ask Thee to take them out of the world, but to keep them from the evil one" (John 17:15). In the book of Revelation, the great hour of trial is the time when the last plagues will be poured out upon "those who dwell on the earth," namely, those who have accepted the mark of the beast rather than the seal of God (Rev. 16). This text seems to suggest that God's faithful people will not be removed from the earth when the judgments of God are poured out; Christ promises to be with them and protect them during that hour of trial (cf. Dan. 12:1).

Jesus' counsel to the church (3:11). Jesus promises the church that he is coming soon. In view of the nearness of Christ's coming, the church is counseled to **hold what you have, that no one take your crown.** William Barclay provides a list of people in the Bible who lost their place to someone else because they were found unworthy of the task God had given them.[58] Esau lost his place to Jacob (Gen. 25:34; 27:36); Reuben lost his place to Judah (Gen. 49:4, 8); Saul lost his place to David (1 Sam. 16:1, 13); Judas lost his place to Matthias (Acts 1:25); and the Jews lost their place to the Gentiles (Rom. 11:11). It is a real tragedy when God opens a door and gives a person a task, then finds that he or she renounces the call. He then removes that person and gives the task to somebody else.[59]

The promise to the overcomer (3:12). Jesus promises to make the overcomer in the church in Philadelphia a **pillar in the temple of my God.** In 1 Timothy 3:15, "the church of the living God" is "the pillar and support of the truth." Paul names Peter, James, and John as pillars of the early church (Gal. 2:9). A pillar is fixed in the temple as support. The metaphor of being a pillar in a temple "conveys the idea of stability and permanence."[60] The faithful overcomers are promised eternal security in Christ, for they **will never go out of it.**

These overcomers receive another promise: *I will write upon him the name of my God and the name of the city of my God, the new Jerusalem which descends out of heaven from my God, and my new name.* The fulfillment of this promise is described in Revelation 21:2 and 10. John saw later in the vision the faithful 144,000 who have the names of Christ and the Father written on their foreheads (14:1). Those who have the name of God belong to God and are under his protection (Rev. 22:4). In addition, the name of the new Jerusalem will be written upon the faithful. According to Ezekiel, the name of the new city would be: "The LORD is there" (48:35). In the new Jerusalem, the overcomers will experience the everlasting presence of God: "Behold, the tabernacle of God is among men, and he will tabernacle with them, and they will be his peoples, and God himself will be among them" (Rev. 21:3).

Call to hear the Spirit. Even though God's people have little strength, he graciously sets before them a door of opportunities. The enemy of God and his people can try to shut that door, but Jesus possesses the key to the heavenly storehouse. When he opens a door, nobody is able to shut it. He is in control. God's people, although weak, need to hold what they have, that spark of their faithfulness, trusting God and allowing him to work in them and through them. In such a way, no one will be able to take their crown from them.

Historical application. The church in Philadelphia fits aptly into the period of the eighteenth and nineteenth centuries which was characterized by a great revival of Protestantism (although various dates have been suggested for the beginning and ending of this period). Various movements revived genuine faith in the saving grace of Christ as a personal Savior, which resulted in restoring the spirit of Christian fellowship and self-sacrifice. With "little strength" (3:8), the church of this period was indeed a missionary church driven by a strong desire to bring the gospel to the entire world. This period was a time of great advancement of the gospel, such as had not been experienced ever before in Christian history.

CHRIST'S MESSAGE TO THE CHURCH IN LAODICEA (3:14–22)

[14]To the angel of the church in Laodicea write:

Thus says the Amen, the faithful and true witness, the beginning of God's creation: [15]I know your works, that you are neither cold nor hot. I would that you were cold or hot. [16]Thus, because you are lukewarm and neither cold nor hot, I am about to vomit you out of my mouth. [17]Because you say, "I am rich, and have become wealthy, and have need of nothing," and you do not know that you are wretched and miserable and poor and blind and naked, [18]I counsel you to buy from me gold refined in fire that you may be rich, and white garments that you may clothe yourself, so that the shame of your nakedness may not be exposed, and eyesalve to anoint your eyes so that you may see. [19]As many as I love, I discipline and reprove; therefore, be zealous and repent. [20]Behold, I am standing at the door and knocking; if anyone hears my voice and opens the door, I will come in to him and eat supper with him and he with me. [21]To the one who overcomes I will grant to sit with me on my throne, as I also overcame and sat with my Father on his throne. [22]The one who has an ear, let him hear what the Spirit says to the churches.

NOTES

3:14 *Laodicea.* Laodicea (modern Eski-hisar) was forty-five miles southeast of Philadelphia and some forty miles east of Ephesus. Because of its favorable location on the system of Roman roads, the city became one of the greatest commercial and financial centers of the ancient world. Laodicea was enormously wealthy and proud of it. When around A.D. 60 it was devastated by an earthquake, its citizens were so rich and independent that, according to the Roman historian Tacitus, they refused imperial help and rebuilt the city using their own resources (*Annals* 14.27). Most of the city's wealth came from the clothing manufacturing industry and banking transactions. Laodicea was widely known for a fine quality of soft and glossy black wool used in the production of different kinds of garments and carpets which were exported all over the world. This commercial prosperity made the city a great banking center where a large quantity of gold was stored.

In addition, Laodicea was famous for its medical school, which had a reputation throughout the ancient world for its treatment of eye diseases by the means of the eyesalve made from "Phrygian powder" mixed with oil. The commercial, financial, and industrial prosperity and success filled the wealthy citizens of Laodicea with a spirit of pride, which evidently also pervaded the church: "I am rich, and have become wealthy, and have need of nothing" (Rev. 3:17).

The beginning of God's creation. Greek *archē* can have a variety of meanings: "beginning [in point of time]," "origin," "source," or "ruler." The same word is used by Paul in Colossians 1:18 where Christ is "the beginning" of creation; "all things were created by him and for him" (Col. 1:16; cf. John 1:3). The fact that Laodicea was near Colossae, and that Paul urged the Colossians to let the Laodiceans read his letter to them, suggests that the Laodiceans were quite familiar with the description of Jesus as "the beginning of God's creation." The translation of the word either as "source" and "origin" or "ruler" would be in agreement with the context.

3:15 *Cold or hot.* The Greek *psuchros* may mean "icy cold" (cf. Sirach 43:20 speaks of a cold north wind freezing the water to the point of ice). The Greek *zestos* means "boiling hot." The verb *zeō*, "to boil," is usually translated as "fervent" (cf. Acts 18:25; Rom. 12:11).

3:16 *You are lukewarm.* Most scholars have interpreted this concept in light of the geographical background of the city. For all its wealth and prosperity, Laodicea's great problem was poor water. About six miles north of the ancient city stood the city of Hierapolis. Bubbling springs of hot mineral water came down off the mountainside, and much of this water was used for medicinal purposes. Since Laodicea had no natural water supply, it used water from these hot springs via a six-mile-long aqueduct; by the time the water reached the city, it had become lukewarm and, although good enough to bathe in, it was distasteful to drink and was not useful for healing the sick.[61]

3:17 *Poor.* The Greek *ptōchos* means "extremely poor," "poor like a beggar."[62]

3:18 *The shame of your nakedness.* Nakedness in the ancient world was regarded as being under judgment and severe humiliation (cf. 2 Sam. 10:4–5; Isa. 20:4; Ezek. 16:37–39; Nah. 3:5; Rev. 17:16). To put a garment on the naked person was to cover his shame (Luke 15:22; Rev. 16:15). To be dressed in fine robes, on the other hand, was regarded as a token of great honor (cf. Gen. 41:42; 2 Kings 25:29; Esther 6:6–11; Dan. 5:29).

3:19 *Repent.* See *Notes* on Revelation 2:5.

3:20 *Knocking.* The present tense suggests an ongoing action of continual knocking.

Eat supper. The Greek *deipneō* means "to dine." The word refers to the evening meal which was "the principal meal and the usual occasion for hospitality."[63] On the basis of the sacral meals from Greco-Roman religious practice, David Aune suggests that the door on which Christ knocks reflects the fact that Christian homes in the first century "were commonly used as gathering places of worship." Yet Aune is aware that the passage addresses Christians as individuals, not as a congregation. The meal to be shared by Jesus and the worshiper might, in his view, be "the Lord's Supper, but it probably is a meal intended to be shared only by two, Jesus and the worshiper."[64] Since the individual Christian, rather than a congregation, appears in this text, the meal referred to is most likely a meal of fellowship.

3:21 *Overcomes.* See *Notes* on Revelation 2:7.

To sit with me on my throne. The ancient Near Eastern thrones were like couches.[65] Thus to be seated at the right hand of the king on his throne was regarded as the highest honor (cf. 1 Kings 2:19; Ps. 110:1; 1 Esdras 4:29).

EXPOSITION

To the church of Laodicea, Jesus identifies himself with three titles. First, Jesus is *the Amen.* The word "amen" comes to us from Hebrew via Greek and basically means "in truth"; according to Barclay, it was used "to affirm and to guarantee a statement as absolutely true and trustworthy."[66] This title reminds one of Isaiah 65:16 where God is called "the God of truth" (in Hebrew, "God of *'amēn*"). In the gospels, Jesus often begins his statement with, "Truly, truly, I say to you" (*amēn* in Greek; cf. John 1:51; 3:3, 5, 11).

Next, Jesus is depicted as *the faithful and true witness.* He is the witness that we can fully rely on. This is most likely what Paul had in mind when he said, "For as many as are the promises of God, in Him they are yes; therefore also through Him is our Amen to the glory of God through us" (2 Cor. 1:20). Finally, Jesus is *the beginning of God's creation*; that is, he is the origin of this world and has absolute authority over it. To the self-sufficient church in Laodicea, Christ introduces himself as "the 'Amen' of God in faithfulness and in true witness, the only one who has absolute power over the world because he is the source and origin of all creation."[67] His faithful testimony exposes the true condition of the church falling away from him. Therefore, when he speaks, the church is to listen and obey.

Jesus' appraisal of the church (3:15–17). Jesus' appraisal of the church in Laodicea begins with a very serious charge: *I know your works, that you are neither cold nor hot. I would that you were cold or hot.* This is followed by a very serious threat: *Thus, because you are lukewarm and neither cold or hot, I am about to vomit you out of my mouth.* This imagery was derived from the water supply of the city. Laodicea was supplied with water from the hot springs of Hierapolis which was approximately six miles from Laodicea. By the time the water reached Laodicea, it had become lukewarm and, although good enough to bathe in, was distasteful to drink.

Jesus prefers that the church be either hot or cold. The lukewarm condition denotes a compromise. The Laodiceans are divided between Christ and the world. Their lukewarm condition indicates that they have fallen into the status of indifference and self-sufficiency. They have lost their original enthusiasm and zeal for spiritual matters (cf. 3:19). Their lukewarm condition provides "neither refreshment for the spiritually weary, nor healing for the spiritually sick."[68] It appears that there is more hope for an antagonistic and opposing spirit than for the attitude of compromise and indifference. Christ detests a divided loyalty and service: "No man can serve two masters" (Matt. 6:24; Luke 16:13).

The Laodiceans are not condemned for apostasy or heresy. Jesus finds no serious sin in them. Yet, he finds no good thing to say about them. They are not even persecuted. Their main problem is indifference. It appears that they have been infected by the city's pride and self-sufficiency as expressed through their attitude: *I am rich, and have become wealthy, and have need of nothing.*

The city of Laodicea prided itself on its material wealth, clothing trade, and popular eyesalve. This spirit evidently crept into the church; the Laodicean Christians were putting their trust in their own wealth. Yet they may have regarded it as a "blessing from God," thus being deceived as to their "true spiritual condition."[69] This reminds us of the boast of Ephraim in the Old Testament: "Surely I have become rich, I have found wealth for myself; in all my labors they will find in me no iniquity, which would be sin" (Hos. 12:8). While the church in Smyrna appears poor, yet in reality is rich (Rev. 2:9), the Laodiceans think that they are rich, while in reality are poor in their spiritual pride. *You do not know that you are wretched and miserable and poor and blind and naked.* They are blind to their own condition and think themselves the opposite of what they really are: spiritually they are extremely poor (as the Greek text indicates), naked, and blind. The one who does not know, and the one who does not know that he knows not, are both in the same precarious position.

Jesus' counsel to the church (3:18–20). The fact that Christ is about to spew the lukewarm Laodiceans out of his mouth indicates that they still have an opportunity to repent (cf. 3:19). Jesus' counsel to the church corresponds to the Laodiceans' self-deceptive condition. First, Jesus counsels them *to buy from me gold refined in fire that you may be rich.* The fact that the Laodiceans are urged *to buy* suggests that they have to give something in exchange for what they can receive. They have an evident need to give up their pride and self-sufficiency. The New Testament text that helps us understand what Jesus meant by offering to the Laodiceans *gold refined in fire* is 1 Peter 1:7, where it stands figuratively for faith which has been tested: "That the proof of your faith, being more precious than gold which is perishable, even though tested by fire, may be found to result in praise and glory and honor at the revelation of Jesus Christ." A person may have wealth, but wealth cannot buy and secure happiness and spirituality.

Christ further admonishes the church "to buy" from him **white garments** in order to cover **the shame of your nakedness.** The white garments are a frequent symbol of salvation and right standing before God in the book of Revelation (cf. Rev. 3:4–5; 6:11; 7:9, 13–14). The bright and clean robes are "the righteous deeds of the saints" (Rev. 19:8). "He has clothed me with garments of salvation," Isaiah acclaimed. "He has wrapped me with a robe of righteousness" (Isa. 61:10). The white robes of salvation are evidently both present reality and future promise (cf. Rev. 3:4–5). To be clothed in white robes is to be rescued from the humiliating position of nakedness and the shame of sin. When the prodigal son returned home, the best robe was put on him to cover the shame of his nakedness (Luke 15:22). Robes are significant to God's end-time people during the battle of Armageddon: "Blessed is the one who watches and keeps his garments so that he does not walk naked and they see his shame" (Rev. 16:15; cf. Matt. 22:11–14). The Laodiceans need the garments of Christ's saving righteousness to cover their wretched and miserable condition of nakedness.

What this church needs above all, however, is **eyesalve to anoint** their **eyes,** so that they may see and understand their true spiritual condition. This is evidently what the church in Laodicea needs the most. Only when their eyes are opened will the Laodiceans be able to see that they are not what they claim to be. The author of Psalm 119 prayed: "Open my eyes that I may behold" (119:18). In the same way, Paul prayed for the Christians in Ephesus that God would give them "a spirit of wisdom and of revelation in the knowledge of Him. I pray that the eyes of your heart may be enlightened, so that you may know what is the hope of His calling, what are the riches of the glory of His inheritance in the saints" (Eph. 1:17–18). What the Laodiceans need is the discerning and working influence of the Holy Spirit in their lives.

The Laodiceans are not left in a hopeless situation; they are still given an opportunity to repent. **As many as I love, I discipline and reprove; therefore, be zealous and repent.** This is a direct allusion to Proverbs 3:12: "For whom God loves He reproves, even as a father, the son in whom he delights" (cf. Job 5:17). Christ loves the Laodiceans, and in his love he disciplines and corrects them. Paul says that we are "disciplined by the Lord in order that we may not be condemned along with the world" (1 Cor. 11:32). The purpose of divine discipline is further explained by the author of Hebrews:

> My Son, do not regard lightly the discipline of the Lord, nor faint when you are reproved by Him. For those whom the Lord loves He disciplines, and He scourges every son whom He receives. It is for discipline that you endure; God deals with you as with sons; for what son is there whom his father does not discipline? But if you are without discipline, of which all have become partakers, then you are illegitimate children and not sons....All discipline for the moment seems not to be joyful, but sorrowful; yet to those who have been trained by it, afterwards it yields the peaceful fruit of righteousness. (Heb. 12:5b–11)

It is especially interesting that of the seven churches, only the Philadelphians and Laodiceans are explicitly told that they are loved by Christ. Christ loves his faithful people; even those not faithful are likewise the subject of his love. This love is expressed, however, in the form of discipline and rebuke with the purpose of making them zealous (which is equivalent to "hot") to repent. Repentance is turning around and breaking with the present situation. Barclay points to a cryptic statement from the apocryphal book *Acts of Peter* allegedly made by Jesus: "Except ye make the right hand as the left hand, and the left hand as the right hand, and that which is upwards as that which is downwards, that which is before as that which is behind, ye shall not know the Kingdom of God." Barclay further explains,

> When does the right become the left, the left the right, and that which is before that which is behind? Obviously when a man turns round. When does that which is upwards become as that which is downwards? When a man is, so to speak, stood on his head, that is, when he begins to see the world the other way round, when his values are reversed, when the things he thought important become unimportant, and when the things he disregarded become the most important things in life. Repentance means the reversal of the direction of life in order to face God.[70]

This is the way the Christians in Laodicea are urged to repent.

Christ's love for the Laodiceans is best illustrated in the impressive picture of Christ standing at the door: ***Behold, I am standing at the door and knocking; if somebody hears my voice and opens the door, I will enter in to him and eat supper with him and he with me.*** This scene reminds us of the lover from the Song of Solomon, knocking on the door of his beloved and pleading with her to let him enter (5:2–6). "In the Near East the sharing of a common meal indicates the forming of a strong bond of affection and companionship. As such it became a common symbol of the intimacy to be enjoyed in the coming messianic kingdom."[71] In their blind self-sufficiency, the Laodiceans put Christ out of their lives. Their religion was not Christ-oriented. Leon Morris observes: "Up till this point the letter has been addressed to the church as a whole, but now there is a change. *If anyone* is an appeal to the individual. Even if the church as a whole does not heed the warning, some individuals may."[72] Jesus is standing before the door of the human heart and asking to be invited in for a meal of mutual and intimate love. He does not break in. The lukewarm and halfhearted Laodiceans must make their own choice because it may soon be too late.

The promise to the overcomer (3:21). Jesus makes a promise to the overcomer in the church in Laodicea: *I will grant to sit with me on my throne, as I also overcame and sat with my Father on his throne.* Here we find the reality of the Christian's status in Christ. This promise to the Laodiceans includes all other promises. As Jesus Christ has already been exalted on the throne of the universe at the right hand of the Father, so God "raised us up with him, and seated us with him in the heavenly places in Christ Jesus" (Eph. 2:6). This picture becomes much clearer if we keep in mind that in the ancient Near East the throne "was more like a couch than a single seat."[73] God's faithful people have been promised a share with Jesus on his throne. They are *already* elevated in the heavenly places (cf. Rev. 1:6; 5:9–10). Yet the final fulfillment of the promise to the overcomer to share the throne with Christ will be realized at the Second Coming (cf. Rev. 20:4–6).

Call to hear the Spirit. The message to the church in Laodicea is directed to all who put their trust in their material and temporal prosperity—those in a condition of self-sufficiency who believe that their material prosperity is a given favor from God. When Christians today, like the church in Laodicea, look lukewarm and feel halfhearted in their relationship with Christ, the best solution is to take the advice offered by Jesus: "I counsel you to buy from me gold refined in fire that you may be rich, and white garments that you may clothe yourself, so that the shame of your nakedness may not be exposed, and eyesalve to anoint your eyes so that you may see" (Rev. 3:18).

What the Laodiceans need above all is eyesalve to clearly discern their real spiritual condition. The fact that they are free from apostasy or heresy, that no serious sin is found among them, and that they have a very positive opinion of themselves is not a guarantee of their relationship with Christ. Jesus longs to become the focus of all the church's attention—the center of its life, worship, activities, and behavior.

Even though the church as a whole is in a condition of self-sufficiency and halfhearted service to God, the call for repentance is directed to each member. Jesus is waiting for individuals to respond. This is what will bring revival and reformation to the lukewarm and halfhearted church of Laodicea.

Historical application. Although the message to the Laodiceans primarily had a local application in John's time, the church in Laodicea was evidently also set as a model for the Christian church of the last period of earth's history. This idea is supported by verbal and conceptual parallels between the message to Laodicea and the final warning to Christians living at the threshold of the battle of Armageddon (Rev. 16:15). This last church appears to be the most troubled one; it goes through the motions of great political, religious, and secular upheavals and faces challenges that no previous generation of Christians did. Yet it is a half-hearted and self-sufficient church, characterized by lukewarmness and a struggle with the issues of its authenticity. In such a way, the message to the ancient church in Laodicea is especially appropriate to the life and experience of Christians living in the concluding period of the world's history.

A RETROSPECT ON REVELATION 2–3

In examining the seven messages originally sent to the Christian congregations in the Roman province of Asia, we have observed several things. First, the messages of the exalted and glorified Christ were presented in language and images that those Christians could understand. In order to reach the hearts and make a lasting impact on those first-century Christians, Jesus used the events from history, Old Testament scenes and concepts, and things from everyday life. These messages had a transforming significance for those Christians, for they reflected their daily reality and addressed their particular needs and circumstances.

Second, all of the messages begin alike and conclude alike. Each message introduces Christ and concludes with an appeal to listen to the Holy Spirit. In between is a special message suited to the actual condition and need of each of the churches as a result of the scrutinizing discernment of the exalted Christ. Jesus had full knowledge of the life situation and needs of each church. He knew, for instance, that the Ephesians were backsliding in love. He knew that the Smyrnians were suffering and in constant fear of the future. He knew the circumstances in which the Pergamenians lived, and everything about the divided church in Thyatira. He knew that the Sardians were spiritually dead, and all about the open door of opportunities for the spiritually weak Philadelphians. Finally, he knew the self-sufficiency and blindness of the Laodiceans. He knew everything about all of them. Nothing could escape his discerning eyes that read the secrets of the human heart. If the churches wanted to know how to live and make a decisive "turning around" in their religion, they needed only to listen to the messages of Christ.

Christians are called to see the relevance of these messages today and apply them to their own life situations and needs. Each of the messages concludes with a personal appeal: "The one who has an ear, let him hear what the Spirit says to the churches." Every Christian living in any place or time is urged to give heed to these messages. The Jesus who knew the situations and needs of those first-century Christians in the province of Asia is still the same Christ. Through these seven messages to the churches, he speaks to the situations and needs of every Christian today.

Third, every appeal to the churches also contains a promise. Jon Paulien observes some important points that deserve to be stressed.[74] He notices a movement of spiritual decline or degeneration in the seven churches. The first three churches were generally faithful, although some in these churches were not behaving as Jesus would have them to do. So a wayward number in the first three churches were "bad" people. They were heretics in the church. The fourth church, Thyatira, was a divided church and had two phases in its faithfulness to Christ. On the other side, in the fifth and sixth churches, namely, Sardis and Philadelphia, the remnant were God's portion of the church. The majority were out of harmony with the gospel. When it comes to Laodicea, nothing good can be said; the church was self-sufficient and indifferent. While the church in Ephesus had left its first love, it was still faithful to God. Laodicea was different. It did not even care about the threat: "I am about to vomit you out of my mouth."

On the other side, along with the evident spiritual decline, there is an increase in promises to the churches. Each church receives more promises than did the preceding one. To the church in Ephesus the tree of life was promised (2:7). The church in Smyrna was promised a crown of life and escape from the second death

(2:10–11). The third church, Pergamum, received three promises: the hidden manna, a white stone, and a new name (2:17). Thyatira received the promise of authority over the nations—rulership over the nations with an iron scepter that dashes them into pieces—and the morning star (2:26–28). Those in the church of Sardis, the fifth of the churches, were promised that they would walk with Jesus, be dressed in white, have their names not blotted out of the book of life, be acknowledged before the Father, and be acknowledged among the angels (3:4–5). Those in Philadelphia were promised that they would be kept from the hour of trial, would be the pillars in the temple, would never leave the temple, and that they would have written on them the name of God, the name of the city of God, and God's new name (3:10–12). However, the last of the seven, Laodicea, was given only one promise—to sit with Jesus on his throne (3:21). In reality, this promise incorporates all other promises given to the churches. To sit with Jesus on his throne is to have everything. So, each church is in decline when compared with its preceding one. Yet each receives more promises than the one before.

This increase in promises, along with the spiritual decline in the churches, reminds one of exactly what Paul meant when he said that where sin increases, grace abounds all the more (Rom. 5:20). Ellen G. White urges us to keep in mind that "the church, enfeebled and defective though it be, is the only object on earth on which Christ bestows his supreme regard. He is constantly watching it with solicitude, and is strengthening it by his Holy Spirit."[75] Christ makes every effort to lead his church to recognize its own condition and break the chains of pride and self-sufficiency which bind it. The church's only hope is in Christ. It is only through his grace that God's church will finally meet its Lord and Savior at the "wedding supper of the Lamb" (Rev. 19:5–9).

Finally, the seven messages to the churches cannot be read apart from the rest of Revelation. It actually appears that the prophetic portion of the book, beginning with chapter 4, builds on these seven messages. Here Christ presents himself as the One who can provide for all the needs of his people. He knows his people because he walks among them and cares for them. As the church of God is facing the eschatological trial and looks forward to the Second Coming, the promise of the exalted Christ is still like the sound of a trumpet: "Stop being afraid! I am the first and the last, and the living One, and I was dead and behold, I am living for ever and ever, and I have the keys of Death and Hades" (Rev. 1:17–18). Jesus is faithful to the promise that he gave on the Mount of Olives: "Behold, I am with you always, even to the end of the age" (Matt. 28:20).

ENDNOTES

1. For a more complete description of Ephesus and its significance in the ancient world, see Aune, *Revelation 1–5*, 136–141; Barclay, *Letters to the Seven Churches* (New York, NY: Abingdon, 1957), 11–17.

2. Barclay, *Letters to the Seven Churches*, 13–14.

3. Aune, *Revelation 1–5*, 138.

4. Barclay, *Letters to the Seven Churches*, 16.

5. Ibid., 17.

6. Ibid.

7. Beasley-Murray, 73.

8. Barclay, *Letters to the Seven Churches*, 19.

9. Fritz Rienecker, *A Linguistic Key to the Greek New Testament* (Grand Rapids, MI: Zondervan, 1976), 815.

10. Barclay, *The Revelation of John*, 1:62.

11. Barclay, *The Mind of Jesus* (San Francisco, CA: Harper & Row, 1976), 43.

12. Beale, 231.

13. Irenaeus *Against Heresies* 1.26.3; 3.11 (*The Ante-Nicene Fathers*, 1:352, 426–429).

14. Hippolytus *Refutation of All Heresies* 7.24 (*The Ante-Nicene Fathers*, 5:115).

15. Hughes, 37.

16. On the subject of eating food sacrificed to idols, see Aune, *Revelation 1–5*, 191–194.

17. See Fiorenza, *The Apocalypse*, 48–50; for a fuller treatment of the subject, see *Aune, Revelation 1–5*, 148–149.

18. Barclay, *Letters to the Seven Churches*, 24.

19. Kenneth Strand, "'Overcomer': A Study in the Macrodynamic of Theme Development in the Book of Revelation," *Andrews University Seminary Studies* 28.3 (1990): 237–254.

20. Charles, 1:53–54.

21. Thomas, *Revelation 1–7*, 139.

22. Barclay, *The Revelation of John*, 1:92.

23. Hughes, 37.

24. Barclay, *The Revelation of John*, 1:68.

25. Hughes, 36.

26. Mounce, 89.

27. Beale, 231.

28. For a fuller treatment of the subject, see Aune, *Revelation 1–5*, 162–164, 168–172.

29. Morris, 63.

30. Mounce, 93–94; Aune, *Revelation 1–5*, 166.

31. Aune, *Revelation 1–5*, 166.

32. J. M. Ford, 395.

33. Barclay, *The Revelation of John*, 1:83.

34. Ibid., 1:89.

35. Charles, 1:60.

36. See further Barclay, *The Revelation of John*, 1:15–20.

37. See Swete, 35–36.

38. Cf. 2 Maccabees 2:4–8 (*The Oxford Annotated Apocrypha*, 265); 2 Baruch 6:1–9 (Charlesworth, *The Old Testament Pseudepigrapha*, 1:623).

39. 2 Baruch 29:8 (Charlesworth, 1:631); Sibylline Oracles 7:149 (Charlesworth, 1:413).

40. Barclay, *The Revelation of John*, 1:90.

41. Barclay, *Letters to the Seven Churches*, 50.

42. Barclay, *The Revelation of John*, 1:92.

43. Ibid., 1:93.

44. Barclay, *Letters to the Seven Churches*, 48–49.

45. Barclay, *The Revelation of John*, 1:102.

46. J. M. Ford, *Revelation*, 403.

47. Beasley-Murray, 92.

48. Barclay, *Letters to the Seven Churches*, 61.

49. Barclay, *The Revelation of John*, 1:111.

50. Ramsay, 275.

51. Mounce, 109.

52. Archibald T. Robertson, *Word Pictures in the New Testament* (Grand Rapids, MI: Baker, 1960), 6:314.

53. Beale, 273.

54. Barclay, *The Revelation of John*, 1:152.

55. Ibid., 1:122.

56. Ibid., 1:120.

57. Ibid., 1:125.

58. Ibid., 1:133.

59. Ibid.

60. Mounce, 120–121.

61. See Stanley E. Porter, "Why the Laodiceans Received Lukewarm Water (Revelation 3:15–18)," *Tyndale Bulletin* 38 (1987), 143–149.

62. Rienecker, 821.

63. Swete, 64.

64. See Aune, *Revelation 1–5*, 254.

65. Barclay, *The Revelation of John*, 1:148.

66. Barclay, *Letters to the Seven Churches*, 96.

67. Johnson, 457.

68. Mounce, 125.

69. Johnson, 458.

70. Barclay, *The Mind of Jesus*, 44.

71. Metzger, *Breaking the Code*, 46.

72. Morris, 83.

73. Barclay, *The Revelation of John*, 1:148.

74. Paulien, The Bible Explorer, 2.3.

75. White, *Selected Messages*, 2:396.

THE OPENING OF THE SEALED SCROLL

THE ENTHRONEMENT OF CHRIST (4–5:14)
    The Heavenly Throne Vision (4:1–11)
    The Sealed Scroll (5:1–14)

THE SEVEN SEALS (6–8:1)
    The Opening of the Seven Seals (6:1–17; 8:1)
    The Sealed Saints and the Great Multitude (7:1–17)

THE SEVEN TRUMPETS (8:2–11:19)
    The First Six Trumpet Plagues (8:2–9:21)
    The Open Little Scroll (10:1–11)
    The Two Witnesses (11:1–14)
    The Seventh Trumpet (11:15–19)

"Behold, the Lion from the tribe of Judah,
who is the Sprout of David, has overcome so that
he is able to open the scroll and its seven seals."

OVERVIEW
REVELATION 4–5

Revelation 4–5 begins the second major division of the book of Revelation. Having observed the vision regarding "the things which are"—namely, the messages to the seven churches (1:9–3:22)—John is now to be shown "the things which must take place after these things" (4:1; cf. 1:19). Thus, the visions of Revelation 4–22:5 concern the things to take place following the time of John and the seven churches. Before providing the panoramic survey of the history of the church and world in the symbolic opening of the seven seals and the blowing of the seven trumpets, however, and in harmony with the "identification-description" strategy of Revelation, John first describes Christ's unique qualification for the task of opening the seals (on this literary strategy, see the "Introduction").

While in chapters 1:9–3:22 Jesus is seen as walking in the midst of the churches on the earth (cf. 1:12; 3:1), with chapter 4 the scene shifts to heaven. There, in the dazzling splendor of the heavenly throne room, all attention is focused on the glorious throne surrounded by heavenly beings who are assembled for a special occasion. The magnificent liturgy is interrupted for a moment, and the entire focus is on a scroll sealed with seven seals at the right hand of God. John understands that nobody in the entire universe is "worthy" to open that remarkable scroll. Finally, a Lamb/Lion-like figure, "the Sprout of David," who appears "as if having been slain," is found worthy to open the scroll. When he takes the scroll from the right hand of God, a series of anthems of praise sound throughout the universe.

The centerpiece of chapters 4–5, the seven-sealed scroll also appears to be the central feature of the second major division of the book (chaps. 4–11). The arrangement of this entire section seems to revolve around that mysterious scroll. This is evident from the fact that while chapter 5 introduces the scroll folded and sealed with seven seals, which nobody in the entire universe can unseal and unfold, chapter 10 portrays an opened scroll given to John by a mighty angel—the contents of which the revelator had to communicate to the churches. Between chapters 5 and 10 are symbolic scenes of the opening of the seven seals and the blowing of the seven trumpets which describe the events and conditions preparatory to the opening of the sealed scroll.

It thus appears that Revelation 4–5 is the pivotal section of the whole book. These two chapters set the stage for what follows. A knowledge of their contents is important for an understanding of the rest of the book of Revelation. Therefore, one must first define the scene that Revelation 4–5 portrays along with the meaning and significance of the sealed scroll in the scene. Later I demonstrate how the sealed scroll defines the structural arrangement of not only chapters 4–11 but the rest of the book as well.

THE ENTHRONEMENT OF CHRIST

It appears that Revelation 4–5 describes a specific, decisive event in the history of the universe. Some questions might be rightly asked: Which event is in view here? What is the purpose and role of the sealed scroll within that event? Compelling evidence leads us to believe that these two chapters describe the exaltation of the glorified Christ, following his ascension to heaven, on the heavenly throne at the right hand of the Father.

SPRINGBOARD PASSAGE: REVELATION 3:21

Revelation 3:21 provides the first argument for the enthronement-ceremony view. Evidently this text functions as the springboard passage concluding the section of the messages to the seven churches and introducing what follows (see the "Introduction" of this commentary). If we follow the springboard text pattern, it appears that the clue for understanding the entire scene of Revelation 4–5 may be found in the summary statement of the seven churches: "To the one who overcomes, I will grant to sit with me on my throne, as I also overcame and sat with my Father on his throne" (3:21). This statement functions as the introductory text for Revelation 4–7.[1]

Hence, Revelation 3:21, in which Christ promises the overcomer (as a present ongoing experience) the future reward of sharing his throne—just as he overcame and sat with the Father on his throne (as a past event)—is "the springboard passage" of the scene of chapters 4–5 and should be taken as the best starting point for the interpretation of the entire scene. As Jon Paulien observes, the central themes of Revelation 4–5 are the Father's throne (chapter 4), Christ's overcoming (5:5), and his joining the Father on his throne (5:6–14). "Not until Revelation 7 are the redeemed explicitly permitted to join in the rejoicing and the worship of the heavenly court (7:9–12). Just as the reward of the saints is related to Christ's in Revelation 3:21, so the two throne scenes of Revelation 5 and 7:9ff. are related, although equally separated chronologically."[2]

Thus, while the scene of Revelation 4–5 with regard to the enthronement of Christ serves as the elaboration of the latter part of 3:21, the scene of 7:9–17 describes the fulfillment of its first part with regard to the overcomers who will join Christ on his throne. Paulien concludes: "Between the two throne scenes is chapter 6. Therefore, the seals of chapter 6 correspond to the assertion of 3:21 ('to the one who overcomes'); they span the time from the overcoming of the Lamb to the reward of the sealed."[3] Therefore, it appears that the seals of chapter 6 have to do with the ongoing period in which God's people are in the process of overcoming until they have joined Christ on his throne.

THE ENTHRONEMENT CEREMONY

The second argument for the enthronement-ceremony view is that the context and language of Revelation 4–5 are similar to those of Old Testament prophetic references to the coming, ideal Davidic king (or king of Davidic lineage). As the exegetical analysis shows, all the key terms and phrases (including the throne, "at the right hand," "the Lion from the tribe of Judah," "the Shoot of David," and "worthy") are deliberately and appropriately chosen in describing the scene of Revelation 5. They all seem to have a common denominator—the exalted office of honor and rulership.[4] In the Old Testament prophetic books, these terms are used frequently with reference to the future ideal king of Davidic lineage who would sit on the throne of David. They are used in Revelation 5 in terms of the fulfillment of the Old Testament promise with regard to the exaltation of Jesus Christ, the promised Davidic descendent, on the throne of the universe.

It appears that the description of the scene in Revelation 5 is patterned after the Old Testament coronation and enthronement ceremony (cf. 2 Kings 11:12–19; 2 Chron.

23:11–20). In the Old Testament, the enthronement ceremony had two stages: the coronation, which was performed in the temple, was followed by the enthronement, which was performed in the royal palace. The enthronement consisted of the investiture of the new king with royal emblems (2 Kings 11:12), followed by the rite of anointing, which was the essential element of the coronation ritual (cf. 2 Sam. 2:4; 5:3; 1 Kings 1:34, 39; 2 Kings 23:30). Anointing signified divine election and the coming of the Spirit of God who took possession of the anointed king (cf. 1 Sam. 10:10; 16:13). The reigning king thus became the Lord's messiah (cf. 1 Sam. 24:7, 11; 26:9, 11, 16, 23; 2 Sam. 1:14–16; 19:22; Lam. 4:20). ("Anointed" is a translation of the Hebrew "Messiah.")

The coronation ceremony concluded with joyful acclamation to the new sovereign by the assembled crowd—both the dignitaries of the nation and the people (1 Kings 1:34, 39; 2 Kings 11:12, 14). In offering acclamation in honor of the newly crowned king, people recognized the king's authority and submitted to it. After the coronation ritual in the sanctuary, the assembled crowd would leave the sanctuary and go to the royal palace where the new king took his place on the throne (cf. 1 Kings 1:46; 2 Kings 11:19), accompanied by the tumultuous joy of the crowd (2 Kings 11:20).

When Revelation 5 is compared with Old Testament coronation accounts, several parallel details can be detected. First, the two parts of the ancient enthronement ceremony (the first in the sanctuary and the second in the royal palace) in Revelation 5 merge into one and the same event. This can be explained based on the fact that in Revelation the temple and palace are not differentiated but are one entity, as is seen later in this chapter. Then, the investment of the king with a scroll/"testimony" parallels the taking of the scroll by the Lamb (Rev. 5:7). Finally, the joy of the enthronement is particularly prominent in Revelation 5 where the newly enthroned Christ is hailed with the imperial acclamation: "You are worthy!"

Further analysis of Revelation 4–5 confirms that a coronation event is intended. In chapter 4, the stage is set for the preparation for the enthronement of a ruler. In the heavenly throne room (with the dazzling splendor of precious stones, a rainbow, thunder, and lightning), all attention is focused on the brilliant throne surrounded by the four living creatures (an exalted angelic order) and the twenty-four elders (redeemed humanity, as shown later). The unceasing acclamation to "the One sitting on the throne" expresses the expectant atmosphere of the splendid moment. While the interior of the temple/palace is in the foreground in chapter 4, in chapter 5 it moves into the background. Another event takes precedence: all attention is focused on the taking of the sealed scroll by the Lamb and is followed by the rapturous glorification and worshiping of "the One sitting on the throne" and of the Lamb. It is particularly significant that it is the taking of the sealed scroll, rather than its opening, that causes the joy and invokes the acclamation of the heavenly beings.

Some interesting parallels can be drawn between chapters 4 and 5. First, the "sitting" on the throne by the "One" in chapter 4 equates to the possessing of the sealed scroll by the Lamb, presumably Christ, in chapter 5. Second, in chapter 4 God is proclaimed worthy to receive glory, honor, and power because he created all things (4:11); in chapter 5, Christ is proclaimed worthy to take the sealed scroll and open its seals because he was slain (5:9). Then, by virtue of taking the scroll, Christ is worthy to receive "power and wealth and wisdom and might and honor and glory and blessing" (5:12). It equates to the taking of rulership. This interpretation appears to be in harmony with the most natural understanding of the text as intended by its author.

Thus is displayed the very moment when the resurrected Christ, in the heavenly temple/palace, approached the throne and took the sealed scroll from the throne at the right side of God as the symbol of the transference of all authority and sovereignty Satan tried to claim. Then Christ sat upon the throne of the universe at the right hand of the Father and received the adoration and shouts of acclamation which belong only to royalty.

THE TIME OF THE SCENE OF REVELATION 4–5

When does this ascension and assumption of authority actually take place? Numerous New Testament texts testify that the exaltation of Christ upon the heavenly throne at the right hand of the Father occurred after his sacrificial death, resurrection, and ascension to heaven (Acts 2:32–36; 13:33–34; Rom. 8:34; Eph. 1:20–22; Heb. 1:3; 10:12; 12:2; 1 Pet. 3:21–22)—that is to say, at Pentecost. (Revelation 5:6 mentions that the Holy Spirit is sent into all the earth, the event that took place at Pentecost; cf. Acts 2:32–36.) G. R. Beasley-Murray notes: "Despite the declaration in 4:1, that John is now to view 'what must take place after this,' it is evident that the victory of Christ has already taken place in his cross and resurrection, that he has ascended the throne of God, and that his reign has begun."[5]

How does one explain, then, that although Christ already sat down with the Father in his throne (cf. Rev. 3:21), the actual sitting on the throne is missing in Revelation 5? How is it that Christ and the throne, although closely related, appear to be separated and distinct throughout most of the book? Why is it not until the establishment of the eschatological kingdom that the divine throne becomes the royal prerogative and the ruling seat of Christ (Rev. 22:1, 3; cf. 7:17)? It appears that Revelation 5 must be understood within the general New Testament concept of "already" and "not yet" or inaugurated and consummated eschatology. The scene of Revelation 5 inaugurates Christ into his royal ministry. He is *already* King of the universe, exercising his sovereignty "with all authority in heaven and on the earth" (Matt. 28:18; cf. Rev. 2:27). According to Paul, "he must reign until he has put all his enemies under his feet" (1 Cor. 15:25). This reign of Christ is the subject of Revelation 6–11. The subjugation of all rebellion has *not yet* taken place, however, but belongs to the future judgment (cf. 1 Cor. 15:24–28). Hence, John reserves Christ's sitting on the throne for the end. Although the enthronement of Christ marks the beginning of the end, the consummated eschatological concept is absent in Revelation 5 and is reserved for the end of the book.

REVELATION 4–5 AND THE JUDGMENT SCENE VIEW

A popular view suggests that Revelation 4–5 describes a judgment scene. Those who hold this view believe that Revelation 4–5 builds especially on Daniel 7:9–14. Some parallels with Daniel are evident: the presence of more than one throne (Dan. 7:9; cf. Rev. 4:4), God sitting on the radiating throne (Dan. 7:9b; cf. Rev. 4:2–3), the presence of innumerable heavenly beings (Dan. 7:10b; cf. Rev. 5:11), the mention of the book(s) (Dan. 7:10b; cf. Rev. 5:1), the Son of man receiving dominion (Dan. 7:13–14; cf. Rev. 5:6–9), and the presence of the saints (Dan. 7:14; cf. Rev. 5:9). Despite the evident parallels, however, nothing in the text indicates that Revelation 4–5 is a judgment scene.

First of all, no judgment language appears in Revelation 4–5. While the language of judgment is often used in the rest of the book (e.g., Rev. 6:10; 11:18; 14:7; 16:5; 17:1; 18:10, 20; 19:2; 20:4, 12–13), it is deliberately avoided in Revelation 4–5. The only appearance of judgment language in the first half of the book is found in Revelation 6:10; this text makes clear that from the perspective of chapters 4–5, the judgment has not taken place yet. The martyrs underneath the altar cry to God: "How long, O Lord, holy and true, will you not judge and avenge our blood on those who dwell on the earth?"

The usage of key terms such as "at the right hand," "worthy," "the Lion from the tribe of Judah," and "the Sprout of David" signify not judgment but royalty. The acclamations of glory, honor, power, blessing, and might (Rev. 4:11; 5:13) do not fit into a judgment scene, but are directed toward a royal dignitary who rules on the throne or is about to be seated there. Those joyful shouts of adoration are not heard in the judgment scenes of the Bible (cf. Dan. 7:9–14; Rev. 20:11–15) or in Jewish apocalyptic literature. They simply do not harmonize with a judgment atmosphere.

Finally, in both biblical and Jewish literature, the judgment scene includes the opening of the "books." In Revelation 5 there is only one book, the sealed scroll, and no mention is made of its opening. It is its taking, not its opening, by Christ that causes the explosion of joy, adoration, royal acclamations, and worship from the heavenly beings (Rev. 5:7–14). The opening of the judgment "books" is reserved for the end of Revelation, where the final judgment is described in clear judgment language (Rev. 20:11–15).

Judgment action may not be entirely excluded from the enthronement, however. It should be noted that ancient enthronement ceremonies also had judgment significance. The king was regarded as both ruler and judge (cf. 1 Kings 3:16–28; 7:7; Prov. 31:9). Thus, the Old Testament enthronement ceremonies were usually followed by judgment action when a newly enthroned king would proceed to punish those who had proven themselves to be disloyal and rebellious, and bestow favorable benefits on loyal adherents (1 Kings 2; 16:11; 2 Kings 9:14–10:27; 11:1, 13–16). In Isaiah 11:1–5, "the Sprout from the stump of Jesse" is endowed by the Spirit of God with wisdom and understanding so that he is able to judge righteously. This is comparable to the prayer for understanding to judge the people rightly which was offered by the newly crowned king Solomon (cf. 1 Kings 3:8–11). According to Psalms 2 and 110, an anointed and enthroned king exercises authority to reign by judging those who are rebellious (cf. Ps. 2:7–11 and Rev. 19:15–16).

By the very event of Christ's enthronement, the faithful ones are endowed with the right to be "a kingdom and priests to our God; and they will reign upon the earth" (5:9–10; cf. 7:9–17). Yet the actions of the newly enthroned Christ following the enthronement ceremony (portrayed in the opening of the seven seals) are "preliminary judgments" which occur on the earth in sequence: war, slaughter, famine, and pestilence. As shown with reference to chapter 6, the concepts of war, famine, pestilence, and wild beasts recall the covenant curses in the Pentateuch (cf. Lev. 26:21–26) and their execution in the context of the Babylonian exile (Jer. 14:12–13; 21:6–9; 24:10; 29:17–18; Ezek. 6:11–12; 33:27–29). These concepts became technical terms for the covenant "woes" by which God punishes apostasy and disloyalty to the covenant (Jer. 15:2–3; Ezek. 5:12–17; 14:12–23; Hab. 3:12–16).[6] The coronation of Christ in Revelation 5 thus marks the beginning of the execution of judgment.

Hence, even though Revelation 5 is not a judgment scene, subsequent judgment follows. Thus, when in Revelation 5 Christ is installed on the heavenly throne (which is also the throne of judgment [Rev. 20:11–15; cf. Dan. 7:9–10]), he assumes both the royal and judging offices (cf. John 12:31–32). His worthiness, and his "seven horns and seven eyes which are the seven spirits of God" (Rev. 5:6), signify his ability and right to both rule and judge. The destiny of humankind was placed in his hand when he approached the heavenly throne and took the sealed scroll.

Some comments are necessary with regard to the popular view that Revelation 4–5 describes the investigative judgment scene of 1844.[7] First, the foregoing arguments do not support any judgment-scene view with regard to Revelation 4–5. Second, if Revelation 4–5 describes the investigative judgment scene of 1844, then everything that follows Revelation 5, including the seven seals, the seven trumpets, and the ministry of the two witnesses of Revelation 11, would occur after the year 1844. A careful analysis of Revelation 6–11 does not support such an idea. Furthermore, the discussion of the literary arrangement of Revelation in the introduction to this commentary shows that the structural composition of the first half of the book focuses on the Christian era, rather than on the eschatological period. The evidence clearly supports the view that Revelation 4–5 describes the enthronement of the resurrected Christ at the right hand of the Father (cf. Dan. 7:13–14; Phil. 2:6–11), the event which occurred at Pentecost (Acts 2:32–36), as the most satisfactory interpretation. We would expect, then, that the material following Revelation 5 covers history throughout the Christian era from the first century until the Second Coming.

THE SEALED SCROLL OF REVELATION 5

If Revelation 4–5 describes the scene of the exaltation of the resurrected Christ upon the throne of the universe at the right hand of the Father (and the evidence strongly supports such a view), what, then, is the role and meaning of the sealed scroll pictured in the enthronement? In order to provide an adequate answer, it is necessary to determine the appropriate Old Testament background of the entire scene of Revelation 5.

THE COVENANT BOOK AND THE ENTHRONEMENT CEREMONY

Our search for the Old Testament motif in which the scroll is related to the throne brings us to Deuteronomy 17:18–20. The text shows that the first duty of the Israelite king when he took the throne was to make for himself a copy of the law on a scroll. This "law," God's Covenant Book, was evidently what we know today as the book of Deuteronomy. Its contents were written by Moses in a scroll and placed in the sanctuary in the custody of Levites (Deut. 31:9, 24, 26). It was from this master copy of Deuteronomy that the newly crowned king had to make a copy of the scroll for himself at his enthronement. The king was to keep the scroll throughout his life, to read and study it constantly, and to obey diligently all its instruction.

The Covenant Book played a very important role in the history of Old Testament Israel and its kings. When an Israelite king took his seat on the throne, he was presented with a copy of the Covenant Book. We read, for instance, how at the coronation of the first Israelite king (Saul), Samuel "told the people the rights and duties of the kingship, and he wrote them in a book and laid it up before the Lord" (1 Sam. 10:25). At his enthronement, according to 2 Kings 11:12, the Judean king Joash was brought to a special place reserved for the king in "the house of the Lord" where he was invested with the royal emblems of "the crown and the testimony." Both the crown and "the testimony" are seen as tokens of kingship. They signified the right to rule.

In the Old Testament, the testimony is always used with reference to the law and God's instruction (Exod. 31:18; 32:15; Pss. 19:7; 119:13–16, 35–36, 143–144). The testimony was clearly the exposition law of the book of Deuteronomy (cf. 4:45; 6:17, 20), or "the book of this law" from Deuteronomy 17:18. It is especially interesting that the young prince Joash was proclaimed king after having the crown put on his head and a copy of the Covenant Book placed in his hand. Also, in 2 Kings 23, we see the young king Josiah taking the scroll of Deuteronomy and learning from it.

By taking his seat on the throne, the new king would begin to reign (1 Kings 16:11; 2 Kings 13:13). The possession of the scroll of the Covenant and the ability to open it and read it demonstrated his right to rule and to deal with any crisis that he might encounter. On the other hand, the scroll was a constant reminder that he was responsible to God, the Great King, for the exercise of his power. The royal throne that he occupied was in fact "the throne of God" (1 Chron. 29:23) or, more explicitly, "the throne of the kingship of God over Israel" (1 Chron. 28:5). The Israelite king was a co-ruler with God honored to sit at his right hand (Ps. 110:1; cf. 80:17).

While performing his royal duties, the king of Israel was to be God's representative and the covenant mediator. By possessing the Covenant Scroll, he assumed the responsibility of reading its contents to the people of his kingdom on certain occasions. Above all, his duty was to instruct the people of its contents through special agents. Thus we read, for instance, of the great reform under the faithful King Jehoshaphat, who sent a team of princes and Levites, and "they taught in Judah, having the book of the law of the LORD with them; they went about through all the cities of Judah and taught among the people" (2 Chron. 17:7–9, RSV).

Throughout the Old Testament, the Covenant Book played a decisive role in the life and destiny of the people of Israel. Although the foregoing coronation of King Joash (2 Kings 11:12) is the only explicit reference showing that the Israelite kings followed the regulations of Deuteronomy 17:18, some indirect references suggest that the lives of the faithful kings were governed by the instructions of the Covenant Book. Each throne succession was, at the same time, the renewal of the covenant relationship between God, the Great King, and his people.

A significant moment in the history of Israel came with David whom the Lord had "appointed to be the prince over his people" (1 Sam. 13:14). God made a covenant with David, promising him the perpetuity of his dynasty (2 Sam. 7:1–17). "The LORD swore to David a sure oath from which he will not turn back: 'One of the sons of your body I will set on your throne'" (Ps. 132:11, RSV). In order to experience the fulfillment of this promise, David and his descendants were to live according to the covenant as regulated by the Covenant Book: "If your sons keep my covenant and my testimonies which I shall teach them, their sons also for ever shall sit upon your throne" (Ps. 132:12, RSV). In his final address to Solomon, David urged him to "keep the charge of the LORD your God, walking in his ways and keeping his statutes, his commandments, his ordinances, and his testimonies, *as it is written in the law of Moses*, that you may prosper in all that you do and wherever you turn; that the LORD may establish his word which he spoke concerning me" (1 Kings 2:3–4, RSV, emphasis supplied; cf. 1 Chron. 22:13).

THE SEALING OF THE COVENANT BOOK

The subsequent history of Israelite kingship shows that only a small number of Israel's kings followed the instructions of God with regard to the Covenant Book. The historical books clearly show that God's ideal of the king obeying the Covenant Book was very rarely realized. The collapse of the Kingdom of Israel is described as a result of the breaking of the covenant with God (2 Kings 17:7–23). The situation in Judah was not seen as any more promising.

The messages of the prophets in the period before the Exile were essentially indictments of Judah and her kings for breaking the covenant. This period is described as one of great religious apostasy which seemed to start with the obvious failure of such kings as Ahaz to live according to the Davidic covenant (cf. 2 Chron. 28:1–27; Isa. 7–12). During the reign of Manasseh and his successor Amon, the Covenant Book was entirely forgotten. The Josiah reform (2 Kings 23) did not change the course of Judah's kings, and one may well wonder whether most of the people underwent any change in heart at all. It was on the eve of the Exile that Jeremiah was called to announce threatening judgments against the unfaithful king who sat on "the throne of David" (Jer. 13:13; 22:2; 29:16; 36:30). The impending judgments were unavoidable. The exile to Babylon thus marked the termination of the Davidic kingship and the Davidic dynasty.

Particularly significant is the fact that it was prior to and at the Exile that the prophets announced the sealing of God's revelation. The first announcement appears in Isaiah, the book which from the outset testifies of the great apostasy of the people of Judah and her kings: "Bind up the testimony, seal the law among my disciples" (Isa. 8:16). We see here that the sealing and binding, and the testimony and the law, are parallel. The testimony stands for "the book of the law," namely, the book of Deuteronomy, deposited "by the side of the ark of the covenant of the LORD your God" (Deut. 31:26) and with which the Israelite king was invested at his enthronement (2 Kings 11:12). The visions were now to be sealed because of the people's refusal to accept them. Isaiah refers later to this sealed Covenant Book when he compares his visions with "the words of the sealed book" which no one could read because it was sealed (Isa. 29:11). "The sealed book" refers clearly to "the testimony" mentioned in Isaiah 8:16 with a command to be sealed. The figurative language of the text refers to a scroll that is rolled up, tied with string, and sealed. The context of the passage suggests the symbolic "sealing" of God's revelation as a result of divine action:

> Stupefy yourselves and be in a stupor,
>   blind yourselves and be blind!
> Be drunk, but not with wine;
>   stagger, but not with strong drink!
> For the LORD has poured out upon you a spirit of deep sleep,
> and has closed your eyes, the prophets,
>   and covered your heads, the seers.
> And the vision of all this has become to you like the words of a book that is sealed. When men give it to one who can read, saying, "Read this," he says, "I cannot, for it is sealed." And when they give the book to one who cannot read, saying, "Read this," he says, "I cannot read." And the Lord said:
> "Because this people draw near with their mouth
>   and honor me with their lips,
>   while their hearts are far from me,
>   and their fear of me is a commandment of men learned by rote;
>   therefore...the wisdom of their wise men shall perish,
>   and the discernment of their discerning men shall be hid."
>   (Isa. 29:9–14, RSV)

This passage indicates that the "sealing" had to do with an inability of human beings to discern and comprehend the revealed will of God. The "sealing" in Isaiah was clearly the result of the unwillingness and unreadiness of the people of Israel to adhere to God's revelation given through both Moses and the prophets.

That God's revelation might be sealed with regard to people is explicitly stated in the book of Daniel, which was written during the Exile: "The words are shut up and sealed until the time of the end" (Dan. 12:9, RSV; cf. 8:26; 12:4). The sealing here clearly implies the concealment of God's revelation, namely, predictions and his plans of judgment and salvation, for a certain period of time.

Jewish sources provide enough evidence that the Jews of John's day believed on the basis of the above-mentioned Old Testament texts that the unwillingness of Israelites to pay heed to the Covenant Book had caused its sealing. Such an idea is first found in the Jewish community in Qumran. An interesting fragment containing a *pesher* on Isaiah 29:10–11 shows that Qumranians evidently understood that the sealing implies the cancellation of Yahweh's revelation to people:

> *Is 29:10–11* [For] ₁the Lord pours [upon] you [a breath] of languor and will blinker [your eyes – the prophets – and] ₂he will cover your heads – the seers – . For you [any vision] will be [like the text of a] ₃[sea]led [book :] they give it to someone who can read, tellin[g him: Please read this,] ₄[and he answers: I cannot because] it is sealed.[8]

The idea of "the sealed book of the Law [Torah]" is also found in *The Damascus Rule:*

> And concerning the prince it is written, *"He shall not multiply wives to himself"* (Deut 17:17); but David had not read the sealed book of the Law which was in the ark (of the Covenant), for it was not opened in Israel from the death of Eleazar and Joshua, and the elders who [or because they] worshipped Ashtoreth. It was hidden and (was not) revealed until the coming of Zadok. [9]

This peculiar passage indicates that the Qumran sect held that the "book" of the Torah which evidently related to the kingship regulation of Deuteronomy 17:14–20 could be sealed due to the lack of kingship in Israel; here in the text it was "sealed" in the ark during the period from Joshua to the rise of Zadok to the priesthood—the high priest in David's time[10] (i.e., during the period "when there was no king in Israel"). The "sealing," which evidently must be taken symbolically, was ascribed exclusively to the sin and unfaithfulness of the national leaders. With the rising of the Davidic kingship, the scroll was presumably "unsealed."

Jewish rabbis believed that the disloyalty of the Hebrew kings and their unwillingness to follow the Covenant Book provoked its "sealing." Such an idea is already expressed in the Targums, where the people's rejection of the law in the time of Isaiah became the ground for the command of the prophet: "Prophet, guard the testimony, do not testify among them, for they do not attend. Seal and hide the law; they do not wish to learn from it."[11] The "sealing" was in the synagogue associated with the threat of the departure of the Shekinah and going into the Exile.[12] According to the same source, a task of Yahweh's "servant the Messiah" would be "to open the eyes of the house of Israel who are as blind as the Torah."[13]

The rabbis also believed that the sealing of the Law began during the reign of king Ahaz, who "caused the sacrificial service to cease, and sealed the Torah, as it is written, 'Bind the testimony, seal the law among my disciples'" (Isa. 8:16). The kings who came after Ahaz—Manasseh, Amon, and Jehoiakim—were equally guilty of rejecting the Law, thus contributing to its sealing.[14] They evidently understood the demise of the Israelite kingship as the divine action of the symbolic "storing" of the Covenant Book and hiding its contents for an appointed time period.

The Babylonian exile and downfall of the monarchy thus in the Jewish mind marked the end of the Davidic kingship wherein the Covenant Book became "sealed." The "sealing" of God's revelation in Isaiah was clearly the result of the unwillingness and unreadiness of the people to adhere to God's revelation given through both Moses and the prophets. The "sealing" of the Covenant Book should not be understood in the sense that people did not have access to learn the will of God, but rather that Israel no longer had a king on the throne of the Davidic lineage. Although later the Jewish people once again had kings, they were not legitimate Davidic descendants. The Old Testament promise with regard to the ideal Israelite king of the Davidic lineage was reserved for a future eschatological time.

CHRIST AS THE TRUE DAVIDIC KING

After the Exile, when the people of Israel no longer had a Davidic king on the throne, they took the shape of a community subject to a divine law under which the authoritative interpreters were the priests rather than the kings. The entire hope of Israel was gradually shifted to the appearance of a future king of the Davidic lineage who would fulfill the role of the ideal and true king of Israel.

It was particularly during the period of the apostasy of Judah's kings and the nation before the Exile that the prophets pointed to the future coming of the ideal Davidic king, the Messiah who would sit upon the throne of David and faithfully instruct the people. According to Jeremiah, the demise of the Israelite kingship in no way annulled the covenantal promise to David: "David shall never lack a man to sit on the throne of the house of Israel" (Jer. 33:17; cf. 23:5), because God was still faithful to his covenantal promise to David (Jer. 33:20–21). During the Babylonian exile, Ezekiel prophesied that in the coming of the Messiah, the covenant promise given to David would achieve its reality: "My servant David shall be king over them; and they shall all have one shepherd. They shall follow my ordinances and be careful to observe my statutes" (Ezek. 37:24, RSV; cf. 34:23–25).

Jewish sources from after the Exile show how the people eagerly awaited the coming of the promised Davidic descendant, the Messiah or Christ ("the Anointed One"). As an ideal king, he would reign on the throne of David and faithfully instruct the people in the Law of God.[15] It was against this Old Testament background of the termination of the Davidic kingship, and in the climate of expectation of the fulfillment of the Old Testament promise among the Jewish people, that John introduced Christ. He is "the Lion from the tribe of Judah, who is the Sprout of David" (Rev. 5:5), who was alone "worthy" to take the sealed scroll as the token of rulership.

As one might expect, the Old Testament promise with regard to the ideal king of the Davidic lineage was fulfilled in the person of Jesus the Messiah in the New Testament (Acts 2:29–36; 13:22–38; Heb. 1:2–13). When after his resurrection Christ was installed upon the heavenly throne at the right side of God, Old Testament prophecy was realized (Acts 2:33–36; 5:31; Rom. 8:34; Eph. 1:20; Col. 3:1; Heb. 1:3, 13; 8:1; 10:12; 12:2; 1 Pet. 3:22). Nathan's promise to David (2 Sam. 7:12–16) was thus consummated in Jesus Christ. He is the descendent of David (Luke 1:27; Rom. 1:3; 2 Tim. 2:8) or "the son of David" (Matt. 9:27; 21:9; Mark 10:47–48; Luke 18:38–39). In Luke, Gabriel announced to Mary that the son she would bear would "be called the Son of the Most High; and the Lord God will give Him the throne of His father David; and He will reign over the house of Jacob for ever; and His kingdom will have no end" (Luke 1:32–33; Acts 13:22–23). In his Pentecost sermon, Peter presented Christ as the legitimate descendent of the throne of David (Acts 2:29–36). In Hebrews, the permanence of the throne of God was accomplished in Christ: "Now the main point in what has been said is this: we have such a high priest, who has taken His seat at the right hand of the throne of the Majesty in the heavens" (cf. Heb. 8:1). In Jesus Christ, all God's promises have found their fulfillment (2 Cor. 1:20).

It appears that Deuteronomy 17:18–20, concerned with the king of Israel and with the scroll of the law, finds its full realization in the nature of the kingship that Jesus manifested in the New Testament. As the Messianic King of the Davidic lineage, he is in the Gospels presented in the role of the great teacher of the Law. For instance, while the gospel of Matthew stresses Jesus' kingly role (Matt. 1:1; 2:2; 25:31, 34; 27:11, 42), Jesus is also the expositor of the "law" in the Sermon on the Mount (chapters 5–7).

According to Luke's account, immediately after baptism, Jesus received the royal anointing from the Holy Spirit and was proclaimed the Son of God. As the Anointed of God, he began his public ministry in the synagogue at Nazareth by standing before the people with the scroll of Scripture in his hands and reading from Isaiah 61:1: "The Spirit of the Lord is upon Me, because He anointed Me to preach the gospel to the poor. He has sent Me to proclaim release to the captives, and recovery of sight to the blind, to set at free those who are downtrodden, to proclaim the favorable year of the Lord" (Luke 4:18–19). After the reading, he concluded: "Today this scripture has been fulfilled in your hearing" (4:21), thus invoking both praise and surprise in the hearers.

THE SEALED SCROLL AS THE SYMBOL OF RULERSHIP

It is against this Old Testament background of the coronation of the Israelite kings, as well as the role that Deuteronomy as the Covenant Book played in the coronation ceremonies and in the history of Israel, that Revelation 5 must be understood. We have already determined that Revelation 4 and 5 describe the enthronement ceremony in the heavenly throne room wherein the resurrected Christ was installed and exalted upon the throne of the universe at the right hand of the Father as co-ruler. The sealed scroll in Revelation must, therefore, have the same meaning and significance as the Covenant Book in the Old Testament enthronements. Now, John tells us that the sealed scroll has been handed to the ideal king of the Davidic lineage, the eschatological "Son" (Rev. 1:13; 2:18; 14:14; cf. Dan. 7:13–14); he is found worthy to take the scroll as a token of kingship and sit on his Father's throne as co-ruler (Rev. 3:21). The symbolic delivering of the sealed scroll into Christ's hands must thus be regarded as "a formal ceremonial act, whereby He was recognized as the Supreme Ruler of the universe,"[16] and the token of inauguration into his universal dominion and the lordship over the world.

This raises an obvious question: Why was it necessary for Christ to receive the scroll of the covenant? We should keep in mind that John wrote his Revelation primarily to readers of his time who apparently were quite familiar with these Old Testament motifs and were in the spirit of expectation for the fulfillment of Old Testament prophecies. He did not want to leave them in any doubt that those Old Testament prophecies had found their fulfillment in the person and ministry of Jesus Christ. He used every possible argument to prove that "all authority in heaven and the earth" was given to Christ (Matt. 28:18). Thus he portrayed the transference of authority to Christ after the Old Testament custom of the enthronement of the Israelite kings of the Davidic lineage.

Christ certainly had no need of a "scroll," as the Israelite kings did, to remind him of covenant duties, just as he had no need to be baptized (which was his anointment) at the beginning of his earthly ministry. In undergoing baptism, however, he gave the response which the whole of Israel was to give: "It is fitting for us to fulfill all righteousness" (Matt. 3:15). The Father declared: "This is My beloved Son, in whom I am well-pleased" (Matt. 3:17). The people of Israel had proved to be disobedient sons, frustrating God; but here was the "Son" in whom the true sonship has been realized.

This explains why Christ is described after the Israelite kingship of the Davidic covenant. The Davidic kings proved to be disobedient sons and unfaithful to the covenant. Yet, where they failed, Christ, the ideal Son of David, succeeded. Therefore, when in Revelation 5 Christ appears on the scene in the symbolic form of a lamb as the only one "worthy" to take the scroll, he responds as the Old Testament kings—and Israel as a nation—were to respond. The throne of David is no longer unoccupied or ineffective but is transferred to the triumphant Christ, who carries out all the plans of God. The scroll of the Covenant is no longer sealed with its contents hidden. Its taking and possession by Christ introduced the coming of the promised kingdom. From that moment on, and in the very presence of Jesus, the kingdom of God manifested itself and keeps manifesting itself.

THE MEANING OF THE SEALED SCROLL

The delivering of the scroll of Deuteronomy, as the Covenant Book, to a newly crowned king in the Old Testament (Deut. 17:18–20; 2 Kings 11:12) seems to be a key motif, and it provides a satisfactory background for the scene of Revelation 5. The scroll functions as a symbol of the installation of the resurrected Christ upon the throne of the universe, signifying his authority and right to rule.

The sealed scroll symbolizes God's promise to give the kingdom to his people. In being handed to Christ, who through his sacrificial death and resurrection has brought the promise regarding the kingdom to its fulfillment (Rev. 5:9–10), the scroll signifies that Christ has been given the lordship as well as the authority and power to reign in that kingdom (Rev. 5:12; cf. Phil. 2:9–11; 1 Pet. 3:22). The reception of the scroll by Christ also signifies the rightful transfer of world dominion to him that was forfeited by sin. Thus, with the scroll, the Father installed Christ as the end-time ruler, transferring to him "the accomplishment of his plan for history."[17] As is discussed later, the sealed scroll is related to the concept of "the mystery of God," the phrase which in the New Testament refers to God's plan to redeem and bring together the entire universe and to establish his eternal kingdom.

Understood in this way, the sealed scroll appears to be the scroll of God's eternal covenant—the revelation of his salvific acts on behalf of humanity. It is a "record of the cosmic controversy,"[18] symbolic of the sum and substance of God's plan and purpose for the human race and the entire universe. It contains the judgments and salvation to be released at the Second Coming. This is exactly what Ellen White meant when she said that the sealed scroll is "the roll of the history of God's providences, the prophetic history of nations and the church. Herein was contained the divine utterances, His authority, His commandments, His laws, the whole symbolic counsel of the Eternal, and the history of all ruling powers in the nations. In symbolic language was contained in that roll the influence of every nation, tongue, and people from the beginning of earth's history to its close."[19]

THE CONTENTS OF THE SEALED SCROLL IN REVELATION 5

Compelling evidence indicates that the sealed scroll is closely related to the book of Revelation itself. First of all, the content of the book is referred to as an *apokalupsis,* which has the literal sense of "an uncovering." This term evidently refers to "a disclosure of what previously had been concealed."[20] Thus, this term might well indicate that Revelation is a disclosure of God's message that was formerly sealed or kept hidden, until the appointed time, due to human disloyalty and unfaithfulness to God. John precisely wanted to tell his readers that the prophesied time had come and that the sealed divine revelation was about to be disclosed due to the "worthiness" of the true descendant of David. Hence the instruction given to John at the end of the book: "Do not seal up the words of the prophecy of this book" (22:10).

Second, the close link between the scroll of Revelation 5 and the book of Revelation is further supported by striking parallels between Revelation 1 and 4–5. Revelation 5 describes Christ as taking the scroll from the right side of God who is the "Lord God, the Almighty, who was and who is and who is coming" (Rev. 4:8; cf. 11:17), which is the name of Yahweh, the Old Testament covenant God. In chapter 1, the revelation is given to Jesus Christ by God who is likewise identified as "the Lord

God, 'who is and who was and who is to come, the Almighty'" (Rev. 1:8; cf. 1:4). In both texts, "the seven spirits" are before his throne (Rev. 1:4; 4:5; 5:6).

Some differences between the two passages appear to be of special importance, however. First of all, while Revelation 5 depicts a sealed scroll which nobody in the universe was able to open and look into (5:1–3), Revelation 1 refers to a book, the contents of which are disclosed (1:1–3; cf. 22:10). Second, while in Revelation 5 the scroll is in the hand of Christ symbolizing his right to rule, in chapter 1 the revelation is handed to Christ to be sent to God's people. Christ conveyed it in symbol through an angel to John, who then "passed on to the church, in the form of 'a book [*biblion*] of prophecy' (22:7, 10, 18, 19), the things that he had seen."[21] As the Old Testament kings were handed a scroll of the Covenant at the enthronement and were to instruct the people through specially chosen instruments, so Revelation, which first signifies Christ's royal authority, is intended for the instruction of churches through especially chosen instruments. It is, after all, to God's people that the entire book of Revelation is addressed and sent.

Although the evidence links the sealed scroll to Revelation, its contents seem to be broader than those of the last book of the Bible. The book itself informs us at the very outset that it has been passed down from God to the church through the chain of mediation: God the Father handed the revelation to Christ, who conveyed it through an angel to John, who passed it on to the church in the form of a scroll (1:11; 22:7, 10). This corresponds remarkably to the scene of Revelation 5 where the newly enthroned Christ takes the sealed scroll from the right side of the Father. The opening of the Covenant scroll by the Israelite kings was an activity practiced after their enthronement. This appears to be one reason why the scene of Revelation 5 says nothing about the opening of the sealed scroll, for the entire focus is on Christ's taking it from the right side of the Father as a part of the enthronement ceremony.

When we reach chapter 10, the picture is completely different. There, we see a mighty angel coming down from heaven with "an opened little scroll" (Rev. 10:2). The little scroll (Gr. *biblaridion*) signifies a small papyrus scroll in comparison with the scroll of normal size in Revelation 5. The fact that this little scroll is open is expressed in Greek with the perfect passive participle. The perfect tense indicates that the contents of the little scroll have been revealed at some previous time. The passive form here functions as the Hebrew divine passive, suggesting the opening as God's action. The main reason for the use of the expression "little scroll" and the emphasis on the fact that it was open may be for the sake of contrasting it with the scroll of chapter 5, which was larger, rolled, and sealed.

According to Revelation 10:7, the sealed scroll is related to the concept of "the mystery of God," a New Testament term which is always used in the eschatological sense.[22] It refers to the whole purpose of God to redeem and bring together the entire universe. It revolves around the full establishment of God's rule and His eternal kingdom, identifying "the citizens who will inhabit it, and those who will be excluded from it"[23] (cf. Rev. 11:15–18). Though hidden for ages, the mystery has been revealed through the preaching of the gospel (Rom. 16:25–26; 1 Cor. 2:6–10; Eph. 3:1–20; 1 Tim. 3:16). This mystery is open to the people of God but closed to those who are outside the kingdom (Matt. 13:11). It appears that only a part of that mystery has been revealed to God's people, however, for the angel commanded John to seal up and not write what the seven thunders said (10:4). The rest is to be revealed at the Second Coming, for "in the days of the sound of the seventh angel, when he is about to sound, then the mystery of God will be completed, as he proclaimed to his servants the prophets" (Rev. 10:7).

All of this might suggest that the little scroll conveyed through the angel to John in chapter 10 contains only a part of God's revelation of his salvific plans and redemptive acts represented by the sealed scroll in chapter 5.[24] It contains the essential divine providence and messages that are profitable for the people of God, which were disclosed to John in symbolic presentation and which John passed on to the church (cf. Rev. 10:8–11).[25] The particular aspect of "the mystery of God" will be revealed in the days of the seventh trumpet. Thus, the final opening of the sealed book as the book of destiny, which is the full revelation of the mystery of God, takes place at the final judgment (Rev. 20:11–15).

ARRANGEMENT OF REVELATION 4–22:5	
Chapters 4–5	The sealed scroll given to Christ by the Father
Chapters 6–9	Preparatory steps for the opening of the sealed scroll
Chapters 10–11	The little scroll as partial disclosure of the sealed scroll's contents by Christ to John through the mighty angel and through John to the churches
Chapters 12–22:5	The revelation of the contents of the little scroll (the ultimate opening of the sealed scroll given in 20:11–15)

In view of everything presented up to this point, Revelation can be seen as the partial disclosure of the divine mystery through John to the people of God. The contents of that mystery, which have been revealed to us through John in terms of the little scroll of chapter 10, are evidently described in Revelation 12–22:5 after "the temple of God that is in heaven was opened, and the ark of the covenant in his temple was seen" (Rev. 11:19). It was there by the ark of the covenant that the Covenant Book was stored (cf. Deut. 31:9, 24–26). The final opening of the sealed scroll with its full disclosure of "the mystery of God" belongs to a future eschatological period of judgment "that will bring history to its foreordained conclusion."[26] The contents of the sealed scroll, which are of importance for God's people with regard to "the things that must soon take place," are disclosed in Revelation 12–22. (See further "A Retrospect on Revelation 10" and "Overview: Revelation 12–22:5.")

ENDNOTES

1. Fiorenza, *Revelation*, 58; Paulien, "The Seven Seals," in *Symposium on Revelation—Book 1*, Daniel and Revelation Committee Series 6 (Silver Spring, MD: Biblical Research Institute, 1992), 201–202.

2. Paulien, "The Seven Seals," 202.

3. Ibid., 203.

4. For a fuller treatment of this section, see Ranko Stefanovic, *The Background and Meaning of the Sealed Book of Rev 5*, Andrews University Seminary Doctoral Dissertation Series 22 (Berrien Springs, MI: Andrews University Press, 1996), 145–195.

5. Beasley-Murray, 110.

6. Paulien, "The Seven Seals," 222–223.

7. E.g., R. Dean Davis (*The Heavenly Court Judgment of Revelation 4–5* [New York: University Press of America, 1992], 22–23, 157–188) and Treiyer (*The Day of Atonement and the Heavenly Judgment*, 474–567) draw parallels between Revelation 4–5 and the heavenly court scenes of Daniel 7, arguing that Revelation 4–5 is a judgment scene along the line of the Day of Atonement. The most recent objections to this view are expressed by Gulley, 59–64.

8. 4Q163 15–16 (Martínez, 189).

9. CD5 2–5 (Vermes, 86). (Italics and bracketed passage in original.)

10. See Vermes, 1; cf., e.g., 2 Sam. 8:17; 15:25–36; 20:25; 1 Chron. 29:22.

11. *The Isaiah Targum 8:16* (Chilton, 20).

12. Ibid., 8:17–18 (Chilton, 20).

13. Ibid., 42:7 (Chilton, 81).

14. The Babylonian Talmud *Sanhedrin* 103b (Epstein, 4/6:703); cf. *The Midrash Rabbah Genesis*, *Lech Lecha* 42.3 (Freedman, 1:342–343); *The Midrash Rabbah Leviticus*, *Shemini* 11.7 (Freedman, 4:144–145); *The Midrash*

Rabbah Ruth, Proem 7 (Freedman, 8:10–11); *The Midrash Rabbah Esther, Proem* 2 (Freedman, 9:12–13).

15. For further reference see Stefanovic, 283–285.

16. Mauro, 171.

17. Roloff, 76, 83.

18. Gulley, 64.

19. Ellen G. White, *Manuscript Releases* 9, Letter 65, 1898 (Silver Spring, MD: Ellen White Estate, 1990), 7.

20. Tenney, 28.

21. Paulien, "The Seven Seals," 217.

22. Günther Bornkamm, "*Musterion*, et al.," in *Theological Dictionary of the New Testament*, ed. G. Kittel and G. W. Bromiley (Grand Rapids, MI: Eerdmans, 1964–1976), 4:817–824.

23. William H. Shea, "The Mighty Angel and His Message," in *Symposium on Revelation—Book 1*, Daniel and Revelation Committee Series 6 (Silver Spring, MD: Biblical Research Institute, 1992), 314–315.

24. As rightly observed by Henry Alford, *The Greek Testament*, 3d ed. (Cambridge: Deighton, Bell, 1866; reprint, Chicago: Moody Press, 1958), 4:654; Alfred Plummer, "Revelation," *The Pulpit Commentary*, 2d ed. (London: Funk & Wagnalls, 1913), 22:163, 273; and Morris, 134.

25. Frederick D. Mazzaferri, *The Genre of the Book of Revelation* (New York: Walter de Gruyter, 1989), 278; Corsini, 132.

26. Paulien, "The Seven Seals," 219; cf. also Strand, *Interpreting the Book of Revelation*, 57.

THE HEAVENLY THRONE VISION
REVELATION 4:1–11

Revelation 4 and 5 constitute a literary and thematic unit. Chapter 4 is the first part of the vision of the sealed scroll; as such, it sets the stage for the scene of Revelation 5. The chapter describes the heavenly throne room and the heavenly hosts therein worshiping and praising God, who is sitting on the throne.

¹After these things I looked, and behold, a door opened in heaven, and the first voice which I heard was as a trumpet speaking to me, saying: "Come up here, and I will show you the things that must take place after these things." ²Immediately I was in the Spirit; and behold, a throne stood in heaven, and upon the throne was One sitting; ³and the One sitting was in appearance like a jasper and a sardius stone, and a rainbow around the throne was in appearance like an emerald. ⁴And around the throne were twenty-four thrones, and upon the thrones were sitting twenty-four elders clothed in white garments and upon their heads were golden crowns. ⁵And from the throne were proceeding flashes of lightning and sounds and peals of thunder; and seven torches of fire were burning before the throne, which are the seven Spirits of God, ⁶and before the throne was something like a sea of glass, like crystal.

And in the midst of the throne and around the throne were four living beings full of eyes in front and back; ⁷the first living being was like a lion, and the second living being like a calf, and the third living being having a face like that of a man, and the fourth living being like a flying eagle. ⁸And the four living beings, each one of them having six wings, are full of eyes around and inside; and they do not have rest day and night, saying:

> "Holy, holy, holy
> Lord God, the Almighty,
> who was and who is and who is coming!"
> [9]And whenever the living beings give glory and honor and thanks to the One sitting on the throne, the One who lives forever and ever, [10]the twenty-four elders fall before the One sitting on the throne and worship the One who lives forever and ever, and they cast their crowns before the throne and say:
> > [11] "You are worthy, our Lord and God,
> > to receive glory and honor and power,
> > Because you created all things
> > and because of your will they existed
> > and were created."

NOTES

4:1 *A door opened in heaven.* In the Greek Old Testament (LXX), the word *thura* ("door") occurs more than two hundred times, many of which relate directly to the sanctuary/temple.[1] The perfect participle of the verb "open" indicates that the door had been opened before John saw it in vision. The door through which John watched the interior of the throne room was most likely the door of the heavenly temple.

There has been debate among some historicist expositors regarding whether the throne room as the setting for the scene of Revelation 4–5 involves the holy place or the holy of holiest of the heavenly temple. Evidence strongly suggests that both apartments are in view due to the fact that both the articles of the holy place of the earthly temple and the throne (symbolized by the ark of the covenant that stood in the most holy place of the earthly temple; cf. 1 Sam. 4:4; Ps. 99:1) are the things that John saw in the throne room. This suggests that no particular apartment is in view in this scene. The curtain that separated the two apartments was removed, so to speak, and the holy and most holy place were coalesced into one throne room. There were only two occasions in the earthly temple in which the entire temple was involved: the inauguration of the sanctuary (Exod. 40; 1 Kings 7–8) and the Day of Atonement (Lev. 16). This would fit the scene of Revelation 4–5 that portrays the inauguration of the heavenly sanctuary and the installment of Christ into both priestly and royal ministry after his death on the cross and resurrection.

The things that must take place after these things. "These things" evidently refers to "the things which are" (Rev. 1:19)—namely, the messages to the seven churches (see *Notes* on Rev. 1:19).

4:2 *The throne.* Undoubtedly, the Old Testament concept of the throne of God as a symbolic expression of his sovereign majesty and ruling authority took its imagery from the earthly throne in ancient times. When a ruler took his seat on the throne, he had royal power. God is often described as sitting on the throne in heaven (1 Kings 22:19; Ps. 47:8; Isa. 6:1; Ezek. 1:26; Dan. 7:9), reigning in overwhelming majesty and glory (Pss. 93:1–2; 97:1–9; 99:1–5) and surrounded by the hosts of heavenly beings (1 Kings 22:19; Isa. 6:1–3; Ezek. 1:4–24; Dan. 7:9–10). The Ark of the Covenant is regarded as the throne of God, invisibly present on the earth (cf. 1 Sam. 4:4). The throne of God is one of the items in heaven most frequently appearing in the book of Revelation (it is mentioned in 16 of its 22 chapters). It is found in the beginning of the book (1:4) and at the end (22:3). Sometimes the throne is used as a reference for God; for instance, "a voice from the throne" could mean "God is saying" (cf. 16:17; 19:5), or "before the throne" could mean "before God" (7:9; 14:3). In the new Jerusalem, "the throne of God and of the Lamb" (Rev. 22:3; cf. Rev. 22:1) signifies the ultimate subjection of the powers of Satan and the abiding presence of God among his saved people (Rev. 21:3; cf. Ezek. 43:7).

4:3 *In appearance like a jasper and a sardius stone, and a rainbow around the throne was in appearance like an emerald.* Identification of these three precious stones is very problematic. Jasper, sardius, and emerald are mentioned by Plato as representative of precious stones.[2] They are among the precious stones that adorned the king of Tyre (Ezek. 28:13) and are found on the breastplate of the High Priest in the Old Testament, which had inscribed on it the names of the tribes of Israel (Exod. 28:17–20). They are also found among the foundation stones of New Jerusalem (Rev. 21:19) which are inscribed with the names of the twelve apostles (21:14). As J. Massynberde Ford observes, sardius (ruby in NASB) and jasper are the first and last of the stones on the breastplate of the High Priest, representing Reuben, the eldest, and Benjamin, the youngest, of Jacob's sons. The emerald (turquoise in NASB) as the fourth stone in the list represents Judah,[3] which is particularly significant in light of the title "the Lion from the tribe of Judah" (5:5).

4:4 *Twenty-four elders.* In addition to appearing in chapters 4 and 5 (4:4, 10; 5:8, 11, 14), the twenty-four elders are mentioned several other times in the book (7:11, 13; 11:16; 14:3; 19:4). Since the author of Revelation never identifies the elders, their identity is left open and ambiguous. Throughout the book, they are portrayed as sitting upon thrones surrounding the throne of God, clothed in white robes, and having crowns upon their heads (4:4; 11:16). They continually worship and give praise to God (4:10, 11; 5:8–10, 14; 11:16–18; 19:4); they bring to God the prayers of the saints (5:8); and on two occasions one of them explains to John what he does not understand in the visions (5:5; 7:13–14). They are evidently some kind of heavenly beings. Different views on their identity have been proposed.[4] The one most widely accepted suggests that the twenty-four elders must be understood as angels since they are in heaven rather than on the earth.[5]

Evidence strongly indicates, however, that the twenty-four elders are redeemed and glorified humanity rather than angels. First of all, angels are never called elders in either the Bible or Jewish literature; they are never described as sharing God's throne, but rather standing in God's presence. Second, the twenty-four elders wear white garments. The white garments in Revelation relate consistently to the faithful people of God (3:4–5, 18; 6:11; 7:9, 13–14). Angels are never described in Revelation as wearing white robes. Third, the elders also wear golden crowns of victory. In Greek, it is *stephanos*, the victory crown (see *Notes* on Rev. 2:10), rather than the royal crown (Gr. *diadēma*), which represents eternal life and which is the reward to the faithful who overcome (cf. 2:10; 3:11). Paul believed he would receive this crown on the day of the Lord's coming (2 Tim. 4:8). The fact that the twenty-four elders wear the victory crowns suggests that they are not rulers but rather the redeemed who have gained a victory. The *stephanos* crowns are never worn by angels in the Bible. All of these descriptions are limited to the people of God, and they rule out any probability that the twenty-four elders are the heavenly presbyterium consisting either of celestial beings[6] or the righteous figures of the Old Testament.[7]

The number "twenty-four" regarding the elders consists of two sets of twelve. "Twelve" is a crucial number in Revelation. In New Jerusalem, the twelve gates are named after the twelve tribes of Israel, and the twelve foundations have the names of the twelve apostles. It is quite possible that the twenty-four elders are somehow related to the 144,000, a number evidently based on twelve times twelve times one thousand (see *Notes* on Rev. 7:4). In addition, twenty-four different courses of priests in the Old Testament Temple took turns during the services (1 Chron. 24:4–19), and they were called the officers of God (1 Chron. 24:5). The twenty-four elders are continually involved in worship and in presenting the prayers of the saints to God (Rev. 5:8), which is priestly work.

All of these considerations strongly suggest that the twenty-four elders are the glorified saints. They are most likely a symbolic group representing all redeemed and faithful people of God of both the Old and New Testament church; that is, they represent the church in its totality. Their description fits well into the picture of the redeemed in Revelation; white garments, victorious crowns (*stephanoi*), and the sitting upon thrones are all promises given to the people of God. Their sitting on the thrones next to the throne of God (4:4) brings to mind Jesus' promise to the overcomer in Revelation 3:21. That they are at the same time continually involved in the heavenly worship suggests their twofold role as priests and kings (cf. 5:8–10). When did these elders get to the heavenly places? Revelation does not explain it. The fact that no elders are mentioned in the records of Old Testament throne visions suggests that, when John saw them, they were a new group not previously present in the heavenly throne room. Most likely they arrived there somewhere around the time of Jesus' death on the cross. According to Matthew 27:51–53, when Jesus died on the cross "the tombs were opened; and many bodies of the saints who had fallen asleep were raised." The text does not say what later happened to these saints. Paul says that when Christ ascended to heaven after his resurrection, "he led captive a host of captives" (Eph. 4:8). It is quite possible that these resurrected saints ascended with Jesus to heaven as the first fruit of the harvest to represent redeemed humanity in the heavenly places.[8]

4:5 Seven torches of fire were burning before the throne, which are the seven Spirits of God. See *Notes* on Revelation 1:4.

4:6 Four living beings. The four living beings are mentioned several times in the book of Revelation. They are always found in proximity to the throne (4:6; 5:6; 14:3), and they are constantly engaged in worshiping and praising God (4:8–9; 5:8–9, 14; 7:11–12; 19:4). No doubt this imagery is drawn from Ezekiel's vision where the prophet saw the four living beings each having four faces: that of a man, a lion, an ox, and an eagle (Ezek. 1:6–10; 10:14); they are "full of eyes all around" (Ezek. 10:12). Ezekiel definitely identifies them with the cherubim (10:20–22). Also, the four living beings of Revelation 4 bring to mind Isaiah's vision of seraphim with six wings and the acclamations of "Holy, holy, holy, is the Lord of hosts" (Isa. 6:2–3). The proximity of the four living creatures to the throne in both Revelation 4 and Ezekiel 1 and 10 reminds us of the cherubim associated with the ark of the covenant; they were placed there to face each other, and their wings were stretched over the mercy seat (Exod. 25:18–21; 1 Kings 6:23–28). God is often pictured in the Bible as sitting on the throne between the cherubim (2 Kings 19:15; Pss. 80:1; 99:1; Isa. 37:16). All of these factors clearly indicate that the four living beings in Revelation are the exalted angels of God who serve him and are the guardians of his throne; they are involved in leading the heavenly hosts in ceaseless worship and praise. As Henry B. Swete proposes, their forms might suggest everything that is "noblest, strongest, wisest, and swiftest" in nature.[9] They are involved somehow in the manifestation of God's wrath upon the earth (6:1, 3, 5, 7; 15:7).

   4:8 Almighty. See *Notes* on Revelation 1:8.

EXPOSITION

   The seven churches have received from the glorified Christ both the appraisal of their spiritual condition and counsel on how to correct and improve their condition. The scene now shifts from the earth to heaven and from John's time to the future. John now begins describing what seems to be "the heart of the book of Revelation."[10]

   One might also observe that the seven messages are written in the epistolary, straightforward language similar to the one that Paul and other New Testament writers used in writing their letters. The use of few symbols in chapters 2–3 can be easily understood. Such straightforward language was appropriate because the seven messages addressed the present conditions and needs of the local churches in Asia. However, from chapter 4 onward, the visions of the book are described in a complex symbolic language not always easy to interpret. In describing the times and things that lay in the future, John followed the style of the Jewish apocalyptic writings characterized by a peculiar symbolic language.

   4:1–2a John tells his readers that he is caught up in a new vision in which he sees **a door opened in heaven.** The door through which he watches the interior of the heavenly throne room is most likely the door of the temple. He hears the same voice of the glorified Christ that he earlier heard **as a trumpet speaking** (cf. Rev. 1:10). This voice now calls him: **Come up here, and I will show you the things that**

must take place after these things. Earlier in Revelation 1:19, when the trumpet-like voice asked John to write down the visions he saw, he was told that the events he was to see in vision were about "the things which are" from his perspective and the things which will happen afterwards. Now, the same voice is telling him that he will witness the things to take place "*after* these things." Revelation 4:1 thus points back to 1:19, making it clear that the phrase "these things" refers to the situation with the seven churches described in chapters 2 and 3. John is now about to be shown what will happen in the future from his perspective with regard to the church and the world.

John states further that he is ***in the Spirit*** while in the vision. This is the same expression used earlier in his introduction to the vision of the glorified Christ (Rev. 1:10). By this he makes clear that what he sees and hears is not "made by an act of human will" (2 Pet. 1:21) but results from the work of the Holy Spirit.

4:2b–3 Through the open door in heaven, John is taken in vision into the throne room of the heavenly temple. The first thing attracting his attention there is ***the throne***. "Throne" is the key word of Revelation 4; it occurs fourteen times in the chapter and is central to everything that takes place. It stands in the heavenly throne room as a symbolic expression of God's sovereign majesty. All things and activities taking place in chapter 4 are oriented to the throne of God. They are referred to as "upon the throne" (v. 2), "around the throne" (vv. 3, 4, 6; cf. 5:11), "from the throne" (v. 5), "before the throne" (vv. 5–6, 10), or "in the midst of the throne" (v. 6; 5:6). This centrality of the throne in chapter 4 causes one to name the place of the scene described in chapters 4–5 as "the heavenly throne room."

It is not the heavenly throne itself which is described in Revelation 4, however, but rather its majestic surroundings, recalling the throne visions from Isaiah (6:1–3) and Ezekiel (1:4–28). Around the throne is a rainbow (Rev. 4:3), and before it are seven lamps (v. 5) and something like a sea of glass (v. 6). From the throne comes forth lightning, sounds, and thunder (v. 5). Around the throne are twenty-four thrones with the twenty-four elders sitting on them (v. 4) and the four living beings constantly praising God (vv. 6–8).

The next thing John sees is ***One sitting*** upon the throne. The description of the occupant of the throne indicates clearly that he must be God the Father (4:2–3). Since John was to be shown what would happen in the future regarding the church and the world, it was important first to introduce him to the one who is in charge and who holds the future. The throne symbolizes the right to rule. The person sitting on the throne has the royal power and authority to rule over the kingdom.

It is interesting that John makes no attempt to describe God in any human form as was common in the portrayal of God in the Old Testament prophetic visions. Elsewhere in the vision he refers to him as "the One sitting on the throne" (Rev. 4:3, 9, 10; 5:1, 7, 13), although he identifies him twice in the chapter as "Lord God, the Almighty" (4:8) and "our Lord and God" (4:11). John focuses on God's radiant glory, which takes a characteristic form. Human words are incapable of expressing the full glory of God. When Moses asked God to show him his glory, he was told: "You can not see My face, for no man can see Me and live" (Exod. 33:20). Even though it was stated that he spoke to God "face to face," Moses was never shown the fullness of God's glory. John somehow had a similar situation. Instead, John describes God's majestic splendor in terms of the dazzling brilliance of *jasper*, *sardius*, and *emerald*, which are typical of precious stones. This description of God's majesty reminds us of Ezekiel's vision (1:26–28). The dazzling light of the precious stones portrays in symbolic language the majesty and glory of God. The Psalmist describes God as the One who covers himself "with light as with a cloak" (104:2), and Paul says that he "dwells in unapproachable light" (1 Tim. 6:16). As the sign of God's covenant, *a rainbow around the throne* (cf. Ezek. 1:28) provides a firm assurance of God's covenant promise to be with his people and of his faithfulness to that promise (Gen. 9:12–17).

All of these descriptions of the throne room in Revelation 4 parallel the great throne visions of the Old Testament. The prophet Micaiah claimed that he saw "the Lord sitting on His throne, and all the host of heaven standing by Him on His right and on His left" (1 Kings 22:19). Isaiah saw "the Lord sitting on a throne, lofty and exalted" in majesty and glory (Isa. 6:1–3). Daniel saw God sitting on the throne which was "ablaze with flames, its wheels were a burning fire. A river of fire was flowing and coming out from before Him; thousands upon thousands were attending Him, and myriads upon myriads were standing before Him" (Dan. 7:9–10). It seems that the crucial background to the scene of Revelation 4, however, is the throne vision of Ezekiel 1 (vv. 4–10, 13–14, 18, 26–28). The parallels between the two visions are obvious:

REVELATION 4	EZEKIEL 1
the throne with God sitting on it (vv. 2–5)	the throne with God sitting on it (vv. 26–28)
rainbow around the throne (v. 3b)	rainbow around the throne (v. 26)
seven lamps of fire (v. 4b)	torches of fire (v. 13)
flashes of lightning and thunder (v. 5)	flashes of lightning and storm (vv. 4, 13)
four living beings (vv. 6–8)	four living beings (vv. 5–10)
– six wings	– four wings
– faces of a lion, calf, man, and eagle	– faces of a man, lion, bull, and eagle
– "full of eyes around and within" (v. 8)	– "full of eyes all around" (v.18)
spread like a sea of glass (v. 6)	crystal spread (vv. 22–26)

Detailed studies show that in Greek, about one third of the words in Revelation 4 also appear in Ezekiel. Yet John's description of the throne scene incorporates the features of all these great Old Testament throne visions.

It is especially interesting that in Revelation 4 it is the throne, rather than God, that attracts John's attention at the very outset of the vision. God, the Father, is presented simply as the "One sitting on the throne," although he is the object of adoration and worship of the heavenly assembly (Rev. 4:8–11). A nearly identical clause appears in Revelation 20:11, where the throne is the place of final judgment. This phenomenon has been explained as John's reluctance to mention the divine name, just as it was avoided in later Jewish literature. However, four times in the vision John declares "the One sitting on the throne" to be God (Rev. 4:8, 11; 5:9–10), as he does elsewhere in the book. Others suggest that the reason for not mentioning the divine name is the impossibility of expressing the awesomeness of God or the avoidance of the anthropomorphic details of God's appearance. But these arguments are weakened by the fact that John does use anthropomorphic language with reference to God. For instance, the sealed scroll is seen "at the right hand of the One sitting on the throne" (Rev. 5:1); the sinners cannot stand before the face of "the One sitting on the throne" (Rev. 6:16; 20:11). In addition, John occasionally refers to "God sitting on the throne" (Rev. 19:4; cf. 7:10; 12:5). All of these examples indicate that John was not reluctant to use anthropomorphic language when referring to God sitting on the throne.

Apparently the linguistic style here focuses on the throne because it is the divine throne, rather than God as a being, that is central to the scene. This view fits into the context of the vision wherein the throne is clearly the central object of Revelation 4. In addition, it appears that the scene of Revelation 4–5 builds on the concluding statement of 3:21, wherein Christ promises to the overcomer a share in his throne, just as he himself has overcome and has joined the Father on the throne. The scene of chapter 4, in which the divine throne is central, is the prelude to Christ's attaining the Father's throne in chapter 5. The future fulfillment of the promise of the reward to the overcomer to sit with Jesus on the throne is reserved for the Second Coming and is described in chapter 7.

The further significance of the focus on the throne of God in chapters 4 and 5 is found in light of the fact that John wrote to Christians suffering under the persecution initiated by the imperial throne of Rome. The throne of God stands in opposition to "the throne of Satan" (Rev. 2:13; cf. 13:2) and "the throne of the beast" (16:10; cf. 13:2). As Daegeuk Nam states, in the Old Testament the throne of God was regarded as the people's last resort of hope in days of disaster and despair (cf. Ps. 11:1–4; Jer. 17:12–13; Lam. 5:19). In times of impending judgments, the prophets referred to "the throne of God as the ground of their appeal to God and as the prospect of future hope for restoration." The throne of God was the place where those who suffered and were persecuted or unfairly treated could come to present their prayer and obtain deliverance from God; to all of them the divine throne was the "unshakable foundation of their faith and trust in God" (Ps. 9:4–5; cf. Job 23:3).[11] In elaborating upon this Old Testament significance of the divine throne, John endeavors to communicate the clear message to his fellow Christians that the throne of God is the controlling force in this universe.

4:4–8 In proximity to the throne, John sees *twenty-four thrones,* and upon them sitting *twenty-four elders clothed in white garments and upon their heads were golden crowns*. The twenty-four elders are most likely glorified saints—the symbolic representatives of the redeemed and faithful people of God of both the Old and New Testaments. They have not been mentioned before in any Old Testament throne visions. This suggests that when John saw them, they were a new group not previously present in the heavenly throne room. They must have arrived there somewhere around the time of Jesus' death on the cross. They ascended with Jesus to heaven as the first fruit of harvest to represent redeemed humanity in heavenly places.

In Revelation 4–5, the twenty-four elders are seen as representatives of redeemed humanity summoned together with the representatives of other worlds and all creation to be a part of the great ceremony to welcome Jesus back to heaven and set him on throne at the right hand of the Father. The reason John saw them in chapter 4 as seated on the thrones before Jesus was inaugurated in chapter 5 is that they were ushered onto the scene during the setting up of the ceremony. When finally Jesus appeared in the throne room and was enthroned on the heavenly throne at the right hand of the Father, he received worship and acclamations from the angelic hosts together with the representatives of the whole creation assembled in the throne room of the heavenly temple.

Also there are *four living beings*, each having *six wings* and *full of eyes around and inside*, which may symbolize swiftness of movement and great intelligence and discernment. Like the cherubim in Ezekiel's vision (10:20–22), their appearance is respectively that of a lion, an ox, a man, and an eagle, and they are constantly praising God. They are probably an exalted angelic order involved in serving God and leading the heavenly hosts in worshiping and praising God (cf. Isa. 6:2–3; Ezek. 1:6–10; 10:14). As William Hendriksen points out, they are described as having "strength like the lion" (cf. Ps. 103:20), "ability to render service like the ox" (cf. Heb. 1:14), "intelligence like man" (cf. Luke 15:10), and "swiftness like the eagle" (cf. Dan. 9:21), characteristics which in the Bible are ascribed to angels.[12]

Some scholars suggest that Revelation 4 could easily evoke a scene from the contemporary Roman imperial court and cult ceremonial in the minds of the original readers. "Just as the Roman emperor was depicted as surrounded by his friends and advisers when dispensing justice, so is God here seen surrounded by hosts of the exalted angelic order and the representation of the redeemed humanity."[13] In Revelation 4, the heavenly hosts are assembled not for dispensing justice, but for a special occasion—most likely that of the great ceremony of Christ's enthronement on the heavenly throne. As the representatives of humanity, they join those of the entire universe in the shouts of acclamation to the newly enthroned King of the universe.

John adds some additional details in describing the scene in the heavenly throne room: *From the throne were proceeding flashes of lightning and sounds and peals of thunder* (v. 5) that accentuate the splendor of the occasion. In the Old Testament, this phenomenon is always connected with the appearance of God

(Ps. 77:18; Ezek. 1:13). What John could have had more particularly in mind is the description of Mount Sinai at the time of the giving of the Law: "There were thunder and lightning flashes and a thick cloud upon the mountain and a very loud trumpet sound" (Exod. 19:16). Before the throne are **seven torches of fire** which **were burning** and which are explained as **the seven Spirits of God** (v. 5). This refers to the work and activity of the Holy Spirit in its fullness (cf. Zech. 4:2–6). The next phenomenon that catches John's attention is a spread before the throne, **something like a sea of glass, like crystal** (v. 6). "Its crystal surface stretches out before the throne, reflecting the flashing, many-colored light from the throne, furnishing a surface for the activity around the throne, and creating for the Seer an unspeakably heightened sense of the transcendence and majesty of God"[14] (cf. Rev. 15:2).

The description of this scene in the heavenly throne room reaches its conclusion and climax with the ceaseless praise from the four living beings: **They do not have rest day and night, saying: "Holy, holy, holy Lord God, the Almighty, who was and who is and who is coming!"** (Rev. 4:8). This reminds us of the song of the seraphim in Isaiah's vision: "Holy, holy, holy, is the Lord of hosts" (Isa. 6:3).

4:9–11 Whenever the acclamation of **glory and honor and thanks to the One sitting on the throne, the One who lives forever and ever** is heard from the four living beings, the twenty-four elders fall down, lay their crowns before the throne, and worship the One sitting on the throne: **You are worthy, our Lord and God, to receive glory and honor and power, because you created all things and because of your will they existed and were created.** The songs of the elders as representatives of human beings emphatically point to two things. First, they show in a nutshell that the essence of true worship is to recount and celebrate God's mighty acts—the act of creation (the focus of which is in chap. 4) and the act of redemption through the death and resurrection of Jesus Christ (the focus of which is in chap. 5). Second, they show that the end-time drama involves both creation and redemption. The same God who created this world has the power and ability to restore it and provide salvation to lost and suffering human beings.

In addition, the text reflects several ancient practices. The act of the twenty-four elders presenting golden crowns before God sitting on the throne reflects the court ceremonial from Roman times when kings would present their crowns before the all-powerful Emperor in expressing their subordination and homage.[15]

According to E. Schüssler Fiorenza, the acclamation "you are worthy" greeted the "triumphal entrance of the Roman emperor."[16] "Our Lord and God" was the official title of Domitian, the Roman emperor during the time of the writing of the book of Revelation.[17] It was in refusing to acknowledge the emperor as lord and god that the Christians of John's day suffered persecution and death. In contrast to the claim of the Roman emperor, the twenty-four elders, as representatives of redeemed humanity in the heavenly courts, proclaim God as the only worthy one to be called Lord and God of all the universe.

A RETROSPECT ON REVELATION 4

No doubt the scene in Revelation 4 sets the stage for the scene described in chapter 5. We see John observing the majestic splendor of the heavenly throne room portrayed in terms of the dazzling light of the precious stones, a many-colored rainbow, lightning, sound and thunder, and the seven torches of burning fire. Also, the crystal surface of the sea of glass stretches out before the throne and reflects the flashing, many-colored lights from the throne. All attention suddenly focuses on the glorious throne surrounded by the four exalted angels leading the heavenly hosts in worship and praise, and the twenty-four elders as the representatives of redeemed humanity. They are together with the heavenly hosts assembled there in the throne room in the expectant atmosphere to welcome Jesus who is about to be enthroned at the right hand of the Father.

Suddenly, the celebration of the magnificent liturgy subsides for a moment when in chapter 5 the Lamb approaches the throne and takes the sealed scroll from the right side of God. Then follows an explosion of tumultuous joy that reaches a magnificent climax when the whole heavenly assembly falls down before the newly crowned king. This time they are uttering the acclamations of glory and honor both to the One sitting on the throne and to the Lamb (Rev. 5:14). This splendid event and joyful celebration is the subject of the next chapter.

ENDNOTES

1. Paulien, "The Seven Seals," 207.
2. Plato, *Phaedo* 110e (The Loeb Classical Library, 1:378–379).
3. J. M. Ford, *Revelation,* 71.
4. For a list of various views, see Aune, *Revelation 1–5,* 287–292.

5. See Ladd, 75.

6. See Bornkamm, *"Presbus*, et al.," in *Theological Dictionary of the New Testament*, 6:668–669; more recently, Alfred Pala argues that the twenty-four elders are the council of cosmic rulers consisting of representatives of the unfallen worlds, the same as in Job 1–2 ("The Council of Cosmic Rulers," *Perspective Digest* 3.2 [1998], 18–25). However, nowhere does the book show God sitting with them in council or suggest that the elders exercise a judicial office. The *stephanos* crowns they wear suggest that the elders are not rulers exercising their dominion throughout the universe.

7. For a discussion of this view, see André Feuillet, *Johannine Studies* (Staten Island, NY: Alba House, 1964), 194–214.

8. Uriah Smith was among the first expositors to suggest this concept (*The Prophecies of Daniel and the Revelation*, revised ed. [Nashville, TN: Southern Publishing Association, 1944], 408–409).

9. Swete, 71.

10. Thomas, *Revelation 1–7*, 333.

11. Daegeuk Nam, "The 'Throne of God' Motif in the Hebrew Bible" (Th.D. dissertation, Andrews University, 1989), 464–465.

12. William Hendriksen, *More than Conquerors* (Grand Rapids, MI: Baker, 1967), 87; Mounce, 138.

13. Fiorenza, *Revelation*, 59.

14. Mounce, 136.

15. See Aune, *Revelation 1–5*, 308–309.

16. Fiorenza, *Revelation*, 59–60.

17. See Aune, *Revelation 1–5*, 309–311.

THE SEALED SCROLL
REVELATION 5:1–14

Revelation 5 builds on the scene of Revelation 4. Here John sees at the right hand of God, who is sitting on the throne, a scroll that is "written inside and on the back" and sealed with seven seals. He understands that nobody in the entire universe is worthy to open that remarkable scroll. Then, a Lamb/Lion-like figure, "the Sprout of David" which appears "as having been slain," is found worthy to open the scroll because he has conquered. When he has taken the scroll from the right side of the One sitting on the throne, anthems of praise sound throughout the universe.

¹And I saw at the right hand of the One sitting on the throne a scroll written inside and on the back, sealed with seven seals. ²And I saw a strong angel proclaiming with a loud voice: "Who is worthy to open the scroll and to break its seals?" ³And nobody in heaven or on the earth or under the earth was able to open the scroll or to look into it. ⁴And I began to weep much because nobody was found worthy to open the scroll or to look at it. ⁵And one of the elders said to me: "Stop crying! Behold, the Lion from the tribe of Judah, who is the Sprout of David, has overcome so that he is able to open the scroll and its seven seals."

⁶And I saw in the midst of the throne and the four living beings and in the midst of the twenty-four elders a lamb standing as having been slain, having seven horns and seven eyes, which are the seven spirits of God sent into all the earth. ⁷And he came and took the scroll from the right hand of the One sitting on the throne. ⁸And when he had taken the scroll, the four living beings and the twenty-four elders fell down before the Lamb, each having a harp and golden bowls full of incense, which are the prayers of the saints; ⁹And they sang a new song and said:

> "You are worthy to take the scroll and open its seals,
>   for you were slain and purchased for God with your
>   blood from every tribe and tongue and people and nation,
> 10 and you have made them a kingdom and priests to our
>   God, and they will reign on the earth."

11 And I looked, and I heard the voice of many angels around the throne and the living beings and the elders, the number of which was myriads of myriads and thousands of thousands, 12 saying with a loud voice:

> "Worthy is the slain Lamb to receive power and riches
>   and wisdom and strength and honor and glory and blessing!"

13 And every creature which was in heaven and on the earth and under the earth and on the sea and all things which are in them, I heard saying:

> "To the One sitting on the throne and to the Lamb
>   be blessing and honor and glory and might for ever and ever!"

14 And the four living beings kept saying: "Amen!" And the elders fell down and worshiped.

NOTES

5:1 *At the right hand.* The Greek *epi tēn dexian* has generally been translated as "in the right hand," mainly because it has been held that John drew this imagery from Ezekiel 2:2–10 where the prophet saw a scroll in the outstretched hand of God. Revelation 5:1 would, accordingly, depict God holding a scroll in his right hand. The phrase *epi tēn dexian* appears nowhere else in the Bible, and it occurs very rarely in Greek literature. Its occasional appearance in the literature from the first up to the seventh century A.D. suggests that *epi tēn dexian* is an idiom corresponding to the English "at the right hand." The phrase thus has primarily to do with the right side rather than the right hand (as a member of the body). It means that the sealed scroll was seen by John as being on the throne at the right hand of God.[1]

A scroll. In the first century A.D., the Greek word *biblion* was a common word for a scroll (a roll of a book), but was also used for documents of any form including codices (separate sheets bound together), writings, letters, and legal documents, regardless of the writing material (such as papyrus, tablet, or parchment). Evidence indicates that the sealed *biblion* of Revelation 5 is of a scroll form. First, codices did not originate until the second, or perhaps the late first, century A.D.[2] Second, John himself indicates that he has a scroll rather than a codex in mind when he describes the sky as vanishing like a *biblion* which was rolled up (Rev. 6:14). Finally, the phrase "inside and on the back" is an appropriate expression for a scroll, unlike a book; "inside" refers to the inside of the scroll before it is unrolled, and "the back" to its back side after being unrolled.

Written inside and on the back. This reading of the phrase is rightly taken as the correct one. However, it is quite possible to link "and on the back" with "sealed with seven seals" ("written inside, and on the back sealed with seven seals"). Although grammatically possible, such a reading is less likely, for the phrase "written inside and on the back" refers to a relatively rare ancient practice. Ancient scrolls were usually written on only one (the inner) side; the back (outside) was often left blank. Sometimes, however, the writing on the inner side was carried over onto and completed on the back. Documents containing writing on both sides of the parchment, called *opisthographos*, were not rare in the first and second centuries A.D.[3] At least two documents written on both sides are mentioned in the Old Testament: "the two tablets of the testimony," which Moses brought down from the mountain (Exod. 32:15), and the scroll that Ezekiel saw spread before him which "had writing on the front and on the back" (2:9–10).

The phrase "written inside and on the back" may just as well refer to the so-called "double document" which was well known and widely used in John's time. The double documents consisted of two copies of the text on the same sheet: the upper half of the papyrus was rolled up and tied with a thread to protect the document against alteration or tampering; and the lower half was left untied, which enabled its holder to consult it at any time. The folded, tied portion was designated as the inner text and the lower untied portion as the outer text.[4] It is hard to determine whether the phrase "written inside and on the back" refers to a scroll document that was inscribed in full on its inner and reverse sides or to a double document of a scroll form. The context of Revelation 5 does not indicate that one part of the scroll was sealed and another one unsealed. The mention of the little scroll in Revelation 10 might even refer to the unsealed outer text of a double document.

Sealed. The scroll of Revelation 5 was further described as being "sealed with seven seals"; this was in accordance with the common practice of sealing documents in the ancient world. In order to protect the contents of legal documents (such as deeds of sale, contracts, wills, and letters), a seal impression was normally made with a signet or ring at the end of the written content. The sealing thus functioned in place of a signature, indicating authenticity, validity, authority, ratification, or protection of the document. In order to protect the contents against an inappropriate disclosure, the document would be tied with threads, and then the seal was impressed at the knots on bullae (a blob of clay, wax, or some other soft material) which kept the papyrus scroll folded (Job 38:14). An unbroken impression would indicate that the sealed document had not been opened. Only the owner could break the seals and disclose the contents.

The practice of sealing was common in ancient Israel. In Jeremiah's account of a transaction, "the deed of sale" was sealed before the witnesses and as such had legally binding significance (Jer. 32:10–11). Isaiah probably had such a document in mind when referring to "the words of a sealed book, which when they give it to the one who is literate, saying, 'Please read this,' he will say, 'I cannot, for it is sealed'" (Isa. 29:11). While private seals were common among the surrounding nations, in Israel the seals were primarily in the possession of kings and officials. In the Old Testament, affixing a seal was usually seen as an official and legal act, most often performed by a king or his official.

With seven seals. The practice of sealing documents with more than one seal was widespread throughout the ancient Near East in John's day. Archaeologists have brought to light many documents sealed with two to seven or more seals. For instance, Roman law dictated that a will or testament had to be sealed with a minimum of seven seals of witnesses in order to render its contents valid, although some evidence shows that more than seven seals were used on occasion. The same Roman legal system, however, also required that some other documents, including contracts and birth registers, be certified by the signatures of seven witnesses. The seals bore the names of the sealers and could only be opened by them. This shows clearly that the description of the sealed scroll of Revelation 5 conformed to a common type of legal document of John's time. Like any sealed scroll of the time, the scroll of Revelation 5 appears rolled up, tied with a cord, and sealed along the outside edge with seals of wax affixed at the knots. As such, it could not be opened and its contents disclosed until all of the seven seals were broken. The breaking of all seven seals is preliminary and preparatory to the actual opening of the scroll and the disclosure of its contents.[5]

Seven. The fact that the scroll was sealed with seven seals is particularly significant in light of the meaning of the number "seven" both in Revelation and in the Bible as a whole (it appears in nearly six hundred passages, either literally or symbolically). "Seven" is "the only number used symbolically in Scripture to any degree with discernible significance," and "this is the only number which appears to be used symbolically with any consistency in contemporary extra-biblical literature."[6] As is generally accepted, the fundamental ancient and Old Testament idea of the symbolic use of "seven" is "fullness," "completeness," or "perfection." Karl H. Rengstorf explains that its meaning as fullness and totality comes from

> the observation that time runs in periods of seven days. This leads to the linking of seven with a completed period, and from here it is only a step to the equation of the abstract number seven with the concept of what is total or complete. Seven represents a complete whole and is thus the given magnitude by which to give short and pregnant expression to such a totality. The number seven thus bears the character of totality, i.e., of the totality desired and ordained by God.[7]

In the Old Testament, "seven" functions as the sacred number of the covenant between God and his creation, for all "covenant relations and obligations" and the ceremonial system appear to be associated with the number "seven."[8] As an expression of the divine totality, the number "seven" plays an important role in Revelation (it is used 56 times in the book). As the introduction to this commentary shows, the number "seven" seems to play an important part in the structure of Revelation.

5:2 Worthy. In Greek, *axios* means "worthy," "estimable," "deserving," "fit," and "appropriate." By John's time, the concept of "worthy" had developed from a general quality or virtue to a distinctive qualification that would make a candidate suitable or eligible for a high position or office of honor. The outstanding Roman nobleman would be considered worthy of being admired and praised for his outstanding achievements. From the time of John, "worthiness" became the virtue which qualified an emperor to lay his chief claim to rule on the basis of how he could win the affection and loyalty of his subjects. This secular usage with reference to kingship and honor gradually penetrated the religious language of both Jews and Christians. The term was frequently used by Jewish writers with reference to Old Testament kingship and priesthood.[9] In Revelation 4 and 5, the term "worthy" designates a unique qualification for a special position and task which nobody possesses but God. In 4:11, God sitting on the throne is worthy of all honor and glory. In chapter 5, by virtue of his victorious death (v. 5) through which he was able to redeem humanity, the Lamb is pronounced worthy to take the scroll (5:9); he is then worthy to receive all honor and glory of kingship (5:12). Finally, both "the One sitting on the throne" and the Lamb receive honor and worship from all the heavenly and earthly beings (5:13–14).[10]

5:5 *The Lion from the tribe of Judah.* This title goes back to Genesis 49:9 in Jacob's final blessing where Judah was called a victorious lion. The strength, courage, and majestic appearance of the lion, which since ancient times has been named king of beasts, make it a fitting symbol of the victorious Messiah in Judaism. For instance, the apocryphal work 4 Ezra mentions the imposing figure of a lion, which is described as "the Messiah whom the Most High has kept until the end of days, who will arise from the posterity of David."[11] Many other examples show that in Jewish tradition the figure of a lion, interpreted in the light of Genesis 49, signifies the Messianic, royal prerogatives and is linked to the throne of David.[12]

The Sprout of David. This title functions most likely as a clarification of the preceding title designating "the Lion from the tribe of Judah" as the descendant of the king David. This title goes back to Isaiah 11:1, which declares that "a shoot will spring from the stem of Jesse, and a branch from his root" will establish the coming kingdom of peace and righteousness (cf. 11:10). In this passage, "the root" is the origin of the new shoot from the fallen tree of David which has been cut down. Jeremiah speaks of the future when God will fulfill his promise and "raise up for David a righteous Branch [Sprout] and He will reign as king" (Jer. 23:5–6; 33:14–16). Zechariah prophesied of "a man whose name is Branch [or Sprout], for He will branch out from where He is; and He will build the temple of the Lord. Yes, it is He who will build the temple of the Lord, and will bear the honor and sit and rule on His throne. Thus, He will be a priest on His throne, and the counsel of peace will be between the two offices" (6:12–13).[13]

In the above-mentioned Old Testament passages, the "Sprout" is linked to the time when the covenant promise given to David with regard to the perpetuity of his throne (cf. 2 Sam. 7:12–16) would be fulfilled in the coming of a descendant to sit on the throne and rule over the nations. Among the Jewish people in John's time, "the Sprout of David" became the favorite title with reference to the Messiah who would sit and reign upon the throne of David (cf. Luke 1:32–33). In the New Testament, "the Sprout of David" and "the son of David" are well-known titles with reference to Jesus, the Messiah, the king *par excellence.* So Paul expressly cites Isaiah 11:10 as having been fulfilled in Christ (Rom. 15:12). It is particularly interesting that John presents Christ as "the Sprout of David" in the beginning of the principal prophetic part of the book (5:5) as well as in its closing statement (22:16). This was meant to show that the Old Testament promises have been fulfilled in Christ, the Messiah.

5:6 *Seven horns.* In the Old Testament, the horn stands for strength and power. For the Egyptians, God is like the horns of the wild ox (Num. 23:22). In the blessing of Moses, it is with his horns that Joseph will push the people together to the ends of the earth (Deut. 33:17). Hannah's horn is exalted in the Lord and she can stand boldly against her enemies (1 Sam. 2:1). In a special way, the horn is used as a symbol of kingly power. "He will give strength to His king, and will exalt the horn of His anointed" (1 Sam. 2:10). Zedekiah, the prophet, made iron horns as a sign of Ahab's victory over the Syrians (1 Kings 22:11). And in such a way the horn is used symbolically in Revelation (12:3; 13:1; 17:3, 12; cf. Dan. 7–8). "Seven horns" denote the fullness of power or omnipotence.

Seven eyes, which are the seven spirits of God sent into all the earth. This imagery is drawn from Zechariah 4:10, where the prophet sees seven lamps which are "the eyes of the Lord, which range throughout the earth." "Seven eyes" denote omniscience (see *Notes* on Rev. 1:4). In Revelation, this is a symbolic reference to the sending of the Holy Spirit by Christ throughout the world. The Greek word *apostellō* ("to send forth," "to send out") was a technical term among the Jews for sending out an official representative with a special task (cf. Matt. 11:10; Acts 10:17; Rev. 1:1; 22:6).[14] The term here refers to the worldwide mission of the Holy Spirit in the full authority of Christ.[15] This sending and mission of the Holy Spirit is further elaborated in the gospel of John (14:26; 15:26; 16:7–15).

5:7 *From the right hand.* As with the phrase "on the right hand" (5:1), the Greek phrase *ek tēs dexias*, apart from Revelation 5:7, does not occur elsewhere in the New Testament and is very rare in Greek literature. The scarce evidence shows it to mean either "from the right hand" or "from the right side."[16] The meaning of the phrase, however, must be defined on the basis of the earlier idiom "at the right hand" in 5:1. The fact that the sealed scroll was found at the right hand of God suggests that *ek tēs dexias* here means "from the right side."

5:9 *And purchased for God with your blood.* The King James Version (KJV) translates the text in the first person: "thou hast redeemed us to God out of...." The correct reading is important for the identification of the elders and the four living beings. If "us" is original, it would set those singing (the elders and the four living beings) among the redeemed. Textual evidence for the exclusion of "us" (*hēmas*) consists of codex Alexandrinus and an Ethiopic version, while all other Greek manuscripts and versions include the pronoun "us" either before, after, or instead of "for God." The exclusion of "us" from the text is based on the established assertion that Alexandrinus is the best witness. Despite the strong manuscript support for the inclusion of "us," several internal factors favor the text that omits "us" as the preferred reading. For instance, the abrupt switch from the first person in verse 9 to the third person in verse 10 would be very awkward. Also, the fact that the song is sung by both the elders and the four living beings would identify the four living beings as the redeemed saints, an idea not supported by the context.

5:10 *And you made them...and they will reign on the earth.* The KJV translates the text: "And hast made us...and we shall reign on the earth." The reading is based on late inferior texts; the KJV translators have most likely taken it from the Latin Vulgate. It is also possible that the scribes tried to correlate the text with Revelation 1:6 which contains the first-person reading. On the other hand, both the present-tense reading of the verb "to reign" ("they reign") and the future ("they shall reign") have equal manuscript support. The UBS and NA editorial committee of the Greek New Testament and many commentators are in favor of the future tense on the basis of their observation that "codex Alexandrinus mistakenly reads *basileusousin* [the present tense] for the future tense."[17]

EXPOSITION

John is still watching through the open door of the heavenly temple/palace. Suddenly, the celebration of the magnificent liturgy subsides, and all attention focuses on the throne.

5:1 This time John notices *at the right hand of the One sitting on the throne a scroll.* The scroll is seen as lying on the throne to the right hand of God, rather than being held in his right hand. In the ancient Near East, the throne was "more like a couch than a single seat";[18] more than one person could sit on it. It was regarded as the highest honor to sit at the right hand of the king. The sealed scroll is waiting for a worthy candidate to come and take it, and, subsequently, to sit in that place on the throne at the right hand of God. The ability to take and open the scroll would represent the right to rule.

When in Old Testament times the Israelite king took the throne, he received, together with the royal crown, the scroll of the covenant, namely, the book of Deuteronomy (2 Kings 11:12; cf. Deut. 17:18–20; 1 Sam. 10:25). The Covenant Scroll became a symbol of installation upon the throne; in taking it, the newly crowned king would sit on the throne and begin to reign. The possession of the scroll and the ability to open and read it demonstrated the king's right to rule and to deal with any crisis that might occur. At the same time, the possession of the Covenant Scroll signified that the king of Israel was co-ruler with God, the Great King. Thus, for instance, we read in Psalms that the king of Israel sits at God's right hand as his co-ruler (Pss. 80:17; 110:1).

Understanding that the sealed scroll was located *at* the right hand of God upon the throne, rather than *in* his right hand, is important for a correct interpretation of the event. It is particularly significant that, after his ascension, the resurrected Christ was exalted on the heavenly throne "at the right side of God" (Rom. 8:34; Eph. 1:20; Col. 3:1; Heb. 10:12; 1 Pet. 3:22). Thus, he has been given all authority, power, and universal dominion (Eph. 1:20–22; Heb. 1:13; 1 Pet. 3:22). The exaltation of Christ onto the throne at the Father's right hand was the core belief for early Christians (Acts

2:33–36; Heb. 8:1) and was the fulfillment of Old Testament prophecy (Ps. 110:1; cf. Matt. 22:41–45; 26:62–65).

The scroll is described in terms of legal documents of the time. John mentions, first, that the scroll is **written inside and on the back**, which normally implies a great amount of written material. However, the phrase might refer to the two documents written on both sides as mentioned in the Old Testament. We read in Exodus that "the two tablets of the testimony" which Moses brought down from the mountain were "written on both sides; they were written on one side and the other" (Exod. 32:15). Likewise, Ezekiel saw in vision a scroll spread before him which had writing "on the front and back" (2:9–10). In the light of this Old Testament background, the scroll of Revelation 5 being written on both sides evidently refers to God's covenant with his people, on one side, and to a prophetic message, on the other;[19] or, to put it in the New Testament context, the scroll is clearly related to "the Law and the Prophets" (Acts 13:15; cf. Matt. 5:17; John 1:45).

It is also quite possible that the scroll was a so-called "double document" (see *Notes* on Rev. 5:1), a form well known and widely used in John's day. The open part of the scroll was outer text; it was unsealed, and could be consulted any time. The longer portion was inner text, and it was sealed. The sealed portion could be opened only by breaking all of the seals in the appropriate office where the contents could be compared and verified. If the sealed scroll is a double document, then it would explain the role of the little scroll of chapter 10. This little scroll would correspond to the outer visible text of the sealed scroll of Revelation 5. The little scroll's contents are clearly described in Revelation 12–22:5 and give us insights into the sealed scroll of Revelation 5.

The scroll is also said to be **sealed with seven seals.** In ancient Israel, the seals were solely in the possession of the king and his officials. Sealing involved two basic concepts. It could denote a validation or ratification of the contents. It meant that an authority of some kind would have to make a seal impression with a signet or ring at the end of the written content. The sealing impression thus functioned in place of a signature, indicating authenticity, validity, or ratification of the document.

The context of chapter 5 strongly suggests that another concept is involved here, however. "Sealing" in Daniel and Revelation signifies that God's revelation could be "stored" until the appointed time due to people's unfaithfulness and unreadiness to pay heed to it (Dan. 12:4, 9; Rev. 10:4). The scroll in Revelation 5 is sealed for the evident purpose of cloaking its contents and keeping them hidden; because it is sealed, nobody is "able to open the book, or to look into it" (5:3–4). It is not possible to open it and disclose its contents unless all the seals are broken.

The fact that the scroll is sealed with seven seals is particularly significant in light of the symbolic meaning of the number "seven" in the Bible as "fullness," "completeness," or "perfection." First, "seven" expresses the idea of the divine plenitude and totality. Second, the sealing with *seven* seals indicates that the scroll is "perfectly sealed." Although the concealment of the scroll's contents is much emphasized in the text (cf. 5:3–4), the entire context shows clearly that the primary purpose of the strong emphasis on its sevenfold sealing is not just to inform the readers of Revelation that the contents of the scroll are profoundly secret and hidden from human knowledge. The overriding purpose is seen from the fact that in Revelation 5, it is not the reading of the sealed scroll but its opening and the breaking of its seals (5:2, 5, 9) that is the main focus of the section. The sealed scroll itself is not opened in chapter 5, but later in chapters 6–8. The primary purpose of such a strong emphasis on the sevenfold sealing is to contrast the totality of "unworthiness" and inability of all the created beings in the universe with the divine plenitude and totality of "worthiness" and ability of Christ. He alone in the entire universe is equal to God. He may sit on the throne of the universe at the right hand of the Father and as the eschatological sovereign bring the history of this planet to its end.

The context of Revelation 5 indicates that it was because of the human factor, the "unworthiness" and inability of humankind, that the scroll was sealed. The question, "Who is worthy to open the scroll and break its seals?" (5:2), leads to the inevitable conclusion that nobody "in heaven or on the earth or under the earth" has been found worthy to open the scroll and break its seals (5:2–4). This fact is very strongly emphasized. Yet the acclamatory "behold" in Revelation 5:5 initiates the divine "worthiness" and omnipotence in the appearance of "the Lion from the tribe of Judah, who is the Sprout of David" and "the slain Lamb" to take the sealed scroll and open its seals. After the taking of the scroll, Christ is acknowledged as "worthy" to receive the glory and adoration of all the heavenly assembly, which belongs only to royalty (5:11–14).

Strong evidence suggests that the Covenant Book, which signified the right and authority of the Israelite kings to rule as the co-rulers with God on the Davidic throne (Deut. 17:18–20; 2 Kings 11:12), was regarded by the Jews of John's time as having been "sealed" at the demise of the Davidic kingdom during the Babylonian exile. The "sealing" resulted from the "unworthiness" and unfaithfulness of the Israelite kings and the people over whom they ruled (Isa. 8:16; Dan. 12:4, 9). It was waiting for the appearance of the future Davidic descendent who would fulfill the role of the ideal and true king of Israel (see "Overview: Revelation 4–5"). On this Old Testament concept both Jews and Christians built their understanding of the coming Messiah in his capacity as king.

5:2–4 A mighty angel proclaims with *a loud voice, "Who is worthy to open the scroll and to break its seals?"* The question "Who is worthy?" calls for a unique qualification. As A. Yarbro Collins suggests, in the context of the book of Revelation as a whole, "it is clear that the problem facing the heavenly council is the rebellion of Satan which is paralleled by rebellion on earth....The tears of the prophet express the desire of the faithful to have this situation rectified."[20] John understands that *nobody in heaven or on the earth or under the earth* is *able to open the scroll or to look into it* because nobody is found *worthy*. "Worthy" is the key word of the whole chapter. In John's day, it denoted a distinctive qualification that made a candidate fit or eligible for a highly honored office. Such a qualification was based on outstanding achievements such as prowess and bravery that were displayed through success in war. In the context of the throne (as in Rev. 4–5), the word "worthy" denoted a particular quality which would enable a ruler to lay his chief claim to the throne and rulership, and claim the affection and loyalty of his subjects.

Furthermore, in Revelation 5, worthiness signifies a unique qualification possessed by no one but God. In Revelation 4:11, God is proclaimed worthy to receive the royal qualities of honor, glory, and power on the basis of his creatorship. He is on the throne reigning over the universe. In the same way, in chapter 5, countless heavenly hosts shout before Christ, the Lamb: "You are worthy to take the scroll and open its seals" (5:9). They are joined by the acclamation of the four living beings and the twenty-four elders falling down and worshiping: "Worthy is the slain Lamb to receive the power and riches and wisdom and strength and honor and glory and blessing!" (5:12).

When the first-century Christians read these shouts of acclamation which ordinarily were directed only to royalty, and when, then, the twenty-four elders fell down before him who is seated on the throne, casting their crowns before the throne (as Oriental princes did before their overlords), shouting, "You are worthy, our

Lord and God, to receive glory and honor and power" (4:11), and "Worthy is the slain Lamb to receive power and riches and wisdom and strength and honor and glory and blessing" (5:12), it is reasonably certain that scenes from earthly royal and imperial ceremonies passed through their minds.

5:5–6 The weeping John is given an answer to the question: "Who is worthy to open the scroll?" He hears: *Behold, the Lion from the tribe of Judah, who is the Sprout of David, has overcome so that he is able to open the scroll and its seven seals.* The acclamatory "behold" initiates here the divine "worthiness" and omnipotence in the appearance of Christ who is proclaimed to be the only one in the entire universe "worthy" to open the sealed scroll. Although this concept of merit, with reference to the resurrected Christ, is presented in many places in the New Testament (e.g., Acts 2:22–36; Phil. 2:5–11; Heb. 12:2), it is unique in this scene. Christ's victory on the cross has made him worthy, first, to take and unseal the scroll of the Covenant which, because of the unworthiness of the Old Testament Davidic kings, has been sealed and stored. Second, it has entitled him to share the heavenly throne with the Father (Rev. 3:21) and receive a cosmic reign and dominion.

The unique qualification that made Christ worthy of sharing the throne and royal prerogatives with the Father is signified by the fact that he is of royal origin. The two titles given to Christ—*the Lion from the tribe of Judah* (cf. Gen. 49:9) and *the Sprout of David* (cf. Isa. 11:1, 10)—have special significance here. They are great Old Testament prophetic titles with regard to the rising of the ideal king, the descendant of David, upon the throne of Israel: "Behold, the days are coming, says the LORD, when I will raise up for David a righteous Branch, and he shall reign as king and deal wisely, and shall execute justice and righteousness in the land. In his days Judah will be saved, and Israel will dwell securely. And this is the name by which he will be called: 'The LORD is our righteousness'" (Jer. 23:5–6, RSV). In the New Testament, Old Testament prophecies find their fulfillment in the coming of Jesus Christ. When Jesus is referred to with these two titles, he is identified as the Son of David, the Messiah. The Israelite kings were found "unworthy" and unfaithful. Their "unworthiness" was the reason that the covenant scroll was sealed, waiting for a worthy Davidic Son to come and take and open it. Here now is that promised king of the Davidic lineage. He is the true heir to the Davidic throne. In him is found the fulfillment of all the hopes and expectations of God's people, of both the Old and New Testament covenant.

When the first-century Christians read about "the Sprout of David" being the only one "worthy" of approaching the heavenly throne, taking the sealed scroll from the right side of the throne, and, then, together with "the One sitting on the throne," receiving royal acclamation, they no doubt saw in it the fulfillment of Old Testament prophecies. They understood that the promised "day" had come when the promised king, "the Sprout of David," was installed on the heavenly throne.

When John turns to see "the Lion," he actually sees *a lamb standing as having been slain.* While the Lion shows *what* Christ did (he "has overcome"), the Lamb shows *how* he did it. The figure of the lamb here, as in the rest of Revelation, must be understood on the basis of the Old Testament sacrificial concept and ritual, in which the blood of the slaughtered lamb was related to redemption.[21] Here is the main point of the scene. Christ is "worthy" to take the sealed scroll and open it by virtue of his victorious death on the cross through which he was able to redeem humanity and win a triumph over death (5:5–6). It was the cross that made Christ unique and worthy of this honor. By virtue of his victory on the cross, he is now eligible to share the heavenly throne with the Father (3:21).

Christ's unique qualification is supplemented by his further description of *having seven horns and seven eyes, which are the seven spirits of God.* The seven horns and seven eyes signify his divine power and ability to both rule and judge. The fact that the Lamb has *seven* horns and *seven* eyes is especially significant in light of the fact that the scroll is sealed with *seven* seals. The seven horns symbolize Christ's omnipotence and are related to his ability to take and open the seven-sealed scroll. The seven eyes that stand for his omniscience are related to his ability to read the scroll and instruct his people in its contents. The seven spirits denote the fullness of the Holy Spirit who is *sent into all the earth.*

This is the only place in the entire book of Revelation where it is mentioned that the Holy Spirit is sent to the earth (earlier in the book, "the seven Spirits" are seen before God's throne [cf. Rev. 1:4; 4:5]). If Revelation 5 describes the enthronement of Christ which occurred at Pentecost (and all evidence supports this assertion), then the significance of this phrase is obvious. According to John 7:39, the Holy Spirit "was not yet given, because Jesus was not yet glorified." In his Pentecost sermon, Peter explained that the coming of the Holy Spirit to the earth was the result of Christ's exaltation at the right hand of God in the heavenly places (Acts 2:32–36). Since Christ is now exalted on the throne of the universe, the work of the Holy Spirit is unlimited in applying Christ's victorious death on the cross to the lives of human beings and announcing God's kingdom throughout the earth.

5:7 Here comes the climactic moment of the entire vision. ***And he came and took the scroll from the right hand of the One sitting on the throne.*** It is the moment when, in the throne room of the heavenly temple/palace, the triumphant Christ approaches the throne of God and takes the scroll from the throne at the right side of God as the token of kingship and the symbol of transference of all authority and sovereignty to him. Through this act, the Father has committed to Christ the lordship over the world. The Covenant Book, which was sealed and stored because of human unworthiness, is now handed to the triumphant Christ, the promised ideal king of the Davidic lineage, the Lion of the tribe of Judah who is actually the Sprout of David, the eschatological "Son" (Dan. 7:13–14; Rev. 1:13; 2:18; 14:14).

The taking of the scroll denotes symbolically "a formal ceremonial act," whereby Christ is invested with the office of "the Supreme Ruler of the universe" as co-ruler with the Father.[22] Possession of the scroll makes him the legal king over the universe. His ability to open and read the scroll signifies "the active execution of the function of lordship. Jesus Christ is seen here as the end-time ruler who, on the basis of the saving work completed by him, is called to discharge with authority God's plan for the end of history."[23] With this symbolic taking of the sealed scroll, the destiny of all humanity is placed into Christ's hands according to God's eternal decree.

5:8 At the moment Christ ***took the scroll,*** the adoration and cries of acclamation that belong only to royalty are directed to him. We have seen in Revelation 4:9–10 that whenever the royal acclamation of giving "glory and honor and thanks to him who is seated on the throne" is heard, the elders fall down, lay their crowns before the throne, and worship the One sitting on the throne. Here in 5:6–8, the Lamb ("the Lion of the tribe of Judah" or "the Sprout of David") is standing "in the midst of" the throne and the living creatures and "among" the elders (v. 6). When he takes the scroll, the elders and the living creatures again fall down, and this time it is before Christ (5:8–10, 12). This indicates that to be worthy of taking the sealed scroll (5:9) is to be worthy of receiving royal glory, honor, and power (in 4:11); furthermore, it is equal to the taking of rulership which is integrated with "the power and wealth and wisdom and might and glory and blessing" (5:12).

5:9–14 By virtue of his victorious death through which he was enabled to redeem humanity *from every tribe and tongue and people and nation* and make them *a kingdom and priests to our God*, Christ is first pronounced *worthy to take the scroll and open its seals* for he was *slain*. He alone is worthy because of the victory that only he could gain. He is *the living One* who died and is alive *for ever and ever* (Rev. 1:18). W. C. van Unnik states: "He has been tested in his sufferings and has gained the victory. The greatness of his work is described in vv. 9: from all nations he has ransomed slaves and he has made them, former slaves, from all peoples, even pagans (!), to be the holy people of God, priests and kings, the typical prerogative of Israel (Ex 19.5f)."[24] Now, he is pronounced worthy to be worshiped and to receive all the honor and glory of kingship: *Worthy is the slain Lamb to receive power and riches and wisdom and strength and honor and glory and blessing!* (5:12). A logical inference would be that, at this moment, Christ takes his seat upon the throne, at the right hand of the Father. That is to say, in taking the scroll, he takes his seat where the scroll had been.

Particularly interesting is the position of the heavenly beings in the throne room—everybody surrounds the throne and gives royal acclamation to the Lamb (5:11). Thus the centrality of the throne of chapter 4, which was lost at the beginning of chapter 5, becomes emphasized again, gaining new significance. Now, both the Father and Christ, who possesses the scroll, are equally adored by all the heavenly beings surrounding the throne: *To the One sitting on the throne and to the Lamb be the blessing and the honor and the glory and the might, for ever and ever!* (5:13). These are attributes which may only apply to royalty. The fact that Christ is adored here on the same basis as the Father implies their equality, for both are jointly enthroned—as co-rulers—on the throne of the universe.

The rest of the New Testament is replete with texts about Christ who, after his resurrection, was seated "at the right side of God," and has been given authority, power, and universal dominion (Rom. 8:34; Eph. 1:20–22; Col. 3:1; Heb. 10:12; 12:2; 1 Pet. 3:21–22). In his sermon on Pentecost, Peter stated that it was then that Christ began his co-rulership with the Father (Acts 2:33–36). He rules "far above all rule and authority and power and dominion, and every name that is named, not only in this age, but also in the one to come. And he [the Father] put all things in subjection under his feet, and gave him as head over all things to the church, which is his body, the fullness of him who fills all in all" (Eph. 1:21–23). God's people do not need to be afraid of what is to come upon the world, because the Lord is in control.

Now, both the Father and Christ, who possesses the scroll, receive honor and worship from all the heavenly beings: *To the One sitting on the throne and to the Lamb be blessing and honor and glory and might for ever and ever!* (5:13).

A RETROSPECT ON REVELATION 5

Revelation 4 and 5 describe the fourth of the great events in the plan of salvation, namely, the coronation of the ascended and glorified Christ on the heavenly throne at the right hand of the Father after the incarnation and his death and resurrection. Two events are yet to take place: the Second Coming and the subsequent final judgment when God's plan of salvation will be brought to its conclusion. However, the enthronement of Christ seems to be the crucial point in the history of the universe. It is the event that has inaugurated Christ into his royal ministry; it is with Christ's exaltation on the heavenly throne that the victory over sin and Satan is assured. Christ's enthronement "marks the beginning of the end, defines the nature of the end of history, and describes who shall participate in the victory of the Lamb."[25] This is what makes Revelation 4–5 the pivotal section of the entire book of Revelation.

According to van Unnik, Revelation 5 "holds a decisive place in the structure of the whole book; what has been described there cannot be left out or missed, because then the sequel becomes unintelligible."[26] There are at least two reasons why Revelation 4–5 is of such special significance for God's people today. First of all, the enthronement of Christ in the heavenly temple at the right hand of the Father signifies the inauguration of the heavenly sanctuary. Although Revelation puts a strong emphasis on the inauguration of Jesus into his royal role, the epistle of Hebrews describes more particularly the priestly aspect of his exaltation. In Hebrews, as the result of his sacrificial death on the cross and his resurrection, Jesus ascended to heaven, entered within the veil, and subsequently established himself on the throne of God at his right hand (Heb. 1:3, 13; 8:1; 10:12; 12:2). The main point of the book is that "we have such a high priest, who has taken His seat at the right hand of the throne of the Majesty in the heavens, a minister in the sanctuary, and in the true tabernacle, which the Lord pitched, not man" (Heb. 8:1–2). Being seated on the throne qualifies Jesus to be the minister of the heavenly sanctuary. Therefore, the books of Revelation and Hebrews should be studied together. Only then are the two aspects of Christ's ministry combined into one complete picture. They give us full insight into Christ's post-resurrection ministry on behalf of his faithful people.

The second reason why Revelation 4 and 5 are significant for God's people today is the fact that the enthronement of Christ took place at Pentecost. In his Pentecost sermon, Peter stated that the exaltation of Christ on the heavenly throne at the right hand of God opened the door for the coming of the Holy Spirit (Acts 2:32–33). That is to say, the coming of the Holy Spirit was conditioned and preceded by Christ's exaltation. According to John 7:39, the Holy Spirit could come only after Jesus had been glorified. It was Jesus' death on the cross, his ascension, and his subsequent enthronement in the heavenly temple that made the manifestation of the work of the Holy Spirit legitimate and visible. Paul states that when Jesus "ascended on high, he led captive a host of captives, and he gave gifts to men" (Eph. 4:8). The passage that follows identifies these gifts as those of the Holy Spirit (4:11–14). This explains the description of Jesus as the Lamb with "seven eyes, which are the seven spirits of God sent out into all the earth" (Rev. 5:6). "Seven" as the number of fullness corresponds to the seven churches to whom Revelation was originally sent as the symbolic representation of the universal church of God. Although the Holy Spirit is referred to as "the seven Spirits of God" in 1:4 and 4:5, it is only in 5:6 that he is "sent out into all the earth," for it was at Pentecost that the Holy Spirit was sent to the earth. Ellen White makes a significant comment:

> Christ's ascension to heaven was the signal that His followers were to receive the promised blessing. For this they were to wait before they entered upon their work. When Christ passed within the heavenly gates, He was enthroned amidst the adoration of the angels. As soon as this ceremony was completed, the Holy Spirit descended upon the disciples in rich currents, and Christ was indeed glorified, even with the glory which He had with the Father from all eternity. The Pentecostal outpouring was Heaven's communication that the Redeemer's inauguration was accomplished. According to His promise He had sent the Holy Spirit from heaven to His followers as a token that He had, as priest and king, received all authority in heaven and on earth, and was the Anointed One over His people.[27]

This message is of special importance to the people of God living at the close of earth's history. The coming of the Holy Spirit at Pentecost marked the beginning of the expansion of Christ's kingdom. The preaching of the gospel began with the central message about Jesus who had been enthroned as Lord on the heavenly throne. This was the core of early Christian belief (Phil. 2:6–11; Heb. 8:1) and the cornerstone of their preaching (Acts 2:32–36; 5:30–31; Eph. 1:20; Col. 3:1; Heb. 8:1; 10:12; 12:2; 1 Pet. 3:22). The fact that the glorified Lord was in control, ruling on the throne of the universe, motivated their actions and was the source of their faith and courage in the face of persecution and difficult life situations (Acts 7:55–56; Rom. 8:34). The result? Many people responded to their preaching. From that time on and through the presence of Jesus in the ministry of the Holy Spirit, the kingdom of God manifested itself and keeps on manifesting itself.

Let God's people today, therefore, never forget the basics. Let them always keep in mind that the main task of the Holy Spirit is to bear witness to Jesus (John 15:26) and to glorify him (John 16:14). It is only the good news of salvation in Christ that can reach and transform human hearts and lead people to respond to the call of the eternal gospel to fear God, give him glory, and worship him (Rev. 14:7). The crucified, resurrected, and glorified Lord and King is on the throne of the universe. He is with his people—he is in control. Let God's people never forget that keeping the essence of the gospel in mind will bring them full success in preaching the final message to lost and suffering humankind.

ENDNOTES

1. For a more in-depth treatment of the phrase, see Stefanovic, 145–155.
2. Bruce Metzger, *The Text of the New Testament*, 2d ed. (Oxford: Clarendon Press, 1964), 6.
3. Stefanovic, 125–126.
4. Ibid.
5. Ladd, 81.
6. John J. Davis, *Biblical Numerology* (Grand Rapids, MI: Baker, 1968), 116–118.
7. Karl H. Rengstorf, "*epta*, et al.," in *Theological Dictionary of the New Testament*, ed. G. Kittel and G. W. Bromiley (Grand Rapids, MI: Eerdmans, 1964–1976), 2:628; for the symbolic significance of the number "seven" in Greco-Roman antiquity, see Aune, *Revelation 1–5*, 114–115.
8. See Milton S. Terry, *Biblical Hermeneutics* (Grand Rapids, MI: Zondervan, 1890; reprint 1978), 382–383.
9. For a fuller treatment of the section, see Stefanovic, 125–126.
10. Ibid., 167–181.
11. 4 Ezra 12:31–32 (Charlesworth, 1:550).
12. See Stefanovic, 181–184.
13. See further ibid., 184–195.

14. Karl H. Rengstorf, "*apostellō*, et al.," in *Theological Dictionary of the New Testament*, ed. G. Kittel and G. W. Bromiley (Grand Rapids, MI: Eerdmans, 1964–1976), 1:400.

15. Swete, 79; Ladd, 88.

16. See Stefanovic, 152–153.

17. See Metzger, *The Text of the New Testament*, 736.

18. Barclay, *The Revelation of John*, 1:148.

19. Charles H. Giblin, *The Book of Revelation* (Collegeville, MN: Michael Glazier, 1991), 75.

20. Collins, *The Apocalypse*, 39.

21. For a fuller treatment of the concept of Christ as the Lamb in Revelation 5, see Aune, *Revelation 1–5*, 367–373.

22. Mauro, 171.

23. Roloff, 76.

24. W. C. van Unnik, "'Worthy Is the Lamb': The Background of Apoc 5," in *Mélanges bibliques en hommage au R.P. Béda Rigaux*, ed. A. Descamps and A. Halleux, 445–461 ([Gembloux]: Duculot, 1970), 460.

25. Fred B. Craddock, "Preaching the Book of Revelation," *Interpretation* 40 (1986), 276.

26. van Unnik, 445.

27. White, *The Acts of the Apostles*, 38–39.

OVERVIEW
REVELATION 6

Before analyzing each of the seven seals in detail, some points of general matter must be stressed. They are of vital importance for the correct interpretation of Revelation 6.

First, Revelation 6 builds on chapters 4 and 5. The scene of the opening of the seven seals follows the scene described in Revelation 4–5. Everything taking place in chapter 6 is a result of what happened in chapter 5. This is especially significant in light of the fact that Revelation 4–5 describes the enthronement of the resurrected Christ on the heavenly throne and the inauguration into his royal office, the event that took place at Pentecost. Thus, the opening of the seven seals begins with the inauguration and enthronement of Christ. Yet the opening of the sixth seal describes the Second Coming and the events that accompany it (6:15–17). This suggests that the scene of the opening of the seven seals covers the historical era from the ascension of Christ and his elevation to the throne of the universe to the Second Coming, when Christ will return to the earth in his full capacity as king and judge of the world.

Second, the events of Revelation 6 do not describe the contents of the seals themselves. They are, rather, the consequences of Christ's breaking the seals in heaven. The events triggered by the opening of the seven seals, however, all take place on the earth. Neither the breaking of the seven seals nor the events that follow constitute the contents of the sealed scroll of Revelation 5. The scroll was not opened and its contents disclosed until all seven seals were broken.[1] According to George E. Ladd, the breaking of all seven seals is "preliminary to the actual opening of the book and the events of the end."[2] Or, as Kenneth A. Strand explains, the opening of the seven seals represents "the steps or means by which God through Christ prepares the way in history for the opening and reading of...the book of destiny at the judgment in the eschatological consummation" (cf. Rev. 20:12).[3]

THE MEANING OF THE SEVEN SEALS

Many modern commentators believe that the vision of the seven seals must be understood literally as reflecting the first-century situation in the Roman empire characterized by warfare.[4] In this avenue of interpretation, the first seal would symbolize Parthians, the warlike people who during the end of the first century were a constant threat to the Roman Empire. They were always ready to cross the river Euphrates, and several times even defeated the Roman army. The understanding of the other seals follows this avenue of interpretation, suggesting that the seals symbolized the political, civil, and physical disorders that undermined the oppressive power of the Roman Empire.[5] No doubt the first-century Christians believed that they lived at the time of the end and thus found contemporary relevance in Revelation 6.

The aforementioned understanding is problematic in many ways, however. First of all, as George E. Ladd observes, the situation in the late first century in the Roman Empire "was not a time particularly characterized by warfare. In fact, the might of the Roman armies had crushed effective resistance so that peace reigned from Armenia to Spain. The great Pax Romana gave to the Mediterranean world several centuries of peace which the western world has never since experienced. However, it was a peace based on force, and the might of Rome was everywhere represented by the presence of her legions."[6] Second, the literal understanding of the seven seals goes against the symbolic character of the book of Revelation. Many elements in the scene of the seals (such as the white of the horse in the first seal) do not fit into the literal application. Finally, such an understanding does not fit into the theological framework of the entire book. The theological meaning of Revelation 6 is much deeper, for instance, than the warfare between the Parthians and the Roman Empire.

What, then, is the theological meaning of the events of the opening of the seven seals? The key lies in Revelation 5. The scene of the opening of the seven seals thus begins with the enthronement of Christ. When in the Old Testament the newly crowned king took his place on the throne, the destiny of the entire nation was placed in his hands. The Old Testament enthronement ceremonies were usually followed by judgment actions of a newly enthroned king when he proceeded to punish those who had proven disloyal and rebellious; he would also bestow favorable benefits on the loyal adherents (cf. 1 Kings 2; 16:11; 2 Kings 9:14–10:27; 11:1, 13–16). In royal Psalms 2 and 110, which originally referred to the Israelite kings, the anointed and enthroned Davidic king was to exercise authority to reign by judging those who were rebellious (compare Ps. 2:7–11 and Rev. 19:15–16). This judgment aspect is expressed in the vision of the opening of the seven seals.

When at his enthronement in Revelation 5 the exalted Christ received the covenant scroll which represented the covenant relationship between him and his people, the destiny of all humanity was placed in his hands. His faithful ones were endowed with the right to be "a kingdom and priests to our God, and they shall reign over the earth" (Rev. 5:9–10; cf. 1:5–6). Then the action of the newly enthroned Christ, portrayed in the opening of the seven seals, triggered a sequential chain of events on the earth: war and slaughter, famine, and pestilence. It is necessary to determine how the Christians of John's day understood the events of Revelation 6, regardless of the application they could find in it. The biblical background texts are instrumental for the understanding of the significance and meaning of the opening of the seven seals.

THE OLD TESTAMENT BACKGROUND OF THE SEVEN SEALS

Covenant curses. As Jon Paulien observes, the language of Revelation 6:1–8 parallels "the covenant curses in the Pentateuch and their execution in the context of the Babylonian exile."[7] After God brought his people out from the bondage of Egypt, he made a covenant with them that contained certain stipulations. If the Israelites obeyed and cooperated with God, they would receive rewards and blessings. If they did not obey the covenant and continued in their disobedience, however, there would be ultimate consequences to come known as the curses of the covenant (cf. Deut. 28:15–68).

These curses of the covenant are described in the Old Testament in terms of "war, famine, pestilence, and wild beasts," which in Ezekiel are referred to as God's "four severe judgments" (Ezek. 14:21; cf., in Jer. 15:3, RSV, the "four kinds of destroyers"). The root text of these covenant curses is Leviticus 26:21–26:

> If then, you act with hostility against Me
> 　　and are unwilling to obey Me,
> I will increase the plague on you *seven times*
> 　　according to your sins.
> I will let loose among you *the beasts* of the field....

> and I, even I, will strike you seven times for your sins.
> I will also bring upon you a *sword*
>> which will execute vengeance for the covenant;
> and when you gather together into your cities,
>> I will send *pestilence* among you,
>> so that you shall be delivered into enemy hands.
> When I *break your staff of bread,*
>> ten women will bake your bread in one oven,
>> and they will bring back your bread in rationed
>>> amounts [by weight, RSV],
>> so that you will eat and not be satisfied. (emphasis supplied)

Here are described the penalties which God would send upon Israel because of her faithlessness. The parallels between the language used in Leviticus 26 and that of Revelation 6 are obvious: the sevenfold plague—sword, famine, pestilence, and wild beasts. They are all the consequences of disobedience to the covenant. In addition, the famine is described in terms of giving the bread by weight (Lev. 26:26; cf. Rev. 6:6). The same language and concepts are repeated in Moses' farewell speech in Deuteronomy 32:23–25.

The covenant curses were, in the initial phase, preliminary judgments from God on his people. They were intended to wake them from their apostate condition, lead them to repentance, and move them toward a positive relationship with God. What seems clear in the Old Testament is that, in implementing those curses, God used enemy nations, such as Assyria and Babylon. These nations were often used as instruments of God's judgment on his own people. God spoke through Isaiah of Assyria as "the rod of My anger, and the staff in whose hands is My indignation. I send it against a godless nation and commission it against the people of My fury" (Isa. 10:5–6).

The covenant curses, then, may be explained in the following way: when Israel became unfaithful to the covenant, God would remove his protective power, and the enemy nations would come and afflict the people of Israel as a result. They would bring the sword against them. Wild beasts would rob them of their children and destroy their livestock. Pestilence and famine would complete the desolation of the land. If God's people persisted in their sins, the final consequence would take place: exile from the promised land.

Later in Israel's history, "the four severe judgments" (which could come in any order), became widely known and commonly used terms with reference to the judgments for disloyalty to the covenant. They were so well-known and stereotyped that they could not be but understood as the consequence of Israel's persistent refusal to live up to the covenant. Especially in Jeremiah and Ezekiel, they became technical terms for the covenant "woes" by which God punished apostasy, endeavoring to lead the people to repentance (Jer. 14:12–13; 15:2–3; 21:6–9; 24:10; 29:17–18; Ezek. 5:12–17; 6:11–12; 14:12–23; 33:27–29). Failing to repent, both Israel and Judah had to experience the ultimate judgment—the Exile.

David Aune notes a report made by Dio Cassius of the casualties that the Jews suffered during the Bar-Kohba revolt (A.D. 132–135): "Five hundred and eighty thousand men were slain in the various raids and battles [i.e., the *sword*], and the number of those that perished by *famine, disease* and fire was past finding out. Thus nearly the whole of Judaea was made desolate, a result of which the people had had forewarning before the war...and many *wolves and hyenas* rushed howling into their cities" (bracketed phrase inserted by Aune).[8] One can observe all the elements of the Old Testament covenant curses in this description: sword, famine, disease, and wild animals.

In the final phase, when these enemy nations used by God as the executors of judgment overdid the punishment of his people, God reversed the judgments and turned them against these enemy nations, in order to deliver his people. This is what Moses announced in Deuteronomy 32:41–43:

> If I sharpen My flashing sword,
>> and My hand takes hold on justice,
> I will render vengeance on My adversaries
>> and I will repay those who hate Me.
> I will make My arrows drunk with blood,
>> and My sword shall devour flesh....
> Rejoice, O nations, with his people,
>> for He will avenge the blood of His servants,
> and will render vengeance on His adversaries,
>> and will atone for His land and His people.

In his prophecy against the nations, Joel declared that God would judge and punish all nations for what they have done to his people Israel (Joel 3:2–7). Jeremiah prophesied concerning Babylon: "'I will repay Babylon, and all the inhabitants of Chaldea for all their evil that they have done in Zion before your eyes,' declares the Lord" (Jer. 51:24).

This was fulfilled with the Babylonian exile, when God's judgments that had been directed toward his people were now turned against the enemy nations afflicting his people.[9] Zechariah 1:12–15 may be taken as a representative text for this idea:

> Then the angel of the LORD answered and said, "O LORD of hosts, how long will You have no compassion for Jerusalem and the cities of Judah, with which You have been indignant these seventy years?"...So the angel who was speaking with me said to me, "Proclaim, saying, 'Thus says the LORD of hosts, "I am exceedingly jealous for Jerusalem and Zion. But I am very angry with the nations who are at ease; for while I was only a little angry, they furthered the disaster.""'

Similar statements are found in other texts in the prophets (cf. Jer. 50:17–20, 33–34; 51:24; Joel 3:19–21; Zeph. 3:19–20; Zech. 14:3–21).

It is especially important to note that when exercised upon God's people, the covenant curses were "preliminary judgments intended to lead them to repentance. When exercised upon the nations who have shed the blood of His people, they are judgments of vengeance (cf. the fifth seal)."[10]

Paulien concludes that the foregoing texts from the prophets "have sufficient parallels to the seven seals to suggest the possibility, but not the certainty, that the revelator was aware of them as he wrote Revelation 6."[11] The striking parallels between the language of Revelation 6 and the Old Testament covenant/curse passages strongly suggest that the scene of the opening of the seven seals has to do with the New Testament covenant established with Christ and the consequences for breaking it. As David Marshall says, whenever "the gospel is preached and rejected there *are* consequences."[12] This is supported by the fact that in Revelation 5 Christ took the sealed scroll of the covenant as the token of his exaltation on the heavenly throne, the act which represented the covenant relationship between him and his people. His enthronement thus marks the beginning of the execution of the covenant contents.

Zechariah's vision. Another Old Testament passage that helps one to understand the scene of the opening of the seven seals is Zechariah 1:8–17. The prophet saw in vision four different colored horses which are the instruments of divine judgment. While in Revelation 6 the colors of the four horses characterize the works they carry out, it appears that the colors of the horses had no apparent significance in Zechariah's vision. In Zechariah 6, these four horses are described as "the four spirits [or winds] of heaven going forth after standing before the Lord of all the earth" (Zech.

6:5). This may indicate that the four winds of Revelation 7:1–3 are related to the horses of chapter 6 unleashed in a covenant reversal like that of Deuteronomy 32.[13]

Zechariah's vision related to the return of Israel from the Babylonian exile. God's people were punished for their disobedience and unfaithfulness to the covenant. The question, "How long, O Lord?" in Zechariah 1:12 brings to mind the cry of the martyrs under the altar in the scene of the opening of the fifth seal of Revelation 6. To Zechariah, the answer was given: "I am exceedingly jealous for Jerusalem and Zion. But I am very angry with the nations who are at ease; for while I was only a little angry, they furthered the disaster" (Zech. 1:15). His people were punished for their unfaithfulness and sins by the removal of his protective power and their delivery into the hands of their enemies. Now God was ready to restore his people and carry out judgment against their oppressors.

Revelation 6 clearly follows the covenant-curses pattern. The scene portrayed in the opening of the first four seals describes the consequences or preliminary judgments intended to awaken God's people and lead them to repentance and restoration. As Peter says, God's judgment comes first on his people (1 Pet. 4:17). In Revelation 6, God's people are afflicted with severe persecution. In the scene of the opening of the fifth seal, the martyrs underneath the altar cry for vindication: "How long, O Lord, holy and true, will you not judge and avenge our blood upon those who dwell on the earth?" (Rev. 6:10)—a cry strikingly parallel with the one cited above from Zechariah 1:12–15.

In the scene of the opening of the sixth seal, God's wrath turns against the persecutors of his people. The time has come for the judgments to fall on the enemies of God and his people. God's people are rescued and appear before God's throne in the New Jerusalem (7:9–17; cf. chapters 21–22). Their enemies are now to experience severe judgments which are portrayed in the scene of the blowing of the seven trumpets. The seven trumpet plagues (Rev. 8–9) are indeed preliminary to the final and ultimate judgment described in Revelation 16–20.

THE NEW TESTAMENT BACKGROUND OF REVELATION 6

Revelation 6 also parallels the Synoptic Apocalypse, the eschatological discourse of Jesus on the Mount of Olives that is reported to us in Matthew 24, Mark 13, and Luke 21. In that sermon, Jesus describes the events leading up to the time of the end.

His language is very reminiscent of that of John in Revelation 6. There, the seven seals seem to follow closely the literary arrangement of the Synoptic Apocalypse. In addition, many thematic parallels appear between the events of the Synoptic Apocalypse and those accompanying the opening of the seven seals, even though they are not always in the same order. Many commentators have observed these similarities between the structure of Revelation 6 and the Synoptic Apocalypse as recorded in Matthew 24 and Mark 13.[14] The following comparisons show the parallels:

THEME	REVELATION	GOSPEL(S)
the gospel spreading	Rev. 6:1–2	Matt. 24:14; Mark 13:10
war	Rev. 6:3–4	Matt. 24:6–7; Mark 13:7–8; Luke 21:9–10
famine	Rev. 6:5–6	Matt. 24:7; Mark 13:8; Luke 21:11
pestilence	Rev. 6:7–8	Luke 21:11
persecution	Rev. 6:9–11	Matt. 24:9–10; Mark 13:9–13; Luke 21:12–17
heavenly signs	Rev. 6:12–13	Matt. 24:29; Mark 13:24–25; Luke 21:25–26
tribes mourn	Rev. 6:15–17	Matt. 24:30
the Second Coming	Rev. 6:17	Matt. 24:30; Mark 13:26; Luke 21:27

Jesus in describing the experience of God's people between the first century and the Second Coming uses Old Testament language and motifs. Curses are merged with heavenly signs accompanying the "Day of the Lord."[15] The inspired author of Revelation uses a similar design pattern. The parallels between the Synoptic Apocalypse and Revelation 6 indicate that the scene of the opening of the seven seals refers to the events taking place on earth from the time of Christ's exaltation on the heavenly throne until his return to earth.

No doubt the Christians of John's day who believed themselves to be living in the time of the end would have seen the signs of the end—wars, insurrections, civil and economic strife, famines, pestilence, persecution of the faithful, false prophets, the preaching of the gospel—as having been fulfilled in their own time. However, the intention of the inspired author of Revelation apparently extends beyond the first-century situation.

The Synoptic Apocalypse falls mainly into three sections. First, Jesus describes the general realities of the Christian Age between the first century and the Second Coming. It is a time of the proclamation of the gospel and of war, famine, pestilence, and persecution (Matt. 24:4–14). Jesus explains that these are not intended to be the signs of the end (Matt. 24:6–8), but are, rather, constant reminders to every generation of Christians that this earth is not their home and of the soon coming of Christ. The first four seals parallel Matthew 24:4–14; they are concerned with the realities of the entire Christian era and not just the end-time.

In the second section, Jesus talks briefly about a special period of tribulation to follow the destruction of Jerusalem during which God's people will experience heightened persecution (Matt. 24:15–22). In Luke, this period is called "the times of the Gentiles" (21:24). The scene of the opening of the fifth seal clearly parallels this section. Although the persecution began in the apostolic times, the cry of the martyrs underneath the altar points to the period of the tribulation and persecution which Jesus foretold in his sermon on the Mount of Olives, "such as has not occurred since the beginning of the world until now, nor ever shall" (Matt. 24:21).

Third, in Matthew 24:23–31 Jesus explains that this time of tribulation will be "followed by end-time deceptions and heavenly signs leading up to the Second Coming itself."[16] The sixth seal fits well into the period between the great tribulation of the Middle Ages and the Second Coming. This period was introduced with the devastating Lisbon earthquake of 1755, the heavenly signs of the dark day in 1780 and the following night when the moon was red, and the spectacular meteor shower of 1833. These phenomena have been regarded by many as the fulfillment of what Jesus foretold in the sermon on the Mount of Olives when he stated that immediately after the period of the great persecution, "the sun will be darkened, and the moon will not give its light, and the stars will fall from the sky, and the powers of the heavens will be shaken" (Matt. 24:29).

The sixth seal, however, points to future events to take place prior to and in connection with the Second Coming. The silence introduced with the breaking of the seventh seal (Rev. 8:1) evidently takes place after the Second Coming.

Matt. 24:3–14	General signs	Rev. 6:3–8
Matt. 24:15–28	The era of the great tribulation	Rev. 6:9–11
Matt. 24:29–31	The signs of the Second Coming	Rev. 6:12–17

Jon Paulien remarks: "It should be noted that the end-time deceptions are omitted in John's brief description of events to occur at the breaking of the sixth seal. However, these are taken up later in great detail in Revelation 13:17. Thus, the events of the sixth seal are to be understood as contemporary with those depicted in that portion of the Revelation."[17]

THE NATURE OF THE OPENING OF THE SEVEN SEALS

What is the nature of the scene of Revelation 6? The springboard passage of Revelation 3:21, in which it is promised that the overcomer will sit with Jesus on his throne as Jesus overcame and sat with his Father on his throne, provides the clue for understanding the nature of the opening of the seven seals. We observed that Revelation 4–5, which refers to Jesus' overcoming and his subsequent sitting with the Father on his throne, elaborates on the second part of Revelation 3:21. Revelation 7:9–17 describes the fulfillment of its first part with regard to the overcomers who will join Christ on his throne. Since chapter 6 is set between chapters 5 and 7, it appears that the opening of the seven seals corresponds to the statement, "to the one who overcomes," of 3:21. One may conclude that the scene of the opening of the seven seals has to do with "the ongoing period in which God's people are in the process of overcoming" until they finally join Christ on his throne.[18]

Rev. 4–5	Christ overcoming and joining his Father on his throne
Rev. 6	The seals describing the ongoing period in which God's people are in the process of overcoming
Rev. 7	God's people joining Christ on the throne of God (vv. 9–17)

The scene of the opening of the seven seals of Revelation 6 thus must be understood as portraying events occurring on earth between the cross and the Second Coming, "with particular focus on the gospel and the experience of the people of God" in the world.[19] Christ's enthronement at Pentecost marks the beginning of Christ's kingdom spread through the preaching of the gospel. As the gospel is being proclaimed, God's people on earth often fail in faithfulness. The situation and needs in the seven Christian communities in the province of Asia reflect the situation and needs of the whole Christian church throughout history. The seven messages of Revelation 2–3 are sent to warn God's people and wake them from their sinful condition and to bring them to repentance. The ultimate objective is to make them overcomers. Only the overcomers will one day have a share with Jesus on his throne and enjoy all the blessings promised in the messages to the seven churches.

As with the seven churches, besides their general application, the scene of the opening of the seven seals might also be appropriately seen as having their specific applications in different periods in Christian history.[20] Like the message to the church in Ephesus (Rev. 2:1–7), the scene of the opening of the first seal coincided with the Apostolic period that was characterized by general faithfulness when in a short time the gospel spread rapidly throughout the world. The scene of the opening of the second seal may aptly be applied to the period of persecution throughout the Roman Empire (2:8–11). The third seal might be applied to the period that followed which was characterized by a progressive spiritual decline and compromise which led to the Dark Middle Ages (cf. 2:12–17). The fourth seal might apply to the period of the famine for God's Word that followed, resulting in spiritual death which characterized the Christian church throughout the Medieval period. It was the period of spiritual decline and persecution when genuine faith was lost and the loving gospel message was resisted, forgotten, and gradually replaced by tradition. The symbolic scene of the fifth seal had a special meaning for God's people in the time of the severe persecutions during the post-medieval period, especially during the time of the Protestant orthodoxy in the post-Reformation period of the seventeenth and eighteenth centuries. And the sixth seal brings us clearly to the time of the end and leads up to the Second Coming.

So we may conclude that Revelation 6 describes the ongoing process through which God leads his people to become overcomers and have a share with Jesus on his throne.[21] The seven seals are instruments that Christ uses "for the sanctification of His Church and the extension of His kingdom."[22] The Synoptic Apocalypse indicates that the events announcing the Second Coming are given for the purpose of reminding us that the end is near. This is made clear in the conclusion of Jesus' discourse on the Mount of Olives: "Be on guard, that your hearts may not be weighted down with dissipation and drunkenness and the worries of life, and that day come on you suddenly like a trap; for it will come upon all those who dwell on the face of all the earth. But keep on the alert at all times, praying in order that you may have strength to escape all these things that are about to take place, and to stand before the Son of Man" (Luke 21:34–36). The events described symbolically in both the vision of the opening of the seals and Jesus' eschatological discourse on the Mount of Olives are intended to wake up God's people and lead them to repentance.

Christ's promise in Revelation 3:21 still stands. The overcomers will sit one day with Jesus on his throne. In the scene of the opening of the fifth seal, the martyrs under the altar ask: "How long?" And Revelation 7 provides the clear answer: "Not too long!" The day is coming when God will justify his faithful people. They must be patient, however. Before the promise is fulfilled, God's righteous judgment will be poured out on the enemies and persecutors of the saints. These acts of judgment are symbolically portrayed in the blowing of the seven trumpets in Revelation 8–9.

ENDNOTES

1. Fiorenza, *Revelation*, 62.
2. Ladd, 95–96; Fiorenza, *Revelation*, 62.
3. Strand, *Interpreting the Book of Revelation*, 57.
4. Including Charles, 1:160; Caird, 80, 122; Barclay, *The Revelation of John*, 2:4; Morris, 102.
5. See Charles, 1:160; Fiorenza, 62–65.
6. Ladd, 100.
7. Paulien, "The Seven Seals," 222–224; see also Beale, 372–374. The section reflects Paulien's study.
8. See Aune, *Revelation 6–16*, 402; cf. Dio Cassius, *Historiae Romanae* 69.1.2, trans. E. Cary, The Loeb Classical Library (New York: Macmillan, 1914–1927).
9. Paulien, "The Seven Seals," 223.
10. Ibid.
11. Ibid., 223 n. 98.
12. Marshall, 60.
13. Paulien, "The Seven Seals," 224.
14. See, e.g., Milligan, *Lectures on the Apocalypse*, 42–59; Charles, 2:163; Johnson, "Revelation," 472; Ladd, 98–99; however, Milligan, Johnson, and Ladd unsuccessfully, as I see it, pursue the Synoptic Apocalypse parallels through the entire book of Revelation.
15. Paulien, "The Seven Seals," 225.
16. Ibid., 225.
17. Ibid.
18. Ibid., 203.

19. Ibid., 226.

20. *The Seventh-day Adventist Bible Commentary,* 7:775.

21. Paulien, "The Seven Seals," 203.

22. William Hendriksen, *More than Conquerors* (reprint, Grand Rapids, MI: Baker, 1982), 105.

THE OPENING OF THE SEVEN SEALS
REVELATION 6:1–17; 8:1

In Revelation 5, Christ was worthy to take the seven-sealed scroll from the right side of God who was sitting on his throne. With the taking of the scroll, Christ was installed on the heavenly throne and received all authority and right to rule over the universe as co-ruler with the Father. When, in the full capacity of a king, Christ breaks one by one the scroll's seven seals, a series of events occurs on the earth. As we analyze these events in detail, we should keep in mind that the seven seals are not events in themselves; rather, they are the events accompanying the breaking of the seals.

The opening of the seven seals appears in two vivid installments—one of four and the other of three—which differ in form and weight. The opening of the first four seals leads into the scene of the four horsemen (6:1–8); the opening of the last three seals brings us to the approaching time of the end. The fifth and the sixth seals (6:9–17) are separated from the seventh one (8:1) by an interlude of the sealing of the saints (chapter 7), the section which is analyzed in the next chapter of this commentary.

THE FOUR HORSEMEN (6:1–8)

As Christ opens the first four seals, John observes four horses and their riders stepping onto the scene. The four horsemen are evidently concerned with Christians and their response to the gospel of Jesus Christ. The gospel of the kingdom is being preached to all nations of the earth. When, after experiencing the gospel, people reject it, consequences are described symbolically in terms of the sword, famine, and pestilence. The sword, famine, and pestilence of the horses are the preliminary judgments on God's people who reject or disobey the gospel.[1] These judgments have redemptive purposes, however; they are intended to awaken God's people and to steer them toward repentance.

THE OPENING OF THE FIRST SEAL (6:1–2)

> *¹And I looked when the Lamb opened the first of the seven seals, and I heard one of the four living beings saying as with a voice of thunder:"Come!"²And I looked, and behold, a white horse, and the one sitting upon it had a bow, and a crown was given to him, and he went forth conquering and that he might conquer.*

NOTES

6:1 *Come!* Variations of this text exist in ancient manuscripts. The King James Version follows some Greek manuscripts that have the phrase "Come and see!" However, the best Greek manuscripts, including Codex Alexandrinus which shows the least evidence of alteration, have the shorter form, "Come!" as a summons to the four horsemen to come forth one by one upon the scene of action (6:1, 3, 5, 7).

6:2 *White horse.* Three main views exist with regard to the interpretation of the white horse and its rider.

(1) According to many modern commentators, this scene is literal and refers to a military power and conquest in the first century. The white horse and its rider would describe the Parthians, a warlike people who lived on the eastern frontier of the Roman Empire and who were the enemies of and a constant threat to the Romans.[2] "They were famous in war as horsemen for the swiftness of their mobility and their skill in the use of the bow and arrow."[3] The literal interpretation of the preterist view is problematic, however. First, it deprives the scene of its prophetic significance, and it does not fit into the theological framework of the vision of the seven seals. Second, the white of the horse does not fit into the Parthian-view scheme. The seals should be understood symbolically rather than literally.

(2) According to the second view, the rider represents "the Antichrist and the forces of evil" as the opponents of the gospel.[4] The proponents of this view argue that since the other three horses bring plagues, so does this one. They point to the Old Testament passages in which the bow is used as a symbol of the enemies of God's people (cf. Jer. 49:35; 51:3, 56; Ezek. 39:3; Hos. 1:5). They also point to the fact that counterfeit is indeed one of the key themes of the second half of Revelation; chapters 11 and 13 describe the beast conquering God's people in the language which is found in 6:1–2. In addition, they note a number of differences between the rider on the white horse of the first seal and the rider in Revelation 19 who is Christ. All of these points would suggest that the rider in 6:1–2 is the Antichrist.

232

(3) Evidence for the third view overwhelmingly suggests that the rider on the white horse symbolizes the triumphant spreading of the gospel initiated by Christ on the cross and begun at Pentecost. In Revelation, white always, and without any exception, refers to Christ or his followers and is never used with reference to the forces of evil. As George E. Ladd observes, the exalted Christ is portrayed in the book as having "white hair white as wool (1:14); the faithful will receive a white stone with a new name written on it (2:17) and they are to wear white garments (3:4, 5, 18); the twenty-four elders are clad in white (4:4); the martyrs are given white robes (6:11), as is the great numbering throng (7:9, 13); the Son of Man is seen on a white cloud (14:14); he returns on a white horse accompanied by the armies of heaven who are clad in white and ride white horses (19:11, 14); and, in the final judgment, God is seen seated on a white throne (20:11)."[5]

Although the bow is sometimes used in the Old Testament as a symbol of the enemy forces, it is also a weapon of God (Isa. 41:2; Lam. 2:4; 3:12; Hab. 3:8–9; Zech. 9:13). The *stephanos* crown worn by the rider is used in Revelation always with reference to Christ or his people, and it is appropriately worn by Christ in the light of his overcoming on the cross (Rev. 5:5–6) and the victory of his people as they overcome sin by means of his blood and their testimony (Rev. 12:11). It is reasonable to conclude, therefore, that the rider on the white horse symbolizes the spreading of the gospel throughout the world.

And the one sitting upon it [the horse] had a bow. The Old Testament background texts for this imagery are Habakkuk 3:8–9 and Psalm 45:3–5 where God rides a horse with a bow in his hand. Revelation 19:11–12 portrays a white horse and on it a rider called Faithful and True, the victorious Christ, with many crowns of victory.

Crown. The Greek word *stephanos* used here is not the royal crown but the crown of victory—a garland given to winners in the Olympic games (see further *Notes* on Rev. 2:10). It is used in Revelation regularly, with only one exception (9:7), with reference to Christ or his people (2:10; 3:11; 4:4, 10; 6:2; 12:1; 14:14).

EXPOSITION

6:1–2 At the opening of the first seal, John hears a living being speak in a voice of thunder: "Come!" This must certainly be the first of the living beings, the one which looks like a lion (Rev. 4:7), because the voice like thunder is very appropriate for a lion. It calls for **a white horse** whose rider **had a bow, and a crown was given to him.** William Barclay points out that "the white horse is the symbol of the conqueror." A Roman general would ride a white horse to celebrate a triumphant victory.[6] In this dramatic presentation, John is shown, in symbolic language, the victorious spreading of the gospel in the world. The rider on the white horse seems to symbolize "Christ's kingdom and its gradual conquest of the world through the preaching of the gospel by His church."[7] In Revelation 19:11–12, Christ rides a white horse and is going forth to war. As Ladd notes, the white color in Revelation is "consistently a symbol of Christ, or of something associated with Christ, or of spiritual victory."[8]

In the Old Testament, God is sometimes portrayed as riding a horse with a bow in his hand, going forth, conquering his and his people's enemies, and bringing salvation to his people (Hab. 3:8–13; cf. Ps. 45:4–5; Isa. 41:2; Zech. 9:13–16). In Revelation 19, Christ is returning to the earth on a horse and bringing judgment and justice (19:11–16). While in Revelation 19 he wears the diadem crown, which is the royal crown, in chapter 6 he has a crown of victory. This is the crown that in Revelation is almost always used with reference to the overcomer Christ and his overcoming people. With his victorious death on the cross, Christ has overcome and conquered the prince of this world (John 12:31–32; 16:11). By virtue of that death (Rev. 5:5) through which he was enabled to redeem humanity, Christ was pronounced worthy to take the sealed scroll (Rev. 5:9). Now in chapter 6, he wears the crown of victory that he earned at the cross.

Christ is not yet an undisputed ruler of the world, however. Some people still do not accept his lordship and rulership in their lives. He "must reign until He has put all His enemies under His feet" (1 Cor. 15:25). Some rebellious territories are yet to be conquered, and many captives of sin to be set free. When he "delivers up the kingdom to the God and the Father, when He has abolished all rule and all authority and power" (1 Cor. 15:24), then he will wear the royal crown as the King of kings and the Lord of lords (Rev. 19:16).

It was at Pentecost that Christ was enthroned on the throne of the universe (Rev. 5) and all authority was placed in his hands. As Jon Paulien observes, "what was ratified in heaven at the enthronement of the Lamb is now actuated in the experience of his people in the course of human history."[9] Christ's victorious death on the cross and his triumphal exaltation on the heavenly throne made the coming of the Holy Spirit possible (John 7:39). With the coming of the Holy Spirit at Pentecost, the proclamation of the gospel was propelled into motion. It was then that Christ *went forth overcoming and that he might overcome.* This conquering evidently has to do with spiritual matters. Through the Holy Spirit and through the preaching of the gospel by his faithful people, Christ has begun the expansion of his kingdom by conquering and winning human hearts for himself and bringing the gospel into their lives.

As with the message to the church in Ephesus (Rev. 2:1–7), the scene of the opening of the first seal can be applied historically to the church of the apostolic period. However, an important point must be underscored. The conquest of the rider on the white horse in no way ends with the apostolic era or the first century. Rather, it portrays in a general way the ongoing progress of the gospel throughout Christian history beginning in John's day and going through to the Second Coming.[10] Christ will continue the triumphant expansion of his kingdom until the total conquest is achieved. "This gospel of the kingdom will be preached throughout the whole world, as a testimony to all nations; and then the end will come" (Matt. 24:14, RSV).

THE OPENING OF THE SECOND SEAL (6:3–4)

> *³And when he opened the second seal, I heard the second living being saying: "Come!" ⁴And another horse, fiery-red, came forth, and the one sitting upon it was given to take peace from the earth in order that they might slay one another, and a great sword was given to him.*

NOTES

6:4 *Fiery-red*. The Greek word *puros* means "fiery red." Red is the color of blood and oppression. The Moabites saw "the water opposite them as red as blood" (2 Kings 3:22–23). Isaiah describes the sins of Jerusalem as scarlet and red (Isa. 1:18) for their "hands are covered with blood" (Isa. 1:15–23). In Revelation 17, the scarlet color of the beast is linked directly to the prostitute "drunk from the blood of the saints and from the witnesses of Jesus" (Rev. 17:6). The color in the scene of the second seal is appropriate for persecution and bloodshed.

That they might slay one another. This vision brings to mind several Old Testament scenes. We read that at Sinai the Israelites each killed his brother, friend, and neighbor with the sword (Exod. 32:27–29). The scene reminds us also of the Midianites who slew each other with the sword (Judg. 7:22). In his prophecy against Egypt, Isaiah announced that God would stir up the Egyptians so they "will each fight against his brother, and each against his neighbor, city against city, and kingdom against kingdom" (Isa. 19:2). Zechariah prophesied that the enemies of Israel would attack one another when God moves into the situation (14:13). The Greek *sphazō*—"to slay" or "slaughter"—is not a typical word for death in battle. In Revelation, it is normally used with reference to the death of Christ (5:6, 9, 12; 13:8) and his saints, because of their witness to the gospel (6:9; 18:24).

235

EXPOSITION

6:3–4 At the breaking of the second seal, John hears the second living being who calls for a *fiery-red* horse. This living being is probably the one having the appearance of a calf (4:7) as the calf is a symbol of a sacrifice and fits nicely into the context of the scene. The rider of this horse *was given to take peace from the earth in order that they might slay one another, and a great sword was given to him.* The fiery-red color of the horse corresponds to the mission of its rider to remove peace from the earth. The understanding of the white horse and its rider in the scene of the first seal is determinative for the interpretation of the second as well as the rest of the seals. As we can see, the rider on the first horse portrays the conquest of the gospel of Christ and its spread throughout the world. Those accepting the gospel experience great blessing. In Revelation 1:4, God's people are promised grace and peace. This peace is evidently the perfect peace of the gospel as the result of having a relationship with Jesus (John 14:27; 16:33). However, resistance to the gospel message results in a loss of peace. Isaiah stated: "But the wicked are like the tossing sea, for it cannot be quiet, and its waters toss up refuse and mud. 'There is no peace for the wicked,' says my God" (Isa. 57:20–21).

When people reject the love of the gospel, they lose the peace that the gospel brings. This results naturally in opposition and division. Jesus explained it in his eschatological discourse on the Mount of Olives: "Then they will deliver you up to tribulation, and will kill you, and you will be hated by all nations on account of My name. And at that time many will fall away, and will deliver up one another and hate one another" (Matt. 24:9–10; cf. 10:21–22, 34–36).

The New Testament is replete with texts that make clear that the preaching of the gospel always divides people. Jesus warned the disciples when he commissioned them to preach the gospel message: "Do not think that I came to bring peace on the earth; I did not come to bring peace, but a sword. For I came to set a man against his father, and a daughter against her mother, and a daughter-in-law against her mother-in-law; and a man's enemies will be the members of his household" (Matt. 10:34–36; cf. 10:21). This passage defines adequately the symbolic meaning of the scene of the second seal. The rider on the second horse is given a sword and his mission is to take peace from the earth. Jesus stated clearly that his mission was not to bring peace but a sword. The context indicates that the sword symbolizes opposition and division.

Luke's version of Jesus' statement confirms this: "Do you suppose that I came to grant peace on earth? I tell you, no, but rather division" (Luke 12:51–53).

All of this strongly suggests that the rider on the second horse symbolizes the consequences of the rejection of the gospel. The second horse follows the first; it means that whenever the gospel is preached and it has been accepted, persecution follows. As in the Old Testament when the enemies of God's people turned their swords against each other, so today resistance to the gospel divides people and causes them to persecute one another and "hate one another" (Matt. 24:10). The scene of the fifth seal portrays the martyrs who had been "slain because of the word of God and because of the testimony that they held" crying for divine intervention (Rev. 6:9–10). In Greek, the word for "slain" in Revelation 6:9 is the same as that used with reference to the mission of the rider on the fiery-red horse in Revelation 6:4. The text makes clear that these martyrs died because of their faithfulness to the gospel proclamation. And they are told to rest for a while until the time when God will avenge the blood of his faithful witnesses who were unjustly persecuted and killed (cf. Rev. 6:11). At the promised time, Christ himself, with the royal crown on his head, will come with a sharp sword and bring judgment on those who resisted the gospel and treated his faithful people unjustly (Rev. 19:11–16).

THE OPENING OF THE THIRD SEAL (6:5–6)

> *⁵And when he opened the third seal, I heard the third living being saying, "Come!" And I looked, and behold, a black horse, and the one sitting upon it had a balance in his hand. ⁶And I heard as a voice in the midst of the four living beings saying: "A quart of wheat for a denarius, and three quarts of barley for a denarius, and do not harm the oil and the wine."*

NOTES

6:5 *Black*. In Revelation, black is related to darkness; the sun becomes "black as sackcloth" (6:12). In the New Testament, darkness symbolizes the absence of the gospel (e.g., Matt. 4:16; Luke 1:79; John 1:5; 3:19; Acts 26:18; Col. 1:13; 1 John 1:5).

A balance. A balance in the Old Testament functions as the symbol of famine. To eat bread by weight denoted in antiquity the greatest scarcity. The Lord made a threat through Moses that, if the people are disobedient "when I break your staff of bread...they will bring back your bread by weights" (Lev. 26:26). Ezekiel prophesied that during the siege of Jerusalem, its inhabitants would "eat bread by weight and with anxiety, and drink water by measure" (Ezek. 4:16).

6:6 *A quart of wheat for a denarius.* The Greek *choinix* was a dry measure equal to a quart. "A quart of grain" was the daily ration for a man. The denarius was a Roman silver coin equivalent to the average daily wage of a worker.[11] According to Robert L. Thomas, a day's wages was required to obtain the ration during times of famine.[12] Wheat was the main staple food in the ancient world; barley, cheaper than wheat, was for the poor. "This pictures a situation where scarcity prevails, when it would take all that a man could earn—a denarius—to buy enough of the cheapest food for a small family. In ordinary times, a denarius would purchase twelve to fifteen times as much food."[13]

Harm. The Greek word *adikeō* means "to injure" or "to do harm to." It is used elsewhere in the book of Revelation repeatedly for judgment on evildoers (2:11; 9:10, 19) or for persecution of God's people (11:5). It can also be used symbolically as damaging and destroying the earth and plants (7:2–3; 9:4).

EXPOSITION

6:5–6 At the breaking of the third seal, John hears the third living being (most likely the one having a face like a man, 4:7) who calls for *a black horse.* The rider on the third horse holds *a balance in his hand.* The balance points to a time of shortage of food "when the basic commodities of life are measured out at greatly inflated prices" (cf. Lev. 26:26; Ezek. 4:16).[14] The scene of the opening of the third seal portrays a famine condition. A voice which comes from the midst of the four living beings may be that of the Father or Christ himself; it describes the condition of great scarcity in terms of *a quart of wheat for a denarius, and three quarts of barley for a denarius.* A quart of wheat was approximately a daily amount of food for an average person. A person had to spend a denarius—his full day's wage—to purchase enough wheat only for himself to survive. He could spend his whole wage on the much cheaper and inferior barley to feed himself and his family. This illustrates serious food shortage. In the ancient world, a shortage of bread was regarded as a sign of a serious famine.

In Palestine, grain, wine, and oil were three main crops. It has been interpreted by some scholars that while wheat signified the basic part of the diet, the oil and wine were luxuries. However, grain, oil, and wine are mentioned together repeatedly in the Old Testament as representing the ordinary necessities of life (Deut. 7:13; 11:14; 28:51;

2 Chron. 32:28; Hos. 2:8, 22; Joel 2:19). All three of these crops were essential to life in the Bible lands and were not regarded as real luxuries.[15] Because the olive and the vine were much more deeply rooted than grain, which was shallow rooted, they could survive a drought much more easily than grain could. So, while the drought would have damaged and destroyed necessities of the basic diet, the hardship of the famine plague in the scene of the opening of the third seal was limited and partial.

The rider on the black horse must represent symbolically a spiritual famine of the word of God rather than a physical shortage of food. The prophecy of Amos suggests that famine can be spiritual:

> "Behold, days are coming," declares the Lord,
>   "when I will send a famine on the land,
>   not a famine for bread or a thirst for water,
>   but rather for hearing the word of the Lord.
> And people will stagger from sea to sea,
>   and from the north even to the east;
>   they will go to and fro to seek the word of the Lord,
>   but they will not find it.
> In that day the beautiful virgins
>   and the young men will faint from thirst." (Amos 8:11–13)

If the black horse of the third seal is opposite to the white horse of the first seal, which symbolizes the proclamation and the spreading of the gospel, then the opening of the third seal portrays a spiritual famine. Grain would symbolize God's word (cf. Matt. 13:3–30; Luke 8:11). The word of God is the bread of life (Matt. 4:4), or it might also symbolize Jesus himself (John 6:35–58; 1 Cor. 10:16). So, whatever this spiritual famine might mean, the scene of the opening of the third seal has to do with a shortage of God's word and the gospel.

This famine is not fatal, however. The voice also orders that the oil and the wine are not to be harmed. The wine symbolizes God's gracious salvation in Jesus Christ; oil stands for the Holy Spirit. It suggests that even though there might be a shortage of God's word in the world, and that the gospel message is hidden from the people, the Holy Spirit is still at work making salvation available. Thus, whenever and wherever the scene of the opening of the third seal takes place, the text makes clear that despite the fact that the word of God might be somewhat obscured, God is still at work. His salvation is still available to everyone.[16]

THE OPENING OF THE FOURTH SEAL (6:7–8)

⁷And when he opened the fourth seal, I heard the voice of the fourth living being saying: "Come!" ⁸And I looked, and behold, a pale horse, and the one sitting upon it had the name Death, and Hades was following him; and authority over one-fourth of the earth was given to them to kill with the sword and with famine and with pestilence and by the beasts of the earth.

NOTES

6:8 A pale horse. The Greek word *chlōros* is used for green vegetation (Mark 6:39; Rev. 8:7; 9:4). It was used also in ancient times for the appearance of a person who was sick. In the context of the fourth seal, it designates "yellowish green" or "pale." It is a pale, ashen-grey color that resembles "a corpse in the advanced state of corruption."[17]

Death and **Hades.** See *Notes* on Revelation 1:18.

Over one-fourth of the earth. "One-fourth of the earth" in Revelation relates to God's dominion; "the one-third of the earth" refers to Satan's dominion (see further *Notes* on Rev. 8:7).

EXPOSITION

6:7–8 At the breaking of the fourth seal, the fourth living being (most likely the one like a flying eagle, 4:7) calls for *a pale horse,* a color that describes the ashen-grey pallor of a dead body or appearance of a person who is very sick. *The one sitting upon it had the name Death, and Hades was following him.* In Revelation 1:18, Death and Hades, as terrible as they might be, are under Christ's control. Christ is the One who holds the key of Hades. And here, with the opening of the fourth seal, Death and Hades appear as the ultimate consequence of the rejection of the gospel. Death is a natural consequence of the famine which is portrayed in the scene of the opening of the third seal. However, Death and Hades—these two enemies—are temporary. The message of the Bible is that death is a consequence of sin. Death, however, is not an ultimate reality. The book of Revelation makes clear that the day is coming when Death and Hades will have their end in the second death (20:14).

Death and Hades were given *authority over one-fourth of the earth.* The fact that they are *given* authority and power indicates that Death and Hades do not have ultimate power; they are under Christ's control (1:18). The fact that their power is limited to only "one-fourth of the earth" would suggest that each seal is related to one quarter of the earth and that each horseman has authority over a quarter. The four horses parallel the four winds in 7:1 which are related to the four corners of the earth (cf. *Notes* on Rev. 7:1).

Death and Hades are authorized to **kill with the sword and with famine and with pestilence and by the beasts of the earth.** In many places in the Old Testament, sword, famine, pestilence, and the beasts are a series of God's judgments upon his people as the consequence of their sins. God presented to Israel through Moses the penalties which he would send upon them because of their unfaithfulness to him and their disobedience to the covenant. He would send wild beasts to bereave them of their children and destroy their cattle. The sword would avenge their breaking of the covenant. Pestilence would be in their cities. He would "break your staff of bread" and they would eat without being satisfied (Lev. 26:21–26).[18] Ezekiel announced that God would send his "four severe judgments against Jerusalem: sword, famine, wild beasts, and plague" (Ezek. 14:21). They were intended to bring Israel to repentance. Continued disobedience, however, would intensify these judgments, leading to exclusion and exile (Lev. 26:21–26; Deut. 32:41–43). Here John is using a well-known picture of what happens "when God despatches his wrath upon his disobedient people."[19]

The rider on the fourth horse describes the most serious situation. It represents an intensification of the activities of the first three riders. Thus, the first four seals describe the reality of what happens as the consequence of sin, and yet they provide hope in that reality. As terrible as these plagues might be and are, they are not an end in and of themselves. As the Old Testament background texts indicate (Lev. 26; Deut. 32), these plagues are intended to awaken God's people and evoke repentance. Christ is in control; the powers of death are under his authority.

The plagues of the first four seals are just precursors and a foretaste of the final judgment which will be experienced by those who refuse to repent and resist the gospel in their unfaithfulness and disobedience. The day is coming, however, when suffering and death, as the consequences for sin, will come to their end. God's faithful people will then find life in the new world which will be established after the Second Coming (cf. Rev. 21:1–5).

A RETROSPECT ON THE FOUR HORSEMEN (6:1–8)

Clearly, the four horsemen of the first four seals stand for the victorious spreading of the gospel and the consequences of rejecting it. The rider on the white horse portrays the proclamation of the gospel to the world through the faithful church. Whenever the gospel is being preached, division takes place; some accept it and others reject and resist it. The rider on the red horse portrays opposition to the gospel. For those who reject and resist the gospel, a spiritual famine follows that leads to spiritual death. The rider on the black horse portrays the famine for the word of God, while the rider on the pale horse describes the pestilence and death which result from that famine. All these scenes are drawn from the Old Testament, and they contain the permanent truth of what happens when people reject the gospel and choose to live in sin.

Being understood in such a way, the riders on the four horses may portray general realities; that is to say, they describe what each person experiences when confronted with the gospel. When a person hears and accepts the gospel, he or she experiences the fullness of blessing and joy of salvation as a result of the close relationship with Christ. On the other hand, rejection and resistance to the gospel always results in a progressive decline leading to spiritual famine and death.

As Jon Paulien suggests, the riders on the four horses may also depict in particular the experience of the church during the first thousand years of the Christian Era.[20] According to the *Seventh-day Adventist Bible Commentary,* "the scenes revealed when the seals are opened may be regarded as having both a specific and a general application."[21] In the initial stage of the Christian church, which was characterized by general faithfulness, through the preaching of Paul and other apostles, the spreading of the gospel was victorious and triumphant. This period was followed by a progressive spiritual decline leading to the period of the famine for God's word and resulting in spiritual death that characterized the Christian church throughout the Medieval period. It was the period of spiritual decline and persecution when genuine faith was lost and the loving gospel message was resisted, forgotten, and gradually replaced by tradition. Furthermore, as Revelation 11:3–14 indicates, the scene of the four horsemen extends beyond the first millennium. Thus, the riders on the four horses might refer to both the history of the first millennium of the Christian era and the general realities of the entire Christian Age with a focus on its beginning.

The judgments depicted in the opening of the first four seals are partial and preliminary, however. The preaching of the gospel did not end in any way with the first century. The rider on the white horse is still going forth overcoming that he might overcome (Rev. 6:2). The four horsemen are just the precursors of the future reality, when once more at the end of this world's history there will be the great and final proclamation of the gospel (cf. Rev. 14:6–12; 18:1–4). Initiated by the latter rain, the gospel will go into the world and be proclaimed through God's faithful remnant in its full and final power; the whole earth will then be "illuminated with his glory" (18:1). This preaching of the gospel results in acceptance by some and rejection and resistance by others. Then, when the preaching of the gospel is completed and the destiny of every human being decided, the final judgments of God will be unleashed on those who have rejected and resisted the gospel. The covenant curses indicated in the four horses will then be complete and final.

The scene of the riders on the four horses is a strong warning of what will happen to those who reject the gospel. It indicates that ignoring and resisting the gospel message always results in spiritual famine, disease, and death. What the scene further makes clear is that the opportunity to receive the gospel, as well as him who is the central subject of the gospel, will not last forever. Before the very time of the end will come the last proclamation of the everlasting gospel to the inhabitants of the earth (Rev. 14:6–12; 18:1–4). The day is coming, however, when the gospel will not be offered and grace and mercy will not be available any more. But today is ours. "Today if you hear His voice, do not harden your hearts" (Heb. 3:15).

THE OPENING OF THE LAST THREE SEALS (6:9–17; 8:1)

The scenes of the opening of the last three seals differ from the previous four. They have no summons from the living beings and horses and riders. The scene of the riders on the four horses of Revelation 6:1–8 describes the consequences experienced by God's people when they are unfaithful to the gospel of Jesus Christ. However, the opening of the fifth seal (6:9–11) portrays the plea of the slain martyrs for judgment, and the opening of the sixth seal (6:12–17) portrays God's judgments falling on the oppressors and enemies of God's people, the realization of which is described in the scene of the blowing of the seven trumpets. The series is concluded with the opening of the seventh seal (8:1) which results in a silence in heaven.

THE OPENING OF THE FIFTH SEAL (6:9–11)

⁹And when he opened the fifth seal, I saw under the altar the souls of those who had been slain because of the word of God and because of the testimony that they had. ¹⁰And they cried with a loud voice: "How long, O Lord, holy and true, will you not judge and avenge our blood upon those who dwell on the earth?" ¹¹And to each of them was given a white garment, and it was said to them that they should rest for a little while yet, until their fellow servants, that is, their brothers who are about to be killed, might be made complete as they themselves had been.

NOTES

6:9 *The altar.* The Old Testament temple had two altars. The altar of sacrifices was in the outer court outside the temple for the sacrifice of animals in burnt offering. Inside the temple was the altar of incense. The altar in view here is most likely the altar of burnt offering rather than the altar of incense. This is clearly seen in the fact that in the Old Testament temple ritual, the blood was poured out at the base of the altar of burnt offering. "All the blood of the bull he shall pour out at the base of the altar of burnt offering" (Lev. 4:7, 18, 25, 30–34; 8:15; 9:9). The phrase "poured out" is also used in Revelation 16:6 where the blood of saints and prophets is poured out (evidently beneath the altar as verse 7 indicates). Since the altar of sacrifice was not in the temple, but in the outer court, it is clear that the scene portrayed here takes place not in the heavenly temple but on the earth which was symbolized by the outer court of the temple. In the relatively later Jewish tradition, the souls of the righteous were preserved under the throne of glory.[22]

The testimony that they had. The testimony that the faithful martyrs held and suffered for does not refer to "the testimony of Jesus" (Rev. 1:2, 9; 20:4; see *Notes* on Rev. 1:2), as some scholars assert,[23] but to the witness of the martyrs about Christ, the same as referred to elsewhere in the book as "the testimony" or "their testimony" (11:7; 12:11; see *Notes* on Rev. 12:17). Such an understanding fits in the context of the vision of the opening of the seven seals which deals primarily with the proclamation of the gospel and its related consequences.[24] The witnessing of the martyrs in Revelation 6:9 parallels that of the two witnesses in Revelation 11:3–10. It is because of their faithful witness to the gospel that the martyrs have experienced persecution and martyrdom (cf. Rev. 12:11).

6:10 *Avenge.* The Greek word *ekdikeō* ("avenge," "procure justice for someone") is a term implying a legal action. The word is found in Luke 18:3, for instance, where the widow cries to the judge: "Give me legal protection from my opponent" (NIV: "grant me justice against my adversary"). In Luke 18:5 the judge responds: "Because this widow bothers me, I will give her legal protection."

244

This legal aspect is clearly expressed in Revelation 19:2, where God has judged Babylon in that he has avenged the blood from her hand (see also Rom. 12:19).

Those who dwell on the earth. This phrase occurs frequently in the book of Revelation and functions almost as a technical expression for the wicked, namely, those who resist the gospel and persecute God's faithful people (cf. 3:10; 6:10; 8:13; 11:10; 13:8, 14; 17:2). The redeemed saints in Revelation, however, are depicted as "those who dwell in heaven" (Rev. 13:6) and reign in the heavenly places (cf. Rev. 1:6; 5:9–10).

6:11 ***White garment.*** See *Exposition* on Revelation 3:18.

Their fellow servants, that is, their brothers. The connecting *kai* in Greek here most likely functions epexegetically as "that is" or "namely." Thus the text presents two perspectives on a single group.[25]

Might be made complete. The Greek *plēroō* means "to make full," "to fill up," "to bring something to completion," or "to complete." The text could mean either that the *number* of their fellow servants who are about to be killed are to be made complete (as translated by the NASB, NIV, NKJV, NRSV, RSV, and others) or that their fellow servants who are to be killed are to be made complete with reference to character (as KJV seems to suggest). Evidence elsewhere in the book of Revelation supports the latter understanding (cf. Rev. 7:13–14; 19:7–8). Translators usually supply the phrase with the word "number" on the assumption that John held to an idea of a fixed number of martyrs to be completed before time comes to an end. This is based on popular Jewish tradition expressed, for instance, in 1 Enoch: "The hearts of the holy ones are filled with joy, because the number of the righteous has been offered [reached], the prayers of the righteous ones have been heard, and the blood of the righteous has been admitted before the Lord of the Spirits."[26] The author of 4 Ezra asked: "Did not the souls of the righteous in their chambers ask about these matters, saying, 'How long are we to remain here? And when will come the harvest of our reward?' And Jeremiel the archangel answered them and said, 'When the number of those like yourselves is completed.'"[27] A similar idea is found in 2 Baruch: "For when Adam sinned and death was decreed against those who were to be born, the multitude of those who would be born was numbered. And for that number a place was prepared where the living ones might live and where the dead might be preserved. No creature will live again unless the number that has been appointed is completed."[28]

The word "number," however, does not appear in the Greek text of Revelation 6:11. George E. Ladd correctly states: "This statement is surely not to be understood in any mathematical way, as though God had decreed that there must be a certain number of martyrs, and when this number was slain, the end will come."[29] Revelation transcends the popular Jewish understanding. The text states that the martyrs underneath the altar must rest until their fellow servants, that is, their brothers who are about to be killed, might be made complete with reference to character, as they themselves have been made complete or perfect in character.

EXPOSITION

6:9 At the breaking of the fifth seal, John observes *under the altar the souls of those who had been slain because of the word of God and because of the testimony that they had.* The scene depicts God's faithful people who died because of their faith and their faithful bearing of their testimony to the gospel. Their souls are seen as being beneath the altar. This imagery is drawn directly from the Old Testament sacrificial ritual and as such must be understood symbolically. The altar of burnt offering (Lev. 4:7) was the place where the sacrifices were offered and burnt. The most sacred part of the sacrifice was blood which symbolized life. When the blood was poured out, a person or animal died. Because life belonged to God (Lev. 17:11–14), the blood of the slain animals was drained and poured out beneath the altar (Lev. 4:7; 8:15; 9:9). Thus, the faithful martyrs were beneath the altar because "their life-blood had been poured out as an offering to God."[30] In Revelation 16, the blood of the saints and prophets is poured out beneath the altar (16:6–7).

The scene of the fifth seal depicts the image of martyrdom. Using the symbolism drawn from the Old Testament sacrificial ritual, John describes God's faithful people sacrificed as martyrs with their lifeblood poured out as an offering to God. The idea of martyrdom as a sacrifice to God is well-known in the New Testament. Jesus stated that the day would come when those who kill his followers would think they were offering service to God (John 16:2). Paul speaks of himself as "being poured out as a drink offering upon the sacrifice" (Phil. 2:17; cf. 2 Tim. 4:6). Thus, what we have here is a symbolic presentation. The saints under the altar died because of "the word of God and the testimony they held"; that is to say, they died because of their faithfulness to the gospel proclamation (cf. 1:9). When Christ's followers die for their faith and loyalty to God, it may very often appear to be a tragedy. The scene of the fifth seal, however, describes the death of Christ's followers as a triumph—a sacrificial offering made to God.

6:10 The martyrs under the altar cry: *How long, O Lord, holy and true, will you not judge and avenge our blood upon those who dwell on the earth?* This plea reminds us of the blood of Abel, which is described as crying out to God from the ground (Gen. 4:10). Just as Abel's blood cried out to God because of his death, so the martyrs cry out to God because they were unjustly persecuted and died because of their faithfulness to him. "Those who dwell on the earth" are ones hostile to the gospel who viciously persecute God's faithful people (cf. 6:10; 8:13; 11:10; 13:8, 14; 17:2). Although the plea of the slain martyrs is a request for judgment on their enemies, it should not be regarded as a longing for revenge but a plea for legal justice (cf. Luke 18:3, 5). "How long, O Lord, are you going to allow injustice on the earth? How long until you judge and avenge the blood upon those who live on the earth?" This cry "must be seen as a legal plea in which God is asked to conduct a legal process leading to a verdict that will vindicate his martyred saints."[31] As E. Schüssler Fiorenza concludes, this plea is not only for "the vindication of those who are oppressed and slaughtered, but it is also a plea for the vindication of God in the eyes of those who have placed their trust in God."[32]

"How long, O Lord?" has been a perennial cry of God's oppressed and suffering people throughout history. This was the cry of the Psalmist with regard to the wicked who were allowed to afflict and assault the righteous (Ps. 79:1–10). Similar sentiments were expressed by Habakkuk: "O Lord, how long shall I cry for help?" the prophet cried when he witnessed how the heathen nations were allowed to afflict God's people (Hab. 1:1–4). "How long will the holy place be trampled?" was the cry of Daniel in the Exile (Dan. 8:13; 12:6–7). "How long are we to remain here? And when will come the harvest of our reward?" asked the writer of the apocryphal 4 Ezra.[33] The cry: "How long?" of the martyred saints beneath the altar is thus a cry for acquittal in the heavenly court. What can be observed here is that when God's faithful people "uttered this cry, they were bewildered by God's seeming inactivity, but they never doubted the ultimate action of God, and the ultimate vindication of the righteous."[34]

6:11 The prayers of the faithful martyrs are heard by God. *Each of them was given a white garment.* The passive form here functions as the Hebrew divine passive, suggesting God as agent who gives the white garments. The white garments of the saved (Rev. 3:4–5) are the garments of victory, triumph, and faithfulness. Later, John sees the redeemed multitude clothed in white garments before the throne (7:9). They have come out of the great tribulation and washed their garments in the blood of Christ (7:13–14). After having been given the white garments, the martyrs underneath the altar are told *that they should rest for a little while yet.* Again we see the divine passive form here: *it was said to them,* suggesting God's action. The prayers of the faithful martyrs are answered directly by God.[35]

The death of God's faithful people in Revelation is described as resting "for a little while" or resting "from their labors; for their works follow them" (Rev. 14:13). Those who have rejected and resisted the gospel "do not have rest day and night" (Rev. 14:11). The slain martyrs do not come to life until the return of Christ. John sees them later in Revelation 19:2 at the center of the rejoicing, redeemed multitude standing before the throne and praising God for judging Babylon and avenging "the blood of his servants from her hand." Later he also sees the same "souls of those beheaded because of the testimony of Jesus and because of the Word of God" coming to life at the Second Coming and reigning with Christ in the heavenly places for a thousand years (Rev. 20:4). In the meantime, these faithful dead rest under God's watchful care until the day of the resurrection.

The martyrs are told to rest for a little while *until their fellow servants, that is, their brothers who are about to be killed, might be made complete as they themselves had been.* The faithful martyrs were obedient unto the point of death. They are made complete with reference to character. They are clothed in white garments, symbolizing their victory over sin and their faithfulness to God. They have to rest *until their fellow servants, that is their brothers* are complete as well; that is to say, until they reach the same level of obedience and faithfulness. That time is described later in Revelation 19:7–8 where John sees God's people clothed in "fine linen, bright and clean, for the fine linen is the righteous deeds of the saints." They are the ones who "have washed their robes and made them white in the blood of the Lamb" (7:14). It is at that point in time that the prayers of the martyred saints under the altar will be answered, for God will finally execute judgment on the enemies and oppressors of his faithful people.

THE OPENING OF THE SIXTH SEAL (6:12–17)

12And I looked when he opened the sixth seal, and a great earthquake occurred, and the sun became black as a sackcloth made of hair, and the moon became like blood, 13and the stars of heaven fell down to the earth as a fig tree casts its figs when shaken by a strong wind, 14and the sky was parted as a scroll being rolled up, and every mountain and island were moved from their places. 15And the kings of the earth and the magistrates and the

military commanders and the rich and the powerful and every slave and free person hid themselves in the caves and among the rocks of the mountains. ¹⁶And they said to the mountains and the rocks: "Fall on us and hide us from the face of the One sitting on the throne and from the wrath of the Lamb, ¹⁷for the great day of his wrath has come, and who is able to stand?"

NOTES

6:12 *A great earthquake occurred.* In the Old Testament, the coming of the Lord to visit the earth is accompanied by the shaking of the earth. There will be a violent earthquake when he comes to Israel in judgment (Ezek. 38:19–20; Joel 2:10; Amos 8:8). Haggai wrote: "Once more in a little while, I am going to shake the heavens and the earth, the sea also and the dry land" (Hag. 2:6). This concept was very prominent in the Jewish extra-biblical literature.[36] The earthquake of the sixth seal appears to precede the one mentioned in 16:18 of the seventh-bowl plague which shatters end-time Babylon, resulting in its destruction.[37] This one mentioned in 6:12 has been identified by historicist commentators as the Lisbon earthquake of 1755.[38]

The sun became black as a sackcloth made of hair, and the moon became like blood. The Old Testament background text for these phenomena is Joel 2:31 where the prophet predicted that before "the great and awesome day of the Lord comes," "the sun will be turned into darkness, and the moon into blood" (cf. Joel 3:15). Also, Isaiah depicts God darkening the sun and clothing it with sackcloth (Isa. 50:3); the stars will not shine, the sun will be darkened, the moon will not shed its light, and the earth will shake from its place at the wrath of the Lord (Isa. 13:10, 13). The historical fulfillment of this phenomena has been dated by historicist scholars as May 19, 1780, when it was experienced in eastern New York and southern New England.[39]

6:13 *The stars of heaven fell down to the earth as a fig tree casts its figs when shaken by a strong wind.* Apparently John chose this description from Isaiah 34:4, where the host of heaven will wither away and fall down as the leaves fall down from the vine and the figs from the fig tree. In his sermon on the Mount of Olives, Jesus predicted that the stars would fall from the sky and the powers of heaven be shaken (Matt. 24:29). Historicist scholars suggest the historical fulfillment of this phenomenon in the spectacular meteor shower on November 13, 1833.[40]

6:14 *The sky was parted as a scroll being rolled up.* The picture of the sky being rolled up like a scroll is taken from Isaiah 34:4 in a description of the Lord's wrath.

Every mountain and island were moved from their places. Jeremiah speaks of the mountains "quaking and all the hills moved to and fro" (Jer. 4:24). Revelation 6:14 refers most likely to the final earthquake mentioned again in Revelation 16:18, which is distinct and greater than the first one mentioned in 6:12.

6:17 *His wrath.* On the meaning of the wrath (Gr. *orgē*) of God, see *Notes* on Revelation 14:10.

EXPOSITION

6:12–14 The opening of the sixth seal unleashes a series of phenomena which are cosmic in scope: they include a great earthquake, a darkening of the sun and moon, and the falling of the stars. Everything is concluded with an even greater earthquake that moves mountains and islands from their places. The scene consisting of these five elements was very familiar to the Christians of John's time. These phenomena were used in the Old Testament to describe the visitation of God's final judgment to the earth, called the Day of the Lord.

The Day of the Lord is an important eschatological concept that runs throughout the Old Testament prophetic books. It is the occasion when God will finally visit the earth as a result of the unfaithfulness of people to God. God will come to earth in judgment, bringing annihilation to the wicked, on one side, and redemption and deliverance for those who are loyal to God, on the other. The Day of the Lord is described as an event of frightening qualities; it is regularly associated with cosmic upheaval and the shattering and destruction of the earth. All of these are seen as the signs of God's impending judgment (for instance, Joel 2:30–31 and Amos 8:8–9). One might observe that the language John used is reminiscent of Isaiah's prophecy with regard to the day of the Lord:

> For the stars of heaven and their constellations
> Will not flash forth their light;
> The sun will be dark when it rises,
> And the moon will not shed its light....
> Therefore, I shall make the heavens tremble,
> And the earth will be shaken from its place
> At the fury of the Lord of hosts
> In the day of His burning anger. (Isa. 13:10, 13)

Thus, in describing the scene of the opening of the sixth seal, John is using the familiar Old Testament portrayal of the Day of the Lord.

The catastrophic language describing the breaking of the sixth seal is almost identical with Jesus' sermon on the Mount of Olives with reference to his second coming. Immediately after the great tribulation, "the sun will be darkened, and the moon will not give its light, and the stars will fall from the sky, and the powers of the heavens will be shaken" (Matt. 24:29). After this cosmic phenomena, the sign of the Second Coming will appear, initiating the gathering of the saints into God's kingdom.

A question arises: Should these descriptions (found both in Jesus' portrayal of the end of the world and in the scene of the opening of the sixth seal) be understood literally or symbolically? Although the language of the opening of the sixth seal is drawn from the Old Testament, nothing in the text indicates that these signs are intended to be symbolic. On the contrary, the repeated usage of the word "as" or "like" (Gr. *hōs*) in the text appears to be very significant. The sun becomes black *as* sackcloth, the moon *as* blood, the stars of the sky fall *as* do the figs of the fig tree, and heaven splits *as* the papyrus scroll. In Greek, this word "introduces a figurative analogy to an actual event" which is compared with something figurative.[41] This suggests that these heavenly signs are intended to be taken literally.

6:15–17 John states that at the manifestation of these cosmic signs the unrepentant sinners will hide *in the caves and among the rocks of the mountains,* seeking to cover themselves *from the face of the One sitting on the throne and from the wrath of the Lamb, for the great day of his wrath has come, and who is able to stand?* This scene brings to mind Adam and Eve hiding themselves from before God after they sinned (Gen. 3:8). Sin makes a person run away from God. Here in the text we see the language of the Second Coming. The coming of Christ is preceded by a violent earthquake (the same as mentioned later in 16:18), even greater than the first one mentioned earlier in verse 12. The scene of the sixth seal is a direct allusion to Isaiah's prophecy with reference to the Day of the Lord:

> Men will go into caves of the rocks,
> And into holes of the ground
> Before the terror of the LORD
> And the splendor of His majesty,
> When He arises to make the earth tremble.
> In that day men will cast away
>   to the moles and the bats
> Their idols of silver and their idols of gold,
> Which they made for themselves to worship,
> In order to go
>   into the caverns of the rocks
>   and the clefts of the cliffs,
> Before the terror of the LORD
>   and the splendor of His majesty,
> When He arises to make the earth tremble. (Isa. 2:19–21; cf. 2:10)

This language Jesus also used in portraying his return to the earth (Matt. 24:29). He stated that after all of these initial events, the Son of Man will appear on the clouds, "and then all the tribes of the earth will mourn, and they will see the Son of Man coming on the clouds of the sky with power and great glory" (Matt. 24:30; cf. Luke 23:30).

The scene of the sixth seal thus portrays the Second Coming which is described in the Old Testament in terms of the Day of the Lord. The Second Coming is the occasion when God will intervene to punish sin and defend his faithful people. The martyrs underneath the altar are crying for God's intervention. Their persecutors must confront the holy God (cf. Amos 4:12). God is about to judge the sinners and the enemies of his people. Nobody is exempt. All levels of human society are mentioned: *kings of the earth and the magistrates and the military commanders and the rich and the powerful and every slave and free person.* Nobody is able to escape the judgment of God. Revelation 19:18 completes the scene in portraying scavengers of the sky feeding themselves on "the flesh of the kings and the flesh of the commanders of one thousand troops and the flesh of the strong and the flesh of horses and of those sitting upon them and the flesh of all, both free men and slaves, the small and great."

The entire scene ends with the very significant rhetorical question: *Who is able to stand?* This calls to mind the questions which Malachi asked: "Who can endure the day of His coming? And who can stand when He appears?" (Mal. 3:2). Revelation 7 indicates that those who are able to stand the divine day of wrath are the sealed people of God. It assures us that, while the Second Coming and the events accompanying it terrify the wicked, God's faithful people may hold on to the promise: "For the mountains may be removed and the hills may shake, but My loving-kindness will not be removed from you, and My covenant of peace will not be shaken" (Isa. 54:10). When the prophet Nahum asked, "Who can stand before His indignation? Who can endure the burning of His anger?" he got the unequivocal answer: "The Lord is good, a stronghold in the day of trouble, and He knows those who take refuge in Him" (Nah. 1:6–7). Here is the hope for God's people with regard to the future. This is what Revelation 7 is all about.

THE OPENING OF THE SEVENTH SEAL (8:1)

> [1] *And when he opened the seventh seal, there was silence in heaven for about half an hour.*

NOTES

Silence. A number of different explanations have been offered on the meaning of the silence in the scene of the opening of the seventh seal.[42] None has proved to be satisfactory, however. For instance, some think that the silence is connected with the offering of the prayers of the saints (8:3–4).[43] Others hold that this silence corresponds to the silence at the beginning of the creation—that is to say, in Genesis 1:2 all was dark and silent. In the Jewish apocalyptic literature, God turns this earth into silence as it was in the beginning: "And the world shall be turned back to primeval silence for seven days, as it was at the first beginnings; so that no one shall be left."[44] According to others, it is the silence of the astonished universe in the expectation of the judgments of God about to be launched on the wicked (cf. Hab. 2:20).[45]

Some Old Testament texts shed light on the possible meaning of the "silence" in Revelation 8:1. In the prophecies of Habakkuk (2:20), Zephaniah (1:7), and Zechariah (2:13), the inhabitants of the earth are exhorted to keep silence in view of the coming judgment of God from his temple. The anticipation of God's imminent action dominates the scene and forms the basis for the prophetic appeal. The Lord prepares to leave his holy dwelling to visit the earth, and his arrival will drive the wicked into dreadful despair. Richard Bauckham points to the statements from early and later Jewish writings where there is silence in heaven so that the prayers of the saints can be heard and answered in judgment on the wicked.[46] As Joseph J. Battistone states, "John takes the themes of silence, judgment, and the Lord's coming, and forms his own picture based on the vision in heaven. Instead of focusing on the earth, however, the revelator pictures what heaven will be like when God leaves His holy dwelling and heads for earth"[47] to bring his righteous judgment on its inhabitants.

For about half an hour. The meaning of the half hour is enigmatic. It evidently should be understood symbolically to refer to a very short period of time of unspecified length.

EXPOSITION

At the breaking of the seventh seal, ***there was silence in heaven for about half an hour.*** Although it apparently occurs in heaven, the effect of the silence extends down to earth. This picture fits well into the context of the breaking of the seven seals. The silence may function "like a calm after the storm of destruction occasioned by Christ's second coming."[48] The riders on the horses have finished their work, the sealing of God's faithful people is completed, the winds have ceased to blow (Rev. 7:1–3), the great tribulation is over, and the second coming of Christ has taken place. The prayers of God's people (cf. Rev. 6:9–11) are heard, and there is silence in heaven in the light of the final judgment to be executed on rebellious humanity of which the seven last plagues are just a precursor and foretaste (cf. Rev. 15–16). Jewish people of

John's day believed that there would be silence before the new creation which would correspond to the silence before the first creation.[49]

This silence is indeed a dramatic pause which makes the righteous judgments of God about to be executed upon the earth even more impressive. Revelation 6:16–17 indicates that the scene of the breaking of the seventh seal follows the Second Coming. This silence might refer to the millennium (which is a relatively short period of time as compared to eternity) or to the period after the millennium, when God will execute justice on the wicked and create a new world. This silence is an indication that the judgment is about to be executed and the whole universe will be at peace.[50] God's faithful people are about to find their rest (cf. Rev. 7:14–17).

In the broader sense, this silence extends to the subsequent period of eternal peace which the entire universe will enjoy after the triumphant victory over sin as the prevalence of God's love spreads throughout all eternity.

A RETROSPECT ON REVELATION 6:9–17; 8:1

While the four horsemen symbolize the judgments of God on those who claimed to be God's people, the scene of the breaking of the fifth seal introduces what seems to be a crucial theme of the book of Revelation,[51] namely, the situation of God's people in the hostile world. The scene sets on the stage two groups of people: those who persecute and those who are persecuted. John observed the faithful dead who had been slain for their testimony to the word of God. Their cry was for God's intervention and judgment on "those who dwell upon the earth" (6:10). Now God reacts and intervenes.

While the four horsemen could symbolize in particular the judgments of God during the first millennium on those who claimed to be God's people but were unfaithful to the gospel, in the scene of the fifth seal, as Paulien observes, "we see the results of the persecution which have been alluded to in the horsemen, particularly the second. Thus the fifth seal represents a later point in time than the four horsemen themselves. Since the phrase 'How long?' is applied in Daniel 7:21, 25; 12:6–7 to the great tribulation of the Middle Ages, Revelation 6:10 appropriately represents a 'cry' of protest from the martyrs of that same era."[52] The sixth seal brings us to the end of this world's history. It portrays the coming judgment when "those who dwell upon the earth" seek to hide themselves from the wrath of the Lamb, crying in panic, "The great day of his wrath has come, and who is able to stand?" (6:17).

Chapter 7 provides the answer to the above question, telling us that those who will be able to stand on that day are the sealed people of God. It also makes clear that the final judgment poured out on "those who dwell upon the earth" and the destruction of earth cannot come until the sealing of God's people has been completed (7:3). This corresponds to the response given to the martyrs underneath the altar—to wait until their fellow servants are complete as well. The rest of chapter 7 brings us to the time after the millennium and the subsequent period characterized by the silence of the seventh seal. God's people have been vindicated and have finally found their rest.

What about the judgment upon the persecutors of God's people? Revelation 8:2–5 indicates that the prayers of God's suffering people are heard by God. And the scene of the angels blowing the seven trumpets is God's evident response: "Not too long. I am already judging those who viciously assault and persecute my saints." It would be natural to expect that the blowing of the seven trumpets has something to do with the answering of the prayers of the martyrs underneath the altar and the command given to the four angels: "Do not harm the earth or the sea or the trees until we have sealed the servants of our God upon their foreheads" (Rev. 7:3). When the sealing is completed, the judgments of God will be put into action. And Revelation 19:2 brings us to the day to come when the vindicated martyrs will give all glory and praise to God because his judgments are true and righteous for "he has avenged the blood of his servants" (cf. also Rev. 16:5–7).

The cry of slain martyrs underneath the altar—"How long, O Lord?"—is the perennial cry of many Christians living in this world who have had to pay the price for following in the steps of Christ. Just as Jesus was persecuted in this world, so are his followers. Yet if the very worst happens to them, they can still find comfort in the fact that Jesus traced the way. If they have to suffer even to the point of death, they will know that the end is coming when all God's promises will be fulfilled. Jon Paulien states:

> The same Christ who safeguards the churches (Rev 1–3) also sits on God's throne in heavenly places (Rev 4–5). He knows and cares when His people suffer or are forced to walk this life alone because of their faith in Him. It is, therefore, not surprising that God's people throughout the Christian Era have found meaning for their lives in the strange collection of images that make up the apocalyptic portions of the book.
>
> The seals of chapter 6 provide a telling description of Christian life on this earth between the cross and the Second Coming. God's suffering people may at times wonder if reality does not prove their faith an illusion. The glory and the glitter seem

to reside with the opponents of the gospel. But the fact that the grim realities of earth's history and experience follow upon the opening of the seals in heaven demonstrates that these realities are under the control of the Lamb, who is already reigning (Rev 5) and whose perfect kingdom will soon be consummated (11:15–18).[53]

Revelation 6–7 sends a perennial and powerful message to God's oppressed people living between the cross and the Second Coming and experiencing trials and suffering in this world. As David Marshall states, "Revelation does not back away from real life. It portrays life as it really is, but it also gives us hope in that reality."[54] In the midst of the blowing of the winds, as bizarre as they might be, God's people have a firm assurance that Jesus Christ is still on the throne in the heavenly places. Through him, God is in control. His promise given some two thousand years ago is still firm: "I am with you always, even to the end of the age" (Matt. 28:20).

ENDNOTES

1. Paulien, "The Seven Seals," 223–224.

2. Charles, 1:160; Caird, 122; Barclay, *The Revelation of John*, 2:4; Morris, 102.

3. Ladd, 97.

4. Johnson, 473.

5. Ladd, 98.

6. Barclay, *The Revelation of John*, 2:178.

7. Paulien, "The Seven Seals," 229.

8. Ladd, 98.

9. Paulien, "The Seven Seals," 229.

10. Ibid., 230.

11. Charles, 1:166.

12. Thomas, *Revelation 1–7*, 422.

13. Ladd, 100.

14. Mounce, 155.

15. Ladd, 101.

16. Paulien, Bible Explorer 3.3.

17. J. M. Ford, 108.

18. As Barclay (*The Revelation of John*, 2:9) points out.

19. Ibid.

20. See further Paulien, "The Seven Seals," 233–234.

21. *The Seventh-day Adventist Bible Commentary*, 7:775.

22. Cf. The Babylonian Talmud *Shabbath* 152b (Epstein, 2/2:780); see J. M. Ford, 111.

23. Including Mounce, 158 (although he believes that the phrase includes the martyrs' own testimony as well); Gerhard Pfandl, "The Remnant Church and the Spirit of Prophecy," in *Symposium on Revelation—Book 2, Daniel and Revelation Committee Series 7* (Silver Spring, MD: Biblical Research Institute, 1992), 313; Hans K. LaRondelle, *How to Understand the End-Time Prophecies of the Bible* (Sarasota, FL: First Impressions, 1997), 283–286.

24. As observed by H. Strathmann, "*martus*, et al," in *Theological Dictionary of the New Testament*, ed. G. Kittel and G. W. Bromiley (Grand Rapids, MI: Eerdmans, 1964–1976), 4:501–502.

25. Aune, *Revelation 6–16*, 411; cf. Beckwith, 527.

26. 1 Enoch 47:4 (Charlesworth, 1:35).

27. 4 Ezra 4:35–36 (Charlesworth, 1:531).

28. 2 Baruch 23:4–5a (Charlesworth, 1:629).

29. Ladd, 106.

30. Barclay, *The Revelation of John*, 2:11.

31. Joel N. Musvosvi, *Vengeance in the Apocalypse*, Andrews University Seminary Doctoral Dissertation Series 17 (Berrien Springs, MI: Andrews University Press, 1993), 232.

32. Fiorenza, *Revelation*, 64.

33. 4 Ezra 4:35a (Charlesworth, 1:531).

34. Barclay, *The Revelation of John*, 2:14.

35. J. M. Ford, 111.

36. Testament of Moses 10:3–7 (Charlesworth, 1:932); 2 Baruch 70:8 (Charlesworth, 1:645).

37. Paulien, "The Seven Seals," 236; such an understanding has been unsuccessfully (in my view) challenged by LaRondelle, *How to Understand the End-Time Prophecies*, 140–141.

38. See *The Seventh-day Adventist Bible Commentary*, 7:779.

39. See ibid.

40. See ibid., 5:502.

41. Paulien, "The Seven Seals," 237.

42. For the list of various views, see Aune, *Revelation 6–16*, 507–508.

43. Charles, 1:223–224; Barclay, *The Revelation of John*, 2:40–41; J. M. Ford, 130; Morris, 116; Caird, 106–107; Bauckham, *The Climax of Prophecy*, 70–83.

44. 4 Ezra 7:30 (Charlesworth, 1:537).

45. Morris, 117; Ladd, 122–123; Mounce, 178–179; Beale, 446–452.

46. Bauckham, *The Climax of Prophecy*, 71–83; he admits his indebtedness to Charles (1:223–224); the same view is shared by Beale, 451–452.

47. Joseph J. Battistone, *God's Church in a Hostile World* (Hagerstown, MD: Review and Herald, 1989), 108.

48. Paulien, "The Seven Seals," 237.

49. Cf., e.g., 4 Ezra 6:39; 7:29–31.

50. Paulien, "The Seven Seals," 237.

51. See J. P. Heil, "The Fifth Seal (Rev 6:9–11) as a Key to the Book of Revelation," *Biblica* 74 (1993): 220–243.

52. Paulien, "The Seven Seals," 235–236.

53. Ibid., 238–239.

54. Marshall, 67.

THE SEALED SAINTS AND THE GREAT MULTITUDE
REVELATION 7:1–17

The scene of Revelation 7 is inserted parenthetically between the opening of the sixth seal and that of the seventh. The conclusion of the sixth seal brings us to the final events of earth's history which lead up to the Second Coming of Christ. With the approaching judgment, rebellious masses seek to hide themselves from the wrath of the Lamb, crying in panic: "Who is able to stand [on the great day of his wrath]?" (6:17). Revelation 7 appears to respond to that question: those who will be able to stand on that great day are the 144,000 and the great multitude. Chapter 7, accordingly, is divided into two parts: the first concerns the sealed 144,000 (7:1–8), and the second describes the great multitude who are in the presence of God's throne after passing through the time of the great tribulation (7:9–17).

THE SEALED SAINTS (7:1–8)

Revelation 7:1–8 describes the 144,000 as being from the twelve tribes of Israel and being sealed on their foreheads for protection from the eschatological destructions coming upon the earth.

> *[1]After this I saw four angels standing at the four corners of the earth, holding back the four winds of the earth, so that the wind would not blow upon the earth or upon the sea or on any tree. [2]And I saw another angel ascending from the rising of the sun, having the seal of the living God, and he cried with a loud voice to the four angels to whom was given to harm the earth and the sea, [3]saying: "Do not harm the earth or the sea or the trees until we have sealed the servants of our God upon their foreheads." [4]And I heard the number of those who have been*

> sealed, 144,000 sealed from every tribe of the sons of Israel:
> 5from the tribe of Judah 12,000 sealed,
> from the tribe of Reuben 12,000,
> from the tribe of Gad 12,000,
> 6from the tribe of Asher 12,000,
> from the tribe of Naphtali 12,000,
> from the tribe of Manasseh 12,000,
> 7from the tribe of Simeon 12,000,
> from the tribe of Levi 12,000,
> from the tribe of Issachar 12,000,
> 8from the tribe of Zebulun 12,000,
> from the tribe of Joseph 12,000,
> from the tribe of Benjamin 12,000 sealed.

NOTES

7:1 *The four corners of the earth.* This phrase was used in the ancient Near East much as we use "the four points of the compass"[1] today to describe the global significance of an event. Thus Isaiah speaks of gathering the outcasts of Israel and of those dispersed from Judah from the four corners of the earth (Isa. 11:12). Ezekiel envisioned the end coming upon the four corners of the earth (Ezek. 7:2). The four corners in Revelation 7:1 evidently correspond to the four winds subsequently mentioned.

Four winds. Winds in the Old Testament symbolize the destructive forces that are the agents of God. The winds are God's chariots (Jer. 4:13). God comes with his chariots like a whirlwind to execute judgment (Isa. 66:15–16). Jeremiah announced the coming judgment against Jerusalem as "a scorching wind from the bare heights in the wilderness" (Jer. 4:11–12; cf. 23:19–20; 51:1–2). The wind of the Lord went forth in fury falling down on the head of the wicked (Jer. 23:19; 30:23). Hosea spoke of the wind of the Lord coming from the wilderness and destroying the fertility of the land (Hos. 13:15). Daniel saw in vision the four winds of heaven stirring up the great sea from which the four beasts were emerging (Dan. 7:2; cf. 8:8; 11:4). God told Jeremiah that he would send his four winds upon Elam and scatter the people (Jer. 49:36). In Zechariah 6:5–7, the four horses are interpreted as the "four spirits [winds] of heaven"; this might suggest that the four winds of Revelation 7:1 are "another way of referring to the four horsemen of chap. 6."[2] The following statement from the apocryphal book Ecclesiaticus (or Sirach) sheds some light on the figurative meaning of the wind with reference to divine judgment in the Jewish mind: "There are winds that have been created for vengeance and in their anger they scourge heavily; in the time of consummation they will pour out their strength and calm the anger of their Maker."[3]

7:2 *From the rising of the sun.* In the ancient Near East, this phrase was a way of designating the east. In the Old Testament, the east is often used with reference to God. Eden was in the east

(Gen. 2:8). In Ezekiel, it was from the east that the glory of God came to the temple (Ezek. 43:2). In the New Testament, the east is always associated with Christ. The magi saw the star in the east announcing the newborn King (Matt. 2:2, 9). Jesus is called the sunrise (Luke 1:78) and the morning star (Rev. 22:16). Jesus spoke of the sign of the Son of Man appearing in the east (Matt. 24:27–30). Thus "another angel ascending from the rising of the sun" in 7:2 is likely one commissioned by Christ, or it is quite possible that he might be Christ himself.

7:3 ***Until we have sealed the servants of our God upon their foreheads.*** This scene is drawn from Ezekiel 9 which portrays in symbolic language the scene of the destruction of Jerusalem before the Exile. The prophet saw in the vision a heavenly messenger whom he described as "a man clothed in linen with a writing case at his loins." He had been instructed to go through the city and mark the foreheads of those who were faithful, before the slaughter of the inhabitants of Jerusalem was to begin. The executioners were told that none so marked should be touched. The sign on the foreheads distinguished those who were God's own faithful people from others who were unfaithful and idolatrous, providing them with protection from the coming judgment (Ezek. 9:1–11).

The basic ancient idea of sealing is ownership. When anything was sealed, such as a document, it was either for the sake of ratification or the protection of its contents (see *Notes* on Rev. 5:1). This sealing of people in the New Testament denotes identification of those who are God's faithful people. Sealing is something that takes place when a person comes to Christ. Being sealed by the seal of the Holy Spirit is the sign of a genuine Christian who belongs to God and the sign of assurance of salvation. "In him, you also," Paul explains, "after listening to the message of truth, the gospel of your salvation—having also believed, you were sealed in Him with the Holy Spirit of promise, who is given as a pledge of our inheritance, with a view to the redemption of God's own possession, to the praise of His glory" (Eph. 1:13–14; cf. 2 Cor. 1:21–22). "Do not grieve the Holy Spirit of God by whom you were sealed for the day of redemption" (Eph. 4:30). Genuine Christians are the ones whom God recognizes as his own people. This is made clear by Paul: "The firm foundation of God stands, having this seal, 'The Lord knows those who are His,' and: 'Let everyone who names the name of the Lord abstain from wickedness'" (2 Tim. 2:19). Thus the faithful people in Revelation are referred to as being "sealed" (9:4; 14:1; 22:4) because they belong to God as his possession. The seal of God consists of the name of God written upon the foreheads: "I saw, and behold, the Lamb standing on Mount Zion, and with him 144,000 having his name and the name of his Father written on their foreheads" (Rev. 14:1). "They will behold his face, and his name will be on their foreheads" (Rev. 22:4; cf. 3:12).

Jon Paulien notes: "Revelation 7:1–3 does not explicitly limit the sealing to the end-time; it merely focuses on the significance of sealing work in an end-time setting."[4] Revelation 9:4 clearly confirms this assumption. At the time of the final crisis of this world's history, the sealing will take on an additional meaning as a sign of protection, just as in Ezekiel's vision where those marked were protected during the judgment befalling Jerusalem (9:1–7). The following text from the Dead Sea Scrolls indicates that some Jewish groups anticipated the eschatological recurrence of Ezekiel's vision: "But all the rest will be handed over to the sword when the Messiah of Aaron and of Israel comes, just as it happened during the time of the first punishment, as Ezekiel said, 'Make a mark on the foreheads of those who moan and lament' (Ezek. 9:4), but the rest were given to the sword that makes retaliation for covenant violations. And such is the verdict on all members of the covenant who do not hold firm to these laws; they are condemned to destruction by Belial."[5]

The eschatological sealing as a sign of protection parallels also the mark on "the door of the house with the blood of the paschal lamb designed to protect the Israelites from the Exodus plagues, which initiated the liberation of Israel" (Exod. 12:21–23).[6] It is the final ratification of God's people to stand for God in the final crisis. Being sealed, God's people are under the special protection of the Holy Spirit from the destructive forces of the seven last plagues. This is exactly what Jesus meant when he promised to protect the Philadelphians "from the hour of trial that is about to come on those who dwell on the earth" (Rev. 3:10).

While in Revelation God's faithful people are sealed (Rev. 9:4; 14:1; 22:4), those who are opposed to God and the gospel are described as being marked with the name of the beast. As such, they are the property of the beast (13:16–17; 14:9; 16:2; 19:20; 20:4). While the seal of God consists of the name of God upon the foreheads, the mark of the beast consists of the name of the beast upon the forehead or hand (Rev. 13:17). "The reception of the mark of the beast and the seal of God, consisting of the names of the beast and of God, denotes conformity to the character of Satan or God. In the final conflict everyone will bear the image of the demonic or the divine."[7] (On the seal as litmus test in the final crisis, see *Notes* on Revelation 13:16.)

7:4 *I heard the number.* This phrase appears here and in 9:16. While here John learns the number of God's sealed people, in 9:16 he is told that the opponents of God number two hundred million. Both numbers must, of course, be taken symbolically.

144,000. This number is evidently made up of twelve multiplied by twelve and subsequently multiplied by 1,000. Twelve is the number of the tribes of Old Testament Israel; it is also the number of the church built upon the foundation of the twelve apostles (cf. Eph. 2:20). In the New Jerusalem, the twelve gates are named after the twelve tribes of Israel and its twelve foundations have the names of the twelve apostles, thus representing both Old and New Testament Israel. Thus 144 (12 x 12) stands for the totality of Israel, that is to say, the entirety of God's people from both the Old and the New Testament times.

The number 1,000 (Heb. *'eleph*) may have different meanings in the Old Testament. It can be a literal number of exactly 1,000. But it can also denote a tribal subdivision (Num. 31:5; Josh. 22:14, 21; 1 Sam. 10:19; 23:23; Mic. 5:2) or a military unit of about 1,000 soldiers. Israel as a nation was administratively organized into tribal units. In the time of war, however, its army was organized into military units of 1,000 with its subunits (Num. 1:16; 10:4; 31:4–6; 1 Sam. 8:12; 18:13; cf. Exod. 18:21, 25; 1 Sam. 22:7). One thousand was thus a basic military unit in ancient Israel. The phrase "thousands of Israel" is used as a synonym for Israel's army and has the same connotation as "the battalions of Israel."[8] The sealed 144,000 is made up of 144 military units, twelve from each tribe, signifying a totality of Israel with her twelve tribes.[9] John uses battle imagery portraying "the church in its aspect of earthly struggle, the 'church militant.'"[10] Since the 144,000 are about to pass through the great tribulation, it is natural and very appropriate to understand the sealed saints of chapter 7 in terms of a military army organized into the units modeled after ancient Israel's military system.

From every tribe of the sons of Israel. One understanding is that the literal Israel is meant here. Another holds that Israel here refers symbolically to the church as spiritual Israel. The problem with the former view is that the twelve tribes no longer exist. Northern Israel, which was made up of ten tribes, disappeared from history with the Assyrian conquest in the eighth century B.C. (2 Kings 17:5–23). Most of the people belonging to those ten tribes were deported from Palestine and scattered among the nations in the Middle East. In the course of history, they became assimilated into those nations (cf. 2 Kings 17:24–41) or amalgamated among themselves. Thus, since at the time of John only two tribes were still in existence, the twelve tribes no longer represent "a historical but only a theological entity."[11]

Furthermore, the list of the twelve tribes in Revelation 7 differs from any list in the Old Testament:

REVELATION 7	GENESIS 49	NUMBERS 1:5–15	EZEKIEL 48
Judah	Reuben	Reuben	Dan
Reuben	Simeon	Simeon	Asher
Gad	Levi	Judah	Naphtali
Asher	Judah	Issachar	Manasseh
Naphtali	Zebulun	Zebulun	Ephraim
Manasseh	Issachar	Ephraim	Reuben
Simeon	Dan	Manasseh	Judah
Levi	Gad	Benjamin	Benjamin
Issachar	Asher	Dan	Simeon
Zebulun	Naphtali	Asher	Issachar
Joseph	Joseph	Gad	Zebulun
Benjamin	Benjamin	Naphtali	Gad

The list of parallels in the order of the tribes is different—Judah comes first as opposed to Reuben, the eldest son of Jacob. As Douglas Ezell observes: "Judah is never listed first in any of the Old Testament tribal listings (Gen. 49; Ezek. 48). This displacement is easily explained when it is remembered that the Lamb, the Messiah, came from the tribe of Judah (Rev. 5:5–6). He is the head of this expanded circle of the people of God."[12]

Dan and Ephraim are omitted, and the tribes of Joseph and Levi are included, even though the Old Testament does not mention a tribe of Joseph. In reality, Joseph, as the favorite son of Jacob, received a double portion in such a way that his two sons Manasseh and Ephraim became the heads of the tribes. Israel actually had thirteen rather than twelve tribes. The thirteenth was the tribe of Levi, the priestly tribe, which never received the inheritance. The tribes of Dan and Ephraim in the Old Testament are described as apostate. In his deathbed speech to his sons, Jacob spoke of Dan as "a serpent in the way, a viper by the path, that bites the horse's heels, so that his rider falls backward" (Gen. 49:17). In the tribal stage of Israel's history, the tribe of Dan set for themselves a graven image (Judg. 18:27–31). During the time of divided monarchy, Dan became one of the centers of idolatrous worship that competed with the Temple in Jerusalem (1 Kings 12:29–30; 2 Kings 10:29). An interesting reference to Dan is found in Jeremiah: "From Dan is heard the snorting of his horses; and at the sound of the neighing of his stallions the whole land quakes; for they come and devour the land and its fullness" (Jer. 8:16). These texts were understood by later Jewish rabbis to refer to the Antichrist which would come from the tribe of Dan.

In the same way, Ephraim became for the prophets a symbol of Israel's apostasy and idolatry (Hos. 4:17; 8:9–11; 12:1; cf. 2 Chron. 30:1, 10). The Psalmist described Ephraim as "archers equipped with bows, yet they turned back in the day of battle; they did not keep the covenant of God" (Ps. 78:9–10). At the time of Isaiah, Ephraim confederated with Syria against Judah (Isa. 7:2–9), thus siding with the enemies of God's people. It is most likely that, because of the tradition, John omitted Dan, as well as Ephraim, from the list of the tribes, and included the tribe of Levi which was not counted among the twelve tribes in the Old Testament. It seems clear, then, that John had the church in view, not literal Israel. In the New Testament, the Christian church is the new and true Israel of God (cf. Rom. 2:28–29; 9:6–8; Gal. 3:29; 6:16; James 1:1) and the recipient of all the privileges and promises previously given to Old Testament Israel.

EXPOSITION

7:1 Further in the vision, John sees *four angels standing at the four corners of the earth, holding back the four winds of the earth.* This "holding" by the four angels might contrast to the "calling out" of the four horsemen of chapter 6. The fact that the four living beings call for the four horses to come forth suggests that the four angels holding the four winds may be the four living creatures who are, as we saw earlier, the exalted angels (Rev. 4:6–7).

These angels are evidently God's agents assigned to restrain the destructive forces, which are symbolized in terms of the four winds, from destroying the earth, the sea, or any tree. The earth and the sea denote universality. In chapter 10, we find the mighty angel standing on the sea and on the earth (10:5). Woe to the earth and the sea because Satan has come down to them (12:12). God is the creator of the heaven, the earth, and the sea (14:7). In chapter 7, the earth and the sea apparently have a negative symbolism. It is particularly interesting that the earth and the sea are the localities from which the two beasts of Revelation 13 come. The trees here symbolize life on the earth. So we find in this text the impending end-time disasters and events to come upon the earth, which are universal in nature.

7:2–3 John sees further *another angel ascending from the rising of the sun, having the seal of the living God.* This angel coming from the east is in ultimate control. The concept of "the rising of the sun" found elsewhere in the New Testament is associated with Christ. The fact that this angel commands the four angels of the higher rank, presumably cherubim, suggests that he is the commander of the heavenly hosts; in the book of Revelation the commander of the heavenly angels is Michael (12:7), and Michael is evidently Jesus Christ. There is no doubt that in the appearance of this angel we have the presence of Jesus himself.

This angel commands the four exalted angels not to loose those destructive forces *until we have sealed the servants of our God upon their foreheads.* Several things can be observed here. First of all, Christ is presented as the One who is in full charge and control of the timing of the last events. He will not allow the final events to move into action until God's people are sealed.

Second, before the end-time great tribulation comes, God's faithful people are to be sealed on their foreheads in order to be protected. The primary purpose of the sealing of God's people is to give them the assurance of salvation. In receiving Christ and surrendering to him, a person receives the seal of God's ownership and is sealed by the Holy Spirit (2 Cor. 1:21–22; Eph. 1:13–14; 4:30). The presence of the Holy Spirit is the sign that such a person belongs to God as his own possession. Paul summarizes the seal of God in these words: "God knows his own" (2 Tim. 2:19). The sealing corresponds evidently to the washing of the robes, making them white in the blood of the Lamb (Rev. 7:14; 22:14). The sealing is, thus, the symbolic sign of a real or genuine Christian. Sealing is what distinguishes such a person from others. Ezell states: "Thus, from John's day to the end, God's sealing of His own through the offer of the gospel continues for the whole period from the cross and resurrection until the end. Those who have the seal of God upon their foreheads (Rev. 7:3) will be able to stand on the great day of wrath."[13]

In the final crisis of this world's history, the sealing will gain an additional meaning and significance: it is a final ratification of God's people to stand for God in the final crisis. Beatrice S. Neall notes:

The seal of God is intended to protect the saints from demonic powers who torture men so that they seek death rather than life (Rev. 9:4–6). Also the saints are protected from the seven last plagues, which fall only upon the beast-worshipers (16:2). The seal, then, protects the saints from defeat by the enemy and the judgments of God. It does not protect them from the wrath of the beast (13:15, 17). Similarly, the mark of the beast protects its followers from the persecution of the beast, but not from the wrath of God (14:9–11).[14]

In the same vein, Hans K. LaRondelle explains:

> God's servants are already in possession of the spiritual seal of the Holy Spirit received in their baptism into Christ. They are therefore "in Christ." But only *after* God's end-time servants have been tested concerning the mark of the beast and found to be loyal unto death will they receive from His angels the unique apocalyptic "seal" as the mark of divine approval and shield against the forces of death and destruction.[15]

As the end draws near, God's faithful remnant must proclaim the final gospel message to the world. After that, they must pass through the final events of this world's history, referred to as "the great tribulation." During that time of crisis, they will need the special protection of the Holy Spirit. It is then that they will experience the fulfillment of Christ's promise given to the Philadelphians: "Because you have kept the word of my endurance, I will also keep you from the hour of trial that is about to come on those who dwell on the earth" (Rev. 3:10). Just as all Israelites having the doors of their house marked with the blood of the paschal lamb were protected from the Exodus plagues (Exod. 12:21–23), and as the marked faithful in Ezekiel's vision were protected during the judgment befalling Jerusalem (9:1–11), so the Holy Spirit will provide a special protection for Christians in the eschatological hour of trial.

Revelation 7 clearly indicates that God's people are sealed not in order to be exempt from that hour of trial—they evidently suffer hunger, thirst, and the scorching heat of the fourth plague (Rev. 7:16; cf. 16:8–9)—but to be brought safely through it (cf. Rev. 7:14). Whatever this sealing is, it is evidently a process through which every Christian must pass, and which reaches a climax and a new significance just before the Second Coming. The sealing of Revelation 7 should be understood as the final closing of the sealing process on the earth, when the preaching of the gospel will come to its close and grace will be available no longer.

Finally, the text suggests that until that hour of trial comes, the wicked are partially protected alongside the righteous. Because the wicked persecute God's faithful people, they experience the judgments of the seven trumpets as the foretaste of the final destruction. The preliminary judgments of the blowing of the seven trumpets, however, are partial and incomplete. But when the hour of the great trial comes and the people of God are fully sealed and identified as his own, and as such protected, the restraining angels will release the destructive forces of the final plagues (Rev. 16). Then the wicked will experience the full force, severity, and universality of the final disasters which will fall upon the earth. As Peter declared: "The Lord knows how to rescue the godly from temptation, and to keep the unrighteous under punishment for the day of judgment" (2 Pet. 2:9).

7:4–8 John hears that the number of God's sealed people is *144,000 sealed from every tribe of the sons of Israel.* Both the number and Israel must be understood symbolically with reference to the church as the true Israel of God. In the New Testament, the followers of Christ constitute the new Israel as the people of God. For instance, when James sent greetings "to the twelve tribes who are dispersed abroad" (James 1:1), he had the church in mind. Paul called the Christians in Galatia "the Israel of God" (Gal. 6:16) who are Abraham's seed and the heirs of the promises of God (Gal. 3:29). In another place, he explained that "they are not all Israel who are descended from Israel" (Rom. 9:6–8). This agrees with the words of Jesus who made it clear that the twelve apostles have replaced the twelve tribes of Israel (Matt. 19:28). In describing God's end-time people in terms of Old Testament Israel, John was thus in agreement with the general New Testament concept according to which the followers of Jesus Christ are the true Israel of God, the recipients of all the privileges and promises which were formerly given to the Israel of old.

The symbolic description of the sealed saints as being 144,000—12,000 from each tribe—is especially important for the correct identification of this group as well as the group which is later referred to as a great multitude (7:9). The context shows that the 144,000 must be taken as a symbolic rather than a literal number. The number here "does not denote a numerical limitation of those who are sealed," but rather their "final perfection."[16] God's sealed people are now standing on the threshold of the great tribulation that is about to come on the inhabitants of the earth (Rev. 3:10). They are about to engage in the greatest of all battles in the history of this planet. It is quite appropriate to expect that John would portray them as the great army of Jesus Christ organized into military units after the model of ancient Israel's army in the time of war (cf. Num. 1:16; 31:3–7). Each tribe here has twelve military units consisting of 1,000 soldiers, a total of 144 units.

The 144,000 sealed saints are portrayed here as an organized army under the leadership of Jesus Christ. Their number stands for the totality of Israel ready to enter the battle of the great day of God Almighty against Satan and his army. Later in the vision, John sees another army, the opponents of God and enemies of his people, who are ready for the battle, and he hears their number which is two hundred million (9:16).

The number 144,000 designates symbolically the end-time true and faithful followers of Jesus Christ as the Israel of God. The tribes of Dan and Ephraim are excluded from the list. In the Old Testament both tribes are described as apostate. This suggests that the unfaithfulness of these two tribes may account for their exclusion from the list of tribes of the eschatological Israel. The 144,000 are the true Israel, pure and without spot (Rev. 14:1–5). They "have washed their robes and made them white in the blood of the Lamb" (7:14). They are later described as those "who have not been defiled with women, for they are virgins. They are the followers of the Lamb wherever he goes. They were redeemed from men as firstfruits to God and to the Lamb, and in their mouth a lie was not found; they are blameless" (14:4–5). The unfaithfulness and apostasy demonstrated by the tribes of Dan and Ephraim have no place among God's faithful people who are to pass through the time of the great tribulation. They are sealed and thus protected by God. Only Christ's victorious people will stand that day in the presence of God's throne (as the fulfillment of the promise given in Rev. 3:21) and receive their eternal inheritance (Rev. 7:14–17).

The 144,000 are the end-time saints—the representatives of all of God's faithful people through the centuries. The final crisis through which they are to pass is symbolic of what God's people have experienced since the death of Abel.

THE GREAT MULTITUDE (7:9–17)

The first part of Revelation 7 responded to the question with regard to those who would be able to stand the wrath of God and the Lamb; the following section points to those who have passed through the great tribulation and participate in eschatological salvation.

⁹*After these things I looked, and behold, a great multitude which no one could count, from every nation and tribe and people and tongue, standing before the throne and before the Lamb, clothed in white robes and palm branches in their hands.* ¹⁰*And they were crying with a loud voice saying:*

"Salvation to our God sitting on the throne and to the
  Lamb."

¹¹*And all the angels were standing around the throne and the elders and the living beings, and they fell on their faces before the throne and worshiped God,* ¹²*saying:*

"Amen! Blessing and glory and wisdom and thanksgiving
  and honor and power and might to our God forever and
  ever. Amen!"

¹³*And one of the elders answered and said to me: "These clothed in the white robes, who are they and from where have they come?"* ¹⁴*And I said to him: "My Lord, you know." And he said to me: "These are the ones coming out of the great tribulation, and they have washed their robes and made them white in the blood of the Lamb.*

¹⁵*Therefore, they are before the throne of God,*
  and serve him in worship day and night
   in his temple,
 and the One sitting on the throne will tabernacle
  over them.
¹⁶*They will not hunger anymore nor thirst anymore*
  nor will the sun fall upon them nor any heat,
¹⁷*because the Lamb who is in the midst of the throne*
  will shepherd them
  and lead them to springs of the water of life;
 and God will wipe away every tear from their eyes."

NOTES

7:9 *I looked, and behold, a great multitude which no one could count.* On the surface, this group is distinct from the 144,000 previously mentioned. While the first group is numbered and consists of the twelve symbolic tribes of Israel, of the second it is said that nobody can count the throng, and it consists of the redeemed from "every nation and tribe and people and tongue." The evidence, however, suggests that the 144,000 and the great multitude are one and the same group.

This view is based on the fact that John uses a special literary technique that comes into play here. According to this literary technique, what John first *hears* in the vision and what he subsequently *sees* is actually one and the same thing. What he sees is actually the further explanation of what he heard before. For instance, in the prologue of the book, John hears "a loud voice as of a trumpet" behind him (1:10); when he turns around, he does not see a trumpet but Jesus walking in the midst of the seven lampstands (1:12–13). In chapter 5, he hears that the Lion from the tribe of Judah has overcome; when he turns to see the lion, he sees the Lamb as having been slain (5:5–6). Later in chapter 17, he hears of "the great prostitute sitting on many waters"; what he later sees is "a woman sitting on a scarlet beast" whose name is Babylon (17:1–5). In the last vision, John first hears of "the bride, the wife of the Lamb," but he actually sees "the holy city Jerusalem" in its glory symbolized by precious stones (21:9–12).

This literary technique is the clue for understanding these two groups of God's people in chapter 7. John first hears the number of 144,000 as God's embattled, sealed people on the earth. Then, in 7:9–14, when he sees this same group, they appear to him in actual fact as a great multitude that no one can number. We concur with those scholars who rightly conclude that the 144,000 and the great multitude are the same group of God's people in their different roles and circumstances.[17]

Herman Hoeksema explained that

> the numberless throng and the 144,000 are not a different class of people, but principally the same. This is shown in the first place, by the fact that the great tribulation is one of the main ideas in both passages, that which speaks of the 144,000 and that which is now under discussion. In fact, both passages find their reason, the reason why they are revealed, in the coming of that great tribulation upon the church. The purpose of both passages evidently is to reveal to the church their precarious position in the world, and nevertheless their safety over against that great tribulation. The only difference is that the 144,000 still confront that tribulation, while the numberless throng have already passed through it. It is very evident that it is the same throng: the one pictured as in the midst of the great tribulation, or rather, as standing on the verge of passing through it, and the other pictured as already having experienced it and having overcome. It is, therefore, the same multitude, only in different states, at different periods, and therefore from different points of view. In the first part they are upon the earth; in the second part they are already in glory in the new economy of the kingdom which is completed. In the first they are in tribulation; in the second they have already passed through that tribulation.[18]

Palm branches in their hands. Palm branches are a symbol of triumph and victory. When, under the leadership of the Maccabees, Jerusalem was freed from the religious oppression of Antiochus Epiphanes, the people celebrated the victory with palm branches and harps and psalms.[19] At the time of Jesus' triumphant entry into Jerusalem, the crowd greeted him waving palm branches (John 12:13). Here in Revelation 7, the redeemed are portrayed as celebrating the victory by waving palm branches.

7:14 *The great tribulation.* This phrase is first used in Daniel 12:1: "And there will be a time of distress [in the Greek Old Testament, "tribulation"] such as never occurred since there was a nation until that time; and at that time your people, everyone who is found written in the book, will be rescued." It is probably the same time of crisis from which Christ promised to preserve the Philadelphians: "Because you have kept the word of my endurance, I will also keep you from the hour of trial that is about to come on those who dwell on the earth" (Rev. 3:10). This hour of trial or the great tribulation is described in detail in Revelation 13:11–17, and in chapters 15–18.

EXPOSITION

7:9–14 In the first half of the chapter, John heard the number of 144,000 as God's sealed people. When he turns around to see them, he actually sees *a great multitude which no one could count.* On the surface, the great multitude and the 144,000 appear to be two distinct groups. A closer look, however, suggests that they are one and the same group of God's redeemed people in different roles, circumstances, and periods, and from different points of view. Hoeksema says: "In the first part they are upon the earth; in the second part they are already in glory in the new economy of the kingdom which is completed. In the first they are in tribulation; in the second they are already passed through that tribulation."[20] They are not in need of the protection of the divine sealing any longer.[21]

In viewing the multitude, the revelator notes that they are from *every nation and tribe and people and tongue.* This brings to mind the "kingdom of priests" described earlier as the people from every nation, tribe, people, and tongue (Rev. 1:6; 5:9). As that title was drawn from the Old Testament and transferred to those in Christ, so this numbering of the tribes is a symbolic description of the followers of Christ. Here we have the completion of God's servants mentioned in the scene of the opening of the fifth seal (6:11).

We can see that the 144,000 standing on the threshold of what is known as "the great tribulation" (7:14) or "the hour of trial" (3:10) are ready to engage in the greatest war in the history of humankind. In the breaking of the seven seals, John depicts the trials and tribulation of God's faithful people throughout history until the return of Christ to this earth. The great tribulation through which God's end-time people have to pass is the climax of the trials and tribulations that God's people have endured from John's day through to the end. The 144,000 are therefore portrayed as the militant people of God, the true Israel divided into the twelve tribes and organized into military units patterned after Old Testament Israel's army. They are sealed for the purpose of being protected from the righteous judgments of God that are about to fall on the wicked.

The great tribulation itself is portrayed not in Revelation 7 but later in Revelation 13:11–17 and chapters 15–18. John is interested here not in the tribulation itself but rather in the question raised earlier by the wicked: "The great day of his wrath has come, and who is able to stand?" (Rev. 6:17). The answer to the question is clear: the great multitude standing before the throne of God. They and the 144,000 are the same group. While earlier portrayed as the militant group standing on the threshold of the great tribulation, ready to wage war, now they are referred to as *the ones coming out of the great tribulation* (Rev. 7:14). The great tribulation is behind, and the battle is over. That is why God's faithful people are no longer organized into military units, but are portrayed as a rejoicing crowd returning from the battle and celebrating the triumphant victory.

The great multitude is seen clothed in *white robes and palm branches in their hands.* Both the white robes and the palm branches are signs of triumph and victory. The white robes remind one of Roman generals and soldiers clothed in white robes celebrating their triumphs after a successful war.[22] The scene also reminds us of the palm branches used for festive joy and celebration of military victory. Here we have the fulfillment of the promise given to the overcomers in Sardis that they would walk before Christ clothed in white garments (3:4–5; cf. 3:18). The great multitude is said to *have washed their robes and made them white in the blood of the Lamb* (7:14). As the blood of the paschal lamb on the door of the house protected the Israelites from the Exodus plagues, just before they were delivered from the Egyptians, so the blood of the Lamb, Christ himself, provides the deliverance of the eschatological Israel (cf. Rev. 22:14). Their triumph is a result of Christ's great victory achieved on the cross. The great promise given in Revelation 3:21 has now come to its realization. The overcomers from all ages have their share with Christ on his throne.

The shout of the redeemed crowd before the throne reveals that their triumph is not a result of their own efforts and achievement: *Salvation to our God sitting on the throne and to the Lamb.* The redeemed multitude say nothing about their own achievement. It is God who protected and preserved them through the hours of their trials and distresses. Their victory is, therefore, the result of what Christ has done for them rather than what they have achieved for themselves. William Barclay puts it in the following way:

The shout of the triumphant faithful ascribes salvation to God. It is God who has brought them through their trials and tribulations and distresses; and it is his glory which now they share. God is the great savior, the great deliverer of his people. And the deliverance which he gives is not the deliverance of escape but the deliverance of conquest. It is not a deliverance which saves a man from trouble but one which brings him triumphantly through trouble. It does not make life easy, but it makes life great. It is not part of the Christian hope to look for a life in which a man is saved from all trouble and distress; the Christian hope is that a man in Christ can endure any kind of trouble and distress, and remain erect all through them, and come out to glory on the other side.[23]

In Revelation 7:10–12 we have a replay of the hymn of Revelation 5:9–14. Its purpose may be to show that in Revelation 7 we have the fulfillment of the promise given in 3:21.[24] Because of his death on the cross, Christ "purchased for God" with his blood "from every tribe and tongue and people and nation," and made them "a kingdom and priests to our God, and they shall reign over the earth" (5:9–10). The redeemed in Revelation 7, "from every nation and tribe and people and tongue," recognize that their salvation is not their merit but a result of what Christ has done for them (7:9–10).

The scene of Revelation 7 refers to the experience of God's people throughout the history of the great controversy between good and evil. The sealed 144,000 and the great multitude of God's people clothed in the white robes, having passed through the great tribulation, relate in a special way to the martyrs underneath the altar in the scene of the opening of the fifth seal. These martyrs clothed in white garments were told to rest for a little while until their fellow brothers who were about to be killed might be made complete (6:11). The 144,000 and the great multitude portray God's oppressed and persecuted people who are now ultimately made complete.

7:15–17 In these three verses John summarizes what he describes later in chapters 21–22. We have here the first glimpse into the glorious reward of the redeemed. They ***are before the throne of God, and serve him in worship day and night in his temple.*** In the final scenes of earth's history, while in fear of the judgment the unrepentant seek to hide "from the face of the One sitting on the throne and from the wrath of the Lamb" (Rev. 6:16), the redeemed are seen standing "before the throne and before the Lamb" (Rev. 7:9). This portrayal of the redeemed before the throne of God attending him in his temple calls to mind Revelation 1:6 and 5:10, where the redeemed are referred to as kings and priests to God. It also reminds us of Revelation

20:6 where they are portrayed in their role as priests reigning with Christ in the heavenly kingdom after the Second Coming. In Revelation 7:15, they serve God in his temple, which evidently functions as the governing center of the entire universe. The redeemed here seem to be members of God's council in heaven, participating in the governmental affairs of the universe.

And the One sitting on the throne will tabernacle over them. (The New International Version translates the text by saying that God "will spread his tent over them.") The idea here is that God will spread the tent of his presence over his people. This calls to mind the presence of God among the people of Israel in the wilderness, when he tabernacled among them in the appearance of the pillar of cloud and the pillar of fire. The presence of God in the midst of ancient Israel provided them with supreme shelter from the scorching heat and storm, and from hunger and thirst. God spoke through Ezekiel: "My dwelling place also will be with them; and I will be their God, and they will be My people" (Ezek. 37:27). The text also reflects the prophecy of Isaiah concerning the cleansing of the daughters of Zion and the restoration of Mount Zion: "for over all the glory will be a canopy. And there will be a shelter to give shade from the heat by day, and refuge and protection from the storm and the rain" (Isa. 4:2–6). What we have here in Revelation 7 is the ultimate fulfillment of the divine purpose. **They will not hunger anymore nor thirst anymore nor will the sun fall upon them nor any heat.** Isaiah prophesied a few centuries earlier: "They will not hunger or thirst, neither will the scorching heat or sun strike them down; for He who has compassion on them will lead them, and will guide them to springs of water" (Isa. 49:10). Scorching heat, hunger, thirst, and tears are among the trials that characterize the plagues of the great tribulation (cf. Rev. 16). In Revelation 7 God is sheltering his people from spiritual wilderness—the great tribulation. Their wilderness wandering is over.

Because God's presence provides shelter, they will no longer experience the trials of life, no more tears and death, because **God will wipe away every tear from their eyes.** Here comes true what Isaiah anticipated: "He will swallow up death for all time, and the Lord will wipe tears away from all faces, and He will remove the reproach of His people from all the earth; for the Lord has spoken" (Isa. 25:8). At the end of the book John exclaims: "Behold, the tabernacle of God is among men, and he will tabernacle with them, and they will be his peoples, and God himself will be among them, and he will wipe away every tear from their eyes, and there shall no longer be the death, neither sorrow, nor crying, nor pain will be any longer there, for the first things have passed away" (Rev. 21:3–4).

Revelation 7:15 also recalls when Jesus tabernacled in the flesh among people, and when they "beheld His glory" (John 1:14). In his presence was no place for pain, tears, and death. This was what the two sisters, Martha and Mary, understood after their brother Lazarus died: "Lord, if You had been here, my brother would not have died" (John 11:21, 32). The presence of Christ with his people on the new earth is a firm guarantee of a life characterized by freedom from pain, tears, death, or any other trials (cf. Rev. 21:4).

The visible presence of Christ will **shepherd** the redeemed and **lead them to springs of the water of life.** David E. Aune observes that both in the Bible and Greek literature the relationship between a king and his people is likened to a shepherd and his flock (cf. Isa. 44:28; Jer. 3:15; Nah. 3:18).[25] Ezekiel prophesied that God would set over Israel "one shepherd, My servant David, and he will feed them; he will feed them himself and be their shepherd" (34:23). "And My servant David will be king over them, and they will all have one shepherd; and they will walk in My ordinances, and keep My statutes, and observe them" (Ezek. 37:24). This prophecy will be fulfilled with Christ. In the New Testament, he is frequently called the Good Shepherd (Matt. 25:32; John 10:1–16; Heb. 13:20; 1 Pet. 2:25; 5:4). Christ shepherds his people here in Revelation 7:17.

Another prophecy from Isaiah now reaches its fulfillment: "Then my people will live in a peaceful habitation, and in secure dwellings and in undisturbed resting places" (Isa. 32:18). There on the peaceful plains and beside the living streams of the heavenly country, "God's people, so long pilgrims and wanderers, shall find a home."[26]

A RETROSPECT ON REVELATION 7

The obvious purpose of Revelation 7 is "to alert the church to its need to get ready for the final conflict. The winds of strife are about to begin their work of devastation. There is no time for delay. At the same time, the restraining of the winds shows God's mercy in giving his people time to prepare. There is also assurance in the sealing message. The seal itself is the guarantee that the saints are secure. Once they are sealed their characters are inviolable, not subject to change, no matter how severe the temptation. The mathematical perfection and symmetry of the 144,000 indicates that God's plan for His Israel is perfectly realized, in spite of the events that rock the church and the world (6:12–17)."[27]

The book of Revelation does not support the idea that God has two different groups of people on the earth.[28] Elsewhere in the book, John the revelator indicates clearly that he has only one people in mind when he refers to them as God's servants (1:1), the remnant (12:17), the saints (14:12), and the wife of the Lamb (19:7–8; cf. chapter 12).[29] The two groups of the redeemed people of God in chapter 7, namely, the 144,000 and the great multitude, are clearly related. They are the same people seen in two stages of their history and in their different roles. They are first depicted as the church militant standing on the threshold of the great tribulation, sealed in order to be protected from the plagues that are to fall upon the enemies of God and his people.[30] Then, they are portrayed as the church triumphant coming victoriously out from the great tribulation. The war is over and their victory complete. Now they are standing before the throne of God receiving their eternal reward.

The main question that Revelation 7 deals with is not regarding *who* the 144,000 are, but rather *what* they are. They are not a select group of God's people separated from the larger body and granted special privileges not available to the rest of God's faithful people. Neall states: "They are not the first ones to be sealed; saints were sealed in Paul's day. They are not the first to be without guile and blameless. They are not the first to be persecuted, or to follow the Lamb, or to be redeemed from the earth, or to 'sing a new song unto the Lord.' John's eightfold description of the 144,000 found in Revelation 14:1–5 indicates that they share a common heritage with the saints of all ages."[31]

In this way the book of Revelation is in agreement with the overall teaching of the New Testament that in God's kingdom there are no clans, cliques, or ranks; no privileges are available to some and not to others. Revelation 7 does not present the idea that the final generation of God's people would reach "a level of holiness never reached before" by God's people.[32] In God's plan of salvation, everything is due to the grace of God. "For by grace you have been saved through faith; and that not of yourselves, it is the gift of God; not as a result of works, that no one should boast" (Eph. 2:8–9). Salvation is the result of what Christ has accomplished on the cross rather than one's own holiness and works.

God's criterion for salvation has been the same for all generations. John the Revelator makes clear that God's faithful end-time people are those who "have washed their robes and made them white in the blood of the Lamb" (7:14; cf. 12:11). It is Christ's victory on the cross that has made them victorious (12:11); and it is through his protection (7:2–3) that they will triumphantly come out from the great tribulation (7:14). Neall also makes these interesting observations:

> The question regarding a state of sinlessness depends upon whether sin is defined as *act* or *nature*. The last living generation of God's people should certainly be free from sinful acts; however, they do not lose their sinful, corruptible nature until they put on incorruption at the Second Advent (1 Cor. 15:53).
>
> In the book of Revelation the saints are always *conquering* (marked by the present tense in the Greek); only Christ *has conquered* (the aorist tense). Even during the seven last plagues the saints are still *conquering* the beast and its image (15:2, Greek). They still contend with the enemy without and within. Their greatest sin, which they must overcome *during* the tribulation, is lack of faith. Yet they are *conquering*, not being conquered. They are victorious in the struggle with evil. They are perfect in character—they choose only God's will—while they are still conscious of having to overcome their sinful nature. However, they stand sealed and spotless through the merits of the Lamb. (7:14)[33]

At this point, Ellen White warns God's people against being involved in "controversy over questions which will not help them spiritually, such as, Who is to compose the hundred and forty-four thousand? This those who are the elect of God will in a short time know without question."[34] In another place she urges the faithful: "Let us strive with all the power that God has given us to be among the hundred and forty-four thousand."[35]

Whichever view one might have, one lesson must certainly be drawn from the vision of the sealed saints before the throne of Revelation 7. As the vision of the opening of the seven seals shows, the faithful people of God often face unpleasant life experiences and trials for the sake of the gospel. The events of Revelation 6 are triggered by the activity of Christ in heaven. This indicates that heaven and earth are closely linked; nothing happens on earth without the knowledge of the One enthroned in heaven who reigns over the universe. The book of Revelation states clearly that God provides power, protection, and guidelines for those who surrender themselves unreservedly to the One who died for them on the cross of Calvary and who reigns in the heavenly places. Sin can be overcome only through him, who is indeed the true Overcomer.

As God's faithful people are about to pass through the final conflict, they have a firm assurance that God will shelter and comfort them during the time of the great tribulation as he protected and comforted his people throughout history. The future might at times look gloomy. Yet the resurrected Christ is in control. He is the source of strength and hope to the redeemed during their earthly sojourn until he, their Lord and King, comes again and dwells with them forever (Rev. 7:15).

ENDNOTES

1. Johnson, 478.

2. See Mounce, 165, n. 1.

3. Ecclesiasticus 39:28–31 (*The Oxford Annotated Apocrypha*, 180).

4. Paulien, "Seals and Trumpets," 198.

5. 4Q267 19:10b–14 (*The Dead Sea Scrolls*, trans. Michael Wise, Martin Abegg, Jr., and Edward Cook, 58).

6. Fiorenza, *Revelation*, 66; J. M. Ford, 122.

7. Beatrice S. Neall, "Sealed Saints and the Tribulation," in *Symposium on Revelation—Book 1*, Daniel and Revelation Committee, Series 6 (Silver Spring, MD: Biblical Research Institute, 1992), 255.

8. Boring, *Revelation*, 131.

9. For further arguments in support of this view, see Aune, *Revelation 6–16*, 443. Bauckham suggests that the census in Revelation 7 is for military purposes, the assertion that is confirmed, in his view, by the context of the chapter and Revelation 14:3–4, where, as he sees, the 144,000 are exclusively adult males who practice sexual abstinence, an ancient requirement for holy warriors ("The List of the Tribes in Revelation 7 Again," *Journal for the Study of the New Testament* 42 [1991]: 104).

10. Boring, *Revelation*, 131.

11. Fiorenza, *Revelation*, 67. Aune points to the fact that "Josephus, writing at the end of the first century A.D. reckoned with the existence of twelve tribes in his day (*Ant.* 11.133) and that the widespread Jewish eschatological hope of the regathering of the twelve tribes of Israel was certainly based on the assumption of their actual existence in the world" (*Revelation 6–16*, 442).

12. Ezell, 60–61.

13. Ibid., 59.

14. Neall, "Sealed Saints and the Tribulation," 256.

15. Hans K. LaRondelle, *Chariots of Salvation: The Biblical Drama of Armageddon* (Washington, DC: Review and Herald, 1987), 171.

16. Ernst D. Schmitz, "*dōdeka*," *The New International Dictionary of New Testament Theology*, ed. Colin Brown (Grand Rapids: Zondervan, 1978), 2:695.

17. E.g., Charles, 1:201; Swete, 99; Beckwith, 539; Ladd, 116–117; Harrington, 98, 101; Beasley-Murray, 139–141; Giblin, 91–92; Ezell, 59–61.

18. Herman Hoeksema, 267.

19. 1 Mac. 13:51 (*The Oxford Annotated Apocrypha*, 256); 2 Mac. 10:7 (*The Oxford Annotated Apocrypha*, 281).

20. Herman Hoeksema, 267.

21. Swete, 99.

22. Barclay, *The Revelation of John*, 2:26–27.

23. Ibid., 2:27.

24. Paulien, The Bible Explorer, 3.5.

25. Aune, *Revelation 6–16*, 477.

26. Ellen G. White, *The Great Controversy* (Mountain View, CA: Pacific Press, 1911), 675.

27. Neall, "Sealed Saints and the Tribulation," 278.

28. Ibid., 275–278.

29. Ibid.

30. Ladd, 116.

31. Neall, "Sealed Saints and the Tribulation," 276.

32. Ibid.

33. Ibid., 277.

34. Ellen G. White, quoted in *The Seventh-day Adventist Bible Commentary*, 7:978.

35. Ibid., 7:970.

The vision of the seven trumpets is one of the most perplexing subjects in the book of Revelation and in the entire New Testament. Before we examine each of the trumpets in detail, it is necessary to discuss some questions of general matter. What are the seven trumpets all about? What is the nature of the trumpets in the Bible? When is the time of the blowing of the seven trumpets? In order to provide adequate answers, we discuss this question in light of both Old and New Testament concepts of the blowing of trumpets in relation to God's people.

THE NATURE OF THE BLOWING OF THE SEVEN TRUMPETS

In both the Old and New Testaments, the blowing of the trumpet symbolizes "the intervention of God in history."[1] In the Old Testament, the life of ancient Israel was closely connected with the blowing of trumpets. For instance, a trumpet sounding could be the summons to battle (Judg. 3:27; 6:34; Jer. 51:27), an announcement at the coronation of an Israelite king (2 Sam. 15:10; 1 Kings 1:34, 39; 2 Kings 9:13; 11:14), a call for gathering the people (Num. 10:2–7; 1 Sam. 13:3–4; Neh. 4:20; Joel 2:15–16), and a warning of approaching danger (Jer. 4:5, 19–21; 6:1–17; Ezek. 33:3–6; Amos 3:6).

In most cases in the Old Testament, however, trumpets were used in the context of the temple liturgy and holy wars (Lev. 25:9; Num. 10:9–10; Josh. 6:4–20). Used in the religious ritual service, the blowing of the trumpet was also "a part of their [Israel's] organization as the Lord's army on tour of duty"[2] (Num. 31:6; 2 Chron. 13:12–15; 29:26–28; Ezra 3:10). The key Old Testament text for the meaning of the trumpets is Numbers 10:8–10:

> The priestly sons of Aaron, moreover, shall blow the trumpets; and this shall be for you a perpetual statute throughout your generations. When you go to war in your land against the adversary who attacks you, then you shall sound an alarm with the trumpets, that you may be *remembered* before the LORD your God, and be saved from your enemies. Also in the day of your gladness and in your appointed feasts, and on the first days of your months, you shall blow the trumpets over your burnt offerings, and over the sacrifices of your peace offerings; and they shall be as a *reminder* of you before your God. I am the LORD your God. (emphasis supplied)

As this text indicates, trumpets were sacred instruments and were, as a rule, blown by priests to call on God to remember his people. Or, it is better to say that they provided Israel with the assurance that God remembered them when their adversaries attacked them and that he would protect and deliver them. "You shall sound an alarm with the trumpets, that you may be remembered before the Lord your God, and be saved from your enemies" (cf. 2 Chron. 13:14–15; emphasis supplied). Whether seeking forgiveness from sins in the sanctuary or fighting against enemies, the priest blew the trumpets. God then responded by remembering his people, forgiving their sins, and delivering them from their adversaries who have been viciously harassing them. This concept of "remembering" before God is crucial for an understanding of the theological meaning of the seven trumpets in Revelation 8–9.

Trumpet blasts in the Old Testament designated the appearance of God in relation to the most important events in Israel's history. In the giving of the law at Sinai, the Israelites experienced thunder and lightning, a thick cloud on the mountain, and "a very loud trumpet sound" (Exod. 19:16; 20:18). The loud trumpet blast caused the destruction of Jericho (Josh. 6:4–16). This trumpet sound is an integral part of the Day of the Lord concept in the Old Testament. "It will come about also in that day that a great trumpet will be blown" and it will summon the exiles scattered among the nations to worship God in Jerusalem (Isa. 27:13). Trumpet blowing will announce the approaching Day of the Lord (Joel 2:1; Zeph. 1:16). At that day, "the Lord God will blow the trumpet, and will march in the storm winds of the south" (Zech. 9:14).

This concept continues in the New Testament. Apart from Revelation 8–11, trumpets are associated with the end-time appearance and intervention of God. In his sermon on the Mount of Olives, Jesus spoke of the great trumpet sound when God's elect are gathered together (Matt. 24:31). Paul spoke of the day when at the last trumpet sound the corruptible will put on incorruption (1 Cor. 15:51–53). A very loud trumpet blast will accompany the second coming of Jesus (1 Thess. 4:16–17). In the book of Revelation, the trumpet sound is a signal of the appearance of God in the person of Christ (1:10; 4:1).

The vision of the blowing of the seven trumpets of Revelation 8–11 should be understood against these Old and New Testament backgrounds. In other words, the blowing of the seven trumpets is a series of interventions by God in response to the prayers of his people. In order to explain this, it is necessary to bear in mind the scene of the opening of the fifth seal, in which the slain saints underneath the altar plea to God for vengeance and judgment: "How long, O Lord, holy and true, will you not judge and avenge our blood *on those who dwell on the earth*?" (6:10; emphasis supplied). Their prayers are not a longing for revenge but a plea for justice and deliverance.[3] As Revelation 8:2–5 shows, the prayers of the saints are heard by God.

After that, John observes the seven angels standing before God's throne to receive seven trumpets. Their mission is to announce a new series of woes being sent to earth. John sees afterwards another angel take the golden censer with the incense mingled with the prayers of the saints, and the angel fills it with fire from the altar. Then he throws it to the earth, and there followed "thunder and voices and flashes of lightning and an earthquake" (Rev. 8:5). Then, one after another, the seven angels blow their trumpets. God *remembers* the saints. The seven trumpets are evidently God's response to the suffering of his people. God's wrath kindles judgments on those who have been oppressing them. Revelation 8:13 states clearly that the trumpets are for "*those who dwell on the earth*," which links the trumpet judgments to the prayers of the saints in Revelation 6:10. The objects of both texts are clearly "those who dwell on the earth."

The text indicates that even though catastrophic in nature, the seven trumpets are not natural calamities and disasters. They are rather a manifestation of the presence and reality of Almighty God in history. They reveal God's reaction to the injustice and harm being done to his people. As bizarre as they might appear, the seven trumpet plagues are under the control of the One who died on the cross of Calvary and reigns in the heavenly places over the universe. Jesus Christ is the Lord of history, and he is in full control of the powers of this world that viciously oppress his people. As one works through the seven trumpets one by one, he or she can still see and feel the presence of the God of the covenant with his people.

As was shown earlier, the scene of the opening of the seven seals is concerned with the progress of the preaching of the gospel in the world, and with those who reject it. The events triggered by the successive opening of the seven seals affect those who profess to be God's people, but are faithless and disloyal. Regarding the seven trumpet woes, John makes it very clear that they are not directed against humanity in general but only against those "who do not have the seal of God upon their foreheads" (Rev. 9:4) and who are elsewhere in the book referred to as "those who dwell on the earth" (6:10; 8:13; 11:10; 13:8, 14; 17:2). These are the ones who have been hostile to the gospel and have persecuted and oppressed God's faithful people.

Thus, the seven trumpet plagues are concerned exclusively with those who do not have the seal of God on their foreheads. Those who are on God's side are evidently not affected by these trumpet plagues. They may have some share in the suffering of the wicked, because God has promised to deliver *through* the trials rather than *from* them. They have a strong assurance of God's presence with them in the time of trial. The Almighty God hears their prayers and cares for them as he deals with their oppressors.

It is, therefore, very appropriate to conclude that Revelation 8–11 is the portrayal of God's dealing with different movements and forces in history that have viciously persecuted and harmed his people. The judgments symbolically portrayed in the seven trumpet plagues are God's response to the suffering of his saints and their plea: "How long will you not judge and avenge our blood on those who dwell on the earth?" (Rev. 6:10). The message of the blowing of the seven trumpets is clear and unequivocal: "Not too long! God is already judging the enemies of his people." As Revelation 16 indicates, the day is coming when full judgment will be poured out on the wicked, of which the plagues of the seven trumpets are just a foretaste.

The scene of the blowing of the seven trumpets in Revelation 8–11 also has a redemptive aspect. If the series of seven seals designates the ongoing period in which God leads his people through the process of overcoming, then, in the light of chapter 7 and verse 9:4, we may conclude that Revelation 6 portrays the process of sealing that runs throughout the Christian age, from the cross to the Second Coming. The events of the opening of the seals are intended to wake up those who profess to follow Christ and bring them to repentance. We saw earlier that sealing in the New Testament referred to the work of the Holy Spirit on the hearts of people (2 Cor. 1:22; Eph. 1:13; 4:30). His work leads them into relationship with God, who accepted them and recognized them as his own possession (2 Tim. 2:19). That is what the sealing is all about. It is the process through which God helps his people become overcomers of sin. The sealing of Revelation 7 is clearly the final closing of the sealing on the earth,[4] after which the preaching of the gospel will come to its completion and grace will no longer be available.

On the other hand, as we observed above, the seven trumpet woes portray judgments on those who have rejected the gospel and have failed to receive the seal of God on their foreheads. In other words, these people have rejected the transforming power of the Holy Spirit on their hearts and the opportunity to be recognized and accepted by God. They have chosen instead to be enemies of God and oppressors of his people. However, as Leon Morris states, "human wickedness does not go unnoticed in heaven."[5] The wicked experience God's judgments in the seven trumpet plagues, which are in reality the foretaste of the ultimate plagues of Revelation 16 and the final judgment described in Revelation 20.

It would be wrong, however, to regard the trumpet woes as retributive. They rather have a twofold purpose. They are intended to bring people to repentance. At the same time, they are also intended to be "a divine warning that time for repentance is rapidly running out."[6] The wicked still have an opportunity to repent (cf. Rev. 11:13), for intercession still takes place and the door of grace is not yet closed. The sounding trumpets and the subsequent plagues are the preliminary judgments and have redemptive purposes. Each trumpet blast is designed to humble people and drive them to repentance, even though that purpose is not achieved (Rev. 9:20–21). It is the failure to repent which makes the pouring out of the last bowl of plagues inevitable and unavoidable.

THE TIMING OF THE SEVEN TRUMPETS

The next question that deserves our serious attention is with regard to the time of the blowing of the seven trumpets. John clearly shows that the blowing of the seventh trumpet brings us to the Second Coming. According to Revelation 10:7, in "the days of the sound of the seventh angel, when he is about to sound, then the mystery of God will be completed." At the sound of the seventh trumpet, heavenly voices are heard saying: "The kingdom of the world has become the kingdom of our Lord and of his Christ and he will reign forever and ever" (Rev. 11:15).

That the seventh trumpet refers to the time of the end is also clear from Revelation 11:17 where God is referred to as the One "who is and who was, because you have taken your great power and begun to reign." Earlier in the book he is designated as "the One who is and who was and who is coming" (1:8; 4:8). In 11:17 he is no longer the God "who is coming," because he has already come and has realized his kingdom. This indicates clearly that the conclusion of the blowing of the seven trumpets brings us to the very end of history, just as the conclusion of the seven seals does.

When then does the blowing of the seven trumpets begin? The clue lies evidently in the introductory section of the scene of the blowing of the seven trumpets (8:2–5).[7] John first observes seven angels with the seven trumpets commissioned to herald a new series of woes to be sent upon the inhabitants of the earth. Afterwards he sees another, unspecified angel with a golden incense censor standing at the altar. This is undoubtedly the altar of burnt offering which was located outside the Hebrew temple. The angel is given much incense to offer upon the altar of incense before the throne with the prayer of the saints. After receiving it, he administers the incense.

This introductory scene is built on a special service in the Hebrew temple—the daily sacrifice known as *tamid,* as portrayed in the *Tamid* tractate of the *Mishnah.*[8] In the *tamid* evening service, the end of the daily sacrifice was announced by the blowing of trumpets. After the sacrificial lamb had been placed upon the altar of burnt offering and the blood of the sacrifice poured out at the base of the altar, the assigned priest would have taken the golden incense censor inside the temple and offered incense upon the golden altar in the holy place. During the time that he was in the holy place, the people in the court were waiting quietly in prayer. At the moment the priest came out to bless the people, the seven priests blew their trumpets, marking the end of the daily sacrifice ceremony. The first-century readers of Revelation were well familiar with this Old Testament ritual practice.

This opening scene of Revelation 8:2–5 helps us to locate in time the scene of the blowing of the seven trumpets of Revelation 8–11. The seven trumpet blasts clearly follow Jesus' sacrificial death on the cross. The cross is the central theme of Revelation 5, where Jesus is portrayed as the slain sacrificial Lamb worthy to take the sealed book. The blowing of the seven trumpets signifies that the sacrifice has been made once for all. In the cross there is the offer of both grace and judgment. Grace is for those who believe; these are saved and are already with Christ in the heavenly places.

But for those who reject and oppose the gospel, judgment has already begun. This concept permeates the entire book of Revelation.

Thus, the scene of the blowing of the seven trumpets begins with the cross, as does the scene of the opening of the seven seals of Revelation 6. The conclusions of both scenes bring us to the time of the end. It is, therefore, reasonable to conclude that both the seven seals and the seven trumpets refer to the same period of history between the cross and the Second Coming. A comparison between the two series confirms such a conclusion:

THE SEVEN SEALS	THE SEVEN TRUMPETS
The four horsemen	The first four trumpets
The fifth and sixth seals	The first and second trumpet woes
The interlude (chapter 7): The sealing of God's people	The interlude (chapters 10–11): the little scroll, the measuring of the temple, and the two witnesses
The seventh seal: silence in heaven before the final judgment	The third trumpet woe (the seventh trumpet): the time has arrived for the judgment and reward to be given to God's servants

This comparison shows significant parallelism. First, both the trumpets and the seals are arranged in groups of four and three; the first four differ from the last three in form and weight. The opening of the first four seals brings on the scene the four horsemen (6:1–8), and the last three trumpets designate the three "woes" (cf. 8:13; 9:12; 11:14). Another point of parallelism is found in the fact that both the seals and the trumpets are interrupted by interludes. Between the opening of the sixth and the seventh seal is inserted the vision of the sealed saints with the purpose of providing the answer to the question of who can stand on the last day (chapter 7). Likewise, between the sixth and the seventh trumpet sound is inserted the vision of the angel with the open scroll, the measuring of the temple, and the witnessing and fate of the two witnesses (chapters 10–11). Thus, Revelation 7 might be the clue for understanding chapters 10–11; while the purpose of chapter 7 is to answer the question raised in 6:17 regarding who will be able to stand in the day of God's wrath, chapters 10–11 seem to provide the answer to the question regarding the task of the church in that troublous period. Finally, both the seventh seal and the seventh trumpet refer to the time before the execution of the final judgment.

Strong textual evidence shows clearly that the scene of the blowing of the seven trumpets concerns the Christian Era rather than the time of the end. First, the introductory sanctuary scene of 8:3–5 indicates that intercession is still in process. Next, the interlude between the sixth and seventh trumpets indicates that the preaching of the gospel is still in progress before the sounding of the seventh trumpet (cf. 10:11; 11:3–14). Also, 9:20–21 indicates that during the sixth trumpet there is still an opportunity for repentance. Finally, 11:19 strongly suggests that the activities in the Holy of Holiest in the heavenly sanctuary are not in view in the first eleven chapters of the book. All of these are strong indications that the events of the blowing of the seven trumpets concern the Christian Age rather than the time of the end after the cessation of the intercession in heaven.

It would thus be correct to understand that both scenes—the opening of the seven seals and the blowing of the seven trumpets—cover the same period of Christian history (although not sequentially) from the cross up until the time of the end. However, whereas the scene of the opening of the seals portrays the progress of the gospel in the world and its effect on those who profess to be God's people but are faithless and disloyal, the vision of the blowing of the seven trumpets portrays the judgment of God on those who reject the gospel, "who do not have the seal of God upon their foreheads" (Rev. 9:4), and who viciously oppress and persecute God's faithful people.

ENDNOTES

1. Barclay, *The Revelation of John*, 2:42.
2. Desmond Ford, 2:407.
3. Battistone, 110.
4. Paulien, "Seals and Trumpets," 198.
5. Morris, 119.
6. Battistone, 111.
7. I am indebted to Jon Paulien for the ideas in this section (The Bible Explorer, 3:7).
8. *Mishnah Tamid* 4.1–5.6 (Danby, 585–587); see also Emil Schurer, *The History of the Jewish People in the Age of Jesus Christ*, rev. ed. (Edinburgh: T. & T. Clark, 1979), 2:299–308.

THE FIRST SIX TRUMPET PLAGUES
REVELATION 8:2–9:21

The Lamb's breaking of the seventh seal and the subsequent silence in heaven (Rev. 8:1) are followed by a new phase of John's vision. The new episode portrays a series of trumpet soundings which herald strange events falling upon the inhabitants of the earth. This section is divided into two parts: the introductory heavenly scene (Rev. 8:2–6) and the subsequent effectuation of the seven trumpet plagues. The seven trumpets are arranged like the seven seals into groups of four and three. The first four trumpets (8:7–13) differ from the last three trumpet "woes" in form and weight. The sixth trumpet (9:13–21) is separated from the seventh one (11:15–19) by an interlude (chapters 10–11:14).

THE INTRODUCTORY SCENE: THE PRAYERS OF THE SAINTS (8:2–6)

Revelation 8:2–6 serves as the introduction to the section of the blowing of the seven trumpets. It presents seven heavenly angels commissioned to herald a new series of woes about to be sent upon the inhabitants of the earth. But before the angels blow their trumpets, the prayers of God's people are offered with incense. This section provides the reader with the key to the interpretation of the seven-trumpet vision.[1]

> *2And I saw the seven angels who stand before God, and seven trumpets were given to them. 3And another angel came having a golden censer and stood at the altar, and much incense was given to him that he might offer it with the prayers of all the saints on the golden altar which is before the throne. 4And the smoke of the incense with the prayers of the saints ascended before God from the hand of the angel. 5And the angel took the censer and filled*

it with the fire from the altar and cast it to the earth; and there were peals of thunder and voices and flashes of lightning and an earthquake. And the seven angels who had the seven trumpets prepared themselves that they might sound.

NOTES

8:2 *The seven angels.* The definite article suggests that the identity of these seven angels, as a specific group, was well-known to the readers of John's day. The problem is that the seven angels who stand before God are not mentioned earlier in the Bible. However, Isaiah mentions "the angel of His presence" (Isa. 63:9), and Luke 1:19 speaks of Gabriel who stands in the presence of God. Jewish tradition identified seven angels who stood before God as Uriel, Raphael, Raguel, Michael, Saraqael, Gabriel, and Remiel.[2] Many scholars believe that John refers to these seven angels. Yet these angels "are missing from the heavenly company described in Revelation 4–5."[3] Whoever they might be, the seven angels in Revelation 8–9 are a special class of heavenly beings. Their position before God characterizes their readiness for service; in the Old Testament, the phrase "stand before God" really means "whom I serve" (cf. 1 Kings 17:1; 18:15; 2 Kings 3:14; 5:16). It is quite possible that these seven angels are the same angels who later pour out the seven last plagues (chapters 15–16).

Trumpets. Trumpets played a major part in the national life of ancient Israel. A number of Hebrew words in the Old Testament can be translated as "trumpet," *shophar* and *chatsotserah* being the most frequent. *Chatsotserah* trumpets were the instruments of the priests; they were usually made of hammered metals. They were blown by priests for different purposes (Num. 10:2–10) such as calling people together (Num. 10:3) or sounding the alarm in times of war (Num. 10:9), at celebrations or religious festivals (Num. 10:10), and in the temple services (2 Chron. 5:12–13; 13:12–14). Gideon used these trumpets to terrorize the enemy into panic (Judg. 7:19–20). *Shophar* trumpets (Exod. 19:16; Lev. 25:9; Josh. 6:4; Judg. 3:27), which were usually made of ram's horn, are the most frequently mentioned instruments in the Old Testament. *Shophar* was a signaling instrument (Judg. 3:27, 6:34; 1 Sam. 13:3; Isa. 18:3; 27:13; Jer. 4:5, 19; 51:27; Joel 2:1). Its function was to make noise rather than music. Both the *shophar* and the *chatsotserah* were regarded as sacred instruments. In the eschatological visions of the Old and New Testaments, *shophar* (Gr. *salpinx*) became an appropriate signal heralding the end-time coming of God in judgment.

Were given. The passive verb construction used here is most likely the Semitic divine passive, a form commonly used in the Bible with a purpose to avoid using God's name, and when from the context an indefinite agent can be identified as God (see *Notes* on Rev. 9:1). It would mean, in this case, that it was God who gave the trumpets to the angels.

8:3 The ***golden censer*** was a "firepan" in the Solomon temple (cf. 1 Kings 7:50; 2 Chron. 4:22; Jer. 52:18–19) as well as in the Second Temple.[4]

The altar. The text does not specify which altar is in view here. It is likely the altar of burnt offering (which was located outside the Old Testament temple setting) as distinguished from the golden altar of incense, mentioned later in the verse, which was before the throne. In the Old Testament temple, the golden altar of incense was "in front of the veil that is near the ark of the testimony, in front of the mercy seat that is over the ark of the testimony" (cf. Exod. 30:6–7). See further *Notes* on Revelation 6:9.

8:5 The angel took the censer and filled it with the fire from the altar and cast it to the earth; and there were peals of thunder and voices and flashes of lightning and an earthquake. This scene reflects the temple scene described in the *Mishnah*, stating that during the *tamid* ritual, when the priests officiating in the holy place reached the place between the porch and the altar of incense, one of them took the shovel and threw it down. The noise of the shovel was so loud that no one in Jerusalem could hear the voice of his neighbor.[5] According to the same tractate, the sound of the shovel could be heard as far away as Jericho.[6]

EXPOSITION

8:2 With Revelation 8:2 a new phase of the vision begins. John observes **seven angels** standing before God with **seven trumpets,** prepared to herald a new series of woes to be sent to the earth and its inhabitants. Before the angels blow the trumpets, a new symbolic scene catches John's attention. This introductory scene of the blowing of the seven trumpets sets the tone for the series of the seven trumpets.

8:3–5 John sees another angel with **a golden censer** standing in close proximity to **the altar** of burnt offering. After receiving much **incense**, the angel administers the incense by offering it with **the prayers of all the saints on the golden altar** of incense before the throne. This scene is built on the Old Testament cultic system, in which the end of the daily sacrifice was announced by the blowing of trumpets.[7] After the sacrificial lamb had been placed upon the altar of burnt offering and the blood of the sacrifice had been poured out at the base of the altar, the assigned priest would have taken the golden censor and offered incense upon the golden altar inside the temple. After offering the incense, the priest came out to bless the people who were waiting quietly in the court. At that moment, the seven priests blew their trumpets, marking the end of the daily sacrifice ceremony.

The angel in Revelation 8 receives the incense with the prayers of the saints at the altar of burnt offering. This is especially significant in light of the fact that in the scene of the opening of the fifth seal, the slain saints beneath the altar of burnt offering pray for judgment on "those who dwell on the earth" (6:10). Here in Revelation 8:3–4, these prayers of the saints are mentioned again in the angel's offering of the incense upon the altar before the throne of God. According to Revelation 5:8, this incense represents the prayers of the saints; these are evidently the prayers for justice and judgment of the saints under the altar in the scene of the opening of the fifth seal. *And the smoke of the incense with the prayers of the saints ascended before God from the hand of the angel.* Here is a firm assurance that the prayers of the saints beneath the altar reach "the throne of grace" and are heard by God in the heavenly places.

Suddenly the scene changes. *And the angel took the censer and filled it with the fire from the altar and cast it to the earth.* This is reminiscent of the scene from Ezekiel's vision in which the man clothed in linen takes coals of fire from between the cherubim; the man then scatters them over Jerusalem as a token of divine judgment because of the abominations committed in it (Ezek. 10:1–2). In light of this Old Testament background, the throwing of coals of fire down upon the earth in Revelation 8:5 symbolizes judgment action. The action of the angel here reminds one of Jesus' statement: "I have come to cast fire upon the earth" (Luke 12:49).

It is particularly interesting that fire comes to the earth from the very altar on which the prayers of the saints were offered. Likewise, as Robert L. Thomas notes, the censer which normally served to offer incense now becomes "a symbol of judgment in response to the prayers."[8] This symbolic scene shows that it is in answer to the prayers of the saints that God's seven trumpet judgments fall upon the earth and its inhabitants. It conveys the assurance that God's people are not forgotten and that their prayers have been heard and are answered.[9]

The throwing of fire to the earth is followed by the manifestation of divine wrath in the form of *peals of thunder and voices and flashes of lightning and an earthquake.* These are the symbols of the appearance of God, much like his appearance on the Mount of Sinai with fire, thunder, lightning, and earthquake (Exod. 19:16–19). This phenomenon represents the answer to prayer which God is about to give to his people. He is preparing to bring his righteous judgments and vengeance upon those who viciously harassed and oppressed the faithful.

8:6 The presentation of the incense on the golden altar (8:3) and the throwing of fire to the earth serve as signals to the seven angels to blow their trumpets and herald the woes about to be sent upon the earth and its inhabitants. This is a further indication that the trumpet judgments are affected by the prayers of the saints in the scene of the fifth seal: "How long, O Lord, holy and true, will you not judge and avenge our blood upon those who dwell on the earth?" (6:10). God is responding to these prayers in judging "those who dwell on the earth" (8:13). This again reminds us of the plagues of Egypt: "I have surely seen the affliction of My people who are in Egypt, and have given heed to their cry" (Exod. 3:7).

The plagues of Egypt, when Pharaoh refused to allow Israel to go, are, for the most part, the main source from which John drew his ideas and descriptions of the seven trumpet woes. Like the plagues of Egypt, so the trumpet woes are judgments against the enemies of God's people leading to the deliverance of the oppressed faithful.[10] We now analyze each of these events in detail.

THE FIRST FOUR TRUMPETS (8:7–12)

The seven angels are ready to blow their trumpets (8:6). At each trumpet sound, a chain of events takes place on the earth. In light of Revelation 8:2–6 as previously discussed, these events must be understood as a series of interventions of God in history in response to the prayers of his people.

THE FIRST TRUMPET (8:7)

> **[7]And the first angel sounded his trumpet; and there were hail and fire mixed with blood, and they were hurled down to the earth; and a third of the earth was burned up, and a third of the trees were burned up, and all green grass was burned up.**

NOTES

8:7 *Hail and fire mixed with blood.* This phrase recalls the seventh plague of the Exodus; hail mixed with fire was God's judgment upon the Egyptians and had a devastating effect (Exod. 9:23–25). Another major source for this imagery is the prophecy of Ezekiel against Gog; hail and fire mixed with blood were God's executive judgment on this enemy of Judah (Ezek. 38:22–23). Although fire (Ps. 80:14–16; Jer. 21:12–14; Ezek. 15:6–7) or hail (Isa. 30:30; Ezek. 13:11–13) are sometimes used in judgment against Israel for forsaking the covenant, the images of hail mixed with fire in the Old Testament are God's consistent weapon of judgment on the nations that were in opposition to God and his people (cf. Ps. 18:12–14; Isa. 10:16–19; 30:30; Ezek. 38:22–23).

A third. The events triggered by Christ's opening of the first four seals evidently affect one fourth of the earth. Each horse has authority over one fourth of the earth (cf. 6:8). In the same way, it appears that the four angels of 7:1 have control over four quarters of the earth. The trumpet plagues, however, affect one third of the earth (8:7–12; 9:15, 18). In the prophecies of Ezekiel and Zechariah, judgments against apostate Israel are described in terms of plagues affecting one third after another of the nation (Ezek. 5:12–13; Zech. 13:8–9). In Revelation 12:4, the tail of the great red dragon in heaven—Satan himself (cf. 12:9)—swept away a third of the stars of heaven and threw them to the earth, meaning that one third of the angels followed him and were under his control. Especially interesting is that the symbolic Babylon is split into three parts as God brings his judgments against it (Rev. 16:19). It would be very appropriate to conclude that the phrase "the third part" of the trumpets in Revelation 8–9 denotes a portion of Satan's kingdom experiencing divine judgments.[11]

The trees and *all green grass*. In the Old Testament, symbols of trees (Pss. 1:3; 52:8; 92:12–14; Isa. 61:3; Jer. 11:15–17; 17:7–8; Ezek. 20:46–48) and green grass (Ps. 72:16; Isa. 40:6–8; 44:2–4) are used figuratively with reference to Israel as God's covenant people. The New Testament writers confirm the association. For instance, John the Baptist compared the apostate leaders of the Jewish people to trees that did not bear good fruit (Matt. 3:10). Likewise, Jesus used tree symbolism in referring to the Jewish people as the green tree (Luke 23:28–31) and as a fig tree that did not bear fruit (Luke 13:6–9; cf. Matt. 7:17–19; 21:18–19).

EXPOSITION

8:7 As the first angel blows his trumpet, *hail and fire mixed with blood* are hurled down upon the earth. In the Old Testament, hail and fire are God's weapons of judgment used against those who oppose him and oppress his people. In the first place, they recall the seventh plague of hail and fire that devastated the entire land of Egypt, destroying every plant and tree of the field (Exod. 9:23–25), for the refusal to let the Israelites go. It also brings to one's mind the prophecy of Ezekiel where God fights against Gog, the enemy nation from the North, through the use of hail and fire mixed with blood (38:22). Thus, hail and fire accompanied by much bloodshed are God's means of intervention in judgment, particularly for those nations which oppress his people.

The effect of this trumpet blast on the earth is that *a third of the trees was burned up, and all green grass was burned up.* In the Old Testament, trees and green grass often symbolize Israel as God's people. Fire destroying vegetation fitly symbolizes God's weapons of judgment used against his own people when they became unfaithful to the covenant and are, thus, equated with the opponents of God. Jeremiah called the nation of Judah "a green olive tree, beautiful in fruit and form," which the Babylonians would destroy with fire (11:16). Ezekiel prophesied that God would kindle a fire for unfaithful Jerusalem which would consume "every green tree in you as well as every dry tree" (20:47).

In addressing the Jewish leaders, John the Baptist announced that any who did not bear good fruit would be cut down as a tree and thrown into the fire (Matt. 3:10; cf. 7:17–19). The key text for understanding the tree symbolism in the first trumpet scene is found in Jesus' prophecy about the inhabitants of Jerusalem: "For if they do these things in the green tree, what will happen in the dry?" (Luke 23:31). It is clear that Jesus referred here to himself as the green tree, and to apostate Jews as the dry trees. When Jesus was treated in such a way as the green tree, what hope had the nation that was dry due to its opposition to and rejection of Jesus? Most biblical scholars maintain that Jesus referred here to the destruction of Jerusalem by the Romans in A.D. 70, the very event that he described in his eschatological discourse on the Mount of Olives.

This biblical evidence leads one to conclude that the first trumpet blast portrays the consequences visited upon those who rejected and crucified Jesus and opposed the gospel. Both the people and their leaders were held responsible for those acts. As God's covenant people, they had full access to the promises of God. However, a sizable number of them became opponents to the gospel and persecutors of God's new covenant people. Now, they are the first ones to experience the consequences of rejecting the covenant.

The Bible states clearly that judgment begins at the house of God (1 Pet. 4:17; cf. Ezek. 9). Just as in the Old Testament "hail and fire" symbolized the divine judgments that would fall on the enemies of Israel, so in the scene of the first trumpet, "hail and fire mixed with blood" portray in symbolic language the divine judgment poured upon God's own people who rejected his covenant and became the oppressors and persecutors of the followers of Christ. In the destruction of the Jewish nation with its capital city Jerusalem in A.D. 70, many of the Jews were "burnt up." For the Jewish people, this event still remains one of the bitterest chapters in their history.

THE SECOND TRUMPET (8:8–9)

8And the second angel sounded his trumpet; and something like a great mountain burning with fire was cast into the sea; and a third of the sea became blood, 9and a third of the creatures which were in the sea, which had life, died, and a third of the ships were destroyed.

NOTES

8:8 *A great mountain burning with fire.* A mountain in the Old Testament often represents a kingdom or empire (Pss. 48:1; 78:68; Isa. 2:2–3; 13:4; 31:4; 41:15; Jer. 51:24–25; Ezek. 35:2–3; Obad. 8–9). In the prophetic vision of Daniel, God's kingdom is described in terms of a great mountain (Dan. 2:35b, 44; cf. Isa. 65:25). Jon Paulien observes that in the judgment passages of the Old Testament, "mountains as representing nations are always the object of God's judgments, never the agents" (Isa. 41:15; 42:15; Ezek. 35:2–7; 38:20; Zech. 4:7).[12] Jeremiah's prophecy of judgment against Babylon is of special interest: "'Behold, I am against you, O destroying mountain, who destroys the whole earth,' declares the Lord. 'And I will stretch out My hand against you, and roll you down from the crags, and I will make you a burnt out mountain'" (Jer. 51:25; cf. 51:42, 63–64). In Revelation 18:8, John described the destruction of spiritual Babylon as being "burned with fire, because the Lord God who judges her is strong."

Was cast into the sea. The destruction of ancient Babylon is described in the prophecy of Jeremiah as its sinking into the sea: "The sea has come up over Babylon; she has been engulfed with its tumultuous waves" (Jer. 51:42). "And it will come about as soon as you finish reading this scroll, you will tie a stone to it and throw it into the middle of Euphrates, and say: 'Just so shall Babylon sink down and not rise again'" (Jer. 51:63–64). John the revelator used the same language in describing spiritual Babylon: "And a strong angel took up a stone like a great millstone and threw it into the sea, saying, 'Thus will Babylon the great city be thrown down with violence, and will not be found any longer'" (Rev. 18:21).

8:9 *A third.* See *Notes* on Revelation 8:7.

EXPOSITION

8:8 As the second angel sounds his trumpet, ***something like a great mountain burning with fire was cast into the sea.*** "Mountain" symbolizes a kingdom. The "*great* mountain" of Revelation 8:8 has to do with a *great* kingdom. The scene of the second trumpet is built entirely on the description of the fall of ancient Babylon in the prophecy of Jeremiah. The prophet predicted that God would judge Babylon, a "destroying mountain, who destroys the whole earth" (Jer. 51:25a), for "their evil that they have done in Zion" (Jer. 51:24). Babylon is to be judged by God; it becomes a burning mountain (Jer. 51:25b) which is thrown into the sea and becomes covered by it (Jer. 51:42, 63–64). The falling of the "great mountain" in Revelation 8:8 reminds us of the fall of "Babylon the great" described later in Revelation (cf. Rev. 14:8; 18:2).

Texts in Jeremiah about the fall of Babylon provide the clue for understanding the scene of the second trumpet plague. At the time of the writing of the book of Revelation, "Babylon" was used with reference to the great Roman Empire. Because it destroyed Jerusalem and its temple, it was to suffer its own fate.[13] Both Peter and John used "Babylon" as the cryptic name for Rome (1 Pet. 5:13; Rev. 17:18). It appears, therefore, that Christians who saw in Rome the new Babylon could easily identify the symbolic burning mountain of the second trumpet as the prophecy of the downfall of the Roman Empire as the enemy of God's people. Jon Paulien states: "Although Rome was used by God as the executor of His covenant on the Jewish nation, its hostility toward Christ and his people and its persecution of the church called for its ultimate downfall."[14] This great destroying mountain has now become a subject of God's judgment. Edwin R. Thiele explained it in the following way:

> After the fall of Jerusalem and the end of the Jewish state, the next scene of judgment is one on a much broader and vaster scale....The second trumpet calls for some terrible, fiery, destructive force to fall into the troubled seas of the ancient world and to turn their turbid waters into blood. After the fall of Jerusalem came the fall of Rome....The empire of the Caesars was doomed. The ax of divine retribution must fall. Like flames of fire from heaven came Genseric the Vandal, Alaric the Goth, and Attila the Hun, leaving in their wake scenes of ruin, desolation, carnage, and blood. Irresistible and destructive as a flaming mountain, the hordes of barbarians fell upon the peoples of Rome, till all the empire was involved in a grand and irretrievable catastrophe. Rome was gone and justice again had had its way.[15]

8:9 The burning mountain sinking into the sea turns the sea into **blood**, leaving one **third** of the marine life dead and one third of the ships destroyed. This brings to mind the first Egyptian plague in which the waters were turned into blood and the fish were destroyed. The sea in the Old Testament is often the symbol for people in their opposition to God (Isa. 17:12–13; 57:20; Jer. 51:41–42; Dan. 7:2–3, 17).[16] As conveyers of wealth, **ships** symbolize a nation's pride in its self-sufficiency[17] (cf. Rev. 18:17–19). The second trumpet thus describes the downfall of the Roman Empire and "the devastation of its economic and social order."[18]

In conclusion, the plagues of the first two trumpets affect two powers—the Jewish nation and the Roman Empire. These two hostile nations united together in their opposition to God and participated in the crucifixion of Christ. Thus they are the first to experience God's judgments. The judgment began with God's household—those under the covenant who later worked in opposition to Jesus. It spread to those who joined the Jews in putting Jesus to death, and subsequently oppressed and persecuted the church in the first century of the Christian era.

THE THIRD TRUMPET (8:10–11)

[10]And the third angel sounded his trumpet; and a great star burning like a torch fell from heaven, and it fell upon a third of the rivers and upon the springs of water. [11]And the name of the star is called "Wormwood"; and a third of waters became wormwood, and many people died from the waters, because they were made bitter.

NOTES

8:10 *A great star.* Stars in the Bible often symbolize angels. In Job 38:7, angels are called stars. The same is true in Revelation (cf. 1:20; 9:1). In Revelation 12:4, Satan pulls a third of the stars of heaven down to earth. These stars are evidently the angels who were thrown out of heaven with Satan (12:9). The "great star" fallen from heaven reminds us of Isaiah 14:12–15 which mentions a "star of the morning" falling from heaven; this evidently refers to Lucifer and his rebellion against God. Jesus spoke of Satan as falling from heaven like lightning (Luke 10:18). To the Jewish people, the stars symbolized "divine beings, who by disobedience could become demonic and evil."[19] The "great star" falling from heaven at the third trumpet sound is a symbol of Satan himself in his rebellion against God (cf. Rev. 12:9–10). It is the same fallen star symbolically portrayed in Revelation 9:1 and identified in 9:11 as "the angel of the abyss."

The rivers and *the springs of water.* Springs in the Bible are often a symbol of spiritual nourishment. Isaiah announced that Israel would "joyously draw water from the springs of salvation" (Isa. 12:3). Solomon stated: "The teaching of the wise is a fountain of life" (Prov. 13:14). God rebuked the people of Israel through Jeremiah for forsaking him, "the fountain of living waters," and hewing for themselves "broken cisterns that can hold no water" (Jer. 2:13). The Psalmist compares a man who has delight in the Word of God with "a tree firmly planted by streams of water" (Ps. 1:3; cf. Jer. 17:7–8). A strong symbolism of the rivers and springs of water is reflected in Jesus' statement at the Feast of Tabernacles: "He who believes in Me, as the Scripture said, 'From his innermost being will flow rivers of living water.' But this He spoke of the Spirit, whom those who believed in Him were to receive" (John 7:38–39). Jesus used the rivers and springs of water as a symbol of the spiritual nourishment of the Word of God which a person receives when the Holy Spirit comes into his or her life. In the conclusion of the book of Revelation, John quotes Christ's offer to give spiritually thirsty people an opportunity to drink from the fountain of the water of life (Rev. 21:6).

A third. See *Notes* on Revelation 8:7.

8:11 *Wormwood.* Wormwood (Gr. *apsinthos*) is the name for the group of herbs *artemesia absinthium* in the Near East, notorious for its bitterness (Deut. 29:17–18; Lam. 3:19). Although wormwood was not poisonous, poisonous effects were often associated with it (cf. Deut. 29:18;

Jer. 9:15; Amos 6:12). Because idolatrous Israel forsook God and rejected his word (Jer. 8:9), God threatened through Jeremiah to give them wormwood to eat and poisoned water to drink (Jer. 9:13–15; cf. 8:14). The same threat was made against the prophets, because from them "pollution has gone forth into all the earth" (Jer. 23:15). Wormwood in the Old Testament was a symbol of divine punishment for apostasy, as well as of suffering and sorrow.

EXPOSITION

8:10 At the trumpet sound of the third angel, John sees *a great star burning like a torch* falling down from heaven upon the rivers and the fountains of water, polluting them with bitterness and bringing death to many people. Stars in the Bible frequently symbolize angels. The fact that this star is referred to as *great* indicates that we are dealing with a character which is superior to the angels. It certainly reminds us of the star of the morning falling down from heaven in Isaiah 14:12, as well as the words of Jesus: "I was watching Satan fall from heaven like lightning" (Luke 10:18). This great falling star burning like a torch is clearly a symbolic reference to Satan, the head of the fallen angels, who once had been in the presence of God and after his rebellion was thrown down from heaven to the earth (cf. Rev. 12:9–10).

The great star falls on *the rivers and upon the springs of water.* The rivers and springs of water symbolize spiritual nourishment—the word of God and salvation—for spiritually thirsty people. The scene of the third trumpet shows Satan's involvement in polluting the source and streams of truth and salvation through human religious teachers and leaders, causing them to have a deadly poisonous effect.

8:11 The name of the falling great star is Wormwood. Its falling on the fresh waters turns a third of them into *wormwood.* "Wormwood is a symbol of bitterness through sin and apostasy."[20] The falling of the star and the defiling of the fresh water supplies are thus symbols of apostasy and perverted gospel teaching. As a consequence of that apostasy, *many among people died from the waters, because they were made bitter.* As Paulien states, when the sources of spiritual life are polluted by apostasy and false teaching, "the immediate result is the spiritual death of some who drink" from these water supplies.[21] The Old Testament writers make clear that when God's people turn their backs on God and the covenant, they are given wormwood to eat and poisoned water to drink (Jer. 8:14; 9:13–15; 23:15). The falling of the star and the defiling of the fresh water supplies are thus the symbols of apostasy and perverted truth. Commenting on this concept, Thiele stresses:

Here a remarkable, revolutionary transformation is depicted. The once pure, life-giving fountains become contaminated and corrupt as the death-star Wormwood falls upon them, and henceforth men die rather than live as they partake of the polluted waters. The pure church is a clear stream and a life-giving fountain. When the enemy enters that church it becomes corrupt. Henceforth it is a scourge rather than a blessing to men. Satan rather than Christ is in control, and the church is to take over complete control, a savor of death unto death instead of life unto life.[22]

If the first two trumpet sounds deal with the fall of the Jewish nation and the Roman Empire responsible for the death of Christ, then the scene of the blowing of the third trumpet has to do with the period in history following the fall of the Roman Empire. This period, often referred to as the Dark or Middle Ages, witnessed great spiritual decline and apostasy, when the mainstream of the church departed from the apostolic gospel and perverted the sound teaching of the Bible. The gospel truth was replaced with church tradition and dogma. The church promoted sinful actions contrary to the Bible; people were led astray from the simplicity of the gospel. Those who resisted the apostasy and the seducing influences of the institutional church experienced rejection and persecution.

The early Christians were warned of the coming apostasy. Jesus spoke of false prophets who would seduce the disciples with their deceptive teachings (Matt. 24:4–5, 11, 23–24). In his farewell address to the elders in Ephesus, Paul predicted the coming apostasy in the church (Acts 20:26–31). Similar predictions are found in other portions of the New Testament (1 Tim. 4:1–2; 2 Tim. 4:3–4; 2 Pet. 2:1–3; 1 John 1:18–19; 4:1; Jude 3–4). The inevitable apostasy is also the regular theme of the messages to the seven churches of Revelation 2–3. Particularly significant for the understanding of the scene of the third trumpet is Paul's prediction of the coming apostasy in 2 Thessalonians 2:1–12. Paul makes clear that the coming apostasy was delayed by "the restrainer," apparently the Roman Empire. The fall of Judaism and especially Rome as "the restrainer" opened the door to the tide of prevailing medieval apostasy. The consequence of that apostasy was the spiritual death of many who drank of that polluted and poisonous water. This is clearly the situation portrayed symbolically in the scene of the third trumpet.

THE FOURTH TRUMPET (8:12)

¹²And the fourth angel sounded his trumpet; and a third of the sun and a third of the moon and a third of the stars were stricken, so that a third of them became darkened and the day did not brighten for a third of it, and the night likewise.

NOTES

8:12 *A third.* See *Notes* on Revelation 8:7.

Became darkened. The symbolic meaning of darkness in the Bible has its roots in creation, when God created the heavenly bodies of the sun, moon, and stars with the purpose of giving light to the earth (Gen. 1:14–18). As the sources of light, the brightening of the sun and moon in the Old Testament is a token of God's favor and blessing on his people (Isa. 30:26). Darkening these sources of light functions as the reversal and undoing of the creation.

Darkening of the heavenly bodies in the Old Testament prophecies is a consistent symbol of the appearance of God in judgment. For instance, Ezekiel prophesied against Egypt: "'And when I extinguish you, I will cover the heavens, and darken their stars; I will cover the sun with a cloud, and the moon shall not give its light. All the shining lights in the heavens I will darken over you and I will set darkness on your land,' declares the Lord GOD" (Ezek. 32:7–8).

Isaiah portrayed the judgment against Babylon on the day of the Lord in a similar way: "For the stars of heaven and their constellations will not flash forth their light; the sun will be dark when it rises, and the moon will not shed its light" (Isa. 13:10). In his judgment prophecy against Israel, Amos described the day of the Lord as a day of darkness rather than light (Amos 5:18). For Joel it will be "a day of darkness and gloom, a day of clouds and thick darkness" (Joel 2:2), when "the sun and moon [will] grow dark, and the stars [will] lose their brightness" (Joel 2:10; 3:15). Jesus spoke of the darkening of the celestial bodies in connection with his second coming to the earth in judgment (Matt. 24:29; Mark 13:24–25; cf. Isa. 13:10).

In the New Testament, light and darkness are the symbols of good and evil. Darkness is often linked with supernatural powers (Eph. 6:12; Col. 1:13; 1 Pet. 2:9; Rev. 16:10). For Paul, light and darkness stand parallel to Christ and Belial (2 Cor. 6:14–15). Paul states further, "The god of this world has blinded the minds of the unbelieving, that they might not see the light of the gospel of the glory of Christ" (2 Cor. 4:4). Through the transforming influence of the gospel, God repeats his work of creation: "For God who said, 'Light shall shine out of darkness,' is the One who has shone in our hearts to give the light of the knowledge of the glory of God in the face of Christ" (2 Cor. 4:6). Jesus is the true light which enlightens those living in the world (John 1:9). "I am the light of the world; he who follows Me shall not walk in darkness, but shall have the light of life" (John 8:12). "I have come as light into the world, that everyone who believes in Me may not remain in the darkness" (John

12:46; cf. Luke 1:79). In preaching the gospel message to the people in Galilee, Jesus was fulfilling Isaiah's prophecy: "The people who were sitting in darkness saw a great light, and to those who were sitting in the land and shadow of death, upon them a light dawned" (Matt. 4:16). It is through the gospel of Christ that the believers are rescued from the domain of darkness and brought into God's marvelous light (Col. 1:13–14; 1 Pet. 2:9). Those who reject the gospel light and stay in darkness bring God's judgment upon themselves (cf. John 3:19).

EXPOSITION

8:12 The fourth trumpet plague strikes the heavenly bodies, *a third of the sun and a third of the moon and a third of the stars,* with the result that *a third of them became darkened and the day did not brighten for a third of it, and the night likewise*. The scene described here is reminiscent of the ninth plague, the plague of darkness, on Egypt (Exod. 10:21–23). In his prophecy against Egypt, Ezekiel envisioned the coming of a renewed plague on the land which is described in terms of the plague of darkness in Exodus (Ezek. 32:7–8). Darkening of celestial bodies in the Old Testament prophetic books is a consistent symbol of the appearance of God in judgment (cf. Isa. 13:10; Ezek. 32:7–8; Joel 2:10; 3:15).

As was the case with the previous three trumpets, the fourth trumpet scene must also be understood as a symbolic representation of God's judgment against apostate humanity, rather than a literal darkening of the sky. As the absence of light, "darkness" is the lack of spiritual understanding and insight that results from the absence of the gospel (cf. Isa. 8:20; 60:1–2; Matt. 4:16). Darkness in the Old Testament is a consistent symbol of judgment for sin and apostasy. The prophet Micah uses this imagery in describing the apostasy of the prophets in Judah: "Therefore it will be night for you— without vision, and darkness for you—without divination. The sun will go down on the prophets, and the day will become dark over them" (Mic. 3:6).

Light in the New Testament stands for the gospel. Jesus himself is the ultimate source of spiritual life. He is the true light that enlightens everyone in the world (John 1:9). Only through him can human beings be rescued from the domain of darkness and brought into God's marvelous light (Col. 1:13–14; 1 Pet. 2:9). Darkness is the absence of the gospel; it is a symbol of sin. When people reject the gospel light for darkness, they bring God's judgment upon themselves: "And this is the judgment, that the light is come into the world, and the men loved the darkness rather than the light" (John 3:19). What Jesus made very clear is that darkness is the consequence of ignoring and denying the gospel. It is in this sense that the symbolism of darkness of the fourth trumpet plague must be understood.

The apostasy of the third trumpet is further developed in the fourth trumpet scene.[23] While the third trumpet scene depicts in symbolic language the consequences of the spiritual decline and apostasy of the medieval Christian church, the fourth trumpet scene portrays the deepening of the prevailing darkness in the world in the period that followed the Dark Ages. In the first stage, the vibrant generation of the Reformers who emphasized the simplicity and purity of the gospel was succeeded by so-called Protestant scholasticism characterized by theological polemics and controversies. During this period, the Christian life became less a personal relationship with Christ and more a matter of membership in the official church.

Next, the intellectual revolution of the Age of Enlightenment, or the Age of Reason, that characterized Europe from the sixteenth through the eighteenth centuries, ended the rule of Christian faith over the Western mind. This new phenomenon rejected traditional religion and led to the outgrowth of rationalism, skepticism, humanism, and liberalism. Its final product was the birth and rise of secularism. Despite many positive elements of secularization in the Western World (on science, politics, religious liberty, arts, and education), its negative effects on Christianity overshadowed its positive effects. With its materialistic orientation, denial of any supernaturality, and skepticism toward faith of any kind, secularism replaced the authority of the Bible and Christian faith with human reason. This negative aspect of secularism gradually degenerated Christian faith and life into lifeless formality and spiritual lethargy and robbed millions of the hope of salvation.

The fourth trumpet might thus be understood as describing the temporal darkening of the spiritual sources of the true light, namely, the Bible gospel, under the prevailing influence of secularism. The best way to understand the judgment of the fourth trumpet is as the obliteration of the gospel of Christ as the only source of spiritual life.[24] The particular effect of the fourth trumpet plague is the partial darkness ("third") of the sources of spiritual light. The deepening of that darkness and its dreadful consequences become more evident in the scenes of the fifth and sixth trumpets.

THE FIRST TWO WOES (8:13–9:21)

The first four trumpet plagues are given in pairs. The first two trumpets deal with the Jewish nation and the Roman Empire, the two nations that crucified Christ. The next two trumpets deal with apostate Christianity and the dread consequences of that apostasy. These four trumpets were intended primarily to be the divine warnings that precede the woes of the three remaining trumpets which are about to come upon the unfaithful, that is, "those who dwell on the earth" (8:13).

THE VULTURE'S WARNING (8:13)

13And I looked, and I heard a vulture flying in midheaven, saying with a loud voice: "Woe, woe, woe to those who dwell on the earth because of the rest of the trumpet sounds of the three angels who are about to sound."

NOTES

8:13 *A vulture*. The Greek word *aetos* may mean both "a vulture" and "an eagle." The *aetos* here in 8:13 is probably the vulture (cf. Rev. 19:17–18). In the Old Testament, the vulture is a symbol of impending judgments and disaster (cf. Deut. 28:49; Ezek. 32:4; 39:17; Hos. 8:1). Habakkuk described the invading Chaldeans as vultures "swooping down to devour" (Hab. 1:8). The vulture mentioned in Revelation 8:13 also evokes Jesus' words with regard to the Second Coming: "Wherever the corpse is, there the vultures will gather" (Matt. 24:28; Luke 17:37).

Woe, woe, woe. This is the first of the seven occurrences of "woe" (Gr. *ouai*) in Revelation (8:13; 9:12; 11:14; 12:12; 18:10, 16, 19) which correspond to the seven beatitudes of the book (see *Notes* on Rev. 1:3).

Those who dwell on the earth. This phrase in Revelation always refers to the unbelievers. See *Notes* on Revelation 6:9.

EXPOSITION

The four trumpet plagues are now completed. John sees next **a vulture flying in midheaven**, announcing with a loud voice the doom to be brought in the remaining three trumpet plagues, in the form of the threefold **woe, woe, woe** for **those who dwell on the earth.** The scene is reminiscent of the judgment oracle against Israel announced by Hosea: "Put the trumpet to your lips! Like an eagle the enemy comes against the house of the LORD, because they have transgressed my covenant, and rebelled against my law" (Hos. 8:1).

The scene here also bears verbal parallels to Revelation 14:6–7, which portrays the angel *flying in midheaven* announcing **with a loud voice** the warning message to *those who dwell on the earth*. The vulture in the Bible is a symbol of impending judgments. The picture of the vulture flying in midheaven announcing the fearful woes is intended to make an impact on the reader of the fearful judgments about to come (cf. Rev. 19:17). The three fearful woes that the vulture announces come as the three remaining angels, one after another, sound their trumpets.

In the book of Revelation, "those who dwell on the earth" designates the wicked in their hostility to God's people and the gospel (cf. 3:10; Rev. 8:13; 11:10; 13:8, 14; 17:8). Although the first four trumpets were "woes" themselves, they were mainly the divine warnings to the wicked. The scene is now moving from the divine warnings to the manifestation of the demonic woes. They are now to be unleashed. The next two trumpet plagues represent "spiritual torment and death" which result from demonic activities on "those who persist in resisting the divine invitation to repent."[25]

In the three remaining trumpet plagues, there is an intensification of divine judgments on those who are spiritually dead as the result of apostasy and persisting in hostility toward the gospel. The worst is yet to come upon "those who dwell on the earth."

THE FIFTH TRUMPET (9:1–12)

> [1]*And the fifth angel sounded his trumpet; and I saw a star fallen from heaven to the earth, and the key of the pit of the abyss was given to him.* [2]*And he opened the pit of the abyss, and smoke came up from the abyss like smoke of a great furnace, and the sun and the air became darkened by the smoke of the abyss.* [3]*And locusts came out of the smoke on the earth, and power was given to them as scorpions of the earth have power.* [4]*And it was said to them not to hurt the grass of earth nor any green thing nor any tree, except the men who do not have the seal of God upon their foreheads.* [5]*And it was given to them not to kill them, but that they should be tormented for five months; and their torment was as the torment of a scorpion when it stings a person.* [6]*And in*

those days people will seek death and they will in no way find it, and they will long to die, and death will flee from them. ^{7}And the appearance of the locusts was similar to horses prepared for battle, and upon their heads were as crowns of gold, and their faces were like human faces. ^{8}And they had hair as the hair of women, and their teeth were as of lions, ^{9}and they had breastplates as breastplates of iron, and the sound of their wings was as the sound of chariots of many horses running into battle. ^{10}And they had tails like scorpions and stings, and authority in their tails was to torment the people for five months. ^{11}They have a king over them, the angel of the abyss, whose name in Hebrew is Abaddon, and in Greek his name is Apollyon. ^{12}The first woe has passed; behold, two woes are coming after these things.

NOTES

9:1 *A star fallen from heaven.* See *Notes* on 8:10. This is apparently the same star mentioned in the third trumpet (8:10–11), and later identified as "the angel of the abyss" (Rev. 9:11). A. Yarbro Collins observes that "the star falling from heaven to earth evokes the story of the fall of Satan, one of the most glorious angels," in his rebellion against God (Rev. 12:7–10; cf. Isa. 14:12; Luke 10:18).[26] "Fallen" is in the perfect tense, which indicates that the star had fallen before the fifth trumpet was blown.

The pit of the abyss. The word "abyss" is used first in Genesis 1:2 with reference to the chaotic condition of the earth before the creation: "And the earth was formless and void, and darkness was over the surface of the deep ["abyss" in the LXX]" (cf. Gen. 7:11). In Jeremiah 4:23–30, it is used to refer to desolated and uninhabited Palestine during the Exile. The abyss came to be a bottomless subterranean cavern where the disobedient hosts of heaven and the kings of the earth were confined as prisoners for a period of time, after which they would receive their punishment (Isa. 24:21–22). Elsewhere in the New Testament, the abyss or the bottomless pit (Gr. *abyssos*) is described as a dark and chaotic prison abode of the fallen angels, the demons, who are under God's control (Luke 8:31; 2 Pet. 2:4; Jude 6; Rev. 20:1, 3). In Revelation it is the place from which the beast arises (Rev. 11:7; 17:8). The abyss is also the place of Satan's imprisonment during the millennium (Rev. 20:1–3) until he receives his final punishment in the lake of fire (20:10).

Was given to him. The passive form here ("was given") functions as the Hebrew divine passive. It was very common in the Judaism of the time. Jews believed that God's name was too sacred to be uttered except in rare circumstances. When talking about God or his actions, they usually used what is called the divine passive. For instance, "You are blessed," meant clearly, "God has blessed you." The divine passive form is used often in the book of Revelation. The fact that the fallen star was given the key of the abyss meant that the key was given to him by God.

9:2 *Became darkened*. See *Notes* on Revelation 8:12.

9:3 *Locusts*. Locusts in the Old Testament are used as another symbol of judgment. Locust plagues were God's judgment against the apostate nations, such as Babylon (Jer. 51:14) and Egypt (Exod. 10:4–15). They were also God's instrument of judgment against Judah for failing to obey the covenant. Joel describes them in connection with the day of the Lord as armies marching to battle, while the earth quakes and the heavens tremble (Joel 2:4–10). "The land is like the garden of Eden before them, but a desolate wilderness behind them" (Joel 2:3).

The locusts of the fifth trumpet must be understood as symbolic. This is evident first because these locusts have the power of scorpions (9:3, 5); they have tails like scorpions and poisonous stings (9:10). Second, locusts normally attack plants; the locusts of the fifth trumpet, however, hurt not plants but people. Finally, their description as armies advancing like a cloud, darkening the sky, and sounding like the rattle of chariots is drawn from Joel's vision of the locust invasion on Judah as a judgment from God (cf. Joel 2:2–10). The fact that the locusts of the fifth trumpet come out from the abyss, the prison abode of the demonic forces, suggests that they are the symbols of demonic forces which were temporarily confined, and are now unleashed to do their harmful work.

9:4 *The grass of earth nor any green thing nor any tree*. Grass and green trees in the Bible are frequent symbols for God's people (see further *Notes* on Rev. 8:7). The fact that the fifth trumpet plague does not affect the grass and green trees (because the vegetation is sealed) but only "the men who do not have the seal of God upon their foreheads" supports such an understanding of the symbolism used here.

9:5 (also v. 10) ***For five months*.** This period has been variously interpreted. It has been suggested that the life span of locusts is five months. The harm of this plague would therefore include one entire generation of locusts.[27] Another attempt to explain the "five months" is through historical interpretation based on the day/year principle. All of these proposals are problematic, however. A search for the Old Testament background to the fifth trumpet scene takes us to the Genesis Flood story, which is the only place in the Old Testament where a five-month period is mentioned. Interestingly enough, it is mentioned there twice, just as in the scene of the fifth trumpet (Gen. 7:24; 8:3). It is most likely that John describes the demonic locusts harming the earth and its inhabitants for five months after the Flood story.

9:10 *Tails like scorpions and stings*. As William Barclay explains, scorpions are lobster-like insects up to six inches in length. With lobster-like claws they clutch their prey. With the curved claw at the end of its long tail, the scorpion strikes its prey, injecting it with poison.[28]

***Authority in their tails was to torment the people*.** The demonic locusts torment people by the stings of their tails. Isaiah uses the metaphor of the tail with reference to the prophets who deceive people with their false teaching (Isa. 9:14–15). In Revelation 12:4, the tail of the great red dragon, Satan himself (cf. 12:9), sweeps away a third of the stars of heaven, presumably the angels. Satan's tail most likely symbolizes the persuasion and deception with which he misled the heavenly beings to rebel against God and to follow him (cf. Rev. 12:9). It is in this sense that the symbol of the tail in the scene of the fifth trumpet must be understood (cf. Rev. 13:13–14).

9:11 *Whose name in Hebrew is Abaddon, and in Greek his name is Apollyon.* The Hebrew *Abaddon* means "destruction." In the Old Testament, Abaddon refers to the place of destruction associated with death and Sheol (cf. Job 26:6; 28:22; Ps. 88:11; Prov. 15:11; 27:20). John designates Abbadon as the personification of destruction. *Apollyon* is the Greek equivalent to Abbadon, which means "the one who destroys" or "the destroyer." The Destroyer is an appropriate name for Satan, who is evidently the king of these demonic locusts, and who in Matthew 12:24 is named "the ruler of the demons" (cf. Matt. 25:41; Rev. 12:9). Jesus describes him as a thief who comes to steal, kill, and destroy (John 10:10). The name Destroyer fits perfectly the nature and character of his activity on the earth (cf. 12:12–17).

EXPOSITION

9:1–2 At the sound of the fifth trumpet, John observes *a star fallen from heaven to the earth.* This is apparently the same fallen star of the third trumpet, "the great star" named Wormwood which had poisoned the rivers and the fountains of water, causing the spiritual death of those drinking from the fresh water supplies. This fallen star represents Satan and his falling from heaven to earth, also identified as *the angel of the abyss* (Rev. 9:11; cf. Isa. 14:12; Luke 10:18; Rev. 12:7–10). The star falling from heaven to earth evokes the fall of Satan, one of the most glorious angels. To him was given *the key of the pit of the abyss.* The abyss is the dark prison where demonic forces are confined (cf. Luke 8:31; 2 Pet. 2:4). It represents the headquarters of the demonic forces of darkness. The powers of evil, however, do not have their own freedom of movement. According to Revelation 1:18, Christ is in possession of the keys of Hades; the demonic forces are under his control (see *Notes* on Rev. 1:18). It is he who authorizes Satan to unlock the abyss and open it. These powers of evil are now given a chance to do their harmful work.

The fallen star opens the abyss from which a cloud of dense smoke emerges *like smoke of a great furnace.* Smoke is another symbol of judgment in Revelation (cf. 14:11; 19:3). *Like smoke of a great furnace* is a reminder of the smoke from the destruction of Sodom and Gomorrah which is described as going up "like the smoke of a furnace" (Gen. 19:28). Likewise, the presence of God at Sinai was associated with smoke ascending "like the smoke of a furnace" (Exod. 19:18). The smoke coming out of the abyss in the fifth trumpet creates thick darkness in the sky. In the fourth trumpet there was a partial darkness, which now becomes total; *the sun and the air became darkened by the smoke of the abyss.* This reminds us of the darkness that fell on Egypt which was so thick that people could not see each other or move from their place (Exod. 10:22–23). Whatever this darkness might mean, the fifth trumpet plague is special and very frightening.

9:3 Next John sees a terrible invasion of *locusts* emerging from the smoke ascending from the abyss. This indicates that the smoke coming up from the abyss is not ordinary smoke, but an exceptionally huge cloud of locusts that blocks the sun to the point of total darkness. The locusts of the Egyptian plague darkened the sky (Exod. 10:15). Joel spoke of the locust plague that caused the darkening of the heavenly bodies (Joel 2:2–10). These Old Testament scenes suggest that the deepening of the darkness of the fourth trumpet plague is caused by the gigantic cloud of locusts coming out from the abyss. Darkness is the obscuring of the gospel. When the people reject the gospel as the source of life, they are tormented by evil forces as a result (cf. John 3:18–21).

Locusts are also a symbol of judgment in the Old Testament. The locusts coming up from the abyss in the fifth trumpet scene are not ordinary insects. Instead of attacking plants (as locusts normally do), these locusts have the power of scorpions and they attack and torment people. Their leader is the angel of the abyss, Satan himself (Rev. 9:11). The clue for this symbolism is found in Luke 10:17–20: "And the seventy returned with joy, saying, 'Lord, even the demons are subject to us in Your name.' And he said to them, 'I was watching Satan fall from heaven like lightning. Behold, I have given you authority to tread upon serpents and scorpions, and over all the power of the enemy, and nothing shall injure you. Nevertheless do not rejoice in this, that the spirits are subject to you, but rejoice that your names are recorded in heaven.'" Jesus used snakes and scorpions here as metaphors for demons or evil spirits. It is quite possible that John the revelator had Christ's statement in mind in describing the locust invasion of the fifth trumpet. This leads one to conclude that the locusts of the fifth trumpet are demonic forces—what Paul calls the power of darkness and wickedness (Eph. 6:12)—abiding in the abyss as their prison abode.

9:4–6 The demonic locusts are now unleashed to harm the face of the earth. They are not able to harm those who are sealed, however, but only those *who do not have the seal of God upon their foreheads* (cf. 9:10). This sealing is portrayed in Revelation 7. Those who are sealed are the ones whom God knows and recognizes as his own (2 Tim. 2:19). They are protected and will not be harmed by these demonic attacks; the gospel protects those who are with Christ from the harm of the demonic powers. The assurance that Jesus gave to the twelve is still firm: "I have given you authority to tread upon serpents and scorpions, and over all the power of the enemy, and nothing shall injure you" (Luke 10:19).

The demonic locusts are not allowed to kill people but only permit *that they should be tormented.* The fifth trumpet plague is not physical, but spiritual and mental. The unleashed demonic locusts cause unbearable psychological torture and suicidal anguish. *In those days people will seek death and they will in no way find it, and they will long to die, and death will flee from them* (Rev. 9:6; cf. 8:3). Job speaks of someone who longs for death that does not come (Job 3:21). Likewise, Jeremiah speaks of the day when men will choose death rather than life (8:3).

The given period of this demonic torment is *five months.* This reminds us of the Genesis Flood that lasted and harmed the earth for five months (Gen. 7:24; 8:3). During this period, Noah and his family were under special protection, and the waters of the great Flood could not harm them. This Flood motif is reflected here in the scene of the fifth trumpet. Like Noah and his family, so the genuine believers are under special protection from the plague of the demonic locusts harming the earth and its inhabitants for "five months."

9:7–10 Having described the origin and mission of the demonic locusts, John next provides a detailed description of their appearance. In describing them, he uses the words "as" and "like." The demonic locusts appear like *horses prepared for battle* (cf. Joel 2:4); they wear what looks like crowns of gold; they have faces like humans, hair like women's hair, and teeth like a lion (cf. Joel 1:6); their scaly exterior is like iron breastplates; the noise of their wings is like the noise of battle chariots (cf. Joel 2:4–5).

It is uncertain whether John intended every detail of this description to be interpreted. The grotesque language is very much reminiscent of Joel's prophecy about the invasion on the day of the Lord:

> Their appearance is like the appearance of horses;
> And like war horses, so they run.
> With a noise as of chariots
> They leap on the tops of the mountains,
> Like the crackling of a flame of fire consuming the stubble,
> Like a mighty people arranged for battle.

Before them the people are in anguish;
All faces turn pale.
They run like mighty men;
They climb the wall like soldiers;
And they each march in line,
Nor do they deviate from their paths.
They do not crowd each other;
They march everyone in his path,
When they burst through the defenses,
They do not break ranks.
They rush on the city,
They run on the wall;
They climb into the houses,
They enter through the windows like a thief.
Before them the earth quakes,
The heavens tremble,
The sun and the moon grow dark,
And the stars lose their brightness. (Joel 2:4–10)

It is self-evident that the description of the demonic locusts is drawn from Joel's vision, although many of the details come from John. This description of the frightening appearance of the demonic locusts is intended, on one hand, to portray in a vivid way the bizarre character of evil powers and the awesomeness of their harm. On the other hand, this symbolic presentation is intended to make an impact on readers with a warning. The evil powers have been restrained for a long time. The day has come, however, when the powers of darkness are to be unleashed to exercise their activity as never before in history.

The demonic locusts are further said to have **tails like scorpions and stings, and authority in their tails was to torment the people for five months.** They torment people by their sting (cf. 9:3). The tail is a symbol of deception by means of persuasion which Satan uses to mislead human beings to rebel against God and follow him (cf. Rev. 12:4). The prophets teaching false instruction in Isaiah are referred to as the tail (Isa. 9:14–15). The harm done by the demonic locusts is obviously not military, but rather ideological. (As is shown later, destructive philosophies have caused tremendous damage to Christian faith and conduct.)

9:11 In contrast to natural locusts (cf. Prov. 30:27), these scorpion-like demonic locusts have as their king **the angel of the abyss.** His name is given in two languages:

in Hebrew it is **Abaddon** ("destruction"), and in Greek **Apollyon** ("destroyer"). This king of the demonic locusts is evidently Satan himself, the fallen star from heaven (Rev. 9:1), who has been given authority over the abyss and who still has dominion over the earth. Paul calls him "the prince of the power of the air" (Eph. 2:2). The Destroyer is his name, which appropriately defines his work of destroying and hurting (cf. John 10:10). He "prowls about like a roaring lion, seeking someone to devour" (1 Pet. 5:8). His followers are "the destroyers of the earth" who themselves will be destroyed by God at the sound of the seventh trumpet (Rev. 11:18). His special work is that of organizing the forces of evil in preparation for the most decisive battle against God and his people in the history of this planet. This preparation for the final battle is described in the sixth trumpet.

We noticed earlier that the first four trumpets are in pairs. The wormwood plague of the third trumpet describes in symbolic language the great apostasy of the Dark Middle Ages. The darkening of the sources of light of the fourth trumpet describes the subsequent Age of Enlightenment in Europe from the sixteenth through the eighteenth centuries. This period was characterized by the rise of rationalism, skepticism, humanism, and liberalism, with its final product of secularism and its negative effects on Christianity. The fifth trumpet plague is evidently the result of the spiritual decline and apostasy portrayed in the third and fourth trumpets. It appears that the situation in the world would have been totally different had the church remained faithful to the gospel.

Thus the fifth trumpet refers to the spiritual condition in the secular world and the consequences of such conditions from the eighteenth century to our time. As Hans LaRondelle explains, "traditional God-centered theology was replaced by a man-centered philosophy, in which man is accountable only to himself."[29] The oppressive rule of the church was replaced by the atheistic philosophy expressed in various forms, such as deism, relativism, nihilism, nationalism, and communism. The fact is that human beings try to live life apart from God. The secular-minded have become alienated from God, from others, and from themselves.[30] On one hand, atheistic philosophy has created in people the agony of emptiness and meaninglessness of life.[31] In the symbolic scene of the fifth trumpet we can observe the despair of the secular man and woman: no God, no future, and no meaning of life. It stands in contrast to green grass and trees that are nourished by water.

On the other hand, atheistic philosophy unleashed the demonic forces. Despite having separated themselves from God, secular people still have a longing for spiritual values to fill the emptiness of their lives. However, resistance to the transforming power of the gospel provides an opportunity for Satan to fill this emptiness. The smoke from the demonic abyss may be observed, for instance, in the various movements within Christianity that are promoting religion based largely on emotions, which has taken the place of the religion of mind and conduct. Yet this demonic smoke can equally be observed in the widespread New Age movement and the growing activities of Islam.

The only security from demonic harm is found in Christ. The scene of the fifth trumpet warns against any religion which is apart from Christ. When Israel in the time of the prophet Amos chose the life of sin and "turned justice into poison, and the fruit of righteousness into wormwood" (Amos 6:12), God brought swarms of locusts upon their land. This might explain what the scene of the fifth trumpet describes. Because the people have resisted and rejected the transforming power of the gospel and have rather chosen darkness (as described in the third and the fourth trumpet), the demonic locust torment resulted. Paul warned the Christians of his day, "Do not be deceived, God is not mocked; for whatever a man sows, this he will also reap" (Gal. 6:7).

9:12 John concludes the scene with a warning to the reader that the fifth trumpet plague is just the *first woe*. Two woes are yet to come. The wicked are to experience more dreadful sufferings, of which the fifth trumpet plague has only been a prelude.

THE SIXTH TRUMPET (9:13–21)

> [13]*And the sixth angel sounded his trumpet; and I heard a voice from the horns of the golden altar which is before God, [14]saying to the sixth angel who had the trumpet: "Release the four angels who are bound at the great river Euphrates." [15]And the four angels, the ones who were prepared for the hour and day and month and year, were released that they might kill a third of humankind. [16]And the number of the army of horsemen was two hundred million; I heard the number of them. [17]And thus I saw the horses in the vision and those sitting upon them, having breastplates of fire and hyacinth and sulphur; and the heads of*

the horses were as heads of lions, and out of their mouths were coming fire and smoke and sulphur. [18]From these three plagues were killed a third of humankind, from the fire and the smoke and the sulphur coming out of their mouths. [19]For the authority of the horses is in their mouths and in their tails, for their tails are like snakes, having heads and with them they cause harm.

[20]And the rest of the people, the ones who were not killed by these plagues, did not repent of the works of their hands, so as not to worship the demons and the idols of gold and of silver and of brass and of stone and of wood, which can neither see nor hear or walk; [21]and they did not repent of their murders or their sorceries or their fornication or their thefts.

NOTES

9:13 *The golden altar which is before God.* The golden altar here is evidently the altar of incense before the throne mentioned earlier in Revelation 8:3–4 (see *Notes* on Rev. 8:3), and which in the Old Testament temple was "in front of the veil that is near the ark of the testimony, in front of the mercy seat that is over the ark of the testimony, where I will meet with you" (cf. Exod. 30:6).

9:14 *The great river Euphrates.* In the Old Testament, the Euphrates, called the great river (Gen. 15:18; Deut. 1:7; Josh 1:4), stood for the boundary that separated God's people from their enemies. Regions beyond the Euphrates were regarded as the symbol of the archenemies of God and Israel—Assyria and Babylon (Isa. 7:20; Jer. 46:10). The attack of these enemy nations on Israel is described in Isaiah as destructively abundant waters of the Euphrates overflowing its banks and sweeping over the land of Judah, reaching up even to the neck, namely, Jerusalem (Isa. 8:7–8). This is the sense in which John uses the symbol of the river Euphrates.

The Euphrates was also the eastern boundary of the Roman Empire beyond which lay the Parthian empire, the rise of which was a constant threat to the Empire. Since the text mentions the invasion of the horsemen from beyond the river Euphrates, some modern commentators argue that they symbolize the much feared Parthian armies.[32] The Roman armies were three times defeated by them (in 53 and 35 B.C. and A.D. 62), which created anxiety among Romans of possible destruction from this eastern power. Even the Jewish apocalyptic writings anticipated an eschatological invasion from the Parthian forces:

> In those days, the angels will assemble and thrust themselves to the east at the Parthians and Medes. They will shake up the kings (so that) a spirit of unrest shall come upon them, and stir them up from their thrones; and they will break forth from their beds like lions and like hungry hyenas among their own flocks. And they will go up and trample upon the land of my elect ones, and the land of my elect ones will be before them like a threshing floor or a highway.[33]

This text shows how the apocalyptic writer applied the prophecy of Ezekiel against Gog (Ezek. 38–39) to the Parthians who lay beyond the Euphrates. Many scholars today find it highly unlikely that John's prophecy concerns a literal Parthian invasion.[34] It is hard to see this prophecy fulfilled with reference to the Roman Empire, because it embraces the entire world. Also, the size of an army of 200,000,000 horsemen (Rev. 9:16) indicates that John did not have a literal Parthian invasion in mind. It appears that in communicating the prophecy of the eschatological demonic invasion, he utilizes Ezekiel's prophecy against Gog and the much familiar first-century Roman anxiety. G. R. Beasley-Murray states: "For the army he awaits is more terrible by far than any human army. It is a supernatural, indeed an infernal, host."[35]

The four angels. The four angels "who are bound at the great river Euphrates" are evidently the same four angels of Revelation 7:1–3. While in Revelation 7 the four angels are holding firmly the four winds of the earth, so that the wind should not blow upon the earth, the four angels in Revelation 9 restrain the armies of the horsemen. While in Revelation 7:3 they are ordered not to harm the earth until the servants of God have been sealed, in the scene of the sixth trumpet they are released "that they might kill the third part of humankind" (9:15, 18). It appears that the destructive winds restrained by the four angels in Revelation 7:1–3 correspond to the horsemen, presumably the demonic forces described in the scene of the sixth trumpet (Rev. 9:16–19).

9:15 *The four angels...were released.* The passive form here ("were released") functions as the divine passive (see *Notes* on Rev. 9:1).

9:16 *Horsemen.* The description of the horsemen suggests that they are the same as the demonic locusts of the fifth trumpet, but under different circumstances. First of all, the appearance of the demonic locusts was like horses prepared for battle (9:7, 9). The demonic locusts came out of the abyss (9:2–3), while the horsemen come from the river Euphrates, the symbolic boundary between God's people and their enemies (see *Notes* on Rev. 9:14). Both have breastplates (9:9, 17). Furthermore, the power of both the locusts and the horses is in their tails (9:10, 19). While the locusts had teeth like that of lions, the heads of the horses looked like the heads of lions (9:8, 17). The harmful activity of the horsemen of the sixth trumpet suggests a further intensification of the destructive demonic activity as divine judgments that began with the coming of the locusts in the fifth trumpet.

Two hundred million. Literally, "two myriads of myriads," or, twenty thousand times ten thousand. The figure here is doubtlessly symbolic, representing a countless multitude,[36] such as the chariots of God in Psalm 68:17, in contrast to the 144,000 sealed saints of Revelation 7.

9:17–18 *Fire and smoke and sulphur.* The combination of fire, smoke, and sulphur in the Bible is always linked with judgments on the wicked. In destroying Sodom and Gomorrah, the Lord rained sulphur and fire out of heaven, so that their smoke ascended like the smoke of a furnace (Gen. 19:24, 28; Luke 17:29). Elsewhere in the Old Testament these elements are used for punishing the wicked (Ps. 11:6; Isa. 34:9–10; Ezek. 38:22). In Revelation, the receivers of the mark of the beast will be "tormented with fire and sulphur before the holy angels and before the Lamb. And the smoke of their torment ascends forever and ever" (Rev. 14:10–11). These three elements are used for the destruction of Satan and his forces in the lake of fire at the final judgment (Rev. 20:10; cf. 19:20; 21:8). The text of 9:17b–18 seems to indicate a chiastic arrangement:

> **A** from their mouths
>> **B** were coming out
>>> **C** fire and smoke and sulphur.
>>>> **D** From these three plagues were killed the third part of humankind,
>>> **C'** from the fire and the smoke and the sulphur
>> **B'** coming out
> **A'** from their mouths.[37]

9:19 *Mouths.* According to 9:18, the people are killed by fire, smoke, and sulphur issuing from the horses' mouths. The mouth as a symbol in Revelation refers to a mighty weapon in the spiritual battle between good and evil. From Christ's mouth proceeds a sharp two-edged sword (1:16) with which he makes war against the unrepentant (2:16; 19:15, 21). If somebody tries to harm the two witnesses, fire proceeds out of their mouths and kills their enemies (11:5). On the other side, the symbolic mouth is the weapon of Satan and his associates in their activities against God's people. From the mouth of the dragon proceeds water to destroy the woman, presumably the church (12:15). The sea beast of Revelation 13 is given "a mouth to speak great things and blasphemies" (13:5). "And he opened his mouth in blasphemies against God, to blaspheme his name and his tabernacle, namely, those who dwell in heaven" (13:6). In preparation for the final battle between the forces of light and darkness, John saw "coming out of the mouth of the dragon and out of the mouth of the beast and out of the mouth of the false prophet, three unclean spirits like frogs" persuading the kings of the world to unite for the final war of the earth's history (16:13–14). All of this suggests that the battle between the forces of good and evil in the book of Revelation is verbal rather than physical in character.

Tails. See *Notes* on Revelation 9:10.

EXPOSITION

In the scene of the blowing of the fifth trumpet, the horse-like demonic locusts were prepared for battle (9:5) under the leadership of the angel of the abyss named Destroyer, who was Satan himself (9:11). Their activities are restrained, however, for they were not allowed to kill people but only to torment them for five months (9:7). The situation is now changing; the demonic forces are given total freedom to exercise their destructive activities against the earth and its inhabitants.

9:13–16 When the sixth angel sounds his trumpet, John hears a voice coming from *the horns of the golden altar which is before God.* This remark about the heavenly voice coming from the altar of incense is especially important in light of the plea of God's oppressed people for deliverance, in the scene of the fifth seal (Rev. 6:9–10). In Revelation 8:3–5, their prayers are offered on the altar of incense before the throne, and judgment is poured out as a result. The mentioning again of the altar of incense—the same altar upon which the prayers of the oppressed saints were offered—suggests that the prayers of God's people are still remembered.[38] The scene of the sixth trumpet represents an advance in divine response to the prayers of God's oppressed people.

Two things come to light from the text. First, the heavenly voice commands the sixth angel to *release the four angels who are bound at the great river Euphrates.* The text shows further that these angels restrain the demonic forces from destroying the earth (9:16–19). This scene reminds us of the four angels holding the destroying winds who are restrained from harming the earth until the sealing of God's people has been completed (Rev. 7:1–3). The obvious parallels between 7:1–3 and 9:13–16 link the two scenes: in both scenes, binding and loosing are associated with four angels; the participants in both scenes are numbered—God's people in chapter 7 and the demonic hordes in the scene of the sixth trumpet; and only these scenes use the phrase "I heard the number" (7:4; 9:16). These strong parallels place the two scenes into the same time setting—the preparation for the final battle.

That the four angels in Revelation 9 are confined to the river Euphrates is especially important. The Euphrates in the Old Testament marks the border between God's people and their enemies; it is the place from which the threat to God's people comes. It is at the symbolic river Euphrates that the four angels restrain the demonic army organized against God's people. The demonic forces are under the sovereign control of God Almighty.

The second thing to observe is that the demonic forces have no freedom to act until the time set for them by God. The four angels are said to have been *prepared for the hour and day and month and year.* This can be understood as "a divinely-appointed *moment* in time."[39] This releasing of the angels must be understood as a divine passive; in other words, it is God who allows them to act. The unleashing of the demonic forces had already begun with the sound of the fifth trumpet. The demonic locusts were allowed to torment the wicked for "five months"; they were restrained from destroying and killing them, however (9:3–6). Here, in the scene of the sixth trumpet, the demonic cavalry completes a widespread killing. The time is coming when God will remove the restraints, thus making it possible for the demonic forces to exercise their activity as never before in history, and carry out his judgments on the inhabitants of the earth.

The number of the horsemen of the demonic army is *two hundred million.* The phrase *I heard the number of them* relates evidently to "I heard the number of those who have been sealed" of Revelation 7:4, and the numbering of the 144,000 sealed people of God. These demonic horsemen are, thus, the demonic counterfeit of God's people.[40] Both groups, God's sealed people and Satan's hosts, are prepared for the final battle of this world's history.

9:17–19 As in the scene of the fifth trumpet, after having described the mission of the demonic hordes, John next provides a detailed description of their appearance. He describes the horses and the riders in the same way as he does the demonic locusts in the scene of the fifth trumpet. In describing their frightening appearance, he uses again the words "as" and "like." The demonic army is equipped with materials from the lake of fire: fire, smoke, and sulphur (Rev. 19:20; 20:10; 21:8). The riders wear fiery red, smoky blue, and sulphurous yellow breastplates. These colors correspond to the fire, smoke, and sulphur issuing from the mouths of the horses. The combination of these three elements in the Bible is the symbol of God's judgment on the wicked. The horses' heads look like those of lions. This grotesque language has been intended, as in the case of the fifth trumpet, to portray the bizarre character of the demonic activity and to make an impact on the readers.

The power of these demonic horses to kill lies in *their mouths and in their tails.* The tails here in the scene of the sixth trumpet are related to the tails in 9:10 which suggests that the sixth trumpet is an extension of the fifth. The sixth trumpet intensifies the demonic activities that began with the fifth trumpet. Whereas the source of the demonic locusts' power was in their tails, causing only torture, here both the tails and the mouths are in action in preparation for the final battle against God's people, causing both torture and death. The consequence of this plague is that *a third of humankind* is destroyed.

The demonic horses use their tails to torment and harm. *Their tails are like snakes, having heads and with them they cause harm*. In Revelation 12:9, Satan is designated as "the old serpent" with the ability to sweep away "a third of the stars of heaven," presumably the angels. Isaiah refers to the prophets teaching false instruction as the tail (Isa. 10:14–15). We can see that the tail is a symbol of deception and false teaching which Satan uses to lead human beings to turn from God and follow him.

While the demonic horses torment people with their tails, they kill with their mouths from which fire, smoke, and sulphur are issuing. This reminds us of the three demons coming from the mouth of Satan and his associates in the scene of the final Armageddon battle (cf. Rev. 16:13–14). In Revelation 12:15, it is from the mouth of the dragon that water proceeds to destroy the woman. It brings to mind also the sea beast of Revelation 13 to whom is given "a mouth to speak great things and blasphemies." "And he opened his mouth in blasphemies against God, to blaspheme his name and his tabernacle, namely, those who dwell in heaven" (13:5–6).

All of this suggests that the final conflict between the forces of light and darkness will not be military, but spiritual. The character of that conflict will be verbal and ideological—a battle for mind by means of persuasion rather than physical force. This is the kind of warfare that Paul had in mind when he wrote: "For though we walk in the flesh, we do not war according to the flesh, for the weapons of our warfare are not of the flesh, but divinely powerful for the destruction of fortresses. We are destroying speculations and every lofty thing raised up against the knowledge of God, and we are taking every thought captive to the obedience of Christ" (2 Cor. 10:3–5; cf. Eph. 6:10–12).

9:20–21 John concludes the entire scene with this observation: *And the rest of the people, the ones who were not killed by these plagues, did not repent.* The sixth trumpet plague affects "a third part" of humankind who suffer terrible torment and massacre (9:15, 18). "The rest of humankind" who survived the demonic destruction refuse to repent. The plague does not soften their hearts. In their helpless and hopeless situation they continue in their course of worshiping *the demons and the idols of gold and of silver and of brass and of stone and of wood, which can neither see nor hear nor walk.* This language is borrowed from Daniel 5:23, where the worshiping of idols of "silver and gold, of bronze, iron, wood and stone, which do not see, hear or understand" resulted in the fall of Babylon (also Ps. 115:4–7).

Furthermore, the wicked *did not repent of their murders or their sorceries or their fornication or their thefts.* Paul describes these sins as the product of idolatry (cf. Rom. 1:18–32; Rev. 21:8; 22:15). Having been taken together, these vices are the fruit of worshiping the demons. The wicked are tormented by the demons, yet they continue to serve them. God does not want anyone to experience judgment but to repent and turn to him (2 Pet. 3:9). The wicked will perish if they refuse to repent, however (Luke 13:3, 5).

The scene of the sixth trumpet brings us clearly to the time of the end. It portrays the preparation for the battle of Armageddon, which is described later in the book (Rev. 16:12–16). It points to the last crisis of the world which, as the end draws near, will be characterized by the intensification of demonic activities. The people who are without the seal of God are unprotected against the demonic powers and from the deceptive doctrines and ideologies of symbolic Babylon. Desmond Ford writes: "The multitudes who have rejected the blood of the atonement, the incense of Christ's righteousness, the refreshment from the divine rivers and fountains, and the light from heavenly orbs, have no protection against the doctrine of devils, and ultimately no protection against the devils themselves."[41]

The failure of the wicked to repent signals the approaching cessation of intercession and the gathering for the final battle between Christ and his army and Satan and his army (Rev. 16:12–16). It is during these intensive demonic activities that God makes a special effort to reach human hearts in offering the everlasting gospel to the inhabitants of the earth (Rev. 14:6–13). His mercies are still available. He hopes that sin-hardened hearts will respond and make a decisive turnaround. This last proclamation of the everlasting gospel is described in the interlude between the sixth and the seventh trumpets (Rev. 10–11:14) as well as in the portrayal of the three angels flying in midheaven with the warning messages to the inhabitants of the earth (Rev. 14:6–13).

A RETROSPECT ON REVELATION 8–9

The vision of the blowing of the seven trumpets portrays in symbolic language a series of interventions by Almighty God in history in response to the prayers of his oppressed and harassed people portrayed in the scene of the fifth seal: "How long, O Lord, holy and true, will you not judge and avenge our blood upon those who dwell on the earth?" (Rev. 6:10). The introductory scene to the seven trumpets (Rev. 8:2–5) shows that the prayers of God's people have been heard in heaven. The answer sent to them is unequivocal and definite: "Not too long." The purpose of the events symbolically portrayed in the blowing of the seven trumpets is to affirm to God's people that God is already judging "those who dwell on the earth" (Rev. 8:13), who have viciously oppressed and persecuted his faithful people.

We observed that the first four trumpet plagues are divine warnings and have redemptive purposes. They are intended to bring the wicked to repentance and warn them that the time for repentance is rapidly running out, and the door of mercy will close forever. The declaration of the vulture's threefold woe forms the transition between the warning judgments of the first four trumpet plagues and the demonic woes of the last three trumpets on those who are spiritually dead in their rejection and persistent hostility to the gospel.

The scene of the sixth trumpet is strikingly parallel to the scene of the four angels restraining the destroying winds and the sealing of the 144,000 of God's people in Revelation 7:1–3. Jon Paulien summarizes these parallels:

> In both sections binding and loosing are related to four angels. In both sections a people are being numbered: in Revelation 7 the people of God; in Revelation 9 their demonic counterparts. And these are the only two places in Revelation containing the cryptic words: 'I heard the number [*ēkousa ton arithmon*].' If probation remains open through the sixth trumpet and then closes with the sounding of the seventh, the sixth trumpet is the exact historical counterpart of Revelation 7:1–8. It is the last opportunity for salvation just before the end.[42]

As in the case of the opening of the seven seals, there is an interlude between the scenes of the sixth and seventh trumpets. The interlude between the opening of the sixth and seventh seals answers the decisive question raised in the scene of the opening of the sixth seal regarding those who would be able to stand on the day of the wrath of God (Rev. 6:17). The interlude inserted between the sixth and the seventh trumpets is likewise related to what is taking place in the scene of the sixth trumpet. First of all, it declares the speedy end of earth's history at the sound of the seventh trumpet (Rev. 10:7).[43] Second, it refers to the time of intensive preparation and the great gathering for the battle of Armageddon. The four angels at the river Euphrates who have been restraining the four destructive winds are being released. This indicates that the sealing of God's people is in the process of its completion (Rev. 7:1–3). The released angels are ready to unleash the restrained winds, let them blow with their full force to "harm the earth and the sea," and bring earth's history to its end.

One serious question deserves an answer: What about God's people living in that period of the great preparation for the final battle before the end? John does not leave his readers with any uncertainty. As in the opening of the seven seals, the interlude between the scenes of the sixth and the seventh trumpets provides the answer to the question. While the followers of Christ are under special care and protection as the angels are in full control of the destructive winds (Rev. 7:3–8), they are commissioned to a special mission in spite of facing "fierce opposition and suffering"[44] (Rev. 10–11:14). Their commission to preach God's final message to the world is portrayed in the symbolic eating of the opened little scroll (Rev. 10), and their experience in preaching the gospel to the world is portrayed in the scene of the two witnesses (Rev. 11). The purpose of the interlude is to awaken God's people and provide them with a firm assurance of the ultimate triumph of the gospel as they approach the final days of earth's history.

ENDNOTES

1. Roloff, 106.

2. See 1 Enoch 20:2–8 (Charlesworth, 1:22–23); cf. Tobit 12:15 (*The Oxford Annotated Apocrypha*, 73).

3. Robert L. Thomas, *Revelation 8–22: An Exegetical Commentary* (Chicago: Moody Press, 1992), 7.

4. *Mishnah Yoma* 5 (Danby, 167).

5. *Mishnah Tamid* 5.6 (Danby, 587).

6. Ibid., 3.8 (Danby, 585).

7. As portrayed in the *Mishnah Tamid* 5.6 (Danby, 587).

8. Thomas, *Revelation 8–22*, 12.

9. Ladd, 126.

10. Thomas, *Revelation 8–22*, 13.

11. Paulien, *Decoding Revelation's Trumpets*, 370.

12. Ibid., 388.

13. Cf. 4 Ezra 3 (Charlesworth, 1:528–529); 2 Baruch 10:1–3; 11:1; 67:7 (Charlesworth, 1:623, 625, 644); Sib. Oracles 5:137–154, 160–161 (Charlesworth, 1:396–397).

14. Paulien, *Decoding Revelation's Trumpets*, 389.

15. Edwin R. Thiele, *Outline Studies in Revelation*, Class Syllabus (Berrien Springs, MI: Emmanuel Missionary College, 1949), 168; Paulien, *Decoding Revelation's Trumpets*, 386.

16. Paulien, *Decoding Revelation's Trumpets*, 386.

17. Ibid.

18. LaRondelle, *How to Understand the End-Time Prophecies*, 182.

19. Barclay, *The Revelation of John*, 2:47; cf. 1 Enoch 86:1; 88:1; 90:24 (Charlesworth, 1:63–64, 70); Test. of Solomon 6:2; 8:1–2; 20:14–17 (Charlesworth, 1:967, 969–970, 983).

20. Desmond Ford, 2:440.

21. Paulien, *Decoding Revelation's Trumpets*, 398.

22. Thiele, 170.

23. Paulien, *Decoding Revelation's Trumpets*, 415.

24. Ibid.

25. Desmond Ford, 2:442.

26. Collins, *The Apocalypse*, 60.

27. Barclay, *The Revelation of John*, 2:51; Mounce, 155; Morris, 126.

28. Barclay, *The Revelation of John*, 2:51.

29. LaRondelle, *How to Understand the End-Time Prophecies*, 189.

30. Paulien, Bible Explorer 3.12.

31. LaRondelle, *How to Understand the End-Time Prophecies*, 189.

32. E.g., Swete, 121; Barclay, *The Revelation of John*, 2:53; J. M. Ford, 153–154; Sweet, 172; Collins, *The Apocalypse*, 62.

33. 1 Enoch 56:5–8 (Charlesworth, 1:39); as pointed to by Ladd, 135.

34. Including Caird, 122; Mounce, 200–201; Harrington, 143; Ladd, 135; Beasley-Murray, 164; Fiorenza, *Revelation*, 72.

35. Beasley-Murray, 164.

36. Bauer, 661.

37. As pointed to by Aune, *Revelation 6–16*, 540.

38. Morris, 129–130.

39. LaRondelle, *How to Understand the End-Time Prophecies*, 193.

40. Paulien, "Seals and Trumpets," 196.

41. Desmond Ford, 2:458.

42. Paulien, "Seals and Trumpets," 196.

43. Ezell, 51.

44. LaRondelle, *How to Understand the End-Time Prophecies*, 194.

Revelation 10–11:14 is inserted between the sixth and the seventh trumpets as a sort of interlude. In the vision of the seven seals, an interlude occurs between the sixth and the seventh seals, portraying the sealing of God's people and the great redeemed multitude standing before God's throne. The seven-trumpet series follows the same pattern. The interlude between the sixth and seventh trumpets portrays the strong angel with the open little scroll (10:1–11) and the two witnesses (11:1–14). Just as Revelation 7 answers the question raised in the scene of the sixth seal (6:17), the interlude between the sixth and seventh trumpets seems to provide the answer to a question, as G. R. Beasley-Murray suggests: "What is the task of the Church in these troublous times?"[1] Thus Revelation 10–11:14 describes the experience of God's people in the world and their role with reference to the preaching of the gospel as the final days of earth's history approach their close.

Revelation 10 contains two parts: a portrayal of a strong angel with the open little scroll (10:1–7) followed by the angel's commission to John to prophesy concerning the nations (10:8–11).

THE LITTLE SCROLL (10:1–7)

The description of the sixth trumpet plague is completed. The angels at the Euphrates River—where the four winds are being held so that the sealing of God's people could take place (cf. Rev. 7:1–3)—are released (9:14); it is now time for the great gathering for the battle of Armageddon. The reader intuitively expects to hear the sounding of the seventh trumpet. Instead, the sequence of the last two trumpets is interrupted. The reader's attention shifts to a scene that is of quite a different character from the rest of the trumpets.

¹*And I saw another strong angel coming down from heaven, clothed in a cloud, and the rainbow was over his head, and his face was like the sun, and his feet like pillars of fire,* ²*and he had in his hand an opened little scroll. And he placed his right foot on the sea and his left on the land,* ³*and he cried with a loud voice as a lion roars. And when he cried, the seven thunders uttered their voices.* ⁴*And when the seven thunders spoke, I was about to write; and I heard a voice from heaven saying: "Seal up the things which the seven thunders spoke, and do not write them."* ⁵*And the angel whom I saw standing on the sea and on the land lifted up his right hand toward heaven* ⁶*and swore by the One who lives forever and ever, who created heaven and the things which are in it, and the earth and the things which are in it, and the sea and the things which are in it, that there will no longer be time,* ⁷*but in the days of the sound of the seventh angel, when he is about to sound, then the mystery of God will be completed, as he proclaimed to his servants the prophets.*

NOTES

10:1 *Another strong angel.* The "strong angel" here seems to correspond to the "strong angel" of Revelation 5:2; both are referred to as "strong" or "mighty" (Gr. *ischuros*) and are associated with the heavenly scrolls. It appears that the designation of the angel in 10:1 as "another" denotes that he is not one of the seven who blew the trumpets. He has a different mission. In the Old Testament, the angel sent by God functions in the authority of God (cf. Gen. 31:11–13; Exod. 3:2–6; Judg. 13:6, 21–22). The description of this strong angel parallels in some detail the description of the glorified Christ in Revelation 1:13–15, leading some expositors to view him as Christ himself.[2] Although the appearance of this angel is described in terms of deity, it seems he is not Christ himself. This assertion is based on the fact that Christ in Revelation is never referred to as an angel. So one may ask why we should view this strong angel as Christ and not the other "strong" angel in Revelation 5:2. What seems clear in the book, however, is that an angel commissioned by Christ functions like Christ himself. For instance, in Revelation 22:6–16 the angel articulates the words of Jesus. Thus it is frequently hard to distinguish between the appearance of the angel sent and commissioned by Christ and the appearance of Christ himself. It is reasonable to assume that the Christ-like figure of Revelation 10 is a special angel of exalted rank, functioning in the full representation and authority of Christ.[3]

10:2 *A little scroll.* The Greek word *biblaridion* denotes a small papyrus scroll (see *Notes* on Rev. 5:1). Originally the term *biblion* was used for a little scroll (as a diminutive of *biblos*). Later, this diminutive meaning of *biblion* vanished, and by the time of John the word *biblaridion* was used instead for a scroll of a smaller size. *Biblos* and *biblion* gradually came to have the same meaning; they were used synonymously and often interchangeably with reference to a scroll regardless of its size. A careful analysis of *biblos, biblion,* and *biblaridion* in Revelation shows that John the revelator does not have a consistent pattern in using these words. For instance, in Revelation 20 *biblos* and *biblion* are used interchangeably for the book of life; in 20:12 it is the *biblion* of life (cf. 13:8; 17:8; 21:27), but in 20:15 it is the *biblos* of life (cf. 3:5). Especially interesting is that in Revelation 10:2 the little scroll is called *biblaridion*, and in verse 8 it is called *biblion*. This shows clearly that in Revelation there is no consistent or purposeful use of one or the other form of the word for the scroll. The probable reason for the use of the diminutive *biblaridion* in Revelation 10 and the emphasis on the fact that it was opened may be for the sake of contrasting it with the scroll of Revelation 5, which was large and was closed and sealed.

A number of recent studies have argued persuasively that the scroll of Revelation 5 and the little scroll in chapter 10 are identical.[4] The fact that both scrolls are associated with a "strong angel" suggests that the two scrolls are closely related. Also, the sealed scroll can be opened only after all the seals have been broken. The events of the breaking of the seven seals and the judgments of the seven trumpets are thus preliminary and preparatory to the opening of the sealed scroll. The disclosure of the scroll's content must come after Revelation 10. The mention of the ark of the covenant at the conclusion of the blowing of the seventh trumpet in Revelation 11:19 and at the beginning of a new vision starting with Revelation 12 suggests Revelation 12–22:5 to be the disclosure of the real little scroll's content (see "Overview: Revelation 12–22:5"). However, the little scroll of Revelation 10 is referred to as the *biblaridion*, suggesting that it may be a portion of the larger *biblion* of chapter 5. This would further suggest that the open little scroll of Revelation 10 held by a strong angel is only a partial disclosure of the divine revelation that had been sealed (cf. Isa. 8:16; 29:9–14; Dan. 12:4, 9) and which is portrayed figuratively in the image of the seven-sealed scroll in Revelation 5.

The close link between the two scrolls and the book of Revelation has already been discussed in detail (see "The Contents of the Sealed Scroll in Revelation 5" in "Overview: Revelation 4–11:19") and will not be repeated here. Revelation 4–10 appears to be arranged to follow the chain of transmission described in Revelation 1:1–3 where Jesus receives the revelation from God (chap. 5). Jesus discloses this message to John through his angel (10:1–10). Finally, John is ordered to communicate to the churches the revelation disclosed to him as the word of prophecy (10:11), the contents of which are given in Revelation 12–22:5 (see "A Retrospect on Revelation 1:1–8"). Some commentators have interpreted the opened scroll of Revelation 10 to be the book of Daniel which was sealed to human understanding "until the end of time" (Dan. 12:4, 9).[5] As described in the *Notes* on Revelation 10:6, a number of common parallels between Daniel 12 and Revelation 10 suggest a close link between the contents of the two chapters, including the oaths of the angel in Daniel 12:7 and of the strong angel in Revelation 10:5–7, respectively. This suggests the close relation of the opened little scroll to the sealed prophetic portion of Daniel with reference to the time of the end. It is disclosed to God's end-time people in Revelation 12–22:5 with the purpose of helping them prepare for the end-time events that are to take place on earth. However, the content of the little scroll of Revelation 10 is not limited to the prophetic portion of the book of Daniel, because its content is broader than that of the book of Daniel.

Opened is the perfect passive participle. The perfect tense indicates that the little scroll has been opened at some previous time. The passive form here functions most likely as a divine passive (see *Notes* on Rev. 9:1), suggesting the opening of the scroll as a divine act. The fact that the angel later lifts up his right hand toward heaven in swearing the oath suggests that he holds the little scroll in his left hand.

10:3 *The seven thunders.* The concept of the seven thunders of Revelation 10 is one of the most mysterious in the book of Revelation. The definite article used ("*the* seven thunders") suggests that the concept was familiar to the Christians of John's day. It appears that Psalm 29 is the key background text for the image of the seven thunders, where the sevenfold voice of God set in action is referred to as the voice of thunder (29:3–9). A later Jewish tradition held that "the voice of Yahweh on Sinai was heard as seven thunders."[6] In the Old Testament, when God speaks and acts in power, it is often portrayed as the sound of thunder (Job 26:14; 37:5; Ps. 18:13; cf. 1 Sam. 7:10). Before the cross in John 12:28–29, the voice of God speaking to Jesus was perceived by the attending crowd as the sound of thunder. It is especially interesting that "this passage is followed by a reference to the judgment of the world and the expulsion of its ruler," Satan himself (12:30–31).[7] In the rest of the book of Revelation, thunder functions as the revelatory forewarning with regard to divine activities in judgment: thunder acts as the forewarning to the breaking of the seven seals (4:5; 6:1), to the trumpet plagues (8:5), to the warfare between the dragon and the woman leading to the seven last plagues (11:19), and to the conclusion of earth's history leading to the final judgment (16:18).

10:6 *There will no longer be time.* The phrase is a literal translation of the Greek, *hoti chronos ouketi estai.* The Greek language has two basic words, *kairos* and *chronos*, which are translated as "time." Broadly speaking, *kairos* denotes a point of time, a fixed or a definite period, a season (cf. Matt. 11:25; 12:1; Acts 3:19; Rom. 3:26; 5:6). *Chronos*, on the other hand, implied duration of a period, a space of time (cf. Matt. 25:19; Acts 13:18; Gal. 4:4; Rev. 20:3), although the two terms often overlap and are synonymous.[8] (NIV translates *chronos* and *kairos* of Acts 1:7 and 1 Thess. 5:1 as "times" and "dates," respectively.) Many scholars understand the phrase as "there will be no more delay." This translation has been contested by David Aune, who argues that "delay" is an inappropriate translation of *chronos* here because it "assumes that eschatological events have been postponed"; rather, the phrase means that "'the time will be up' and the eschatological events will begin to unfold."[9]

A striking resemblance between Revelation 10:1–7 and Daniel 12:4–7 suggests that the *chronos* of Revelation 10:1 should be understood in light of Daniel 12:4–9 which reads as follows in the NIV translation:

"But you, Daniel, close up and seal the words of the scroll until the time of the end. Many will go here and there to increase knowledge." Then I, Daniel, looked, and there before me stood two others, one on this bank of the river and one on the opposite bank. One of them said to the man clothed in linen, who was above the waters of the river, "How long will it be before these astonishing things are fulfilled?" The man clothed in linen, who was above the waters of the river, lifted his right hand and his left hand toward heaven, and I heard him swear by him who lives forever, saying, "It will be for a time, times and half a time. When the power of the holy people has been finally broken, all these things will be completed." I heard, but I did not understand. So I asked, "My lord, what will the outcome of all this be?" He replied, "Go your way, Daniel, because the words are closed up and sealed until the time of the end."

Several parallels exist here, suggesting that Revelation 10 follows up on Daniel 12. First of all, there is the command to seal up the words of the scroll until the time of the end (Dan. 12:4; cf. Rev. 10:4). Next, there is a question: "How long will it be before these astonishing things are fulfilled?" It is followed by a raising of the hands toward heaven and the swearing of an oath by the One who lives forever that "it would be for a time, times and half a time," the time of "the abomination of desolation" (Dan. 12:11; cf. Rev. 10:5–6), namely, the Antichrist's persecution of the saints. Daniel was told that the end would certainly come when this prophesied time is completed. In Revelation 6:9–11, the slain martyrs under the altar cry for deliverance and vindication: "How long, O Lord, before you vindicate us?" They are told to wait for a short time (*eti chronon mikron*). In Revelation 10:6, however, God's people are given the promise that there will be no more time (or "delay," as in Matt. 24:48; 25:5; Heb. 10:37). The time is coming when at the sound of the trumpet of the seventh angel, "the mystery of God will be completed, as he proclaimed to his servants the prophets" (Rev. 10:7), Daniel in particular. God is about to fulfill his promise to vindicate and deliver his suffering yet faithful people.

Seventh-day Adventists often refer to the statement of Ellen G. White for their understanding of the *chronos* of Revelation 10:6, which is in line with the foregoing observations: "This time, which the angel declares with a solemn oath, is not the end of this world's history, neither of probationary time, but of prophetic time, which should precede the advent of our Lord. That is, the people will not have another message upon definite time. After this period of time, reaching from 1842 to 1844, there can be no definite tracing of the prophetic time. The longest reckoning reaches to the autumn of 1844."[10]

10:7 *The mystery of God.* "The mystery of God" in the Bible refers to God's purpose with reference to the future, which he has revealed through his specially chosen agents, the prophets. In Daniel 2, God revealed mysteries to king Nebuchadnezzar with reference to what will take place in the latter days (Dan. 2:28–29) to bring the earth's history to an end and establish his eternal kingdom in the world (2:44–45). These mysteries were concealed from the wise men in Babylon (2:27). That God reveals his mysteries with reference to the future by means of the prophets is also stated by Amos: "Surely the Lord God does nothing unless He reveals His secret counsel to His servants the prophets" (3:7). In the New Testament, "the mystery of God" stands for the whole purpose of God in the world to establish his eternal kingdom. Paul explained that the mystery of God "has been kept secret for long ages past," but has been made known through the preaching of the gospel (Rom. 16:25–26; Eph. 3:4–12; Col. 1:26–27). This mystery is revealed to God's people (Matt. 13:11; 1 Cor. 2:6–8; Eph. 1:9), who have now become "the stewards of the mysteries of God" (1 Cor. 4:1; Eph. 3:7). It remains a closed mystery to the unbelievers, however—to those who are outside the kingdom.

This mystery of God is symbolically portrayed in the image of the sealed scroll of Revelation 5. Its disclosure will take place at the sound of the trumpet of the seventh angel: "When he is about to sound, then the mystery of God will be completed, as he proclaimed to his servants the prophets." This disclosure of "the mystery of God" is described in Revelation 20:11–15, in the scene of the final opening of the book of destiny at the eschatological judgment that will bring the history of this planet to its foreordained conclusion.

EXPOSITION

10:1-2a John now sees *another strong angel coming down from heaven.* The magnificent appearance of this angel indicates that he comes from the very presence of God. He is *clothed in a cloud.* Clouds in the Bible are associated with the appearance of God; in Revelation, the cloud is associated with the coming of Jesus (1:7; 14:14–16). The angel also has *the rainbow* over his head as the sign of God's covenant (Gen. 9:12–17), which is a part of the glory of the throne of God (Ezek. 1:28; Rev. 4:3). The rainbow is most likely created by the light of the angel's face shining through the cloud.[11] The phrase *His face was like the sun* is the description of Jesus' face on the Mount of Transfiguration (Matt. 17:2; cf. Rev. 1:16). Feet *like pillars of fire* recall those of the glorified Christ which "were like burnished bronze, as if refined in a furnace" (Rev. 1:15; cf. Dan. 10:6). The angel's feet like pillars of fire are reminiscent of the pillar of fire that led Israel during their wilderness journey to the promised land (Exod. 14:19). Finally, the voice of the angel is as the roar of a lion (10:3), which in the Bible is the voice of God (Jer. 25:30; Hos. 11:10; Joel 3:16; Amos 1:2; 3:8). This divine-like heavenly messenger is a legitimate representation of Christ, sent and commissioned directly by him with a special message.

This strong angel seems to correspond to the "strong angel" of Revelation 5:2 who called for someone to open the scroll sealed with seven seals (the designation "another" angel is evidently for the purpose of distinguishing him from the seven trumpets' angels, the same as in 8:3). In Revelation 5:2 he is seen in heaven, and now he is down on the earth holding in his hand *an opened little scroll.* Several things may be noted here. First, the little scroll is seen by John as already opened when the angel descends from heaven and appears to him. It was most likely opened in heaven before the angel was sent with the message to the earth.[12] Second, given the emphasis that the scroll is seen opened implies that it was previously closed and sealed and its contents kept hidden (see *Notes* on Rev. 5:1). Finally, the Greek text suggests that the opening of the little scroll is a divine act. It is not the angel who opened the scroll, for the scroll was given to him by Christ after Christ had opened it.

It appears that the little scroll of Revelation 10 is related to the sealed scroll of Revelation 5 which Christ was worthy to take from the right side of God and break its seals.[13] The fact that it is referred to as "little" suggests that it may contain only a portion of the sealed scroll, the portion which is essential and profitable for God's people as it applies to the final events of earth's history. This little scroll is evidently very important, though, because we later learn that its contents have to do with the experience of God's people in the world in the last days. This experience is portrayed in vivid language in the second half of the book of Revelation (chapters 12–22). The disclosure of the scroll's contents comes after Revelation 10. Revelation 12–22:5 thus proves to be a disclosure of the divine revelation which has been only partially disclosed to John in symbol and which he further conveyed to the church. The final opening of the sealed scroll and the complete disclosure of its contents belongs to the future eschatological period that will bring history to its foreordained conclusion, as described in Revelation 20:11–15.

10:2b–4 The angel places **his right foot on the sea and his left on the land.** The land and the sea taken together may represent the whole earth. This suggests the universality and worldwide dimension of the message about to be proclaimed by the angel. It is especially interesting that, in Revelation 13, it is out of the sea and out of the land that the beasts come, causing universal apostasy and rebellion against God.

The angel then cries out with **a loud voice** that sounds like the roar of a lion. In the Bible, the voice of God speaking in prophecy of the impending judgment is likened to the roaring of a lion (Jer. 25:30; Hos. 11:10; Joel 3:16; Amos 1:2; 3:4). Of special significance is the text from Amos: "A lion has roared! Who will not fear? The Lord God has spoken! Who can but prophesy?" (Amos 3:8). In Revelation, when a "strong angel" announces a divine message, it is always done in a loud voice (cf. 5:2; 7:2; 14:7,

9, 15; 18:2). This leads to the conclusion that the strong angel of Revelation 10 is a representation of the voice of God with a special message for his people.

The angel's roaring cry is immediately followed by the sound of **the seven thunders.** The sound of thunder in the Bible is a symbol of the voice of God manifested in mighty actions and warning of his activities directed to the people dwelling on the earth. The plurality of the thunders in Revelation 10 as seven must be understood against the biblical concept of the number seven as a symbolic expression of divine fullness and totality (see *Notes* on Rev. 5:1). The seven thunders, whatever they are, seem to symbolize the fullness of divine forewarning with reference to the divine actions about to take place before the time of the end.

The sound of the seven thunders is not just a thundering, because John hears them speak articulately.[14] The content seems very important for the church, for John is about to write it down. He is prohibited to do that, however, for a voice from heaven instructs him otherwise: **Seal up the things which the seven thunders spoke, and do not write them.** This voice, which can be either that of the Father or of Christ himself, commands John not to write down what the seven thunders have uttered and not to communicate it to the churches. This prohibition seems strange, for elsewhere in the book John is always instructed to write down what he sees and hears (Rev. 1:11, 19; 14:13; 19:9; 21:5) and not to "seal the words of the prophecy of this book, for the time is near" (Rev. 22:10). So, this prohibition must be very unusual and significant.

The Bible teaches that some things are relevant and of special importance to God's people; they are revealed and disclosed to them with the purpose of warning them and helping them prepare for future events (cf. Rev. 1:1–3). Some things remain a mystery, however; they are not revealed to God's people, for the knowledge of them belongs only to God. "The secret things belong to the Lord our God, but the things revealed belong to us and to our sons forever, that we may observe all the words of this law" (Deut. 29:29). Paul had a similar experience when he was caught up to the third heaven and "heard inexpressible words, which a man is not permitted to speak" (2 Cor. 12:4). As Richard Bauckham states, "the seven thunders are not the prophetic revelation given to him [John] to communicate, whereas the content of the little scroll is."[15]

10:5–7 At that moment, the angel raises his right hand and swears his oath by God the Creator that **there will no longer be time.** In portraying this act of raising a hand to swear the oath, John refers clearly to Daniel 12, which provides a clue for understanding this time concept. There in Daniel 12:5–7, in responding to the question regarding how long it will be before the persecution of the saints is completed, the heavenly messenger swears an oath by raising his hands toward heaven by him who lives forever that it would be for "a time, times, and half a time. When the power of the holy people has been finally broken, all these things will be completed" (Dan. 12:7, NIV). Until this time has come, God's people must wait patiently. Revelation 10 clearly echoes Daniel 12 with an exception that the phrase "there will no longer be time" replaces "a time, times, and half a time" period.

In the book of Revelation, there is the perennial plea of God's oppressed people calling for vindication: "How long, O Lord, holy and true, will you not judge and avenge our blood upon those who dwell on the earth?" (Rev. 6:10). They were told to wait for a short time (Rev. 6:11). Now in Revelation 10:7, God's people are assured by means of an oath sworn to the eternal Creator God that "there will no longer be time." The author of Hebrews states that God's promise, confirmed with an oath, is unchangeable and certain (Heb. 6:17–18). It means that God is faithful to his promise and will certainly bring it to its fulfillment. The angel's swearing of the oath provides the church with a strong assurance that God is firmly faithful to his promise. There is no more delay; the time of the end, prophesied by Daniel, is now "irrevocably set into motion."[16] God is about to deliver and vindicate his faithful saints and bring earth's history to its end.

Further on in the oath, the angel announces that *in the days of the sound of the seventh angel, when he is about to sound, then the mystery of God will be completed, as he proclaimed to his servants the prophets.* This announcement is introduced with a strong adversative *"but."* The time of the end from Daniel is about to be set into motion, but the end of the world has not yet come. It is at the sound of the trumpet of the seventh angel that the end will come. The sealed time prophecies of Daniel will be unsealed and "the mystery of God" will be revealed as it was proclaimed by the prophets, Daniel in particular.

The mystery referred to here is regarding the gospel of the kingdom; the term in the New Testament refers to all of God's purposes in the world, his plan of redemption, and his dealings with the sin problem. This mystery has puzzled all creatures in the universe, and was presented in the symbolic portrayal of the sealed scroll in Revelation 5. The contents of the scroll were sealed for the ages (Rom.

16:25–26; Col. 1:26–27), and nobody in the entire universe, but Christ, was able to open and read it. By virtue of his triumphant and sacrificial death on the cross, Christ has been found able to open the sealed mystery and carry out the purpose of God concerning the earth and humanity.

Because of Christ and through what he has done on the cross, a part of that mystery has been revealed to God's people through the gospel (Rom. 16:25–26; Eph. 1:9; 3:4–12; Col. 1:26–27). Likewise, the things referring to the future—those profitable for God's people—are revealed through John in the symbolic portrayal of the little scroll, the contents of which are described in Revelation 12–22. God's people are shown the things to happen in the future not to satisfy their curiosity but to help them to prepare for the last-day events. The full completion of the mystery of God is reserved for the future: "But in the days of the sound of the seventh angel [not the sixth], when he is about to sound, then the mystery of God will be completed" (cf. Rev. 11:15–18). It is then that everything having to do with the full establishment of God's everlasting kingdom, including both its inhabitants and those who are excluded,[17] will be open before the entire universe (Rev. 20:11–15). God will then "bring to light the things hidden in the darkness and disclose the motives of men's hearts; and then each man's praise will come to him from God" (1 Cor. 4:5). All of God's purposes for the world with reference to the establishment of the kingdom, as proclaimed through the prophets, will then come to their conclusion.

THE EATING OF THE SCROLL (10:8–11)

Following the angel's solemn announcement (10:5–7), attention shifts to the prophet himself. It is interesting that in this section, John, who has been a somewhat passive spectator, begins to take an active role in the visions given to him.

> *[8]And the voice which I had heard from heaven again spoke to me, saying: "Go, take the scroll which is opened in the hand of the angel standing on the sea and on the land." [9]And I went to the angel, telling him to give me the little scroll. And he said to me: "Take and eat it, and it will make your stomach bitter, but in your mouth it will be sweet like honey." [10]And I took the little scroll from the hand of the angel and ate it, and it was sweet like honey in my mouth; and when I ate it, my stomach was made bitter. [11]And they*

said to me: "You must prophesy again concerning many peoples and nations and tongues and kings."

NOTES

10:10 *Sweet like honey in my mouth; and...my stomach was made bitter.* John's bittersweet experience parallels the visionary experiences of Jeremiah and Ezekiel. Jeremiah said to God: "Thy words were found and I ate them, and thy words became to me a joy and the delight of my heart" (Jer. 15:16, RSV). However, as the prophet digested the divine message, he experienced its bitter effect: "I have become a laughing stock all day long; everyone mocks me. For each time I speak, I cry aloud; I proclaim violence and destruction, because for me the word of the Lord has resulted in reproach and derision all day long" (20:7b–8; cf. 15:17–18). In a similar way, Ezekiel saw in his vision a scroll in God's hand. He was instructed to take and eat the scroll and to go and speak to the people. Upon consuming the scroll, the prophet discovered that it was in his mouth "sweet as honey" (Ezek. 2:10–3:4). The prophet was further instructed that in proclaiming the message, he would experience its bitter effect (cf. Ezek. 3:5–11). In both cases, the eating of the scroll symbolized the commission to proclaim a God-given message to a rebellious and unresponsive people. The bitter effect of the eating symbolizes a disappointment that the prophet experienced in giving the message which resulted in constant opposition.

10:11 *Concerning many peoples.* The word translated here as "concerning" is the Greek preposition *epi*; when used with the dative case (as it is here), it generally means "concerning," "about," "in regard to" (cf. John 12:16; Acts 26:6; Heb. 11:4), and "against" (cf. Luke 12:52–53). Scholars generally hold that the meaning of the preposition here is "concerning." It brings to mind Jeremiah 46:1 where the word of the Lord came to Jeremiah "concerning the nations" (Jer. 46:1).

Peoples and nations and tongues and kings. This classification is reminiscent of the book of Daniel (3:4, 7, 29; 4:1; 5:19; 6:25; 7:14). Mention of "peoples and nations and tongues and tribes" occurs several times in Revelation (5:9; 7:9; 11:9; 13:7; 14:6; 17:15), which stresses the universal nature and worldwide scope of the proclaimed message. In 10:11, "kings" are included instead of "tribes," which suggests that God's word is superior to the highest rank in human authority.[18]

EXPOSITION

10:8–11 The same voice from heaven that ordered John earlier to seal up the message of the seven thunders (10:4) now instructs him to take the little scroll from the angel's hand. When John does so, the angel further instructs him to *eat* the scroll. Before John can communicate the message that God has commissioned him to preach, he has to assimilate it completely.[19] Only then is he able to proclaim the message with full conviction.

The scroll in John's mouth tastes **sweet like honey,** but is **bitter** in his stomach, as the angel told him it would be. The sweetness of the message of the God-given word is a recurring concept in the Bible. To the psalmist, the judgments of God were "sweeter also than honey and the drippings of the honeycomb" (Ps. 19:10). "How sweet are Your words to my taste! Yes, sweeter than honey to my mouth!" (119:103). Jeremiah exclaimed: "Your words were found and I ate them, and Your words became for me a joy and the delight of my heart" (Jer. 15:16).

In a similar manner, the scroll eaten by Ezekiel was in his mouth "sweet as honey" (Ezek. 3:3). When it is received, God's word is sweet, giving joy and delight to the heart. The gospel is always the "good news" about the God who loves, cares, and is in control. It often becomes bitter for God's messenger, however, who may experience disappointment in some way in proclaiming the message.

After the bittersweet experience, John is commissioned to prophesy again **concerning many peoples and nations and tongues and kings.** The content of the scroll becomes the prophetic revelation given to John which he has to communicate to God's people.[20] The revelator has already prophesied earlier. He thought that his ministry was accomplished. He anticipated the immediate conclusion of earth's history with the blowing of the seventh trumpet, believing the mystery of God to be completely finished. However, he is told that the end is not yet; there is a delay in the coming of Jesus. Before the end comes, there will be the final "prophesying," or proclamation, of the everlasting gospel message (cf. Rev. 14:6–12). This prophesying concerns many peoples, nations, tongues, and kings; that is, it is worldwide in scope. Such an understanding is supported by Revelation 14:6, in which John sees in vision a symbolic angel flying in midheaven preaching the eternal gospel "to those who dwell on the earth, and every nation and tribe and tongue and people." The concept of prophesying concerning nations reminds us of Jesus' end-time sermon on the Mount of Olives: "And this gospel of the kingdom shall be preached in the whole world for a witness to all the nations, and then the end shall come" (Matt. 24:14). This final proclamation of the gospel will evidently bring the end of all things and the closing of this world's history (cf. Matt. 24:14; Rev. 14:14–20).

It appears that Revelation 11:1–14 provides the clue to what is going on in Revelation 10. It makes clear that John's visionary, bittersweet experience is intended to explain in a symbolic portrayal what God's last-day people will experience in fulfilling the task of preaching the gospel to the world in the last days. First, Revelation 11:1–2 provides a clue to the content of the final gospel message that is to be prophesied to all nations before the sounding of the seventh trumpet. It is the message of the restoration of the heavenly temple and its services in the context of judgment. This would perhaps explain to some extent the reason for the bitterness that God's people will experience. Then, Revelation 11:3–14 seems to illustrate the bitter experience of God's people in the proclamation of the final gospel message in the symbolic portrayal of the two witnesses prophesying to "those who dwell upon the earth" (11:10), "the peoples and tribes and tongues and nations" (11:9). (The extensive portrayal of the same is given in Rev. 14:6–12.) The fate of the two witnesses seems to illustrate the bitterness of eating the scroll.

This confirms the view that the contents of the little scroll have to do with the experience of God's people in the last days. The church lives in a world that is hostile to the gospel. In proclaiming the final gospel message, God's people will experience the bitterness of hostility and persecution. Robert H. Mounce, who argues that the contents of the little scroll are a message for the church, explains further: "It is *after* the eating of the book that John is told he must prophesy again, this time concerning many peoples, nations, tongues, and kings (Rev. 10:11). This begins with chapter 12. The sweet scroll which turns the stomach bitter is a message for the church. Before the final triumph believers are going to pass through a formidable ordeal. As the great scroll of chapter 5 outlined the destiny of all mankind, so the little scroll unveils the lot of the faithful in those last days of fierce Satanic opposition."[21]

There is a sense of divine compulsion in the charge given to John. He *must* prophesy again. The prophecy relates to many peoples and nations. It is the final act in the great drama of God's creative and redemptive activity. The meaning of history comes into sharp focus at the end point in time. John's mission is to lay bare the forces of the supernatural world that are at work behind the activities of men and nations. Mounce states: "His prophecy is the culmination of all previous prophecies in that it leads on to the final destruction of evil and the inauguration of the eternal state."[22]

At this stage we can conclude that Revelation 10 has to do with the time of the end between the close of Daniel's prophecies and the Second Coming. It is the time period between when "there will no longer be time" and when the seventh trumpet is about to sound. That period is marked by the final proclamation of the everlasting gospel. As Revelation 12–14 shows, that period is marked by Satan's decisive determination to win for himself the allegiance of the inhabitants of earth. It is during that period before the end that God makes his final effort, through the church, to warn the inhabitants of the earth and bring them to repentance. This final proclamation of the gospel message is portrayed in the symbolic presentation of the three angels flying in the midst of heaven proclaiming the everlasting gospel "to those who dwell on the earth" (Rev. 14:6–12).

A RETROSPECT ON REVELATION 10

With Revelation 10 the chain of transmission of the divine revelation from God through John to the church has been concluded (cf. Rev. 1:1). The revelation began with the Father who handed it to the newly enthroned Jesus Christ in the symbolic form of the sealed scroll (Rev. 5). After further developments, Christ communicated it through his angel to John in the symbolic form of the open little scroll (Rev. 10:1–11). This suggests that in chapter 10 we have a revelation of a portion of the sealed scroll of Revelation 5 as it applies to the final events of the earth's history. After receiving the open scroll, John was commissioned to communicate its message, the things which he had seen in visions (1:11, 19), to the people as the prophetic word (10:11). The whole purpose of the divine revelation is "to show to his servants the things which must soon take place" (Rev. 1:1); in other words, it is to prepare God's people to understand God's purpose for them as history approaches its end.

One question remains unanswered: What are the contents of the portion of the sealed scroll of Revelation 5 that is disclosed to God's people in the symbolical presentation of the little scroll in Revelation 10? Scholars have expressed many different views on this question. One thing that seems clear in the rest of Revelation is that Revelation 12:1 is a completely new beginning. The fact that this new beginning is introduced with the manifestation of the ark of the covenant whereby the sealed scroll has been stored (see "Overview: Revelation 4–5") suggests that Revelation 12–22:5 is comprised of the contents of the little scroll (the part of the sealed scroll which is disclosed to God's people). Its contents "consist of a whole complex of events" that lead to the establishment of God's kingdom,[23] that involve the ultimate "defeat of Satan's rebellion, the judgment of the earth and the salvation of the faithful."[24] The second half of the book clearly portrays the bitterness that God's people will experience in the last days because of their faithfulness to the proclamation of the final message to the world. This agrees with what we have concluded earlier, that the contents of the little scroll have to do with the experience of God's people in the last days. This information is revealed so that God's people will be found ready and prepared when these things take place.

The rest of the sealed scroll, the things not profitable to God's people, are not disclosed until the eschatological consummation of earth's history (Rev. 20:11–15). It is then, at the sound of the trumpet of the seventh angel, that "the mystery of God will be completed, as he proclaimed to his servants the prophets." The sealed scroll will then finally be opened and its contents disclosed before the entire universe.

History shows that it has always been a constant temptation for many to delve into the things God never intended to be revealed to us. Revelation 10 makes clear, first of all, that some things are of special importance for God's people, those which God finds appropriate to reveal to his people. All things with reference to the future that are profitable for salvation and entry into the kingdom are revealed to God's people through the prophetic word. Everything else goes beyond God's intention; humans are unable to penetrate the secrets that God has reserved for himself. "The secret things belong to the Lord our God, but the things revealed belong to us and to our sons forever, that we may observe all the words of this law" (Deut. 29:29).

The second point in Revelation 10 is that there are some things which remain concealed from human beings and are known only to God. For instance, Jesus said clearly that the exact time of his second coming is known only by God (Matt. 24:36). After the resurrection, the disciples asked Jesus: "Lord, is it at this time You are restoring the kingdom to Israel?" Jesus made it clear that they were not "to know times or epochs which the Father has fixed by His own authority" (Acts 1:7). Then he revealed that what mattered was that they receive the Holy Spirit and be involved wholeheartedly in the spreading of the gospel.

Christians must be aware that any time setting for the Second Coming, or drafting of detailed prophetic charts with dates and sequential events, is contrary to God's will. If there had been a need for time setting or prophetic charts, God would have provided them in the prophetic word. However, God knew in his wisdom that they never work for good, but are rather destructive to Christian faith, resulting in an abandonment of hope in the soon coming of Christ and the kingdom. Many attempts to make detailed prophetic charts should better be replaced by analyses of geographical charts for the purpose of reaching those who are still unreached for Christ (cf. Acts 1:7–8). What

God's people have to keep in mind is the gospel that they are commissioned and entrusted to proclaim, for "there will no longer be time" (Rev. 10:6).

Seventh-day Adventist Christians have seen in Revelation 10 a special prophetic significance for their life and mission. In John's bittersweet experience they have seen what is known as the great disappointment experienced by the Millerite movement in 1844. Under the leadership of William Miller, a Baptist lay preacher and revivalist, a large group, gathered from different Protestant denominations, concluded mistakenly that the Second Coming would occur in the fall of 1844. The expectation grew as the believers shared the message they believed and made thorough preparation for the end. When the coming of Christ did not take place, the disappointed Millerites experienced in different ways the bitter taste of the message they believed and shared. Although disappointed, some of them found in John's visionary experience the explanation of their disappointment. In John's eating of the scroll they saw the symbol, and even the prophecy, of their own experience.

Since then, in Christ's commission to John to "prophesy again" to many people, nations, tongues, and kings, Adventists have seen the commissioning of God's end-time church to proclaim the message of the Second Coming "to those who dwell on the earth, and to every nation and tribe and tongue and people" (Rev. 14:6). When the proclaimed gospel message is heard by the whole world, then the end will come and earth's history will reach its conclusion (Matt. 24:14).

ENDNOTES

1. Beasley-Murray, 168.

2. See, e.g., *The Seventh-day Adventist Bible Commentary* (7:796–797) which follows the statement of Ellen White that the strong angel of Revelation 10 "was no less a personage than Jesus Christ" (see ibid., 7:971); Shea shares a similar view, "The Mighty Angel and His Message," 283–291. For a different view, see LaRondelle, *How to Understand the End-Time Prophecies*, 196–197.

3. On a different view, see Shea, "The Mighty Angel and His Message," 289–291.

4. E.g., Mazzaferri, 295–296; Bauckham, *The Climax of Prophecy*, 243–266.

5. See *The Seventh-day Adventist Bible Commentary*, 7:797.

6. See Aune, *Revelation 6–16*, 560.

7. As noticed by J. M. Ford, 159.

8. C. H. Pinnock, "Time," in *The International Standard Bible Encyclopedia*, 2d ed. (Grand Rapids, MI: Eerdmans, 1988), 4:852.

9. Aune, *Revelation 6–16*, 568.

10. White, quoted in *The Seventh-day Adventist Bible Commentary*, 7:971.

11. Charles, 1:259; Barclay, *The Revelation of John*, 2:54.

12. Shea, "The Mighty Angel and His Message," 288.

13. E.g., Mazzaferri, 295–296; Bauckham, *The Climax of Prophecy*, 243–266.

14. Mounce, 209.

15. Bauckham, *The Climax of Prophecy*, 260.

16. LaRondelle, *How to Understand the End-Time Prophecies*, 197.

17. Shea, "The Mighty Angel and His Message," 314–315.

18. Morris, 140.

19. Mounce, 214.

20. Bauckham, *The Climax of Prophecy*, 260.

21. Mounce, 216.

22. Ibid., 217.

23. Ladd, 109.

24. Collins, *The Apocalypse*, 39–40.

THE TWO WITNESSES
REVELATION 11:1–14

Most commentators consider Revelation 11:1–14 one of the most difficult passages of Revelation to interpret. This section is very important because it seems to provide additional information with regard to what goes on in the previous section (10:8–11). One must keep in mind, then, that Revelation 11 is a part of the sixth trumpet in the same way as is chapter 10. The chapter has two parts: the measuring of the temple (11:1–2) and the two witnesses (11:3–14).

THE MEASURING OF THE TEMPLE (11:1–2)

We observed in Revelation 10:8–11 how John turned from passive spectator to active participant in the vision. He has eaten the little scroll and assimilated its contents. Afterwards, he is commissioned to prophesy again concerning many peoples. What is the message to be proclaimed to the world? It appears that the opening of the following section gives us the clue.

> *¹And a measuring reed like a staff was given to me, saying: "Rise and measure the temple of God and the altar and those who worship in it. ²And exclude the outer court and do not measure it, for it has been given to the nations; and they will trample the holy city for forty-two months."*

NOTES

11:1 *A measuring reed.* The Greek word *kalamos* ("reed") denotes a plant with a hollow stalk that grew in the Jordan valley. The reed was straight and long (it could reach to the height of more than ten feet), and as such it was suitable to use as a measuring rod.

Measure. The Greek word *metreō* ("measure") in a figurative sense may mean to evaluate or judge. The New Testament passages which are characterized by the word *metron* or *metreō* refer to "the judicial work of God in the Last Judgment"[1] (cf. Matt. 7:2; Mark 4:24). The word used for the measuring process in Revelation 11:1 also occurs in 2 Corinthians 10:12 with reference to some members of the church in Corinth who were measuring or evaluating themselves by themselves.

In Old Testament times, measuring involved judgment with regard to who would live and who would die. For example, David "defeated Moab, and measured them with the line, making them lie down on the ground; and he measured two lines to put to death and one full line to keep alive" (2 Sam. 8:2). It is in this sense that the measuring process in Revelation 11 must be understood.

Kenneth Strand suggests that the only Old Testament background which adequately explains the measuring process specified in Revelation 11:1 is Leviticus 16. He shows persuasively how the measuring of the temple, altar, and worshipers has its most complete thematic parallel with the description of the Israelite Day of Atonement ritual.[2] On that day, atonement was made for the priests themselves, the sanctuary, the altar, and the congregation (cf. Lev. 16:33). The only other place in the Bible where the sanctuary, the altar, and the people are mentioned together is here in Revelation 11:1–2. "With the exception of the omission of the priesthood in Revelation 11:1, the same three elements under review are common to both passages: temple, altar, and worshipers. The fact that that one particular omission is made is perfectly logical, for Christ as NT [New Testament] High Priest, would need no atonement (or 'measuring') made for himself."[3] Strand further observes a commonality in the order or sequence of the three items in both texts. "In both cases, the movement is from sanctuary/temple *to* altar *to* worshipers."[4] Strand concludes with the following observation:

> The parallel in Revelation 11:1 certainly embraces, too, a "measuring" in the spiritual, rather than physical, sense. This is obvious from the context, wherein the "temple" and "altar" refer to heavenly entities, not a physical temple in the city of Jerusalem (cf. the general use of temple imagery in Revelation, as e.g., in 4–5, 8:3–5, 11:19, etc.). And the "measuring" of worshipers is itself terminology that has spiritual, not physical, implications.[5]

The temple of God. The Greek word used here is *naos* which in Revelation refers to the innermost part of the temple, the most holy place. *Naos* is distinguished from *hieron* (not occurring in Revelation), which refers to the entire temple complex, including the courts and the temple property (cf. Matt. 4:5; John 2:14). Thus in the gospels Jesus is always found teaching in the *hieron* (Matt. 26:55; Luke 21:37; John 7:28).

Several views have been suggested with regard to the meaning of the temple which is measured in Revelation 11:1. (1) The most popular view is that the temple represents the Christian church, or God's people (cf. 1 Cor. 3:16). The vulnerability of this view is seen in the fact that although the word "temple" occurs frequently in Revelation, it never symbolizes the church. John is very consistent in distinguishing between the temple and God's people ("the temple, the altar, and those who worship in it"; cf. Rev. 7:17; 15:8). (2) Another view holds that John refers to the temple in Jerusalem. This avenue of interpretation overlooks the fact that the temple in Jerusalem had been destroyed some twenty years before Revelation was written, and was not in existence in John's day (ca. A.D. 90). (3) It is most likely that John refers to the measuring of the temple in heaven. For John there is a real temple in heaven, as he constantly refers to it or to its articles of furniture in his visions (3:12; 7:15; 11:19; 14:17; 15:5–8; 16:1, 17). It is also noteworthy that the expression "the temple of God" is consistently used in the book to refer to the heavenly temple (3:12; 11:19; cf. 7:15).

The altar. Although the text does not specify which altar is in view here, it is undoubtedly the altar of incense. It cannot be the altar of burnt offering which was located outside the Old Testament temple setting, in the outer court (John was explicitly instructed not to measure the outer). In the Old Testament temple, the golden altar of incense was "in front of the veil that is near the ark of the testimony, in front of the mercy seat that is over the ark of the testimony" (cf. Exod. 30:6). It is the same golden altar associated with the prayers of the saints that are heard by God in Revelation 8:3–6.

11:2 Exclude. The Greek *ekballō exōthen* means literally "to throw out," "to cast out." The word is used here in the sense of "to exclude" the outer court from the measuring of the temple and its precincts, in the same way as it is used in John 9:34–35 with regard to the excommunication of the blind man from the synagogue (cf. 3 John 10).

The outer court. The temple in Jerusalem was divided into two courts. The inner court consisted of three precincts: the Court of the Priests, the Court of the Israelites, and the Court of the Women. The outer court was the Court of the Gentiles. It was an uncovered yard outside the temple building separated from the inner court by a barrier. Gentiles were allowed to enter this part of the temple, but they were not allowed to pass beyond the barrier under the penalty of death. There were marker tablets with a warning that any Gentile who would pass beyond that point was responsible for his own death.

Nations. The Greek *ethnoi* means "nations" or "Gentiles." In Revelation, these are forces hostile to God and his people, and are in opposition to the preaching of the gospel (Rev. 11:2, 18; 14:8; 16:19; 18:3, 23; 19:15; 20:3, 8).

Trample. The Greek *pateō* means "to tread underfoot," "to trample." The word is used metaphorically in Revelation 14:20 and 19:15 in reference to the trampling of the wicked under the wrath of God (cf. Isa. 63:3). In the Old Testament, the expression refers often to the oppression of God's people by enemy nations (Isa. 63:18; Jer. 12:10). The trampling imagery is especially prominent in the book of Daniel with reference to the fourth beast, representing the Roman Empire, which trampled its prey underfoot (Dan. 7:7, 19, 23), and the activities of the little horn which arose out of the ten horns of the fourth beast (Dan. 8:9–13); such persecution was directed particularly "against the saints of the Most High," persecuting for "a time, times, and half a time" (Dan. 7:25). Jesus prophesied that Jerusalem would "be trampled under foot by the Gentiles, until the times of the Gentiles be fulfilled" (Luke 21:24). The trampling of the holy city for the forty-two months evidently corresponds to the forty-two months of the activities of the sea beast of Revelation 13:1–10. Thus the trampling of the holy city is identical to the activities of the sea beast.

Forty-two months. The time designation of forty-two months is mentioned only here and in 13:5 with reference to the symbolic sea beast and its activities in persecuting God's people. This period is evidently the same as the 1,260 days (11:3; 12:6) and "a time and times and half a time" (12:14). The parallel between Revelation 12:6 and 14 indicates that a time and times and half a time and the 1,260 days refer to the same period of the persecution of the woman. If these three time designations refer to the same period, where then does this designation come from? It is undoubtedly taken from Daniel (7:24–25 and 12:7), where the phrase exclusively refers to the period of the activities of the symbolic little horn in oppressing and persecuting the saints of God. John takes over the prophecy from Daniel and develops it further in the symbolic Antichrist sea beast in Revelation 13:1–10, in which the forty-two months corresponds to the time, times, and half a time of Daniel—that is, one year (360 days), two years (720 days), and half a year (180 days, thus totaling 1,260 days).[6]

The most plausible interpretation understands these time designations (repeated in one way or another in chapters 11 and 12–13) not as a literal time period of forty-two months, but as referring to the prophetic period of more than twelve centuries, known as the Middle Ages, during which the church, like Israel at the Exodus, suffered the hardship of its "wilderness" pilgrimage (cf. Rev. 12:6, 14). It was the time when the Bible was held in obscurity and those who followed its teachings usually were condemned and persecuted. LeRoy E. Froom observed that among the historicist interpreters there is disagreement "as to when to begin and when to end the 1,260-day period of the Antichrist, but they were all united in the conviction that a period of 1,260 years had been allotted to him, and that it was drawing toward its close."[7] The dates commonly suggested for the beginning of the period have included the years 455, 508, 538, 606, and 756. The subject has been treated extensively by Hans LaRondelle, who concludes that the period designations of the forty-two months, a time and times and half a time, and the 1,260 days apply to the period of 1,260 actual years, however, "without being dogmatic about precise date-fixings in church history."[8] However, on the basis of day-year symbolism in biblical prophecy, in which the prophetic day stands for a literal year,[9] Seventh-day Adventists have traditionally held A.D. 538 as the year when the church—having liberated itself from Arian dominion—established itself as an ecclesiastical power. Thus that, as such, marks the beginning of this prophetic period. The year A.D. 1798—when the events of the French Revolution shook the church's religious-political oppressive power—would thus mark the end of the forty-two months/1,260–days period.[10]

However, it appears that all three time designations have both quantitative and qualitative significance. The forty-two months might point, first of all, to the three and a half years of Elijah's witnessing (cf. Luke 4:25; James 5:17) during the great apostasy and persecution in the days of the pagan queen Jezebel, when the sky was shut for three and a half years (Rev. 11:3, 6). It further points to the three and a half years of Jesus' life of witnessing in "the sackcloth" of rejection and humiliation. An exact dating of Jesus' ministry is not possible from the synoptic gospels; however, the gospel of John refers to three Passovers (2:13; 6:4; 13:1). Since his ministry began several months before the first Passover, it has been generally regarded that Jesus' earthly ministry spanned about three and a half years. This would be in agreement with Daniel's prophecy of a half week that is generally interpreted to be a reference to Jesus' life and ministry (Dan. 9:27). Thus the forty-two months would, on one level, relate the church's experiences to the experience of Elijah during the great apostasy in Israel. On the second level, the followers of Christ are going through what Jesus went through during his three and a half years of life of faithful witnessing. Jesus stated: "If they persecuted Me, they will also persecute you" (John 15:20).

Whatever the time designation of forty-two months might refer to, in Revelation it is always associated with the wicked who, for a long period, held dominion over God's faithful people, oppressing and persecuting them (cf. Rev. 11:2; 13:5). On the other hand, the 1,260 is always associated with the faithful, designating the period assigned to God's people who, although oppressed and persecuted, are under the special protection of God as they bear their witness to the gospel in the world (cf. Rev. 11:3; 12:6).

EXPOSITION

11:1 John was given a measuring reed like a rod with instructions to measure *the temple of God and the altar and those who worship in it.* Centuries earlier, Ezekiel watched in vision a divine figure measuring carefully every part of the temple (Ezek. 40–42). Measurement is the preliminary groundwork to building. In Ezekiel's vision the temple was measured for the purpose of being restored (cf. Ezek. 39:25–29). The visionary scene was intended to motivate the Israelites to repent of their sins and turn back to God. The temple was destroyed because of Israel's unfaithfulness and apostasy. The symbolic act of measuring the temple was a firm message of assurance to the people that God was committed to restoring the temple and once again being Israel's God and making Israel his people (cf. Ezek. 39:25–29, the introductory text to the subsequent measuring of the temple). The rebuilding of the temple must be understood as God's new attempt to restore his relationship with Israel (cf. 43:7–11).

At least two things may be observed in Ezekiel's text. First, the measuring of the temple came on the tenth day of the first month, which was the Day of Atonement. It was on that Day of Atonement that God came with the promise to restore the temple and bring his people back into relationship with himself. Second, the measurement in Ezekiel's vision was with reference to three things: the temple itself (Ezek. 40:3–43:12), the altar of sacrifice (43:23–27), and the people (44–48:35). It is in the context of Ezekiel's vision that the measuring of the temple in John's vision must be understood.

When John speaks of the measuring of the temple and its altar, he does not refer to the actual reconstruction of the Jerusalem Temple that had ceased to exist by the time Revelation was written. For John, there is a real temple in heaven. The heavenly temple is the most central concept in the book of Revelation. It is perceived by John as the dwelling place of God where his throne is located and from which he rules over the universe. Furthermore, it is the center of all divine activities—the place where all strategies and decisions with regard to the earth are made. Thus there is strong hostility toward the heavenly temple by antagonistic enemy powers opposing God (cf. Rev. 13:6).

John's act of measuring also involves the worshipers. In Jesus Christ, God's saved people are made "a kingdom and priests to our God" (Rev. 5:10; cf. 1:6). According to Paul, Christians are raised with Christ and made to sit with him in the heavenly places (Eph. 2:6). God's saved people are already elevated in the heavenly places and participating with Jesus in his glory. Their prayers are offered "on the golden altar" from which they ascend before God (Rev. 8:3–4).

How then do we understand this measuring of the heavenly temple and its altar and worshipers in John's visionary experience? In the light of Ezekiel's background, this measuring has to do with restoration of the temple with reference to the people. We observed that in Ezekiel's vision the measurement and restoration involves the temple, the altar, and Israel. Kenneth Strand notes that these three elements are also mentioned in Leviticus 16:16–19, 30–31 with reference to the Day of Atonement.[11] We observed already that the Day of Atonement was also the time of the measuring of the temple in Ezekiel. It thus appears that these two Old Testament background texts are the key for understanding what is taking place in Revelation 11:1.

The Day of Atonement was the most solemn day of the Jewish sacred calendar, when the sanctuary was cleansed from all sins that were accumulated during the year. It is a sort of final day of "measuring" within the Israelite cultic year. As Kenneth Strand notes, that day had an atmosphere of "final judgment about it, for on that day separation was to take place: the people were to 'afflict' themselves, and 'whoever is not afflicted on this same day shall be cut off from his people' (Lev. 23:28–29, RSV)."[12]

In Revelation, a distinct line of division is drawn on the basis of worship: those who fear, worship, and serve God (cf. 11:18; 14:7; 15:4; 19:10), and those who worship the dragon and the beast (cf. 13:4, 8, 12, 15; 14:9–11; 16:2; 19:20). On that distinction is based the recognition of the two groups in the book. In 2 Samuel 8:2, it is especially illustrated how measuring is involved in judgment regarding who lives and who dies.

So, the measuring of the saints in Revelation has figurative meaning, bearing a strong sense of evaluation in judgment. It has to do with deciding between those who serve God and those who do not. All of this takes place before the righteous can receive their reward and the wicked their condemnation (Rev. 11:18).

Comparing the interludes between the sixth and seventh seals and the sixth and seventh trumpets suggests that the measuring of Revelation 11:1 is related to the sealing of God's people (Rev. 7:1–4). As J. Massynberde Ford notes, "just as the sealing of the elect preceded the seventh seal," so "measuring the holy and excluding the outsiders precedes the seventh trumpet."[13] The measuring and sealing must be placed side by side, for both portray the divine work of grace in human lives. The measuring, however, is for the purpose of deciding who is to be sealed—namely, those who belong to God and are faithful to him. These will be protected during the time of the final tribulation.

11:2 The voice from heaven instructs John to *exclude the outer court and do not measure it, for it has been given to the nations.* The outer court of the temple in Jerusalem was the place outside the temple building where the Gentiles were allowed to worship. The fact that the court mentioned here was "given to the nations [or the Gentiles]" suggests that John had this outer court in mind. It is excluded from the measuring because it is given to the nations, or the Gentiles, which in Revelation are forces hostile to God and his people (cf. Rev. 11:18). The outer court is evidently in contrast to the temple of God in heaven and the worshipers. It seems to represent the forces (elsewhere in the book referred to as "those who dwell on the earth"—Rev. 3:10; 6:10; 8:13; 11:10; 13:8, 14; 17:2) that are hostile to God and the gospel, viciously persecuting God's faithful people, and are excluded from the kingdom.

It is noteworthy that the exclusion is a part of the measuring. The measuring divides the genuine Christians from those who profess Christianity but are apostate. As in the case of Ezekiel's measuring of the temple, no foreigner who was "uncircumcised in heart and uncircumcised in flesh" was allowed to enter the temple (Ezek. 44:9). So in John's vision the Gentiles are excluded. They do not belong to the community of believers. Only the worshipers of God are measured: those saints whose prayers, offered "on the golden altar," ascend before God (Rev. 8:3–4). Similar exclusion is mentioned in the last part of the book in connection with the measuring of the new Jerusalem (Rev. 21:15–17), which functions as the temple of the new earth (Rev.

21:2–3). The unfaithful are excluded from the reward of the new Jerusalem and are found outside the temple-city (21:27). "*Outside* are the dogs and the sorcerers and the fornicators and the murderers and the idolaters and everyone who loves and practices the lie" (Rev. 22:15).

The giving over of the outer court to the nations, or the Gentiles, signifies that they **will trample the holy city for forty-two months.** The starting point for the understanding of this image is Jesus' prophecy that "Jerusalem will be trampled under foot by the Gentiles, until the times of the Gentiles be fulfilled" (Luke 21:24). Luke 21:24 and Revelation 11:2 have a common denominator: the trampling of the holy city by the nations or the Gentiles. The forty-two months equates to "the times of the Gentiles" that are permitted to oppress God's people for a limited time. The trampling of Jerusalem referred to by Jesus has become the prototype[14] of the oppression and persecution that God's people have experienced from the powers that are hostile to God and the gospel. Revelation 11:18 speaks of the angry nations that "destroy the earth." Their hostility has a limit, for a time will come when those who destroy the earth will themselves be destroyed (cf. Rev. 19:20–21).

It appears that both Luke 21:24 and Revelation 11:2 have a common background in the book of Daniel. In the symbolic image of the fourth beast, Daniel portrayed the powerful Roman Empire that would trample underfoot the conquered nations (Dan. 7:7, 19, 23). The prophet further described the little horn that arose subsequently out from among the ten horns of the fourth beast. This power, hostile to God, is said to "speak against the Most High and oppress his saints" for a time, times, and half a time (Dan. 7:25, NIV), or three and a half years. The further activities of this enemy power described in Daniel 8:9–13 are characterized by trampling the holy place and its worshipers.

It is in this sense that the trampling of the holy city in Revelation 11:2 must be understood. "The holy city" stands for God's people who are oppressed and persecuted by the Antichrist. This oppression is similar to the trampling of Jerusalem "under foot by the Gentiles" (Luke 21:24), in contrast to "the great city" of Revelation 11:8. The activities of this persecuting power are described in Revelation 13:1–10 in the symbolic presentation of the sea beast who has his worshipers referred to as those "who dwell on the earth" (Rev. 13:8, 12, 14). This oppressive power is also the one described in Daniel 7:25; the time given to it is the forty-two months (Rev. 13:5) historically fulfilled during the Middle Ages (usually dated from A.D. 538 to A.D. 1798). During this period the beast "opened his mouth in blasphemies against God, to blaspheme his name and his tabernacle, namely, those who dwell in heaven [the worshipers of Christ]" (13:6).

Revelation 13:1–10 provides the key for understanding the trampling of the holy city by the Gentiles during the forty-two months. One thing becomes clear: the context of Revelation 11 indicates that literal time is not intended here. The forty-two months allotted to the nations or Gentiles represents a specific period of about 1,200 years during which God's faithful people will endure hardship and suffering because of their faithfulness to Christ. It seems clear that Daniel 7–9, Revelation 11:2–13, and Revelation 13:1–10 are related and must be understood in connection with each other.

THE TWO WITNESSES (11:3–14)

It is important to bear in mind that Revelation 11:3–14 is the conclusion of the interlude between the sixth and seventh trumpets. It builds on the preceding section of Revelation 10:8–11:2 by providing further information with regard to Revelation 10:8–11, namely, the experience of God's people in the hostile world as they bear witness to the gospel.

> **³And I will commission my two witnesses, and they will prophesy for 1,260 days clothed in sackcloth. ⁴These are the two olive trees and the two lampstands standing before the Lord of the earth. ⁵And if anyone wants to harm them, fire comes out of their mouths and devours their enemies; and if anyone would want to harm them, he must be killed. ⁶They have authority to shut heaven, lest it give forth rain during the days of their prophecy; and they have authority over the waters to turn them into blood, and to strike the earth with every plague as often as they want. ⁷And when they complete their witness, the beast coming up from the abyss will make war with them, and will conquer them and kill them. ⁸And their dead body will be on the street of the great city, which is spiritually called Sodom and Egypt, where also their Lord was crucified. ⁹And those of the peoples and tribes and tongues and nations will behold their dead body for three and a half days, and they will not permit their dead bodies to be placed in a tomb. ¹⁰And those who dwell on the earth will rejoice over them and**

make merry, and they will send gifts to one another, because these two prophets tormented those who dwell upon the earth. [11]*And after three and a half days the breath of life from God entered them, and they stood up on their feet, and a great fear fell on those beholding them.* [12]*And they heard a great voice from heaven saying to them: "Come up here!" And they went up to heaven in the cloud, and their enemies beheld them.* [13]*And at the same hour there was a great earthquake, and a tenth of the city fell, and 7,000 people were killed in the earthquake; and the rest of the people became afraid and gave glory to the God of heaven.* [14]*The second woe has passed; behold, the third woe is coming quickly.*

NOTES

11:3 *I will commission.* Literally, "I will give" (Gr. dōsō), meaning that the two witnesses have been given divine authority. The phrase is a Hebraic construction meaning, "I will commission."[15]

My two witnesses. The Greek word *martus* means both "witness" and "martyr" (see *Notes* on Rev. 1:5). A number of suggestions have been offered with regard to the identity of the two witnesses: the Law and the Prophets, the Law and the Gospel, Moses and Elijah, or two prophets who would function as Moses and Elijah in the last days. Most persuasive are the ones which identify the two witnesses as the Bible or as the people of God.

According to the former, the two witnesses represent the Bible, both the Old and New Testaments. Jesus made clear that the Old Testament does "bear witness" of him (John 5:39; cf. Luke 24:25–27, 44). Likewise, the New Testament bears witness to the life, work, and words of Jesus and his sacrificial death and his post-resurrection ministry on behalf of his people. Furthermore, the message of God is presented in Revelation as the word of God and the testimony of Jesus (Rev. 1:2, 9). If anyone wishes to harm the two witnesses, they have authority to devour their enemies with fire, to shut heaven lest it give forth rain, to turn the waters into blood, and to strike the earth with every plague (Rev. 11:5–6). In the Old Testament, it is the Word of God, through Moses, that brought the plagues on Egypt (Exod. 7–11). In Jeremiah 5:14, the Word of God is as fire in Jeremiah's mouth. The Word of God through Elijah also shut the sky and there was no rain in the land for three and a half years (1 Kings 17:1). It is noteworthy that the end of Revelation presents a threat to anyone who tampers with "the word of prophecy" of the book of Revelation (22:18–19). In the light of such an understanding, the killing of the witnesses (Rev. 11:7–10) would mean the rejection of the Bible by the people for a time. Their resurrection would signify a renewal of interest in the Bible message.

Another view suggests that the two witnesses represent the people of God.[16] In the New Testament, witnessing is the primary task of God's people. Jesus often referred to his disciples as witnesses (cf. John 15:27; Luke 24:48). Before his ascension, Jesus made this clear to his disciples: "You shall receive power when the Holy Spirit has come upon you; and you shall be My witnesses both in Jerusalem, and in all Judea and Samaria, and even to the remotest part of the earth" (Acts 1:8; cf. 2:32; 3:15; 5:32). According to Jesus, the preaching of the gospel before the end is "for a witness to all the nations" (Matt. 24:14). In Revelation, witnessing is the reason why God's people are persecuted (2:13; 6:9; 12:11; 17:6; 20:4). It is the church that bears witness to Jesus (Rev. 17:6; 20:4).

As the foregoing shows, evidence suggests that the two witnesses stand for the people of God, namely, the church (of both Old and New Testament Israel). On another level, they may equally symbolize the Bible as "the word of God and the testimony of Jesus." These two identifications should not be seen as necessarily exclusive. It is through the preaching and teaching of the church that the Word of God is manifested. The two witnesses should thus be understood as representing God's people in their kingly and priestly function (cf. Rev. 1:6; 5:10),[17] whose primary task is like that of Joshua, Zerubbabel, Moses, and Elijah—to bear prophetic witness to the apostate world.[18] For Seventh-day Adventists, it is especially interesting that Ellen White's understanding of the two witnesses is given in this twofold sense. While on one occasion she stated that the "two witnesses represent the Scriptures of the Old and the New Testament,"[19] on another she stated that the "church will yet see troublous times. She will prophesy in sackcloth....They are to be His witnesses in the world, His instrumentalities to do a special, a glorious work in the day of His preparation."[20]

1,260 days. See *Notes* on Revelation 11:2.

11:4 *The two olive trees and the two lampstands standing before the Lord of the earth.* Here is a reference to Zechariah 4. The prophet saw in vision the lampstand with seven lamps flanked by two olive trees with two olive branches sprouting from the olive trees. These two trees are said to represent "the two anointed ones, who are standing by the Lord of the whole earth" (4:14). In Zechariah 4, these "two anointed ones" are Joshua, the high priest, and Zerubbabel, the governor of Judea, who brought about the restoration of the temple. While Zechariah saw only one lampstand, John takes both the olive trees and the two lampstands to represent the two witnesses in their royal and priestly roles (cf. Rev. 1:6; 5:10).

11:7 *When they complete their witness* refers to the end of the 1,260 days that the two witnesses have spent clothed in sackcloth.

The beast coming up from the abyss. This beast is often identified with the beast "coming up out the sea" of Revelation 13:1–10, because it, like the beast coming up from the abyss, wages war with the saints and it overcomes them (Rev. 13:7; cf. Dan. 7:21). In addition, it is noteworthy that the beast of Revelation 13 has a dominant power over God's people during the forty-two months, which in Revelation 11 is the period of the prophesying of the two witnesses. The statement "when they complete their witness" (Rev. 11:7) indicates that it is after the period of the forty-two months, or 1,260 days, that the beast coming out from the abyss of Revelation 11 engages in war against the two witnesses and kills them. The beast coming up from the abyss probably is not Satan who is represented by the dragon in Revelation (Rev. 12). Since beasts represent political powers in the book of Daniel, the beast from the abyss must be understood as a kind of political or religious power that dominates the world or a part of it.

Having understood the two witnesses to be the Scriptures, Seventh-day Adventists have interpreted the beast from the abyss as the French Revolution. The death of the witnesses has been interpreted as the great attack on the Bible in the context of the French Revolution, which came right after the prophetic period of the 1,260 days. Ellen White devoted the entire chapter 15 of *The Great Controversy* to this interpretation. The French Revolution was a period of terror when antireligious and atheistic sentiments swept the country, resulting in the rejection of Christianity and the Bible, and the rising tide of atheism and secularism with all hostility toward the Word of God throughout the world. If the two witnesses symbolize the Bible, this historical interpretation seems appropriate. Since the time of the French Revolution, the church has witnessed the most widespread and triumphant spread of the gospel throughout the world.

Although such a historical application is quite tenable, it is not without significance that the understanding of the two witnesses is not restricted to the Bible. The books of Revelation and Daniel never restrict the attack of the evil powers against the Bible as a book, but rather extends it to God's faithful people as they preach the word of God and the testimony of Jesus. It is against the saints that the evil powers wage war (cf. Dan. 7:21; Rev. 12:17; 13:7). It is the people of God and the powers of evil persecuting them that John had in mind in describing the scene of the two witnesses and their prophetic witnessing.

The abyss. See *Notes* on Revelation 9:1.

11:8 *Their dead body.* The Greek has the collective singular noun, *to ptōma autōn* ("the dead body of them") here and in verse 9, where it is used again before switching back to the plural. The same is found in verse 5 with reference to the mouth. This suggests the corporate nature of the two witnesses, which is especially significant in the light of the understanding of the two witnesses as the people of God. As G. K. Beale observes, while they are "one witnessing 'body' of Christ who witness,...they are also many witnesses scattered throughout the earth."[21]

The great city. The Old Testament is replete with references to the great cities (including Nineveh, Tyre, and Babylon) where God was opposed and his people were harassed. This great city is in contrast to the "holy city" of Revelation 11:2 (cf. Dan. 9:24; Rev. 21:2, 10; 22:19). The great city in Revelation refers consistently to Babylon as the symbolic end-time evil power that stands in opposition to God (cf. 14:8; 16:19; 17:18; 18:10, 16, 18–19, 21). See further *Notes* on Revelation 14:8. Seventh-day Adventists have traditionally believed that France manifested all the characteristics of this "great city" toward the close of the 1,260-year prophetic period.

Sodom and Egypt, where also their Lord was crucified. Jerusalem, as the professing city of God, was in the days of her apostasy frequently equated with Sodom by the prophets (Isa. 1:9–10; 3:9; Jer. 23:14; Ezek. 16:48–58). Both Sodom and Egypt are in the Old Testament renowned for their wickedness and as places where God's people "lived as aliens under persecution."[22] Sodom stands for all-inclusive sin and total moral degradation (Gen. 18:20–21; 19:4–11). On the other hand, Egypt is known for its arrogance and atheistic self-sufficiency as the oppressor of God's people. That attitude was first expressed in the arrogant words of Pharaoh at the Exodus: "Who is the Lord...? I do not know the Lord"

(Exod. 5:2). The prophet Ezekiel mentions "the pride of Egypt" (Ezek. 32:12). In the prophecy of Amos, Israel became like Sodom and Egypt; she will therefore be punished accordingly (Amos 4:10–11).

11:10 *Those who dwell upon the earth.* See *Notes* on Revelation 6:10.

Send gifts to one another. This exchange of gifts (a common custom in the ancient Near East) reminds one of the Jewish feast of Purim, when the Jews celebrated their deliverance by "rejoicing and sending portions of food to one another and gifts to the poor" (Esther 9:22; cf. Neh. 8:10–12).[23]

11:13 *There was a great earthquake.* The clause occurs also in Revelation 6:12 with reference to the sixth seal. This suggests that the "great earthquake" mentioned in 11:13 is the same one described upon the opening of the sixth seal.

The rest of the people became afraid and gave glory to the God of heaven. Several arguments suggest that genuine repentance is displayed here. First, "Fear God and give him glory" (Rev. 14:7) is a call for repentance. Second, giving glory to God throughout the Bible (Luke 17:18; John 9:24; Acts 12:23; Rom. 4:20; 1 Pet. 2:12) and in Revelation suggests a positive attitude toward God (Rev. 15:4; 16:9; 19:7). What one reads in Revelation 11:13 is the opposite of what one finds in Revelation 9:20–21 and 16:9.

EXPOSITION

11:3 The voice from heaven that earlier commissioned John to prophesy concerning many nations, and which subsequently ordered him to measure the temple, the altar, and the worshipers, now makes an announcement: ***And I will commission my two witnesses, and they will prophesy for 1,260 days clothed in sackcloth.*** "I will give" means that the two witnesses will be given the divine authority and power to prophesy. Their prophesying is related to Revelation 10:11, in which John is commissioned to prophesy concerning many nations. Revelation 11:3–14 clearly shows that the commission to prophesy given to John is extended to the church to be faithful witnesses of the gospel. This signifies the commission given by Jesus to the disciples: "You shall receive power when the Holy Spirit has come upon you; and you shall be My witnesses both in Jerusalem, and in all Judea and Samaria, and even to the remotest part of the earth" (Acts 1:8).

The number of witnesses in Revelation 11 recalls the law of the two witnesses of ancient Israel's legal system (Deut. 19:15; cf. Num. 35:30; Deut. 17:6; Heb. 10:28), which prescribes two as the number of witnesses for the Jewish legal court system. In order to establish something to be true, two witnesses had to have corresponding and corroborative testimonies (cf. Matt. 18:16; 2 Cor. 13:1; 1 Tim. 5:19). Jesus said to the Pharisees: "Even in your law it has been written, that the testimony of two men is true" (John 8:17). According to this practice, Jesus commissioned the disciples as his witnesses by sending them two by two (Mark 6:7; Luke 10:1), and the early church continued the same practice (Acts 13:2; 15:39–41). Thus the testimony borne by the two witnesses in Revelation 11 suggests the seriousness and importance of the message they proclaim. The world cannot reject the prophetic witnessing without suffering serious consequences and judgment.

The period of the prophesying of the two witnesses—"1,260 days"—is the same period designated to the Gentiles to trample and oppress God's people (cf. Rev. 11:2; 12:6, 14; 13:6). While in the book of Revelation the forty-two months are allotted to the wicked, 1,260 days is the period used with reference to God's people. As mentioned earlier with reference to Revelation 11:2, it seems that literal time is not intended here, but a specific period of more than 1,200 years during the Middle Ages—usually dated A.D. 538 to A.D. 1798—when God's people experience the bitterness of intense hardship and persecution in bearing their witness for Christ. This is clearly signified by the clothing being worn by the two witnesses during the time of their faithful witnessing. They are dressed in sackcloth, which in the Old Testament is the usual garb of prophets in their prophetic office (Isa. 20:2; Zech. 13:4; cf. Matt. 3:4). And this evidently has something to do with the bitter effect experienced in sharing the gospel message in Revelation 10:8–11.

11:4–6 The voice from heaven gives John several clues for the identification of the two witnesses. First, they are **the two olive trees and the two lampstands standing before the Lord of the earth.** John points clearly to Zechariah's vision where the two olive trees are said to represent "the two anointed ones, who are standing by the Lord of the whole earth" (Zech. 4:14). They refer to Joshua the high priest and Zerubbabel the governor, who were in the business of restoring the temple. In referring to Zechariah 4, John indicates that the activity of the two witnesses resembles the roles of Joshua and Zerubbabel. They embrace both the priestly and royal roles. It is especially significant that the two witnesses are related to the restoration of the temple (cf. Rev. 11:1–2). Just as the Holy Spirit worked through those anointed ones in restoring the temple and its services in Jerusalem (Zech. 4:6), so the two witnesses are used by the Holy Spirit as the bearers of the gospel message throughout the world. This message is centered in the theme of the restoration of the heavenly sanctuary and God's love and activity in the world.

Although experiencing the bitterness of opposition and persecution during the period of their prophetic activity, these two witnesses are evidently not powerless and destroyed. *If anyone wants to harm them, fire comes out of their mouths and devours their enemies; and if anyone wants to harm them, he must be killed.* This fire coming from their mouths recalls, first of all, Elijah's calling of fire down from heaven to devour the soldiers who were repeatedly sent by king Ahaziah to arrest the prophet (2 Kings 1:9–14). It also brings to mind God's words that became fire in Jeremiah's mouth, devouring the rebellious and unfaithful people (Jer. 5:14). *They have authority to shut heaven, lest it give forth rain during the days of their prophecy.* Here is another allusion to Elijah's prophetic activity during the great apostasy and absence of the word of God in Israel. It refers to the terrible drought that Elijah prophesied to king Ahab (1 Kings 17:1); the sky was shut and there was no rain in the land for a period of three and a half years (cf. Luke 4:25; James 5:17). The two witnesses also *have authority over the waters to turn them into blood, and to strike the earth with every plague as often as they want.* This evidently reflects the plagues of Egypt initiated by Moses when Pharaoh refused to let the Israelites leave Egypt. As a result, the land of Egypt was stricken with every kind of plague (Exod. 7–11).

The language used in the description of the two witnesses indicates that the roles and activity of the witnesses resemble, first of all, "the anointed ones" at the time of the rebuilding of the temple in Jerusalem, namely, Joshua the priest and Zerubbabel the governor. Second, their role and activity resemble those of Moses and Elijah, who met Jesus on the Mount of Transfiguration and talked to him with regard to what Jesus was to experience at the end of his life in Jerusalem (cf. Luke 9:31). The prophet Malachi predicted the coming of Elijah before the coming of the Day of the Lord (Mal. 4:5–6). However, these two witnesses are to be understood not as Moses and Elijah returning to the earth, but as symbolical figures. Their witnessing activity is modeled on the prophetic roles and activities of two of the greatest prophets in Israel's history, Moses and Elijah. The same divine power that accompanied the prophetic activity of the two greatest prophets, as well as Joshua and Zerubbabel, will be manifested in the witnessing of these two symbolic figures representing God's chosen agents of witnessing.

Who, then, are the two witnesses of Revelation 11? Evidence indicates that they might symbolize either the Bible as the word of God ("the word of God and the testimony of Jesus"), or God's people as they bear witness on behalf of the gospel in the world. It would seem, therefore, very appropriate to understand the two witnesses of Revelation 11 as the people of God in their royal and priestly roles (cf. Rev. 1:6; 5:10) as they bear their prophetic witness to the Word of God. Their witnessing recalls Jesus commissioning his disciples and sending them two by two as his witnesses (Mark 6:7; Luke 10:1). The seriousness and importance of witnessing was based on the Old Testament law which required two witnesses with corresponding and corroborative testimonies in order to make their witness valid (Deut. 19:15; John 8:17; Heb. 10:28).

11:7–10   The two witnesses have been given the determined period for their prophetic witnessing. After they complete their witnessing while clothed in sackcloth during the 1,260 days, *the beast coming up from the abyss will make war with them, and will conquer them and kill them.* Who is this beast coming from the abyss that wages war against the two witnesses? We saw earlier that the abyss or the bottomless pit stands for the abode of the fallen angels, the demons (cf. Luke 8:31; 2 Pet. 2:4; Jude 6). It is the place from which the demonic locusts come out attacking people in the scene of the fifth trumpet (Rev. 9:1–11). This suggests the demonic origin of the beast that attacks the two witnesses. In Revelation 13, the beast "coming up out the sea" has a dominant power over God's people during the forty-two months. It is after the period when the two witnesses have completed their prophetic witnessing that the beast coming up from the abyss makes war with them. Revelation 17:8 mentions another beast that comes out from the abyss and upon which the harlot Babylon sits. The beast waging war against the two witnesses, and harassing and persecuting them, is an authority endorsed and backed up by Satan himself. Seventh-day Adventists have generally identified the killing of the two witnesses with the atheistic assault against the Bible and the abolishment of religion during the French Revolution that came right at the conclusion of the prophetic 1,260-year period.

The two witnesses lie dead and publicly exposed *on the street of the great city.* The original Greek has "the dead body of them," which shows that the two witnesses are a single individual; they are never separated. In ancient times, it was a disgrace and the greatest tragedy to leave dead bodies exposed and deprived of burial (cf. 1 Kings 13:22; Ps. 79:3; Jer. 8:1–2; 14:16). The two witnesses are rejected by the world together with the message they have preached. Now they suffer a terrible indignity in death. The great city is *spiritually called Sodom and Egypt.* In other words, the great city where the witnesses are martyred integrates the wickedness and moral degradation of Sodom (Gen. 18:20–21; 19:4–11) with the atheistic arrogance and self-sufficiency of Egypt (cf. Exod. 5:2). Both cities were places where God's people "lived as aliens under persecution."[24]

The great city is further identified as **where also their Lord was crucified**. What happens to these two witnesses is "what has already happened to their Lord in Jerusalem."[25] Their opponents are those that Jesus faced earlier. Just as Jerusalem rejected Jesus and put him to death, so this great symbolic city—professing Christians under the control of political power—persecutes God's people.

The dead bodies of the witnesses lay exposed and unburied for **three and a half days**—a day for every year of their witnessing clothed in sackcloth. This period also corresponds to the time Jesus spent in the tomb. During this period the two witnesses remain exposed on the streets of the great city while men of **the peoples and tribes and tongues and nations** are gloating over their corpses, refusing them a proper and respectful burial. The reference to "the peoples and tribes and tongues and nations" recalls the commission to John to prophesy to "many peoples and nations and tongues and kings" (Rev. 10:11). They are evidently the same people. Here we seem to have a description of the bitterness that John tasted after eating the little scroll (cf. Rev. 10:8–11). God's people often experience painful bitterness because their witnessing is met with rejection and scorn.

Those who dwell on the earth rejoice over the bodies of the witnesses, make merry, and exchange gifts as the expression of their celebration. "Those who dwell on the earth" in Revelation is always a reference to the wicked. They are evidently "the peoples and tribes and tongues and nations" of Revelation 11:9. Here, they are celebrating the death of the witnesses **because these two prophets tormented those who dwell upon the earth.** This torment was evidently expressed in "troubling men's consciences over their sinfulness" and wickedness.[26] The gospel expressed through God's witnessing people "has always harassed the consciences of evil men."[27] To king Ahab, the prophet Elijah was a "troubler of Israel" (1 Kings 18:17) and his enemy (1 Kings 21:20). Ahab also hated the prophet Micah because he did not prophesy good concerning him, but evil (1 Kings 22:8, 18). When Paul was preaching to Felix the governor of "righteousness, self control, and the judgment," the frightened Felix refused to listen to Paul any longer and sent him away (Acts 26:25). And Jesus announced to his disciples: "You will be hated by all on account of My name" (Mark 13:13). The Word of God always "brings torment to those who hear the Word without surrendering to it."[28]

11:11–13 The celebration is now over. After three and a half days, *the breath of life from God entered them, and they stood up on their feet.* The breath of life is here the reference to Genesis 2:7; it is God who brings the witnesses back to life. This scene of bringing to life the two witnesses recalls Ezekiel's vision of the valley of the dry bones—the prophecy of the restoration of Israel from the Babylonian exile. To their enemies, Israel is seen as having been slain. As Ezekiel prophesied, the breath came into the dead bodies, and they came to life and stood on their feet (Ezek. 37:1–10). Whenever the world thinks it has silenced the voice of the faithful witnesses that "tormented them," vindication is always portrayed symbolically in the resurrection and ascension of the two witnesses. As Desmond Ford states, "the righteous may be knocked down, but they are not knocked out."[29] Applying it historically, one of the consequences of the French Revolution was a great revival of interest in the Bible manifested particularly in the establishment of the great Bible societies and numerous missionary societies during the time that followed. Two witnesses thus came back to life and the stage was set for a widespread preaching of the gospel—more than at any time in history. Bringing them back to life engenders *a great fear* on their enemies who earlier rejoiced over their disgraceful death.

A voice from heaven summons the resurrected witnesses. *And they went up to heaven in the cloud, and their enemies beheld them.* Their enemies are identified earlier as "the peoples and tribes and tongues and nations" (11:9) and "those who dwell on the earth" (11:10). The ascension of the witnesses recalls Jesus' ascension to heaven on a cloud after his resurrection (Acts 1:9). We know that both Elijah and Moses were raised to heaven (2 Kings 2:11; Jude 9). The witnesses, having completed their prophetic witnessing, are now miraculously raised to heaven in the cloud. Their exaltation from the humiliated condition they had been in adds to the terror in the hearts of the earth dwellers.

The preaching of the gospel, however, has not come to an end yet; in Revelation 14:6, John sees the three angels proclaiming the final gospel message to "those who dwell on the earth, and to every nation and tribe and tongue and people." The text points to the final proclamation of the gospel toward the close of this world's history.

And at the same hour there was a great earthquake taking place when the witnesses are raised to heaven. This earthquake, like the one of the sixth seal, signals the beginning of the time of the end and the final events of this world's history. "The symbol of an earthquake is used repeatedly in Scripture to portray the turmoil and upheaval that characterize the world immediately preceding the second advent (see Mark 13:8; Rev. 16:18)."[30] The earthquake causes the destruction of *a tenth of the city*, bringing death to *7,000 people.* This city is evidently "the great city" figuratively called Sodom and Egypt, which, in Revelation 18, is called Babylon. The 7,000 people killed in the collapse of the great city represents the totality of the hardened unbelievers.[31] It reminds us of the 7,000 who remained faithful during the ministry of Elijah (1 Kings 19:18). In Romans 11:4–5, this number stands for the totality of the remnant of Israel. Here only a partial collapse of the great city of Babylon takes place; its total destruction occurs in Revelation 18.

The earthquake, along with the partial collapse of the great city, creates a positive effect on the surviving people. *And the rest of the people became afraid and gave glory to the God of heaven.* It seems that genuine repentance is in view here. That brings to mind the confession made by king Nebuchadnezzar in giving glory to the God of heaven after experiencing divine judgment (Dan. 4:34–37). The survivors of the collapse of the great city seem to give the response that the first angel of Revelation 17 calls for: "Fear God and give him glory" (Rev. 14:7). This suggests that the vindication of the two witnesses (Rev. 11:11–13) parallels the proclamation of the eternal gospel of the first angel of Revelation 14. It thus seems clear that the main focus of Revelation 11 is the proclamation of the gospel through the church. As earth's history approaches its close, the gospel will be proclaimed once more in mighty power and be accepted by many people.

11:14 John concludes the section with this statement: *The second woe has passed; behold, the third woe is coming quickly.* The first and second woes were related to the blowing of the fifth and sixth trumpets, respectively. It is natural, therefore, to understand the sounding of the seventh trumpet as the third woe that is ready to take place, which brings us to the completion of God's mystery (cf. Rev. 10:7).

A RETROSPECT ON REVELATION 11:1–14

Revelation 11:1–14 concludes the interlude between the blowing of the sixth and seventh trumpets. In chapter 10 we were left with the commission to John to prophesy concerning many peoples (Rev. 10:8–11). Revelation 11:1–14 provides some additional information with regard to the content of the message that the church via John was commissioned to prophesy to the world at the end time (11:1–2), along with an explanation of the bitter experience that the proclamation of the gospel brings upon those who proclaim it (11:3–13).

Revelation 11:1–2 indicates that the restoration of the heavenly sanctuary and its services, with reference to the preparation of the saints for the Second Coming, lies at the heart of the final gospel proclamation. The restoration of the sanctuary, the altar, and the worshipers has to do with God's government over the universe. During the history of sin on this earth, God's character and the way he treats his subjects have been under constant attack. The restoration of the sanctuary message is meant to vindicate God's character before the entire universe, to restore his rightful rulership, and to establish the kingdom. It further involves the restoration of the gospel message with regard to the atoning work of Christ and his righteousness as the only means of salvation.

The restoration of the sanctuary message also includes the preparation of God's people for the kingdom. This preparation involves the restoration of their mental, physical, and spiritual aspects of life. Revelation 11:1–2 indicates that the proclamation of the everlasting gospel message that the church has been commissioned to "prophesy" in the final stage of this world's history will be in the context of the restoration of the heavenly sanctuary. The experience of God's people as they proclaim the gospel message is further described in the portrayal of the witnesses in the following section.

Revelation 11:3–14 describes symbolic bitterness and pain which God's people experience as they proclaim the gospel message to the world. Although Seventh-day Adventists have interpreted this section of Revelation as having been fulfilled during the period of the Middle Ages and in the context of the French Revolution, its significance for God's end-time people goes beyond this temporal and geographical location. This scene of the two symbolic witnesses, whoever they might be, shows that God had in the past and still has in the present his saints who are faithful to the commission to bear witness to the gospel in the world. He uses them as he used Moses at the Exodus, Elijah during the great apostasy in Israel, and Joshua and Zerubbabel at the post-exilic time of the rebuilding of the temple in Jerusalem.

In bearing witness to the world, God's servants often experience harassment and persecution. But whatever may happen to them in "the great city," God's people experience what has already happened to their Lord in Jerusalem. To be with him and speak of him is the primary commission of the church. "This is because the function of the church's prophetic ministry to the world is to bring into universal effect what Jesus achieved in his own prophetic witness, death and resurrection."[32] God's adversaries may harass and persecute God's faithful witnesses in an attempt to silence them, and it may appear that the foes have won the victory. But the prophecy makes it clear that we are approaching a time when we will see the gospel being proclaimed once more in mighty power and the glory of God. This final proclamation will illuminate the whole earth with the glory of the gospel message (cf. Rev. 18:1).

ENDNOTES

1. See Kurt Deissner, *"metron,"* in *Theological Dictionary of the New Testament*, 4:633–634.

2. Strand, "An Overlooked Old-Testament Background to Revelation 11:1," 322–325.

3. Ibid., 324.

4. Ibid., 322.

5. Ibid., 322–323.

6. See Jacques B. Doukhan, *Secrets of Daniel: Wisdom and Dreams of a Jewish Prince in Exile* (Hagerstown, MD: Review and Herald, 2000), 108–110.

7. LeRoy E. Froom, *The Prophetic Faith of Our Fathers* (Washington, DC: Review and Herald, 1948), 2:794–795.

8. LaRondelle, *How to Understand the End-Time Prophecies*, 258.

9. On the year-day symbolism in biblical prophecy, see Alberto R. Timm, "Miniature Symbolization and the Year-day Principle of Prophetic Interpretation," *Andrews University Seminary Studies* 42.1 (2004): 149–167.

10. See C. Mervyn Maxwell, "Roman Catholicism and the United States" (pp. 72–77), and "Some Questions Answered—Dates: Their Historical Setting" (pp. 125–132), in *Symposium on Revelation—Book 2*, Daniel and Revelation Committee Series 7 (Silver Spring, MD: Biblical Research Institute, 1992). The most recent affirmation of A.D. 538 as the starting point for the 42-months/1,260-days prophetic period is given by Alberto Timm ("A Short Historical Background to A.D. 508 and 538 as Related to the Establishment of Papal Supremacy," a paper presented at the Michigan Conference Bible Prophecy Symposium, Camp Au Sable, August 2006) and Heinz Schaidinger, "History Behind the Prophecy of the 1260 Days: The Beginning of the Time Period in 538 AD," unpublished paper, Bogenhofen Seminary, March 2008).

11. Strand, "An Overlooked Old-Testament Background to Revelation 11:1," 322–325.

12. Ibid., 322–323.

13. J. M. Ford, 177.

14. Hughes, 121.

15. Charles, 280.

16. Convincing arguments for such a view are offered by Bauckham, *The Climax of Prophecy*, 273–283.

17. Frederick F. Bruce, "The Revelation to John," *A New Testament Commentary* (Grand Rapids, MI: Zondervan, 1969), 649; Fiorenza, *Revelation*, 78.

18. Beale, 573.

19. White, *The Great Controversy*, 267.

20. White, *Testimonies for the Church* (Mountain View, CA: Pacific Press, 1948), 4:594–595.

21. Beale, 594.

22. Ibid., 591.

23. See Bauckham, *The Climax of Prophecy*, 281–282.

24. Beale, 591.

25. Johnson, 506.

26. Thomas, *Revelation 8–22*, 96.

27. Mounce, 227.

28. Desmond Ford, 495–496.

29. Ibid., 496.

30. *The Seventh-day Adventist Bible Commentary*, 7:804.

31. Beale, 603.

32. Bauckham, *The Climax of Prophecy*, 280.

THE THIRD WOE: THE SEVENTH TRUMPET
REVELATION 11:15–19

The starting point for understanding the scene of the blowing of the seventh trumpet is Revelation 10:5–7, in which the mighty angel raises his right hand and swears his oath by God the creator that "there will no longer be time." The angel provides the church with strong assurance that the end time prophesied by Daniel (12:5–10) will soon run its course and that God is about to deliver and vindicate his faithful saints and bring earth's history to a close. With a strong adversative "but," the angel also makes it clear that the end would not come until the sound of the trumpet of the seventh angel: "But in the days of the sound of the seventh angel, when he is about to sound, then the mystery of God will be completed, as he proclaimed to his servants the prophets" (Rev. 10:7).

The seventh trumpet sounds the end of earth's history, and now the revelation of "the mystery of God," which has puzzled all creatures of the universe and the contents of which were sealed for ages (Rom. 16:25–26; Col. 1:26–28), has been brought to the world through Christ. This mystery was symbolically portrayed in the scroll sealed with seven seals (Rev. 5), the portion of which has been disclosed to the church through John in the symbolic little scroll in Revelation 10. It is through the church that God wants to bring the good news of that mystery to the world (Eph. 3:9–11). The symbolic portrayal of the witnessing of the two witnesses in Revelation 11 shows that for 2,000 years there has been the proclamation of that mystery of God to the world. However, in the final days of this world's history, as the wicked are preparing themselves for the battle of Armageddon, God's people will be involved in the great proclamation of the gospel, which is presented symbolically as the three angels proclaiming the everlasting gospel to the inhabitants of the earth (Rev. 14:6–12).

The proclamation of the gospel will be completed at the sound of the seventh angel. It seems clear, therefore, that the blowing of the seventh trumpet denotes the end of the time of grace when all final events will be set in motion. Now, at the sound of the seventh trumpet, the time has arrived for "the mystery of God," which has been partially disclosed and proclaimed through the church, to be completed.

> *15And the seventh angel sounded his trumpet; and there were loud voices in heaven saying:*
>> *"The kingdom of the world has become the kingdom of our*
>>> *Lord and of his Christ*
>>> *and he will reign forever and ever."*
> *16And the twenty-four elders who were before God sitting on their thrones fell on their faces and worshiped God, 17saying:*
>> *"We give thanks to you, Lord God, the Almighty,*
>>> *who is and who was,*
>> *because you have taken your great power*
>>> *and begun to reign;*
> *18And the nations were enraged,*
>> *and your wrath came*
> *and the time for the dead to be judged*
>> *and to give the reward to your servants the prophets*
>>> *and the saints*
>> *and those who fear your name,*
>>> *the small and the great ones,*
> *and to destroy the destroyers of the earth."*
> *19And the temple of God that is in heaven was opened, and the ark of the covenant in his temple was seen; and there came flashes of lightning, voices, peals of thunder, an earthquake, and great hail.*

NOTES

11:15 *Our Lord and of his Christ.* The phrase is borrowed from Psalm 2:2 where the kings and rulers of the earth conspire together against "the Lord and his Messiah," namely, the king of Israel.

11:16 *The twenty-four elders.* See *Notes* on Revelation 4:4.

11:17 *Almighty.* See *Notes* on Revelation 1:8.

11:18 *Nations.* See *Notes* on Revelation 11:2.

The nations were enraged, and your wrath came. In Greek, the verb "to be enraged" or "to be angry" (*orgizō*) and the noun "wrath" (*orgē*) belong to the same word group of the stem *org–*. Thus here in the text, God's wrath is the response to the wrath of the nations.

To destroy the destroyers of the earth. In Greek, *diaphtheirō* means "to destroy" or "to corrupt." In coining the phrase "to destroy the destroyers of the earth," John could have had the Old Testament pre-flood account in mind. The original reading of Genesis 6:11–13 in both Hebrew and Greek is as follows: "But the earth was corrupted [destroyed, Gr. *ephtharē*] before God, and the earth was filled with iniquity. And the Lord God saw the earth, and it was corrupted [being destroyed, Gr. *katephtharmenē*]; because all flesh had corrupted [destroyed, Gr. *katephtheire*] its way upon the earth. And the Lord God said to Noe, 'A period of all men is come before me; because the earth has been filled with iniquity by them, and behold, I destroy [Gr. *kataphtheirō*] them and the earth'" (LXX 6:12–14).[1] The text shows that because the antediluvian people were "destroying" the earth, the Lord decided to destroy them from the earth. This "destroying" of the earth had to be understood as the filling of the earth with iniquity (Gen 6:12, 14). According to 1 Corinthians 3:17, the destroyers of the temple of God will be destroyed. The destruction of the destroyers of the earth in Revelation 11:18 is a clear reference to the end-time Babylon described in Revelation 19:2 as corrupting (or destroying, Gr. *phtheirō*) the earth with immorality, which is a further reference to Revelation 17:1–6. Jeremiah referred to historical Babylon as the "destroying mountain, that destroys the whole earth" (in the Greek OT: *to oros to diephtharmenon, to diaphtheiron pasan tēn gēn*; Jer. 28[51]:25). This is the sense in which the destroyers of the earth in Revelation must be understood.

11:19 *The temple of God.* The Greek *naos* here refers to the innermost part of temple, the most holy place. That the innermost part is in view here is further indicated by the appearance of the ark of the covenant located in the most holy place of the temple. For more on the meaning of *naos* in Revelation, see *Notes* on Revelation 11:1.

EXPOSITION

11:15 The seventh trumpet signals the consummation of all things and the completion of "the mystery of God" (Rev. 10:7). At the moment it is blown, John hears loud voices in heaven declaring the triumph of God and the transfer of dominion and rulership to God and his Christ (namely, his Messiah or anointed one) over the world: ***The kingdom of the world has become the kingdom of our Lord and of his Christ and he will reign forever and ever.*** Here is the fulfillment of what God's faithful people in every generation have yearned and prayed for: "Thy kingdom come" (Matt. 6:10). This earth that has been under the dominion and rule of the usurping power and in rebellion against God will finally come back under God's dominion and rule. The text brings to mind the prophecy given by Daniel to king Nebuchadnezzar: "In the days of those kings the God of heaven will set up a kingdom which will never be destroyed, and that kingdom will not be left for another people; it will crush and put an end to all these kingdoms, but it will itself endure forever" (Dan. 2:44).

The establishment of God's eternal kingdom on the earth, which is the central theme of the book of Revelation (11:17; 12:10; 19:6; 22:5), involves "the wresting of authority from all hostile powers, including the godless nations of earth, and the exercise of all authority by the *Lord and his Christ*."[2] In Revelation 5, in the formal ceremonial act of symbolically taking the sealed scroll, Christ was recognized as the co-ruler with the Father, reigning at his right hand on the heavenly throne over the entire universe. As the end-time ruler, he was entrusted with the authority to carry out "God's plan for the end of history."[3] The destiny of all humanity was placed into Christ's hands. His co-rulership was to last until his enemies were made "a footstool for your feet" (Ps. 110:1). "For he must reign until He has put all His enemies under His feet" (1 Cor. 15:25). When finally the enemies are subjected, "then comes the end, when He hands over the kingdom to the God and Father, and when He has abolished all rule and all authority and power…. When all things are subjected to Him, then the Son Himself also will be subjected to the One who subjected all things to Him, so that God may be all in all" (1 Cor. 15:24, 28).

11:16–18 Following the declaration of the heavenly hosts, the twenty-four elders, as representatives of redeemed humanity, fall down before the throne in worship and sing a hymn of thanksgiving to God for taking his great power and reigning. God is referred to as the ***Lord God, the Almighty, who is and who was.*** While earlier in the book God is identified as the "Lord God, the Almighty, who is and who was and who is coming" (1:8; 4:8), this time the third item, "who is coming," is omitted. His coming is no longer in the future, because he has already come and has taken his ***great power and begun to reign.***

The hymn sung by the twenty-four elders outlines the events that follow God's taking the kingdom and which are portrayed in the remaining chapters of Revelation. First, ***the nations were enraged*** against God and his people. This is an allusion to Psalm 2, which speaks of the nations raging against the Lord and his anointed one (Ps. 2:1–2; cf. Rev. 11:15b) and God's response of wrath (2:12; cf. vv. 8–12). The anger of the nations in Revelation 11:18 is the result of their opposition to the kingdom and God's rule. It will climax in the battle of Armageddon, when the nations of the world will unite in their anger to oppose the establishment of God's kingdom. The anger of the nations against God and his people is described in detail in Revelation 12–13.

To the wrath of the nations, God responds with wrath: ***And your wrath came.*** This outpouring of God's wrath is for the purpose of ending the rebellion of the wicked against God. This is portrayed in detail in Revelation 14–18. ***The time for the dead to be judged*** shows that the judgment includes both positive and negative aspects. Its positive aspect includes the giving of ***the reward to your servants the prophets and the saints and those who fear your name, the small and the great ones,*** which will occur at the Second Coming (Rev. 19:1–10; chapters 21–22). The phrase "who fear the Lord, the small and the great ones" is borrowed from Psalm 115:13, denoting the faithful believers from every socio-economic level.[4] Judgment has also a negative aspect with regard to ***the destroyers of the earth,*** who are to be destroyed. This expression brings to mind the identification of the antediluvians in Genesis 6:12–14 as the destroyers of the earth who did so by "filling the earth with iniquity." Just as the antediluvian destroyers of the earth had to be destroyed with the earth, so will be the fate of the end-time destroyers of the earth. This suggests that Revelation 11:18 does not refer to ecological concerns of destroying the earth by modern technology, a rather contemporary view, but to the activities of end-time Babylon filling the earth with sins which have "accumulated unto heaven, and God has remembered her unrighteous acts" (Rev. 18:5). This assertion is further supported by the fact that Jeremiah identifies historical Babylon as the "destroying mountain, who destroys the whole earth" (Jer. 51:25). In Revelation 19:2, end-time Babylon is judged because she has corrupted (or destroyed) the earth with her immorality (cf. Rev. 17:1–6). The eradication of Satan and his hosts is the final act in the drama of the great controversy between good and evil (Rev. 19:11–20:15).

11:19 The vision ends with the opening of the temple of God in heaven, its innermost part, enabling John to see ***the ark of the covenant in his temple*** accompanied by ***lightnings and voices and thunder and earthquakes and great hail*** which represents the manifestation of the divine presence (Rev. 4:5; 8:5; 16:18; cf. Exod. 19:16–19; 20:18; Deut. 5:22–23). The mention of the Ark of the Covenant at the beginning of the new vision has special significance. First of all, it has to do with the disclosure of the contents of the little scroll that John received in Revelation 10, because it was by the Ark of the Covenant that the Book of the Covenant was stored (as will be discussed in the introductory section to Rev. 12–22:5).

The second reason for mentioning the Ark of the Covenant is to prepare readers for the chapters which concern God's faithfulness to his end-time church.[5] In the Old

Testament, the Ark of the Covenant was the symbol of God's continuing presence with his people and the assurance of his promise. As the ark of the covenant was the reminder to Israel of God's loyal love during their wilderness journeys and battles, so the reference to the ark of the covenant in Revelation 11:19 is a reminder to God's end-time people of his love and covenant promise to be with them through all the trials that they will experience in the closing period of earth's history.[6] Whatever trials are to come, God will stay faithful as he promised to carry out "his covenant promises and destroy the enemies of his people.[7]

A RETROSPECT ON REVELATION 11:15–19

The portrayal of the blowing of the seventh trumpet provides a summary of what will happen at the time of the end immediately prior to the Second Coming, as described in detail in the second half of the book of Revelation (chapters 12–22). It shows us that the events of the end will be the final triumph of God's rule in this world. It guarantees the fulfillment of the promise given in response to the plea of the saints in the scene of the fifth trumpet: "How long, O Lord, holy and true, will you not judge and avenge our blood upon those who dwell on the earth?" (Rev. 6:10). The establishment of God's eternal kingdom and his rule over the world denotes the vindication of God's saints and satisfies their perennial longings and expectations.

ENDNOTES

1. Translated by Lancelot C. L. Brenton, *The Septuagint with Apocrypha: Greek and English* (Peabody, MA: Hendrickson, 1986), 7.
2. Ladd, 161.
3. Roloff, 76.
4. Mounce, 338.
5. Johnson, 510.
6. Ibid.
7. Mounce, 233.

THE CONTENTS OF THE SEVEN-SEALED SCROLL

The Dragon and the Woman (12:1–17)
The Two Beasts (13:1–18)
God's Final Message to the World (14:1–20)
The Seven Last Plagues (15–16:21)
Prostitute Babylon and the Resurrected Beast (17:1–18)
The Judgment of Babylon (18:1–24)
The Two Suppers (19:1–21)
The Millennium and the Final Judgment (20:1–15)
The Restored Earth (21–22:5)

"And the dragon was angry at the woman,
and went away to make war with the remaining ones
of her offspring, the ones keeping the commandments
of God and having the testimony of Jesus."

The third and last major section of the book of Revelation begins with chapter 12. As we have seen in the introduction to this commentary, the book is well structured. An analysis indicates that its first half covers the Christian era from the time of Christ's ascension to the heavenly places until his return to the earth. The second half of the book (Rev. 12–22:5) focuses in particular on the time of the end and the final events of this world's history. It appears that Revelation 11:18 provides in detail the outline of the main themes and movements of the second half of Revelation.

SPRINGBOARD PASSAGE: REVELATION 11:18

The function of the springboard passages in the book of Revelation has been discussed earlier in this commentary. The springboard passage functions both as the concluding statement of the preceding section and as the introduction of the section that follows (e.g., Rev. 1:20; 3:21; 6:16–17; 12:17). Thus, we have seen, for instance, how the concluding statement of the section of the seven churches (Rev. 3:21) is the key for understanding Revelation 4–5. In the same way, the concluding statement of the seven seals (Rev. 6:17) functions as the introduction to Revelation 7. Now this literary technique is employed in Revelation 11:18 which not only concludes the vision of the blowing of the seven trumpets, but also introduces the second half of the book.

The springboard passage of Revelation 11:18 contains five basic statements which outline the structure of the second half of the book of Revelation and summarize the themes of its major portions: "the nations were enraged," "your wrath came," "the time for the dead to be judged," "to give the reward to your servants," and "to destroy the destroyers of the earth." The last two substatements obviously explain the preceding one: "the time for the dead to be judged." In other words, the judging of the dead involves the giving of the reward to God's servants, on one side, and the destroying of the destroyers of the earth, on the other.

Each statement provides a summary and defines the themes of the main sections of the second half of the book, as shown in Table 1. The parallels between Revelation 11:18 and Revelation 12–22:5 are evidently not accidental. Revelation 11:18 provides an outline of the structure of the last half of the book and summarizes its main sections and themes. Revelation 12–22:5 is thus an elaboration of Revelation 11:18.[1]

TABLE 1

REVELATION 11:18	REVELATION 12–22:5
the nations were enraged	Revelation 12–14 describes the anger of the nations expressed in the activity of Satan and his allies, the sea beast (13:1–10) and the land beast (13:11–18), who are setting themselves up against God and his people. During this time, God is making the last appeal to the nations for repentance (14:6–13) through the proclamation of the gospel.
your wrath came	The seven last plagues (chapters 15–16) and judgment on Babylon (chapters 17–18) are the means by which "the wrath of God" is completed (Rev. 15:1) on the nations that have been oppressing and harassing his people.
the time for the dead to be judged	Revelation 19–22 describes this time and the reward and punishment which follow.
to give the reward to your servants	Revelation 19:1–10 and chapters 21–22 are about rewarding God's people in terms of the new earth and the new Jerusalem.
to destroy the destroyers of the earth	Revelation 19:11–20:15 portrays the destruction of those who destroyed the earth at the Second Coming (19:11–21) and at the final judgment after the millennium (20:1–15)

Another significant point comes to light here. The fact that Revelation 11:18 is part of the scene of the seventh trumpet (and, as such, outlines the second half of the book) suggests that what follows will deal with the final events leading up to the Second Coming. Jon Paulien remarks that Revelation 11:18 tells us that the second half of Revelation focuses on the time of the end.[2] According to Revelation 10:7, "in the days of the sound of the seventh angel, when he is about to sound, then the mystery of God will be completed, as he proclaimed to his servants the prophets." Revelation 12–22 thus should be understood as the completion of God's mystery when the preaching of the gospel and the history of this world will be brought to their end.

APPEARANCE OF THE ARK OF THE COVENANT: REVELATION 11:19

With Revelation 12:1 begins a completely new vision in the book. We have observed that the vision of the seven trumpets concluded with the opening of the most holy place of the heavenly temple. The opening of the most holy place enabled John to see "the ark of the covenant in his temple" (11:19). The appearance of the ark of the covenant here seems to be very significant, because it was by the ark of the covenant in the most holy place of the Old Testament temple that the scroll of the covenant was stored (cf. Deut. 31:24–26). In the context of the book of Revelation, the seven-sealed scroll has all the characteristics of the Old Testament book of the covenant that was stored by the ark of the covenant (cf. Deut. 31:9, 24–26). This suggests that the appearance of the ark in the heavenly sanctuary at the beginning of the completely new section of Revelation has something to do with the disclosure of the contents of the sealed scroll of Revelation 5, the book of God's eternal covenant. Only a portion of the sealed scroll was revealed to John in Revelation 10 in the symbolic form of the little scroll. John now passes on to the churches the contents of the sealed scroll that were disclosed to him (see further *Notes* on Rev. 10:2).

In this new vision, the appearance of the ark of the covenant is evidently linked to the revelation of a portion of the sealed scroll because its appearance is accompanied by "lightning, voices, peals of thunder, an earthquake, and great hail." These phenomena also accompanied the giving of the law at Mount Sinai (Exod. 19:16–19; 20:18; Deut. 5:22–23). Here we have an announcement of the disclosure of God's plans with regard to the future portrayed in the manner of the giving of the law at Sinai. Therefore, it is very appropriate to understand the second half of Revelation (chapters 12–22:5) as the disclosure of what was portrayed symbolically in the little scroll of Revelation 10. As we have seen, the little scroll of Revelation 10 contains just a portion of the seven-sealed scroll of Revelation 5 as it applies to the final events of earth's history. In his providence, God has found it important to disclose the contents of the little scroll to his end-time people to help them prepare for the events that are about to take place on the earth at the time of the end.

David Aune observes the verbal and structural parallels with Isaiah 66:6–7, which he sees as further evidence that Revelation 11:19 is the starting point for the vision of Revelation 12:[3]

> Hark, an uproar from the city!
>> A voice from the temple!
> The voice of the LORD,
>> rendering recompense to his enemies!
> Before she was in labor
>> she gave birth;
> before her pain came upon her
>> she was delivered of a son. (Isaiah 66:6–7, RSV)

In both texts, the scene of a woman giving birth to a son is preceded by a divine action from the temple to render judgment on the unfaithful.

Thus, in conclusion, Revelation 12–22:5 reveals the contents of the little scroll of chapter 10 which seems to be just a portion of the sealed scroll of Revelation 5 that was revealed to John in a symbolic presentation, and which he further conveyed to the church. The remaining portion of the sealed scroll that John was commanded to seal up and not to convey to the church (10:4) is to be disclosed after the Second Coming, when "in the days of the sound of the seventh angel, when he is about to sound, then the mystery of God will be completed" (10:7).

COUNTERFEIT MOTIFS IN REVELATION 12–22:5

Crucial to the understanding of the main theological themes of the second half of Revelation is the counterfeit motif, including counterfeits of persons, messages, the mark of the identification of true worshipers, and the city. The main focus of the first eleven chapters of the book is on the three persons of the Godhead who are referred to at the very outset of the book as "the One who is and who was and who is coming" (presumably God the Father), "the seven Spirits" (denoting the fullness and universality of the work of the Holy Spirit), and Jesus Christ (Rev. 1:4). They are also mentioned together at the enthronement of Christ in Revelation 4–5.

Their salvific activities on behalf of humanity are implicit throughout the rest of the book.

Revelation 12–22:5 focuses on Satan's endeavor to prevent God's plans for the world and to urge the inhabitants of earth to side with him. He will, as Paulien states, "place in motion a massive counterfeit of the true God" and his salvific activities.[4] His efforts to deceive the inhabitants of the earth are portrayed in the book as antitheses to God and his activities: the satanic trinity (chapters 12–13) functions as the antithesis of the three persons of the Godhead (1:4–5; chapters 4–5), the mark of the beast (13:15–16) as the antithesis of the seal of God (7:1–3; 14:1), the three demonic messages (16:13–14) as the antithesis of the three angels' messages (14:6–12), and the woman-city of Babylon (chapters 17–18) as an antithesis of New Jerusalem (chapters 21–22).

Counterfeit Trinity. Chapters 12 and 13 introduce the major actors in the scene of the second half of Revelation: the dragon (Rev. 12) and his two allies—the sea beast (Rev. 13:1–10) and the earth beast (13:11–17). Together they make up a satanic trinity as an antithesis to the Trinity of the Godhead. Throughout the rest of the book they are inseparably associated in the activities of deceiving people to turn from God and put themselves into the service of Satan (cf. Rev. 16:13–14; 19:20; 20:10).

The first entity in that triune league is Satan who in Revelation 12–13 is presented as the antithesis of God the Father, seeking equality with God and leading war against him. He functions as the leader of the group, authorizing others and giving them orders. (See Table 2.)

TABLE 2

DRAGON/SATAN	GOD THE FATHER
His place is in heaven (12:3, 7–8)	God's dwelling place is in heaven (Rev. 4–5)
He has a throne (13:2b; cf. 2:13)	He has a throne (Rev. 4–5; 7:9–15; 19:4)
Gives power, throne, and authority to the sea beast (13:2, 4)	Gives power, throne, and authority to Christ (Matt. 28:18; Rev. 2:27; 3:21; chapters 4–5)
He is worshiped (13:4a)	He is worshiped (Rev. 4:10; 15:4)
He is destroyed forever (20:9–10)	He lives and reigns forever (Rev. 4:9; 5:13; 11:15)

Such parallelism suggests the intention of the inspired author to show that in the satanic league the sea beast functions as an antithesis of Jesus Christ, imitating his life and ministry on the earth. The sea beast acts in the full authority and power of the dragon, just as Jesus acts in the authority of the Father (cf. Matt. 28:18). (See Table 3.)

TABLE 3

THE SEA BEAST	JESUS CHRIST
Comes from water to begin his activity (13:1)	Comes from water to begin his ministry (Luke 3:21–23)
Resembles the dragon (12:3; 13:1)	"He who has seen me has seen the Father" (John 14:9)
Has ten diadems (13:1)	Has many diadems (Rev. 19:12)
Has ten horns upon his heads (13:1)	The Lamb with seven horns (Rev. 5:6)
Receives power, throne, and authority from the dragon (13:2, 4)	Receives power, throne, and authority from the Father (Matt. 28:18; Rev. 2:27; chaps 4–5)
Forty-two months of his activity (13:5)	Three and half years of his ministry (as the Gospel of John indicates)
He was slain (13:3)	He was slain (Rev. 5:6)
Came back to life (13:3)	Resurrected (Rev. 1:18)
Received worship after his mortal wound was healed (13:3–4, 8)	Received worship after his resurrection (Matt. 28:17)
Was given universal authority over the earth after the healing of his mortal wound (13:7)	"All authority has been given to Me in heaven and on earth" (Matt. 28:18) after the resurrection
"Who is like the beast?" (13:4)	Michael ["Who is like God?"] (Rev. 12:7)
Global target (over all nations, tribes, tongues, and peoples; Rev. 13:7; cf. 17:15)	Global target (over all nations, tribes, tongues, and peoples; Rev. 5:9; 10:11; 14:6)

The earth beast reveals himself as a counterfeit of the work of the Holy Spirit. He functions in the full authority of the sea beast (Rev. 13:3) in the same ways as the Holy Spirit represents Jesus Christ acting in his full authority (cf. John 14:26; 15:26; 16:13). (See Table 4.)

TABLE 4

THE EARTH BEAST	THE HOLY SPIRIT
Called the false prophet deceiving people (16:13; 19:20; 20:10)	Called the Spirit of truth guiding people to salvation (John 16:13; Rev. 22:17)
Lamb-like (13:11)	Christ-like (John 14:26; 16:14)
Exercises all the authority of the sea beast (13:12a)	Exercises all the authority of Christ (John 16:13–14)
Directs worship to the sea beast (13:12b, 15)	Directs worship to Christ (Acts 5:29–32)
Performs great signs (13:13; 19:20)	Performs great signs (Acts 4:30–31)
Brings fire down from heaven (13:13)	Comes in fire at the Pentecost (Acts 2)
Gives life/breath to the beast's image (13:15)	Gives life/breath of life (Rom. 8:11)
Applies the mark on the hand or forehead (13:16)	Applies the seal on the forehead (2 Cor. 1:22; Eph. 1:13; 4:30)
Received worship after his mortal wound was healed (13:3–4, 8)	Received worship after his resurrection (Matt. 28:17)

The book concludes with God's ultimate triumph over the satanic trinity who will find a definite and ultimate end in the lake of fire (Rev. 19:20; 20:10).

Counterfeit Seal. Before the final crisis, God's people are sealed on their foreheads (Rev. 7:1–3). While the faithful receive God's seal, their enemies receive a symbolic mark on the hand or forehead known as "the mark of the beast" (Rev. 13:16–17). This mark functions as the counterfeit of the seal of God, and its acceptance indicates an antithesis to God's command—obedience to God is replaced by obedience to the beast.[5] In the same way as the followers of Christ bear the symbolic seal of God's possession and their loyalty, the worshipers of the beast bear the symbolic mark of ownership and loyalty to Satan (13:16–17; 14:9; 16:2; 19:20; 20:4). While the seal of God consists of the name of God upon the forehead, the mark of the beast consists of the name of the beast upon the forehead or hand (Rev. 13:17). The forehead stands for the mind, and the right hand stands for the deed and action. "Both rival powers wish to control the mind and behavior. The followers of the Lamb all have the name of God upon their foreheads, whereas the followers of the beast have the mark on the forehead (indicating belief and allegiance) or the hand only (indicating forced

379

obedience without mental assent)."[6] Since the sealing signifies the working process of the Holy Spirit on human hearts (cf. 2 Cor. 1:21–22; Eph. 1:13–14; 4:30), the intention of the inspired author is to show that the placing of the mark of the beast is spurious to the work of the Holy Spirit.

Counterfeit Message. Revelation 14:6–12 reveals three angels proceeding from God with a threefold gospel message urging the inhabitants of the earth to repent and worship the living God, announcing the demise of spiritual Babylon, and warning against any association with her. Revelation 16:13–14 portrays three demonic counterparts proceeding from the mouth of the satanic trinity with a false gospel message to the inhabitants of the earth. They summon the unrepentant to join the satanic trinity against God and his faithful people for the great day of God Almighty. The three demonic angels of the sixth plague are Satan's last attempt to mirror the work of God, for they appear to be the counterpart of the three angels of Revelation 14, and their messages are described by John as the antitheses to the warning messages that the three angels proclaim.

Counterfeit City. Finally, Revelation 17 portrays the end-time apostate religious system, called Babylon, as a prostitute—a seductive woman-city dominating the secular and political powers of the world. What seems particularly interesting is that in depicting New Jerusalem, the bride of the Lamb (Rev. 21:10–22:5), John essentially repeats the description of Babylon in Revelation 17–18. It is noteworthy to observe the antithetical parallels between the two cities in Table 5.[7]

The verbal and conceptual similarities between the descriptions of the two women-cities are hardly accidental. They indicate that end-time Babylon, portrayed as the prostitute woman who dominates the world, functions as the unholy antithesis to New Jerusalem, the bride of the Lamb. Babylon represents earthly hopes and dreams; the heavenly Jerusalem represents the fulfillment of all dreams, hopes, and longings of God's people from the beginning. As G. R. Beasley-Murray notes, "Revelation as a whole may be characterized as *A Tale of Two Cities*."[8]

It is especially interesting that both explanatory descriptions are given to John by the same seven-bowl angel. This makes the contrast between the two cities even more evident. "It is over the ruins, so to speak, of the proud, evil, and corrupted Babylon, that New Jerusalem comes, from heaven, pure and radiant with the glory of God."[9] Revelation 17–18 thus continues with the main theme of the eschatological part of

Revelation (chapters 12–22)—Satan's counterfeiting of God's salvific activities in the closing days of earth's history.

TABLE 5: PARALLELS OF THE TWO CITIES

BABYLON	NEW JERUSALEM
The Setting of the Visions	
"And one of the seven angels	"And one of the seven angels
who had seven bowls	who had seven bowls full of the seven last plagues
came and spoke with me saying:	came and spoke with me saying:
'Come here, I will show you...	'Come, I will show you
the great prostitute...	the bride,
with whom the kings of the earth have committed fornication...'	the wife of the Lamb.'
And he carried me away in the Spirit into a wilderness.	And he carried me away in the Spirit to a great and high mount,
And I saw..." (17:1–3)	and showed me
"the great city" (17:18)	the holy city,
"Babylon" (17:5)	Jerusalem,
"sitting on many waters,"	descending out of heaven
"...on a scarlet beast" (17:1, 3)	from God" (21:9–10)
The Description of the Two Women/Cities	
"And the woman was clothed	"Having the glory of God.
in purple and scarlet, and adorned	Her radiance was like
with gold and precious stones and	a precious stone, like a jasper stone
pearls." (17:4)	sparkling." (21:11)
She holds a golden cup in her hand filled with abominations (17:4)	She offers the water of life, bright as crystal (22:1)
"The dwelling place of demons	"The tabernacle of God is among men" (21:3)
and a prison of every unclean spirit and...of every unclean bird and...of every unclean and hated beast" (18:2)	"Nothing unclean will enter into it, no one who practices the abomination and the lie,

"Those...whose names are not written in the book of life... will marvel seeing the beast" (17:8)	but only those who are written in the book of life of the Lamb [will enter into it]" (21:27)
The nations and the kings (17:15) will "give their power and authority to the beast" (17:13)	The nations and the kings "will bring their glory into it" (21:24)

The Fate of the Two Cities

"It is done" (16:17); God will give to Babylon the cup of the wine of fury of his wrath (16:19)	"It is done" (21:6) God will give freely to the thirsty from the fountain of the water of life (21:6)
"In one day her plagues will come, death and mourning and famine, and she shall be burned with fire" (18:8).	"And no longer shall there be death, neither sorrow...nor pain" (21:4)
"The light of a lamp will never shine in you any longer" (18:23)	"The nations will walk by its light" (21:24) "The Lamb is its lamp" (21:23) "The Lord God will illumine them" (22:5)
Babylon "adorned with gold and precious stones and pearls" is brought to ruin (18:16–17).	Jerusalem has "the glory of God. Her brilliance was like a precious stone, like a jasper stone sparkling" (21:11)
Babylon reigns as a queen (18:7), but with her inhabitants is doomed to destruction (18:8)	"The throne of God and of the Lamb will be in it, and his servants will serve him" (22:3)
Babylon is "thrown down with violence and will never be found any longer" (18:21)	"The Lord God shall illumine them; and they will reign forever and ever" (22:5)

ENDNOTES

1. Paulien, *What the Bible Says About the End-Time*, 108.

2. Ibid.

3. Aune, *Revelation 6–16*, 662.

4. Paulien, *What the Bible Says About the End-Time*, 111.

5. Neall, "Sealed Saints and the Tribulation," 257.

6. Ibid., 256.

7. Adapted from Roberto Badenas, "New Jerusalem—The Holy City," in *Symposium on Revelation—Book 2*, Daniel and Revelation Committee Series 7 (Silver Spring, MD: Biblical Research Institute, 1992), 256; also Aune, *Revelation 17–22*, 1144–1145.

8. Beasley-Murray, 315.

9. Badenas, 255.

THE DRAGON AND THE WOMAN
REVELATION 12:1–17

Revelation 12 begins the third and last major section of the book of Revelation: a revealing of the contents of the little scroll (Rev. 10). Chapters 12–13 set the stage for the great climax of earth's history; they introduce the actors who will play the major roles in the final battle. The chiastic structure demonstrates that these chapters form the central portion of the book. Chapter 12 consists of three scenes: the birth of the child (12:1–6); the expulsion of Satan from heaven, which functions as a sort of interlude (12:7–12); and the dragon's persecution of the woman and her child (12:13–17).

THE WOMAN, THE CHILD, AND THE DRAGON (12:1–6)

John is again in the Spirit in a new vision. Before describing the final battle between God and his faithful people and Satan and his followers, he explains the underlying root cause for the hostility about to flood God's end-time faithful remnant people (cf. 12:17). The images employed here in the scene are completely different from those in the first half of the book.

> *¹And a great sign was seen in heaven: a woman clothed with the sun, and the moon under her feet, and on her head a crown of twelve stars, ²and she was pregnant and was crying out with birth pains and she was tormented to give birth. ³And another sign was seen in heaven, and behold, a great red dragon, having seven heads and ten horns and upon his heads seven crowns. ⁴And his tail dragged the third of the stars of heaven and cast them to the earth. And the dragon stood before the woman who was about to give birth, so that when she gave birth to her child he might devour him. ⁵And she gave birth to a son, a male child, who is about to*

shepherd all the nations with the rod of iron; and her child was caught up to God and to his throne. ⁶And the woman fled into the wilderness, where she had there a place prepared by God, so that they might nourish her for 1,260 days.

NOTES

12:1 *A great sign.* The Greek word *sēmeion* ("sign" or "mark" and "miracle") is in the gospel of John used in reference to Jesus' miracles. It is used seven times in Revelation; it refers four times to the miracles performed by Satan's allies to deceive the world at the time of the end (Rev. 13:13–14; 16:14; 19:20). Here and in 12:3 and 15:1, however, the word seems to mean a striking visual scene that captures one's attention.

A woman. Some commentators (primarily Roman Catholics) argue that the woman of Revelation 12:1 is Mary, the mother of Jesus. This avenue of interpretation fails to recognize the symbolic nature of the book of Revelation. What takes place in the rest of the chapter is contrary to what could have been said about Mary (especially if the literal interpretation is in view here). As G. K. Beale notes, "the woman is persecuted, flees into the desert" where she is nourished for 1,260 days, and "has other children, who are described as faithful Christians."[1] However, a woman is often used as the symbol for the people of God in both the Old (Isa. 54:5–6; Jer. 3:20; Ezek. 16:8–14; Hos. 1–3; Amos 5:2) and New (2 Cor. 11:2; Eph. 5:25–32) Testaments. In addition, the figure of Israel as a travailing woman appears often in the Old Testament (e.g., Isa. 26:17–18; 66:7–9; Jer. 4:31; Mic. 4:10). J. Massyngberde Ford observes: "Although the woman may be an individual, a study of the OT background suggests that she is a collective figure, like the two witnesses. In the OT the image of a woman is a classical symbol for Zion, Jerusalem, and Israel."[2] The symbol of a pure and faithful woman consistently stands for God's people faithful to him elsewhere in Revelation (Rev. 19:7–8; 22:17), while a prostitute symbolizes the apostate and unfaithful (Rev. 17–18). This evidence suggests that the remarkable woman of Revelation 12 symbolizes the people of God; and this interpretation fits into the context of the entire scene of Revelation 12 (cf. Rev. 12:17).

Crown of twelve stars. The crown on the head of the woman in Revelation 12:1 is *stephanos*, the garland or the crown of victory (see *Notes* on Rev. 2:10) promised repeatedly to the victorious faithful people in Revelation (2:10; 3:11).

12:2 *Crying out.* The Greek *krazō* is not limited to association with ordinary childbirth. In the Greek translation of the Old Testament (the Septuagint), it is often used for crying out to God (cf. Pss. 22:5; 34:6; 107:6, 13). The phrase in Revelation is used with reference to the cry of the martyrs to God for a vindication (Rev. 6:10).

She was tormented. The Greek *basanizō* means "to torment." The word is never used in the Bible or Greek literature "with reference to a woman suffering birth pain."[3] In the New Testament, *basanizō* is normally used with reference to the suffering of punishment, trial, and persecution (Matt. 8:6, 29; 14:24; Mark 5:7; 6:48; Luke 8:28; 2 Pet. 2:8). In Revelation, it is used only of torment inflicted by demonic powers (9:5) or by God (11:10; 14:10; 20:10).

12:3 *A great red dragon.* The word "dragon" (Gr. *drakōn*) refers to the mythological figures of the ancient Near East, such as the sea monsters of Leviathan and Rahab. In the Old Testament, these two sea monsters are used metaphorically with reference to the evil enemy powers that oppressed Israel and were defeated and crushed by God. Thus, for instance, the Pharaoh of the Exodus is referred to both as Leviathan (Ps. 74:14) and Rahab (Ps. 89:10; Isa. 30:7; 51:9–10). Isaiah spoke of the day when God would "punish Leviathan the fleeing serpent" (Isa. 27:1). In Jeremiah, Babylon is equated with a devouring monster (Jer. 51:34). Ezekiel spoke of the Pharaoh of Egypt as "the great monster that lies in the midst of his rivers" (Ezek. 29:3; 32:2). In addition, the image of the seven-headed monster was a well-known concept in the ancient Orient.[4] In Revelation 12:9, the dragon is identified as "the ancient serpent, who is called the Devil and Satan, the one who deceives the whole world." This is an allusion to the temptation account in Genesis 3, where, through deceiving the first human pair, the serpent brought sin on the earth. It is against this Old Testament background of the dragon that John portrays the figure of the archenemy of God and his people. On the meaning of red as the color of oppression and bloodshed, see *Notes* on Revelation 6:4.

Seven crowns. The seven crowns on the heads of the dragons are royal crowns (Gr. *diadēma*, "diadem"). See further *Notes* on Revelation 2:10.

12:4 *Tail.* See *Notes* on Revelation 9:10.

The stars of heaven. The stars in Jewish tradition stood for divine beings who, because of their rebellion against God, could become demonic and evil. See *Notes* on Revelation 8:10.

12:6 *1,260 days.* The parallel between Revelation 12:6 and 14 provides solid evidence that the two-time designation, "a time and times and half a time" and "one 1,260 days," refers to the same period, that of the persecution of the woman by the dragon (see *Notes* on Rev. 12:14). This period of the woman in the wilderness corresponds to the forty-two months of the trampling of the holy city by the Gentiles (Rev. 11:2) and the 1,260 days allotted to the two witnesses to prophesy in sackcloth (Rev. 11:3–6). While in Revelation the forty-two months are allotted to the oppressive anti-God powers (cf. 11:2; 13:5), the 1,260 days is the period used with reference to God's people (cf. 11:3; 12:6). It appears that these time designations in Revelation have qualitative as well as quantitative significance. Seventh-day Adventists have regarded A.D. 538 as the year when the church established itself as an ecclesiastical power to mark the beginning of this prophetic period, and A.D. 1798 as the year to end it. On the meaning and significance of the period, see further *Notes* on Revelation 11:2.

EXPOSITION

12:1–2 John sees ***a great sign*** in heaven. The reference to the sign as "great" indicates that John sees something special and remarkable. This sign is ***a woman clothed with the sun, and the moon under her feet, and on her head a crown of twelve stars.*** The word "sign" used here for the woman suggests that this is not a literal woman, but that she is a symbol.[5] This symbol was very familiar to the readers of Revelation in John's day, for the Old Testament portrays the covenant people of Israel as the wife of God. In the same way, the New Testament refers to the followers of Christ in terms of the wife or bride of Christ. Isaiah spoke with reference to Israel: "Your husband is your Maker, whose name is the Lord of hosts" (Isa. 54:5). Paul calls the "Jerusalem above" the "mother" of God's people on the earth (Gal. 4:26).

The association of the woman in Revelation 12:1 with the sun, moon, and twelve stars is a strong allusion to Joseph's dream in which the sun, moon, and eleven stars (Joseph is evidently the twelfth) represent Jacob, his wife, and his sons as the patriarchs of the twelve tribes of Israel that descended from them (Gen. 37:9–10). The portrayal of the woman evokes the description of Solomon's bride, who was "beautiful as the full moon, as pure as the sun" (Song of Sol. 6:10). Isaiah speaks of God: "He has clothed me with garments of salvation, He has wrapped me with a robe of righteousness" (Isa. 61:10). The crown on the head of the woman that John sees is the garland or the crown of victory (Gr. *stephanos*) promised repeatedly to God's faithful people in the book of Revelation (2:10; 3:11).

It is in this sense that the description of the woman of Revelation 12 should be understood. The brightness of her appearance comes from the light of the glory of the gospel (cf. 2 Cor. 4:6; Rev. 1:16), while she is standing on the Old Testament revelation that reflected the light of the gospel.[6] The crown with twelve stars signifies the twelve tribes of Israel and the twelve apostles, indicating the continuity between the Old Testament people of God and the Christian church. The remarkable woman in Revelation 12:1 symbolizes the people of God of both the Old and New Testaments, the bride of Christ (Rev. 12:17; cf. 19:7–8; 22:17). "She appears in her true heavenly and glorious character despite her seemingly fragile and uncertain earthly history."[7]

This remarkable woman is **pregnant** and is about to give birth. She **was crying out in birth pains and she was tormented to give birth.** Jesus illustrated the grief of the disciples over his death with a woman in travail who "has sorrow" and "gives birth" (John 16:21–22). The metaphor of Israel as a woman in pain giving birth appears frequently in the Old Testament (e.g., Isa. 66:7–9; Jer. 4:31; Mic. 4:10). The language which John uses in describing the birth pains of Revelation 12 echoes Isaiah 26:17–18:

> As the pregnant woman approaches the time to give birth,
> She writhes and cries out in her labor pains,

> Thus were we before Thee, O Lord.
> We were pregnant, we writhed in labor,
> We gave birth, as it were, only to wind.
> We could not accomplish deliverance for the earth
> Nor were inhabitants of the world born.

The celestial woman of Revelation 12 apparently represents Old Testament Israel with her twelve tribes bringing into being the Messiah. Just as a woman experiences birth pains in delivering a child, so did Israel in preparing for the coming of the promised Offspring. As Revelation 12:4 indicates, the intensity of the woman's pain was caused by being tormented by the dragon in preparation for the birth of the child: "And the dragon stood before the woman who was about to give birth, so that when she gave birth to her child he might devour him." Tormenting the woman was evidently part of Satan's plan to destroy the covenant people and prevent the birth of the offspring of the woman (Gen. 3:15).[8] This is the way in which the tormenting of the woman should be understood, for the word "torment" used here was never used by the Greeks "with reference to a woman suffering birth pains."[9]

Isaiah 26:18 states that ancient Israel could not bring "deliverance for the earth"; this was accomplished only by Jesus Christ.[10] What we find in Revelation 12 is the transition from Israel as the people of God of the old dispensation to the Christian church as the people of God of the new dispensation. Revelation 12:13–17 indicates that just as the woman Israel often experienced torment while preparing for the coming of the Messiah, the church is tormented in preparation for the coming of Christ.

12:3–5 John now describes the second character in the drama—namely, the tormentor of the woman. He sees *another sign* in heaven; this sign is evidently related to the first one in Revelation 12:1. This sign is *a great red dragon.* According to Revelation 12:9, the dragon stands for Satan, whose frightening appearance John portrays in terms of the ancient mythological figures which in the Old Testament are used as symbols of the evil powers that oppress God's covenant people. Red is the color of oppression and bloodshed (cf. Rev. 6:3–4; 2 Kings 3:22–23; Rev. 17:3–6), and it denotes the oppressive character of Satan against the church.

The dragon is described as *having seven heads and ten horns and upon his heads seven crowns.* On the basis of Revelation 17:9–11, as William G. Johnsson suggests, the seven heads of the dragon "represent kingdoms through which Satan has worked to oppress God's people throughout the ages"[11] with the intent of preventing the coming of the offspring of the woman. Horns are a symbol of political powers (cf. Rev. 17:12). The ten horns of the sea beast are the ten horns of the fourth beast from Daniel, where they symbolize the kingdoms which follow the breaking up of the Roman Empire into ten parts (Dan. 7:7, 23–24; cf. Rev. 17:12). The seven crowns on the heads of the dragon suggest Satan's false claim of full authority and power in opposition to the true "King of kings and Lord of lords" who wears "many crowns" (cf. Rev. 19:12–16). The dragon primarily symbolizes Satan acting behind the power of pagan Rome, attempting to destroy Christ and, subsequently, his followers. The ten horns of the dragon suggest that Satan's work against the church will continue in a significant measure throughout the period following the breaking up of the Roman Empire.

The tail of the dragon *dragged the third of the stars of heaven and cast them to the earth.* This reminds us of Daniel 8:10 where it is said that the enemy of God and his people "grew up to the host of heaven and caused some of the host and some of the stars to fall to the earth, and it trampled them down." Stars in Revelation symbolize angels (Rev. 1:20). In addition, Revelation 12:7–9 makes it quite clear that those "stars of heaven" the dragon dragged down with his tail are the fallen angels who joined Satan in his rebellion against God, and which were "cast down with him" to the earth (12:9). In the scene of the fifth trumpet, Satan is behind the demonic locusts that torment people with the stings of their tails (cf. Rev. 9:1–11). We can see that the tail is a symbol of deception by means of the persuasion that Satan has used to mislead others to rebel against God and to follow him (cf. Rev. 12:9). John introduces Satan here in the seductive role in which he is portrayed throughout the rest of the book of Revelation (13:13–14; 18:13–16; 20:7–10).

Next, John sees the dragon standing *before the woman who was about to give birth, so that when she gave birth to her child he might devour him.* This standing of the dragon ("the ancient serpent" in 12:9) before the woman refers to the great hostility of the serpent toward the woman, and the enmity between the serpent's seed and the woman's seed, as announced in Genesis 3:15. Revelation 12:5 presents Satan's bruising of Christ's heel. Satan's primary effort to destroy Christ at the moment he was born continued until the end of Jesus' ministry.

The child is finally born. John does not leave his readers in any doubt that this child is anybody else but the promised Messiah, Jesus Christ. He is the one who is

to shepherd all the nations with the rod of iron. John alludes here to the royal Psalm 2:7–9 where the Davidic king is the anointed one to whom God speaks: "You are my son, today I have begotten you. Ask of me, and I will make the nations as your heritage, and the ends of the earth as your possession. You shall break them with a rod of iron" (RSV).

Revelation 12:5 also echoes the prophecy of Micah, about the "ruler in Israel" to be born in Bethlehem: "'His goings forth are from long ago, from the days of eternity.' Therefore, he will give them up until the time when she who is in labor has borne a child....And He will arise and shepherd His flock in the strength of the Lord, in the majesty of the name of the Lord His God" (Mic. 5:2–4).

Now, the true Davidic king is born, and in him all the promises with reference to the Davidic king have found their definite fulfillment (cf. Rev. 5:5). Revelation 19:15–16 depicts him in the role of "King of kings and Lord of lords" to shepherd the nations with a rod of iron.

Without any reference to his life and death, John depicts Christ as being **caught up to God and to his throne** where his rule begins in the heavenly places. This omission of the earthly life of Jesus may be explained, as William Barclay suggests, on the basis of the fact that, throughout the book, "John's interest is not in the human Jesus but in the exalted Christ, who is able to rescue his people in the time of their distress."[12] It is after his ascension that the church faces the outburst of Satan's wrath. This outpouring of Satan's wrath against the church is the subject of 12:6 and 13–17.

12:6 (and v. 14) After Christ's ascension to heaven, the church comes under a severe attack by Satan. The woman flees **into the wilderness,** where she is nourished for **1,260 days.** The wilderness is the **place prepared by God** for the woman. The scene is similar to Israel's escape from Pharaoh and the Egyptians (Exod. 13:17–16:21) to the wilderness where God cared for Israel and provided them with manna as nourishment for their sustenance. Robert H. Mounce explains: "To the Jewish people the wilderness spoke of divine provision and intimate fellowship."[13] As a model of Israel's wilderness experience, John portrays God's people as cared for and nourished spiritually by God during the time of their wilderness hardship and the severe oppression that they experience in the world. God's care of the woman in the wilderness is evidently intended to assure "the suffering Christians that no matter how fierce the trials they may be called upon to bear, He is watching over His church and will sustain them."[14]

The period of "1,260 days" of the woman in the wilderness corresponds to the period of the prophesying of the two witnesses in sackcloth (Rev. 11:3–6). The parallel between Revelation 12:6 and 14 shows that the "1,260 days" is the same as "a time and times and half a time" of Revelation 12:14. This links Revelation 12 to the prophecy of Daniel, where "a time and times and half a time" is the period of the activities of the little horn (7:24–25; 12:7). It seems clear that in portraying the woman in the wilderness, John points to the oppression of God's people from the persecuting power of the little horn in Daniel's prophecy during the authoritarian ecclesiastical rule of the Middle Ages. Furthermore, the time allotted to the nation or Gentiles to trample the holy city is forty-two months (Rev. 11:2), which is the time designation used with reference to the dominion of the sea beast over the earth in Revelation 13:5–8. It appears that all of these time designations refer to one and the same time period. On one hand, it is the time of the dominion of evil with the oppression and persecution of God's people. On the other hand, God's people, although banished to the wilderness, dressed in sackcloth, oppressed, and persecuted, are surviving under the protection of God and bearing their faithful witness for Christ and the gospel.

All of these time periods designate three and a half years. As discussed earlier (with reference to the trampling of the holy city by the nations and the prophetic activity of the two witnesses in Rev. 11), it seems that these three and a half years are not intended to be a literal period. They refer rather to a specific period of approximately twelve hundred years of the medieval ecclesiastical oppressive rule (usually dated from A.D. 538 to A.D. 1798) during which God's faithful people who were few in number experienced intense hardship and suffering because of their faithfulness to Christ. This period, however, does not extend to the Second Coming, for it is *after* the 1,260 days that Satan focuses on the woman's descendants.[15]

The theological importance of these time designations seems to be John's primary focus in the text. According to the gospel of John, the three and a half years is the period of Jesus' earthly ministry characterized by rejection and humiliation from the side of those whom he came to save. In other words, what the followers of Christ experience in the world is essentially what Jesus himself experienced "clothed in sackcloth" during his life of faithful witnessing. He made clear to his followers that "if they persecuted Me, they will also persecute you" (John 15:20). "He who does not take his cross and follow after Me is not worthy of Me" (Matt. 10:38).

THE WAR IN HEAVEN (12:7–12)

Revelation 12:7–12 is a sort of interlude interrupting the further description of the dragon's persecution of the woman. It is placed between the account of Christ's ascension to heaven and the woman's escape to the wilderness, and the later description of Satan's attack on the Church. Its purpose is to provide some particular information on the activities of the dragon and his hostility against the woman and her descendants.

> **⁷And there was war in heaven; Michael and his angels had to fight against the dragon. And the dragon and his angels fought back, ⁸and he was not strong enough, nor was found there a place for them any longer in heaven. ⁹And the great dragon, the ancient serpent, who is called the devil and Satan, the one who deceives the whole world, was cast down to the earth, and his angels were cast down with him. ¹⁰And I heard a loud voice in heaven saying:**
>
> **"Now the salvation and the power**
> **and the kingdom of our God**
> **and the authority of his Christ has come,**
> **because the accuser of our brothers**
> **has been cast down,**
> **the one who accuses them before our**
> **God day and night.**
> **¹¹And they overcame him by the**
> **blood of the Lamb**
> **and by the word of their testimony,**
> **and they did not love their life to the point of death.**
> **¹²For this reason rejoice heavens**
> **and those who dwell in them;**
> **woe to the earth and the sea,**
> **for the devil has come down to you**
> **having great anger,**
> **knowing that he has little time."**

NOTES

12:7 *Michael.* Michael (Heb. *mikā'ēl*, "Who is like God?") is mentioned five times in the Bible. In the book of Daniel he is the commander or "the chief prince" of the angels who fights the battle against the princes of the kingdoms of Persia and Greece (10:13, 21), who are identified as Satan. In Daniel 12:1, Michael is "the great prince" who protects God's people in the final days of earth's history. In Jude 9 he is "the archangel," and here in Revelation 12:7 he is the commander of the heavenly army.[16]

12:9 *The ancient serpent.* See *Notes* on Revelation 12:3.

The devil and Satan. The Greek *diabolos* means literally "a slanderer." This word in the Greek is usually used for the Hebrew *śāṭān,* meaning "satan" ("adversary"). This suggests that the two words are synonymous.[17] Satan in the Old Testament is portrayed as the adversary and accuser of God's people in the heavenly counsel (Job 1:6–2:6; Zech. 3:1–2) and as the tempter (1 Chron. 21:1). The Old Testament portrays him as the angel of light who was once in the service of God but who in his pride sought to be higher than God, and because of that was cast out from heaven (cf. Isa. 14:12–15; Ezek. 28:12–17). In the New Testament, Satan is the evil one, the enemy of God and his people. Jesus called him the ruler of this world (John 12:31; 14:30; 16:11) and "a liar, and the father of lies" (John 8:44). In Revelation 12 he is identified as the deceiver of the whole world (12:9; cf. 20:3, 10), and as "the accuser of our brothers" who "accuses them before our God day and night" (12:10). In Revelation 13 he works through his two allies, the sea beast and the land beast, to subvert the entire world by means of deception to render worship to him instead of to God. Finally, Satan and his allies and associates find their end in the lake of fire after the millennium (Rev. 20:7–10).

Cast down. The Greek word *ballō* ("cast out" or "cast down") has a judicial denotation; it is "a technical term for excommunication (cf. John 9:34–35)" and judicial punishment (cf. Matt. 3:10; 13:41–42; John 15:6; Rev. 2:10).[18] With regard to the timing of this casting down of Satan out of heaven, there have been three proposals. Some see the text as a description of the conflict in heaven prior to the beginning of the history of sin on earth. Others see it as a background or a flashback to explain the ongoing story of chapter 12 with the purpose of showing that the conflict on earth is part of a wider drama that started long before the creation of earth. The evidence strongly suggests, however, that 12:7–12 describes the event that took place after the cross. More precisely, 12:10 indicates that the event is related to the enthronement of Christ as portrayed in chapters 4–5. With the casting out of Satan, the kingdom of God and the authority of Christ have come. Here the words of Jesus are fulfilled: "Now the ruler of this world will be cast out" (John 12:31). It is after he had been cast out of heaven that Satan realized that he had little time (12:12), something that he did not realize at the beginning of his rebellion prior to the creation of earth but rather after the cross. It is particularly significant that at the time of his being cast down, Satan was involved in accusing God's people "before our God day and night" (12:10). His activity of "accusing" and his subsequent casting out could obviously not take place prior to the creation of earth but rather after the cross. Verse 11 emphatically states that it was the "blood of the Lamb" that made victory over Satan possible. Also, it was after Satan had been cast out of heaven that he started persecuting the woman during the 1,260-day period of the Middle Ages, something that does not fit any primordial casting out of Satan.[19] Ellen White clearly affirmed such an understanding with this statement: "The casting down

394

of Satan as an accuser of the brethren in heaven was accomplished by the work of Christ in giving up his life."[20]

12:12 ***Little time*** (*oligon kairon echei*) has here a qualitative rather than a quantitative significance, the same as in 17:10. The phrase states that Satan's time is limited and terminated. It stands in contrast to *mikron kronon* ("short time"), which refers to the impending judgment on Satan. See Notes on Revelation 17:10.

EXPOSITION

Revelation 12:7 introduces a new scene that switches from earth to heaven. John is telling us here that the great enmity between the dragon and the woman is a part of the larger drama that is cosmic in scope.

12:7–9 ***There was war in heaven.*** The participants in the war are ***Michael and his angels*** against ***the dragon and his angels***. This war evidently takes place after the child has been taken from earth (12:5). The context indicates that Michael, the commander of the heavenly hosts, is Christ himself (cf. 12:10–11), while Satan is the anti-Christ. Revelation 12:3 points to the fallen angels who joined Satan in his rebellion against God, and who were "cast down with him" to the earth (12:9). This indicates that in his rebellion against God, Satan has won for himself a large number of associates. The battle they fought must be understood to be verbal rather than physical. Both Christ and Satan are described as being engaged in the battle for the allegiance of the heavenly beings. However, as the text tells us further, Satan ***was not strong enough*** to fight back against Christ. Thus, he and his associates lost their place in heaven and free access there. John wants to impress upon readers the fact that Satan, the mighty angel, and the demonic forces are not "strong enough" in their war against Christ and his faithful followers.

Next, John provides the threefold identification of the dragon. First, he is ***the ancient serpent.*** This is the allusion to Genesis 3, where through the serpent Satan deceived Adam and Eve, thus bringing sin on the earth. Second, his name is ***the devil and Satan*** (meaning "slanderer" and "adversary," respectively), who is the adversary of God and his people. Jesus refers to him as "the ruler of this world" (John 12:31; 14:30; 16:11). Peter calls him "your adversary, the devil" (1 Pet. 5:8). In tempting Jesus, Satan stated that the dominion over the earth was given to him, which he could give to whomever he wished (Luke 4:6). In Revelation 12:10 he is referred to as "the accuser of our brothers," "the one who accuses them before our God day and night." This depicts

Satan's accusation before God against Job (Job 1:6–12), as well as his accusation against Joshua, the high priest (Zech. 3:1–2).

Finally, the dragon is identified as the one **who deceives the whole world.** His deception began in the Garden of Eden (Gen. 3:1–7). He has used every device to seduce people and lead them astray to his purposes ever since (2 Cor. 2:11; 11:3, 14; Eph. 6:11). In the rest of the book of Revelation, Satan stands behind all the deception carried out by the powers of this world as the history of this world approaches its end (Rev. 13:11–17; 18:2–3; 19:20; 20:10).

Having been defeated, Satan is **cast down to the earth** together with the angels who have joined him in his rebellion against God. When does this casting down of Satan take place? Revelation 12:10 indicates that the war between Christ and Satan (v. 7) was regarding the transference of authority and rule to Christ (the event described in Rev. 4–5). This evidently did not go without some form of resistance and opposition from Satan. Moreover, Satan stood in open revolt. The phrase "to cast out" denotes excommunication (cf. John 9:34–35) and "judicial punishment" (cf. Matt. 3:10; 13:41–42; John 15:6; Rev. 2:10). This "casting down" of Satan from heaven suggests his excommunication from the heavenly council. It is not his expulsion from heaven when he rebelled against God at the beginning of the history of sin (cf. Isa. 14:15; Ezek. 28:16–18). Between then and Christ's death on the cross, Satan evidently still had access to the heavenly places. We see him attending the assembly of the sons of God before the Lord in the heavenly places (cf. Job 1:6–12) and accusing Joshua, the high priest, before God in the heavenly court (Zech. 3:1–2).

But the situation changed with the death of Christ on the cross where Satan's defeat was assured. It was at the cross that it became clear to the entire universe who God was and the character of his rule. In the same manner, Satan's character was revealed at the cross. Though he had been a murderer from the beginning (John 8:44), it was at the cross that the entire universe came to realize his true character. As a result, Satan was forever excommunicated from the heavenly places; and since then, there was **no longer any place** for him and his angels **in heaven.** Some other New Testament texts speak of Christ's victory over the evil angel hosts at the cross and the subsequent enthronement (cf. Col. 2:15; 1 Pet. 3:22). Jesus referred to Satan's expulsion as legal action, saying that "now the ruler of this world shall be cast out" (John 12:31; cf. Luke 10:18; John 14:30; 16:11). This *now* referred to the death of Jesus on the cross. It is the death of Jesus that marks the casting down of Satan as well as the exultation of Christ on the heavenly throne (cf. John 12:32).

Revelation 12:10 sheds more light on this *now*. It indicates that at Christ's ascension and subsequent exaltation on the heavenly throne (cf. Rev. 5), "the kingdom of our God and authority of his Christ" was set up, and Satan was ultimately expelled from heaven. The cross marks the decisive point in human history, with cosmic meaning and significance, "when God's 'direct rule' replaces Satan's abuse of his powers, and *authority* passes to God's *Christ*."[21] As John Sweet says, "Christ is now enthroned at God's right hand, but on the earth the usurping *authorities* must still be fought" (Rev. 12:17; 1 Cor. 15:24–26).[22]

12:10–12   John hears yet another **loud voice in heaven** announcing with triumphant song God's victory over Satan's rule and the inauguration of God's rule in the world and Christ's kingly authority. This hymn is one of many in Revelation celebrating God's mighty actions on behalf of human beings by redeemed humanity or the twenty-four elders (cf. Rev. 5:9–14; 11:11–15; 15:3–4; 19:1–6). Though John does not provide the identity of the singers, the expression "the accuser of our brothers" suggests a group. They are most likely the twenty-four elders as the representatives of redeemed humanity in the heavenly places.

The hymn begins with the temporal adverb **now.** The word refers, first, to the longed-for time when Satan, **the accuser of our brothers,** is expelled from the heavenly places (cf. John 12:31); second, when **the salvation and the power and the kingdom of our God** replaces Satan's usurping rule and abuse of power; and third, when **the authority** passes to God's Christ, who, after being enthroned on the heavenly throne at God's right hand, rules in the midst of the usurping authorities here on the earth (Rev. 12:17; 1 Cor. 15:25–28).[23] Revelation 12:10 refers to the enthronement of Christ after his death and resurrection and subsequent ascension to the heavenly places, which took place at Pentecost (Acts 2:32–36), as portrayed in Revelation 4–5.

Everything referred to in the hymn—salvation, the inauguration of God's rule in the world, and the reclamation of kingly authority by Christ—have been made possible through the casting down of "the accuser of our brothers," the one **who accuses them before our God day and night.** Here is unveiled the intensity and character of Satan's activity. John told us earlier that the four living beings were giving praise to God "day and night" (Rev. 4:8). This means that while the four living beings, the cherubim, are giving unceasing praises to God "day and night," Satan brings his unceasing accusations against his people "day and night." No wonder that his expulsion from the heavenly places invokes such a great outburst of praises to God and Christ.

Instead of defeating the followers of Christ by accusing "them before our God day and night" (12:10), Satan suffers his own defeat. His accusations rebound against him.[24] The followers of Christ **overcame him by the blood of the Lamb and by the word of their testimony.** In this lies the secret of the victorious life for the followers of Christ. Their victory over Satan comes by virtue of what Christ has accomplished on the cross. The blood of Christ produces the victory. The theme of Revelation is not a military battle (or battles) or some political event (or events), but rather the final conquest of sin and Satan, the conquest led by the slain Lamb. In his blood there is sure victory. Christ's death in Revelation is an event of the past as well as a present reality.

The victory over Satan is also a result of the faithful witness of God's people to Christ and the gospel. Their victory is affirmed further by their loyalty to Christ, which they consider more important than their own lives. Despite hardship and oppression, they have remained faithful and loyal to him even **to the point of death.** This brings to mind Christ's exhortation to his followers in Smyrna: "Remain faithful until death, and I will give you the crown of life" (Rev. 2:10). Paul was fully convinced that "neither death, nor life, nor angels, nor principalities, nor things present, nor things to come, nor powers, nor height, nor depth, nor any other created thing, shall be able to separate us from the love of God, which is in Christ Jesus our Lord" (Rom. 8:38–39).

While Satan's expulsion from heaven arouses great joy among all heavenly beings, it is **woe to the earth and the sea, for the devil has come down to you.** As A. Yarbro Collins explains, Christ's victory over Satan is only partial; he is "defeated in heaven, but he [still] reigns on earth."[25] The earth and the sea together represent the whole earth. This suggests the universality and the worldwide dimension of Satan's activities. This becomes especially significant in light of the fact that in Revelation 13, it is out of the sea and out of the land (in Greek the same word is used for both the earth and the land) that Satan's two allies come, deceiving people to rebel against God. This "woe to the earth" is particularly significant because Satan is filled with **great anger,** *knowing that he has little time.* The first reason for his anger is his expulsion from heaven. Second, Satan's rule over the earth has passed to Christ, inaugurating his eternal kingdom. Satan is obviously a defeated adversary. He was not strong enough to win the battle against Christ in the heavenly places. Furthermore, not only has he suffered defeat in heaven, but he suffers defeat from Christ's followers. He is filled with great fury and anger. Now the earth gets his full attention.

It happens often in life that after a person has experienced humiliation and loss, he pours out his angry feelings against those around him who seem to be weaker. This is exactly what we find here in Revelation 12. Satan is filled with anger because he knows that he has but a short time. He realizes that he has lost the war. The cross has provided strong assurance for that defeat. He now pours out his full anger on the followers of Christ who are faithful and loyal to him "to the point of death." This is the situation in which God's faithful people find themselves as the earth's history approaches its end.

SATAN AND THE SEED OF THE WOMAN (12:13–17)

The interlude provided the reason for Satan's great anger against God's people. Satan realizes his impotence in fighting against Christ. Having failed to overthrow Christ, he turns all his attention on Christ's followers, intending to harm and destroy them. We now return to the scene of 12:6, the description of which is repeated in verses 13–14.

> **¹³And when the dragon saw that he was cast down to the earth, he persecuted the woman that had given birth to the male child. ¹⁴And two wings of a great eagle were given to the woman, so that she might fly into the wilderness, to her place where she is nourished there for a time and times and half a time from the presence of the serpent. ¹⁵And the serpent cast from his mouth water like a river after the woman, in order to make her flooded by the water. ¹⁶And the earth helped the woman, and the earth opened its mouth and swallowed the river which the dragon had cast from his mouth. ¹⁷And the dragon was angry at the woman, and went away to make war with the remaining ones of her offspring, the ones keeping the commandments of God and having the testimony of Jesus.**

NOTES

12:14 *A time and times and half a time.* This time designation occurs first in the book of Daniel (7:25; 12:7). Most interpreters understand the second word as a dual ("two times"); the phrase thus means "a year, two years, and half a year."[26] The parallel between Revelation 12:6 and 14 shows that "a time and times and half a time" and the "1,260 days" are the same time period.

REVELATION 12:6	REVELATION 12:14
"And the woman fled into the wilderness, where she had there a place prepared by God, so that they might nourish her for *1,260 days.*"	"And two wings of a great eagle were given to the woman, so that she might fly into the wilderness, to her place where she is nourished there for *a time and times and half a time* from the presence of the serpent."

On the symbolism and historical dating of this period, see *Notes* on Rev. 11:2.

12:15 *Mouth.* On the meaning of the "mouth" in Revelation with reference to Satan, see *Notes* on Revelation 9:19.

Water like a river. The flood-like river proceeding from the serpent's mouth may stand for at least two things. First of all, it might symbolize Satan's effort to destroy the church by physical force and persecution. The flooding water in the Old Testament is a frequent symbol of evil nations attacking and persecuting the people of Israel (Ps. 69:1–2). Referring to his enemies, the Psalmist stated that if the Lord had not protected his people, the waters would have overwhelmed them and the raging waters would have swept over their soul (Ps. 124:2–5). Isaiah prophesied that the Lord would bring "the strong and abundant waters of the Euphrates" that would sweep on into Judah (Isa. 8:7–8). Jeremiah describes Egypt as "an overflowing torment that floods the land" (Jer. 47:2; cf. 46:7–8). In Revelation, the river Euphrates symbolizes the wicked who support the great harlot Babylon (Rev. 16:12; 17:15).

The flood-like river proceeding from the mouth of the serpent may also symbolize Satan's effort to sweep away the church with deceit and false teaching.[27] In this vein of interpretation, the flooding water would be the "river of deceit."[28] The reference to Satan here as the serpent rather than the dragon, and his mouth, from which the flooding water proceeds, may be an allusion to the serpent in the garden of Eden (Gen. 3:1–7). It must be noted that later in the book, the mouth of the dragon, the beast, and the false prophet are the source from which the three unclean spirits come to gather the world for the battle of Armageddon (Rev. 16:13–14). This would be in line with the description of Satan's activity in Revelation in terms of deceiving the whole world at the time of the end (Rev. 12:9; 13:14; 18:2–3; 19:20; 20:10).

Both of these interpretations are based on strong biblical evidence. As such, they are not necessarily exclusive. Taken together, they refer to the two strategies that Satan used during the symbolic three-and-a-half years of the woman's wilderness pilgrimage in an attempt to harm and destroy the people of God. These two strategies are force and persecution, and deception and false teaching.

12:17 ***The remaining ones.*** The Greek word *loipos* (used here in the plural form) means "remaining" or "rest." The word belongs to a group of several Hebrew and Greek words usually translated as "remnant" in English translations. The "remnant" in the Old Testament is commonly used for a group of Israelites who survived war, destruction, or other calamities, and who were spared to continue as God's chosen people (e.g., Isa. 10:20–22; 11:11–12, 16; Jer. 23:3; 31:7; Mic. 2:12; Zeph. 3:13). The recurring theme of the Old Testament is that when the majority of the people apostatized, a small remnant remained faithful to God (for instance, when God reminded Elijah that there were seven thousand who had not worshiped Baal; 1 Kings 19:18). Some studies have noted that the remnant concept in the Bible applies to three categories of God's people: the historical remnant, the faithful remnant within the historical one, and the eschatological remnant.[29] In Revelation, the word *loipoi* ("the remaining ones") appears only three times with reference to God's people: "the remaining ones" in Thyatira (2:24) and Sardis (3:2), and in 12:17 with reference to God's end-time people, "the remaining ones" of the woman's offspring.[30] The context indicates that "the remaining ones" in 12:17 refer clearly to the eschatological remnant of God's faithful ones who will go through the last events of this earth's history. They are identified as the ones keeping the commandments of God and having the testimony of Jesus (cf. 14:12).

Having the testimony of Jesus. The Greek word *echō* in the New Testament means "to possess" in a sense of "holding fast to what one possesses."[31] This indicates that the remnant in Revelation 12:17 possess "the testimony of Jesus." The expression "the testimony of Jesus Christ" in Greek can be interpreted either as an objective or a subjective genitive. In other words, it may be understood as the testimony about Jesus (Jesus is, accordingly, the object of Christians' witness), or the testimony which Christ himself bears through those who have the gift of prophecy (for instance, through John himself). The context of the book favors the latter. In Revelation 1:2, the testimony of Jesus is "the word of God" that Jesus communicated to John in a visionary presentation. John bears record of the "testimony of Jesus Christ." This suggests that the contents of Revelation are Christ's "testimony" which he gave to his church through John the prophet (see *Notes* on Rev. 1:2).

Revelation 19:10 further defines "the testimony of Jesus" as "the spirit of prophecy" (cf. Rev. 22:9). The role of the prophets in the New Testament is to bear the testimony of Jesus to his people. Thus, "the testimony of Jesus" in Revelation does not refer to the contents of the book of Revelation, which are clearly identified throughout the book as "the words of the prophecy" (1:3; 22:7, 10, 18–19) consisting of "the things that John saw, that is, the word of God and the testimony of Jesus" (Rev. 1:2). Neither does the phrase refer to the church's witness concerning Christ, for in the book the church's witness is always referred to as "the testimony" (cf. Rev. 6:9) or "their testimony" (11:7; 12:11; see further *Notes* on Rev. 6:9). It appears that the expression "the testimony of Jesus" refers either to "the testimony born by Jesus Himself" in his own ministry while he was in the flesh, or to his self-revelation to the church "by the working of the Holy Spirit through inspiring his servants the prophets."[32] The prophets in the New Testament are the bearers of Christ's revelation. It is because of his faithful testimony to "the word of God and the testimony of Jesus" (cf. Rev. 1:2) that John was exiled to Patmos (1:9). Revelation 12:17 indicates that the prophetic revelation did not die with John, for God's end-time people will be in possession of the prophetic gift (cf. Rev. 19:10).

EXPOSITION

12:13–14 The opening words of the text explain why Satan is filled with fury against the church: ***When the dragon saw that he was cast down to the earth, he persecuted the woman.*** The main reason for his anger involves his expulsion from heaven after the transference of authority and rule over the earth from him to Christ (cf. 12:10). This is further evidence that the casting out of Satan from heaven down to earth occurred after the cross. Having suffered defeat by Christ, it is no wonder that he is filled with such great fury against the followers of Christ, who in Revelation 12:17 are referred to as "the remaining ones of her offspring." The rest of the text essentially repeats what was said earlier in verse 6. Only one new detail is added.

The woman was carried on ***two wings of a great eagle*** to ***the wilderness into her place*** for a period of ***a time and times and half a time*** (commonly dated from A.D. 538 to A.D. 1798). The reference to the eagle's wings recalls Old Testament texts which say that when Pharaoh was chasing the people of Israel after they had fled Egypt, God carried them "on eagles' wings" and brought them to himself (Exod. 19:4; Deut. 32:11–12). Also in Isaiah's prophecy, the eagle's wings are associated with the return of Israel from the Exile (Isa. 40:31). Just as God did for Israel both in the wilderness at the time of the Exodus and at the Exile, so in Revelation 12 he does for the woman/church in the wilderness in protecting her and sustaining her that she may remain faithful. From the historical perspective, God's faithful people during the Dark Middle Ages had to hide themselves and live in isolated places in order to escape persecution and the torrent of false teachings.

12:15–16 In order to sweep away the woman, ***the serpent cast from his mouth water like a river after the woman.*** The flood-like river proceeding from the mouth of the serpent portrays in symbolic language Satan's two strategies—persecuting force, and deception and false teachings—for harming God's people during the symbolic three-and-a-half years of the church's wilderness pilgrimage. The reference to the serpent, rather than the dragon, and its mouth brings to mind the deceptive persuasion of the serpent in the Garden of Eden (Gen. 3:1–5). Just as the serpent deceived the first woman, so now Satan attempts to sweep away Christ's people with the flood of deception and false teaching (cf. 2 Cor. 11:3).

However, here comes to fulfillment God's promise to the Psalmist that "a flood of great waters shall not reach him" (Ps. 32:6). ***The earth helped the woman, and the earth opened its mouth and swallowed the river.*** This imagery is drawn from Israel's wilderness experience, when "the earth opened its mouth and swallowed" Korah, Dathan, and Abiram because of their rebellion against Moses' authority and leadership (Num. 16:32; 26:10; Deut. 11:6; Ps. 116:17). It reminds one also of the words from the song of Moses—how God stretched out his right hand, and "the earth swallowed" the Egyptians pursuing Israel (Exod. 15:12). Just as in the past God protected his people from the pursuit of the Pharaoh, and Moses from the vicious rebellion of Korah and his associates, so now he provides protection for his church from Satan's flooding waters of persecution and false, seductive teaching.

12:17 Satan seems very frustrated by his constant failure in attempting to destroy Christ. No wonder he becomes ***angry at the woman.*** One reason for his rage is God's protection over the woman in the wilderness. It is through the church that the kingdom of Christ has been and continues to be manifested. Oscar Cullmann says: "The Church is the earthly center from which the full Lordship of Christ becomes visible."[33] Satan has not been able to harm her. Now he faces ***the remaining ones of her offspring,*** and decides ***to make war*** with them. Jesus Christ is the woman's offspring (cf. Rev. 12:5). The expression "the dragon was angry at the woman" and his decision to wage war with "the remaining ones of her offspring" is a strong allusion to the enmity between the serpent and the woman, and the serpent's offspring and the woman's offspring announced in Genesis 3:15. What John endeavors to impress upon the minds of his readers is that the scene here is a part of the great conflict which began in Genesis 3 and continues through the Bible until the time of the end. The conflict will not last forever, though, for Satan's determination to engage in the final conflict is actually the beginning of his end.

The remaining ones of the woman's offspring are, then, the followers of Christ living in the last period of this earth's history. Revelation 17 indicates that this woman who once was the true church of God will, during end-time events, have a very negative role. She will eventually turn from her faithfulness to oppose God and his true people. This is why God's end-time people in Revelation are referred to not as the woman but rather as "the remaining ones of the woman's offspring." They are identified by two definite characteristics: they are the ones **keeping the commandments of God and having the testimony of Jesus.** This is what makes the end-time followers of Christ the remnant and separates them from the unfaithful. The text indicates that at the end of time, as the whole world renders their allegiance and loyalty to Satan and his allies (Rev. 13:4, 8), God will have a people who will be unreservedly faithful and obedient to him in keeping his commandments and holding to the testimony of Jesus given through the gift of prophecy (cf. Rev. 19:10).

One may agree with Hans LaRondelle's assertion that "to 'have' the testimony of Jesus is not restricted to the end-time church, but is the essential characteristic of Christ's faithful followers during the *entire* Christian age."[34] Such an assertion might be supported by the fact that John himself was the medium through whom Jesus gave his testimony (cf. Rev. 1:2). What John now clearly indicates in Revelation 12:17 is that as Jesus communicated his revelation to the church of his day through the medium of the prophetic ministry, so he will do in the very last days of this earth's history. As Jesus will be with his end-time remnant until the very end, they are characterized by their obedience to him (cf. Rev. 14:12) and their faithfulness to his testimony revealed through the prophetic voice in their midst.

Satan feels frustrated but determined to enter the final conflict against Christ. He is determined more than ever before to win the battle. The text says that Satan **went away** to make war. This may mean that he retreats for a while in order to prepare himself for that war. Being aware of his constant failure, he decides not to be alone but to find associates in planning the strategy. And he finds two allies in the beast that comes from the sea (Rev. 13:1–10) and the beast that comes from the land (Rev. 13:11–17). The three of them form a counterfeit triumvirate in their final battle against Christ and the remnant (cf. Rev. 16:13–16). The strategy and end-time activity of this counterfeit union is described in the following chapter of the book.

A RETROSPECT ON REVELATION 12

The vision of Revelation 12 sets the stage for what comes into play in the second half of the book of Revelation. It introduces what seems to be the central theme of the book, namely, the great controversy between good and evil. It indicates that what takes place on the earth is just a part of what is transpiring on the cosmic scale. What happens to Christians on the earth, as they suffer oppression and hardship due to their loyalty to Christ, is just a part of the great, drawn-out conflict between good and evil. In such a way, an understanding of chapter 12 of the book is a prerequisite for the interpretation of the end-time issues in the context of that great conflict.

With Revelation 12:17, the unrolling of the final events of this earth's history begins. Chapter 12 brings to the scene two main actors in the final drama of this earth's history: the dragon, identified as Satan, and the remnant of the woman's offspring, who are the followers of Christ. As Merrill C. Tenney observes, Revelation treats Satan as a real enemy and takes "his existence for granted, and discloses enough about him to show that he is a very real and fearsome figure."[35] Planet Earth has become the battlefield of the great controversy. Having failed in his effort to destroy Christ and sweep away the church, Satan is filled with fury. He is determined to enter his final battle and win the victory over those who are identified as the remnant of the woman's offspring living at the last period of this earth's history. The last-day events are thus Satan's last attempt to destroy the saints and prevent the accomplishment of God's purpose in the world. This indicates that in the final battle between Christ and Satan, the church is on the front line.

God's triumphant victory over Satan introduces the inauguration of God's rule in the world and Christ's kingly authority. The word used with reference to the inauguration of God's rule and Satan's defeat is "now" (Rev. 12:10). Revelation 5 describes in the symbolic handling of the sealed scroll the transfer of rulership over the earth to Christ. Yet how does one explain Christ's victory over Satan, the inauguration of God's rule in the world, and the freedom from Satan in Christ, in light of the fact that Christ's followers are still oppressed and harmed by Satan? It appears that this concept must be understood within the general New Testament concept of "now" and "not yet." Satan is *already* defeated, and Christ exercises his sovereignty *now* "with all authority in heaven and on the earth" (Matt. 28:18). The subjection of all rebellion has *not yet* taken place, however. It is not until the close of the millennium that Satan and his associates will finally be destroyed (Rev. 20:7–10) and God's universal kingdom will be forever established.

The illustration from World War II given by Oscar Cullmann is very instructive here. After "D-Day," when the Allied forces had defeated the Germans in the decisive battle at Normandy, it became clear that the outcome of the war was just a matter of time. Although the decisive effect of that battle was perhaps not recognized by all, it nevertheless already meant victory. But the war still had to be carried on through to "V-Day," when Germany surrendered and the hostility finally ceased.[36]

Christians find themselves between the Doom's Day of the decisive battle when Christ won victory over Satan at the cross, and the Victory Day of Christ's return to the earth and the final surrender of Satan. Until then, according to Paul, Christ "must reign until He has put all His enemies under His feet" (1 Cor. 15:25). Cullmann argues: *"The hope of the final victory is so much the more vivid because of the unshakably firm conviction that the battle that decides the victory has already taken place."*[37] Thus it is understandable that Satan has realized that he has but "little time" (Rev. 12:12).

In conclusion, Revelation 12 portrays Satan as the archenemy of Christ and his followers. In order to impress upon the reader the character of Satan's activities, John portrays him in a vivid presentation as the dragon of a fearsome appearance. Together with his followers, Satan is in conflict with Christ in such a way that every creature in the universe is affected.[38] Merrill C. Tenney explains that Satan is "the power behind the scenes of this world, the evil intelligence that makes war on the saints of God. The conflict between the Lamb and the dragon shows that the whole historical process can be interpreted in terms of a warfare which does not end in a hopeless dualism, but in a victory for God and for His Christ. The supernatural elements on both sides become increasingly evident as the plot progresses, until at last in the final climax God removes the dragon from the scene of earth by one great cataclysmic judgment."[39]

What Revelation makes clear, however, is that Satan is indeed a defeated enemy. He was defeated in the decisive battle on the cross where his destiny has been definitely decided. During the history of constant oppression, his efforts to destroy and sweep away the church have failed. In this is both the hope and warning for God's people today as they face the last-day events. There is hope for them in knowing that they confront a defeated enemy. But Satan's realization that he has failed too many times makes him angry and cautious. Therefore, he enters the final conflict against Christ's followers, determined more than even before to win the battle. He is preparing himself for that conflict accompanied by two allies, the beast from the sea and the beast from the earth (Rev. 13). This is what the next two chapters of Revelation are all about: the dragon's war against the remnant (chapter 13) and "the remnant's response to the dragon's attack" (chapter 14).[40]

ENDNOTES

1. Beale, 628–629.
2. J. M. Ford, 195.
3. Beale, 628–629.
4. See Johnson, 524; Aune, *Revelation 6–16*, 684–685.
5. Thomas, *Revelation 8–22*, 119.
6. See Morris, 152.
7. Johnson, 514.
8. Thomas, *Revelation 8–22*, 121.
9. Beale, 629.
10. Morris, 152.
11. Johnsson, 17.
12. Barclay, *The Revelation of John*, 2:78.
13. Mounce, 239.
14. Johnsson, 18.
15. Ibid.
16. For a fuller treatment of the Michael concept in both the biblical and Jewish tradition, see Aune, *Revelation 6–16*, 693–695.
17. Charles, 1:325.
18. J. Massynberde Ford, 194.
19. Johnsson, 19–20; *The Seventh-day Adventist Commentary*, 7:809–810.
20. Ellen G. White, quoted in *The Seventh-day Adventist Commentary*, 7:973.
21. Sweet, 201.
22. Ibid.
23. Ibid.
24. Hughes, 140.
25. Collins, *The Apocalypse*, 141.
26. Anthony A. Hoekema, "Time, (Two) Times, and Half a Time," in *The International Standard Bible Encyclopedia*, 2d ed. (Grand Rapids, MI: Eerdmans, 1988), 4:854.
27. Beale, 673.
28. Mounce, 246.
29. See Gerhard F. Hasel, "Remnant," in *The International Standard Bible Encyclopedia*, 2nd ed. (Grand Rapids, MI: Eerdmans, 1988), 4:130.
30. For an extensive treatment of the subject, see *The Seventh-day Adventist Bible Commentary*, 7:813–815.
31. General Conference of Seventh-day Adventists. Committee on Problems in Bible Translation. *Problems in Bible Translation* (Washington, DC: Review and Herald, 1954), 248; Bauer, 331–332.
32. Pfandl, 320.
33. Oscar Cullmann, *Christ and Time* (Philadelphia, PA: Westminster Press, 1964), 154.

34. LaRondelle, *How to Understand the End-Time Prophecies*, 283.

35. Tenney, 175.

36. Cullmann, 84.

37. Ibid., 87. (Italics in original.)

38. Edward Heppenstall, "Sin, Salvation, and the Sanctuary," *Ministry*, March 1977, pp. 13–16.

39. Tenney, 175.

40. Paulien, *What the Bible Says About the End-Time*, 109.

THE TWO BEASTS
REVELATION 13:1–18

The scene of Revelation 12 concludes with the dragon's determination to engage in the final battle against the remaining ones of the woman's offspring (12:17). This section describes the way the dragon moves in his final attempt to wage war against Christ and his followers at the time of the end. In order to fight and possibly win the battle, he finds support in his two allies—the beast from the sea (13:1–10) and the beast from the earth (13:11–18).

THE BEAST FROM THE SEA (13:1–10)

Crucial to a sound interpretation of the following section is an understanding of the organization of its structure. Revelation 13:1–4 introduces the first of Satan's allies in the final crisis by giving his general description in terms of Daniel's vision of Daniel 7. Revelation 13:5–7 provides further identification of the sea beast by describing his activities during the period of forty-two months. Thus, these two passages are parallel in thought.[1] Revelation 13:8 serves as a sort of introduction to the final conflict to occur in the closing days of earth's history, which is described further in 13:11–18.

> *[1]And he stood on the sand of the sea. And I saw a beast coming up out of the sea, having ten horns and seven heads, and upon his horns were ten crowns, and upon his heads were names of blasphemy. [2]And the beast which I saw was like a leopard, and his feet were like those of a bear, and his mouth was like the mouth of a lion. And the dragon gave him his power and his throne and great authority. [3]And one of his heads was as slain unto death, and his mortal wound was healed. And the whole earth marveled after the beast, [4]and worshiped the dragon, because he gave authority*

to the beast, and worshiped the beast saying, "Who is like the beast, and who is able to wage war with him?"

⁵And it was given to him a mouth to speak great things and blasphemies, and it was given to him to exercise authority for forty-two months. ⁶And he opened his mouth in blasphemies against God, to blaspheme his name and his tabernacle, namely, those who dwell in heaven. ⁷And it was given to him to make war with the saints and to overcome them, and authority over every tribe and people and tongue and nation was given to him. ⁸And all those who dwell on the earth will worship him, whose names are not written in the book of life of the Lamb slain from the foundation of the world.

⁹If anyone has an ear, let him hear:

¹⁰If somebody is to go into captivity,
　　　　into captivity he goes;
if somebody kills with the sword,
　　　　with the sword he must be killed.
Here is the endurance and the faith of the saints.

NOTES

13:1 He stood. Most modern translations read "he stood" (Gr. *estathē*) rather than the "I stood" (*estathē*) found in the King James Version which places John on the seashore watching the beast coming out of the water. The reading "he stood" is most likely the correct one, largely because it is based on the early Greek manuscripts, contrary to the King James Version reading which is based on a later Greek text. Accordingly, the phrase "he stood on the sand of the sea" refers to the dragon standing on the seashore awaiting the emergence of his first ally, the beast from the sea.

A beast. The Greek word *thērion* denotes a wild animal, a savage beast, and a being with a bestial nature, including monsters.[2] The description of the beast in Revelation 13:1–2 suggests a picture of a sea monster[3] (see *Notes* on Rev. 12:3). The many-headed monster is mentioned in the book of Psalms (74:13–14). The symbol of the beast which stands for world empires goes back to the book of Daniel (cf. Dan. 7:17, 23). In Revelation, the beast stands as the symbol of the political power through which Satan works actively throughout the earth's history, in general, and in the last days, in particular (Rev. 11:7; 13:1–18; 14:9–11; 15:2; 16:2, 10, 13; 17:3–17; 19:19–20; 20:4, 10).

The sea. Mention of the sea as the source from which the monstrous beast of Revelation 13:1 comes is a clear allusion to Daniel 7:2–3. This is evident from the fact that the composite beast incorporates the characteristics of all four beasts from Daniel's vision (Dan. 7:3–7). In the Old Testament, the sea often symbolizes the abode of the sea monsters (Job 26:12–13; Ps. 74:13–14; Isa.

27:1; 51:9–10; Ezek. 32:2), from which the evil enemy powers come that oppressed Israel (see *Notes* on Rev. 12:3). The symbolism of the sea in Revelation seems to correspond to the abyss (Rev. 11:7; 17:8). In Revelation 17, John refers to the same beast (he has seven heads and ten horns, and is full of names of blasphemy; 17:3, 7, 12). This time he is said to come from the abyss (17:8). This might suggest that the sea and the abyss or the bottomless pit are the same symbolic place from which the beast of Revelation 13:1 comes (on the concept of the abyss as the abode of Satan and the demons, see *Notes* on Rev. 9:1). It is noteworthy that the "many waters" on which the harlot Babylon sits in Revelation 17:1 is parallel to the beast "full of names of blasphemy, having seven heads and ten horns" on which the woman sits (17:3). The waters on which the harlot sits are identified as "peoples and multitudes and nations and tongues," which are evidently the same as the ten horns of the beast (17:12–18). Eugenio Corsini argues that the sea here "represents the cosmic yet historical reality of the bottomless pit."[4] It is reasonable to conclude that the sea from which the beast of Revelation 13:1 comes may be a symbol of the "disturbed and stormy social and political conditions out of which tyrannies commonly arise"[5] (cf. Rev. 17:15).

Ten crowns. The crowns on the horns of the beast are diadems—royal crowns (Gr. *diadēma*, "diadems"). For a fuller explanation of the concept, see *Notes* on Revelation 2:10.

13:3 *Slain.* The word "slain" here in Greek is *sphazō* ("to slay," "to slaughter," "to kill"). The same word in Greek is used with reference to the Lamb (Rev. 5:6, 9, 12; 13:8), which suggests that the mortal wound of the beast's head was like that of the slain Lamb. The same word is also used with reference to the death of God's faithful people as the result of their loyalty to God and the gospel (Rev. 6:9; 18:24). Elsewhere in the New Testament, the word is used in 1 John 3:12 which speaks of Cain who had "slain" his brother Abel.

13:5 *Blasphemies.* Blasphemy in the New Testament refers to the act of claiming equality with God (John 10:33; cf. Matt. 26:63–65) as well as the prerogatives of God alone (Mark 2:7). That the blasphemies of the sea beast have to do with God is evident in Revelation 13:6 where he opens "his mouth in blasphemies against God, to blaspheme his name and his tabernacle, namely, those who dwell in heaven." As George E. Ladd states, the blasphemies of the beast consist of "the derogation of deity by his own claim to self-deification."[6]

Forty-two months. This time period in Revelation is allotted to the oppressive anti-God powers (cf. 11:2; 13:5) in contrast to the 1,260 days consistently used with reference to God's people (cf. 11:3; 12:6). Seventh-day Adventists have regarded A.D. 538 as the year when the church established itself as an ecclesiastical power to mark the beginning of the 1,260-year period. The year A.D. 1798 thus marks the end of this prophetic period. On the symbolism of this prophetic period and its historical application, see *Notes* on Revelation 11:2 and 12:6.

13:8 *Those who dwell on the earth.* See *Notes* on Revelation 6:10.

The book of life of the Lamb. See *Notes* on Revelation 3:5.

13:10 *If somebody kills with the sword, with the sword he must be killed.* This reading of the proverbial statement (found in KJV, RSV, and NASB) is based on some Greek manuscripts, including the fourth-century codex Sinaiticus, and stresses the destiny of the beast as the persecutor. The variant reading is found in the NIV and NEB: "If anyone is to be killed with the sword, with the sword he will be killed." It is based on other Greek manuscripts, including the fifth-century codex Alexandrinus, and stresses the destiny of those who stay faithful to God. Although no satisfactory solution is found, the reading in the KJV, RSV, and NASB is most likely, for it echoes the declaration made by the prophet Jeremiah with reference to the judgment over the apostate people (Jer. 15:2) and Egypt (Jer. 43:11). This corresponds to the proverbial words of Jesus in Matthew 26:52: "All those who take up the sword shall perish by the sword."

EXPOSITION

Frustrated in his efforts to destroy the church, Satan now directs his anger toward the remaining ones of the woman's offspring.

13:1–2 The dragon is now seen standing on *the sand of the sea*, summoning his first ally, to invest him with his power and authority. John subsequently sees *a beast coming up out of the sea*. The reference to the sea as the source from which the beast comes is reminiscent of the vision from Daniel 7 in which the prophet saw the four beasts coming out of the sea (7:3). The beast coming out of the sea in Revelation 13 is described in detail later in Revelation 17, adding supplementary information with regard to the identity of this sea monster.

The physical description of the beast in John's vision is introduced as the various parts of its body emerge from the water. The beast has *ten horns and seven heads.* The horns stand for political powers (Rev. 17:12). The ten horns of the sea beast are related to the ten horns of the fourth beast in Daniel's vision; they symbolize the kingdoms arising after the breaking up of the Roman Empire (cf. Dan. 7:7, 23–24; Rev. 17:12). However, as William G. Johnsson states, the seven heads of the dragon represent "the kingdoms through which Satan has worked to oppress God's people throughout the ages."[7] The beast was active throughout history in one after another of his heads. When one of the heads was mortally wounded, the beast ceased to be active. When in the future that head is healed, the beast would resume his activities. It is significant that the beasts of Daniel 7 have together seven heads and ten horns in total.[8] The sea beast is described as having the same number of heads and horns as the dragon of Revelation 12:3. This implies "the oneness of the dragon and the sea beast in a parody of the oneness of God and Christ. As Jesus Christ and the Father are one, so the dragon and the sea beast are one."[9]

The beast has on its horns **ten crowns** which are the royal diadems of political authority. However, while the dragon had the seven crowns on his heads, the beast has ten crowns on his horns. We saw earlier that the seven crowns on the dragon's heads denote Satan's false claim of full authority and power over the world. The ten crowns upon the horns of the sea beast symbolize the power, throne, and great authority given to him by the dragon (Rev. 13:2) through the political and secular powers of the world (cf. Rev. 17:12–13, 17). This stands in opposition to Christ, "Lord of lords and King of kings" (Rev. 17:14), who wears "many crowns" on his head (19:12).

It is further said that the beast has **names of blasphemy** upon his heads. Likewise the beast of Revelation 17 is described as full of names of blasphemy (17:3). In Revelation 13:6, the beast opened "his mouth in blasphemies against God, to blaspheme his name and his tabernacle, namely, those who dwell in heaven." As Ladd explains, these blasphemies of the beast "are not curses on the divine sovereignty uttered by men under the judgments of God (16:9); they consist of the derogation of deity by his own claim to self-deification."[10] This power claims prerogatives of God and equality with him. This strongly indicates that while this satanic ally is a political power, it is also a religious power working in opposition to God and his people (cf. 2 Thess. 2:3–4). He claims worship and sovereignty over the earth which belongs only to Christ (Rev. 13:3b–4, 12).

The beast of Revelation 13 combines the features and characteristics of all four beasts of Daniel 7, representing the succession of empires that would rule the world. The body of the beast is like that of a leopard, the feet like those of a bear, and the mouth like the mouth of a lion. Several things come to view here. First of all, the image of the composite beast from the sea is based on Daniel's vision. Daniel 7 thus provides the key to identifying the sea beast and his activities. Since in Daniel an image of a beast stands for a ruling power, the description of the sea beast suggests that this ally of Satan must be a sort of ruling power, both political and religious. He is the real successor of all the powers that came before him. The activities of this beast become evident sometime after the breaking up of the Roman Empire as the fourth empire of Daniel 7.

The sea beast receives **power and his throne and great authority** from the dragon who summoned him. As Christ was given authority from the Father (Rev. 2:27), so the sea beast was given authority from the dragon. Satan has already claimed the right over this world. Jesus called him "the ruler of this world" (John 12:31; 14:30; 16:11). In tempting Jesus, he asserted that the dominion over this world "has been handed over to me, and I give it to whomever I wish" (Luke 4:6). This claim to power and authority that he has exercised over the earth throughout history is now handed to the sea beast via the Roman Empire. Through the activities of the first member of the evil triumvirate, Satan himself exercises full power and authority over the earth in the closing days of earth's history.

13:3–4 Having described the appearance of the sea beast in terms of the symbolic little horn from Daniel's vision, John now provides further identification with regard to this sea monster. ***One of his heads was as slain unto death.*** The portrayal of the beast "as slain" is like that of the Lamb "as slain" in Revelation 5:6 (in the Greek text the same word is used to describe the death of each).[11] Thus the mortal wound of the beast's head is like that of the slain Lamb.

The existence of the beast and his activities is identified with his heads. The beast had existed and was active throughout history in one after another of his heads. When one of the heads was mortally wounded, the dominion and activities of the beast temporarily ceased. Thus while here the mortal wound is of one of the beast's heads, in Revelation 13:12 and 14 the beast himself receives the mortal wound and comes back to life. When in the future this head is healed, the beast will resume his former role and activities. Which of the seven heads was wounded to the point of death? Most likely the seventh one, which, according to Revelation 17:9–10, "was not" yet from John's perspective, but which was to come after the Rome of John's day. According to Revelation 13:14, the mortal wound was caused "by the sword."

The beast, however, experiences a resurrection because ***his mortal wound was healed.*** This is spurious to the death and resurrection of Christ. The healing of the mortal wound wins worldwide admiration and awe, for ***the whole earth marveled after the beast.*** This admiration leads them to worship both the beast and the dragon (who has invested the beast with his authority), saying: ***Who is like the beast, and who is able to wage war with him?*** The rhetorical question: "Who is like the beast?" is a parody of "Who is like God?" in the Old Testament (Exod. 15:11; Ps. 35:10; Mic. 7:18). It is especially significant that Christ, while waging war with the dragon in heaven, is referred to as Michael (Rev. 12:7), which in Hebrew means "Who is like God?" Here is another indication that in preparation for the final battle this beast imitates Christ.

The question: "Who is like the beast, and who is able to wage war with him?" implies the answer: no one. This indicates a firm conviction of victorious success in the battle.

13:5–7 After giving the general description of the sea beast in terms of Daniel's vision, John now identifies the beast's activities and character. The beast is given *a mouth to speak great things and blasphemies.* This is an allusion to the activities of the little horn that arises after the fourth beast—the Roman Empire—in Daniel 7:8 and 25. The time allotted to the beast to exercise his authority is *forty-two months.* This is another allusion to Daniel 7:25 which portrays the activities of the symbolic little horn. It is said that he "will speak against the Most High and oppress his saints... for a time, times, and half a time" (Dan. 7:25, NIV), equating to three and a half years. Forty-two months is the period allotted to the nations to trample the holy city in Revelation 11:2 (see the exposition of Rev. 11:2). This period corresponds to the "1,260 days" of the dragon's pursuit of the woman in the wilderness (Rev. 12:6, 13–16). All of this indicates that this political-religious power that will play the key role in the final conflict has more than a 1,200-year-long history in the Medieval period of harming and oppressing God's people. Historicist interpreters have usually marked A.D. 538 as the year when the church established itself as an ecclesiastical power to begin this prophetic period. The year 1798—when the events of the French Revolution and the capture of the Pope shook the church's religious-political oppressive power—would thus mark the end of the forty-two-month period.

The forty-two months of his activities parallel the three-and-a-half years of Christ's ministry in the world—a total of forty-two months characterized by continual rejection and persecution. As during the Medieval period the followers of Christ prophesied "for 1,260 days clothed in sackcloth" (Rev. 11:3), thus they experienced what Jesus did during his three-and-a-half years of faithful witnessing. Jesus stated: "If they persecuted me, they will also persecute you" (John 15:20).

Next, John elaborates on the blasphemous characteristics of the sea beast. The beast opens *his mouth in blasphemies against God, to blaspheme his name and his tabernacle, namely, those who dwell in heaven.* The phrase "those who dwell in heaven" is a reference to God's people in contrast to the wicked who are in the chapter referred to as "those who dwell on the earth" (Rev. 13:8, 12, 14). The followers of Christ are portrayed metaphorically as already reigning with Christ in the heavenly places (cf. Rev. 1:6; 5:9–10). It is of special interest here that God's dwelling or tabernacle is equated with "those who dwell in heaven." This indicates that God's tabernacle is his faithful people seated "with him in the heavenly places, in Christ Jesus" (Eph. 2:6), in spiritual union with him.[12] The blasphemies of this enemy power are directed against both God and his faithful and loyal saints. The beast is allowed *to make war with the saints and to overcome them*. During this period of the symbolic forty-two months, God's people, although oppressed, persecuted, and small in number as compared with the wicked, hold fast to God's word and bear their witness to Christ (cf. Rev. 12:17).

The beast is also given *authority over every tribe and people and tongue and nation*. This giving of authority to the beast is a repetition of Revelation 13:2, where the dragon delegated "his power and his throne and great authority" to the beast. The phrase "every tribe and people and tongue and nation" indicates the same territory to which the end-time gospel is preached in Revelation 14:6. The sea beast thus offers a rival gospel to that of the three angels in Revelation 14.

13:8 Having identified the first of Satan's allies in terms of Daniel's vision and his activity during the forty-two months, John turns the attention of his readers to the time of the end. *All those who dwell on the earth* whose names are not written in the book of life *will worship him.* This statement refers to the time of the end. It introduces the activity that the beast will exercise and the support he will receive in the closing days of earth's history. The same power that has exercised great power and authority in oppressing God's people throughout the course of history will again seek to dominate the world and win allegiance of the entire world at the time of the end. The final conflict will draw a definite line of demarcation between the true worshipers of God—those who have their names written in the book of life—and those who worship the beast, *whose names are not written in the book of life of the Lamb slain from the foundation of the world* (cf. 17:8). This recalls the great warning of the angel flying in mid heaven proclaiming an eternal gospel to "those who dwell on the earth," urging them to fear God and worship him, and warning them not to worship the beast and render their allegiance to him (Rev. 14:6–12). The mention here of "the Lamb slain from the foundation of the world" is very significant. It shows that the only hope of God's people in the final conflict is in the blood of Christ and the salvation that he secured by his death on the cross.

13:9–10 The section closes with an appeal: *If anyone has an ear, let him hear.* This appeal echoes the exhortation which concludes each of Christ's messages to the seven churches in Revelation 2–3. Everybody is urged to pay close attention to what has been said here with reference to the first of Satan's allies. The appeal is followed by the universal warning expressed with two matching proverbial statements:

> *If somebody is to go into captivity, into captivity he goes;*
> *if somebody kills with the sword, with the sword he must be killed.*

The first statement stresses the destiny of God's people. It states that their lives of loyalty and faithfulness will often involve imprisonment and death (cf. Rev. 12:11). But persecution is not the last word; the second statement stresses the destiny of the persecutors of God's people. God's people are not urged to resist but rather are called to endurance. The last word is with God, and he will bring judgment and retribution on the oppressors of his people. Their punishment will be proportionate to the harm and oppression they brought upon God's people (cf. Rev. 18:6–8). Until then, God's people must have **the endurance and the faith.** The phrase **here is** indicates that while in the final crisis the satanic trinity is seeking to win the allegiance of all "those who dwell on the earth," God's people are characterized by their unswerving faithfulness to God with patient endurance and perseverance (cf. Rev. 14:12).

Whom or what does this first of Satan's allies represent? The definite parallel in the description between the sea beast and Christ suggests that this enemy power is the antithesis of Jesus Christ and his activity. Just as Jesus began his ministry by coming out of the water (cf. Luke 3:21–23), so the sea beast begins his ministry by coming out of the sea. The beast is described as one with the dragon, as Jesus is one with the Father (John 14:9). As Christ received the authority of the Father (Rev. 2:27), so the sea beast receives authority from the dragon. Both Christ and the beast wear diadems on their heads (Rev. 19:12), both wield swords (cf. Rev. 1:16), and both have horns (Rev. 5:6). The forty-two months of the beast's activities equate to the three and a half years of Jesus' ministry. Both Christ and the sea beast receive the mortal wound (Rev. 5:6), and subsequently come back to life and rise to greater authority. Both are worshiped after the mortal wound is healed (cf. Matt. 28:17), and both have followers with inscriptions upon their foreheads (Rev. 13:16; 14:1). The exclamation "Who is like the beast?" brings to mind the name of Michael ("Who is like God?") of Revelation 12:7. Finally, both Christ and the sea beast exercise global authority over "every tribe and people and tongue and nation" (cf. Rev. 13:7). This identifies the first of Satan's allies of Revelation 13 as an apostate religious system which counterfeits

Christ's ministry on the earth. The fact that this religious system is presented in the symbol of a beast suggests that its political authority and power is under the guise of religion.

Furthermore, the activities of this power are reminiscent of the activities of the little horn of Daniel 7 which arises after the fourth beast: "And he will speak out against the Most High, and wear down the saints of the Highest One, and he will intend to make alterations in times and in law; and they will be given into his hand for a time, times, and half a time" (Dan. 7:25). Both Daniel 7 and Revelation 13 refer to the power that arises out of the Roman Empire and succeeds it after its breakup. The period of the activities of the little horn (Dan. 7:25) and those of the first sea beast (Rev. 13:5) are both set out in "forty-two months" or 1,260 prophetic days. In other words, the end-time activity of the beast from the sea is preceded by more than 1,200 years of opposition to God and oppression of God's people.

Many interpreters see in the sea beast of Revelation 13 the symbol of imperial Rome in its hostility against the Christians of John's time. The beast's mortal wound is applied to the *Nero revividus* (or Nero resurrected) myth; "the mortal wound" or "is not" period of the beast (cf. Rev. 17:11) would stretch from the suicide of Nero and the healing of the wound to the renewed persecution by emperor Domitian at the end of the first century.[13] It has been demonstrated in the "Introduction" of this commentary that the book of Revelation was meaningful for those to whom it was first directed. Revelation was a letter sent to the Christian congregations of John's day in the Roman province of Asia, addressing their own immediate historical circumstances and situations. One can certainly agree with Johnsson who points out that "the Christians living at the end of the first century would have found contemporary significance in the symbols of Revelation 13."[14] Johnsson further observes:

> A small, illicit sect, they would have seen satanic forces and designs behind the might of imperial Rome, raised against them by Nero and Domitian and to fall ever more heavily in the succeeding 200 years. We notice a strong movement from Romans 13 to Revelation 13. In the former the state is ordained of God, but in the latter it has become an agent of Satan....The combination of religion and state portrayed by Revelation 13 would have evoked echoes of their current experiences.[15]

No matter what applications the Christians of the first century or later may have seen in chapter 13, Revelation itself shows clearly that the fulfillment of the book's prophecy with regard to the sea beast extends beyond John's day. It thus provides the clue for the identification of the sea beast exclusively as the end-time religious-political system. The description of this system as the composite beast based on Daniel 7 and with seven heads (cf. Rev. 17:9–11) suggests that the sea beast stands as a corporate symbol of all oppressive world powers, civil and religious, that oppressed God's people from the establishment of the church at the Exodus down to the Second Coming.[16]

The beast has existed in different periods of history in one of his heads. Each head "is a partial incarnation of satanic power that rules for a given period."[17] Revelation 17 in particular sheds more light on such identification of the sea beast. The angel explains to John that the seven heads of the beast (cf. Rev. 13:1) symbolize seven successive godless world powers that dominated the world throughout history and have persecuted God's people (Rev. 17:9–11). The angel further states that five of those empires (Egypt, Assyria, Babylon, Persia, and Greece) ruled the world before the time of John; the sixth one, Rome, was the world power of John's time; the seventh one is described as a future manifestation from John's perspective. This is followed by the "is not" phase (Rev. 17:11), which is to be identified as the period of the mortal wound (Rev. 13:3).

Finally, in Revelation 17:11, the angel explains to John that the end-time worldwide political power which is in the service of end-time Babylon comes as the eighth head. The eighth head is actually a reappearance of the seventh head at the time of the end after the healing of the mortal wound. John lived in the time of the sixth or Roman head; the seventh was about to appear on the scene, and is described in Revelation 13. We evidently live in the era after the seventh head or the "is not" phase of the beast, for the eighth head—that is, the seventh head after it came back to life—with its united ten kingdoms has not yet come (cf. Rev. 17:12–13); it will appear on the worldwide scene in the final days of this world's history.

The text indicates that the sea beast in Revelation 13 is in the phase of the seventh head as the successor of the pagan Roman Empire (the sixth head; cf. Rev. 17:10). The only historical period following the disintegration of the Roman Empire that fits into this phase of the seventh head is the religious-political oppression of God's people during the Middle Ages. The only religious-political power that matches the description of the sea beast and its activities in Revelation 13 during the Medieval period was the papal ecclesiastical authoritarian rule that, having established itself as an institutional power in the sixth century, dominated the Western world in the name of heaven for more than twelve centuries. Historical records confirm that the first stage of the activities of the sea beast (in the phase of the seventh head)—to make "war with the saints and to overcome them" and to exercise "authority over every tribe and people and tongue and nation"—found its tragic fulfillment during the religious oppression of the Medieval period orchestrated by the Roman papacy. Although such an interpretation seems harsh and unfair in these modern days characterized by ecumenism and religious tolerance, the present does not erase historical realities.

We must acknowledge, however, that applying the seventh head of the sea beast to the Medieval ecclesiastical power alone is inadequate. History depicts similar behaviors and activities by the hierarchy of the Eastern Orthodox Church. Sadly, religious-political oppression was also demonstrated by the newly established Protestant orthodoxy in the Western world during the seventeenth and eighteenth centuries, characterized by religious intolerance.[18] Support for this perspective is ample, yet beyond the scope of this commentary.

The step-by-step breakdown of the Roman Empire following the reign of Constantine gradually ushered in the oppressive ecclesiastical authority which lasted until its demise with the emergence of the modern world. Starting with both the Renaissance humanist skepticism and the Protestant challenge on theological and political fronts, the ecclesiastical authoritarian rule was being seriously undermined. Furthermore, the rise of the urban class was bringing in a challenge of its own to both the aristocratic and ecclesiastic hierarchies. The ensuing Enlightenment Age attacked the entire rationale behind the existing political and religious governance. Continuing in the tradition of the Renaissance spirit, the new thinkers began to secularize society in earnest. What the philosophers advocated in theory, the American and French revolutionaries would eventually put into practice. The liberal philosophers were demanding a quantity of freedoms which the Church and the monarch were not willing to hand out. The establishment of the republican form of government in North America and in Europe and the gradual secularization of society, ranging from education to governance, was progressively ending the religious and political oppression and intolerance of both the Middle Ages and the post-Medieval period.

Furthermore, the emancipation of the masses meant freedom from religious superstition and oppression. Nationalism was elevating the masses to the level of the ruling elite; while destroying the monarchial system, it was also effectively incapacitating the Church for its own needs. The events of the French Revolution (including the demise of the papacy under Napoleon in 1798) that impacted politics and religious liberty are probably the most apparent manifestation of the "mortal wound." But for all practical purposes, it was this long process of political, social, and religious transformation that caused the "mortal wound" and brought the sea beast to the "is not" period (cf. Rev. 17:11). Both the authoritarian oppressive religious-political rule and the traditional God-centered theology that dominated the Western world for centuries were brought to an end, and since have been replaced with the human-centered and materialistic (atheistic) philosophy expressed in various forms.

However, the text says that this mortal wound will be eventually healed, and the beast will come to life once again and will exercise his authority and power in the phase of his eighth head (Rev. 17:11), covering the same territory to which the end-time gospel is preached (cf. Rev. 13:7; 14:6). Revelation 13:8 makes clear that this religious-political system, backed by worldwide secular and political authority and powers, will intensify its activities, particularly in the last days of this world's history. The result will be that "all those who dwell on the earth will worship" the beast and render their allegiance to the satanic triumvirate. This time, however, the resurrected apostate religious-political power will find its ultimate destruction before carrying out its purposes to destroy God's people.

THE BEAST FROM THE EARTH (13:11–18)

Revelation 13:8 refers to the time of the end when the beast from the sea wins the allegiance and worship of the entire world. John now turns his attention to the second of Satan's allies—the beast from the earth. As in the portrayal of the first beast, John gives the general characteristics of the earth beast (13:11), and then moves into a description of its end-time activities (13:12–18).

> **11And I saw another beast coming up out of the earth, and he had two horns like a lamb, and he spoke like the dragon. 12And he exercises all the authority of the first beast before him. And he makes the earth and those who dwell on it to worship the first beast, whose mortal wound had been healed. 13And he performs great signs, that he even makes fire come down from heaven to the earth before the people, 14and he deceives those living on the**

earth by means of the signs which were given to him to do before the beast, telling those who dwell on the earth to make an image to the beast who had the wound by the sword and came back to life. ¹⁵And it was given to him to give breath to the image of the beast, that the image of the beast might speak and cause as many as do not worship the image of the beast to be killed. ¹⁶And he causes all, the small and the great, and the rich and the poor, and the free and the slaves, to receive a mark on their right hand or on their forehead, ¹⁷and that no one may buy or sell except the one who has the mark, that is, the name of the beast, or the number of his name. ¹⁸Here is wisdom: let the one who has understanding count the number of the beast, for it is a human number; and his number is 666.

NOTES

13:11 *Beast.* See *Notes* on Revelation 13:1.

The earth. Earth (Gr. *gē*) here is related to the earth of Revelation 12:15–16 with reference to the dragon's pursuit of the woman into the wilderness, when the earth helped the woman by opening its mouth and swallowing the floodlike river proceeding from the dragon's mouth. The "earth" thus first functions as a positive symbol in Revelation. In the time of the end, however, the "earth" becomes the place of abominations of eschatological Babylon (Rev. 17:5). According to Revelation 19:2, Babylon corrupted or destroyed the earth with her fornication; "it is from the 'earth' [that] the 144,000 must be redeemed (Rev. 14:3)."[19] The association of the earth and the sea in Revelation 13 (as in Rev. 10) might suggest that the earth in 13:11 is the complement of "the sea" mentioned in 13:1. Together they signify the universal and worldwide scope of Satan's end-time activities as the fulfillment of the statement from Revelation 12:12: "Woe to the earth and the sea, because the devil has come down to you having great anger, knowing that he has little time."[20] LaRondelle, in a privately published work, holds that the inference of "the earth" to mean a restricted geographic area (such as Palestine or Asia Minor) or a sparsely settled region (representing America) in contrast to the inhabited area (such as "the sea" in Rev. 13:1) is a conjecture.[21] *The Seventh-day Adventist Bible Commentary*, in keeping with traditional Adventist interpretation, maintains that such an inference may be reasonably assumed.[22]

But. The Greek word *kai* ("and") functions here as an adversative "but."

13:14 *Those who dwell on the earth.* See *Notes* on Revelation 6:10.

13:16 *A mark on their right hand or on their forehead.* The Greek word *charagma* signifies an imprinted or engraved mark, and also a graven image (cf. Acts 17:29). *Charagma* was a technical term for the imperial stamp on commercial documents and the royal impression on Roman coins. The word was also used for branding animals.[23] However, no evidence indicates an ancient practice of placing *charagma* on a person (for instance, for branding the slaves with a mark, the word *stigmata* was used; cf. Gal. 6:17). This suggests a symbolic meaning of the placing of the mark of the beast on the forehead as the identification mark of belonging to the satanic trinity. The seal of God on the foreheads of God's people (Rev. 7:1–4) and the mark on the worshipers of the satanic trinity denote the distinction between the two groups at the time of the end.

What does the mark of the beast symbolize? No doubt the first-century Christians suffering under severe persecutions of the imperial cult would have seen in the certificate of conformity with the popular demand for emperor worship an application of "the mark of the beast." Throughout history, the mark of the beast was understood to mean different things in different times. However, Revelation 13 indicates clearly that the ultimate application of the mark of the beast is set for the time of the end, just prior to the Second Coming. It is in the final crisis that the mark of the beast will become a sign of allegiance for those who worship the satanic trinity, in contrast to those who worship God and obey him in keeping his commandments.

The mark of the beast in Revelation stands in sharp contrast to the seal of God. The basic function of both the seal and the mark is ownership, identity, and protection. Both are thus signs of loyalty to God or the beast, respectively. Revelation 12–14 emphasizes that "in the final crisis the commandments of God will emerge as the standard of loyalty" and obedience.[24] The end-time saints having the divine seal are characterized as those who "keep the commandments of God" (Rev. 12:17; 14:12). The mark of the beast thus seems to be the substitution of obedience to the beast for obedience to God.

It appears that the first four commandments of the Decalogue, in particular ("You shall have no other gods before Me"; "You shall not make for yourself an idol, or any likeness of what is in heaven above or on the earth beneath or in the water under the earth," in order to worship them; "You shall not take the name of the LORD your God in vain"; and, "Remember the Sabbath day, to keep it holy"), will become the test of loyalty to God in the final crisis. These four commandments concern one's relationship with God and worship. According to Revelation 12–14, the issue in the final crisis centers on the relationship with God and proper worship. The two groups at the time of the end are identified as those who worship God versus those who worship the dragon and the beast (Rev. 14:7, 9; cf. 13:8, 12–15). This explains why the sea beast's end-time activities are described as well-planned attacks on these four commandments. The beast's demand for worship, something that is reserved for God alone (13:4, 8), is a direct attack on the first commandment: "You shall have no other gods before me." The raising up of an image to be worshiped (13:14–15) is a direct violation of the second commandment, and the blasphemy of God attacks the third commandment (13:5–6). The demand for receiving the mark of the beast indicates a direct attack on the fourth, the Sabbath commandment.

At this point, caution is necessary with regard to any attempt to limit the receiving of the seal of God on the foreheads in Revelation 7 to the observance of the Sabbath only. Observance of the Sabbath is nowhere explicitly stated as being the seal of God. Sealing in the New Testament signifies unequivocally the presence of the Holy Spirit in human hearts (2 Cor. 1:21–22; Eph. 1:13–14; 4:30; for further discussion, see *Notes* on Rev. 7:3); the sealed person belongs to God as his own possession and is distinguished from other people (cf. 2 Tim. 2:19). This in no way undermines the validity of the Sabbath as the seal of the commandments of God. Meredith Kline demonstrates that the Decalogue in Exodus 20 follows the format of ancient covenant documents which were stamped with a seal of ownership and authority in the center. In such a way, the fourth commandment functions as the seal stamped at the center of the Decalogue.[25] The Sabbath was thus the seal of the ratification of the Sinaitic covenant between God and Israel.

On the other hand, the Hebrew Scriptures define unequivocally the seventh-day Sabbath as the distinctive sign that distinguished the people of Israel from other peoples. The Sabbath was an external sign of belonging to the true God and the special relationship between God and his covenant people (Exod. 31:12–17; Ezek. 20:12, 20). The two versions of the Decalogue given in Exodus and Deuteronomy show that the purpose of the Sabbath was to be a constant reminder to Israel of God as their Creator (Exod. 20:11) and their Savior (Deut. 5:15). It appears that this aspect of the Sabbath is emphasized in Revelation 12–14. Although the issue in the final crisis is not confined just to the Sabbath, the Sabbath will evidently come to be "the litmus test" of loyalty and obedience in the final crisis.[26] When in Revelation 14:6–12 John describes God's final appeal to the inhabitants of the earth, he does so in terms of calling them to worship the true God, the Creator, in the context of the fourth commandment (Rev. 14:7; cf. Exod. 20:11; the editors of the fourth edition of the UBS Greek New Testament admit in the margins that the statement from Rev. 14:7b is an allusion to Exod. 20:11).[27] This appeal to worship the Creator God is followed by the proclamation of the two other angels who announce the fall of Babylon and warn against worshiping the beast and receiving the mark on the right hand or the forehead (Rev. 14:6–11). The urging of people to worship the true God in relation to the Sabbath commandment and warning them not to worship the beast and receive his mark strongly suggests that the mark of the beast functions as the counterfeit to the Sabbath commandment. That the receiving of the mark has something to do with the commandments of God is further confirmed with the concluding text; the worshipers of God are characterized as the ones "who keep the commandments of God and the faith of Jesus" (14:12).

The text seems to indicate that as the Sabbath will be the distinctive sign of obedience to God in keeping his commandments in the final crisis, so the mark of the beast, the counterfeit Sabbath (in contrast to the seventh-day Sabbath) will become the sign of obedience to the beast. The receiving of the mark of the beast will thus stand in direct opposition to obedience to God's commandments. One can certainly agree with William G. Johnsson that "while the nonobservance of the Sabbath- or Sunday-observance is not the 'mark' per se just now, both are integral to its end-time enforcement. The Sabbath, anciently the 'sign' of the people of God (Exod 31:13; Ezek 20:20), will again come to the fore to show the world those who put God first."[28]

13:17 *The mark, that is, the name of the beast, or the number of his name.* Such a reading is supported by the codex Alexandrinus. However, some other important early manuscripts attest the inclusion of the word "or" in the text: the earliest Greek manuscript P⁴⁷ reads as "the mark or the name of the beast or the number of his name," and Sinaiticus reads it as "the mark of the beast or his name or the number of his name." Despite the strong manuscript support for the inclusion of "or," it appears that the reading of Alexandrinus (which is asserted to be the best textual witness) is more accurate. It places "the name of the beast" in apposition to "the mark"; in other words, the mark consists of the name of the beast. This would place the mark of the beast in contrast to the seal of God on the foreheads, consisting of the name of the Lamb and the Father (Rev. 14:1).

13:18 Wisdom (*sophia*) and **understanding** (*nous*, "mind"). The two words occur conjoined again in 17:9 with reference to the identity of the beast upon which the prostitute is seen as sitting. It appears that the call for wisdom alludes to Daniel 12:10 where "those who are wise shall understand" (RSV) the end times shown to Daniel in visions. In the light of Daniel 12:10 and Revelation 17:9, the call for "wisdom" and "understanding" in 13:18 does not refer to a brilliant mental and intellectual ability to calculate the number of the beast by means of a mathematical calculation including *gematria* (see below). In the book, wisdom is a divine attribute (5:12; 7:12). Only through this divinely imparted wisdom will the faithful be able to comprehend and discern the meaning of the satanic number 666 and the true character of the beast.

Count. The Greek word *psēphizō* ("to count," to calculate," "to reckon," "to figure out") means literally "to count with pebbles." The word occurs only here and in Luke 14:28. Its synonym is *logizomai* ("to reckon," "to calculate," "to give careful thought to a matter"). In Luke 14:28, *psēphizō* is used in the sense of "to reckon" or "to count" the cost. Jesus says that if his listeners want to follow him, they must reckon the cost of discipleship. In Revelation 13:18, the word is used in the sense of "to figure out" where the readers are called to probe the cryptic number 666 for its symbolic meaning.[29] **It is a human number**. The Greek *arithmos gar anthrōpou estin* can be translated as "for it is a number of a man" or "for it is a human number" (or "a number of humanity"). The beast in chapter 13 does not refer to an individual or a specific person in history (whether past or future) but a human system that stands in opposition to God; thus *arithmos anthrōpou* means here "a human number." John uses *anthrōpos* in the generic sense also in 21:17 where *metron anthrōpou* means "human measurement." The text suggests that the number of the beast is somehow related to humanity. Thus 666 is a human number in contrast to the divine number 777.

His number is 666 (*hexakosioi hexēkonta hex*). The context seems to suggest that the original readers had an ability to break the code, which must have later been lost. Since the second century, the most popular method utilized in attempting to decipher the cryptic number of 666 has been the technique known as *gematria* (a word derived from the Greek *geōmetria*, meaning "manipulation with numbers")[30] in which each letter of the Hebrew, Greek, or Latin alphabet has its own numerical value (e.g., "A" stood for 1, "B" for 2, "C" for 3, etc.).[31] As a result, numerous conjectures have been made as to the meaning of the number 666. The numerical value may stand for various Roman emperors such as Nero and Caligula,[32] or for others like Muhammad, Napoleon, or Hitler; it may also refer to the inscription of *vicarious filii dei* allegedly inscribed on the papal tiara.

None of these suggestions seems to be convincing for at least five reasons. First, the possibilities of the technique of *gematria* regarding the number 666 are unlimited. Second, John nowhere in Revelation employs *gematria* as the method of identification. Whenever he uses the word "number" (*arithmos*) in the book (5:11; 7:4; 9:16; 20:8), it is never with an intent to be calculated. All the numbers occurring in the book "have figurative significance and symbolize some spiritual reality and never involve any kind of literal gematria calculation."[33] When in the following text John referred to the 144,000 having Christ's "name and the name of his Father written on their foreheads" (Rev. 14:3), he did not intend any sort of mathematical calculation but a symbolic or spiritual understanding of the number. Third, John nowhere in the book refers to a specific individual in history—past, present, or future—but rather to religious or political systems. This is true also of the beast in chapter 13. If the number 666 was intended to be identified with some historical person "by means of such literal calculation, it would be a rare exception from the way numbers are employed elsewhere in the Apocalypse."[34] Fourth, if John wanted readers to figure out the meaning of the number 666 by counting the numerical value of letters, he would certainly point to the language in which the name occurs. Elsewhere in the book, when he wants to point to a specific meaning of a name, he does not let the reader decide the language arbitrarily. Rather, he specifies that the name is "in Hebrew" (9:11; 16:16) or "in Greek" (9:11). Fifth, the context suggests that the number of the beast's name has an eschatological significance and meaning. The readers are called to figure out the meaning of the number 666 in the context of the end-time activities of the earth beast who will cause the world to make the image of the beast and to receive "the name of the beast, or the number of his name" (13:17). In other words, the number 666 is applicable to the beast not prior to but after the healing of its mortal wound. Any application of 666 to historical persons (including Nero or Muhammad) or a medieval title *vicarius filii dei* that was allegedly inscribed on the papal tiara somewhere in the past does not fit the eschatological context in which readers are urged for divine discernment to perceive the character of the beast and protect themselves from the end-time deception.

The number of the beast expressed as 666 is far from being fully understood. It is said to be "a human number" (*arithmos anthrōpou*) rather than a divine one. It consists of the triple six clearly expressed in Greek: **hex**akosioi **hex**ēkonta **hex**. Babylonian mathematics was based on the sexagesimal system, in which the basic counting units were the numbers 6 and 60. (The sexagesimal system has been accepted universally today for the measurement of arcs and angles and for divisions of time.[35]) Furthermore, the number six was also significant to the Babylonian religion.[36] Sixty was the number of Babylonian supreme gods in the pantheon at different times (e.g., Anu and Marduck). (This explains why King Nebuchadnezzar's gold statue was 60 cubits high and 6 cubits wide; Dan. 3:1). A popular amulet worn by Babylonian priests contained a mysterious configuration of numbers in a square as follows:

1	32	34	3	35	6
30	8	27	28	11	7
20	24	15	16	13	23
19	17	21	22	18	14
10	26	12	9	29	25
31	4	2	33	5	36

The total of this sequence of numbers in the amulet both horizontally and vertically is 666. Six is thus the number of Babylon, and, as such, it stands in contrast to the divine number seven (see *Notes* on Rev. 5:1). Being one short of seven, it expresses human imperfection without God, in contrast to the number seven which expresses the completeness and perfection of God.

One might also observe the reference to 666 in 1 Kings 10:14 where 666 talents of gold were listed as King Solomon's annual income. The information is given in the context of when Solomon started going away from God after having married an Egyptian princess. In such a way, 666 as the number of the beast might point to the Christian church as the system that was once faithful to God and which eventually turns away from God and becomes the enemy of God's people at the time of the end.

The further significance to the meaning of the number six as "a human number" in Revelation 13:18 is found in the fact that humanity was created in the height of glory on the sixth day of creation.[37] The full week, however, is not expressed in the number six, but rather in the number seven.[38] The seventh day is the crowning day of the creation week; it expresses the fullness of God's creation and redemption. Six finds its real meaning in seven when human beings lift themselves from the sphere of the mundane and consecrate themselves to God and give all the glory to him for their existence. In such a vein of understanding, as Beatrice S. Neall suggests, the number 666 "represents the refusal of man to proceed to seven, to give glory to God as Creator and Redeemer. It represents man's fixation with himself, man seeking glory in himself and his own creations. It speaks of the fullness of creation and all creative powers without God—the practice of the absence of God. It demonstrates that unregenerate man is persistently evil. The beasts of Rev 13 represent man exercising his sovereignty apart from God, man conformed to the image of the beast rather than to the image of God. Man apart from God becomes bestial, demonic."[39]

In such a context, the number 666 functions as a symbol of the greatest imperfection.[40] It is in this sense that the true meaning of the number of the beast is to be found—meaning that is possible to perceive only through divine discernment.

It is noteworthy that the reference to the number of the beast as 666 is followed by the vision of the sealed saints carrying the name of Christ and the Father on their foreheads (14:1). This suggests that in the text "a contrast is intended between the beast's name and the Lord's name. If the latter symbolizes a purely spiritual reality, which it does, then so does the former. This is true also of the beast's number, since it is synonymous with his name."[41] However, the beast falls short of the divine character that he is counterfeiting.[42] Such an identification of this anti-Christ power "requires the wisdom of divine discernment" more than intellectual cleverness and human calculation.[43] An interpretation along these lines seems to be in harmony with the entire book of Revelation.

EXPOSITION

The dragon, Satan himself, is still standing on the seashore. This time he summons to the scene the second of his allies who joins him and the sea beast in the final and decisive battle in the history of the earth.

13:11 Now John describes the appearance of the second actor in the drama, the **beast coming up out of the earth.** The earth from which the second beast comes is the same earth which helped the woman by swallowing the floodlike river proceeding from the dragon's mouth (Rev. 12:15–16). This suggests a friendly appearance of the second beast that fits his deceptive activities in making the whole earth worship the sea beast. In addition, the fact that Satan's two allies come from the sea and the earth, respectively, indicates the worldwide scope of Satan's end-time activities (cf. Rev. 12:12).

The earth beast is referred to with the same Greek word for "beast" as in the sea beast, suggesting a savage beast. While the sea beast appears with ten monstrous horns, the earth beast appears with **two horns like a lamb.** The symbol of the lamb in Revelation always refers to Christ, which suggests that the reference here is not to any lamb but clearly to *the* Lamb. Thus, the appearance of the earth beast is described in Christ-like terms, suggesting a very positive history of this power, with a religious overtone. The character of the earth beast is opposite that of his appearance, however, for he speaks **like the dragon.** As E. Schüssler Fiorenza notes, "the reference to the horns and the speech of the monster further affirms the assertion that the text does not refer to *any* lamb and dragon, but clearly to *the* Lamb and *the* Dragon."[44] Like the first beast, the second beast functions as the mouthpiece of the dragon in his effort to defeat the church by means of deception. The statement that the earth beast speaks like the dragon (or serpent in 12:9) may refer to the "seductive and deceitful character of the serpent in the Garden of Eden."[45] As the prophets in the Old Testament were the mouthpiece of God, so this end-time power is the mouthpiece of Satan. This is why the rest of the book refers to the earth beast as "the false prophet" (16:13; 19:20; 20:10).

13:12 Having identified the earth beast in general terms, John now moves on to portray his activities in the final crisis. (Note the change in the text from the past tense in verse 11 to the present in verse 12). From now on, we witness the war between the dragon and the remnant of the woman's offspring. The rest of chapter 13 describes "the dragon's war against the remnant," while chapter 14 describes "the remnant's response to the dragon's attack."[46]

The beast from the earth *exercises all the authority of the first beast before him.* This Satanic ally is clearly a parody of the Holy Spirit. He exercises the authority of the sea beast as the Spirit exercises the authority of Christ (cf. John 15:26; 16:13–14). Through the earth beast, the sea beast indirectly exercises the great power and authority that he exercised earlier during the symbolic period of the forty-two months (Rev. 13:5–8). The power and authority exercised by the earth beast is implemented with the two strategies of the sea beast throughout history: deception and coercion. It is apparent that the earth beast represents religious-political power in the service of the sea beast and is hereafter called "the false prophet" (16:13; 19:20; 20:10).[47]

Furthermore, the earth beast *makes the earth and those who dwell on it to worship the first beast, whose mortal wound had been healed.* Again, we see here a counterfeit of the role of the Holy Spirit. In exalting the sea beast and causing people to worship him, the earth beast imitates the Holy Spirit whose role, according to the gospel of John, is to magnify Christ (John 15:26; 16:12–15). It is important to note the change of the tenses here in the text. The phrase "he makes" is in the present tense in the Greek, while "to worship" is in the future tense. "He makes" carries the idea of preparing "the earth and those who dwell on it" to worship the first beast. This "making" of "the earth and those who dwell on it" to worship the first beast includes some sort of activities on the part of the earth beast in the closing days of earth's history. These activities, in their initial stage, evidently include deception and persuasion (cf. Rev. 13:13–14), and, as the final measure, coercion (13:15–17). The friendly earth, which earlier served to help the woman, now engenders allegiance to the first beast and becomes the opposition to the remnant of the woman's offspring.

The reference to the mortal wound of the sea beast seems to be very significant (it is repeated again in verse 14). It appears that the "making" of the earth to worship the sea beast has to do with the healing of the mortal wound. We already noted in Revelation 13:3–4 that the healing of the mortal wound led to worldwide admiration and worship of the sea beast. The healing of the mortal wound plays a decisive role in the preparation of "the earth" and its inhabitants for the final crisis with worldwide rendering of loyalty and worship to the oppressive power of the sea beast.

13:13–15 John now explains the first of the strategies that the earth beast uses in order to make "the earth" worship the sea beast. First, the beast *performs great signs, that he even makes fire come down from heaven to the earth before the people.* The purpose of these great and miraculous signs—of which the greatest sign is bringing fire down from heaven—is to prompt the whole world to worship the sea beast. "Miracles and wonders and signs" characterized Jesus' earthly ministry (Acts 2:22). These miraculous signs performed by the beast remind one of the signs and wonders that the Holy Spirit worked through the apostles in the book of Acts (cf. 2:43; 4:30; 5:12–16). Just as through miraculous signs the Holy Spirit convinced people to accept Jesus Christ and worship him, so this counterfeit Christ "deceives those living on the earth by means of the signs" (Rev. 13:13).

The bringing of fire down from heaven to the earth might be a counterfeit to the day of Pentecost when the tongues of fire came down from heaven upon the disciples (Acts 2:3). However, this fire bears a stronger allusion to the fire that the prophet Elijah called down from heaven (1 Kings 18:38), which demonstrated that Yahweh was the true God of Israel and the only one to be worshiped. Thus, in the second case, the earth beast functions as the counterfeit of Elijah, who, by bringing fire down from heaven, misleads people into worshiping the false god. Whatever this fire might represent, it is effective in counterfeiting the truth and the gospel. All of this is designed to deceive people and persuade them that these great and miraculous signs are the manifestations of divine power.

The strategy of this end-time miracle worker seems to be effective. Through great miraculous signs, the earth beast *deceives those living on the earth by means of the signs.* This deceit is satanic, because the authority to perform these miraculous signs was *given* to the beast by Satan. This idea recalls Paul's prophecy of the lawless one whose coming would be "in accord with the activity of Satan, with all power and signs and false wonders, and with all the deception of wickedness for those who perish, because they did not receive the love of the truth so as to be saved" (2 Thess. 2:8–10).

Through the deception of these great miraculous signs, the earth beast leads deceived people on the earth *to make an image to the beast who had the wound by the sword and came back to life.* Here John introduces a new player to the end-time drama. The expression "the image of the beast" suggests that this new player is like the sea beast, yet different from the earth beast. While the earth beast uses the strategy of persuasion by means of deception, the image of the beast uses force as the means of persuasion. This new player seems to be more a political than a religious power.

Images and idols in the Old Testament are noted for their inability to speak and act (e.g., Pss. 115:4–5; 135:15; Isa. 46:7; Jer. 10:5; Hab. 2:18–19) because of a lack of breath in them (Ps. 135:17; Jer. 10:14; Hab. 2:19). Therefore, the earth beast is delegated to *give breath to the image of the beast.* This brings to mind the giving of the breath of life to the first man (Gen. 2:7). The image of the beast is put into action on the demand of the sea beast, so that *the image of the beast might speak and cause as many as do not worship the image of the beast to be killed.* The whole scenario is based on Daniel 3 which describes King Nebuchadnezzar ordering the people of his kingdom on the threat of death to worship the golden image he had erected. Just as in the time of Daniel the worship of the golden image was enforced by a legislative decree, so at the time of the end the demand to worship the image of the beast will be supported by civil power. Thus the image of the beast and the false prophet will render service to the first beast and force the whole earth to worship him.

Two things are evident here. First, the issue in the final crisis will be worship. Only God is worthy of worship (Rev. 14:7; 19:10; 22:8–9), and to worship anyone else is an affront to him. The two groups in Revelation at the time of the end are identified as those who worship God versus those who worship the dragon and the beast. The final test will not be denial of worship, but rather who is worshiped. Second, the symbol of the image of the beast in relation to the healing of the wound of the beast (Rev. 13:14) indicates the end-time revival of Satan's twofold strategy (deception and coercion) that he has employed throughout the ages. Thus, the symbol of the image of the beast points to "an institution and procedures which will duplicate the form and behavior of the beast power in other ages. That union of church and state which characterizes apostasy, and ever precedes persecution, is again to be made." In other words, the characteristics of the final conflict will be "the ultimate union of professed Christianity with the power of the state, in order to force all men to conform to its decrees."[48]

Whom or what does the earth beast as the second of Satan's allies represent? His identity seems to be very ambiguous. What has been said with reference to the sea beast applies also to the earth beast. As Johnsson points out, "no doubt Christians living at the end of the first century would have found contemporary significance in the symbols of Revelation 13." They most likely saw "elements of the imperial cult behind the land [earth] beast whose efforts were directed toward the exaltation of the sea beast. The combination of religion and state portrayed by Revelation 13 would have evoked echoes of their current experiences."[49] However, as with the sea beast, the fulfillment of the prophecy regarding the activities of the earth beast extends beyond John's day and points to the end of the age. Several things in the text provide the clue for identifying the earth beast as the end-time religious-political system.

First of all, we have observed that the sea beast in its seventh-head-phase activities represents an ecclesiastical religious-political power and system that dominated and ruled the world with political authoritarian power during the religious oppression of the Medieval period. However, the earth beast does not have ancient antecedents like the sea beast. He seems to rise into power after the sea beast has suffered the mortal wound, during the latter's "is not" phase of Revelation 17:11. The earth beast is clearly portrayed in Revelation 13 as an exclusively end-time power.

The origin of this end-time power is depicted in positive terms. The beast arises out of the earth which in Revelation 12, as we saw above, is a positive symbol regarding the church. It is further described as having two horns like a lamb, which suggests positive qualities. Its appearance is thus described as Christlike. It exercises a tolerant authority over the people. At the time of the healing of the mortal wound of the sea beast, however, this lamb-like power begins to speak more like a dragon, and becomes an ally of the dragon. In the latter stage of its activities, this end-time religious-political power exalts the sea beast and causes people to worship him. This parallels Jesus' saying that the role of the Holy Spirit was to magnify *him* (John 15:26; 16:12–15).

Finally, this end-time power is predicted to play a key role in the final crisis. What the second half of Revelation 13 seems to suggest is that the Medieval authority of the first beast once again will be exercised through the earth beast. It appears that the earth beast will even replace the first beast in universal power and authority and will act as the end-time worldwide oppressive power.

It appears that no single religious or political entity in modern history matches the description of the earth beast as does the United States of America. The United

States emerged on the historical arena after the Medieval ecclesiastical system had received its "mortal wound." This nation has become a major dominant power in the world. As the leading democratic world power, it has been admired for its political and religious tolerance and freedoms; yet, as a military and financial powerhouse, it is being highly respected and, by some, even feared. Today, the United States exercises a major role in world affairs. So far, this power clearly resembles the two-horned beast. Speaking in historical terms, what will make this two-horned lamb begin to speak like the dragon is yet to be seen. Revelation 13, however, seems to foretell a key religious-political role for the United States in the final crisis.

Revelation 13:12–14 shows that in exalting the sea beast in the last days, the activities of the earth beast will initially be characterized by great and miraculous signs as the means of persuasion. Later in the book, this end-time religious-political power is referred to as the false prophet (Rev. 16:13; 19:10; 20:10). In Revelation 16:13–14, the false prophet deceives people by means of deceptive signs and miracles to gather them for the battle of Armageddon. It will operate in the very presence of the sea beast, instilling followers in the initial stage with a false gospel characterized by sensationalism based on miracles and emotions that take the place of the religion of the heart and conduct and the transforming influence of the Holy Spirit.

Because of the peculiar nature of the aforementioned end-time activities of the earth beast, one must concur with the observation of William G. Johnsson:

> Let us frankly acknowledge that the full understanding of the fulfillment of this prophecy of the land monster still awaits us....Significant features of the second monster's deceptions are not yet clear, however—especially the miracles that cause many to be led astray, and the "image" to the sea monster. Further, the vision indicates a stage of action which embraces the whole world....How the entire mass of humanity will be drawn into the vortex of deception is not apparent at present.[50]

The reason for such an understanding is that in Revelation 13–18 everything is to be fulfilled on a worldwide scale, and nothing is "localized or nationalized" to any single area or nation.[51] These remarks are not to deny the validity of the application of the earth beast to the United States, but rather to say, as Johnsson further states, that "the full disclosure of the meaning of the land monster still awaits us and that the final deceptive activities of the great controversy, while heavily involving the United States, will be worldwide."[52]

13:16 In the final stage of his activities, however, the earth beast comes to exercise the same intolerance and force that characterized the sea beast during the Medieval times. The image of the beast makes a demand that all earth-dwellers receive *a mark on their right hand or on their forehead.* "The mandate extends to all people of all civic ranks" (*the small and the great*), of all economic strata (*the rich and the poor*), and of all social categories (*the free and the slaves*).[53] Nobody is exempt. In Revelation 7:3, the saints, standing on the threshold of the great tribulation, are sealed on their foreheads. This sets them apart as God's people and protects them from defeat of the enemy and the judgments of God.[54] Just as God marks his faithful people with the seal on the forehead, so Satan marks the followers and worshipers of the beast on their right hand or forehead with the name of the beast.

The mark of the beast functions clearly as the counterfeit of the seal of God (Rev. 7:3; 14:1). Sealing is the symbol of a genuine Christian. The sealed person belongs to God as his own possession (2 Tim. 2:19). The worshipers of the beast bear the symbolic mark of ownership and loyalty to Satan (Rev. 13:16–17; 14:9; 16:2; 19:20; 20:4), just as the followers of Christ have the symbolic seal of God's possession and their loyalty to him. While the seal of God consists of the names of the Lamb and the Father written upon the forehead (14:1), the mark of the beast consists of "the name of the beast, or the number of his name" upon the forehead or hand (13:17). The forehead stands for the mind, and the right hand stands for deeds and actions. Beatrice Neall states: "The reception of the mark of the beast and the seal of God, consisting of the names of the beast and of God, denotes conformity to the character of Satan or God."[55] Since the sealing signifies the working presence of the Holy Spirit in human hearts (2 Cor. 1:21–22; Eph. 1:13–14; 4:30), the placing of the mark of the beast counterfeits the work of the Holy Spirit. The people with the mark of the beast have been brought into this religious system, and they ever serve it with their minds and hearts—some willingly, others reluctantly.

As Neall rightly points out, the demand to receive the mark on the right hand or forehead evokes God's injunction to Israel to bind his commandments as a sign on their hands and frontlets on their foreheads (Deut. 6:8), "which the Jews literally carried out in the wearing of phylacteries. Hence, the mark on the hand or forehead signifies the writing of God's laws into the minds and behavior of his people."[56] This practice was intended to impress upon minds what Jews considered to be the central text of the Hebrew Bible: "Hear, O Israel! The Lord is our God, the Lord is one! And you shall love the Lord your God with all your heart and with all your soul and with all your might" (Deut. 6:4–5). For Jesus these words were a nutshell summary of the first four commandments of the Decalogue (Matt. 22:27–40). This suggests that the demand of the beast to have the mark on the right hand or the forehead stands as an antithesis to God's commandments, the exchange of obedience to the beast for obedience to God.

As Jon Paulien states, Revelation 12–14 shows that "the testing truth for the world" in the final crisis "is centered on the matter of proper worship."[57] The people living at the time of the end will fall into one of two groups: the worshipers of the true God having the seal on their forehead or the worshipers of the satanic trinity having the mark on their right hand or forehead. It is thus the seal and the mark received that distinguish the two groups of worshipers, respectively, in the final crisis.

The sealed worshipers of the true God in Revelation 12–14 are further characterized as those who "keep the commandments of God" (Rev. 14:12; cf. 12:17). Those who have the mark of the beast contrast with those "who keep the commandments of God" (14:9–12). It seems that the mark of the beast "has to do with the violation of the commandments of God," while the seal of God has to do with "the keeping of them."[58] This suggests clearly that in "the final crisis the commandments of God will emerge as a standard of loyalty" to God.[59] The context indicates, however, that not just any of God's commandments but rather the first four commandments of the Decalogue— those which concern one's relationship to God and worship—will become the central issue in the final crisis. The sea beast's activities are portrayed as part of a well-planned strategy arranged against these four commandments (see *Notes* on Rev. 13:16).

Revelation 14:6–12 indicates clearly that the Sabbath, as Johnsson states, "in particular will be the litmus test; one's relationship to it will disclose his basic relationship to God and His law."[60] When the final appeal is made to the earth dwellers to worship the true God (14:7) rather than obey the beast's demand to worship the satanic trinity and receive the mark of the beast (14:9), it is clearly done "in the context of the fourth commandment."[61] Thus the author of Revelation understood the Sabbath to be the crucial issue that concerns proper worship and relationship with God in the final conflict. As the Sabbath is the distinctive sign of obedience by God's faithful people (cf. Exod. 31:12–17; Ezek. 20:12, 20), so the mark of the beast, the counterfeit

Sabbath, is the sign of obedience to the beast. The mark of the beast thus functions as the substitution of God's commandments for human commandments (including the human-established false Sabbath, substituted for the seventh-day Sabbath, which is the distinctive sign of belonging and loyalty to God).

13:17 In order to secure compliance with the demand to receive the mark of the beast on the right hand or on the forehead, the measure is taken that ***no one may buy or sell except the one who has the mark, that is, the name of the beast, or the number of his name.*** The phrase "to buy or sell" might be understood here in either a literal or figurative meaning. It may refer to economic sanctions against those who do not submit to the demands of the power in control, such as the example of the faithful Christians in Thyatira who refused to participate in the activities of the trade guilds (Rev. 2:19–22). On the other hand, the highly figurative context of Revelation 13 suggests the figurative meaning of buying and selling. Revelation 18 describes "the merchants of the earth" who have become wealthy through their business with the great harlot Babylon (18:3, 15). At the judgment of the harlot, those merchants mourn because they are not able to do business with Babylon anymore (18:11–19). "The merchants" are further described in the text as "the great men of the earth" deceived by Babylon's magic spell (18:23). We have already pointed out the relationship between Revelation 13 and 17–18. "The merchants" of Revelation 18 are the figurative commercial salespeople of Babylon who sell and distribute the spiritual merchandise of her corrupt doctrines and policies. In light of Revelation 18, the buying and selling of Revelation 13 might be a symbolic way of expressing the social isolation and hardship that the faithful and sealed followers of Christ will endure at the time when the whole world will be buying Babylon's corrupt doctrines and policies.[62] Those who worship the beast buy Babylon's merchandise and serve her purposes to destroy those who remain faithful to Christ until the point of death.

13:18 In the conclusion of the section, readers are invited to identify the first beast coming out of the sea. ***Here is wisdom: Let the one who has understanding count the number of the beast, for it is a human number; and his number is 666.*** John urges readers here not to exercise brilliant intellectual ability or mathematical skills, but rather to seek divine wisdom and discernment in order to perceive the deceptive character of the beast and to protect themselves from the deception (the same as in Rev. 17:9).[63] John's reference to the beast's number will help the faithful Christians recognize "the true character and identity" of this end-time anti-Christ power.[64] Only through this divinely imparted wisdom will they finally be able to stand as overcomers "over the beast and his image and the number of his name" (15:2).

The number 666 of the beast from the sea is "a human number" (or "the number of humanity"), thus having something to do with human rather than divine characteristics and qualities. It is the typical number of Babylon. Six symbolizes a falling short of the divine ideal symbolized in the number seven. It appears that the triple six—**hex**akosioi **hex**ēkonta **hex** in Greek ("**six** hundred **six**ty **six**")—stands for the satanic triumvirate in contrast to the triple seven of the Godhead in Revelation 1:4–6 (see *Exposition* on Rev. 1:4–6). This leads to the conclusion that the number 666 functions as a parody of the divine name of perfection. Philip E. Hughes states:

> The number six has understandably been regarded as a symbol of man, in that it falls short of seven, which is the divine number. On this basis the threefold six may be understood as indicative of a human or humanistic trinity, that is to say a counterfeit of the divine Trinity, with all the pretensions to supreme power and authority that such a counterfeit implies. It may perhaps be inferred from the context that this pseudo-trinity is that of Satan (the dragon) plus antichrist (the first beast) plus the false prophet (the second beast), who are united in the one diabolical objective, namely, to dethrone the Creator and to enthrone the creature and to substitute the image of the beast for the image of God in man.[65]

The number 666 identifies the true character of the beast from the sea as the end-time power exalting itself against God and claiming the loyalty and worship of the world for itself. The beast is described as carrying "names of blasphemy" (13:1; cf. 17:3). This means that he claims "names and honorific titles which belong to God or Christ alone."[66] He succeeds in deceiving "those who dwell on the earth." Having been deceived, his followers are forced to receive the mark of the beast, which is the name of the beast or the number of his name. The symbolic receiving of the mark of the beast involves the acceptance of the beast's name "on their right hand or on their forehead" (Rev. 13:16–17). As G. K. Beale stresses, to be identified with someone's name is to partake of that person's character.[67]

The followers of Christ, however, are protected from the end-time deception by having the seal of God which contains Christ's "name and the name of his Father written on their foreheads" (Rev. 14:1; cf. 2:17). A person is sealed by the seal of the

Holy Spirit as the sign of a genuine Christian who belongs to God (2 Cor. 1:21–22; Eph. 1:13–14; 4:30). Only the Holy Spirit can endow God's people with spiritual discernment to perceive the deceptive nature of Satan's end-time activities and the ability to withstand them and remain loyal to Christ and render their worship to him. Thus John's call for "wisdom" and "understanding" refers to the mind enlightened by the Holy Spirit rather than to a brilliant mathematical intellect.

A RETROSPECT ON REVELATION 13

Revelation 13 portrays in symbolic language the great preparation for the end-time, worldwide crisis between the forces of Christ and Satan—the battle of Armageddon (further described in Revelation 16:12–16 through chapters 17–18). One thing seems very certain here: Satan himself is depicted as the power standing behind the forces of this world—"the evil intelligence that makes war on the saints of God."[68] Satan is presented as a fearsome figure (12:3), and together with his two allies he engages in the final war in a way that every human being is affected. As Strand states, "*real* people are very much involved in *real* struggles as they choose either loyalty to God and the Lamb or to the antidivine forces."[69]

Beginning with Revelation 12:17, John the revelator makes every effort to warn readers of the book about Satan's firm determination to win the final battle. A careful analysis of the text suggests that the final crisis will be the battle for the minds of people. Beatrice S. Neall notes: "Both rival powers wish to control the mind and behavior. The followers of the Lamb all have the name of God upon their foreheads; whereas the followers of the beast have the mark on the forehead (indicating belief, allegiance) or the hand only (indicating forced obedience without mental assent)."[70] In order to claim the allegiance of the world for himself, Satan prepares a new strategy of deception. Having associated himself with two allies, portrayed symbolically by the sea beast and the earth beast, he will place in motion "a massive counterfeit of the true God"[71] and his saving work on behalf of human beings. The purpose of the counterfeit is to deceive the world. Jesus warned: "For false christs and false prophets will arise and will show great signs and wonders, so as to mislead, if possible, even the elect" (Matt. 24:24). Jon Paulien stresses, "the end-time deception is of such magnitude that even God's faithful people will find themselves troubled by its severity."[72] The battle in the final crisis is clearly not about political events, but rather about "a battle for the mind of every human being on the earth" to side either with God and his faithful people or to choose to follow Satan and his allies.[73]

It is noteworthy to observe a number of verbal and conceptual parallels which exist between Revelation 13 and Daniel 3, including "the image," worship of the image (Dan. 3:5), the death threat for not worshiping the image (Dan. 3:6), universality (Dan. 3:2), and the number "six" with regard to the image (Dan. 3:1). This suggests that while writing Revelation 13, John had Daniel 3 in mind. He tells us that the story of Daniel 3 will be repeated at the time of the end on a worldwide scale, however. What appears very clear is that the true test of the final crisis will be worship. Just as in the case of the three young men in Daniel 3, God will triumphantly intervene in delivering his faithful people and defeating the forces of evil.

It is especially important to keep in mind that the end-time activities of the religious-political power symbolically portrayed in the sea beast are still a matter of future fulfillment. At this point, Hans K. LaRondelle calls for caution:

> We need to realize that Revelation 13:11–17 describes symbolically the final deception of the world in the future. The formation of "the image" of the beast is still an incomplete fulfillment. Also the mark of the beast has not yet been imposed on humanity. This realization should prevent any interpreter from being dogmatic regarding the future fulfillment of Revelation 13:11–17.[74]

At this point a caution is necessary against rash judgments many make when it comes to the identity of the two beasts of Revelation 13. Followers of Christ must manifest not only Christian love but also divine discernment as they proclaim "the everlasting gospel" and warn the world of the deceptive nature of Satan and the two beasts as his allies. Deciphering which group of people, or which individuals, belong to God's people is often impossible for human beings. It is God's prerogative to pass final judgment upon the people. One may apply the same principle of discernment to political and religious establishments as well. Since this earth is the valley of sin in which God himself is working to save human beings from Satan and his allies, and since this world is comprised of human beings who struggle on all levels, including political and religious ones, we must recognize that rarely is an institution entirely evil. In all times and in all institutions God has his agents working for him. The very fact that it takes Satan so much time and so much cunning and planning to deceive men and women indicates that the Holy Spirit works just as hard to counter Satan's counterfeits. As God's duty alone, any passing of judgment by human beings is irresponsible behavior and often hinders the objectives of the gospel.

This does not suggest, however, that we should not identify evil behavior and wrong policies. Christians must remember that their place on this earth is to be light and salt. Only the love of Christ as manifested on the cross of Calvary will move people to accept him, the one who is the only hope and source of life for the human race, and commit their lives in obedience to him.

Three groups of people exist today: those who love the gospel and are committed to God, those who hate the gospel and God, and the vast majority of people who are indifferent to or ignorant of the gospel. The last group is not necessarily against God, nor has it necessarily sided with Satan. However, Revelation 13 makes it clear that as the end of time approaches, polarization will take place, and all will have to make a stand for either God or Satan. One group will worship and fear the true God (Rev. 11:1, 18; 14:7; 19:10), and the other will reject the gospel and worship the dragon and the beast (Rev. 13:4–15; 14:9–11; 16:2; 19:20). The key issue in the final crisis will be centered on the matter of proper worship. Christ's end-time followers will be characterized by their total commitment to God and their readiness to obey his commandments, including the one that points to the true day of worship to God, the Creator and Savior (Rev. 14:7, 14). Those not truly committed to God—those who do not have unreserved love for the gospel—will find themselves completely exposed to the end-time deception and will most likely be deceived.

What matters in the final crisis, accordingly, is love for the truth (2 Thess. 2:10). The deceived world will follow the religious system based on sensationalism and emotional expressions that will take the place of the gospel religion that involves heart and conduct. Love for the truth is the only hope for God's people in the final crisis. We may apply the same principle here for those who did not or will not live in the end time: sooner or later in life we all face issues and make decisions that place us on one side or the other. As the history of this world approaches its end, the book of Revelation appeals to God's people to take the Bible and, in a heart-searching spirit, to study the prophetic word for themselves. This is what Peter had in mind when he wrote: "So we have the prophetic word made more sure, to which you do well to pay attention as to a lamp shining in a dark place, until the day dawns and the morning star arises in your hearts" (2 Pet. 1:19). Total commitment to God and love of the gospel is the secret of victory for God's end-time people in the closing days of this world's history.

ENDNOTES

1. Johnsson, 24.
2. Bauer, 455–456.
3. Johnsson, 23.
4. Corsini, 227.
5. Charles R. Erdman, *The Revelation of John* (Philadelphia, PA: Westminster Press, 1936), 112.
6. Ladd, 223.
7. Johnsson, 17.
8. Ibid., 23.
9. Ezell, 77.
10. Ladd, 223.
11. Fiorenza, *Revelation*, 83.
12. Beatrice S. Neall, *The Concept of Character in the Apocalypse with Implications for Character Education* (Washington, DC: University Press of America, 1983), 137.
13. On the *Nero revividus*, see Bauckham, *The Climax of Prophecy*, 407–423, 441–452; Aune, *Revelation 6–16*, 737–740; for the assessment and criticism of the view, see Strand, "The Seven Heads," 191–200; Paul S. Minear, "The Wounded Beast," *Journal of Biblical Literature* 72 (1953): 93–101.
14. Johnsson, 22; see also Bauckham, *The Climax of Prophecy*, 423–452.
15. Johnsson, 22.
16. As correctly observed by Roy C. Naden, *The Lamb among the Beasts* (Hagerstown, MD: Review and Herald, 1996), 196.
17. Thomas, *Revelation 8–22*, 292.
18. This interpretation was first suggested by John N. Andrews who argued that the eschatological Babylon comprises the whole corrupt Christianity that included altogether the Papal, Greek, and Protestant churches (see Alberto R. Timm, *The Sanctuary and the Three Angels' Messages: Integrating Factors in the Development of Seventh-day Adventist Doctrines,* Adventist Theological Society Dissertation Series, vol. 5 [Berrien Springs, MI: Adventist Theological Society Publications, 1995], 307–308).
19. LaRondelle, *How to Understand the End-Time Prophecies*, 302.
20. Johnsson, 28.
21. See LaRondelle, *How to Understand the End-Time Prophecies*, 302–303.
22. *The Seventh-day Adventist Bible Commentary*, 7:820.
23. Ulrich Wilckens, *"Charagma,"Theological Dictionary of the New Testament*, ed. G. Kittel and G. W. Bromiley (Grand Rapids, MI: Eerdmans, 1964–1976), 9:416–417; Ladd, 185.
24. Johnsson, 30.

25. Meredith G. Kline, *The Structure of Biblical Authority*, 2d ed. (Grand Rapids, MI: Eerdmans, 1975), 120.

26. Johnsson, 30.

27. As rightly observed by Paulien, *What the Bible Says about the End-Time*, 125–126.

28. Johnsson, 30.

29. Bauer, 1098.

30. Aune, *Revelation 6–16*, 771.

31. Irenaeus was the first to calculate "the number of the beast" through the process of gematria (see *Against Heresies* 5:29–30); *The Ante-Nicene Fathers*, 1:558–560.

32. For the application of the number of the beast to Nero, see Bauckham, *The Climax of Prophecy*, 385–407; Aune, *Revelation 6–16*, 770–771; Barclay, "Great Themes of the New Testament: V. Revelation xiii," *Expository Times* 70 (1958–1959): 260–264, 292–296.

33. Beale, 721.

34. Ibid.

35. Joan Oates, *Babylon*, 2d ed. (London: Thames and Hudson, 1986), 185–186.

36. The following ideas are borrowed from Thiele's *Outline Studies in Revelation*, 216–217.

37. Neall, *The Concept of Character in the Apocalypse*, 153.

38. Hoeksema, 475.

39. Neall, *The Concept of Character in the Apocalypse*, 154.

40. Metzger, *Breaking the Code*, 76.

41. Beale, 721.

42. Ibid., 722.

43. LaRondelle, *How to Understand the End-Time Prophecies*, 311.

44. Fiorenza, *Revelation*, 84.

45. Charles, 1:358.

46. Paulien, *What the Bible Says about the End-Time*, 109.

47. Ladd, 183.

48. Desmond Ford, 575.

49. Johnsson, 22; see Bauckham, *The Climax of Prophecy*, 434, 446–448.

50. Johnsson, 29.

51. Desmond Ford, 575.

52. Johnsson, 29.

53. Thomas, *Revelation 8–22*, 179–180.

54. Ladd, 185.

55. Neall, "Sealed Saints and the Tribulation," 255.

56. Ibid., 257.

57. Paulien, *What the Bible Says about the End-Time*, 122. (Original quotation was italicized.)

58. Neall, "Sealed Saints and the Tribulation," 257.

59. Johnsson, 30.

60. Ibid.

61. Paulien, *What the Bible Says about the End-Time*, 126.

62. *The Seventh-day Adventist Bible Commentary*, 7:864.

63. Johnson, 534; Beale, 723.

64. Johnson, 534.

65. Hughes, 154–155.

66. H. Bietenhard, "Name," *The New International Dictionary of New Testament Theology*, ed. Colin Brown (Grand Rapids, MI: Zondervan, 1986), 2:653.

67. Beale, 723.

68. Tenney, 175.

69. Strand, "An Overlooked Old Testament Background to Revelation 11:1," 318.

70. Neall, "Sealed Saints and the Tribulation," 256.

71. Paulien, *What the Bible Says about the End-Time*, 111.

72. Ibid., 113.

73. Ibid., 136.

74. LaRondelle, *How to Understand the End-Time Prophecies,* 311–312.

Revelation 13 portrays the great preparation for the final crisis of earth's history. As the end approaches, both heaven and the forces of darkness intensify their appeals. The satanic triumvirate seeks to deceive people on the earth, leading them to worship the sea beast and Satan. Revelation 14 points to God's activities through his faithful remnant, warning the people of the world that their only hope is in accepting the gospel. The opening part of the chapter identifies and describes God's end-time faithful remnant (Rev. 14:1–5). Revelation 14:6–13 contains the proclamation of God's last warning message to the world. The rest of the chapter portrays in symbolic language the great harvest of the world after the final gospel proclamation is completed (Rev. 14:14–20).

GOD'S REDEEMED PEOPLE (14:1–5)

The opening of Revelation 14 contrasts with chapter 13. While the majority of people living in the end-time succumb to the worldwide deception and render their allegiance to the satanic trinity, God has a true remnant of those who withstand the final conflict and remain loyal to him until the very end.

¹And I saw, and behold, the Lamb standing on Mount Zion, and with him 144,000 having his name and the name of his Father written on their foreheads. ²And I heard a voice from heaven like a sound of many waters and like a sound of great thunder, and the voice that I heard was like harpers playing on their harps. ³And they sing as it were a new song before the throne and before the four living beings and the elders; and no one was able to learn the

**song except the 144,000 who have been redeemed from the earth.
⁴These are those who have not been defiled with women, for they
are virgins. They are the followers of the Lamb wherever he goes.
They were redeemed from men as firstfruits to God and to the
Lamb, ⁵and in their mouth a lie was not found; they are blameless.**

NOTES

14:1 *Mount Zion.* Mount Zion in the Old Testament is seen as the center of God's rule in the messianic kingdom. God spoke to the Psalmist: "I have installed my King on Zion, My holy mountain" (Pss. 2:6; 48:1–2; cf. Isa. 24:23). And Micah prophesied: "The Lord will reign over them in Mount Zion" (Mic. 4:7). Isaiah, Joel, and Obadiah refer to Mount Zion as the place of deliverance for God's people and their final victory (Isa. 59:20; Joel 2:32; Obad. 17). This idea appears again in the New Testament where Mount Zion becomes "the city of the living God, the heavenly Jerusalem" (Heb. 12:22). Jerusalem in Revelation stands in contrast to Babylon (see "Overview: Revelation 12–22:5").

144,000. See *Notes* on Revelation 7:4.

14:3 *They sing as it were a new song.* Some commentators suggest that these singers and harpers are not the 144,000, but rather are angels with a message which only the 144,000 can understand. However, such an understanding overlooks the fact that in Revelation 15:2–3 the 144,000 are clearly the harpers and the singers singing the song of Moses and of the Lamb. In addition, when later (in Rev. 19:1, 6) John hears the redeemed singing in heaven, their voices are like the sound of many waters and like great thunder.

Redeemed. The Greek word *agorazō* means "to buy," "to purchase" (Rev. 3:18, 18:11; cf. 1 Cor. 6:20), or "to redeem" (Rev. 5:9; cf. Rom. 3:24).

14:4 *Defiled.* The Greek word *molunō* means "to defile" (conscience, 1 Cor. 8:7) or "to soil" (robes, Rev. 3:4). The aorist tense in Greek suggests action at a specific point in time. In this case, as the *Seventh-day Adventist Bible Commentary* notes, it refers to "the time when the coalition of religious elements, symbolized by 'women'...will bring every pressure to bear upon the saints" to renounce their loyalty to God and worship the beast. "Any yielding would be an act of defilement."[1]

Women. The symbol of a faithful woman in Revelation is used consistently with reference to God's people (Rev. 12:1; 19:7–8; 22:17), while a prostitute symbolizes the apostate and unfaithful (Rev. 17–18; see further *Notes* on Rev. 12:1). In the Old Testament, the apostasy of Israel from God is often described as adultery. In Revelation, the kings and all the nations of the earth have committed fornication with the great harlot Babylon (Rev. 14:8; 17:2, 4; 18:3, 9; 19:2); by contrast, the 144,000 have "refused to defile themselves" by worshiping the beast but have "kept themselves pure unto God."[2] The plural form "women" refers most likely to the great prostitute Babylon and her daughters (Rev. 17:5).

Virgins. The Greek word *parthenos* usually means "virgin," but it can be used with reference to formerly married persons and widows. It can apply to both men and women.[3] The term is often used metaphorically in the Bible, signifying fidelity to God. The word "virgin," however, does not suggest that there has never been any unfaithfulness; Israel, although often described as adulterous and unfaithful in her relationship with God, is yet often called a virgin when she comes back to God (2 Kings 19:21; Isa. 37:22; Jer. 14:17; 18:13; 31:4; Lam. 2:13; Amos 5:2). In the New Testament, the word is used with reference to the church. Paul was eager to present the Christians in Corinth as "a pure virgin" to Christ (2 Cor. 11:2–3). In Matthew 25:1–3, God's people awaiting the Second Coming are described as ten virgins. The 144,000 are virgins in the sense that they do not defile themselves with the fornication of worshiping the beast, the great harlot Babylon and her daughters, but have rather kept themselves faithful to Christ.[4]

Firstfruits to God. The Greek word *aparchē* is used in the Septuagint for the firstfruits of the harvest offered to God in the sanctuary. The word is used figuratively in the Bible with reference to the redeemed saints set apart for God as his special offering.[5] Thus, for instance, the prophet Jeremiah refers to Israel redeemed from Egypt as "holy to the Lord, the firstfruits of his harvest; all who devoured her were held guilty, and disaster overtook them" (Jer. 2:3, NIV). Here Jeremiah portrays redeemed Israel, the firstfruits of the harvest to God, as distinct from the antagonistic nations who oppressed her and are now to be judged.[6] Similarly, James refers to redeemed Christians as "the first fruits among his creatures" (James 1:18). It appears that the reference to the 144,000 as the "firstfruits to God" in Revelation 14:4 must be understood in light of the idea expressed in Jeremiah 2:3. These 144,000 are redeemed or purchased as the firstfruits of the end-time harvest (the wheat harvest, Rev. 14:14–16), in contrast to "the unbelieving nations about to be judged" (the grape harvest, Rev. 14:17–20).[7]

14:5 *Lie.* "Lie" (*pseudos*) here seems to be more than common untruthfulness; it is "the lying of the antichrist powers" (1 John 1:5–10; 2:21–22).[8] This kind of lie characterizes the activities of the end-time satanic trinity (Rev. 13:14; 16:13–14; 19:20), and is not found in the 144,000 (cf. Rev. 21:27; 22:15).

Blameless. In the Greek Old Testament, the word *amōmos* is a technical term for sacrifices to be offered to God, in the sense of being unblemished and "sacrificially perfect."[9] In the New Testament, the word is used with reference to Christ (Heb. 9:14; 1 Pet. 1:19) and to the lives of Christians who are to be holy and without blemish before God (Eph. 1:4; 5:27; Phil. 2:15; Col. 1:22; Jude 24). The 144,000 are the blameless firstfruits to God, referring not to moral, sinless perfection but to their fidelity to Christ and their refusal to defile themselves when the people in the world renounce their loyalty to God and commit fornication with the great harlot Babylon and her daughters (Rev. 14:8; 17:2, 4; 18:3, 9; 19:2). Beatrice S. Neall explains: "To be *amōmos* is not a quality unique to the 144,000, a state of perfection achieved only by those who go through the great tribulation of the last days. It is God's evaluation of all saints, Old Testament or New, who, like the 144,000 have 'washed their robes and made them white in the blood of the Lamb' (Rev. 7:14). It is this washing, and the walking with the Lamb, that make them *spotless.*"[10]

447

EXPOSITION

14:1–3 In the next stage of the vision, John's attention turns to *the Lamb standing on Mount Zion* and the 144,000 marked with his name and the name of his Father on their foreheads. This echoes what Joel prophesied centuries earlier:

> And it will come about
> That whoever calls on the name of the Lord
> Will be delivered;
> For on Mount Zion and in Jerusalem
> There will be those who escape,
> As the Lord has said,
> Even among the survivors whom the Lord calls. (Joel 2:32)

Here, in fulfillment of Joel's prophecy, John observes a group of people standing on Mount Zion, calling on the name of the Lord. Revelation 14 describes the same group of God's people as that described earlier in Revelation 7. However, while in Revelation 7 they are sealed in order to be able to stand on the great day of God's wrath (cf. Rev. 6:17), and are subsequently seen as standing before the throne of God (7:9), here in Revelation 14 they are standing on Mount Zion. In Revelation, Mount Zion signifies the "eschatological victory of God"[11]—the place of deliverance for God's faithful end-time people. The 144,000 are clearly the remnant of the woman's offspring (Rev. 12:17); as God's end-time sealed people they have passed through the final crisis, and are now with Christ, eternally secure, celebrating the great victory over the forces of darkness.

The 144,000 are seen as having Christ's *name and the name of his Father written on their foreheads.* Just as those serving the beast bear the symbolic mark with the name of the beast on their foreheads, so the 144,000 have the name of the living God on their foreheads. This reception of a name on the forehead signifies "conformity to the character of Satan or God."[12] It was promised that the faithful in Philadelphia would receive "the name of my God and the name of the city of my God, the new Jerusalem which descends from heaven from my God, and my new name" (Rev. 3:12). "The city of my God" is Mount Zion where John sees the redeemed standing with the Lamb. This signifies "their eternal citizenship," which is entirely different from the fate of those who bear the name of the beast on their foreheads (cf. Rev. 13:16–17)[13] and who are identified as "those who dwell on the earth" (Rev. 13:14). Thus the name on the foreheads of the 144,000 denotes their wholehearted commitment to God, and citizenship in heaven, at a time when most people in the world choose to render their loyalty and total commitment to Satan and his allies.

John hears a song being sung by the chorus of the redeemed 144,000 in heaven. The sound of the music is like that *of many waters and like a sound of great thunder* and like *harpers playing on their harps.* In the same way, John later likens the chorus of the redeemed in heaven to the sound of many waters and to the sound of great thunder (Rev. 19:1, 6). The redeemed saints sing *as it were a new song* before the throne; *no one was able to learn the song except the 144,000 who have been redeemed from the earth.* In Revelation 15:3, this new song is called "the song of Moses and of the Lamb," a reference to the special song sung by the people of Israel in celebrating their miraculous deliverance through the Red Sea (Exod. 15). Thus, this new song is one of deliverance and salvation; the 144,000 have come from "the great tribulation" (Rev. 7:14). Now they are portrayed as Israel of old; after having passed through the Red Sea, they are standing on the other side. They have experienced deliverance in the final crisis like no other human beings in history. This is why no other group is able to learn the new song—it is the song of redemption (cf. Rev. 7:14–15). The 144,000 belong to God, and they celebrate their redemption before his throne.

14:4–5 Next, John identifies the 144,000 redeemed saints. They are described as *virgins* who *have not been defiled with women.* This must be understood symbolically. They are virgins in the sense that they have resisted all defiling relationships with the great harlot Babylon, with whom it is said that all the nations of the earth have committed fornication (Rev. 14:8; 17:2; 18:3). Entirely loyal to Christ, *they are the followers of the Lamb wherever he goes.* On earth they put Christ first, choosing to maintain a relationship with him no matter what the cost. Their loyalty has been severely tested, but they have victoriously withstood the end-time deception. Now they are following Christ, and nobody and nothing is able to separate them from his love.

They were redeemed from men as firstfruits to God and to the Lamb. "They were redeemed" is a metaphorical expression for "the release of someone from slavery."[14] That they are "redeemed from men" means that they "no longer belong to the world."[15] They are redeemed at the price of the blood of Christ on the cross of Calvary (Rev. 5:9). In the portrayal of the end-time harvest, the 144,000 are described as the wheat harvest (Rev. 14:14–16). They are redeemed as the firstfruits of the harvest "to God and to the Lamb" (cf. James 1:18). Now, as his special offering, they are brought to his sanctuary on Mount Zion, while the wicked, the grape harvest, are about to experience the judgments of God (Rev. 14:17–20).

The final characteristic of the 144,000 is that *in their mouth a lie was not found.* Several centuries earlier, Zephaniah prophesied: "The remnant of Israel will do no wrong and tell no lies, nor will a deceitful tongue be found in their mouths" (3:13). Lying is one of the characteristics of those who are excluded from the New Jerusalem (Rev. 21:27; 22:15). Paul said of the pagans that they "exchanged the truth of God for a lie" (Rom. 1:25). Complete truthfulness as another characteristic of the 144,000 becomes especially significant in the light of the fact that deception characterizes Satan's end-time activities (2 Thess. 2:9–11; Rev. 13:14; 19:20). While the whole world refusing to "receive the love of the truth so as to be saved" (2 Thess. 2:10) is deceived to believe the lie (2 Thess. 2:11), God's end-time people hold firmly and faithfully to the truth.

Finally, the 144,000 are found *blameless* as the firstfruits of the harvest. Just as Jesus was blameless while he was on this earth (Heb. 9:14; 1 Pet. 1:19), so Christ's end-time followers are seen as blameless (Eph. 1:4; 5:27; Phil. 2:15; Col. 1:22; Jude 24). This blamelessness does not refer to absolute moral perfection, but rather to their fidelity to Christ. To be blameless means to walk with God just as Noah (Gen. 6:9) and Abraham (Gen. 17:1) did. The 144,000 are "the followers of the Lamb wherever he goes" (Rev. 14:4). In the closing days of this world's history, when the majority renounce their loyalty to God and side with the satanic trinity, the 144,000 reflect the true character of Christ as acceptable to God. "Therefore, beloved," Peter wrote, "since you look for these things, be diligent to be found by Him in peace, spotless and blameless" (2 Pet. 3:14). To be found "in peace" means to be "in relationship with Christ" (cf. Rom. 5:1). The 144,000 are fully loyal and in a continuous, close relationship with Christ.

THE MESSAGE OF THE FIRST ANGEL (14:6–7)

In his eschatological discourse, Jesus stated that one sign of the end would be the proclamation of the gospel in the whole world (Matt. 24:14), the fulfillment of which is described in Revelation 14.[16] It indicates that at the time of the end God will send to the inhabitants of the earth his warning message, described in a symbolic portrayal of three angels flying in mid-heaven proclaiming God's everlasting gospel to "those who dwell upon the earth."

⁶And I saw another angel flying in midheaven, having an eternal gospel to proclaim to those who dwell on the earth, and to every nation and tribe and tongue and people, ⁷saying with a loud voice: "Fear God and give him glory, for the hour of his judgment has come, and worship the one who made the heaven and earth and sea and fountains of waters."

NOTES

14:6 *Those who dwell on the earth.* See *Notes* on Revelation 6:10.

14:7 *Fear God.* To fear God (Greek *phobeomai*, "to fear," "to reverence") is a well-known concept in the Old Testament. It conveys the idea of taking God seriously in life by following him and obeying his commandments. Fearing God denotes a relationship with God and full surrender to his will (cf. 1 Sam. 12:14, 24; 2 Chron. 6:31; Neh. 7:2; Job 1:9; Ps. 40:3; Jer. 32:39; 44:10; Hag. 1:12). When, for instance, Israel saw the great power of God against the Egyptians, the people feared him and believed (Exod. 14:31). The servants of God are often referred to as the ones fearing God (Gen. 22:12; 1 Kings 18:3, 12; 2 Kings 4:1; Pss. 22:23; 33:18; Mal. 3:16; 4:2). To fear God is the beginning of wisdom (Ps. 111:10; Prov. 1:7; 9:10). Fearing God results always in right doing (cf. Exod. 18:21; Lev. 19:14, 32; 25:17, 36, 43) and avoiding evil (Job 1:1, 8; Prov. 3:7; 16:6).

Give him glory. Giving God glory is the aftereffect of fearing God. When a person fears God, he lives a life of glorifying God by keeping his commandments. Jesus made it clear to his disciples: "By this is My Father glorified, that you bear much fruit, and so prove to be My disciples" (John 15:8). Jesus himself glorified the Father in accomplishing the work the Father gave him to do (John 17:4). Christians give glory to God when they value themselves as God values them (1 Cor. 6:19–20). In all their endeavors, Christians must glorify God (1 Cor. 10:31). The exhortation "fear God and give him glory" reflects the appeal of Moses to Israel before they entered the promised land—to fear the Lord, to obey him, and to keep his commandments (Deut. 6:13, 17; 10:12–13; 13:4). Elsewhere in the Old Testament, fearing God and obeying him by keeping his commandments always go together (Deut. 5:29; 6:2; 8:6; 17:19; 31:12; Pss. 111:10; 112:1; 119:63; 128:1; Jer. 44:10). According to Solomon, fearing God and keeping his commandments is the first duty of a human being (Eccl. 12:13). It is in the sense of obeying God and his commandments that the giving of glory to God in Revelation 14:7 must be understood. God's end-time people in Revelation are referred to as those who fear God (Rev. 11:18; 15:4; 19:5) and keep his commandments (cf. Rev. 12:17; 14:12).

His judgment has come. The Greek word for "judgment" here is *krisis* and refers primarily to the action of judging (Rev. 16:7; 18:10; 19:2);[17] in contrast, *krima* denotes primarily the result of an action, "verdict," "the sentence of judgment" (cf. Rev. 17:1; 20:4).[18] What has been translated in English as "has come" is in Greek the ingressive aorist pointing to the beginning of an action that took place at a point in time in the past. Some assume that "has come" is to be understood as the so-called prophetic perfect (a past tense used to describe a future event), as, for instance, in Revelation 14:8.[19] The conjunction "for" or "because" (*hoti*) indicates, however, as Gregory K. Beale observes, that the commencement of the judgment is the reason the command is issued to fear God and give him glory. "Those addressed are not warned to give glory *before* the time of punishment arrives but 'because' (*hoti*) the time has arrived."[20] "The hour of his judgment" pointed to by the first angel refers to the judgment, the first phase of which takes place *before* the Second Coming and its second phase (the final judgment) *after* the millennium (Rev. 20). Revelation 14:14–20 indicates that the destiny of every person is to be decided before the Second Coming and the final judgment. Christ will come to bring his reward with him, in order to "give to each as his work is" (Rev. 22:12). The final judgment after the millennium (Rev. 20:11–15) is the executive judgment that carries into execution that which the pre-advent judgment has ascertained. All decisions with reference to those who are included in the Kingdom and those who are excluded from it are brought before the throne at the pre-advent judgment. Jesus makes it very clear that the faithful one does not have a part in the final judgment, having already received "eternal life, and does not come into judgment, but has passed out of death into life" (John 5:24).

Who made the heaven and earth and sea and fountains of waters. This clause echoes the fourth commandment of the Decalogue: "the Lord made the heavens and the earth, the sea and all that is in them" (Exod. 20:11). One may notice the strong verbal parallels with the text in the Septuagint:

Exodus 20:11 LXX: *epoiēse ...ton ouranon kai tēn gēn kai tēn thalassan kai panta ta en autois* ("he made the heaven and the earth and the sea and all things in them").

Revelation 14:7b: *tō poiēsanti ton ouranon kai tēn gēn kai thalassan kai pēgas hudatō* (the one who made the heaven and earth and sea and springs of water).

The editors of the fourth edition of the USB Greek New Testament indicate in the margins that Revelation 14:7b reflects on Exodus 20:11. Thus, the appeal of the first angel to worship the creator God in Rev. 14:7 is given in the context of the fourth commandment of the Decalogue.

EXPOSITION

Having observed the redeemed multitude standing victoriously on Mount Zion, John's attention turns to an angel calling all people to repent before God's judgments fall and mercy is no longer available.

14:6 The first angel is seen *flying in mid heaven* with a warning message to preach to *those who dwell on the earth.* "Those who dwell on the earth" in Revelation are the worshipers of the beast—the ones "whose names are not written in the book of life" (Rev. 13:8). This indicates that the final message is not for God's people but for unbelievers. This message is referred to as *an eternal gospel.* This is especially significant. It indicates that the end-time gospel, while relevant in particular to the people living in the closing period of earth's history, is not a different gospel from that preached by Paul. It is the same and unaltered gospel, the proclamation of which started at Pentecost. It is the good news about Christ, his ministry, his death on the cross and his resurrection, his ascension to heaven, and his subsequent enthronement on the heavenly throne from which he rules as Lord over the universe. It is also about his intercession and judgment, and his soon return to the earth. This everlasting gospel is to be proclaimed and heard in the closing days of this world's history (cf. Matt. 24:14).

This everlasting gospel is worldwide in scope; it is proclaimed to *every nation and tribe and tongue and people.* The reference to "every tribe and people and tongue and nation" is related to Revelation 10:11 where John is commissioned to prophesy again "concerning many peoples and nations and tongues and kings." It becomes evident that the commission given originally to John has a further implication for the church. This worldwide warning comes at the time when the sea beast is given authority "over every tribe and people and tongue and nation" and when all render their service and allegiance to Satan and worship him (Rev. 13:7–8). As Satan's end-time activities are worldwide in scope, so is the end-time gospel message. It is intended to reach people of "every nation and tribe and tongue and people," calling them back to worship the living God. What we actually have here is the fulfillment of Matthew 24:14. "This gospel of the kingdom shall be preached in the whole world as a testimony to all the nations, and then the end will come." In the scene of the three angels is given the final proclamation of the gospel to the world, calling all people back to worship the living God. It is not yet too late. Sinners still have time to repent and find the mercy and grace of God.[21]

14:7 Next John summarizes the content of the end-time gospel being proclaimed by the first angel. This gospel is proclaimed *with a loud voice*, which is a wake-up warning call to the inhabitants of the earth. It consists of two exhortations. The first is to *Fear God and give him glory.* Fearing God and giving him glory have a special meaning in Revelation (cf. 11:13; 14:7; 15:4). While the former designates a right relationship with God, the latter suggests obedience to his commandments. A person comes to fear God after recognizing the Lord's great power and works (Rev. 11:13; 15:4). Fearing God leads one to repentance (16:9; cf. 11:13). Thus, to fear God is to take him seriously, make a decisive turnaround in life, enter into a relationship with him, and be totally committed. God is then glorified through a life characterized by obedience to his commandments. This is what the appeal of the first angel is all about.

People are exhorted to fear God and give him glory because **the hour of his judgment has come.** The judgment referred to here is the first phase of the judgment (the pre-advent judgment) taking place in heaven *before* the Second Coming. This first phase of judgment denotes the action of judging rather than the execution of the judgment to take place *after* the millennium (Rev. 20:11–15). This judging takes place at the same time that the final proclamation of the gospel goes throughout the earth. Both have the same purpose; they draw a clear line of demarcation between those who are on God's side and those who are against him. The first angel's message makes it very clear that everybody living in the closing days of this world's history is held accountable to God with regard to his or her decision to accept or reject the gospel. The book of Ecclesiastes warns: "Fear God and keep His commandments....For God will bring every act to judgment, everything which is hidden, whether it is good or evil" (Eccl. 12:13–14). Paul states that every person must appear before the judgment seat of Christ to be recompensed for what he or she has done, whether good or evil (2 Cor. 5:10). Revelation 14:14–20 clearly indicates that the end-time gospel proclamation and the pre-advent judgment will conclude with the great separation between those who have chosen God and those who are lost. Christ will come "to give to each as his work is" (Rev. 22:12). In other words, as indicated in Revelation 11:18, he comes to give the reward to his servants, on one hand, and "to destroy the destroyers of the earth," on the other.

What is seen in the first angel's message is that the end-time judgment is a part of the everlasting gospel. To God's end-time people the word of judgment is good news. To them, judgment is the time when God will deal with all oppressing and persecuting powers in this world, and when he will finally vindicate his faithful people. This is the judgment which God's oppressed people have longed and prayed for throughout history; it is portrayed symbolically in the perennial plea of the martyred saints underneath the altar: "How long, O Lord?" (Rev. 6:10). The realization that they live in the time of the judgment signals to God's faithful people the "hope and prospect of their everlasting home."[22] To the unfaithful, however, "the word of God's judgment is a thing of terror."[23] To them God sends his end-time gospel in order to move them to repentance, for he does not wish "for any to perish but for all to come to repentance" (2 Pet. 3:9).

The first angel has a second exhortation to the inhabitants of the earth: ***Worship the One who made heaven and the earth and the sea and the fountains of waters.*** Those who fear God and give him glory are those who worship him (cf. Rev. 15:4). The central issue in the final crisis will be worship. Revelation makes clear that the test will not be denial of worship, but rather who is worshiped. At the time of the end, only two groups of people will be in the world: those who fear and worship the true God (11:1, 18; 14:7) and those who hate the truth and are worshipers of the dragon and the beast (13:4–8; 14:9–11). The worshipers of God are identified as those who have their names written in the book of life, while the beast-worshipers are identified as those "whose names are not written in the book of life of the Lamb slain from the foundation of the world" (13:8). The final conflict will draw a definite line of demarcation between the two groups. When the whole world turns to worship the beast and the satanic trinity (Rev. 13:12), God's end-time people are characterized by their total commitment to God and their readiness to obey his commandments, including the one that points to the true day of the worship of God as the sign between God and his people (cf. Exod. 31:13–17; Ezek. 20:12, 20).

If worship is the central issue in the final conflict, no wonder then that God sends his end-time gospel urging the inhabitants of the earth to take him seriously and worship him as the Creator, the only One worthy of worship (Rev. 14:7; cf. 19:10; 22:8–9). The exhortation to worship the true Creator God is especially significant for the end-time generation for at least two reasons. First, the exhortation has become especially relevant in the climate of the rise and popularity of the evolutionary theory that denies the validity of the biblical account of the creation and diminishes God's creative power.

Second, the exhortation to worship God—the maker of "the heaven and the earth and the sea and the fountains of waters"—is an evident allusion to the fourth commandment of the Decalogue. The fourth commandment requests that people keep the Sabbath because "in six days the Lord made the heavens and the earth, the sea and all that is in them, and rested on the seventh day; therefore the Lord blessed the Sabbath day and made it holy" (Exod. 20:11). The parallel between the language of the message of the first angel and that of the fourth commandment suggests that the call to worship God is given in the context of the relation to the fourth commandment. John makes clear that the proclamation of the end-time gospel includes an appeal to worship God in the context of the Sabbath command. This suggests, as Paulien notes, that the Sabbath will be "an integral part of the issue" in the final crisis, although "the issue...is not confined to the Sabbath."[24]

In concluding, the exhortations of the first angel clearly echo "Moses' appeal to Israel just before they entered the promised land"—to fear the Lord, obey him by keeping his commandments, and worship only him (Deut. 6:13, 17; 10:12–13; 13:4).[25] They also conclude the book of Ecclesiastes: "Fear God and keep his commandments, for this is the whole duty of man" (Eccl. 12:13, NIV). Before the conclusion of this world's history, God makes his last appeal to the inhabitants of the earth. It is not yet too late. People still have a chance to turn back to God and find forgiveness in his grace. As the song of the 144,000 indicates, many people will respond to the appeal of the first angel's message: "Who will not fear, O Lord, and glorify Your name? For You only are holy; because all the nations will come and worship before you, because your righteous acts have been manifested" (Rev. 15:4).

THE MESSAGE OF THE SECOND ANGEL (14:8)

A second angel appears on the scene, announcing briefly the fall of end-time Babylon. His proclamation shifts from the positive call to worship the true God made by the first angel to a description of the consequences of unbelief and rejecting the message.

> *[8]And another angel, the second one, followed saying: "Fallen, fallen is Babylon the great, who made all nations drink of the wine of the wrath of her fornication."*

NOTES

14:8 *Fallen, fallen.* The repeated verb "fallen" in Greek is an aorist announcing a future event. The futuristic use of the aorist in the Hebrew prophecy is known as the prophetic perfect in which a future event is described with the past tense as if it has already occurred (cf. Isa. 21:9; Jer. 51:8; Rev. 10:7). Here in the text, the fall of end-time Babylon to take place in the future is announced as if it has already occurred, thus underscoring the prophetic certainty of Babylon's future demise.[26]

Babylon the great. Here is the first mention of Babylon in Revelation. The theological concept of end-time Babylon the great in the New Testament is rooted in the role of ancient Babylon ("the gate of god") in the Old Testament. Babylon is a religious-political power opposing God and oppressing his people. From its beginning, it stands as an incarnation of godless power in opposition to the true God (cf. Gen. 11:1–9). Elsewhere in the Old Testament, Babylon represents the religious system that stands in opposition to the religion of the true God and tries to control the world. As such, it is portrayed as the traditional great enemy of God's people. The prophet Isaiah equates the king of Babylon with Lucifer (Isa. 14:12–14); in other words, Babylon's behavior and attitude towards God and his people become a symbol of Lucifer's behavior. The phrase "Babylon the great" in Revelation is used as a reminder of the self-boasting of Nebuchadnezzar: "Is this not Babylon the great, which I myself have built as a royal residence by the might of my power and for the glory of my majesty?" (Dan. 4:30). This boasting was met with the announcement of God's judgment over the kingdom (Dan. 4:31–32). Babylon was about to meet its end. Toward the close of the first century A.D., among both Jews and Christians, the cryptic name of Babylon was used with reference to Rome (cf. 1 Pet. 5:13).[27]

This theological meaning of end-time Babylon in Revelation is based on the theological denotation of ancient Babylon in the Old Testament. Revelation 17:1–13 describes Babylon in terms of a prostitute woman sitting on "many waters" and the beast. Both the waters and the beast stand for secular and political powers of the world. This indicates that Babylon in Revelation must be something other than the secular and political powers of the world. It rather represents the end-time worldwide religious confederacy made up of the satanic trinity (Rev. 16:19) arrayed against God and his people. Like Babylon of old, end-time Babylon exalts itself above God, taking the place of God (cf. 2 Thess. 2:3–4). Revelation 13 shows that this religious system counterfeits the Godhead. It will unite the apostate religious organizations and bring them into service to the satanic triumvirate in their opposition to God and his faithful people at the time of the end. The hatred that turned ancient Babylon against God and his covenant people will characterize this end-time worldwide confederacy (cf. Rev. 13:6). Revelation 17:2–4 shows that Babylon will make the nations drink of the wine of her fornication. Her activities will be endorsed and backed up by the governing secular and political powers of this world (Rev. 13:12–17). However, Revelation makes clear that Babylon will come to its final end once and for all. At the most critical moment, God will come to save and vindicate his people. John sees this end-time system split into three parts (Rev. 16:19); in other words, the satanic coalition will experience its unavoidable collapse. The description of the collapse of end-time Babylon in Revelation is based on the fall of ancient Babylon. This is the sense in which the theological concept of end-time Babylon the great is to be understood in the book of Revelation.

The wine of the wrath of her fornication. This statement blends two Old Testament concepts into one.[28] First, ancient Babylon is portrayed by the prophet Jeremiah in terms of a prostitute seducing a man into immorality by making him drink wine. Babylon is the "cup of the wine of wrath" in God's hand, urging all nations to drink of it (Jer. 25:15; 51:7). On the other side, Job says of the evil man: "Let him drink of the wrath of the Almighty" (Job 21:20). In Revelation 14:8, the acceptance of Babylon's seductive wine of fornication results in the drinking of God's wine of wrath (cf. 17:2; 18:3); that is, it brings as a consequence the judgment of God (cf. Rev. 14:9–10).

Fornication. The imagery of "immorality" as a symbol of unfaithfulness to God is drawn from the Old Testament (cf. Isa. 57:3–12; Ezek. 16:15, 26–29), and it continues into the New Testament (cf. James 4:4; Rev. 17:1–5). See *Notes* on Revelation 14:4.

EXPOSITION

14:8 The first angel calling people back to worship the true God is *followed* by the second angel who appears on the scene. The fact that this angel is referred to as "the second one" and that he "follows" the first one shows that the two messages are related. Actually, "the message of the second angel of Revelation 14 is the complement of the first. Men and women in all nations, as they are directed to return to the worship of the Creator, must be led to repudiate all systems and schemes, avowedly religious or otherwise, that run counter to allegiance to Christ."[29]

The second angel announces the collapse of end-time Babylon: *Fallen, fallen is Babylon the great!* Babylon is an end-time worldwide religious confederacy made up of the satanic trinity—the dragon, the sea beast, and the earth beast—arrayed against God and his faithful people. As William G. Johnsson suggests, Babylon "represents all human attempts to provide the way of salvation, all those plans and programs that, because they are built alone on human reason and devices, attempt to frustrate the divine plan for the world."[30] In other words, it is a religious system that stands in opposition to the gospel. Whereas the gospel is everlasting, Babylon is short-lived. The repetition of the word "fallen" in the past tense expressing the future occurrence underscores the imminence and certainty of the fall of end-time Babylon. This echoes the very words that the Old Testament prophets used in foretelling the fall of ancient Babylon. "Fallen, fallen is Babylon," Isaiah shouted, "and all the images of her gods are shattered on the ground" (Isa. 21:9). Jeremiah proclaimed: "Suddenly Babylon has fallen and been broken" (Jer. 51:8). In a similar manner, the second angel announces the collapse of end-time Babylon, the worldwide apostate religious system and a confederacy of religious organizations backed by political powers of the world (Rev. 13:12–17). This end-time apostate religious system responsible for oppressing God's people is to meet its end. Its collapse, announced here by the second angel, is described later in Revelation 18.

End-time Babylon has *made all nations drink of the wine of the wrath of her fornication.* This statement echoes Jeremiah's oracle against ancient Babylon: "Babylon has been a golden cup in the hand of the Lord, intoxicating all the earth. The nations have drunk of her wine; therefore the nations are going mad" (Jer. 51:7; cf. 25:15). In a similar way, John portrays end-time Babylon in terms of a prostitute woman seducing the nations into immorality by intoxicating them with the wine of her fornication (cf. Rev. 17:1–2; 18:3). In Revelation 13 we see how Babylon seduces all the nations to side with the satanic trinity by means of deception. It seems that the drinking of Babylon's wine of fornication refers to her seducing the inhabitants of the earth to worship the beast and his image and to receive the mark of the beast upon the right hand or the forehead (Rev. 14:9; cf. 13:11–17; 17:1–6; 18:2–3). The seduced nations associate themselves with Babylon for the purpose of economic security and prosperity (Rev. 18:3, 9–19). As a consequence, they will drink of God's wine of wrath.

While the message of the second angel is an alarm warning the wicked, at the same time it provides a strong assurance to God's end-time people. End-time Babylon, as the worldwide apostate religious system, is a temporary phenomenon. It will soon come to its end. Its collapse is determined and announced. Nobody must be deceived. There is still time to come out of Babylon and worship and serve the true God (Rev. 18:1–4).

THE MESSAGE OF THE THIRD ANGEL (14:9–11)

A third angel with a warning message follows the first two. His warning builds upon the announcement of the second angel. It concerns, in particular, those who, rejecting the message of the first angel to worship the true God, choose rather to worship the beast and receive the mark on their forehead or hand.

> *⁹And another angel, the third one, followed them saying with a loud voice: "If anyone worships the beast and his image, and receives the mark on his forehead or on his hand, ¹⁰he will drink from the wine of the wrath of God which is mixed undiluted in the cup of his wrath, and he will be tormented with fire and sulphur before the holy angels and before the Lamb. ¹¹And the smoke of their torment ascends forever and ever, and they have no rest day and night, those who worship the beast and his image, and whoever receives the mark of his name."*

NOTES

14:9 *A mark.* See *Notes* on Revelation 13:16.

14:10 *The wine of the wrath of God...in the cup of his wrath.* The execution of the wrath of God in the Old Testament is frequently symbolized by drinking wine from the Lord's cup (cf. Job 21:20; Pss. 60:3; 75:8; Isa. 51:17–23; Jer. 25:15–29; 49:12; Ezek. 23:32–34; Obad. 16). A wicked person, it was said, would "drink of the wrath of the Almighty" (Job 21:20). God warned Jerusalem through Ezekiel that she would suffer the same fate as Samaria which had been destroyed:

> You will drink your sister's cup,
> Which is deep and wide.
> You will be laughed at and held in derision;
> It contains much.
> You will be filled with drunkenness and sorrow,
> The cup of horror and desolation,
> The cup of your sister Samaria. (Ezek. 23:32–34)

Isaiah addresses Jerusalem, which underwent the divine judgment, as "you who have drunk from the Lord's hand the cup of His anger" (51:17; cf. also v. 22). This metaphorical expression occurs elsewhere in the Old Testament (Ps. 60:3; Jer. 25:15–29; 49:12–13; Obad. 15–16). The same figure of speech was used by Jesus in referring to his suffering on the cross (Matt. 20:22; 26:39; John 18:11).

Two words for wrath in Greek are used in Revelation 14:10—*thumos* ("anger," "fury") and *orgē* ("wrath"). *Thumos* is a strong or passionate indignation or anger, whereas *orgē* denotes a demonstration of displeasure and righteous indignation. *Orgē* is the usual word for divine wrath in the New Testament (especially by Paul; cf. Rom. 1:18; 3:5; 12:19; Col. 3:6). In Revelation, however, both *thumos* and *orgē* are used for the eschatological wrath of God (Rev. 14:10, 19; 15:1, 7; 16:1, 19; 19:15). The two words are often used together in the Septuagint as well as in Revelation; this is for the purpose of intensifying the reality of God's wrath being manifested in judgment (Rev. 14:10; 16:19; 19:15; cf. Rom. 2:8).

Mixed undiluted. The Greek word *kerannumi* ("to mix") used in conjunction with wine refers to the ancient practice of mixing wine with various spices and herbs to increase its intoxicating power, or of diluting it with water to reduce its strength. Thus, the expression "the wine of the wrath of God which is mixed undiluted in the cup" means that the wine is full strength without having been diluted with water.[31] In other words, the execution of the final wrath of God is in its full strength, not mixed with mercy. Psalm 75:8 is especially significant here: "For a cup is in the hand of the LORD, and the wine foams; it is well mixed, and He pours out of this; surely all the wicked of the earth must drain and drink down its dregs."

14:11 *The smoke of their torment ascends forever and ever.* The idea of fire and sulphur with the smoke ascending "for ever and ever" is drawn from the Old Testament. After God had "rained on Sodom and Gomorrah fire and sulphur" (Gen. 19:24), Abraham saw the smoke ascending from the earth (19:28). Reflecting on that scene, Jude describes the fate of these two cities as experiencing "the punishment of eternal fire" (Jude 7). Isaiah prophesied that God would punish Edom with fire and sulphur; it would become a "burning pitch; it shall not be quenched night and day; its smoke shall go up forever; from generation to generation it shall be desolate" (Isa. 34:8–10). Note that the smoke will arise for ever and ever, and that it lies *desolate* from generation to generation, and will never again rise from its ruins. The smoke ascending for ever and ever of Revelation 14:11 (also 19:3; 20:10) echoes in particular this prophecy of Isaiah regarding Edom. The phrase "forever and ever" does not mean endless burning. No fire burns today in Sodom and Gomorrah and Edom in modern Jordan, although eternal fire was their allotment. As Desmond Ford stresses, "the purpose of fire is to consume, never to preserve."[32] The phrase "for ever and ever" stands for burning which lasts long enough to make the consumption complete, with nothing left to be burned.

EXPOSITION

14:9–10 The third angel continues the theme of the first angel's message. He warns anyone who worships *the beast and his image, and receives the mark on his forehead or on his hand* that *he will drink from the wine of the wrath of God.* The demand to worship the beast and receive his mark in Revelation 13 counterparts the command to worship "the One who made heaven and the earth and the sea and the fountains of waters" in Revelation 14:7. In the final crisis, the mark of the beast on the right hand or the forehead serves as identification for the worshipers of the satanic trinity, as the counterpart to the seal of God. Worship of the beast and the reception of his mark stands as the antithesis to obedience to God's commandments, the substitution of the obedience to the satanic trinity for the obedience of God.

Revelation 13:11–17 shows that by demanding the inhabitants of the earth to receive the mark of the beast, Babylon has made "all nations drink of the wine of the wrath of her fornication" (Rev. 14:8), seducing them to render their allegiance to the unholy triumvirate. All those who consent to drink from Babylon's seductive wine of fornication will become the objects of divine wrath. They will have to drink of God's cup of wrathful wine. The cup of wrath is a symbol of God's judgment on the wicked (cf. Job 21:20; Ps. 75:8; Isa. 51:21–23), the execution of which is portrayed symbolically as the pouring out of the seven last plagues (Rev. 15–16). In pouring out the seven last plagues, "the wrath of God was completed" (Rev. 15:1).

This cup of God's wrath is *mixed undiluted in the cup of his wrath.* This means that the outpouring of the final wrath will be in its full strength, without mercy and grace.[33] The wrath of God, however, is not to be understood as "a human emotion," but rather as a metaphor for the inevitable "reaction of God's holiness" to sin and rebellion.[34] It is God's final response to those who have rebelliously and persistently resisted the gospel, disobeyed the commandments of God, and viciously oppressed his faithful people. George E. Ladd states: "Unless God in his wrath finally purges the world of all evil and rebellion, his Kingdom cannot come. Therefore, in the largest sense of God's redemptive purpose for men, his wrath is a necessary correlative to his love and mercy."[35]

The third angel warns worshipers of the beast that, in addition to drinking from the cup of God's wrath in the pouring out of the seven plagues, they will also *be tormented with fire and sulphur.* The language here recalls the scene of the raining down of "brimstone and fire from the Lord out of heaven" on Sodom and Gomorrah (Gen. 19:24). It reminds us also of the prophecy of Isaiah about the fate of Edom, the enemy of Israel (Isa. 34:8–10). Having been destroyed by God's judgment, Edom would never rise again. In the same way, those who side with the satanic trinity will share the ultimate fate of Sodom and Gomorrah and Edom. God's judgment on them "at the end of time will be as absolute and complete."[36]

Unbelievers will be destroyed *before the holy angels and before the Lamb.* The expression points to the final judgment after the millennium that is described in Revelation 20. While the overcomers in the church of Sardis are promised recognition before the Father and his angels (Rev. 3:5), the unbelievers will have their end in the lake of burning fire before Christ and the angels. The lake of fire burning with sulphur is the symbolic place of punishment for the beast and the false prophet (Rev. 19:20). Likewise, all those who have rejected the call of the gospel and have sided with the satanic trinity will share the ultimate fate of the unholy triumvirate in "the lake of fire and sulphur" where "they will be tormented day and night for ever and ever" (Rev. 20:10).

14:11 The destructive fire burning with sulphur destroys those who have rejected the gospel and worshiped the beast and received his mark; such destruction is final and complete—*And the smoke of their torment ascends forever and ever.* The ascending smoke indicates the completion of the burning. This is much like the smoke that Abraham saw ascending from Sodom and Gomorrah as a sign of divine judgment on these two cities (Gen. 19:28). The extinction of the cities in the valley is used by Old Testament prophets as the model for the fate of ancient Babylon: "Babylon, the beauty of kingdoms...will be as when God overthrew Sodom and Gomorrah" (Isa. 13:19; cf. Jer. 50:40). In describing the destruction of end-time Babylon, John employs the language in which the Old Testament prophets foretold the fate of ancient Babylon. The portrayal of the impending judgment, therefore, must be taken as symbolic of "a fearful and final reality which no man can describe."[37] The imagery of the smoke of the fire burning with sulphur indicates the completion of the final judgment rather than an eternal burning and suffering. The burning fire continues long enough to complete its purpose and leaves nothing to be burned.

The angel further announces that those who worship the beast and receive the mark of his name *have no rest day and night.* This is in contrast to the statement in Revelation 14:13 in which the followers of Christ are promised rest from their labor (cf. 6:11). The worshipers of the beast and his image, however, will never taste that rest. The threat echoes the declaration made to rebellious Israel regarding its rest in the promised land: "Therefore I swore in My anger, 'Truly they shall not enter into My rest'" (Ps. 95:11). The idea of the promised rest continues in the New Testament as rest in the grace of God: "There remains therefore a Sabbath rest for the people of God. For the one who has entered His rest has himself also rested from his works, as God did from His. Let us therefore be diligent to enter that rest, lest anyone fall through following the same example of disobedience" (Heb. 4:9–11). The rest into which God's people enter is eternal; so the unrest of the impending judgment for the unbelievers is eternal. As Philip E. Hughes stated, "From this last judgment there is no reprieve; the sentence of death is irreversible; the destruction permits no recovery."[38]

The grotesque language used in the warning of the third angel is intended to move people to stand firm and render their allegiance to the true God. The beast of Revelation 13 uses fear to make people conform to his demand for worship; but now, with the message of the third angel, that "fear is driven out by a stronger fear."[39] Jesus used this method in warning the twelve: "Do not fear those who kill the body, but are unable to kill the soul; rather fear Him who is able to destroy both soul and body in hell" (Matt. 10:28). Those who respond to the final call of the gospel and worship the true God with obedience to his commandments can escape the fate of the beast and the false prophet.

THE FAITHFUL REMNANT (14:12–13)

In concluding the warning message of the inevitable consequences for siding with the satanic trinity in the final crisis, John presents the characteristics of God's end-time people and their glorious future. Revelation 14:12–13 appears to be John's comment attached as an appendix to the messages proclaimed by the three angels.

¹²Here is the endurance of the saints, the ones who keep the commandments of God and the faith of Jesus. ¹³And I heard a voice from heaven saying, "Write: Blessed are the dead who die in the Lord from now on." "Yes," says the Spirit, "that they may rest from their labors; for their works follow them."

NOTES

14:12 *Faith of Jesus.* The faith of Jesus here is most likely the objective genitive, the same as that in Revelation 2:13 (cf. Mark 11:22; James 2:1); that is, it is the faith in Jesus[40] (see NEB: "remaining loyal to Jesus"). The word "keep" (Gr. *tēreō*) must be understood here to mean "maintain," as in 2 Timothy 4:7: "I have kept the faith." "To keep faith" or "to remain loyal" was a common Greek expression in John's day.[41] The phrase in this text means that the end-time saints keep afresh their living faith in Jesus, which enables them to obey and sustains them "under the severe pressure of persecution"[42] because of their loyalty to Christ.

14:13 *Blessed are the dead who die in the Lord from now on.* This is the second of the seven beatitudes in the book of Revelation (1:3; 14:13; 16:15; 19:9; 20:6; 22:7, 14); see *Notes* on Revelation 1:3.

Their labors. The Greek word *kopos* means "hard work" or "labor to the point of weariness and exhaustion" (cf. Rom. 16:12; 1 Cor. 15:10; Gal. 4:11; 1 Thess. 2:9). See *Notes* on Revelation 2:2.

EXPOSITION

14:12 While the message of the third angel is a warning to unbelievers, to the saints it is a strong impetus to faithfulness and steadfastness. ***Here is the endurance of the saints, the ones who keep the commandments of God and the faith of Jesus.*** The opening part of this statement also appears in Revelation 13:10—"Here is the endurance and the faith of the saints." Apparently, then, the saints of Revelation 14:12 are those of Revelation 13:7 against whom the satanic trinity wages war, and who in Revelation 12:17 are identified as the remaining ones of the woman's offspring who keep "the commandments of God" and have "the testimony of Jesus." They are not called to resistance and protest but to endurance and perseverance. The phrase "here is" means that in the final crisis when most people in the world side with the unholy triumvirate in obedience and allegiance to Satan, God's end-time people— "buffeted by false ideas, assaulted by religious confederacy, and threatened by the civil powers"[43]—remain steadfast and firm in their loyalty to God. They are characterized by their obedience to God in keeping his commandments (cf. Rev. 12:17) and their continuing faithfulness and loyalty to Christ. They maintain an ongoing relationship with Christ. Nobody and nothing in this world can separate them "from the love of God, which is in Christ Jesus our Lord" (Rom. 8:38–39). As Johnsson says, they are not "deceived by the miraculous phenomena associated with the false system of worship; they are resolute in their convictions, not swayed by persuasion or coercion; above all they are loyal to their God, prepared to suffer loss, physical hardship and even death itself to maintain their relationship with Him."[44]

14:13 The second of the seven blessings of Revelation promises a special assurance to those who endure and remain loyal to Christ until the very end. ***Blessed are the dead who die in the Lord from now on.*** When Christ's followers die because of their faith and loyalty to God, it often appears to be a tragedy. However, their death is described in Revelation as rest. This resting of Christ's followers stands in sharp contrast to the sorrowful reality of the followers of the satanic trinity who "do not have rest day and night" (Rev. 14:11). God's faithful servants, however, are promised ***rest from their labors.*** The Greek indicates that the labor from which they rest is not just good hard work, but labor to the point of weariness and exhaustion.[45] Rest is especially sweet after exhaustive, hard labor.[46] This is the same rest promised in the scene of the fifth seal to the martyrs underneath the altar who died because of "the word of God" and "the testimony that they held" (Rev. 6:9).

This suggests that "labors" in Revelation 14:13 refer to the devotion of God's end-time saints to the gospel proclamation on behalf of which they suffered hardship and persecution to the point of death (cf. Rev. 12:11). They rest from their labors but ***their works follow them.*** The "works" here refer evidently to the remnant's obedience to God in keeping his commandments and faith in Jesus (Rev. 14:12). Their endurance lies behind them, and they rest under God's watchful care until the hour of resurrection and coming glory. This is why Christians are urged to be "steadfast, immovable, always abounding in the work of the Lord, knowing that your toil is not in vain in the Lord" (1 Cor. 15:58, NKJV).

THE TWO HARVESTS OF THE EARTH (14:14–20)

The end-time gospel proclamation concludes with a great separation between God's people and the wicked. This section describes that great separation which takes place prior to the Second Coming. John portrays it in terms of a dual harvest: the reaping of grain (Rev. 14:14–16) and the gathering of the grapes to be tread in the winepress (14:17–20).

> ¹⁴*And I saw, and behold, a white cloud, and upon the cloud one sitting like a son of man, having a golden crown upon his head, and in his hand a sharp sickle.* ¹⁵*And another angel came out of the temple crying with a loud voice to the one sitting on the cloud: "Send forth your sickle and reap, for the hour to reap has come, because the harvest of the earth is ripe."* ¹⁶*And the one sitting on the cloud cast his sickle upon the earth, and the earth was reaped.*
>
> ¹⁷*And another angel came out of the temple which is in heaven, he himself also having a sharp sickle.* ¹⁸*And another angel came out from the altar, the one having authority over fire, and he called with a loud voice to the one who had the sharp sickle, saying: "Send forth your sharp sickle and gather the clusters of the vineyard of the earth, because her grapes are ripe."* ¹⁹*And the angel cast his sickle upon the earth, and gathered the vintage of the earth and cast it into the great winepress of the wrath of God.* ²⁰*And the winepress was trodden outside the city, and the blood came out from the winepress up to the bridles of the horses, from 1,600 stadia.*

NOTES

14:14 *Like a son of man.* This expression is drawn from Daniel 7:13. "The Son of Man" was Jesus' favorite title for himself in the gospels. The same phrase, "like a son of man," is used for Christ in Revelation 1:13. This suggests that the figure identified here as "like a son of man" is Christ himself rather than an angel (see *Notes* on Rev. 1:13) as some commentators assume.

A golden crown. The Greek word for the crown here is *stephanos,* which is not a royal crown (*diadēma*) but a crown of victory, the garland (see *Notes* on Rev. 2:10).

14:15 *The temple.* The Greek word *naos* used here refers to the sanctuary or the inner temple, namely, the most holy place. For more on the meaning of *naos,* see *Notes* on Revelation 11:1.

Send forth your sickle. The command to send the sickle in verses 15 and 18 is a direct allusion to Joel 3:13. The command to Christ to reap is expressed in Greek with the verb *pempō* ("to send"). This word is used by Jesus with reference to the eschatological harvest when God will send the sickle to reap the grain (Mark 4:29). According to Matthew 13:39–43, however, "the reapers are angels" who will be sent by the Son of Man to gather the harvest of the earth. In the parable of the net, angels are the ones who separate the wicked from the righteous at the eschatological consummation. The role of the angels as reapers sent by Jesus to gather the righteous for the kingdom is further affirmed in Jesus' eschatological discourse on the Mount of Olives (Mark 13:27; Matt. 24:31). It would thus appear that the sending of the sickle in Revelation 14:15 and 18 implies the sending of the angels to gather the faithful for the kingdom and the wicked for the outpouring of God's final wrath portrayed in terms of the grain and grape harvest, respectively (see the following section for further discussion).

The harvest of the earth. The harvest (with the threshing floor) is a well-known biblical metaphor for the eschatological judgment on the enemies of ancient Israel (cf. Jer. 51:33; Joel 3:13); it can also be used in a positive sense for the gathering of God's people. "O Judah," Hosea cried, "there is a harvest appointed for you, when I restore the fortunes of my people" (Hos. 6:11; cf. Joel 3:1–2). In the teachings of Jesus, the harvest gathers people into the kingdom of God (Matt. 9:37–38; Luke 10:2; John 4:35–38). "When the grain is ripe, he immediately sends the sickle, because the harvest has come" (Mark 4:29, as it reads in the Greek). In the parable of the wheat and tares, Jesus linked the idea of reaping the harvest to the great gathering prior to the Second Coming and the subsequent judgment on the wicked. "The harvest is the end of the age; and the reapers are angels....The Son of Man will send forth His angels, and they will gather out of His kingdom all stumbling blocks, and those who commit lawlessness, and they will cast them into the furnace of fire; in that place there shall be weeping and gnashing of teeth. Then the righteous will shine forth as the sun in the kingdom of their Father" (Matt. 13:39–43). According to John the Baptist, at the harvest Christ "will gather His wheat into the barn, but He will burn up the chaff with unquenchable fire" (Matt. 3:12).[47]

14:18 *The altar.* The altar mentioned here is probably not the altar of incense before the throne, but rather the altar of burnt offering mentioned in Revelation 8:3–5 (see *Notes* on Rev. 8:3). It was underneath this altar, in the scene of the opening of the fifth seal, that the slain saints have been praying for judgment "upon those who dwell on the earth" (6:10). The time has now come for the promise given to the martyred saints to be fulfilled. God is about to judge those who viciously persecuted and oppressed his faithful people.

Send forth your sharp sickle. See *Notes* on Revelation 14:15.

14:19 *The great winepress of the wrath of God.* As William Barclay explains, the winepress consisted of "an upper and a lower trough connected by a channel. The troughs might be hollowed out in the rock or they might be built of brick. The grapes were put into the upper trough that was on a slightly higher level. They were then trampled with the feet and the juice flowed down the connecting channel into the lower trough."[48] The imagery of treading grapes was familiar to the Jewish mind. In the Old Testament, it is used for the execution of divine wrath upon the enemies of Israel. Isaiah portrays God as the warrior returning after executing his wrath upon Edom:

> Who is this who comes from Edom,
> With garments of glowing colors from Bozrah,
> This One who is majestic in His apparel,
> Marching in the greatness of His strength?
> "It is I who speak in righteousness, mighty to save."
> Why is Your apparel red,
> And Your garments like the one who treads in the wine press?

> "I have trodden the wine trough alone,
>
> And from the peoples there was no man with Me.
>
> I also trod them in My anger,
>
> And trampled them in My wrath;
>
> And their lifeblood is sprinkled on My garments,
>
> And I stained all My raiment.
>
> For the day of vengeance was in My heart,
>
> And My year of redemption has come....
>
> I trod down the peoples in My anger,
>
> And made them drunk in My wrath,
>
> And I poured out their lifeblood on the earth." (Isa. 63:1–6)

In a similar way, Jeremiah describes God's judgment on Judah: "The Lord has trodden as in a winepress the virgin daughter of Judah" (Lam. 1:15). John uses this well-known imagery of treading grapes in the winepress to portray the execution of God's disfavor on the wicked in the closing days of this world's history. In Revelation 19, he describes Christ the Warrior "clothed in a robe dipped in blood," treading "the winepress of the wine of the anger of the wrath of God, the Almighty" (19:13–15).

14:20 *Was trodden outside the city.* The expression "outside the city" is an allusion to the prophecy of Joel where the nations are gathered and judged in the valley of Jehoshaphat, which lay outside the walls of Jerusalem (most likely the Kidron valley that separated Jerusalem from the Mount of Olives). The judgment against the nations in Joel's prophecy is initiated with a command: "Put in the sickle, for the harvest is ripe. Come, tread, for the wine press is full; the vats overflow, for their wickedness is great" (Joel 3:13; cf. Zech. 14:2–4). It appears that in this sense and against this Old Testament background John portrays the treading of the winepress of God's wrath outside the city. Drawing on Joel's prophecy which was originally of ethnic and local significance, John reinterprets it, giving it a worldwide fulfillment and significance with regard to the end-time outpouring of divine wrath on the oppressors of God's people.

The blood came out...up to the bridles of the horses. Here John used a hyperbolic expression from the battle that was well known among Jewish people. An interesting statement from 1 Enoch, the Jewish pseudepigraphal book, confirms that this hyperbolic expression was common among Jews in the first century for describing the final judgment: "The horse shall walk through the blood of sinners up to his chest; and the chariot shall sink down up to its top. In those days, the angels shall descend into the secret places. They shall gather together into one place all those who gave aid to sin. And the Most High will arise on that day of judgment in order to execute a great judgment upon all the sinners."[49]

1,600 stadia. A stadion was a distance of about 600 feet. No satisfactory interpretation has been offered for the symbolic meaning of this number. The most common scholarly view holds that 1,600 stadia (about 184 miles, or 300 kilometers) corresponds roughly to the length of Palestine from north to south.[50] Palestine would thus stand for the entire earth which becomes a battlefield completely covered with blood. Another view is based on the symbolic meaning of the number four. Four is the number of the earth (four corners of the earth [Rev. 7:1, 20:8], the four winds of the earth [Matt. 24:31], and the four quarters of the earth [Isa. 11:12]). The symbolic meaning of 1,600 is thus found in the multiplication of four times four hundred. A thousand and six hundred stadia would denote the worldwide scope and significance of the execution of the divine wrath. Perhaps the best explanation is offered by *The Seventh-day Adventist Bible Commentary*: "The main thought is that the enemies of the church of God are to be completely and finally overthrown. Therefore, the church can look forward to full and complete deliverance from all her enemies, and to joyful triumph in the kingdom of God."[51]

EXPOSITION

The end-time proclamation of the everlasting gospel has divided the people of the entire world into two camps: those who have responded to the gospel and worship the true God in the midst of opposition and pressure, and those who have rejected it and have sided with the satanic trinity and worship the beast and Satan. The history of this world is about to be concluded with the coming of Christ and the final judgment when everybody will be given "as his work is" (Rev. 22:12). Prior to that, a great gathering of God's people for the kingdom and the wicked for the outpouring of the wrath of God takes place, which John portrays in terms of two harvests that were familiar to Jewish thought.

14:14–16 John now sees *a white cloud, and upon the cloud one sitting like a son of man.* This recalls the vision in which Daniel saw "one like a son of man" coming on the clouds of heaven who subsequently received the kingdom and universal and everlasting dominion from the Ancient of Days (Dan. 7:13–14). It is more likely, however, that here John had in mind Jesus' prediction about the sign of "the Son of Man coming on the clouds of the sky with power and great glory" (Matt. 24:30). "You shall see the Son of Man sitting at the right hand of Power, and coming on the clouds of heaven" (Matt. 26:64). In the prologue to his book, John announced: "He is coming with the clouds, and every eye will see him" (Rev. 1:7). These references suggest that the one like a son of man sitting on the "white cloud" is Christ about to come victoriously for the purpose of bringing judgment upon the earth. He is portrayed as wearing *a golden crown upon his head.* This crown is a garland, a crown of victory. He carries *a sharp sickle,* a harvest instrument, in his hand and is prepared to reap the harvest of the earth. The proclamation of the gospel has been completed, and it is time for the reaping of the harvest of the earth, for, "when the grain is ripe, he immediately sends the sickle, because the harvest has come" (Mark 4:29; the author's translation).

Next, John sees an angel coming out of *the temple*, a reference to the most holy place of the heavenly temple (cf. Rev. 11:19). This means that the angel comes out from the very presence of God with a message from God himself. He announces that the time for the harvest has arrived. He calls on Christ: *Send forth your sickle and reap, for the hour to reap has come, because the harvest of the earth is ripe.* A similar command is found in Joel's prophecy of judgment against the nations: "Put in the sickle, for the harvest is ripe" (Joel 3:13). In response to the angel's call, Christ swings the sickle to the earth and the earth is reaped.

Jesus made it clear that the harvest comes at the end of earth's history (Matt. 13:39) and prior to the Second Coming. The harvest marks the conclusion of the gospel proclamation. The sins of human beings have reached their full measure. Every person has sided either with God or with the satanic triumvirate. The sealing of God's people has been completed, and probation is closed for those who have persistently opposed and rejected the gospel message. The destiny of every human being has been decided. "The harvest is past, summer is ended, and we are not saved" (Jer. 8:20). Now is the time for the gathering of the redeemed into the kingdom prior to the execution of the wrath of God portrayed symbolically in the pouring out of the seven last plagues on the wicked (Matt. 13:38–43). The gathering of the righteous occurs before Jesus comes on the clouds with great power and glory. He will send his angels, the reapers, to "gather together His elect from the four winds, from the farthest end of the earth to the farthest end of heaven" (Mark 13:26–27; Matt. 24:30–31). This is the meaning of "the firstfruits" mentioned in Revelation 14:4. The redeemed are the firstfruits of the grain harvest (cf. Jer. 2:3). They are sealed (cf. Rev. 7:3–8) and in such a way are distinct from the unbelieving nations about to be judged in the grape harvest (Rev. 14:17–20). The sealed redeemed are under special protection from the wrath of God to be poured out on the wicked (cf. Rev. 7:3; 15:1–6). They are ready now to experience the transformation of their mortal bodies (1 Cor. 15:50–54) and, subsequently, to be taken up in the air to meet Christ coming in glory (1 Thess. 4:17).

14:17–20 The grain harvest of God's people is followed by the execution of God's wrath on the wicked which is portrayed in terms of the treading of the grapes in the winepress. John draws the imagery of two distinct harvests from the prophecy of Joel where the directive "Put in the sickle, for the harvest is ripe" is followed by "Come, tread, for the wine press is full; the vats overflow, for their wickedness is great" (Joel 3:13). Here in Revelation, the grain harvest is followed by the treading of the vintage in the winepress. This figuratively connotes the gathering of God's people for the kingdom and the execution of God's wrath upon those siding with the satanic trinity.

John sees another angel coming *out of the temple which is in heaven, he himself also having a sharp sickle.* This angel also comes from the very presence of God as did the previous one. Next, John sees *another angel* coming out *from the altar, the one having authority over fire.* The identification of this angel is curious enough. First of all, his coming out from the altar links him to the angel mentioned in Revelation 8:3–5 who stands at the altar and offers the prayers of the saints before God's throne. These prayers were the perennial plea of God's oppressed people throughout history for deliverance and judgment on their oppressors and the enemies of the gospel (Rev. 6:9–11). This angel is further identified as the one having "authority over fire," pointing to the scene of Revelation 8:5 where the angel fills the censer with fire from the altar and throws it to the earth; this is followed by the phenomena of "thunders and voices and lightning and an earthquake" as the announcement of approaching divine judgment.

This suggests, then, that the altar from which the angel in Revelation 14:18 comes is the same altar mentioned in the scene of the opening of the fifth seal underneath which the perennial plea for judgment and deliverance of the martyred saints has been ascending before God. Revelation 14 shows that the gospel has been proclaimed, and God's final warning message has been given to the inhabitants of the earth. The sins of the oppressors of God's people have reached their full measure. God's people are sealed and made complete. With the harvest of the righteous, probation closes for the wicked. Grace is no longer available, and there is no opportunity for repentance. The time has come for God to fulfill his promise given to the saints underneath the altar (Rev. 6:11) and deal with the opponents of the gospel and the oppressors of his faithful people.

With special urgency, the angel coming from the altar delivers the divine command to the angel with the sickle to commence the harvest of the wicked: *Send forth your sharp sickle and gather the clusters of the vineyard of the earth, because her grapes are ripe.* Without delay the angel swings his sickle and gathers *the vintage of the earth and cast*[s] *it into the great winepress of the wrath of God.* The casting of the grapes into the winepress of the wrath of God and the trampling underfoot is drawn from Isaiah 63:1–6. John uses the well-known Jewish concept to describe the severity of divine judgment to be executed upon the wicked. This judgment is described in the symbolic portrayal of the pouring out of the seven last plagues in which "the wrath of God was completed" (Rev. 15:1).

The winepress filled with the vintage is now *trodden outside the city.* This city is a reference to the New Jerusalem, the holy city, into which nothing unclean can enter (Rev. 21:27). Here we see the fulfillment of Joel's prophecy which notes that the enemy nations of Israel will be gathered into "the valley of Jehoshaphat. Then I will enter into judgment with them there on behalf of My people and My inheritance, Israel, whom they have scattered among the nations....Put in the sickle, for the harvest is ripe. Come, tread, for the wine press is full; the vats overflow, for their wickedness is great" (Joel 3:2–3, 13).

Just as the enemies of Israel were to be judged in the valley of Jehoshaphat that stood outside the city of Jerusalem, so the enemies of God's end-time people are to experience the outpouring of God's wrath outside the holy city.

As a result of the treading of the vintage, blood is seen as coming from the winepress. The blood rises up to "the horses' bridles" and extends for *1,600 stadia.* This distance is expressed hyperbolically to stress the severity of the execution of God's wrath.[52] It is worldwide in scope and extends to all people on the earth who find themselves outside the umbrella of God's protection. The entire earth looks like a battlefield as the seven last plagues are poured out upon the wicked (cf. Rev. 19:17–19). The grotesque language employed in the portrayal of the pouring out of God's final wrath in the seven last plagues is intended, together with other scenes in Revelation 14, to warn the readers of the seriousness of their decision to respond to the gospel warning proclaimed by the three angels. The only way to escape the fate reserved for the satanic triumvirate and their worshipers is to choose to serve the true God and worship him.

Once again, the purpose of this impressive picture is to drive out the fear of the threat of the beast and the false prophet by a "stronger fear."[53] The day is coming when mercy will no longer be available. Christ will come "clothed in a robe dipped in blood"

(Rev. 19:13) accompanied by the heavenly armies. He will tread "the winepress of the wine of the anger of the wrath of God Almighty. And he has on his robe and on his thighs a name written: 'King of Kings, and Lord of Lords'" (Rev. 19:15–16; cf. Isa. 63:1–6).

A RETROSPECT ON REVELATION 14

Revelation 14 makes it clear that before the end comes and God's judgments are executed, the inhabitants of the earth will witness a final proclamation of the everlasting gospel which will be glorious and worldwide in scope. Its effectiveness will be similar to the proclamation of Elijah on Mount Carmel when many of the apostate in Israel were moved to choose the true God and obey and worship him. The prophet Malachi prophesied that God would send "Elijah the prophet before the coming of the great and terrible day of the LORD" (Mal. 4:5). The proclamation of the final gospel warning to the world will be characterized by the same appeal that marked the preaching of Elijah: "If the Lord is God, follow Him; but if Baal, follow Him" (1 Kings 18:21).

The powerful proclamation of the gospel warning will bring "worldwide ripening" so that the entire earth will be ready for the harvest.[54] In the harvest, those represented by the wheat receive the glorious reward, but those represented by grapes experience the wrath of God (cf. Rev. 11:18).

Revelation 14 is of special significance for God's faithful people living in the closing days of earth's history. Before the end comes and probation closes, God's people are commissioned with the proclamation of the everlasting gospel. It is the same gospel that Paul and the early church preached about Jesus Christ—the One who died, was resurrected, and is sitting on the heavenly throne at the right hand of the Father, bringing the history of this world to its end. He has promised to be with his people always, "even to the end of the age" (Matt. 28:20). He is coming soon. Therefore, a strong appeal implores the church today to uplift Christ as the first and last in proclaiming the final warning message to the world.

Revelation 14:6–12 is of crucial importance for the end-time church of Jesus Christ. It sets forth the church's program, message, and destiny. While it urges the church to preach the everlasting gospel (cf. Matt. 28:19–20), it shows clearly that in the final analysis it is indeed God who will bring the gospel proclamation to its completion.[55] The fact that the angels from heaven, rather than human beings, are mentioned as the ones preaching to the inhabitants of the earth suggests strongly that the final proclamation of the everlasting gospel will be brought to its completion primarily by divine action rather than human effort. When Jesus stated that "this gospel of the kingdom shall be preached in the whole world" (Matt. 24:14), he used the passive form ("shall be preached") rather than the active ("you shall preach") to express it. The passive form here functions as the Hebrew divine passive, suggesting divine action. The final proclamation of the everlasting gospel will be brought to its completion not through human wisdom, efforts, skills, and methods, but through the special activities of the Holy Spirit. Our main task is to "lift up Christ and His Cross as the good news of grace and pardon." It is then that we shall witness the completion of the preaching of the everlasting gospel and then "we shall see One coming in the clouds of Heaven to make an end of sin and death."[56]

ENDNOTES

1. *The Seventh-day Adventist Bible Commentary*, 7:826.

2. Ladd, 191.

3. See Swete, 179; on the celibacy in antiquity, see Aune, *Revelation 6–16*, 818–822. Aune does not enter into discussion on whether the term in Revelation 14:4 should be understood literally or figuratively.

4. Ladd, 191.

5. Aune demonstrates that, in both biblical and Greco-Roman literature, the "first-fruits" refers to sacrifices offered to God/gods (see *Revelation 6–16*, 814–818).

6. Beale, 743.

7. Ibid., 743–744.

8. Neall, *The Concept of Character in the Apocalypse*, 163.

9. Swete, 181.

10. Neall, *The Concept of Character in the Apocalypse*, 166.

11. Ladd, 189.

12. Neall, "Sealed Saints and the Tribulation," 255.

13. Hughes, 158.

14. Aune, *Revelation 6–16*, 818.

15. Morris, 172.

16. Barclay, *The Revelation of John*, 2:109.

17. Mathias Rissi, "*krinō, krisis*," in *Exegetical Dictionary of the New Testament*, ed. Horst Balz and Gerhard Schneider (Grand Rapids, MI: Eerdmans, 1990–1993), 2:318, 320.

18. Herntrich Büchsel, "*krinō*, et al.," in *Theological Dictionary of the New Testament*, ed. G. Kittel and G. W. Bromiley (Grand Rapids, MI: Eerdmans, 1964–1976), 3:941–942; Rissi, "*krima*," in *Exegetical Dictionary of the*

New Testament, 2:317.

19. See Robertson, 6:411; LaRondelle, *How to Understand the End-Time Prophecies,* 339. Aune is obviously struggling with the meaning of the aorist in the text (see *Revelation 6–16*, 827–828).

20. Beale, 753.

21. Ladd, 193.

22. Johnsson, 38.

23. Ibid.

24. Paulien, *What the Bible Says about the End-Time*, 126.

25. LaRondelle, *How to Understand the End-Time Prophecies*, 334.

26. See Aune, *Revelation 6–16*, 829.

27. Cf., Sibilline Oracles 5.137–162 (Charlesworth, 1:396–397); 2 Baruch 11:1; 67:7 (Charlesworth, 1:625, 644); Tertulian *Against Marcion* 3.13 (*The Ante-Nicene Fathers*, 3:332).

28. See Barclay, *The Revelation of John*, 2:111.

29. Johnsson, 35.

30. Ibid.

31. Beasley-Murray, 226.

32. Desmond Ford, 603.

33. Mounce, 275.

34. Ladd, 195.

35. Ibid.

36. Beale, 761.

37. Ladd, 196.

38. Hughes, 164.

39. Desmond Ford, 602–603.

40. Robertson, 6:413; *The Seventh-day Adventist Bible Commentary*, 7:833. Beale struggles with the concept here (see *The Book of Revelation*, 766–767).

41. Aune, *Revelation 6–16*, 837–838.

42. Thomas, *Revelation 8–22*, 213.

43. Johnsson, 39.

44. Ibid., 38.

45. Rienecker, 815.

46. Barclay, *The Revelation of John*, 2:114.

47. For a fuller treatment of the harvest concept, see Aune, *Revelation 6–16*, 801–803.

48. Barclay, *The Revelation of John*, 2:115.

49. 1 Enoch 100:3 (Charlesworth, 1:81).

50. See Ladd, 202.

51. *The Seventh-day Adventist Bible Commentary*, 7:835.

52. Beale, 781.

53. Desmond Ford, 602–603.

54. LaRondelle, *How to Understand the End-Time Prophecies,* 363.

55. Desmond Ford, 593.

56. Ibid.

Revelation 15–18 portrays in vivid language the execution of God's divine wrath in terms of the pouring out of the seven bowl plagues upon the worshipers of the satanic triumvirate (chapters 15–16) and the subsequent judgment on end-time Babylon (chapters 17–18). Before engaging in a detailed analysis of Revelation 15–18, it is necessary to stress some points of general matter that are important for a meaningful interpretation of the text.

THE THEOLOGICAL MEANING OF THE SEVEN LAST PLAGUES

Revelation 15–18 builds on chapters 12–14. The central theme of Revelation 12 is Satan's effort to destroy God's people living between the first coming of Christ and his return to the earth. Revelation 13 focuses on the time of the end. The chapter portrays the anger of the nations against God's faithful remnant. Next, the discussion turns to God's response to the anger of the nations. In chapters 15–18, John elaborates upon the statement "your wrath came" of Revelation 11:18. He describes first the execution of divine wrath in the pouring out of the seven bowl plagues on the followers and worshipers of the satanic trinity (chapters 15–16), and, second, the judgment on the end-time prostitute Babylon (chapters 17–18).

Revelation presents the seven last plagues as the expression of God's final wrath in full strength (Rev. 14:10) for "the world in final rebellion against God."[1] They are referred to as "the last ones," because in them the wrath of God against rebellious humanity reaches its completion (Rev. 15:1). They complete the pouring out of God's wrath portrayed symbolically in the seven trumpet plagues (Rev. 8–9). The plagues of the seven trumpets had redemptive purposes; they were God's judgment mixed with mercy intended to bring rebellious people to repentance, and warn them that the time for repentance was rapidly running out, and that the door of mercy would be closed forever.

The purpose and nature of the seven last plagues, however, is completely different. They denote God's judgments unmixed with mercy. The bowl plagues are executed after the last call for repentance is given (Rev. 14:6–12) and the destiny of every human being has been fixed (cf. Rev. 15:8). The context shows that the seven last plagues are God's final response to the purpose of end-time Babylon to destroy God's faithful people. The Egyptian plagues with the song of Moses celebrating the great deliverance at the Red Sea (Exod. 15), along with the overthrow of ancient Babylon (Jer. 51), are very instructive in regards to the purpose and character of Revelation 15–16. (While four of the bowl plagues strikingly correspond to the plagues inflicted on Egypt at the time of the Exodus, the sixth and seventh plagues are modeled on the motif concerning the fall of ancient Babylon in the Old Testament.)[2] Just as the plagues fell on the land of Egypt, providing deliverance from Egypt to the Israelites, and as the drying up of the Euphrates led to the fall of ancient Babylon, thus providing liberation for the people of Israel from the Exile and subsequently the return to their homeland, so the purpose of the outpouring of the seven last plagues is to deliver God's people from the oppression of end-time Babylon.[3]

The seven last plagues are likewise portrayed as the mighty acts of God on rebellious humanity for the purpose of defeating his enemies and providing liberation for his end-time people from the bondage of Babylon. Although each of the Egyptian plagues increased Pharaoh's stubbornness and hardness of heart, he and his officials had to admit that the plagues were acts from "the finger of God" (Exod. 8:19), and they let Israel go free to the promised land (Exod. 12:31–32).

The vision of the pouring out of the seven last plagues begins with the Exodus scene. John introduces the Exodus motif by portraying God's victorious people standing on the sea of glass singing a song of liberation from Babylon. It is the song of Moses and of the Lamb (Rev. 15:2–4). The suffering of the Israelites under the oppression of the Egyptians becomes in Revelation the foreshadowing of the oppression of God's end-time people under Babylon. Like the Egyptian plagues, these seven last plagues are intended to disclose all the hardness of the hearts of those who have rejected the gospel and sided with the unholy trinity. The refusal of the wicked to repent of their deeds appears three times in the text (Rev. 16:9, 11, 21). The execution of divine wrath corresponds to the way they oppressed and persecuted God's faithful people. Here comes to light the prophecy of Isaiah: "Behold I have taken from your hand the cup of staggering; the bowl of my wrath you shall drink no more; and I will put it into the hand of your tormentors" (Isa. 51:22–23, RSV).

The time has come for Babylon, "who made all nations drink of the wine of the wrath of her fornication" (Rev. 14:8; cf. 17:2), to be given "the cup of the wine of the fury of his [God's] wrath" to drink (16:19). The execution of the plagues on Babylon is appropriate to Babylon's sins and her oppression of God's people. Babylon will reap the consequences of what she has sown. "Pay her back as she has given, and pay her double according to her works, in the cup which she has mixed, mix a double portion for her" (Rev. 18:6).

The Exodus motif in the background of the seven last plagues suggests a rather positive character of the execution of God's final wrath on rebellious humanity. G. R. Beasley-Murray notes:

> The judgments of the Lord on the land of Egypt are but pale anticipations of the greater judgments which are to fall on the kingdom of the beast, and the emancipation from Egypt is far surpassed by the redemption of the Lamb, as the saints rejoice in the resurrection glory and sing of the turning of the nations to God (15:2ff.). The duality of exodus as judgment and redemption is maintained in chapters 15–16, and to ensure that this is understood by the reader, the positive element of redemption is placed first.[4]

Hans LaRondelle observes that the God who will accomplish the final liberation of his people from Babylon is the same "I AM" of the historical deliverance from Egypt. As Moses was his agent in the infliction of the plagues on Egypt and in bringing his people to the promised land, so Christ—the new Moses—functions as God's end-time agent in the execution of the seven last plagues on spiritual "Egypt" or "Babylon," liberating his people and bringing them into the promised land.[5]

The text does not indicate clearly whether the seven last plagues are to be understood as literal or figurative. In dealing with the seven seals and trumpets, the symbolic meaning is obvious. Any figurative meaning of the first four plagues is not. While the first four plagues are evidently literal, the last three—which shift from nature to humanity—are to be understood as spiritual in their effect.[6] Whether intended to be literal or figurative, the last plagues represent the terrible experience that the wicked will undergo after the close of probation.

THE TIMING OF THE SEVEN LAST PLAGUES

The next question to be addressed concerns the timing of the execution of the seven last plagues. Revelation 15:7–8 shows clearly that Revelation 16 deals with the time after everyone's eternal destiny has been determined. The temple is said to be closed so that "no one was able to enter"; thus, the intercession has been completed in the heavenly sanctuary, and grace is no longer available.

Why then is the execution of the last plagues necessary? The reason is found in the underlying theme of the book of Revelation: the wicked must face the righteous judgments of God. In the scene of the opening of the fifth seal, the martyred saints cry out for vindication. Their cry symbolizes the perennial plea of God's people throughout history for deliverance from rebellious humanity. It is now in the pouring out of God's final wrath that the prayers of God's oppressed people are being answered. The wicked must experience the righteous judgments which are appropriate to their sins (cf. Rev. 16:5–7). The suffering inflicted by the plagues, however, does not turn them from their wickedness to repentance. On the contrary, they continue to oppose God.

Revelation 15–18 assures the end-time saints that God is in control in the final crisis, and that he will be with and by his faithful people during that most frightening moment of history "that is about to come on those who dwell on the earth" (Rev. 3:10). LaRondelle states: "Terrible as they will be, the seven last plagues carry a comforting and reassuring message for God's people. The divine Deliverer, who rescued ancient Israel from Egypt and Babylon, will intervene again. He will deliver His new-covenant, remnant people from the worldwide apocalyptic Egypt and Babylon and take them to the New Jerusalem above."[7]

THE TRUMPETS AND THE SEVEN LAST PLAGUES

Students of the book of Revelation have observed some striking similarities between the seven trumpets and the seven last plagues. The following comparison demonstrates the self-evident parallelism between the two series:

	THE SEVEN TRUMPETS	THE SEVEN BOWLS
	Introductory temple scene (8:2–6)	Introductory temple scene (15:5–16:1)
1st	Earth (8:7)	Earth (16:2)
2nd	Sea (8:8–9)	Sea (16:3)
3rd	Rivers and fountains (8:10–11)	Rivers and fountains (16:4)
4th	Sun, moon, and stars (8:12)	Sun (16:8–9)
5th	Darkness from the abyss, locusts (9:1–11)	Darkness over the throne of the beast (16:10–11)
6th	The River Euphrates (9:14–21)	The River Euphrates (16:12–16)
7th	Loud voices: the kingdom has come and Christ reigns (11:15–16)	A loud voice: It is done (16:17–21)

Despite these similarities, evident differences make clear that the seven trumpets and the seven last plagues are not the same. First, the introductory section of Revelation 8:2–5 shows that the blowing of the seven trumpets occurs while the intercession is still in progress and grace is still available. The bowl plagues affect humankind after the intercession is completed; the temple is said to be closed so that "no one was able to enter" (Rev. 15:7–8). Second, in the trumpets the plague terror is limited and partial. The trumpet plagues affect some of the people of Satan's kingdom (Rev. 8:7–12). However, no restriction is imposed on the bowl plagues that are evidently global in scope. Their terror affects the whole earth (cf. Rev. 16:3), harming the worshipers of the unholy triumvirate while sparing God's faithful people. (Revelation 7:16 indicates, however, that God's people will suffer hunger, thirst, and the scorching heat of the fourth plague.) Third, while the seven trumpet plagues had redemptive purposes, the seven last plagues are punitive (15:1; 16:2). They disclose the hardness of the unbelief of the wicked, who despite the severity of the plagues are not willing to abandon their idolatry (16:9–11). Finally, the trumpet blasts involve relatively long periods (9:5, 15; 11:2, 11); no such time is mentioned with reference to the bowl plagues which most likely fall during a very short period. We observed that the blowing of the seven trumpets has to do with the period of history from the time of John to the Second Coming; the seven last plagues come at the end of history, immediately before the Second Coming.

How, then, can the striking similarities between the seven trumpets and the seven last plagues be explained? The basic differences are in their purpose and nature.

The bowl plagues are still future events; their execution comes at the end of history. The trumpets precede the bowl plagues; they are a series of divine interventions throughout Christian history. They occur while the gospel is still being preached, and people are being saved and brought into a relationship with Christ. The trumpet plagues thus must be regarded as preliminary judgments—God's reaction to the wickedness of those who do not have the seal of God on their foreheads and who reject the gospel (9:4). Their purpose is to awaken repentance in the world hostile to God's people. The bowl plagues fall on rebellious humanity when intercession and grace are no longer available to the impenitent. Accordingly, the trumpet plagues and the bowl plagues are not the same, for the former are the foretaste and forewarning of the future visitation of God's wrath in its fullness with the seven final plagues (Rev. 16) and the final judgment described in Revelation 20.

Jon Paulien observes an interesting parallel between the blowing of the seven trumpets of Revelation 8–11 and the story of the battle at Jericho from Joshua 6.[8] The Israelites, together with the priests carrying the trumpets, marched around the city for seven days. For six days, they marched once each day. Then on the seventh day they marched around the city seven times. At the end, there was a great blowing of the seven trumpets, causing the fall of the city. This Old Testament background is very illustrative of what takes place in Revelation 8–11. The seven trumpet blasts of Revelation are parallel to the sevenfold blowing of the trumpets at Jericho. In this analogy, the seven bowl plagues should be understood as a part of the blowing of the seventh trumpet. They are evidently God's response to the anger of the nations announced in the seventh trumpet blast (Rev. 11:18).

ENDNOTES

1. LaRondelle, *The Good News about Armageddon* (Hagerstown, MD: Review and Herald, 1990), 7.

2. LaRondelle, "Contextual Approach to the Seven Last Plagues," in *Symposium on Revelation—Book 2*, Daniel and Revelation Committee Series 7 (Silver Spring, MD: Biblical Research Institute, 1992), 143–144.

3. Fiorenza, *Revelation*, 70; Boring, 175.

4. Beasley-Murray, 233.

5. LaRondelle, "Contextual Approach to the Seven Last Plagues," 138.

6. Johnson, 549.

7. LaRondelle, "Contextual Approach to the Seven Last Plagues," 149.

8. Paulien, The Bible Explorer, 3.8.

evelation 12–13 portrayed the anger of the nations (Rev. 11:18) against God's faithful remnant, while Revelation 14 portrayed God's final warning message to the nations. Now, the discussion turns to God's response to the anger of the nations. Chapters 15–16 describe the execution of divine wrath in terms of the pouring out of the seven bowl plagues on the followers and worshipers of the satanic trinity.

PREPARATION FOR THE SEVEN LAST PLAGUES (15:1–8)

This section is a continuation of Revelation 14:14–20. It portrays the preparation for the execution of God's final wrath on the wicked in the outpouring of the seven last plagues. Before the execution of the plagues, John sees the victorious saints celebrating the great deliverance after having passed through the final crisis (15:2–4). Revelation 15:2–4 appears to function as the springboard passage. It serves both as the conclusion of chapters 12–14 and as the introduction to the seven last plagues.[1]

¹And I saw another sign in heaven, a great and marvelous one: seven angels having seven plagues, the last ones, for in them the wrath of God was completed.
²And I saw something like a sea of glass mixed with fire, and those who had overcome the beast and his image and the number of his name, standing on the sea of glass having harps of God.
³And they sing the song of Moses, the servant of God, and the song of the Lamb, saying:

"Great and marvelous are your works,
 Lord God the Almighty;
righteous and true are your ways,

>   **King of the nations.**
> **⁴Who will not fear you, O Lord,**
>   **and glorify your name?**
> **For you only are holy,**
>   **because all the nations will come**
>   **and worship before you,**
> **because your righteous deeds have been**
>   **manifested.”**

⁵And after these things I looked, and the temple of the dwelling of the testimony was open in heaven. ⁶And the seven angels having the seven plagues came out of the temple, clothed in pure and shiny linen and girded around their breasts with golden girdles. ⁷And one of the four living beings gave to the seven angels seven golden bowls filled with the wrath of God who lives forever and ever. ⁸And the temple was filled with smoke of the glory of God and from his power, and no one was able to enter the temple until the seven plagues of the seven angels were completed.

NOTES

15:1 *Sign in heaven.* As in Revelation 12:1, the Greek *sēmeion* here means a striking visual scene that captures one's attention. See *Notes* on Revelation 12:1.

The wrath of God. The Greek word used here is *thumos* ("anger," "fury"), denoting a strong or passionate indignation or anger (see *Notes* on Rev. 14:10).

15:3–4 *The song.* The song that John heard the redeemed singing on the sea of glass is almost entirely composed of phrases from the Old Testament: "Great and marvelous are your works" (cf. Ps. 111:2–3); "Righteous and true are your ways" (cf. Deut. 32:4; Ps. 145:17); "King of the nations" (cf. Jer. 10:6–7); "Who will not fear you, O Lord, and glorify your name?" (cf. Jer. 10:7); "For you only are holy" (cf. 1 Sam. 2:2); "All the nations will come and worship before you" (cf. Ps. 86:9; Jer. 16:19).

Almighty. See *Notes* on Revelation 1:8.

15:5–8 *The temple.* The Greek word used here is *naos* which in Revelation refers particularly to the innermost part of temple, the most holy place, where God's throne is located. For more on the meaning of *naos* in Revelation, see *Notes* on Revelation 11:1.

15:7 *One of the four living beings.* The four living beings, who are probably an order of exalted angels, are somehow involved in the manifestation of God's wrath upon the earth (6:1, 3, 5, 7; 15:7). See *Notes* on Revelation 4:6.

Golden bowls. In the Old Testament, golden bowls (Gr. *phialē*) are the vessels used in the temple for incense and offerings to God (cf. 1 Kings 7:40, 45, 50; 2 Kings 12:13; 25:15; cf. Rev. 5:8). The golden bowls in Revelation 15–16 are most likely the same as "the cup of wine" of the wrath of God in Revelation 14:10.

EXPOSITION

15:1 A new striking scene captures John's attention. He sees *seven angels having seven plagues.* These seven angels are most likely the same angels who blew trumpets (chapters 8–9) to announce the plagues which were the preliminary judgments intended to bring sinners to repentance. There they were given the trumpets as the instruments of judgment; now they are given the bowls. The seven last plagues are said to be *the last ones, for in them the wrath of God was completed.* The visitation of the seven last plagues completes the divine warnings to the rebellious world. The sins of human beings have reached their full measure. Up to now, God's wrath has always been softened with mercy. Here the situation changes. The wicked have to experience the final wrath of God in its full strength, without mercy and grace (cf. Rev. 14:10). Here is the fulfillment of the threat of the third angel to those who have chosen to drink from Babylon's seductive wine of fornication. They have to drink from the cup of God's wrath. It is from this final wrath of God, as described in the scene of the opening of the sixth seal, that the wicked seek to hide themselves in the caves and rocks of the mountains (Rev. 6:16–17). The last plagues are poured out upon the unrepentant in anticipation of the final judgment.

15:2–4 While the followers and worshipers of the satanic trinity are the subject of God's final wrath, the saints are under God's watchful care and protection. The final plagues evidently do not harm them. John sees them standing on a spread that looks like *a sea of glass.* The sea of glass in Revelation 4:6 is located before the throne of God in the heavenly throne room. This corresponds to what John saw in Revelation 7, where the redeemed coming out of the great tribulation are standing before the throne of God in the heavenly temple (Rev. 7:9–15). While in chapter 4 the sea of glass looked clear like crystal, this time it is *mixed with fire.* The sea of glass is reflecting the colorful display of God's glory expressed with lightning and the "seven torches of fire" burning before the throne (Rev. 4:5). This new detail is intended to heighten the dazzling splendor of the scene in the heavenly throne room.[2]

The redeemed are also seen as having *harps of God* and singing *the song of Moses, the servant of God, and the song of the Lamb.* Harps are instruments of praise to God (Rev. 5:8; 14:2). The song of the redeemed is a song of praise to God for great deliverance and for judgment on their enemies. The song of Moses is the song of deliverance sung by the people of Israel as they were standing at the Red Sea watching the destruction of the Egyptians (Exod. 15). The great deliverance at the Exodus is here the pattern for the great deliverance of God's people in the final crisis.

A significant difference exists between the Exodus event and Revelation 15–16, however. While in Exodus the song comes after the plagues were inflicted upon Egypt and the Israelites were liberated from bondage, in Revelation 15 the song of Moses and the Lamb is placed before the manifestation of the seven last plagues, showing that the positive element of redemption in Revelation 15–16 comes before the negative element of the judgment.[3] God's end-time people emerge victoriously from the great tribulation after having their loyalty severely tested. They have "washed their robes and made them white in the blood of the Lamb" (Rev. 7:14). Now, just as the people of Israel praised the Lord at the sea after he delivered them from the Egyptians, so the redeemed praise God for delivering them from the unholy trinity and from those who sided with and worshiped them. Their deliverance and salvation is a result of what Christ has done on their behalf at the cross. This suggests that there is one song, rather than two, that is sung by the redeemed in celebration of the great deliverance wrought by Christ on behalf of his faithful followers.

According to Revelation 14:3, only the redeemed are able to sing that song of salvation. They have experienced deliverance in the final crisis as have no other human beings in history. They have remained steadfast in their loyalty to Christ and obeyed God's commandments, refusing to side with the satanic trinity and worship the beast and receive the number of its name. Now they celebrate their victory over the satanic trinity which John portrays in terms of Israel's celebration at the Red Sea.

The song of the redeemed praises the **Lord God the Almighty** for his **great and marvelous** works, and his **righteous and true** ways on behalf of his people. What comes to light here is that the redeemed saints do not know of any of their own achievements or merits.[4] The entire song is about the Almighty God of the covenant, the great deliverer of his people. He is the one who protected and preserved them during the hours of their trials and distresses, and "it is his glory which now they share."[5] The victory of God's faithful remnant, therefore, is the result not of their human achievement but of God's great and marvelous works and his righteous and true ways. The rest of the song is a clear allusion to Revelation 14:7: ***Who will not fear you, O Lord, and glorify your name? For you only are holy, because all the nations will come and worship before you, because your righteous deeds*** *have been manifested.* It shows that the redeemed saints have accepted the eternal gospel message of the three angels. They have separated from Babylon and her sins. Therefore, they do not "receive of her plagues" (Rev. 18:4).

15:5–7 Next, John sees that *the temple of the dwelling of the testimony was open in heaven.* While the heavenly temple is the place where God's mercy and grace can be found, in Revelation it is also the place from which divine judgments emanate when people reject the gospel. The heavenly temple is referred to as "the dwelling of the testimony" because the law of God was located in the most holy place of the Old Testament tabernacle. *The seven angels having the seven plagues* emerge from the most holy place of the heavenly temple "to show that no person or nation can with impunity defy the Law of God."[6] The angels with the plagues come from the very presence of God as his avenging commissioners. It is God who executes his righteous wrath as the answer to the prayers of his people. The seven last plagues are his response to the anger of the nations intent upon destroying his faithful people (cf. Rev. 13:11–17).

The angels are clothed in *pure and shiny linen and girded around their breasts with golden girdles.* Their appearance is described in the manner of the glorified Christ in the introduction of the book (Rev. 1:13). This link with the description of the glorified Christ suggests that the angels come with the authority of Christ who has commissioned them. One of the four living beings gives to the angels seven *golden bowls filled with the wrath of God.* These are the temple bowls of offering to God. In Revelation 5:8, the golden bowls are full of incense, representing the prayers of God's people that the twenty-four elders offer to God (cf. Rev. 8:3–5). This time, however, the golden bowls of intercession become the instruments of destruction, full of the wrath of God to be poured out on the wicked. Mercy has ceased for those on whom the divine wrath will be executed. The execution of the wrath of God has been initiated by the prayers of God's faithful people.[7]

15:8 At the moment the angels receive the bowls of the wrath of God, the heavenly temple is filled with the *smoke of the glory of God and from his power, and no one was able to enter the temple until the seven plagues of the seven angels were completed.* This reflects the scene of the dedication of the tabernacle in the wilderness (Exod. 40:34–35) and Solomon's temple (1 Kings 8:10–11). On both occasions, the cloud of the glory of the Lord filled the building structure so that the services could not be held. Here, the heavenly temple—the very place where intercession for human beings has been made—is now filled with the cloud of the glory of God so that nobody can enter. Probation has closed and intercession on behalf of sinners no longer exists. The sinners must experience the fullness of the final wrath of God which is unmixed with mercy and grace as the consequence of their persistent resistance and opposition to the gospel.

THE EXECUTION OF THE FIVE LAST PLAGUES (16:1–11)

The time has come for the seven angels to pour out the bowls of the wrath of God upon rebellious humanity. God's people are sealed, and the winds are to be unleashed (cf. 7:1–3). What earlier has been described as the cup of wine of the wrath of God (14:10) and the treading of the winepress (14:17–20) is now portrayed symbolically as the pouring out of the seven plagues. The enemies of God's end-time people are now to experience the full visitation of the wrath of God unmixed with mercy and grace. "For the great day of his wrath has come, and who is able to stand?" (Rev. 6:17).

> *¹And I heard a loud voice from the temple saying to the seven angels, "Go and pour out the seven bowls of the wrath of God upon the earth.*
>
> *²And the first one went and poured out his bowl upon the earth, and a bad and malignant sore came on the men who had the mark of the beast and who worshiped his image.*
>
> *³And the second one poured out his bowl into the sea, and it became like the blood of the dead, and every living soul died in the sea.*
>
> *⁴And the third one poured out his bowl into the rivers and the fountains of waters, and they became blood. ⁵And I heard the angel of the waters saying:*
>
> *"You are righteous, who is and who was, the holy One,*
> *because you have judged these things,*
> *⁶because they poured out the blood of saints and prophets,*
> *and you have given them blood to drink;*
> *they deserve it."*
>
> *⁷And I heard the altar saying, "Yes, Lord God the Almighty, true and just are your judgments."*
>
> *⁸And the fourth one poured out his bowl upon the sun, and*

it was given to it to burn people with fire. ⁹And the people were burned with great heat, and they blasphemed the name of God who had authority over these plagues, and they did not repent to give him glory.

¹⁰And the fifth one poured out his bowl upon the throne of the beast, and his kingdom became darkened, and they gnawed their tongues because of the pain, ¹¹and they blasphemed the God of heaven because of their pains and because of their sores, and they did not repent of their works.

NOTES

16:1 *The temple.* The Greek word used here, as in 15:5–8, is *naos*; it here refers most likely to the most holy place, where God's throne is located. See *Notes* on Revelation 11:1.

16:2 *A bad and malignant sore.* The Greek word *helkos* ("sore," "boil") here is used in the Greek translation of the Old Testament (LXX) for the boils of the sixth plague that struck Egypt (Exod. 9:10–11). The same word is used with reference to the affliction that came upon Job, causing great pain and suffering (Job 2:7), so that he "took a potsherd to scrape himself while he was sitting among the ashes" (Job 2:8). They are described as "sore boils" affecting the entire body from the sole of the foot to the crown of the head (Deut. 28:35; Job 2:7). A plague of this kind is often used as punishment for sin (Deut. 28:35; 2 Kings 5:25–27; 2 Chron. 26:16–21).

16:5 *The angel of the waters.* This angel is not mentioned elsewhere in the book of Revelation. The pseudepigraphal book of 1 Enoch mentions "the angels who were in charge of the waters" (66:2). However, it is uncertain whether this is the sense in Revelation 16:5. The expression most likely refers to the angel who poured his bowl into the water supplies, turning them to blood.

16:6 *They deserve it.* The Greek *axioi eisin* ("they are worthy") most likely means "they deserve it" (as RSV, JB, and NIV translate it).

16:7 *The altar.* This is most likely the altar of burnt offering underneath which the martyred saints cried for judgment on their enemies in the scene of the opening of the fifth seal (see *Notes* on Rev. 6:9). It is less likely that John had in mind here the altar of incense from which the prayers of the saints ascend to God in Revelation 8:3–4, for this altar is referred to as "the golden altar" (Rev. 8:3; 9:13). See *Notes* on Revelation 8:3.

Almighty. See *Notes* on Revelation 1:8.

EXPOSITION

16:1 *A loud voice* from the most holy place of the heavenly temple commands the angels to *pour out* their bowls on the wicked. This voice coming from the most holy place is likely to be the very voice of God. The angels are commissioned directly by God as his avenging commissioners. The wicked have "poured out" the blood of God's people (Rev. 16:6); therefore, the bowl plagues are now poured upon them.

16:2 The first angel pours out his bowl upon the earth. As a result, *a bad and malignant sore* afflicts the human beings. The first bowl plague recalls the boils of the sixth plague that struck Egypt (Exod. 9:10–11; Deut. 28:27). Just as the boils afflicted only Egyptians and not the Israelites, so the malignant sore of the first of the last plagues afflicts only those having *the mark of the beast and who worshiped his image.* The same are identified as the recipients of the rest of the bowl plagues. Thus the seven last plagues are the visitation of God's wrath against those who have sided with the unholy trinity. They are the oppressors who have tried to destroy God's people (Rev. 13:15–17; 16:5–6). The first bowl plague carries out the threat proclaimed by the third angel with regard to anyone who "worships the beast and his image, and receives the mark on his forehead or on his hand"; it warns that such a one "will drink from the wine of the wrath of God which is mixed undiluted in the cup of his wrath" (Rev. 14:9–10).

16:3–7 The second and third angels pour out their bowls into the water. The second angel pours out a bowl into *the sea*, which immediately becomes like the *blood of the dead, and every living soul died in the sea.* The third angel pours his bowl into *the rivers and the fountains of waters, and they became blood.* This brings to mind the first of the Egyptian plagues when the waters of the Nile were turned to blood (Exod. 7:17–21). These two bowl plagues parallel the second and third trumpet plagues which affect and pollute only the third part of the water supplies and destroy the third part of everything living in them (Rev. 8:8–11). This time no mention is made of any proportion; these bowl plagues are complete in their effect. Without water to drink, rebellious humanity will not survive. In the bowl plagues there is an intensification of the divine wrath executed on the enemies of God's people unlike the trumpet plagues which were just the forewarning and preliminary visitation of God's wrath.

Next, John hears *the angel of the waters* who poured his bowl into the waters and turned them into blood. He declares the appropriateness of God's judgments on the wicked, echoing the song of the redeemed in Revelation 15:3. The wicked have readily *poured out the blood of saints and prophets.* They delighted in viciously persecuting God's faithful people. Now, they are given *blood to drink.* The execution of the plagues on the wicked is appropriate to their sins.

At that moment John hears **the altar saying, "Yes, Lord God the Almighty, true and just are your judgments."** This altar is most likely the altar of burnt offering mentioned in the scene of the opening of the fifth seal from which the prayers of the saints have been ascending to God: "How long, O Lord, holy and true, will you not judge and avenge our blood upon those who dwell on the earth?" (Rev. 6:10). They were told to wait for a little while until an appointed time when their prayers would be answered. Here, the voice from the altar affirms that the prayers of God's people are finally answered in the plagues. God is beginning to execute the fullness of his disfavor against the oppressors of his people. Justice is being completely vindicated.

16:8–9 The fourth angel pours out his bowl upon **the sun, and it was given to it to burn people with fire.** At the sounding of the fourth trumpet, a partial diminishing of the intensity of the sun caused partial darkness on the earth (cf. Rev. 8:12). However, the fourth plague is as others entire in its effect—the intensity of the heat of the sun is enormously increased. As a result, **the people were burned with great heat.** The plague, however, does not cause them to change their ways; they go on to curse **the name of God who had authority over these plagues, and they did not repent to give him glory.** These people recognize God's hand in the execution of the plagues. Yet instead of repenting, they blaspheme the name of God as does the beast they have sided with (Rev. 13:6). They rebelliously blame God for the consequences of their own actions. This parallels what Paul stated of the ungodly people of his time: "For even though they knew God, they did not honor [glorify] Him as God, or give thanks; but they became futile in their speculations, and their foolish heart was darkened" (Rom. 1:21).

16:10–11 The fifth angel pours out his bowl upon **the throne of the beast.** While the first four plagues have affected humanity in general, the fifth plague strikes the very seat of Satan's authority. It is Satan who delegated to the sea beast its throne and great authority (cf. Rev. 13:2). The beast has exercised authority over the earth through the assistance of the earth beast. They have caused the earth dwellers to side with the satanic trinity (Rev. 13:12). However, even the very seat of the beast cannot withstand the force of the plagues. This scene recalls the sixth Egyptian plague that affected even Pharaoh's magicians who "could not stand before Moses because of the boils" (Exod. 9:11). The terror of the plague brings chaos on the **kingdom** of the beast which becomes completely **darkened.** This supernatural darkness parallels the ninth plague which affected the whole land of Egypt with total and intense darkness (Exod. 10:21–23). The authority of the beast suffers great humiliation before the eyes of the earth dwellers. They begin to realize the impotence of the unholy trinity to protect them from the effect of the plagues.

The darkness of the fifth plague intensifies the terror of the unrepentant in such a way that the people *gnawed their tongues because of the pain.* The terror and pain of each plague increasingly hardens their hearts. Even the awful and unbearable plagues do not cause the wicked to repent. Instead, *they blasphemed the God of heaven because of their pains and because of their sores, and they did not repent of their works.* In rejecting God's warning message (Rev. 14:6–12), the wicked have refused the last opportunity to repent. Intercession has been completed in the heavenly sanctuary, and "no one was able to enter" it (Rev. 15:8). The wicked continue to oppose God until it is too late to return to him. They have firmly set their minds against God. Thus, they become fertile soil for the great and final deception that will draw the entire world into the great battle between God and Satan, the deception which is portrayed in the scene of the sixth plague (Rev. 16:13–14).

THE SIXTH PLAGUE (16:12–16)

The sixth plague differs from the five previous plagues in that it introduces the consummation of earth's history. It portrays the preparation for the coming final battle between Christ and his faithful people and Satan and the worshipers of the beast.

> [12]*And the sixth one poured out his bowl upon the great river Euphrates, and its water was dried up, in order that the way of the kings from the rising of the sun might be prepared. [13]And I saw coming out of the mouth of the dragon and out of the mouth of the beast and out of the mouth of the false prophet three unclean spirits like frogs; [14]for they are spirits of demons performing signs, which go out to the kings of the whole inhabited world to gather them for the battle of the great day of God the Almighty. [15]"Behold, I am coming as a thief. Blessed is the one who watches and keeps his garments so that he does not walk naked and they see his shame." [16]And he gathered them to the place which is called in Hebrew "Armageddon."*

NOTES

16:12 *The great river Euphrates.* The Euphrates in the Old Testament, called "the great river" (Gen. 15:18; Deut. 1:7; Josh. 1:4), is the boundary that separated God's people from their enemies, Assyria and Babylon (see *Notes* on Rev. 9:14). It was the place from which the archenemy nations would invade Israel. The imagery of the river Euphrates seems to be particularly important because of the prominence of Babylon in Revelation. The Euphrates flowed through the ancient city of Babylon. As such, it was an integral part of the city, nurturing its crops and providing water for the city's inhabitants. Without that river, Babylon could not survive. The concept of the Euphrates seems to be very important in Revelation because of the prominence of the imagery of Babylon in the last portion of the book (see *Notes* on Rev. 14:8). Revelation 17 indicates that the river Euphrates must be understood symbolically. The prostitute Babylon sits on "many waters" (17:1). Jeremiah 51:13 shows that the expression "many waters" by which Babylon was located is another reference to the Euphrates River. The angel explains to John that the waters on which the prostitute Babylon sits symbolize the national powers of the world—"peoples and multitudes and nations and tongues" (Rev. 17:15); they will be in service to end-time Babylon and in opposition to God and his people.

Its water was dried up. The drying up of the waters in the Old Testament often symbolizes a mighty action of God on behalf of his people. It was so with the Red Sea (Exod. 14:21–22) and the Jordan River (Josh. 3:14–17). Regarding Babylon, God threatened through Jeremiah: "I shall dry up her sea and make her fountain dry" (Jer. 51:36). In Isaiah, it is God "who says to the depth of the sea, 'Be dried up, and I will make your rivers dry'" (Isa. 44:27), in order to restore his people to their land. Elsewhere in the Old Testament, the drying up of the waters by God is preparatory to the gathering of God's people and bringing them back to their land (cf. Isa. 11:15–16; 51:10–11; Zech. 10:10–11).

The drying up of the Euphrates River in Revelation 16:12 particularly echoes God's judgment on ancient Babylon as announced by the Old Testament prophets. Isaiah spoke of God promising to dry up the waters of the Euphrates to enable Cyrus to enter the city and conquer it (Isa. 44:27–28). Jeremiah prophesied that the collapse of Babylon would be the result of the drying up of the Euphrates River (Jer. 50:35–38; 51:36–37). However, the fall of Babylon, the oppressor of God's people, was not an end in itself. Its collapse served God's purpose to deliver his people Israel from their oppressor and to bring them to their homeland to rebuild Jerusalem and Judea: "Thus says the Lord of hosts: 'The people of Israel are oppressed, and the people of Judah with them; all who took them captive have held them fast, they refuse to let them go. Their Redeemer is strong; the Lord of hosts is his name. He will surely plead their cause, that he may give rest to the earth, but unrest to the inhabitants of Babylon'" (Jer. 50:33–34, RSV).

The agent in these events was to be Cyrus the Persian (Isa. 44:26–28; 45:1–5, 13), who was for this reason designated as God's messiah, the anointed one (Isa. 45:1), and "my shepherd" (44:28). God bestowed on this pagan king these most honorable titles (Isa. 45:4) that were later reserved for the Messiah of Israel. Cyrus was God's chosen one who would conquer Babylon by drying up the river Euphrates and providing deliverance for God's people in exile. "He will build My city and let My exiles go free" (Isa. 45:13; cf. 44:28). Thus, as Hans LaRondelle stresses, in "his work of deliverance Cyrus served as a type of the Messiah's mission of liberation."[8]

The historical fulfillment of these prophecies was later recorded by the famous Greek historian Herodotus[9] and confirmed in modern times by the Cyrus Cylinder.[10] According to Herodotus, Cyrus the Persian captured Babylon by drying up the Euphrates River which flowed through the city. When he approached Babylon, he discovered that the walls and defenses were too strong and that the city had supplies for many years to come. Cyrus used a section of his soldiers to divert the incoming water flow of the river, when it was low, into a lake. According to Daniel 5, it was that night when Babylon was having a drinking celebration that the Persians entered the city on the dry riverbed underneath the city walls in a surprise attack, conquering the overconfident defenders of Babylon. Later, Cyrus issued the decree allowing Israel to return to their homeland and rebuild Jerusalem and the temple. It seems clear that John used the real historical scene in order to symbolically portray God's final judgment on end-time Babylon which would initiate the deliverance of God's end-time people from their oppressors.

The kings from the rising of the sun. The phrase "the rising of the sun" is the ancient reference to the east (see *Notes* on Rev. 7:2). "The kings from the rising of the sun" is an allusion to Cyrus the Persian and his allied forces. Isaiah predicted that God would raise up Cyrus, his messiah (Isa. 44:28; 45:1), who would come "from the east" (Isa. 41:2; 46:11) or "from the rising of the sun" (Isa. 41:25) against Babylon. God spoke through Isaiah: "I have aroused him [Cyrus] in righteousness, and I will make all his ways smooth; he will build My city, and will let My exiles go free" (Isa. 45:13). LaRondelle states: "While coming from the east, Cyrus invaded Babylon from the north."[11] Why, then, is the plural form "kings" used in Revelation? Cyrus was the commander in chief of the allied forces of the *kings* of Media and Persia (Jer. 51:11, 28). The drying up of the waters of the Euphrates opened the way to Cyrus and his allied forces—"the kings from the rising of the sun"—to capture and overtake Babylon, to take over her world government (cf. Dan. 5:28), and to set Israel free to return to their homeland (cf. Ezra 1:1–4).

In the New Testament, the phrase "the rising of the sun" or "east" is often used metaphorically with reference to Jesus Christ; he is called the sunrise (Luke 1:78) and the morning star (Rev. 22:16). Jesus describes his return to the earth as from the direction of the rising sun (Matt. 24:27–31). In Revelation 7:2, the angel with the seal of God comes from the rising of the sun (see *Notes* on Rev. 7:2). Who then are these kings from "the rising of the sun"? The fact that they are referred to as coming "from the rising of the sun" suggests that they must be somehow related to Christ. Hans LaRondelle argues that they are God's unfallen angels "presented as celestial warriors—kings who will come to wage war against all the world's kings (Rev. 19:14)."[12] In his view, the saints will have a passive rather than an active role in the final conflict. "The saints will participate in Christ's victory, not in his battle."[13] C. Mervyn Maxwell suggests that Revelation 16:16–17 indicates that both God the Father and Christ will "arrive on the scene as the kings from the east."[14]

However, John the revelator provides the clue to their identity. Revelation 19:11–19 describes two opposing armies in the final conflict: Christ the Warrior and his armies against "the beast and the kings of the earth and their armies" (Rev. 19:19; cf. 16:13–16; 19:11–16). Christ is referred to as "Lord of lords and King of kings" and is accompanied by those who are "called and elect and faithful" (Rev. 17:14; cf. 19:16). The titles "called," "chosen," and "faithful" in the New Testament are consistently used with reference to God's people (cf. Rom. 1:6–7; 1 Cor. 1:2; 1 Pet. 2:9). The epithets "lords" and "kings" must be taken with reference to the saints who are elsewhere in Revelation identified as kings and priests (Rev. 1:6; 5:10; cf. 20:4, 6). They are in Revelation 7 symbolically portrayed as an eschatological army organized into 144 military units of 1,000 (7:2–8) ready to engage in the last battle (see *Notes* on Rev. 7:4). They are referred to as "the armies which are in heaven" (19:14) because the 144,000 in Revelation are seen as already being in the heavenly places (cf. Rev. 14:1; 15:2; 19:1–5). In Revelation 15:2, they are described as "those who had overcome the beast and his image and the number of his name." Those who oppose God in the book are always referred to as "those who dwell on the earth" (see *Notes* on Rev. 6:10). The saints as Christ's "armies which are in heaven" thus stand in opposition to "the kings *of the earth*" who are under the leadership of the satanic trinity (Rev. 16:14; 19:19) whose symbolic number is "two hundred million" (Rev. 9:16). If "the kings of the earth" are the secular and political powers of the world in service to the satanic trinity in the final battle, then "the kings from the rising of the sun" are evidently Christ—"King of kings and Lord of lords"—and his armies of the saints fighting against the satanic confederacy and providing their final and ultimate deliverance (Rev. 19:14–16). That the saints are both Christ's army and those to be delivered in the final crisis is not the only anomaly in the book. In 19:7–9, the saints are described as both the bride of the Lamb and the guests at the wedding.

16:13 *Mouth.* On the meaning of the "mouth" with reference to Satan in Revelation, see *Notes* on Revelation 9:19.

The false prophet. The false prophet is mentioned here and in Revelation 19:20 and 20:10, where he is always found in tandem with the dragon and the sea beast. Revelation 19:20 describes the false prophet as the one who performed signs in the presence of the sea beast by which he deceived those having the mark of the beast and worshiping his image. This feature depicts the religious character and activities of the second beast of Revelation 13; the earth beast does great signs, deceiving those living on the earth by means of the signs given to him to perform before the beast (Rev. 13:13–14). Thus the works of the false prophet and the earth beast are identical. The earth beast is no longer mentioned in the book after chapter 13 but is referred to as the false prophet—a member of the satanic trinity. The false prophet is another name for the earth beast in its new role; he is in league with "the image of the beast," deceiving people to side with the satanic trinity and worship the sea beast (Rev. 13:15–17). This new designation of the earth beast is used for the purpose of expressing the deceptive character and activity that characterize false prophets in the Bible (cf. Matt. 7:15; 24:24; 2 Pet. 2:1; 1 John 4:1; 2 John 7).

16:14 *Spirits.* The Greek word *pneuma* means both "spirit" and "breath."

Almighty. See *Notes* on Revelation 1:8.

16:15 *Blessed is the one who watches and keeps his garments.* This is the third of the seven beatitudes of the book of Revelation (see *Notes* on Rev. 1:3). F. F. Bruce points to a passage from the *Mishnah* which indicates that the captain of the temple in Jerusalem made his rounds of the precincts by night to check the members of the temple police guarding the temple. If anyone was caught asleep at his post, his clothes were stripped off and burned, and he was sent away naked in disgrace.[15] This custom might shed some light on the meaning of the text.

Naked and they see his shame. Nakedness in the ancient world was regarded as severe humiliation (see *Notes* on Rev. 3:18). A defeated army would be severely humiliated by having their garments stripped off and being led naked into captivity. Isaiah prophesied that Assyrians would lead the captives of Egypt "naked and barefoot, with buttocks uncovered, to the shame of Egypt" (Isa. 20:4). In Revelation, God will judge end-time Babylon by making her "desolate and naked" (Rev. 17:16). In the Old Testament, this was a token of divine judgment. Ezekiel prophesied that in judging idolatrous Israel, God would strip off their clothes and "expose their nakedness before their enemies" (Ezek. 16:37–39). In his oracles against Nineveh, Nahum announced that God would take off the clothing of the people of Nineveh and "show to the nations your nakedness, and to the kingdoms your disgrace" (Nah. 3:5).

16:16 *The place which is called in Hebrew "Armageddon."* The term "Armageddon" (in Greek *harmagedōn*) occurs only here in Revelation. The name of the place is very uncertain, and the word "Armageddon" difficult. The text says that it is a Hebrew term. The word combines *har* ("mountain") and *magedōn*. *Magedōn* occurs three times in the Septuagint (Josh. 12:22; Judg. 1:27; 2 Chron. 35:22) and *mageddōn* once in 2 Kings 9:27 with reference to Megiddo; so the name Armageddon means "the mountain of Megiddo." Megiddo was a well-known fortress-city located in the northern part of Israel in the plain of Esdraelon at the foot of the Carmel ridge between the Mediterranean Sea and the Sea of Galilee. Since the city stood in the Valley of Jezreel or Esraelon on the great highway from Egypt to Damascus, providing a natural passage for the invasion of Palestine, it was a very important strategic site. Its vicinity was one of the famous battlefields which witnessed the greatest and most decisive battles in the history of Israel. At Megiddo, Barak and Deborah defeated Sisera and his army (Judg. 5:19–21), Ahaziah was shot by Jehu (2 Kings 9:27), and Josiah was killed by Pharaoh Neco (2 Kings 23:29–30; Zech. 12:11). Some other significant battles probably occurred there including the victory of Gideon over the Midianites (Judg. 7) and the defeat of Saul by the Philistines (1 Sam. 31:1–7).

The problem, however, is that Megiddo was located in a plain rather than on a mountain. There is no Mount of Megiddo. Different suggestions have been offered on the matter. The view which is most likely is that "the mountain of Megiddo" refers to Mount Carmel, which lay close to Megiddo.[16] Mount Carmel hosted one of the most significant battles in Israel's history—the battle in which the prophet Elijah defeated the prophets of Baal (1 Kings 18). It appears that this spiritual battle stands behind the battle of Armageddon of Revelation 16:16. The allusion to the Carmel event may already be observed in Revelation 13:13–14 where the earth beast brings fire "down from heaven to the earth before the people"; this reminds one of the fire that the prophet Elijah called down from heaven (1 Kings 18:38), which demonstrated that the Lord was the true God of Israel to be worshiped.

William H. Shea points to further parallels between the battle of Armageddon of Revelation 16 and 1 Kings 18.[17] For instance, just as Elijah had Ahab summon all Israel to Mount Carmel for the contest, so the satanic trinity calls its followers to Armageddon. The apostate religious system involved in the battle of Armageddon is represented by the great harlot in Revelation 17–18, corresponding to the Israelite queen Jezebel who was the main player in the Mount Carmel scenario. The main role in gathering forces to Armageddon, according to Revelation 16:13, will be played by the false prophet. This is the first time the term "false prophet" occurs in the book. In the Mount Carmel event, 850 false prophets were on Mount Carmel to oppose Elijah. Just as the prophets of Baal were slaughtered by Elijah (1 Kings 18:40), so the followers of the satanic trinity will be defeated in a similar way with the sword coming from Christ's mouth (cf. Rev. 19:21).

All of this suggests that, in portraying the final battle between Christ and the forces of darkness, John had in mind this event from Israel's past. The name of Armageddon must be taken symbolically. It does not refer to any geographical territory either in Palestine or elsewhere, but rather to the final worldwide spiritual conflict in which the satanic trinity and its forces will suffer total and final defeat by Christ and his armies.

EXPOSITION

16:12 The sixth angel pours his bowl on ***the great river Euphrates, and its water was dried up.*** The symbolic drying up of the Euphrates River evidently results in the collapse of end-time Babylon, the oppressor of God's end-time people. The imagery is drawn entirely from the fall of ancient Babylon, the religious and political enemy of Israel in the Old Testament. Hans LaRondelle remarks: "The perspective of the future fall of Babylon is based on the fall of ancient Babylon as its ordained type. The theological essentials remain the same while the ethnic and geographic restrictions are removed by giving them cosmic-universal proportions."[18]

With the destruction of ancient Babylon, God desired to deliver his people from their oppressors and to bring them from captivity back to their homeland (Jer. 50:33–34). The drying up of the Euphrates thus functioned as "the preparation for Israel's deliverance."[19] Just as the sudden drying up of the Euphrates River led to the collapse of ancient Babylon (Isa. 44:27–28; Jer. 50:35–38; 51:36–37), so the symbolic drying up of "the great river Euphrates" is preliminary to the collapse of end-time Babylon. The idea assures the church of Christ of "the certainty of the fall of end-time Babylon."[20] As the collapse of ancient Babylon was the fulfillment of prophecy, so will be the collapse of end-time Babylon.

John the revelator makes clear that the Euphrates here must be understood figuratively. He later explains in 17:15 that the Euphrates River on which end-time Babylon dwells (17:1; cf. Jer. 51:13) symbolizes the national powers of the world—"peoples and multitudes and nations and tongues" who would be in the service of end-time Babylon (Rev. 17:18). The Euphrates River thus represents the people of the world and "their civil authorities who support the religious authority of Babylon in the last days."[21] The symbolic drying up of the Euphrates signifies, accordingly, that the secular powers and nations of the world that are in service to end-time Babylon will withdraw their support for this religious system.

Unfortunately, John does not explain what will cause the secular powers to withdraw their allegiance from Babylon and turn against her (cf. Rev. 17:15–16). It seems clear, however, that the situation comes to the fore in preparation for the sixth plague. The proclamation of the everlasting gospel by the three angels certainly prepares the way for that. However, a sudden change in attitude must evidently come as a result of the realization of Babylon's impotence to protect her followers from the unbearable terror of the plagues. The nations of the earth become disillusioned with Babylon's impotence to protect herself, for even the very seat of Satan's authority is struck by the plagues (Rev. 16:10–11). Meanwhile, the faithful are under God's protective power and are evidently not harmed by the plagues. The disillusioned nations will unitedly withdraw their support from Babylon and turn it into such hostility that they will completely destroy Babylon (cf. Rev. 17:16–17). This is the sense in which the drying up of the river Euphrates must be understood.

The collapse of Babylon, however, is not an end in itself. The drying up of the Euphrates prepares the way for *the kings from the rising of the sun.* Here is a reference to Christ ("King of kings and Lord of lords") and his armies consisting of the saints—the ones who are "called and elect and faithful" (Rev. 17:14), and who are kings and priests (Rev. 1:6; 5:10)—to fight against the world confederacy under the leadership of the satanic trinity. What we have here is the end-time confederacy of the saints ready to be directly engaged in battle against the confederacy of evil agencies under the leadership of Satan himself. "At that time shall arise Michael, the great prince who has charge of your people. And there shall be a time of trouble, such as never has been since there was a nation till that time; but at that time your people shall be delivered, every one whose name shall be found written in the book"

(Dan. 12:1, RSV). Christ comes to help his end-time people and deliver them from the oppression of Babylon.

The scene of Revelation 16:12 elaborates further upon the famous conquest of ancient Babylon by Cyrus the Persian and his allied forces. Cyrus is referred to by Isaiah as God's messiah (Isa. 45:1) and as coming "from the rising of the sun" (Isa. 41:25; cf. 41:2; 46:11). The drying up of the river Euphrates provided the way for Cyrus and his armies to overtake and destroy ancient Babylon, the oppressor of God's people of Israel. The destruction of Babylon by Cyrus initiated the deliverance of God's people from captivity and the return to their homeland (Isa. 45:13; Jer. 50:33–38; 51:36–37). John uses this well-known incident to illustrate the preparation for the final battle between Christ and Satan. The book of Revelation takes Cyrus's capture of Babylon and subsequent liberation of Israel as a guarantee of what Christ with his armies will do in overthrowing end-time Babylon and thus providing ultimate deliverance for his people (Rev. 19:1–19).[22]

16:13–14 John now turns our attention to the forces that array themselves against Christ and his end-time people in preparation for the final battle. He sees the satanic trinity—the dragon, the beast, and the false prophet—and *three unclean spirits* coming from their *mouth.* Here is a new designation of the earth beast of Revelation 13:11–17 as *the false prophet*, a deceptive character who misleads people. These are the main characteristics of false prophets in the Bible. H. B. Swete describes false prophets as persons "who falsely interpret the Mind of God. True religion has no worse enemies, and Satan no better allies."[23] The earth beast, in the role of a false prophet, is seducing people to side with and worship the satanic trinity instead of God. As the time of Christ's first coming witnessed intense demonic activities on a scale never previously encountered, so it shall be in the closing days of earth's history.[24] In his sermon on the Mount of Olives, Jesus warned his followers that as the time of the end approached, "false prophets will arise, and will show signs and wonders, in order, if possible, to lead the elect astray" (Mark 13:22; cf. Matt. 24:24; 2 Pet. 2:1).

The three unclean spirits proceeding from the mouths of the satanic trinity resemble *frogs.* As unclean animals, frogs stand for uncleanness. Uncleanness is indeed the characteristic of end-time Babylon (the name designates the satanic triumvirate). Babylon is full of "abominations and the unclean things of her fornication" (Rev. 17:4). She is "the dwelling place of demons and a prison of every unclean spirit" (Rev. 18:2).

The unclean spirits appearing as frogs remind us of the frog plague in Egypt (Exod. 8:1–15). What is especially significant with regard to the Egyptian frog plague is that it was the last plague which Pharaoh's magicians were able to reproduce in imitating the miracles of Moses through their deceptive artistry, thus confounding the minds of both Pharaoh and the Egyptians.[25] In other words, the frogs were the last deception with which the magicians could influence and persuade Pharaoh to oppose God and not to take seriously his message given through Moses. The three frog-like demons of the sixth plague are Satan's last attempt to counterfeit the work of God, for they appear to be the evil counterpart of the three angels of Revelation 14. Furthermore, the message they send to the earth dwellers is the antithesis of the warning message proclaimed by the three angels.

The frog-like demons proceed from the mouths of the satanic trinity. This indicates that they are Satan's powerful agents of propaganda who will make persuasive deceptions in the final battle. The three frog-like demons are the very "breath" of the satanic trinity in the last deception. Satan is determined to win the victory in the final crisis, and he enables the demonic spirits to perform miraculous *signs.* This clearly reminds us of Revelation 13:13–14. Miraculous signs are a part of Satan's end-time deception to persuade people to side with the satanic trinity rather than the true God.

The purpose of the end-time miraculous deception performed by the frog-like demons in the final crisis is to persuade *the kings of the whole inhabited world to gather them for the battle of the great day of God the Almighty.* Deception is Satan's method of persuasion (cf. Rev. 13:13–14; 20:7–9). This recalls the "deceiving spirit" which enticed king Ahab to refuse the message sent to him from God and to go into the battle (1 Kings 22:21–23). The satanic trinity here sends three demonic angels with the false gospel to persuade the secular and political authorities and powers of the world to side with them against God and his people for the great day of God Almighty. It appears that spiritualism will become part of the final deception "that is to sweep the world."[26] Ellen G. White admonishes Christians:

> Fearful sights of a supernatural character will soon be revealed in the heavens, in token of the power of miracle-working demons. The spirits of devils will go forth to the kings of the earth and to the whole world, to fasten them in deception, and urge them on to unite with Satan in his last struggle against the government of heaven. By these agencies, rulers and subjects will be alike deceived. Persons will arise pretending

to be Christ Himself, and claiming the title and worship which belong to the world's Redeemer. They will perform wonderful miracles of healing and will profess to have revelations from heaven contradicting the testimony of the Scriptures.[27]

16:15   In the midst of this graphic portrayal of the great preparation and gathering for the final battle, John suddenly inserts the direct words of Jesus who makes earnest appeals to his people to be ready and not to be deceived: ***Behold, I am coming as a thief.*** This coming of Jesus is in connection with the final battle. Jesus' appeal to his end-time people is "to orient their lives in the present toward the coming eschatological reality."[28] By means of deceptive persuasion, the satanic trinity will be able to gather the secular and political powers of the world. However, as Cyrus unexpectedly triumphed over ancient Babylon (cf. Dan. 5), so will the intervention of Christ prevail over end-time Babylon: "The day of the Lord will come just like a thief in the night. While they are saying, 'Peace and safety!' then destruction will come upon them suddenly...and they shall not escape" (1 Thess. 5:2–3). Jesus often warned of the unexpectedness of the final crisis and his coming (cf. Matt. 24:42–44; Luke 21:34–35).

Christ urges his followers toward spiritual alertness for this great critical period in the world's history. They need to stay spiritually awake and watchful and remain ready, for the day of God Almighty can come at any moment. They are like soldiers dressed and on alert. Jesus admonished his followers in the conclusion of his speech on the Mount of Olives: "Be on guard, that your hearts may not be weighted down with dissipation and drunkenness and the worries of life, and that day come on you suddenly like a trap; for it will come upon all those who dwell on the face of all the earth. But keep on the alert at all times, praying in order that you may have strength to escape all these things that are about to take place, and to stand before the Son of Man" (Luke 21:34–36). "Therefore, be on the alert...in case he should come suddenly and find you asleep. What I say to you I say to all, 'Be on the alert!'" (Mark 13:35–37).

In this critical time, Christ's followers will be characterized by spiritual alertness. As Robert H. Mounce states, they will not be "taken by surprise as a soldier who, when the alarm is sounded, must run away naked because he has misplaced his clothing,"[29] or as a guard, caught asleep by the captain at the temple gate, who would have his clothes burned and be sent away naked in disgrace (see *Notes* on Rev. 16:15). Therefore, each Christian is urged to keep his garment ***so that he does not walk naked and they see his shame.*** This admonition reminds one of a similar appeal that Jesus made to the church of Laodicea to have "white garments that you may clothe yourself, so that the shame of your nakedness may not be exposed" (Rev. 3:18). Garments stand for "the righteous deeds of the saints," that is, the requirement for participation in meeting Christ (Rev. 19:7–9; Matt. 22:11–14). They symbolize uncompromising loyalty and faithfulness to Christ (Rev. 3:4–5; 6:11; 7:9, 13–14; 19:8). On the other hand, nakedness denotes the compromising attitude toward Babylon under her deceptive persuasion (cf. Rev. 17:2; 18:3). In defeating Babylon, God will make her "desolate and naked" (Rev. 17:16), as the token of the severe humiliation of the defeated army (cf. Isa. 20:4). Those who compromise with Babylon will have an obvious share in the humiliation of Babylon. Only those clothed spiritually in the robe of Christ's righteousness will be able to stand firm at "the hour of trial that is about to come on those who dwell on the earth" (Rev. 3:10).

16:16 John shows that the demonic deceptive miracles will achieve a success beyond any prediction or expectation. In refusing the true gospel, people "will believe a lie which comes as a strong over-mastering delusion" which is accompanied by "miraculous wonders" (cf. 2 Thess. 2:9–12).[30] Satan is able to persuade the religious and secular powers of the world and gather them *to the place which is called in Hebrew "Armageddon"* ("the Mountain of Megiddo"). Bruce M. Metzger correctly observes that because of the historical significance of Megiddo as "the scene of frequent and decisive battles in ancient times (Judg. 5:19–21; 2 Kings 9:27; 23:29), it would appear that John is using familiar language to symbolize the final great conflict between the forces of good and the forces of evil, a battle in which evil will be defeated— not by armaments but by God's incarnate Word, Jesus Christ (19:13)."[31] The religious and secular powers are all unified and organized into one army under the leadership of the satanic trinity for the battle on the great day of God Almighty. This brings to mind the text from Psalm 2:2: "The kings of the earth take their stand, and the rulers take counsel together against the Lord and against His Anointed." The battle of Armageddon echoes the well-known conflict on Mount Carmel between the prophet Elijah and the prophets of Baal (1 Kings 18). The issue to be resolved once and for all on Mount Carmel was to identify the true God: "If the Lord is God, follow him; but if Baal, follow him" (1 Kings 18:21).

The same matter will have to be resolved in the great showdown battle of Armageddon: Is the true Trinity or the spurious satanic trinity to be followed and worshiped? The battle will finally resolve the issue that Satan introduced in the beginning: Who is the legitimate ruler of the universe? This indicates further that the final battle of Armageddon is not a military battle but a spiritual one—the battle for the minds of people. Its conclusion will be like that of the Carmel conflict at the time of Elijah when the assembled people on Mount Carmel recognized that "The LORD, He is God; the LORD, He is God" (1 Kings 18:39).

Revelation 16:12–16 does not portray the actual battle, but only the preparation and great gathering of the religious and political powers of rebellious humanity to Armageddon. The actual battle follows the sixth plague and is described in Revelation 16:17–19:21. John sees later "the beast and the kings of the earth and their armies gathered to make war" against Christ coming from heaven as King of kings and Lord of lords accompanied by his army consisting of the saints (Rev. 19:19; cf. 17:14). The battle will conclude with a total defeat of the beast and his armies (19:20–21) by the one who is indeed the legitimate King of kings and Lord of lords (Rev. 19:16).

THE SEVENTH PLAGUE (16:17–21)

This section concludes the vision of the seven last plagues. With the seventh plague, readers are brought to the very beginning of the battle of Armageddon.

> **¹⁷And the seventh one poured out his bowl into the air, and a loud voice came out of the temple from the throne, saying: "It is done." ¹⁸And there were flashes of lightning and voices and peals of thunder, and a great earthquake occurred, such as has not been ever since human beings came upon the earth, so powerful was the great earthquake. ¹⁹And the great city was split into three parts, and the cities of the nations fell. And Babylon the great was remembered before God to give her the cup of the wine of the fury of his wrath. ²⁰And every island fled away, and the mountains were not found. ²¹And great hailstones about a talent in weight came down from heaven upon the people, and the people blasphemed God for the plague of the hail, because its plague was extremely great.**

NOTES

16:17 The temple. On the meaning and significance of the heavenly temple (Gr. *naos*) in Revelation, see *Notes* on Revelation 11:1, 19.

The throne. See *Notes* on Revelation 4:2.

16:18 *A great earthquake.* This earthquake is evidently distinct from the one mentioned at the opening of the sixth seal (Rev. 6:12) coming prior to this one. See *Notes* on Revelation 6:12.

16:19 *Three parts.* See *Notes* on Revelation 8:7.

Babylon the great. See *Notes* on Revelation 14:8.

The cup of the wine. See *Notes* on Revelation 14:10.

16:21 *Great hailstones about a talent in weight came down from heaven upon the people.* Hailstones are often God's weapons of judgment in the Old Testament. The destructive hailstones of the seventh Egyptian plague devastated the land (Exod. 9:24–25). Hailstones were God's weapon against the five Amorite kings in the battle under Joshua; more people were killed by the hailstones than by the sword (Josh. 10:11). Ezekiel prophesied of God sending "a torrential rain, with hailstones, fire, and brimstone" against Gog and Magog (Ezek. 38:22). God asked Job: "Have you seen the storehouses of the hail, which I have reserved for the time of distress, for the day of war and battle?" (Job 38:22–23). Isaiah and Ezekiel speak of a flooding rain and great hailstones which God will send in judgment against the unfaithful (Isa. 28:2; 30:30; Ezek. 13:10–14). Each hailstone of the seventh bowl plague was about "a talent in weight." An exact measure of a talent is uncertain; it varied "among different peoples and at various times."[32] It could be from fifty to over one hundred pounds. The hailstones of the seventh plague were clearly of enormous size and, consequently, of devastating effect.

Extremely great. In order to show the severity of the seventh plague, John uses the Greek word *sphodra* ("extremely," "very much") which is used nowhere else in the book.

EXPOSITION

16:17–18 The seventh plague proceeds from the very presence of God. The last of the seven angels pours out his bowl upon the air. At that moment a loud voice issues *out of the temple from the throne.* This recalls Revelation 16:1 where "a loud voice from the temple" commissions the seven angels to pour out their bowls. The voice comes from the throne of God located in the temple in heaven (cf. Rev. 4–5). The temple and the throne are inseparable in the book of Revelation. The throne stands as the controlling force in the universe. It signifies the very presence of God and his sovereign authority over the creation. In Revelation it stands in opposition to the throne of Satan (Rev. 2:13; 13:2) and the throne of the beast (Rev. 16:10). The fact that this loud voice comes from the throne of God suggests that God himself is speaking.

The divine voice announces: *It is done.* This is a repetition of the "It is done!" of Calvary which announced the victory over Satan and the beginning of the time of the end (John 19:30). This time the same voice of Christ proclaims the conclusion of earth's history and the final victory over Satan and the powers of darkness. Once more this voice will be heard in Revelation (21:6). It will announce the eradication of sin and the glorious beginning of the everlasting kingdom of God.

At that moment, there were *flashes of lightning and voices and peals of thunder.* In Revelation, this phenomenon is always associated with the throne of God (cf. Rev. 4:5; 8:5; 11:19). In addition, *a great earthquake occurred, such as has not happened ever since humans came upon the earth, so powerful was the great earthquake.* Earthquakes in the Old Testament are used to describe the visitation of God's final judgment upon the earth, referred to as the Day of the Lord.

16:19 The severe earthquake shatters *the great city*, splitting it into *three parts.* The term "great city" is a reference to Babylon (cf. Rev. 17:18; 18:10). Satan's kingdom in Revelation consists of three parts. End-time Babylon is made up of the union of the satanic trinity. In experiencing divine judgments, it splits into three parts: the dragon, the sea beast, and the earth beast. The unity of the satanic trinity is shattered. After Babylon is split, *the cities of the nations fell.* The nations in Revelation denote the political and secular powers of the world that supported end-time Babylon and frustrated God's work on the earth. The breakup of end-time Babylon leads to their unavoidable collapse.

And Babylon the great was remembered before God to give her the cup of the wine of the fury of his wrath. This anticipates Revelation 18:5–6 where God has remembered Babylon's iniquities and punishes her with "the cup which she has mixed," and he mixes a double portion for her. It also recalls Revelation 14:10 where all those who worship the beast and his image and receive the mark are threatened to drink "from the wine of the wrath of God which is mixed undiluted in the cup of his wrath." What we see here is that Babylon "who made all nations drink of the wine of the wrath of her fornication" (Rev. 14:8; 17:2; 18:3) is given by God "the cup of the wine of the fury of his wrath." Revelation 14:19 portrays the execution of judgment on Babylon and all those who have chosen to side with her.

16:20–21 The severe earthquake sinks *every island* and *the mountains.* This reminds us of the scene of the opening of the sixth seal in which "every mountain and island were moved from their places" (Rev. 6:14). The author of Hebrews pointed to the final shaking of the creation, "in order that those things which cannot be shaken may remain," namely, the kingdom of God (Heb. 12:26–28). Finally, *great hailstones about a talent in weight came down from heaven upon the people.* Here we have another portrayal of the manifestation of God's judgment drawn from the Old Testament. Just as God sent hailstones to destroy the enemies of Israel (cf. Josh. 10:11; Ezek. 38:22), so in this case we see the manifestation of the full and final judgment on the enemies of God's end-time people.

However, these exceedingly great hailstones do not produce any change in the wicked. Those on whom these hailstones fall *blasphemed God for the plague of the hail, because its plague was extremely great.* This is the recurring theme of Revelation 16; those on whom the last plagues fall respond by cursing God and refusing to repent of their evil deeds (16:9, 11, 21). This is understandable in light of the fact that probation has closed and intercession is no longer available (cf. Rev. 15:8). The end has come, and a definite line of demarcation has been set between those who followed God and those who were in opposition to him. There is no longer any opportunity for repentance.[33] The unrepentant sinners are beyond their ability to return. In the scene of the sixth seal, they are portrayed as seeking to hide themselves from God's face on "the great day of his wrath" (Rev. 6:16). It is impossible for even this "extremely great" plague to change their attitude toward God and cause them to return to him.

A RETROSPECT ON REVELATION 15–16

The purpose of Revelation 15–16 is "to reveal God's pre-ordained plan for the triumph of His faithful ones."[34] The seven last plagues are portrayed in Revelation as God's final response to the wrath of end-time Babylon in its attempts to destroy God's faithful people. Chapters 15–16 portray a vivid picture of the consequences the world will reap as a result of the abandonment of the law of God and his plans for human beings. The violation of the divine law results in the destruction of the violators. Paul wrote: "Do not be deceived, God is not mocked; for whatever a man sows, this he will also reap" (Gal. 6:7). Those who have been destroying the earth will experience their own destruction (Rev. 11:18). However, although Revelation pictures the end as a series of terrifying events, Paulien states that "these events are in the control of One who cares deeply for the human race, One who loves the human race so much that He was willing to die for it (Rev. 5:5–12)."[35]

The climax of the seven plagues is the battle of Armageddon. As LaRondelle points out, "Armageddon is Heaven's response to the cries of the Israel of God for deliverance from the Babylonian oppressor."[36] The battle of Armageddon guarantees that the powers of this world which stand in opposition to God will finally meet their end as the answer to the prayers of God's suffering people (cf. Rev. 6:9–10). The preparation for the final battle is described in the scene of the sixth plague, while the battle itself is described in Revelation 16:17–19:21.

Significant to the understanding of the true character of the battle of Armageddon is the interlude of Revelation 16:15. In the midst of the graphic portrayal of the great preparation for the battle of Armageddon, and right before the description of the final battle, John inserts a forewarning and appeal of Jesus to his church: "Behold, I am coming as a thief. Blessed is the one who watches and keeps his garments so that he does not walk naked and they see his shame" (16:15). The warning is inserted for the purpose of providing a firm assurance to God's people as they face the final deception. Christ's end-time followers will be at the very center of the battle of Armageddon. They must keep in mind that the climactic event of the final crisis is the return of Jesus. The coming of Christ in glory and majesty is to be "the focus of the expectation" of God's end-time people.[37] Jesus urges them to prepare themselves spiritually and to be found faithful and ready for the critical event in this world's history.

It is of crucial importance for God's end-time people to understand the true character of the final battle in order to prepare themselves for it. Christ's warning to his end-time people in Revelation 16:15 shows clearly that the nature of the final battle in which they will be involved is not a political and military battle, but rather a theological and spiritual one. It is not a battle for economic interest. Hans LaRondelle states: "War predictions of a purely secular nature, detached from Christ and the divine plan of salvation, are no part of the Old Testament covenant prophecies or the NT [New Testament] Armageddon war. Yahweh war never was a *secular*, political struggle between nations."[38] Armageddon is "the battle for the mind [and intellect] of every human being on earth."[39] Paul describes the nature of Christian warfare: "For though we walk in the flesh, we do not war according to the flesh, for the weapons of our warfare are not of the flesh, but divinely powerful for the destruction of fortresses. We are destroying speculations and every lofty thing raised up against the knowledge of God, and we are taking every thought captive to the obedience of Christ" (2 Cor. 10:3–5).

Revelation portrays the final battle as part of the cosmic conflict between Christ and his arch-antagonist "the Devil and Satan, the one who deceives the whole world" (Rev. 12:9). The instigator of the battle of Armageddon is the same Satan who originated war in heaven, lost it there, and, in constant frustration, became enraged "at the woman, and went away to wage war with the remaining ones of her offspring, the ones keeping the commandments of God and having the testimony of Jesus" (Rev. 12:17). The battle of Armageddon represents his firm determination and last attempt to destroy God's people and prevent the establishment of God's kingdom on the earth. Paul made clear that Satan's activities in the final days will include persuasion which uses "all power and signs and false wonders, and with all the deception of wickedness for those who perish, because they did not receive the love of the truth so as to be saved" (2 Thess. 2:9–10). Ellen White gives a warning:

> The "time of trouble, such as never was," is soon to open upon us; and we shall need an experience which we do not now possess and which many are too indolent to obtain. It is often the case that trouble is greater in anticipation than in reality; but this is not true of the crisis before us. The most vivid presentation cannot reach the magnitude of the ordeal. In that time of trial, every soul must stand for himself before God.[40]

Christ's followers need spiritual discernment as they face the deceptions of the final crisis.

Armageddon is a battle in which all the people of the earth must give allegiance to either God or Satan. The ultimate issue will be regarding who God is, as it was on Mount Carmel. What God did on Carmel he will do once again in the final battle; he will win the triumphal victory over the oppressor of his people. However, as LaRondelle states, "the *ultimate* purpose of Christ's return is not the destruction of Babylon" but the final establishment of "God's rulership in eternal peace and justice on the earth."[41]

ENDNOTES

1. Beale, 784.
2. Mounce, 286.
3. Beasley-Murray, 233.
4. Barclay, *The Revelation of John*, 2:120.
5. Ibid., 2:27.
6. Ibid., 2:121.
7. Morris, 185.
8. LaRondelle, *Chariots of Salvation*, 115.
9. See Herodotus, *History* 1.191. Trans. George Rawlinson. Great Books of the Western World (Chicago: Encyclopaedia Britanica, 1952), 6:43.

10. The document describes Cyrus' capture of Babylon in the following way: "Without any battle, he [god Marduk] made him [Cyrus] enter his town Babylon, sparing Babylon any calamity" (J. B. Pritchard, *Ancient Near Eastern Texts Relating to the Old Testament*, 3d ed. [Princeton, NJ: Princeton University Press, 1969], 315). See a discussion of the subject by William H. Shea, "The Location and Significance of Armageddon in Rev 16:16," *Andrews University Seminary Studies* 18 (1980), 157–158.

11. LaRondelle, *Chariots of Salvation*, 116.

12. Ibid., 120; idem, *The Good News about Armageddon*, 24–25, 120–121.

13. LaRondelle, "Contextual Approach to the Seven Last Plagues," 149.

14. Maxwell, 443.

15. Bruce, 657; cf. *Mishnah Middoth* 2.1.

16. Shea, "The Location and Significance of Armageddon," 160.

17. Ibid., 161.

18. Hans K. LaRondelle, "Armageddon: Sixth and Seventh Plagues," in *Symposium on Revelation—Book 2*, Daniel and Revelation Committee Series 7 (Silver Spring, MD: Biblical Research Institute, 1992), 384.

19. LaRondelle, *The Good News about Armageddon*, 16.

20. LaRondelle, *Chariots of Salvation*, 119.

21. Paulien, *What the Bible Says about the End-Time*, 133.

22. *The Seventh-day Adventist Bible Commentary*, 4:265.

23. Swete, 207.

24. Desmond Ford, 2:571.

25. Beale, 832.

26. Desmond Ford, 571.

27. White, *The Great Controversy*, 624.

28. Boring, *Revelation*, 178.

29. Mounce, 301.

30. Desmond Ford, 571.

31. Metzger, *Breaking the Code*, 84.

32. Mounce, 304, n. 40.

33. Beale, 845.

34. LaRondelle, *How to Understand the End-Time Prophecies*, 390.

35. Paulien, *What the Bible Says about the End-Time*, 149.

36. LaRondelle, *Chariots of Salvation*, 144.

37. Ladd, 214.

38. LaRondelle, "Armageddon: Sixth and Seventh Plagues," 390.

39. Paulien, *What the Bible Says about the End-Time*, 136.

40. White, *The Great Controversy*, 622.

41. LaRondelle, *Chariots of Salvation*, 121. For further study regarding the interpretation of the battle of Armageddon, see Hans K. LaRondelle, *Chariots of Salvation* and "Armageddon: Sixth and Seventh Plagues."

For an understanding of the spiritual significance and meaning of the final battle, see Jon Paulien, *What the Bible Says about the End-Time* (Hagerstown, MD: Review and Herald, 1994), 131–150; C. Mervyn Maxwell, *The Message of Revelation*, God Cares 2 (Boise, ID: Pacific Press, 1985), 428–451; and Hans K. LaRondelle, *The Good News about Armageddon* (Hagerstown, MD: Review and Herald, 1990).

Revelation 16:19, which announced the collapse of "Babylon the great," functions as a springboard passage. While concluding the section of the seven last plagues, it also introduces Revelation 17–18. As such, Revelation 16:19 provides the clue for understanding Revelation 17–18, which quite evidently is the elaboration of the springboard passage. It describes how God's judgments will be executed on end-time Babylon.

Whenever a new power is mentioned elsewhere in the book, its description is given first in general terms. Following this pattern, Revelation 17 provides a description of end-time Babylon for the purpose of showing the reason for judgment upon her; Revelation 18 describes the judgment upon this end-time apostate religious system and her demise.

PROSTITUTE BABYLON (17:1–6A)

Two times John has announced the collapse of end-time Babylon without identifying it (Rev. 14:8; 16:19). Now he provides the description and identification of Babylon in terms of a prostitute in her seductive role at the time of the end.

> *¹And one of the seven angels who had seven bowls came and spoke with me saying: "Come, I will show you the judgment of the great prostitute sitting on many waters, ²with whom the kings of the earth have committed fornication, and those dwelling on the earth became drunk with the wine of her fornication." ³And he carried me away in the Spirit into a wilderness. And I saw a woman sitting on a scarlet beast full of names of blasphemy, having seven heads and ten horns. ⁴And the woman was clothed in purple and scarlet, and adorned with gold and precious stones and pearls, having in her*

hand a golden cup filled with abominations and the unclean things of her fornication, ⁵and upon her forehead was a name inscribed, which is a mystery: "Babylon the great, the mother of prostitutes and of the abomination of the earth." ⁶And I saw the woman drunk from the blood of the saints and from the witnesses of Jesus.

NOTES

17:1 *Sitting on many waters.* The expression is taken from Jeremiah 51:13 where the phrase "on many waters" denotes specifically the Euphrates River. The meaning of the symbol is provided in Revelation 17:15 (see *Notes* on Rev. 16:12). It is important to realize that "sitting on many waters" changes into "sitting on a scarlet beast" (17:3) and later into "seven mountains on which the woman is sitting" (17:9). Here again John employs the "I heard" and "I saw" technique. John first *hears* something in the vision, and what he subsequently *sees* is actually the same thing, yet different. It appears that what he sees is a different facet of what he heard before (see the "Introduction" of this commentary). Thus, in chapter 17, he first hears of "the great prostitute sitting on many waters"; what he later sees is "a woman sitting on a scarlet beast" (17:4–5). This suggests that waters, the beast, and the seven mountains all refer to the same thing, namely the secular and political power of the world.

17:1–2 *The great prostitute...with whom the kings of the earth have committed fornication.* Fornication in the Old Testament is used often as a metaphor for the alliance between apostate cities and nations. Thus, for instance, Isaiah called Tyre a city that played "harlot with all the kingdoms on the face of the earth" (Isa. 23:17). Nahum announced the judgment of Nineveh "because of the many harlotries of the harlot...who sells nations by her harlotries, and families by her sorceries" (Nah. 3:4). The language of fornication is often used with reference to the relationships between Israel and the surrounding nations. Isaiah mourns: "How the faithful city has become a harlot" (Isa. 1:21). Jeremiah speaks of Israel as "a harlot with many lovers" (Jer. 3:1; cf. Hos. 3–4; Mic. 1:7). Ezekiel mentions Israel playing the harlot with "many nations" including the Egyptians, Assyrians, and Chaldeans (Ezek. 16:26–29; 23:3–30). Furthermore, it appears that John's description of the great prostitute in 17:1–6 reflects the image of the figure of queen Jezebel which served as a model for Jeremiah's portrayal of faithless Jerusalem (Jer. 4:30; cf. 2 Kings 9:30).[1] The portrayal of the union between end-time Babylon and the governing political powers of the world in Revelation 17–18 builds on this Old Testament imagery.

17:2 *Those dwelling on the earth.* See *Notes* on Revelation 6:10.

17:3 *"Woman sitting on a scarlet beast."* The symbol of the beast stands for political powers that stand in service to end-time Babylon in the last days (see *Notes* on Rev. 13:1).

Blasphemy. Blasphemy in the New Testament refers to the act of claiming equality with God (John 10:33; cf. Matt. 26:63–65) as well as the prerogatives of God alone (Mark 2:7). See further *Notes* on Revelation 13:5.

17:5 *Upon her forehead was a name inscribed.* This may reflect the Roman custom for prostitutes in the public brothels to wear a frontlet with their name.[2] Jeremiah mentions "a harlot's forehead" (or "a harlot's brow" in RSV; Jer. 3:3). It also recalls the inscription "Holy to the Lord" on the high priest's miter in the Hebrew sanctuary ritual (Exod. 28:36–38).

A mystery. The word "mystery" here might be either a part of the inscription on the woman's forehead ("Mystery Babylon") or a prefix to the title. The latter seems to be more likely, indicating that Babylon is to be understood, not in a literal sense, but rather as a cryptic name and a mystery now to be revealed. Only those endowed with divine discernment are able to grasp the full meaning of the name.

Babylon the great. See *Notes* on Revelation 14:8.

EXPOSITION

17:1–2 One of the seven angels who executed the plagues of the wrath of God on the wicked summons John to view *the judgment of the great prostitute.* This angel is most likely the seventh-bowl angel who announced the collapse of Babylon (Rev. 16:19). This suggests that what the angel is about to explain to John in Revelation 17–18 elaborates upon what was portrayed in the sixth plague (Rev. 16:12–16). The same angel later summons John to show him the bride of Christ, the New Jerusalem (Rev. 21:9). Robert H. Mounce points out that when the great prostitute with all her seductive attractiveness and glamour "is exposed and destroyed, then the Bride of Christ will be seen in all her beauty and true worth."[3]

What does this woman prostitute represent? In Revelation 17:5, John identifies her as "Babylon the great." Babylon in the Old Testament is a symbol of oppression and of rebellion against God. John uses the figure of Babylon to portray the prevailing apostate religious system in the world allied with the state and its related authorities at the time of the end (cf. Rev. 17:18). George E. Ladd correctly observes that "the city had a historical manifestation in first-century Rome, but the full significance of the wicked city is eschatological."[4] End-time Babylon is a worldwide religious confederacy with the satanic trinity—Satan, the sea beast, and the earth beast or false prophet—arrayed against God and his faithful people and supported by the secular and political powers (cf. Rev. 13:12–17).

In portraying this end-time apostate religious system in Revelation 17, John uses many references to ancient Babylon in the Old Testament.[5] The prostitute Babylon is seen as *sitting on many waters.* This expression is taken from Jeremiah where the prophet describes ancient Babylon as dwelling by the many waters of the river Euphrates, greatly multiplying its wealth: "O you who dwell by many waters, abundant in treasures, your end has come" (Jer. 51:13). The angel later explains to John that the waters on which the prostitute sits have a deeper meaning; they figuratively refer to the secular powers of the world, "peoples and multitudes and nations and tongues" (Rev. 17:15), which at the time of the end will be in service to Babylon and opposing God and his people. The fact that the prostitute sits on these secular powers (cf. Rev. 17:3, 9, 15) signifies that she has dominion and control over them. As Ladd states, first-century "Rome could be said to be seated on many waters in the sense that she drew her strength and sovereignty from her conquest of many nations; but it will be even more true of eschatological Babylon, who will seduce all the world to worship that which is not God."[6]

The angel further explains that this prostitute is the one **with whom the kings of the earth have committed fornication** (also in Rev. 18:3, 9). "The kings of the earth" stand here for the governing political powers of the world that will place their authority and influence into the service of the end-time apostate religious system called Babylon. Their relationship with Babylon is referred to in terms of sexual fornication. Babylon will apparently act through these political powers "to gain control of those inhabitants of earth who have not already voluntarily submitted to her."[7]

The language of fornication is often used by the prophets in the Old Testament with reference to the illicit relationships of Israel with surrounding apostate and disobedient nations (cf. Jer. 3:1–10; Ezek. 16:26–29; 23:3–30). "You have played the harlot with the nations," shouted Ezekiel (23:30). Revelation 17 builds on this Old Testament concept to portray the adulterous alliance of end-time Babylon with the political powers of the world for economic benefits. The political powers of the world will be seduced by Babylon's arrogance and glamorous wealth and luxury. Babylon promises them safety and security.

The adulterous wine of Babylon that first seduces the political powers of the world also affects **those dwelling on the earth** who follow their lead and in turn become **drunk with the wine of her fornication** (also in Rev. 18:3). In drunkenness a person cannot reason and think clearly, and this usually results in bad decisions. End-time Babylon will gain control over the nations of the world by means of deception.

17:3 The angel now takes John **in the Spirit into a wilderness** to witness the divine judgment about to be executed upon prostitute Babylon. Four times John has said that he was "in the Spirit" (cf. 1:10; 4:2; 17:3; 21:10). This indicates that what he sees and hears is not "made by an act of human will" but through the revelation of the Holy Spirit (2 Pet. 1:20). First, John encountered the risen Christ "in the Spirit on the Lord's day" (1:10–18). Second, he witnesses the enthronement of Christ "in the Spirit" in chapters 4–5. Third, John in vision is taken into the wilderness "in the Spirit." And finally, he will be taken "in the Spirit" to a mountain to view the bride-city of the Lamb (21:9–10). The wilderness in 17:3 seems to be a very appropriate setting for judging end-time Babylon. It was where the "red dragon having seven heads and ten horns" pursued the woman/church during the 1,260 prophetic days (Rev. 12:6, 14), but she was there protected by God. The place of the church's persecution is now the setting for the judgment on Babylon. In the course of the vision, John sees *a woman sitting on a scarlet beast.* Earlier in Revelation 17:1, the prostitute was said to sit "on many waters." This reflects her relationship with the nations of the earth (cf. Rev. 17:15). Here she is seen sitting on the beast, reflecting her relationship with the political powers of the world.[8] Through fornication and drunkenness, the governing secular and political powers of the world have been seduced to enter into union with end-time Babylon. The fact that Babylon sits upon the waters and the beast indicates that this end-time religious system has gained control over the secular and political powers of the world. Yet, she is also dependant on them to enforce her plans and purposes.

The scarlet color reinforces the "terrifying appearance of the beast."[9] It associates the beast of Revelation 17 with the red dragon of Revelation 12:3, reflecting an intimate relationship between this end-time political power and Satan.[10] Scarlet, or red, is the color of blood and oppression (cf. 2 Kings 3:22–23; Rev. 6:4). Isaiah describes the sins of harlot Jerusalem as scarlet and red (Isa. 1:15–23) for their "hands are covered with blood" (Isa. 1:15). The scarlet color of the beast is linked directly to the prostitute "drunk from the blood of the saints and from the witnesses of Jesus" (Rev. 17:6).[11] The color is very appropriate for the oppressive character of the beast in relation to God's people.

The language used for the beast upon which Babylon sits is remarkably similar to the description of the sea beast in Revelation 13. The beast of Revelation 17 is described as *having seven heads and ten horns.* In Revelation 12, the dragon is portrayed as having seven heads and ten horns (12:3), chasing after the woman in the wilderness. In Revelation 13, the sea beast—having seven heads and ten horns (13:1), and full of blasphemies against God and his people (13:6–7)—acts in the full authority of the dragon (13:2). He persecutes and oppresses God's people during the forty-two months (13:5–6) of the dragon's pursuit of the woman in the wilderness (Rev. 12:6, 13–16). It is upon the resurrected beast of Revelation 13 that end-time prostitute Babylon sits. This suggests that the religious system of Revelation 17, which will play the key role in the final conflict, is a continuation of the political-religious power that has a long history of harming and oppressing God's people. This oppressing religious power is now to receive judgment.

17:4–6a The great prostitute displays all power and splendor. She is *clothed in purple and scarlet,* and lavishly *adorned with gold and precious stones and pearls* (also in 18:16). John's portrayal of the woman Babylon evokes in particular the image of Jezebel, an ancient Phoenician princess who became a queen of Israel by marrying king Ahab and who led Israel into apostasy. It also echoes the language of Jeremiah concerning the faithless believers. The symbolic city of Jerusalem is portrayed as dressed in scarlet and decorated with ornaments of gold whose lovers turn against her (Jer. 4:30). Her appearance is also almost identical to the bride-city in Revelation 21 (see "Overview: Revelation 12–22:5"). This suggests that the prostitute in chapter 17 has a religious pedigree.

The scarlet of the woman's dress corresponds to the scarlet color of the beast upon which she sits (17:3). As a color of blood and oppression, scarlet is a very fitting imagery of the character of this religious system which is "drunk from the blood of the saints and from the witnesses of Jesus" (17:6). In ancient times, "purple was often used for royal garments" (cf. Judg. 8:26; Esther 8:15; Song of Sol. 3:10; Dan. 5:7).[12] The prostitute states arrogantly: "I sit as a queen" (Rev. 18:7), for she has dominion and rules over the secular and political powers of the world. In ancient times, the scarlet dress and lavish decoration were worn by a prostitute for seduction (Jer. 4:30). Also, harlot cities in the Old Testament are characterized by wealth and prosperity combined with splendor and luxury (Isa. 1:21–22; Jer. 51:13; Ezek. 16:10–13; Nah. 2:9).

End-time Babylon's jewelry consists of gold and precious stones and pearls. The precious stones with their qualities of radiant light, beauty, and permanence are used consistently in the Bible to describe the visible presence of God.[13] However, Babylon's costly and luxurious adornment is the "expression of arrogance and a desire to dominate" the earth.[14] The gold and precious stones and pearls adorn New Jerusalem in her glory (Rev. 21:11). This suggests prostitute Babylon to be an antithesis to the New

Jerusalem, the bride of the Lamb. The luxurious appearance of Babylon also stands in sharp contrast with the appearance of the bride of the Lamb clothed in "fine linen, bright and clean," which represents "the righteous deeds of the saints" (Rev. 19:8).

In her hand the prostitute holds *a golden cup.* A golden cup promises the most delicious drink. The cup that end-time Babylon holds, however, is filled with unclean things offering *abominations and the unclean things of her fornication.* Jeremiah speaks of Babylon as "a golden cup in the hand of the Lord, intoxicating all the earth. The nations have drunk of her wine; therefore the nations are going mad. Suddenly Babylon has fallen and been broken" (Jer. 51:7–8). End-time Babylon is said to make all the people drunk with the cup of her fornication for the purpose of worshiping the beast (cf. Rev. 14:8; 17:2; 18:3).

On the forehead of the prostitute John sees an inscription, which is a divine mystery: *Babylon the great, the mother of prostitutes and of the abomination of the earth.* Babylon is a cryptic name for the end-time worldwide religious confederacy made up of the dragon, the sea beast, and the earth beast. This satanic triumvirate will unite all false and apostate religious systems, the act that makes Babylon "the mother of prostitutes" of the earth. As such, it stands here as an antithesis of the heavenly Jerusalem which is "our mother" (Gal. 4:26). Babylon cannot be identified as Imperial Rome, for it is not a political but rather a religious system dominating political powers of the world at the conclusion of this world's history. As name stands for character, this end-time religious power has the character of Babylon in the Old Testament. Babylon in the Old Testament stands for the beginning of the rebellion against God, and its ambition has been to reach heaven "in order to usurp the place and the ruling power of God (Gen. 11:4; Isa. 14:13–14; Jer. 51:53)."[15] As such, it became the archetypal source of all rebellion and resistance to God throughout history.[16] The children of Babylon in Revelation have the mark with the name of the beast on their foreheads (Rev. 13:17), while the offspring of the woman of Revelation 12 have the name of God written on their foreheads (Rev. 14:1).

It appears that the description of the woman of Babylon in chapter 17 has an even deeper intention. Her appearance mimics that of the high priests in the Old Testament sanctuary ritual. Her purple and scarlet dress adorned with gold, precious stones, and pearls brings to mind the attire of the high priest that included the purple and scarlet colors as well as gold and precious stones (Exod. 28:4–35). The cup that she holds in her hand may parallel the drink offering officiated in the sanctuary (cf. Exod. 29:40–41; 30:9; Lev. 23:13). The inscription on her forehead functions as an antithesis to the title "Holy to the Lord" engraved on a plate on the high priest's miter (Exod. 28:36–38). These allusions suggest that the imagery of the woman of Babylon of chapter 17 refers to an end-time religious institution rather than a political or secular entity. She becomes Satan's powerful tool to seduce the world into apostasy at the end of time, just as the Babylon of old.

End-time Babylon has a long history of persecuting the faithful followers of Christ. John sees her as **drunk from the blood of the saints and from the witnesses of Jesus.** This element evidently points to the persecution of the saints in Revelation 13:14–17. The mother of all rebellion is responsible for the death decree in the final crisis. She who makes all people drunk with her immorality is herself drunk with the blood of the saints who laid down their lives in faithful testimony to Jesus and the gospel. The judgment of Babylon denotes God's answer to the plea of God's oppressed people symbolically portrayed in the scene of the fifth seal: "How long, O Lord, holy and true, will you not judge and avenge our blood upon those who dwell on the earth?" (Rev. 6:10). God is about to judge their oppressors for shedding their blood on the earth.[17]

THE RESURRECTED BEAST (17:6B–18)

Revelation 17:1–6a describes in general terms the end-time apostate power, Babylon, providing some background to explain its function. Now, beginning with 17:6b, John provides detailed information especially with reference to the identity of the beast upon which prostitute Babylon sits and regarding the beast's function at the time of the end.

And seeing her I marveled with great marvel. [7]And the angel said to me:"Why do you marvel? I will show you the mystery of the woman and of the beast which carries her, which has seven heads and ten horns. [8]The beast which you saw was, and is not, and is about to come up out of the abyss, he departs into destruction, and those dwelling on the earth, whose names are not written in the book of life from the foundation of the world, will marvel seeing the beast because he was and is not and will come. [9]Here is the mind with wisdom.The seven heads are seven mountains on

which the woman is sitting. And they are seven kings; ¹⁰*five have
fallen, one is, another has not yet come, and when he comes it
is necessary for him to remain a little while.* ¹¹*And regarding the
beast which was and is not, he himself is an eighth and is one of
the seven, and departs into destruction.* ¹²*And the ten horns which
you saw are ten kings, which have not yet received a kingdom, but
they receive authority as kings with the beast in one hour.* ¹³*They
are of one mind, and they give their power and authority to the
beast.* ¹⁴*They will make war with the Lamb, and the Lamb will
overcome them, for he is Lord of lords and King of kings, and those
with him are called and elect and faithful."*

¹⁵*And he said to me: "The waters which you saw, where the
prostitute is sitting, are peoples and multitudes and nations and
tongues.* ¹⁶*And the ten horns which you saw, and the beast, they
will hate the prostitute and make her desolate and naked, and will
eat her flesh and will burn her up with fire.* ¹⁷*For God has put into
their hearts to do his purpose, and to do it with one mind, that
is, to give their kingdom to the beast, until the words of God are
fulfilled.* ¹⁸*And the woman whom you saw is the great city which
rules over the kings of the earth."*

NOTES

17:8 *The abyss.* See *Notes* on Revelation 9:1. On "the beast coming up from the abyss," see
Notes on Revelation 11:7. A. Yarbro Collins relates the beast and its ascension from the abyss with the
demonic locusts ascending from the abyss in Revelation 9. They have the same function.[18]

17:9 *Here is the mind with wisdom.* See *Notes* on Rev. 13:18.

Seven mountains. The Greek *oros* here means "mountain" rather than "hill" as used by some
translators (such as the NIV) who believe that the city of Rome—known as the city on seven hills—is
in view here. Most modern commentators argue that this is undeniable evidence that the great harlot
of Revelation 17 is Imperial Rome, because Rome was widely known in the first century as the city
that lay on seven hills. The context does not indicate that Rome is intended here, however, because
John immediately explains that the mountains on which the prostitute sits are used metaphorically
for "seven kings" (Rev. 17:9–10). In the Old Testament, "kings" often mean "kingdoms" (cf. Dan.
2:37–38; 7:17). It is therefore hard to see any literal connection between the seven hills of Rome and
the seven successive kingdoms.

The mountain is used frequently as a symbol of a kingdom or empire in the Old Testament, but
never as a symbol of an individual ruler[19] (see *Notes* on Rev. 8:8). In addition, the seven mountains
and seven heads are consecutive rather than parallel together (cf. Rev. 17:10–11).[20] A question

arises: If the prostitute represents the city of Rome located on the seven hills, why then does it require any special divine wisdom for an understanding of the symbolism? (Rev. 17:9). As Johnson states, "whenever divine wisdom is called for, the description requires theological and symbolical discernment, not mere geographical or numerical insight" (cf. 13:18).[21] The great prostitute, observes George E. Ladd, "sits upon a succession of empires. She found her embodiment in historical Babylon, in the first century in historical Rome, and at the end of the age in eschatological Babylon....No simple identification with any single historical city is possible. The woman has formed an adulterous connection in every epoch of her history with the then existing world power."[22] In the same vein is Alan Johnson: "Babylon is an eschatological symbol of satanic deception and power; it is a divine mystery that can never be wholly reducible to empirical earthly institutions. It may be said that Babylon represents the total culture of the world apart from God, while the divine system is depicted by the New Jerusalem. Rome is simply one manifestation of the total system."[23]

7:10 *Seven kings.* Several modern expositors interpret the seven kings as Roman Emperors: five have fallen (Augustus, Tiberius, Caligula, Claudius, and Nero), one ruled in John's time (Vespasian), and the seventh, Titus, would be the one to come. The eighth one that was not yet would be Domitian as the returned Nero. This vein of interpretation involves several problems. The first Imperial Emperor was Julius Caesar, not Augustus. Even if we start with Augustus, the problem remains. In order to have seven plus one king, the scholars leave off the list Galba, Otho, and Vitelius because of the shortness of their reign. Starting with Augustus and excluding the three emperors, this interpretation makes Vespasian (A.D. 69–79) the emperor in power at the time of the writing of Revelation. However, evidence seems to indicate that John wrote during the reign of Domitian (A.D. 81–96).[24] Yet three times it is said that the beast "is not" in the time of the writing of the book of Revelation but that he will come sometime in the future before the end (Rev. 17:8, 11).

The "*Nero redivivus*" myth view—which applies "the mortal wound" or the "is-not" period of the beast to the suicide of Nero, and the healing of the wound to the renewed persecution by emperor Domitian at the end of the first century—has been refuted by many scholars.[25] A. Yarbro Collins makes the following remarks: "John's probable expectations with regard to historical events were not fulfilled. It is unlikely that he considered the emperor Domitian, reigning in John's time, to be the returned Nero....There is no good reason to doubt that John wrote during the time of the king he said 'is'—the sixth. If Domitian were considered the returned Nero, John would have been writing under the eighth king."[26]

Another interpretation is that the seven kings stand for a series of seven successive world powers or empires that have oppressed God's people throughout history from the establishment of God's church with Israel down to the Second Coming. There are two different views on the application of the seven heads/kings. Some authors have recently suggested that the sequence of the heads/kings should be viewed from the end times rather than from John's perspective.[27] In this avenue of interpretation, the five kings that were fallen are Babylon, Medo-Persia, Greece, Imperial Rome, and religious Rome (the sea beast of Rev. 13); the sixth king is the beast of Revelation 11 (the

French revolution); the seventh one is the lamb-like beast of Revelation 13; and the eighth one is the revived religious Rome (the beast of Rev. 17). The main point of departure this view takes is the interpretation of the head/king identified with the present "is." This commentary argues that the sixth head/king which "is" must be understood from John's viewpoint at the time of the writing of Revelation;[28] in other words, the angel identified the heads/kings to John, and it must have had meaning for John when he wrote. Thus the five that have fallen can be listed as follows:

- Egypt was the world power and oppressed Israel.
- Assyria was responsible for destroying the northern kingdom of Israel and scattering the ten tribes throughout the Middle East.
- Babylon destroyed Jerusalem and took the people of Judah into the exile.
- Medo-Persia in the days of Queen Esther almost annihilated the Jews.
- Greece through Antiochus Epiphanes oppressed the Jewish people and tried to destroy their religion.

The kingdom that ruled the world and oppressed the church during the time of John was Imperial Rome. The seventh kingdom to come from John's perspective referred to medieval ecclesiastical Christianity represented in the sea beast that was mortally wounded in Revelation 13:1–10. The eighth kingdom refers to the healing of the mortal wound of the beast that will appear on the world scene before the end of the age.

This interpretation provides the most satisfactory explanation of the succession of empires and fits nicely into the context of Revelation 17–18. All of these kingdoms have in common the combination of religion and state, and all have been responsible for oppressing God's people and attempting to destroy them.

To remain a little while (Gr. *oligon auton dei meinai*). This expression obviously has a qualitative rather than a quantitative significance, just as Satan has realized that "he has little time" (*oligon kairon echei* 12:12). In other words, Satan's time is limited. It stands in contrast to the *mikron kronon* ("short time") of 20:3 appointed to Satan with reference to the impending judgment on him.

17:11 *The beast which was and is not.* The expression "was" and "is not" was "an epitaph used widely in the ancient world" to mean "who lived" and "who no longer lives."[29]

17:12 *Ten kings.* Some modern commentators who argue for the *Nero redivivus* view interpret the ten kings as ten Parthian satraps invading from the east under the leadership of a revived Nero assisting to regain his power in the empire.[30] This avenue of understanding is weakened by the fact that there were not ten but fourteen Parthian satraps. John makes it clear that they were a future reality from his perspective; they "have not yet received a kingdom." They will receive it at the eschatological appearance of the beast. We must keep in mind that some prophetic fulfillment will be understood only at the time of its fulfillment. The imagery of the "ten kings" can best be understood in this way. At this point, one might agree with Isbon T. Beckwith who, in my view, correctly identifies the ten horns as "purely eschatological figures representing the totality of the powers of all nations on the earth which are to be made subservient to Antichrist."[31]

17:16 *Eat her flesh.* Eating somebody's flesh in the Old Testament is a savage action of an enemy. David complained of the wicked coming upon him to devour his flesh (Ps. 27:2). Micah spoke against the wicked rulers in Israel who ate the flesh of God's people (Mic. 3:2–3; cf. Jer. 10:25).

Burn her up with fire. In the Old Testament, burning with fire is the punishment for a terrible act of immorality. If a man took a wife and also her mother, all three were to be burned with fire (Lev. 20:14). It is also the punishment reserved for a priest's daughter found guilty of sexual immorality (Lev. 21:9). In portraying the punishment of end-time Babylon, John uses the motif of the punishment for sexual immorality from the laws of Moses and combines it with Ezekiel's portrayal of the judgment executed upon prostitute Jerusalem (Ezek. 16:38–41; 23:22–29).

EXPOSITION

17:6b–8 John is astonished **with great marvel** at the extraordinary appearance of the woman. However, he does not state the reason for his astonishment. For one thing, it could be that he was told earlier that he would witness the judgment of the prostitute, but now he views her in all seductive splendor and triumph. It is possible, however, that the real reason for John's astonishment could be that this seductive woman seems somehow familiar to him. The fact that he sees her in the desert (17:3) could remind him of the other woman in the wilderness who he saw previously in the vision in Revelation 12. This latter woman in the wilderness signified the church faithful to God during the period of "a time, times, and half a time" (12:13–14). Thus, it may be that the symbols of what appear to be two different women may actually seem to refer to the same religious entity in different times and circumstances. The true church that was faithful to and served God in the past will at the time of the end compromise the faith and oppose God and his people. It is no surprise then, that John is filled with great astonishment when he sees the woman of Babylon. This would explain why God's end-time people in Revelation are referred to as the remaining ones of the woman's offspring (12:17) rather than the woman. The woman who once was the true church of God will at the time of the end turn from her faithfulness to opposition against God, culminating in the attempt to destroy his faithful people—the remnant—"the ones keeping the commandments of God and having the testimony of Jesus" (12:17).

The angel responds to John's amazement by promising to explain to him **the mystery of the woman and of the beast which carries her.** This seems rather surprising, for John is perplexed with the mystery of the prostitute, and yet the angel promises to also explain the mystery of the beast. The mystery involves both the woman and the beast; it refers to the intimate relationship between Babylon and the beast. The two are inseparable, for she derives her character and power from the beast.[32] Understanding the identity of the beast is key to understanding the true nature of end-time Babylon.

The angel explains to John that the scarlet beast on which Babylon sits is the one that *was, and is not, and is about to come up out of the abyss.* The identification of the beast as the one who "was, and is not, and is about to come up" is a parody of the title of God as the One "who was and who is and who is coming" in Revelation 4:8 (also 1:4, 8). This title refers to the covenant name of Yahweh. The reference to God as "the One who is and who was and who is coming" refers to "the eschatological 'visitation' of God"; so the beast who "was, and is not, and is about to come up out of the abyss" also refers to the beast in his end-time activity and role.[33]

The tripartite formula indicates that the beast passes through three phases of his existence. The beast's past/present/future phases are to be identified with the seven heads. Thus, throughout its existence, the beast exercises oppressive rule through one of its heads during different periods of history.[34] As Robert L. Thomas observes, "each head of the beast is a partial incarnation of satanic power that rules for a given period."[35] First, the beast "was." This points most likely to the sea beast with seven heads and ten horns in Revelation 13. One of his heads—the seventh one (cf. Rev. 17:10)—was wounded to the point of death. The beast temporarily disappears from the scene, yet he survives. Now, he "is not"; namely, the beast is not active on the scene—he is dead—for some time. Then, he will return from the dead after the mortal wound has been healed; he appears again before the time of the end in "renewed fury" against God.[36]

The fact that the beast comes up from the abyss suggests its relation to the beast of Revelation 11:7 which killed the two witnesses. We saw earlier that the abyss or the bottomless pit is the abode of demons (cf. Luke 8:31; 2 Pet. 2:4; Jude 6). This suggests the demonic origin of the beast on which the prostitute Babylon sits. In this context, the abyss functions as the place of the dead, the underworld (cf. Rom. 10:7). Descending into the "abyss" would represent the receiving of the mortal wound of the beast and his subsequent disappearance from the world scene.[37] In the end times, this beast will come up from the abyss with full satanic manifestation (cf. 2 Thess. 2:8–12).

Yet he will appear for only a short time before he ***departs into destruction*** together with the prostitute Babylon sitting upon him. "And the beast was captured, and with him the false prophet who performed the signs before him, by which he deceived those who received the mark of the beast and who worshiped his image; these two were cast alive into the lake of fire burning with sulphur" (Rev. 19:20).

This remarkable appearance of the beast causes ***those dwelling on the earth, whose names are not written in the book of life from the foundation of the world,*** to ***marvel seeing the beast.*** This is a repetition of Revelation 13:3–4 where "the whole earth marveled" at seeing the sea beast reappear after his mortal wound was healed. "And all those who dwell on the earth will worship him, whose names are not written in the book of life of the Lamb slain from the foundation of the world" (Rev. 13:8). Only those who have their names written in the book of life will be able to withstand the deception. The parallel in the wording between Revelation 13:8 and 17:8 confirms the view that the beast upon which end-time prostitute Babylon sits is the same religious-political power of Revelation 13:1–9 that has a long history of persecuting the faithful followers of Christ.

When this religious-political power revives in full strength after centuries of quiescence during which it did not persecute God's people, it will cause the inhabitants of the world to marvel and be filled with awe for the beast ***which was and is not and will come***. Although worldwide, religious-political unity seems inconceivable in the modern world, many will put themselves into the service of Babylon, albeit for a short time (cf. Rev. 17:10).

17:9–10 With the statement ***Here is the mind with wisdom,*** the angel is saying, "Here is the wisdom which calls for understanding of the things you see." Wisdom here refers to a spiritual insight to understand the true nature of things. The understanding of the beast calls for spiritual discernment rather than brilliant mental and intellectual activity. It can only be imparted to the believer by the Spirit. This wisdom was required earlier with regard to the understanding of the cryptic number of the sea beast (Rev. 13:18). Only through this divinely imparted wisdom, the faithful will be able to discern and comprehend the true character of this end-time ungodly power.

The angel first explains that the existence of the beast and his activities are identified with his heads. The beast has been active throughout history through its successive heads. ***The seven heads are seven mountains on which the woman is*** *sitting.* The expression "on which the woman is sitting" suggests that the mountains are the same as "many waters" (Rev. 17:1) and "a scarlet beast" (Rev. 17:3), representing the secular and political power of the world.

In order to avoid any misunderstanding, the angel immediately goes on to explain that the seven mountains on which the woman sits are *seven kings,* which is another expression for world powers or empires (cf. Dan. 7:17). The seven mountains stand for seven successive world powers that dominated the world throughout history and "through which Satan has worked to oppress God's people throughout the ages."[38] Thus the great prostitute "finds her support from the beast who appears in history in a succession of secular godless kingdoms."[39] The five that have fallen are evidently the empires which ruled the world before the time of John: Egypt, Assyria, Babylon, Persia, and Greece; the sixth *one is* the Rome of John's time; the entity that *has not yet come* is still a future manifestation from John's perspective. Regardless of the application the first-century reader could see here in the text, John is obviously referring not to imperial, but rather to eschatological, Babylon. This worldwide political power will *remain a little while,* that is, it is doomed to destruction for Christ's coming will bring the ultimate and definite victory over the forces of darkness (cf. 2 Thess. 2:8).

17:11 The angel explains further that *the beast which was and is not* (cf. Rev. 17:8) on which the woman sits *is an eighth and is one of the seven.* This worldwide political power, which is in the service of Babylon during the final crisis, comes as the "eighth in the sense that he [it] is distinct from the other seven."[40] Yet it is one of the seven, most likely the seventh one that came after Rome (Rev. 13), the one referred to as the little horn in Daniel 7:21–25 arising out of Rome to make war against the saints. That the beast "was and is not" suggests that he was dead at a point in time and subsequently returned from the dead.[41] It is a parody of Christ "who was put to death yet came back to life and now is alive forevermore" (Rev. 1:18; 2:8; cf. 5:5).[42] Thus, in the eighth head, the seventh head reappears at the end of the age and exercises authority and power greater than ever before. This end-time political power functions much like the previous seven in history as the oppressive power of the world in all ages.[43] We evidently live in the era of the seventh head, for the eighth head with its united ten kingdoms has not yet ascended from the abyss, but will appear on the worldwide scene in the end. He will appear for a time, and then the beast will go into eternal *destruction* (Rev. 19:20) before he can carry out his purpose to destroy God's people.

17:12–13 Next, the angel provides the identification of the ten horns of the beast upon which prostitute Babylon sits: ***The ten horns which you saw are ten kings, which have not yet received a kingdom.*** This is an allusion to Daniel 7:7 and 24. The ten kings compose a very powerful confederacy of nations of the world. Their identity is not specified in the text and no indication of their previous history is mentioned. Should we seek their identity in such political powers as NATO, G8, or United Europe? Or, do they stand for the totality of nations in the world that will put themselves into the service of the beast? Only time will tell which if any of these views was correct. Since the text does not reveal their identity, all we can conclude at this point is that they will emerge at the very end of time after the healing of the mortal wound of the beast. They will ***receive authority as kings*** over the world together ***with the beast in one hour,*** that is, for a very short time. Thus this political union is of the eighth head, the time of the final crisis. What the text clearly states is that the ten kings are integrally connected with the beast. They collectively ***have one purpose, and they give their power and authority to the beast.*** Whoever or whatever these ten kings are, they evidently "constitute the last phase of the beast's power."[44] They represent an end-time unity of the governing political powers of the world which will submit to the authority of the Satanic trinity. The ten kings will become the backbone in the creation of the religious-political confederacy in the final crisis. The beast will use them to enforce his plans and purposes.

17:14 The ten kings will ***make war with the Lamb.*** This climactic battle takes place not at this point, but rather in Revelation 19:11–21. This reaffirms the idea that the final battle in the great eschatological showdown is against Christ and his faithful people, those who are ***called and elect*** by God and also who have remained ***faithful*** in the midst of the fiercest persecution. The final battle is clearly theological rather than political; it is a spiritual rather than a military battle. Babylon's aim to defeat God's people will be reversed to her own defeat: ***And the Lamb will overcome them.*** Revelation 17:14 provides the answer to the question: "Who is able to wage war with him [the beast]?" (Rev. 13:4).[45] It is the Lamb, for he is ***Lord of lords and King of kings.*** Revelation 17:14 thus provides in a nutshell what is described in more detail in Revelation 19:17–21. The final battle will result in the triumph of Christ and the ultimate destruction of the worldwide confederacy that loyally supported Babylon in opposition to God and his faithful people.

17:15–16 The angel now identifies the waters upon which end-time Babylon dwells—the river Euphrates itself—as *peoples and multitudes and nations and tongues.* In the Old Testament, water is often used figuratively for the enemies of God's people (Pss. 18:4; 124:2–5; Isa. 8:7–8; Jer. 47:1–2). The waters upon which Babylon sits symbolize the governing secular and political powers of the world which will unite and render their allegiance to the end-time religious system known as Babylon. This popular support will last but for a short time.

In the final stage the picture suddenly and dramatically changes. The drunken prostitute's lovers, *the ten horns*, and *the beast* that have loyally supported Babylon now awaken from their drunkenness and turn against their mistress. The language here echoes closely Jeremiah's prophecy concerning the faithless Jerusalem:

> And you, O desolate one, what will you do?
> Although you dress in scarlet,
> Although you decorate yourself with ornaments of gold,...
> Your lovers despise you;
> They seek your life (4:30).

The very powers that have up to this point loyally supported Babylon now withdraw their support and turn against her. It appears that we have an elaboration of the sixth plague here. The river Euphrates upon which Babylon has been sitting now dries up (Rev. 16:12). The political and secular powers that enabled Babylon to dominate the world suddenly withdraw their support and turn against her. The reason for such a sudden reversal is not explained here. The context of chapter 16 indicates that most likely the deceived governing political powers of the world have become disillusioned with Babylon's impotence to protect herself from the plagues falling on the world (cf. Rev. 16:10–11, 19) and have unitedly withdrawn their loyal support from her. They have turned to such antagonism and hostility that they will *hate the prostitute* and bring her to ruin.[46] This recalls the Old Testament prophecies according to which, in the eschatological state of turmoil, the enemies of God's people turn against each other (Ezek. 38:21; Hag. 2:22; Zech. 14:13).[47]

The disillusioned worldwide political powers will make Babylon *desolate and naked, and will eat her flesh.* This savage act is driven by extreme hostility and hatred (cf. Ps. 27:2; Mic. 3:3). The impassioned lovers have become the hostile haters. They *will burn her up with fire.* These cruel acts remind one of the prophecies of

Ezekiel about judgment falling upon prostitute Jerusalem:

> I shall gather all your lovers....So I shall gather them against you from every direction and expose your nakedness to them that they may see all your nakedness.... Thus I shall judge you, like women who commit adultery or shed blood are judged; and I shall bring on you the blood of wrath and jealousy. I shall also give you into the hands of your lovers, and they will tear down your shrines, demolish your high places, strip you of your clothing, take away your jewels, and will leave you naked and bare.... And they will burn your houses with fire and execute judgments on you in the sight of many women. Then I shall stop you from playing the harlot. (Ezek. 16:37–41)
>
> Behold I will arouse your lovers against you....They will remove your nose and your ears....Your survivors will be consumed by the fire. They will also strip you of your clothes and take away your beautiful jewels....And they will deal with you in hatred, take all your property, and leave you naked and bare. And the nakedness of your harlotries shall be uncovered. (Ezek. 23:22–29)

In both Ezekiel and Revelation, former lovers are responsible for the punishment of the prostitute.

Interestingly, the punishment for the prostitute is the death penalty by burning with fire rather than death by stoning—the regular form of punishment for sexual immorality in the Old Testament (Deut. 22:20–24; cf. John 8:5). Burning by fire was the form of punishment reserved for a priest's daughter who was involved in prostitution (Lev. 21:9). The fact that the fate of the prostitute Babylon is stated in terms of burning by fire rather that stoning is a further indication that the woman of chapter 17 denotes a religious rather than political entity, that once was the true church faithful to God but at the time of the end will turn into a power that opposes God and his faithful people.

We see in this scene in Revelation the pattern of Satan's kingdom: each power destroys its predecessor (Babylon destroyed Assyria, Persia destroyed Babylon, etc.). Finally the battle of Armageddon "breaks this cycle." God himself steps into the action and brings the history of oppression to its end.[48]

17:17 The angel further explains that it was God who has brought about the destruction of Babylon. *For God has put into their hearts to do his purpose, and to do it with one mind, that is, to give their kingdom to the beast, until the words of God are fulfilled.* In believing that they are working out the purposes of the beast, the united governing political powers are, in fact, unconsciously carrying out God's purposes to bring judgment upon Babylon.[49] This echoes Paul's statement that "God will send upon them a deluding influence so that they might believe what is false, in order that they all may be judged who did not believe the truth, but took pleasure in wickedness" (2 Thess. 2:10–12). Regarding Revelation 17:17, William Barclay observes: "The truth behind this is that God never loses control of human affairs. In the last analysis God is always working things together for good."[50] It is God who permits the end-time powers to come together to serve Babylon. When he withdraws, however, the united powers "immediately turn against Babylon and destroy her."[51] God is in full control here and the wicked can do no more than he allows.[52] The final crisis will bring God's purposes to an ultimate conclusion.

17:18 We saw that in the image of a prostitute seducing the people of the world and dragging them into illicit relationships, John portrays the end-time worldwide religious confederacy based on the evil religious system empowered by Satan himself. This religious system is now to be judged. John reverses the metaphor from a prostitute to a great city. ***The woman whom you saw is the great city which rules over the kings of the earth.*** Prostitute Babylon and the great city Babylon are the same entity. They symbolize the same end-time religious system that stands in opposition to God. Divine judgment is now set into motion against this end-time religious system. This judgment is described in Revelation 18 in terms of the destruction of the ancient city of Babylon that has grown wealthy through economic trade.

A RETROSPECT ON REVELATION 17

Revelation 17 elaborates the motif of the drying up of the river Euphrates in the sixth plague that causes the fall of end-time Babylon (Rev. 16:12). The first portion of the chapter identifies Babylon the great as a seducing prostitute dwelling "on many waters" and riding on the resurrected beast of Revelation 13:1–10. This religious power/system stands behind the end-time persecution and oppression of God's people. Babylon's dominating influence on the inhabitants of the earth will be achieved through cooperation with the governing secular and political powers of the world. Yet, Revelation 17:14–17 indicates that the drying up of the Euphrates symbolizes the withdrawal of support for Babylon when the dominating secular and political powers of the world, realizing that they were deceived, turn against it and destroy it.

Revelation 17 deals in more detail with the theme of Satan's final grasp for world dominion through the resurrected beast of Revelation 13:1–10. Remarkably, end-time Babylon is portrayed in Revelation 17–18 as the unholy antithesis to the New Jerusalem in Revelation 21:10–22:5. In his depiction, John employs the language that he later uses with regard to the New Jerusalem, the bride of the Lamb.[53] The illicit relationship between the governing secular and political world powers and prostitute Babylon is contrasted with the love relationship between the Lamb and New Jerusalem, his bride. The antithetical parallels drawn between the descriptions of the two cities appear in a chart in the "Overview: Revelation 12–22:5."

The verbal and conceptual parallels between the two visions are hardly accidental. First of all, both explanations of the two cities are provided to John by the same seven-bowl angel. Both begin with an invitation: "Come, I will show you…" (Rev. 17:1; 21:9). Then the subsequent "And he carried me away in the Spirit…" (Rev. 17:3; 21:10) is followed by John viewing prostitute Babylon and New Jerusalem, the bride of Christ, respectively. Just as New Jerusalem is the seat of God's rule over the earth, denoting his presence with his people, Babylon is perceived as the seat of the end-time apostate system denoting Satan's aspiration to dominate the world.

Next, the antithetical parallels are evident in the descriptions of the two woman-cities. The costly and lavishly luxurious adornment expresses the self-glorification and corruption of Babylon. It is for the purpose of seducing the governing secular and political powers to enter into an illicit relationship with her (Rev. 17:4–5); on the other hand, the radiant light and beauty that adorns New Jerusalem expresses God's glory for the purpose of attracting people to salvation and the kingdom of God (Rev. 21:11, 23–24). Babylon is the dwelling place of demons and all uncleanness (Rev. 18:2); New Jerusalem symbolizes "the tabernacle of God…among men" (Rev. 21:3). A definite line of demarcation between those associated with the two cities is drawn on the basis of having one's name written in the book of life (cf. Rev. 17:8; 21:27).

Finally, an acute distinction is made regarding the fates of the two cities. Both are introduced with a declaration—"It is done!"—announcing that God will give Babylon the cup of wine of the fury of his wrath to drink (Rev. 16:19), and that God will give freely to the thirsty from the fountain of the water of life (Rev. 21:6). Babylon, adorned with all her faded glory, is together with its inhabitants doomed for destruction (18:8), darkness (18:23), and ruin (18:6–7) so that it "will never be found any longer" (18:21);

New Jerusalem offers to her inhabitants a life of safety and security "forever and ever" (22:5). Roberto Badenas observes that "it is over the ruins, so to speak, of the proud, evil, and corrupted Babylon, that New Jerusalem comes, from heaven, pure and radiant with the glory of God."[54]

Revelation 17–18 thus continues the main theological theme of the eschatological part of Revelation (chapters 12–22). It involves Satan's counterfeit of God's salvific activities in the closing days of earth's history: the counterfeits of the three persons of the Godhead, the final gospel message, the mark of the identification of the genuine worshipers of God, and now a counterfeit city. By identifying Babylon as the counterfeit New Jerusalem, the city of Christ, John endeavors to draw the contrast between the two last-day major religious systems.

As God's gift to humanity, New Jerusalem stands for the system of salvation founded by God. It signifies the presence of God among human beings, giving life with joy and happiness, and giving the future with hope. Babylon, on the other hand, signifies the religious system established by Satan, characterized by a separation from God, suffering, and death, without any hope for the future. While New Jerusalem represents God's method of redemption, "Babylon represents all human attempts to provide the way of salvation, all those plans and programs that, because they are built alone on human reason and devices, attempt to frustrate the divine plan for the world."[55] While New Jerusalem stands as the expression of God's grace, Babylon represents a futile human endeavor to obtain salvation apart from God.

John makes it very clear that the religion of Babylon—regardless of the city's appearance and attractiveness—deprives human beings of safety and security both in the present life and in the future. The only hope for lost humanity is to look "for the city which has foundations, whose architect and builder is God" (Heb. 11:10). This city of grace "represents the reconciliation of mankind with God, the realization of the everlasting covenant."[56] The redeemed have come "to Mount Zion, and to the city of the living God, the heavenly Jerusalem, and to myriads of angels, to the general assembly and church of the first-born who are enrolled in heaven, and to God, the Judge of all, and to the spirits of righteous men made perfect, and to Jesus, the mediator of a new covenant, and to the sprinkled blood, which speaks better than the blood of Abel" (Heb. 12:22–24).

ENDNOTES

1. See Hans K. LaRondelle, "Babylon: Anti-Christian Empire" in *Symposium on Revelation—Book 2*, Daniel and Revelation Committee Series 7 (Silver Spring, MD: Biblical Research Institute, 1992), 159–163.

2. As suggested by Charles (*A Critical and Exegetical Commentary on the Revelation of St. John*, 2:65) and Swete (*The Apocalypse of St. John*, 217); cf. Seneca *Controversiae* 1.2.7 (The Loeb Classical Library 1:66–69); Juvenal *Saturae* 6.123 (The Loeb Classical Library, 93).

3. Mounce, 307.

4. Ladd, 222.

5. Barclay, *The Revelation of John*, 2:136.

6. Ladd, 222.

7. *The Seventh-day Adventist Bible Commentary*, 7:850.

8. Ladd, 223.

9. Mounce, 309.

10. Ladd, 223.

11. Beale, 853.

12. Mounce, 309.

13. Badenas, 257.

14. Roloff, 197.

15. LaRondelle, *How to Understand the End-Time Prophecies,* 346.

16. Johnson, 554.

17. Beale, 848.

18. Collins, *The Apocalypse*, 72–73.

19. Strand, "The Seven Heads," 186.

20. See ibid., 187–191.

21. Johnson, 558.

22. Ladd, 228.

23. Johnson, 554.

24. Strand, "The Seven Heads," 187–191.

25. Minear, 93–101; Strand, "The Seven Heads," 191–200.

26. Collins, *The Apocalypse*, 122.

27. Including William H. Shea, "The Identification of the Seven Heads of the Beast in Revelation 17," unpublished paper, n.d.; LaRondelle, *How to Understand the End-Time Prophecies*, 410–417; Maxwell, 471–476, although he sees the sixth head/king as Christian Rome.

28. See Strand, *Interpreting the Book of Revelation*, 55–56.

29. Aune, *Revelation 17–22*, 940.

30. E.g., Charles, 71–72; Barclay, *The Revelation of John*, 2:141–142; Beasley-Murray, 258; Mounce struggles with this view (p. 317); Aune identifies the ten kings as Roman client kings (see *Revelation 17–22*, 951).

31. Beckwith, 700.

32. Ladd, 226.

33. Aune, *Revelation 17–22*, 939–940.

34. Ladd, 226; LaRondelle, *How to Understand the End-Time Prophecies*, 409.

35. Thomas, *Revelation 8–22*, 292.

36. Mounce, 312.

37. *The Seventh-day Adventist Bible Commentary*, 7:854.

38. Johnsson, 17.

39. Ladd, 229.

40. Mounce, 316.

41. Collins, *The Combat Myth in the Book of Revelation*, 174; Aune, *Revelation 17–22*, 940; both Collins and Aune assert that the phrase here refers to the Nero *redivivus* myth.

42. Mounce, 312.

43. Desmond Ford, 561.

44. Ibid., 671.

45. Beale, 880.

46. LaRondelle, *The Good News about Armageddon*, 17.

47. Ladd, 233.

48. William S. LaSor, *The Truth about Armageddon* (New York: Harper & Row, 1982), 140.

49. Thomas, *Revelation 8–22*, 305.

50. Barclay, *The Revelation of John*, 2:149.

51. Paulien, *What the Bible Says about the End-Time*, 146.

52. Morris, 196.

53. For the list of parallels, see Aune, *Revelation 17–22*, 1144–1145.

54. Badenas, 255.

55. Johnsson, 35.

56. Badenas, 271.

THE JUDGMENT OF BABYLON
REVELATION 18:1–24

Revelation 17 describes the end-time apostate religious power, named "Babylon the great" (17:5), in terms of a prostitute seducing the governing secular and political powers of the world with the wine of her fornication. The text explains that the fall and complete destruction of Babylon results from the withdrawal of support by the secular and political powers after recognizing that they have been deceived. They turn against Babylon and destroy it completely. The destruction of end-time Babylon is introduced in Revelation 17:16–17, and it is depicted in terms of the ancient practice of punishing a prostitute with fire as prescribed in the laws of Moses (cf. Lev. 20:14; 21:9; Ezek. 16:38–41; 23:22–29).

Chapter 18 continues to follow the theme of the previous chapter. It describes the judgment of end-time Babylon in greater detail. It explains how this end-time apostate religious system is brought to her end. This time the fall of Babylon is portrayed in terms of the collapse of a rich commercial city—ancient Babylon in particular—that has grown wealthy through economic trade. Ancient cities were known as centers of commerce and the storehouses of wealth. In portraying the demise of spiritual Babylon, John uses language that the prophets Isaiah (chapters 13 and 47) and Jeremiah (chapters 50–51)[1] employed in predicting the destruction of ancient Babylon, and Ezekiel in reference to Tyre (Ezek. 26–28). Here in Revelation 18, as G. K. Beale points out, the judgment of historical Babylon becomes a type of the judgment of end-time Babylon.[2]

CALL TO SEPARATE FROM BABYLON (18:1–8)

Babylon has filled up her cup of abomination. The time is now that "Babylon the great was remembered before God to give her the cup of the wine of the fury of his wrath" (Rev. 16:19). Before she is judged, however, God's people are exhorted to cut all ties with this end-time apostate religious system dominating the world and to turn back to God, so as to escape Babylon's fate.

¹*After these things I saw another angel coming down from heaven having great authority, and the earth was illuminated with his glory. ²And he cried with a strong voice saying:*
"Fallen, fallen is Babylon the great,
    and has become the dwelling place of demons
  and a prison of every unclean spirit
    and a prison of every unclean bird
    and a prison of every unclean and hated beast,
    ³*because of the wine of the wrath of her fornication*
      all nations have drunk,
  and the kings of the earth have committed
    fornication with her,
  and the merchants of the earth have become wealthy
    through the power of her luxuries."
⁴*And I heard another voice from heaven saying:*
"Come out of her, my people,
    that you might not share in her sins,
  and that you might not receive of her plagues,
    ⁵*because her sins have accumulated unto heaven,*
    and God has remembered her unrighteous acts.
    ⁶*Pay her back as she has given,*
    and pay her double according to her works,
    in the cup which she has mixed, mix a double
      portion for her;
    ⁷*as much as she has glorified herself*
    and lived luxuriously,
    give torture and mourning to her,
because she says in her heart,
    'I sit as a queen, and am not a widow,
    and I will never see mourning.'
    ⁸*Therefore, in one day her plagues will come,*
    death and mourning and famine,
and she shall be burned with fire,
    because the Lord God who judges her is strong."

NOTES

18:2 *Fallen, fallen.* See *Notes* on Revelation 14:8.

Babylon the great. See *Notes* on Revelation 14:8.

Has become the dwelling place of...every unclean bird and...unclean and hated beast.
The text reflects the Old Testament oracles against Edom (Isa. 34:11–15), Nineveh (Zeph. 2:13–15), and, in particular, ancient Babylon. Isaiah prophesied that when God destroyed Babylon, its ruins would become the habitation of all kinds of wild birds and animals:

> Desert creatures will lie down there,
> And their houses will be full of owls,
> Ostriches also will live there, and shaggy goats will frolic there.
> Hyenas will howl in their fortified towers
> And jackals in their luxurious palaces. (Isa. 13:21–22; cf. 34:11–15)

Similarly, Jeremiah prophesied against Babylon:

> The desert creatures will live there along with jackals,
> The ostriches also will live in it,
> And it will never again be inhabited
> Or dwelt in from generation to generation. (Jer. 50:39)
> And Babylon will become a heap of ruins, a haunt of jackals. (Jer. 51:37)

18:3 *The wine of the wrath of her fornication.* See *Notes* on Revelation 14:8.

The merchants of the earth. See *Notes* on Revelation 18:11.

18:6 *Pay her double* (Gr. *diplōsate ta dipla* means "double the double"). The double recompense is a well-known Old Testament concept; according to the law of Moses, anyone responsible for stolen property had to repay it twice over (Exod. 22:4, 7, 9). The idea of rendering double for one's deeds is often used by the prophets as an idiom expressing punishment or reward in full measure.[3] Isaiah declared that Jerusalem "received of the Lord's hand double for all her sins" (Isa. 40:2). "Instead of your shame you will have a double portion....Therefore they will possess a double portion in their land" (Isa. 61:7). Jeremiah prophesied with regard to Israel: "I will first doubly repay their iniquity and their sins, because they have polluted My land" (Jer. 16:18). "Let those who persecute me be put to shame....Bring on them a day of disaster, and crush them with twofold destruction" (Jer. 17:18). God spoke through Zechariah that he would "restore double" to Judah when he delivers them from their enemies (Zech. 9:12). Many scholars think that the word "double" does not mean that the punishment was twice as much as the wrongdoing, but an exact equivalent.[4] This would suggest, according to Meredith G. Kline, that "Babylon's iniquities were to be balanced by their equal weight of punishment in God's scales of justice."[5]

18:8 *The Lord God who judges her.* The word "judges" is in the aorist participle, suggesting action taking place in the past. Babylon has been judged; the investigation has been completed, the sentence pronounced, and the execution is about to take place.

EXPOSITION

18:1   John sees *another angel coming down from heaven* with a divine message. He is not the interpreting angel of Revelation 17, but another angel coming from God with *great authority* to proclaim a special message. The entire *earth was illuminated with his glory.* Notwithstanding the gloom of his proclamation, this angel is the messenger "of the gospel. He comes, not to gloat over the fallen, but to announce the triumph of God's purposes and the final liberation of God's people from all oppression."[6] The glory of the angel outshines the charming glory of Babylon. His glorious appearance and loud voice are meant to draw the attention of the earth dwellers to God's last appeal to leave the apostate religious system and turn to God so as to escape what is about to befall the unrepentant. His proclamation is a call to separate from Babylon and turn to God (Rev. 18:4), bringing to an end the proclamation of the warning messages of the three angels of Revelation 14.

18:2–3   The angel announces with *a strong voice* the collapse of the end-time counterfeit apostate religious system: *Fallen, fallen is Babylon the great.* This announcement echoes the words of Isaiah 21:9: "Fallen, fallen is Babylon; and all the images of her gods are shattered on the ground." It also repeats the warning message of the second angel (Rev. 14:8). In all cases, the fall of end-time Babylon is portrayed as already being accomplished even though it is to happen in the future.[7] The repetition of the word "fallen" and the past tense in the future use is for the purpose of assuring God's people that the fall of end-time Babylon is imminent and certain.

In describing the certainty of Babylon's desolation, John borrows well-known prophetic language with reference to the desolation of ancient Babylon (cf. Isa. 13:19–22; Jer. 50:39; 51:37). Babylon has become the dwelling place of *demons* and every *unclean spirit* and *every unclean bird*, and *every unclean and hated beast*. No human being will live there any longer. The downfall and collapse of end-time Babylon is as certain as the destruction and devastation of ancient Babylon. The portrayal of the destruction of Babylon as the end-time apostate and oppressive religious system in terms of the collapse of the ancient city of Babylon seems to be remarkably significant. Gregory K. Beale notes:

> The assurance of worldwide Babylon's fall in the future is rooted in the fact that the fall of old Babylon was predicted in the same way, and the fulfillment came to pass; John believes that God will continue to act in the future as he had acted in

the past. The prophecy and fulfillment of Babylon's past fall is viewed as a historical pattern pointing forward to the fall of a much larger Babylon.[8]

As the fall of ancient Babylon was good news for Israel, so the fall of end-time Babylon is good news for God's end-time people.

The cause of Babylon's fall is threefold: First, with *the wine of the wrath of her fornication* she has made all nations drunk (Rev. 14:8; 17:2). This points to the seductive activities of end-time Babylon, deceiving the people to accept her religious demands.[9] Second, Babylon has seduced *the kings of the earth* to commit *fornication with her* (cf. 17:2; also in 18:9). This refers to the illicit relationship of the governing political powers of the world with the end-time apostate religious system. Finally, she has made *the merchants of the earth* wealthy through *the power of her luxuries* (also in Rev. 18:15). Here is a new aspect of Babylon's influence that was not mentioned earlier: while Revelation 17 focuses on the political aspect of the unity between the end-time apostate religious system and the world's governing secular and political powers, the text here explains the motivation for economic security standing behind that end-time unity. The intoxicating influence of Babylon's wine of fornication blinds the world's secular and political powers to "Babylon's own ultimate insecurity and to God as the only source of real security."[10]

18:4–5 In the midst of the announcement of the demise of Babylon, John hears *another voice from heaven* exhorting God's people to leave Babylon: *Come out of her, my people, that you might not share in her sins, and that you might not receive of her plagues*. This call echoes the appeal of the prophet Jeremiah to the Jews in Babylon: "Flee from the midst of Babylon, and each of you save his life! Do not be destroyed in her punishment, for this is the Lord's time of vengeance; he is going to render recompense to her" (Jer. 51:6; also 50:8; 51:45).

Apparently many sincere and God-fearing people are still wavering in Babylon. This recalls the story of Lot (Gen. 19). Though he did not participate in the sins of Sodom, he was identified with it. Just before the city was destroyed, he was urged to leave it; otherwise he would have shared in the city's destruction. In a similar way, God sends a last appeal to his people to come out of Babylon before it is destroyed. Leon Morris states: "In a sense this appeal is the key to the whole chapter. John is not gloating over the city's downfall. He is appealing to Christians to see the realities of the situation and act accordingly."[11] This is the last opportunity for people to turn to

God and escape the fate of Babylon and all those associating themselves with her.

Babylon is to be exited **because her sins have accumulated unto heaven.** This echoes the appeal made by Jeremiah to the Israelites in Babylon: "For her judgment has reached to heaven and towers up to the very skies" (Jer. 51:9). Paul explains that the stubborn and unrepentant are storing up wrath for themselves "in the day of wrath and revelation of the righteous judgment of God, who will render to every man according to his deeds" (Rom. 2:5–6). The sins of Babylon are unaccountable. She has long rejected the gospel and despised God's patience and grace; however, **God has remembered her unrighteous acts** so as to execute his righteous judgment upon her.

18:6 Suddenly the angel changes the theme. He has just made an appeal to God's people to leave Babylon; now he announces the divine sentence on her: **Pay her back as she has given.** This principle of retribution echoes the Old Testament announcements of judgment upon ancient Babylon: "O daughter of Babylon," shouted the psalmist, "you devastated one, how blessed be the one who repays you with the recompense with which you have repaid us" (Ps. 137:8; cf. 28:4). Jeremiah spoke: "Repay her according to her work; according to all that she has done, so do to her; for she has become arrogant against the Lord, against the Holy One of Israel" (50:29). The punishment of Babylon fits her crime. This principle Jesus stressed in his Sermon on the Mount: "The measure you give will be the measure you get" (Matt. 7:2, RSV).

The punishment of end-time Babylon is described further in terms of the Old Testament legal concept of the double recompense: **Pay her double according to her works, in the cup which she has mixed, mix a double portion for her.** Babylon is found guilty, and she will receive the punishment in full measure,[12] equivalent to her crime. Thus God's promise given through Jeremiah regarding ancient Babylon will be fulfilled in the fate of end-time Babylon: "'I will repay Babylon and all the inhabitants of Chaldea for all their evil that they have done in Zion before your eyes,' declares the Lord" (Jer. 51:24).

18:7–8 Verse 7 restates the principle that the "punishment fits the crime" with reference to Babylon:[13] To the degree that **she has glorified herself and lived luxuriously, give torture and mourning to her.** Babylon is to be judged according to her sins. Her sins are vain self-glorification and luxury that make her arrogantly boast: *"I sit as a queen, and am not a widow, and I will never see mourning."* This boasting of end-time Babylon evokes the arrogant boasting of ancient Babylon:

> You said, "I shall be a queen forever."
> These things you did not consider,
> Nor remember the outcome of them.
> Now, then, hear this, you sensual one,
> Who dwells securely,
> Who says in your heart,
> "I am, and there is no one besides me.
> I shall not sit as a widow,
> Nor shall I know loss of children."
> But these two things shall come on you
> > suddenly in one day:
> Loss of children and widowhood.
> They shall come on you in full measure
> > In spite of your many sorceries,
> > In spite of the great power of your spells. (Isa. 47:7–9)

In glorifying herself, Babylon assumes and claims the prerogatives of God; for in Revelation, glory belongs only to God (Rev. 14:7; cf. 15:4; 19:1). Arrogant self-glorification and self-sufficiency are the basis for the condemnation and punishment of end-time Babylon. Her self-glorification is initially dimmed by the glory of the angel illuminating the whole earth (Rev. 18:1) as the precursor of the ultimate judgment to be executed on her. *Therefore, in one day her plagues will come.* As it was for ancient Babylon (cf. Isa. 47:9), so the time for the judgment of end-time Babylon is set. The plagues are undoubtedly the seven last plagues of Revelation 16. In contrast to the arrogant boasting in verse 7, Babylon will receive *death and mourning and famine, and she shall be burned with fire.* The burning of Babylon with fire refers probably to Revelation 17:16. This end-time apostate religious system—which "opposes and exalts himself above every so-called god or object of worship, so that he takes his seat in the temple of God displaying himself as being God" (2 Thess. 2:4)—will learn the real truth that *the Lord God who judges her is strong.*

LAMENT FOR BABYLON (18:9–24)

This section contains a series of three mournful lamentations over the destruction of Babylon by those who licentiously cooperated with her. These laments are expressed in the form of ancient dirges or funeral laments. Each concludes in the same way: "Woe, woe, the great city...for in one hour [your judgment has come]" (18:10,16–17a, 19). These "dirges function as announcements of sudden and unexpected judgment."[14] The section concludes by summoning heaven and the faithful to rejoice over Babylon's destruction (18:20–24).

> [9]*And the kings of the earth who committed fornication and lived luxuriously with her will cry and mourn over her when they see the smoke of her burning,* [10]*standing at a distance because of the fear of her torment, saying:*
>
> "Woe, woe, the great city,
> > Babylon the strong city,
>
> for in one hour your judgment has come."
>
> [11]*And the merchants of the earth cry and mourn over her, because nobody buys their merchandise any longer,* [12]*merchandise of gold and silver and precious stones and pearls and fine linen and purple and silk and scarlet, and every kind of citron wood and every vessel of ivory and every vessel of precious wood and brass and iron and marble,* [13]*and cinnamon and spice and incense and myrrh and frankincense and wine and olive oil and fine flour and wheat and cattle and sheep, and of horses and chariots and slaves and souls of men:*
>
> [14]*"And the fruit for which your soul longed*
> > *has gone from you,*
>
> *and all luxurious and splendid things*
> > *have perished from you,*
> > *they will never find them any longer."*
>
> [15]*The merchants of these things, who have become wealthy from her, will be standing at a distance because of the fear of her torment, crying and mourning,* [16]*saying:*
>
> "Woe, woe, the great city,
> > *which was clothed in fine linen and purple*
> > > *and scarlet,*
> > *and adorned with gold and precious stones*
> > > *and pearls,*
>
> [17]*for in one hour such great wealth*
> > *has been laid waste."*
>
> *And every shipmaster and everyone who sails by ship and*

sailors and as many as make their living by the sea, stood at a distance ¹⁸and cried observing the smoke of her burning, saying: "What city is like the great city?" ¹⁹And they threw dust on their heads and were crying out, weeping, and mourning, saying:

"Woe, woe, the great city,
     in which all who have ships in the sea
     became rich through her wealth,
for in one hour she became desolate.
²⁰Rejoice over her, heaven,
     and saints and apostles and prophets,
because God has executed judgment for you on her."

²¹And a strong angel took a stone like a great millstone and threw it into the sea, saying:

"Thus will Babylon the great city
     be thrown down with violence
     and will never be found any longer.
²²And the sound of harpists and musicians
     and flutists and trumpeters
     will never be heard in you any longer,
and every craftsman of any craft
     will never be found in you any longer,
and the sound of a mill
     will never be found in you any longer,
²³and the light of a lamp
     will never shine in you any longer,
and the voice of the bridegroom and of the bride
     will never be heard in you any longer;
because your merchants were the great men
     of the earth,
because by your magic spell all the nations
     were deceived,
²⁴and in her the blood of prophets and saints
     was found
     and of all those who have been slain on the earth."

NOTES

18:9 *The kings of the earth who committed fornication and lived luxuriously with her.* See *Notes* on Revelation 17:1–2.

18:9, 10 ***They see the smoke of her burning, standing at a distance.*** This scene recalls Genesis 19:28 which describes Abraham witnessing the smoke ascending from Sodom and Gomorrah, "like the smoke of a furnace," as a sign of divine judgment on these two cities. The destruction of the cities in the valley is used by Old Testament prophets as the model of the fate of ancient Babylon: "Babylon, the beauty of kingdoms...will be as when God overthrew Sodom and Gomorrah" (Isa. 13:19). "'As when God overthrew Sodom and Gomorrah with its neighbors,' declares the Lord, 'no man will live there, nor will any son of man reside in it'" (Jer. 50:40). This suggests that in describing the destruction of end-time Babylon, John employs the language in which Old Testament prophets foretold the fate of ancient Babylon.

18:11 ***The merchants of the earth.*** These merchants are said to be "the great men of the earth" (Rev. 18:23; cf. Isa. 23:2, 8). The merchants of the earth might be understood here either literally or figuratively. They might be the governing economic or commercial leaders of the world whose financial and material support has contributed to the success of Babylon the great; they may also stand for figurative "merchants"—the commercial salespeople of "the spiritual merchandise of Babylon, those who have sold her doctrines and policies to the kings and peoples of earth."[15] The latter fits into the highly figurative context of Revelation 18 and is favored by this commentary.

18:17 ***Every shipmaster.*** The figurative context of Revelation 18 suggests figurative shipmasters, just as with "the merchants of the earth" (see *Notes* on 18:11).

18:23 ***Magic spell.*** The Greek *pharmakeia* ("sorcery," "magic spell") is the word from which we get the word "pharmacy." The word is used only here and in Paul's list of vices in Galatians 5:20. The related word *pharmakon* ("sorcery") is used in Revelation 9:21, 21:8, and 22:15. Isaiah mentions sorcery and magic spells as being among the sins of ancient Babylon that brought about her fall (Isa. 47:9, 12).

EXPOSITION

The divine retribution of end-time Babylon will bring great sorrow and mourning to those who cooperated with this apostate religious system and participated in her sins. The rest of the chapter describes mournful lamentations by the governing political powers of the world (18:9–10) and the figurative commercial salespeople of Babylon (18:11–19). Their lamentations do not reflect any grief for Babylon herself, but rather for their personal loss caused by her destruction.

18:9–10 The fall of end-time Babylon afflicts first ***the kings of the earth who committed fornication and lived luxuriously with her***. The kings of the earth denote the end-time governing political powers of the world who have put their authority and influence into the service of Babylon (cf. 17:1–2). Babylon apparently acted through them to gain control of those inhabitants of the world who did not voluntarily submit themselves to her. The political powers were seduced by Babylon's arrogance and glamorous wealth and luxury. Babylon promised them safety and security. Now they realize how they were deceived by those false promises when they see *the strong city* destroyed. Babylon's destruction means their own imminent loss of political power. As Abraham centuries earlier watched the smoke ascending from Sodom and Gomorrah as a sign of divine retribution on those two cities in the valley (Gen. 19:28), so the political powers of the world witness the demise of end-time Babylon. They stand at a distance in fear of their own torment and *cry and mourn over her when they see the smoke of her burning.* The words *your judgment has come* suggest that in the defeat of Babylon the political powers of the world will perceive God's righteous judgment. Babylon's destruction is as certain as the destruction of Sodom and Gomorrah (cf. Isa. 13:19; Jer. 50:40). Their mourning is an expression of the realization that they must share in Babylon's fate. The repetition of the time designation *in one hour* (also in vv. 17 and 19) suggests the speed with which Babylon is overthrown.[16] It relates to Revelation 17:12 where "one hour" denotes a very brief time when the ten kings turn against end-time Babylon and destroy her.[17]

18:11–17a The fall of Babylon also afflicts *the merchants of the earth* who traded with her and have grown rich from her excessive luxuries. These "great men of the earth" (Rev. 18:23) are the figurative commercial retailers of Babylon who sell and distribute the spiritual merchandise of "her corrupt doctrines and policies."[18] Their grief reflects their selfish motives. The destruction of Babylon means "an end to the flow of corrupt goods that have been sold and distributed in her name, and by which she has deceived the world,"[19] for *nobody buys their merchandise any longer.* Verses 12–13 give a long list of figurative merchandise in terms of gold and silver, precious stones, fine and costly garments, luxurious articles of decoration, fragrances, foods, domestic animals, and slaves. They stress the comprehensiveness of Babylon's "corrupt doctrines and policies."[20] This catalogue of merchandise is not unlike the list of luxurious items mentioned in the doom song over Tyre (Ezek. 27:5–24). *All luxurious and splendid things* (v. 14) in which Babylon has taken delight are gone.

18:17b–19 The last group of mourners are *every shipmaster and everyone who sails by ship and sailors and as many as make their living by the sea.* The figurative language here is borrowed from Ezekiel's vision of the fall of Tyre:

> The sailors, and all the pilots of the sea
> Will come down from their ships;

> They will stand on the land,
> And they will make their voice heard over you
> And will cry bitterly.
> They will cast dust on their heads....
> In their wailing they will take up a lamentation for you
> And lament over you:
> "Who is like Tyre...?" (Ezek. 27:29–32)

The merchants and shipmasters have shared in the wealth and luxury of end-time Babylon. They stand at a distance watching the city burning and lamenting: *"What city is like the great city?"* This rhetorical question parallels "Who is like the beast?" (Rev. 13:4). It is the parody of "Who is like God?" (Exod. 15:11; Ps. 35:10; Mic. 7:18). The sea people express the intensity of their grief by throwing *dust on their heads.* Their grief and mourning are purely selfish, however, because they *became rich through her wealth. In one hour* Babylon has become *desolate* and all their wealth is gone.

18:20 While the fall of Babylon is bad news for the enemies of God, it is good news for God's people. Both heaven and the saints are summoned to *rejoice* because *God has executed judgment for you on her.* The rejoicing called for here is portrayed as taking place in Revelation 19:1–10. This call for rejoicing echoes the words of Jeremiah with regard to the fall of Babylon: "Then the heavens and the earth, and all that is in them, shall sing for joy over Babylon; for the destroyers shall come against them out of the north, says the LORD. Babylon must fall for the slain of Israel, as for Babylon have fallen the slain of all the earth" (Jer. 51:48–49, RSV).

End-time Babylon is found responsible for unjustly accusing God's faithful people and inducing the secular and political powers of the world to destroy them and shed their blood (Rev. 18:24). The judgment upon the end-time apostate religious system is God's solution to save his oppressed and persecuted people. It further declares God's ultimate triumph over Satan and his evil forces.

18:21–23a In the final stage of the vision, John again makes the point that in the end evil must be completely destroyed. In a symbolic presentation, John sees a strong angel taking *a stone like a great millstone* and throwing it into the sea with this comment: *Thus will Babylon the great city be thrown down with violence and will never be found any longer.* The picture of throwing the stone into the sea as a symbolic act of Babylon's destruction is borrowed from Jeremiah 51:59–64. The word of God ordered Jeremiah to attach a stone to the book which described the destruction of Babylon and to throw it into the Euphrates: "Just so shall Babylon sink down and not rise again, because of the calamity that I am going to bring upon her" (Jer. 51:64). This reaffirms the ultimate and complete destruction of end-time Babylon as was the desolation of historic Babylon. The angel's action also evokes the language of Matthew 18:6: "Whoever causes one of these little ones who believe in Me to stumble, it would be better for him to have a heavy millstone hung around his neck, and to be drowned in the depth of the sea." Babylon has been found guilty of using her power and seduction to lead people, even "the little ones," into sin.[21]

The desolation of Babylon is vividly portrayed in the cessation of all the city's activities: no more music, no everyday business or domestic activities such as craftsmanship and food production (18:22); never again will light shine in it nor wedding rejoicing be heard (18:23). In portraying this desolated condition, John uses several Old Testament prophecies of the collapse of the apostate cities. For instance, Ezekiel prophesies against Tyre: "So I will silence the sound of your songs, and the sound of your harps will be heard no more" (Ezek. 26:13). Jeremiah announced the desolation of Jerusalem: "I will take from them the voice of joy and the voice of gladness, the voice of the bridegroom and the voice of the bride, the sound of the millstones and the light of the lamp" (Jer. 25:10).

18:23b–24 The section ends with the indictment on Babylon and reasons for her destruction. First, *your merchants were the great men of the earth.* This suggests the arrogant attitude of the figurative commercial salespeople of Babylon who have placed themselves into the service of Babylon. They were mainly responsible for selling and distributing Babylon's "corrupt doctrines and policies."[22] Their greatness resulted from their illicit association with Babylon which led them to self-exaltation and pride. The second reason for the indictment against Babylon is that by its *magic spell all the nations were deceived.* Magic arts are a sort of special demonic activity at the time of the end (cf. Rev. 9:21). By means of the wine of her fornication and magic arts, Babylon has been very successful in deceiving people. Signs are the means used by the earth beast (under the auspices of the sea beast) to deceive and seduce the earth dwellers to receive the mark of the beast and side with the satanic trinity in the final crisis (Rev. 13:14; 19:20).

Finally, Babylon is also indicted because *in her the blood of prophets and saints was found and of all those who have been slain on the earth.* This reflects

Jeremiah's prophecy against ancient Babylon: "Babylon must fall for the slain of Israel, as for Babylon have fallen the slain of all the earth" (Jer. 51:49, RSV). The end-time apostate religious system, Babylon, is found responsible for unjustly accusing and severely persecuting God's faithful people and shedding their blood (Rev. 18:24). It has even become drunk with the blood of those who have been killed (Rev. 17:6). It is the blood of God's suffering people that has cried for vindication and justice, as symbolically portrayed in the scene of the fifth seal: "How long, O Lord, holy and true, will you not judge and avenge our blood upon those who dwell on the earth?" (Rev. 6:9–11). The destroyer of the saints is now judged. "'I will repay Babylon and all the inhabitants of Chaldea for all their evil that they have done in Zion before your eyes,' declares the Lord" (Jer. 51:24). In the judgment of this end-time apostate and persecuting power, the prayers of God's suffering people will finally be answered (as stressed in Rev. 19:1–2).

A RETROSPECT ON REVELATION 18

With Revelation 18 ends the theme introduced in Revelation 17:14–17—the withdrawal of popular support for Babylon by the governing secular and political powers of the world after they realize that they were deceived. Former supporters will turn against Babylon and destroy it completely. In the judgment of end-time Babylon, the wrath of God is his response to the anger of the nations announced at the sound of the seventh trumpet. The time has come for the destroyers of the earth to be destroyed (Rev. 11:18). The certainty of the judgment on Babylon is accentuated in the repeated announcement of Babylon's fall throughout the book (cf. 14:8; 16:19; 17:16; 18:2, 21). The readers of Revelation are repeatedly reminded that, in the end, the enemy of God and the oppressor of God's people will be completely defeated.[23]

One purpose of Revelation 16–18 is to provide God's oppressed people throughout Christian history with the firm assurance that their unjust suffering will come to an end and that God will judge his and their enemies (cf. Rev. 18:6, 20, 24; 19:2–3). The bad news for the enemies of God is good news for God's oppressed people. To them, the destruction of Babylon means guaranteed deliverance from suffering and oppression. The future might be vague and uncertain, and the description of the final events frightening, yet he is in control. He will judge with justice the enemies of the gospel and usher in the kingdom of eternal joy. Kenneth Strand expresses it in the following way:

In Scripture there is assurance that God has always cared for His people: that in history itself He is ever present to sustain them, and that in the great eschatological denouement He will give them full vindication and an incomprehensibly generous reward in life everlasting. The book of Revelation picks up and expands beautifully this same theme, and thus Revelation is not by any means some sort of offbeat apocalypse that is out of tune with biblical literature in general; it conveys the very heart and substance of the biblical message. Indeed, as Revelation emphatically points out, the "Living One"—the One who conquered death and the grave (1:18)—will never forsake His faithful followers and that even when they suffer martyrdom they are victorious (12:11), with the "crown of life" awaiting them (see 2:10; 21:1–4; and 22:4).[24]

The announcement of Babylon's downfall is a strong wake-up call to God's people to break off personal identification with any religious system that is not in line with the gospel. Many sincere people are still wavering in Babylon for different reasons. They may be deceived by "a form of godliness" (2 Tim. 3:5) manifest in many religious systems. Some religious systems can take and use "the name of Christ and even rejoice in the Spirit," and yet be systems that have their "power coming from below."[25] Some are in Babylon even without being aware of this. Others think that they are not in Babylon, yet they might be identified with her. A person can speak against Babylon, and take the name of Christ, and yet have the mark of the beast on the forehead (cf. Matt. 7:21). Being a member of a group that teaches the true gospel does not guarantee that one is on God's side. The appeal of grace to every Christian is to examine and test by the word of God the religious system to which he or she belongs.

The conclusion of the gospel proclamation is God's end-time appeal to the earth dwellers to turn to him and escape what is about to befall Babylon and its worshipers: "Come out of her, my people, that you might not share in her sins, and that you might not receive of her plagues" (Rev. 18:1–4). As Revelation 19:1–10 shows, many will respond to this call.

ENDNOTES

1. For a list of parallels with Jeremiah, see Aune, *Revelation 17–22*, 983.
2. Beale, 901.
3. Ladd, 238.
4. Beckwith, 715; J. M. Ford, 297–298; Hughes, 191; Beale, 901.
5. Kline, 177.

6. Caird, 222.

7. Ladd, 236; Aune, *Revelation 6–16*, 829.

8. Beale, 893.

9. Ibid., 895.

10. Ibid., 896.

11. Morris, 210.

12. Ladd, 238.

13. Beale, 902.

14. LaRondelle, *How to Understand the End-Time Prophecies*, 429.

15. *The Seventh-day Adventist Bible Commentary*, 7:864.

16. Beale, 907.

17. Ibid.

18. *The Seventh-day Adventist Bible Commentary*, 7:864.

19. Ibid.

20. Ibid.

21. Sweet, 274.

22. *The Seventh-day Adventist Bible Commentary*, 7:864.

23. Morris, 196.

24. Strand, "The Seven Heads," 206.

25. Paulien, The Bible Explorer, 5.4.

THE TWO SUPPERS
REVELATION 19:1–21

Revelation 19 falls into two distinct parts. Verses 1–10 describe the tumultuous joy of the heavenly beings as a reaction to Babylon's doom and also announce the wedding supper of the Lamb. Verses 11–21 describe the coming of Christ as the warrior/king escorted by his heavenly army to complete the destruction of the evil forces and rescue God's people. This is followed by a call to the birds of the sky to participate in a gruesome feast of the great supper of God.

THE WEDDING SUPPER OF THE LAMB (19:1–10)

In Revelation 18:20 the call was given to rejoice over the destruction of end-time Babylon: "Rejoice over her, heaven, and saints and apostles and prophets, because God has executed judgment for you on her." Revelation 19:1–10 portrays a spontaneous outpouring of joy and the giving of praises to God. It functions as a sort of interlude between the scenes of the judgment of Babylon (Rev. 17–18) and the appearance of the warrior/king Christ to fight on behalf of his people, bringing her ultimate destruction (Rev. 19:11–21).

> *¹After these things I heard something like a loud voice of a great multitude in heaven saying:*
> *"Hallelujah!*
> *Salvation and glory and power to our God,*
> *   ²because his judgments are true and righteous;*
> *for he has judged the great prostitute*
> *   who corrupted the earth with her fornication,*
> *and he has avenged the blood of his servants*
> *   from her hand."*

³*And they said a second time:*
  "Hallelujah!
  Her smoke ascends forever and ever!"
⁴*And the twenty-four elders and the four living beings fell*
down and worshiped God sitting on the throne, saying:
  "Amen! Hallelujah!"
⁵*And from the throne a voice came, saying,*
  "Praise our God all his servants,
  those who fear him, small and great."
⁶*And I heard something like a voice of a great multitude and*
like a voice of many waters and like a voice of strong
thunders saying:
  "Hallelujah,
  because our Lord God the Almighty began to reign.
  ⁷*Let us rejoice and be glad and give glory to him,*
  because the wedding of the Lamb has come,
  and his wife has prepared herself;
    ⁸*and it was given to her to clothe herself in fine linen, bright*
        and clean,
  for the fine linen is the righteous deeds of the saints."
⁹*And he said to me, "Write: Blessed are those who are invited*
to the wedding supper of the Lamb." And he said to me, "These
are the true words of God." ¹⁰*And I fell before his feet to*
worship him. And he said to me, "See that you do not do this; I
am a fellow servant of you and your brothers who have the
testimony of Jesus. Worship God! For the testimony of Jesus is
the spirit of prophecy."

NOTES

19:1 *Hallelujah.* Except for four times in Revelation 19, this word appears nowhere else in the New Testament. "Hallelujah" is a compound Hebrew word of *halal* ("to praise") and *Yah* ("Yahweh"), meaning to "praise God" (the Greek equivalent is given in verse 5: "praise God"). The word occurs twenty-four times in the Psalms (e.g., Pss. 111:1; 112:1; 113:1; 146:1). The original Hebrew form is here transliterated into Greek. The word was adopted by early Christians and became a very common expression in religious vocabulary for giving praises to God.[1]

19:2 *Corrupted.* See *Notes* on Revelation 11:18.

Fornication. See *Notes* on Revelation 14:8.

552

He has avenged the blood of his servants. The text refers to a legal action: God has judged Babylon in avenging the blood of his servants from her hand (see *Notes* on Rev. 6:10).

19:3 *Her smoke ascends forever and ever.* The ascending smoke indicates the completion of the burning. See *Notes* on Revelation 14:11.

19:4 *The twenty-four elders.* See *Notes* on Revelation 4:4.

The four living beings. See *Notes* on Revelation 4:6.

19:6 *Almighty.* See *Notes* on Revelation 1:8.

Began to reign. The phrase in Greek is most likely an ingressive aorist denoting the beginning of the action.

19:7 *The wedding of the Lamb.* The wedding metaphor appears frequently in the Scriptures. Jesus used the wedding motif with regard to his relationship with his disciples (Mark 2:19). The wedding supper is also a motif in his parables about the coming kingdom, including the parable of the wedding of the king's son (Matt. 22:1–14) and that of the ten virgins (Matt. 25:1–13). Paul speaks of himself as betrothing the church like a pure virgin to Christ (2 Cor. 11:2). On the symbolism of the woman with reference to God's people, see *Notes* on Revelation 12:1 and 14:4.

His wife has prepared herself. In the Old Testament, Israel is often described in terms of a bride (cf. Isa. 61:10; 62:5; Jer. 2:32; Hos. 2:19–20). The preparation of the Lamb's bride in Revelation 19 must be understood in the context of the ancient Hebrew wedding.[2] The Hebrew wedding usually began with the betrothal at the house of the bride's father, where the groom paid the dowry. The two were, afterwards, considered husband and wife. The groom then returned to his father's house to prepare the place where he and his bride would live. During that time, the bride stayed at her father's home preparing herself for the wedding. When both the place and the bride were ready, the bridegroom would return to take the bride to his father's house where the wedding ceremony was to take place (cf. Matt. 25:1–10). The preparation of the Lamb's bride in Revelation 19:7 reflects a typical Hebrew wedding setting.

19:8 *The righteous deeds.* The meaning of the Greek word *dikaiōmata* (the plural form) is somewhat vague here. It seems to refer to "regulations," "requirements," or "statutes" (cf. Luke 1:6; Rom. 1:32; 2:26; 8:4; Heb. 9:1, 10).[3] In Romans 5:18, the word contrasts with *paraptōma* ("an act of transgression") and refers to the act of the righteousness of Christ.[4] The plural form of the word occurs in Revelation 15:4 as God's "righteous deeds" in judging the nations. It appears that the correct translation of the word here is "the righteous deeds" which are in harmony with the requirements of the laws of God (cf. Rev. 12:17; 14:12). "The righteous deeds [*dikaiōmata*] of the saints" obviously stand in contrast to the unrighteous deeds (*adikēmata*) of prostitute Babylon (Rev. 18:5).

19:9 *Blessed.* See *Notes* on Revelation 1:3.

19:10 *The testimony of Jesus.* See *Notes* on Revelation 1:2 and 12:17.

The spirit of prophecy. This expression is used only here in the entire New Testament. The Jewish and early Christian literary sources indicate, however, that "the spirit of prophecy" was not a new phrase coined by John, but rather that it was in current usage among the first-century

Jewish people.[5] The phrase refers to the Spirit who speaks through those who have been called to be prophets to declare the message revealed and entrusted to them by God. The expression "the testimony of Jesus is the spirit of prophecy" must be understood as the testimony that Jesus either bore in his own life and ministry, or through those who have the spirit of prophecy, much as he did through the prophets in ancient times (cf. 1 Pet. 1:11–12; see *Notes* on Rev. 1:2 and 12:17). William Barclay explains: "We can define the true prophet as the man who has received from Christ the message he brings to men, and whose words and works are at one and the same time an act of witness to Christ."[6] Many other scholars share this view.[7] Hans LaRondelle, following a few scholars, argues that "the testimony of Jesus" refers to the historic testimony of Jesus that he bore in his life. The term "the spirit of prophecy" is not restricted to a chosen group of believers; it rather embraces all faithful Christians who "have" the testimony of Jesus.[8]

The context shows, however, that the expression "the spirit of prophecy" is not to be a possession of all Christians, in general, but "only of those who have been called by God to be prophets."[9] Richard Bauckham explains: "Probably a distinction is to be drawn between the special vocation of the Christian prophets to declare the word of God within the Christian community, and the general vocation of the Christian community as a whole to declare the word of God in the world. The former will then subserve the latter. The Spirit speaks through the prophets to the churches and through the churches to the world. However, as far as specific references to the Spirit go, those we have so far examined concern exclusively the Spirit's inspiration of Christian prophecy addressed to the churches. For the Spirit's activity in the church's missionary role in the world, we must turn to a distinct category of references to the Spirit."[10] In the same line is David Aune, and many others, who hold that the phrase should be understood to refer to "the power that allows certain individuals to have visionary experiences and gives them revelatory insights not available to ordinary people."[11]

In addition, the context of the book shows that "the testimony of Jesus" is not just the historic testimony of Jesus, but that "the testimony of Jesus" is for the purpose of showing "the things which must soon take place" (Rev. 1:1). This fact is especially emphasized in Revelation 22:6: "The Lord God of the spirits of the prophets sent his angel to show to his servants the things which must soon take place."[12]

EXPOSITION

19:1–3 While the destruction of end-time Babylon prompts a lament among Babylon's allies, it also provokes an explosion of joy in heaven in celebration of God. John hears the sound of *a great multitude in heaven* shouting: *"Hallelujah! Salvation and glory and power to our God."* This multitude is probably the same "great multitude" who are in heaven shouting: "Salvation to our God sitting on the throne and to the Lamb" (Rev. 7:9–10); it also brings to mind "the new song that the Lamb's followers sing on Mount Zion" (Rev. 14:1–3; 15:2–4).[13] This multitude in heaven is made up of those who have been able to stand in the great day of God's wrath (Rev. 6:17). Now they celebrate the mighty acts of God, praising him for having executed his **true and righteous** judgments on end-time Babylon and for having taken his power and begun to reign. This recalls the words from the song of Moses and the Lamb sung by the saved standing on the sea of glass in Revelation 15:3–4.

The reason for this rejoicing is twofold. First, God **has judged** the great prostitute Babylon since she **corrupted the earth with her fornication.** This refers to the activities of Babylon described in Revelation 17:1–6. Second, what was announced in Revelation 11:18 is fulfilled: Babylon as the destroyer of the earth is destroyed. The rejoicing over Babylon's destruction is not an expression of vengeance or revenge, but rather of gratitude to God for the salvation of his people. However, this salvation is made possible only after the persecuting enemy power has been removed and God's people have come out of Babylon.

The second reason for the rejoicing of the heavenly choruses is that, in punishing Babylon, God **has avenged the blood of his servants from her hand.** The text implies a legal action: God has judged Babylon in avenging the blood of his servant. This end-time apostate religious power is found responsible for oppressing God's faithful people and shedding their blood (Rev. 18:24). Here is a strong allusion to Revelation 6:9–11 where the suffering saints beneath the altar long for vindication and justice in the scene of the fifth seal. "How long, O Lord, holy and true, will you not judge and avenge our blood upon those who dwell on the earth?" It is reasonable to assume that these oppressed saints are at the center of this rejoicing multitude before the throne of God.[14] Their rejoicing reveals a sense of relief after the great deliverance in the final crisis.

Those of the saved multitude now shout a second "Hallelujah" because Babylon's **smoke ascends forever and ever!** Here is the fulfillment of what was earlier announced in Revelation 14:11. The ascending of the smoke forever and ever is another way of saying that Babylon will never again "rise from her ruins" just as Edom of old never did (cf. Isa. 34:8–10).[15] The destruction of the oppressor of God's people will be definite and irreversible.

19:4 The rejoicing multitude is joined by **the twenty-four elders and the four living beings.** As we have seen, the twenty-four elders are most likely the glorified saints; in the heavenly places they are a symbolic representation of the redeemed and faithful people of God, from both the Old and New Testaments (cf. Rev. 4:4). The four living beings are probably an exalted angelic order involved in service to God and leading the heavenly hosts in worship and praise (cf. Rev. 4:6–8). In contrast to the majority of people on the earth who turn their backs on God, here we see the representation of both heaven and earth joined in giving praises to God for his mighty works of deliverance and judgment. With *Amen! Hallelujah!* they express their agreement with the heavenly choruses in adoring God for the salvation of his people.

19:5–6 At this point, an invitation from God's throne calls upon the servants of God: *Praise our God all his servants, those who fear him, small and great.* This invitation fulfills what was announced with the seventh trumpet in regard to the giving of the reward to the saints who fear God's name, "the small and the great ones" (Rev. 11:18). The phrase "who fear him [the Lord], the small and the great ones" is borrowed from Psalm 115:13, denoting the faithful believers from every socio-economic level.[16]

The song of the redeemed multitude praising God for his victory over their enemies reaches a crescendo with a new exclamation of "hallelujah." This time they rejoice not over the destruction of end-time Babylon but because *our Lord God the Almighty began to reign.* Here is the development of the announcement made with the seventh trumpet sound: "We give thanks to you, Lord God, the Almighty, who is and who was, because you have taken your great power and begun to reign" (Rev. 11:17). The collapse of the end-time apostate religious power means the beginning of God's reign over the earth in the fullness of his power and authority. As George E. Ladd points out, "the reign of God has in fact not yet been fully established" at this point; "it awaits the return of Christ, the chaining of Satan, and the inauguration of Christ's messianic reign" after the millennium.[17]

19:7–8 At this point, the song of the redeemed turns into a call for rejoicing at the wedding of the Lamb: *Let us rejoice and be glad and give glory to him, because the wedding of the Lamb has come.* The much-awaited union of Christ with his bride—the church—at the Second Coming is expressed in terms of "the wedding of the Lamb." This union between the Lamb and his bride stands in stark contrast to the illicit relationship between prostitute Babylon and her lovers portrayed in the previous chapters.[18] The invitation expressed as "rejoice and be glad" is found only in one other place in the New Testament. In the Sermon on the Mount, Jesus made a promise to his oppressed and persecuted followers in the world: "Rejoice and be glad, for your reward in heaven is great" (Matt. 5:12).[19] The giving of the reward promised by Christ is portrayed in Revelation as "a great wedding feast in which the Lamb and his bride celebrate" their long-awaited union.[20] The Lamb's bride is made up of those who heeded the call to come out of Babylon and not be partakers in Babylon's sins. They have kept themselves undefiled from the adulteration and impurity of Babylon and suffered because of that. Now they are partakers of the Lamb's wedding supper.

This joining of Christ with the people whom he has purchased on the cross is the focus of the entire book of Revelation. Everything in the book moves toward that climactic triumph. The wedding supper does not occur at this point; Revelation 19 only announces that the time for the wedding supper has come, as a parallel to another supper—"the great supper of God" portrayed in Revelation 19:17–19.[21] The union between Christ and his church is developed in Revelation 21. George E. Ladd explains:

> It must be again emphasized that John does not describe the marriage supper; he only proclaims that the time has come. The actual event is nowhere described; it is a metaphorical way of alluding to the final redemptive fact when "the dwelling of God is with men. He will dwell with them, and they shall be his people, and God himself will be with them" (Rev. 21:3). This is why John can apply the same metaphor of the bride prepared for her husband to the new Jerusalem which comes down from heaven to dwell among men (Rev. 21:2), and why the angel can refer to the new Jerusalem "as the bride, the wife of the Lamb" (Rev. 21:9). As Jerusalem is frequently used in Scripture to represent the people of God (Matt. 23:37), so in the vision of the new world, the people of God and their capital city—the church and the new Jerusalem—are so closely connected that the same figure—the bride—is used for both.[22]

The Lamb's bride *has prepared herself* for this much-awaited union with Christ. The text shows the church actively participating in her preparation, rather than waiting in passiveness. Here we have an allusion to the ancient wedding practice. Christ left his Father's house in heaven to come down to the earth to betroth his bride—the church—for himself. At Calvary, he paid the dowry for his bride. Afterwards, he returned to his father's house to prepare a place for her (cf. John 14:1–3). In the meantime, his bride remains here on the earth. While waiting, she is preparing herself, just as the Hebrew bride in ancient times stayed at her father's home preparing herself for the wedding. When both the place and bride are ready, then the wedding—the Second Coming—will take place. Paul speaks of Christ's love for his church and his giving himself up for her, so that when he comes "he might present to Himself the church in all her glory, having no spot or wrinkle or any such thing; but that she should be holy and blameless" (Eph. 5:27). John wrote: "Everyone who has this hope in him purifies himself just as he is pure" (1 John 3:3, NIV). Here in Revelation 19:7–8, the apostle announces that the church has now prepared herself and is ready for the wedding. The moment has finally arrived for Christ, the bridegroom, to leave his Father's house and to come down to the earth to join his beloved bride, the church, and take her to the place prepared for her.

The bride's preparation is described in terms of arraying herself *in fine linen, bright and clean* (cf. Rev. 7:14). Daniel prophesied that at the time of the end "many shall purify themselves, and make themselves white, and be refined" (Dan. 12:10, RSV). "Bright" indicates a radiant whiteness which denotes glorification (cf. Matt. 13:43), and "clean" reflects the church in all her purity, loyalty, and faithfulness.[23] Fine linen is mentioned several times in Revelation. In this text, however, it is especially significant in that it represents *the righteous deeds of the saints*. "Righteous deeds are the natural and inevitable result of a righteous character" produced by a victorious Christian life developed by the grace of the indwelling Christ (cf. Gal. 2:20; James 2:17–20).[24] The bride's linen dress stands in sharp contrast to the purple and scarlet clothing and lavish adornment of the great harlot Babylon (Rev. 17:4). Both the church and Babylon "are clothed in their deeds and character"[25]; while the church's robe symbolizes righteous deeds and Christ-like character, Babylon's robe symbolizes unrighteous deeds and Satan-like character (cf. Rev. 18:5). G. R. Beasley-Murray notes that "Revelation as a whole may be characterized as *A Tale of Two Cities*, with the sub-title, *The Harlot and the Bride*."[26]

Although the church's preparation includes her active participation, the text shows that the church does not put on her own works. John states that the Lamb's bride *was given* to array herself in bright and clean linen. The fact that the bride "was given" to clothe herself with fine linen indicates that it was not her own righteous deeds that make up a gown of meritorious works or self-righteousness.[27] The white robes are not self-made or self-earned, but are supplied by Christ and are given to God's redeemed people. The righteous deeds are thus Christ's gift to his people. This concept is emphasized elsewhere in Revelation. Christ invited the Christians in Laodicea to "buy" from him white garments "at the cost of total commitment,"[28] so as to clothe themselves and cover the shame of their nakedness (Rev. 3:18). The slain martyrs underneath the altar in the scene of the fifth seal were given white garments as a token of their obedience to God (Rev. 6:11). Revelation 7:9–14 shows that the white and clean robes of the redeemed are the result of having them washed in the blood of the Lamb. That is why they shout before the throne: "Salvation to our God sitting on the throne and to the Lamb" (Rev. 7:10). In Revelation 19:7 the redeemed are called to *give glory to him*, showing that their redemption is entirely the result of what Christ has done for them, rather than what they have achieved for themselves. Such an idea is confirmed in the prophecy of Isaiah: "I will rejoice greatly in the Lord, my soul will exult in my God; for He has clothed me with garments of salvation, He has wrapped me with a robe of righteousness, as a bridegroom decks himself with a garland, and as a bride adorns herself with her jewels" (Isa. 61:10). Revelation 19:8 reflects on this passage from Isaiah. It indicates that the robe of salvation and righteous deeds is granted to the redeemed by God, and not made by them.[29] It is a product of their intimate relationship with Christ (cf. Eph. 5:24–27).

19:9–10 The angel summons John to write: *Blessed are those who are invited to the wedding supper of the Lamb.* This is the fourth of the seven beatitudes in Revelation (1:3; 14:13; 16:15; 19:9; 20:6; 22:7, 14). It certainly evokes the saying of the man dining with Jesus at the table: "Blessed is everyone who will eat bread in the kingdom of God" (Luke 14:15). Jesus spoke of many coming from the east and west, and sitting "at the table with Abraham, Isaac, and Jacob, in the kingdom of heaven" (Matt. 8:11). This joyous banquet expresses the fulfillment of Jesus' promise to his disciples at the last supper: "I say to you, I will not drink of this fruit of the vine from now on until that day when I drink it new with you in My Father's kingdom" (Matt. 26:29). John was instructed to write this beatitude to remind God's people that even though they might be experiencing hardship and suffering, they are blessed because of the call to the wedding supper of the Lamb.

To assure both John and the readers of the book of the certainty and reliability of this beatitude, the angel adds a statement: *These are the true words of God.* God's people are provided here with a solemn confirmation of the certainty that the invitation to the wedding feast is "the unfailing word of God."[30]

Those who are invited to the wedding supper of the Lamb are unequivocally those who make up the bride of the Lamb. The redeemed saints are both the bride and the invited guests at the wedding supper. These concepts are expressed also in the parables of Jesus (cf. Matt. 22:1–14; 25:1–13). By means of these two imageries, John describes the experience of God's people at the Second Coming from two different perspectives. Herman Hoeksema observes that the figure of the bride is the unified church as a whole, in her marriage with Christ, while the guests are the members of the church who individually responded to the invitation to the feast which the Father has prepared for his Son.[31]

Overwhelmed by joy with what he has just heard, John prostrates himself before the angel's feet to worship him. However, the angel immediately warns him not to do that, reminding him that he is not divine: *I am a fellow servant of you and your brothers who have the testimony of Jesus. Worship God!* This is what Jesus made clear in the desert when he was tempted by Satan: "You shall worship the Lord your God, and serve Him only" (Matt. 4:10). Regardless of how important a person and his message may be, he is not to be worshiped. Only God, "the one who made heaven and the earth and the sea and the fountains of waters" (Rev. 14:7), is to be the object of our worship.

The angel explains further that the testimony of Jesus is *the spirit of prophecy*, that is, as Richard Bauckham states, "the Spirit who speaks through the prophets."[32] According to Ephesians 3:2–6, the prophets are the agents of God's revelation. Their role is to "unpack the mysteries about Jesus Christ," his life and death, his resurrection, his work in heaven, and his return to the earth.[33] Bauckham notes that "the Spirit of prophecy speaks through the Christian prophets bringing the word of the exalted Christ to his people on earth, endorsing on earth the words of heavenly revelations, and directing the prayers of the churches to their heavenly Lord. These are the special functions of the Christian prophets, whom Revelation distinguishes as a special group within the churches" (11:18; 16:6; 18:20, 24; 22:9).[34] John here claims to be one of the prophets; he received a special revelation from God. And he bears witness to "the testimony of Jesus Christ" that was communicated to him in the vision (Rev. 1:2). John does not consider himself to be the last in the prophetic office, however; he indicates that the prophetic ministry will continue in the church after the first century throughout the Christian age. Although this has been the case of the true people of God through the ages, Revelation 12:17 states clearly that God's end-time remnant is characterized by a special possession of the testimony of Jesus given through those who have been called by God to be his prophets. In the end, the church will once more be in possession of the prophetic ministry as it was in the time of John.

"Brothers" is another term for Christ's bride. God's people living in the closing days of this earth's history are given an assurance of God's special care and guidance through the Spirit who speaks through the prophets, just as with God's people of old. It is not just the manifestation of the prophetic gift in their midst, however, but rather their faithfulness to the prophetic message that separates God's people from the unfaithful at the time of the end.

THE GREAT SUPPER OF GOD (19:11–21)

The scene suddenly shifts from the wedding supper to the coming of the warrior/ king Christ at the head of the armies of heaven to confront the armies of the earth under the leadership of the satanic triumvirate and the kings of the earth. Here is the climax of the final battle of Armageddon. End-time Babylon was dealt with in Revelation 18. The rest of Revelation 19 completes this scene that was interrupted by the rejoicing of the redeemed saints over Babylon's destruction and the announcement of the wedding supper of the Lamb (Rev. 19:1–10). The text provides the answer to the question about the fate of those who licentiously cooperated with the end-time apostate religious system and participated in her sins. The time has come for them— as announced in Revelation 14:17–20—to be trod upon in "the winepress of the wine of the anger of the wrath of God Almighty" (Rev. 19:15) and to be devoured by the scavengers of the sky.

> **[11]And I saw heaven opened, and behold a white horse and the One sitting upon it was called faithful and true, and in righteousness he judges and wages war. [12]His eyes are like a flame of fire, and on his head are many crowns; he has a name written on himself which nobody knows except himself, [13]and he is clothed in a robe dipped in blood, and his name is called the Word of God. [14]And the armies which are in heaven were following him on white horses, clothed in fine linen, white and clean. [15]And from his mouth proceeds a sharp sword, that with it he may smite the nations, and he will rule them with a rod of iron, and he treads the winepress of the wine of the anger of the wrath of God the Almighty. [16]And he has on his robe and on his thighs a name written: King of kings and Lord of lords.**

¹⁷And I saw an angel standing in the sun, and he cried with a loud voice, saying to all the birds flying in midheaven: "Come, gather for the great supper of God, ¹⁸that you may eat the flesh of the kings and the flesh of the commanders of 1,000 troops and the flesh of the strong and the flesh of horses and of those sitting upon them and the flesh of all, both free men and slaves, the small and great." ¹⁹And I saw the beast and the kings of the earth and their armies gathered to make war against the one sitting on the horse and against his army. ²⁰And the beast was captured, and with him the false prophet who performed the signs before him, by which he deceived those who received the mark of the beast and who worshiped his image; these two were cast alive into the lake of fire burning with sulphur. ²¹And the rest were killed with the sword of the one sitting upon the horse, the sword having proceeded from his mouth; and all the birds were filled with their flesh.

NOTES

19:12 *His eyes are like a flame of fire.* See *Notes* on Revelation 1:14.

On his head are many crowns. The Greek *diadema* ("diadem") is the royal crown (see *Notes* on Rev. 2:10). It may seem strange that Christ wears many crowns. William Barclay points to 1 Maccabees 11:13 which mentions that when Ptolemy entered Antioch he wore two crowns or diadems—one to show that he was lord of Asia and one to show that he was lord of Egypt. This indicates that in John's time "it was not uncommon for a monarch to wear more than one crown."[35]

19:13 *He is clothed in a robe dipped in blood.* The Old Testament background text for this imagery is Isaiah 63:1–6 (see *Notes* on Rev. 14:19).

19:14 *The armies which are in heaven.* The armies following Christ in the final battle are most likely the saints referred to in Revelation 17:14 as "the called and elect and faithful." See *Notes* on Revelation 16:12.

19:15 *From his mouth proceeds a sharp sword.* See *Notes* on Revelation 1:16.

The winepress of the wine of the anger of the wrath of God. See *Notes* on Revelation 14:19.

The wine of the anger of the wrath of God. See *Notes* on Revelation 14:10.

Almighty. See *Notes* on Revelation 1:8.

19:20 *The false prophet who performed the signs before him.* The false prophet is a new designation for the earth beast of Revelation 13:11–17 as the third member of the satanic trinity. See *Notes* on Revelation 16:13.

19:21 *The birds were filled with their flesh.* This statement reflects the ancient Near Eastern post-combat scene. Disposing one's body to the birds and animals for food signified total defeat and shameful humiliation (Deut. 28:26; 1 Sam. 17:44; 1 Kings 14:11; 16:4; 21:23–24; Ezek. 39:4, 17–21). Furthermore, "to be devoured by the scavengers of the skies constituted one of the curses for disobedience pronounced by Moses...to the people of Israel."[36]

EXPOSITION

19:11–13 Once again John sees *heaven opened* as he did in Revelation 4:1. This time the door in heaven is not open for John to enter, but for Christ to come down to the earth. The warrior Christ is seen here as a Roman general riding on *a white horse* celebrating his triumph and victory,[37] even though the battle has not yet been won. He is called *faithful and true.* To the church in Laodicea, he introduced himself as "the faithful and true witness" (Rev. 3:14). It is necessary to keep in mind that Near Eastern names stand for character.[38] These names ascribed to Christ refer to him as the one whom we can trust and rely on. He is coming to rescue his people according to the prophetic word: "At that time shall arise Michael, the great prince who has charge of your people. And there shall be a time of trouble, such as never has been since there was a nation till that time; but at that time your people shall be delivered, every one whose name shall be found written in the book" (Dan. 12:1, RSV). The same God who has performed marvelous acts for his people in the past gives us the certainty that he is faithful to his promises pertaining to the future. He will stand on behalf of his people to defend them at the time of the end. It is because he is faithful and true that *in righteousness he judges and wages war.* Wars are usually matters of oppression and bloodshed rather than of justice. The war that Christ is about to wage is for the purpose of establishing justice and bringing an end to oppression. It is waged on behalf of his people to deliver them and establish them in the place he has prepared for them.

The warrior Christ's *eyes were like a flame of fire.* This is reminiscent of his description in Revelation 1:14. The imagery signifies Christ's ability to judge; nothing can remain hidden from his penetrating insight. He wears on his head *many crowns.* These are royal crowns, signifying his royal power and authority to exercise judgment. The many crowns on his head stand in contrast to the crowns of the dragon in Revelation 12:3. In Revelation 5, Christ has been given authority to rule, but his rule was limited due to Satan's rebellious claim to dominion on the earth (cf. Luke 4:6). Satan is allowed to continue his rule for a "little time" (Rev. 12:12) until Christ puts his enemies under his feet (1 Cor. 15:25). Now, the downfall of end-time Babylon opens the door for Christ's definite right to rule. He is coming now as "King of kings and Lord of lords" (Rev. 19:16) to destroy "all rule and all authority and power" (1 Cor. 15:24) and become the King and Lord of all the kingdoms of the earth.

He has *a name* inscribed on his thigh *which nobody knows except himself.* What is this name? Paul stated that God highly exalted Christ and "bestowed on Him the name which is above every name," so that "every tongue should confess that Jesus Christ is Lord" (Phil. 2:9–11). Christ is twice referred to in the text as "King of kings and Lord of lords" (Rev. 17:14; 19:16), suggesting that this special name would single out Christ as the only true and universal king in the universe.[39]

The warrior Christ's robe is *dipped in blood.* This description evokes Isaiah's portrayal of God, returning from punishing Edom and clothed in "garments of glowing colors," who is "majestic in His apparel, marching in the greatness of His strength":

> "It is I who speaks in righteousness, mighty to save."
> Why is Your apparel red,
> And Your garments like the one who treads in the wine press?
> "I have trodden the wine trough alone,
> And from the peoples there was no man with Me.
> I also trod them in My anger,
> And trampled them in My wrath;
> And their lifeblood is sprinkled on My garments,
> And I stained all My raiment." (Isa. 63:1–3)

That Christ's robe is stained with blood comes here somewhat as a surprise, for "the combat has not yet begun."[40] It is apparently the blood of Christ's persecuted and faithful witnesses (Rev. 17:6).[41] Jesus is coming to rescue them and avenge their blood, giving them victory over their enemies.

Christ's name is *the Word of God*, which may mean two things. First, it may be an allusion to John 1:1–5, where Christ is the Word of God through whom the heavens and the earth and all that is in them was created. That he is coming to judge the inhabitants of the earth having the name of the Word of God would suggest that he is coming in the full manifestation of the glory and power of God the Creator. Second, "the word of God" in Revelation refers to the prophetic message of assurance to God's people of Christ's presence with them at the time of the end. It is because they bear faithful witness to the word of God that the saints, including John himself (Rev. 1:9), have suffered hardship and severe persecution (cf. Rev. 6:9; 20:4). Now the same Christ, who is the embodiment of the word of God, is coming to provide deliverance for his oppressed and persecuted people and bring the prophetic word to its final and definite fulfillment.

19:14 The victorious Christ is accompanied by *the armies which are in heaven* riding *on white horses, clothed in fine linen, white and clean*. In a literal sense when Christ returns to the earth, he will be accompanied by the heavenly angels (cf. Matt. 24:30–31). This is a clear allusion to Revelation 17:14; this heavenly army is most likely the saints, "the kings from the rising of the sun" (Rev. 16:12), those "called and elect and faithful" (Rev. 17:14), under the leadership of Christ in the final battle of this earth's history. "The fine linen, white and clean" is an allusion to the Lamb's bride clothed in "fine linen, bright and clean" (Rev. 19:8), confirming that God's people are in view here. While in actuality the saints are on the earth awaiting translation (cf. 1 Thess. 4:16–17), spiritually they are already in the heavenly places sharing with Christ his glory (cf. Eph. 2:6). They stand in contrast to those opposing God—those in Revelation who are constantly referred to as "those who dwell on the earth" (cf. Rev. 6:10; 8:13; 11:10; 13:8, 14; 14:6). The saints are now seen "sweeping through the skies on white horses" led by Christ in triumph over their enemies.[42] Even though Christ is accompanied by the armies, he alone administers judgment.[43]

19:15–16 In portraying the rider on the white horse, John depends on the earlier images of Christ in Revelation. He does not want his readers to doubt that the warrior on the white horse is the same Christ described elsewhere in the book of Revelation. *A sharp sword* proceeding from Christ's mouth to strike down *the nations* (cf. Rev. 19:21) is a clear allusion to Revelation 1:16. The sword in the Old Testament is a weapon for executing judgment upon the wicked (Ps. 149:6). With *a rod of iron* he will rule the nations (Ps. 2:9; cf. Rev. 2:27 and 12:5). John evidently wants to show that here is the fulfillment of Isaiah's prophecy of the messianic Sprout from the stem of Jesse who "will strike the earth with the rod of His mouth, and with the breath of His lips He will slay the wicked" (Isa. 11:4). He *treads the winepress of the wine of the anger of the wrath of God the Almighty.* Here is the elaboration of the scene of Revelation 14:17–20, where the fate of the wicked is portrayed metaphorically in terms of the treading of the winepress. These elements indicate that the coming of

Christ in the role of a warrior/king means that the destruction of the evil forces is definite and final.

Finally, Christ has inscribed on his robe and thigh the title *King of kings and Lord of lords.* This title declares the eternal reality of his absolute power and authority over rebellious humanity. The only other place in Revelation where this title is mentioned is Revelation 17:14 where Christ is referred to as the all-conquering Lamb. This indicates that Revelation 19 completes the scene that was introduced in Revelation 17.

⟋ **19:17–19** Now is to be completed the destruction of the end-time confederacy in the final conflict. John sees an angel calling in a loud voice to *all the birds flying in midheaven: "Come, gather for the great supper of God,"* to eat the flesh of the armies of the earth. This imagery is drawn from Ezekiel's vision of judgment on the pagan nations of Gog, where God's victory over the pagan nations is portrayed as a sacrificial feast prepared for the birds of the air and the beasts of the field. God told the prophet: "Speak to every kind of bird and to every beast of the field, 'Assemble and come, gather from every side...that you may eat flesh and drink blood. You will eat the flesh of mighty men and drink the blood of the princes of the earth....You will be glutted at My table with horses and charioteers, with mighty men and all the men of war,' declares the Lord GOD" (Ezek. 39:17–21). The invitation for the birds of prey to participate at the great supper of God stands in sharp contrast to the previous invitation to the wedding supper of the Lamb (Rev. 19:9). The mention of two meals in the same chapter seems very important. While those called to the wedding supper of the Lamb are blessed, the impenitent are threatened to become the ghastly supper of the fowls of the sky. The readers of the text are offered a choice either to accept the gracious invitation to the Lamb's wedding supper, or to number themselves with Christ's opponents and find themselves on "the menu of scavengers."[44]

The birds are invited to *eat the flesh of the kings and the flesh of the commanders of 1,000 troops and the flesh of the strong and the flesh of horses and of those sitting upon them and the flesh of all, both free men and slaves, the small and great*—that is to say, the flesh of all men who have received the mark of the beast (cf. Rev. 13:16). This terrifying scene of scavengers feeding themselves with the flesh of horses and human beings further reflects Ezekiel's vision (39:17–21). "And all the nations will see My judgment which I have executed, and My hand which I have laid on them." The list shows that rebellious humanity who oppose God in the final battle are human beings of every socio-economic level.[45] The picture is also an allusion to the scene of the sixth seal where "the kings of the earth and the magistrates and the military commanders and the rich and the strong and every slave and free person" try to hide themselves from the face of God and the Lamb (Rev. 6:15–17). The parallel between the two texts indicates that the destruction of the wicked occurs in the context of the Second Coming. Babylon, the end-time apostate religious system, is overthrown.

Yet the final battle is not over. John now sees *the beast and the kings of the earth and their armies gathered to make war against the one sitting on the horse and against his army.* This parallels Revelation 17:14 which states that the kings of the earth "will make war with the Lamb, and the Lamb will overcome them." In the scene of the pouring out of the sixth plague, the satanic triumvirate sent their emissaries worldwide to gain the nations and the governing authorities of the world for themselves and their cause (Rev. 16:13–14). Their deceptive influence is so compelling that the governing religious and political authorities form a worldwide confederacy under the leadership of the satanic triumvirate for the purpose of fighting against Christ and his people. They assemble for the final battle at Armageddon (Rev. 16:16) with a full determination to win the combat and defeat Christ and his followers. Their confederacy lasts for only a very short time, however.

19:20–21 The outcome of the final battle is contrary to what the worldwide confederacy has expected. The warrior Christ appears personally on the scene to completely overthrow the worldwide confederacy. Paul states that Christ will bring to destruction the end-time apostate religious system "with the breath of His mouth, and bring to an end by the appearance of His coming" (2 Thess. 2:8). *The beast was captured, and with him the false prophet who performed the signs before him* to deceive people to receive the mark of the beast and to worship his image. The text thus concludes the theme of Revelation 13:13–17. In Revelation 13:4, the worshipers of the beast ask: "Who is like the beast, and who is able to wage war with him?" Revelation 19 provides the answer: Christ, the Lamb and warrior. He brings ultimate defeat to the beast and the false prophet, who are together thrown alive into *the lake of fire burning with sulphur*. The lake of fire is also mentioned in Revelation 20:10–15. It is not a literal, everlasting burning hell, but rather a metaphorical expression describing complete destruction. It is the place of the full and ultimate end to all rebellion against God.

The rest of the people are killed with *the sword* proceeding from the mouth of Jesus. Paul states that those who have not obeyed the gospel of Christ will be destroyed by the glory of Christ's power at the Second Coming (2 Thess. 1:8–10). At this point, the whole earth resembles a battlefield filled with bodies of those killed. The grotesque description of the destruction concludes with the statement that *all the birds were filled with their flesh.* The defeat of the worldwide confederacy of rebellious humanity that gathered against God in the final combat will be total and complete.

The cosmic conflict is about to be concluded: Babylon is destroyed, both of Satan's allies are in the lake of fire, and their supporters are slain, awaiting the final judgment. What about the fate of Satan? Revelation 20 provides the answer to that question.

A RETROSPECT ON REVELATION 19

Chapter 19 of Revelation is a part of the great judgment scene that begins in chapter 17 and ends in chapter 20.[46] The evil powers are destroyed in the reverse order of their being mentioned in the book. The judgment begins with the dragon in Revelation 12, the two beasts in chapter 13, and the prostitute Babylon in chapter 17. Tantamount to the judgment, the ultimate destruction begins, as announced in the seventh-bowl plague (Rev. 16:17–21), with Babylon, the end-time apostate religious system (Rev. 17–18). Next follows the punishment of the beast, the false prophet, and their supporters (Rev. 19:20), and, finally, the destruction of the dragon, Satan himself, in the lake of fire (Rev. 20).

The book of Revelation portrays the second coming of Christ in majesty and glory in several symbolic presentations, each providing a different aspect of the nature of his return to the earth. The first half of Revelation 19 vividly describes the return of Christ in terms of the long-awaited wedding supper. The wedding union, however, is only announced in chapter 19. It is further developed in Revelation 21–22. The second half of chapter 19 describes the return of Christ in the role of a conquering warrior/ king completing the battle of Armageddon introduced in Revelation 16:12–16. Ellen White also affirms that the coming of Christ as the heavenly warrior on a white horse in Revelation 19:11–21 describes the battle of Armageddon: "The battle of Armageddon is soon to be fought. He on whose vesture is written the name, King of kings, and Lord of lords, is soon to lead forth the armies of heaven."[47]

Revelation 19 has consistent shifts with regard to the saints. First, they are the bride of Christ. The wedding signifies the long-awaited union between them and Christ. Then, at the wedding supper of the Lamb, they are the invited guests. Finally, in 19:11–21, the saints are an army on white horses—evidently still dressed in wedding garments. This shifting of metaphors may be the key for unlocking some apparent contradiction in the chapter with regard both to Christ and the saints.[48]

The coming of the warrior Christ marks the end of the end-time apostate religious system that has opposed God and exalted itself "above every so-called god or object of worship" (2 Thess. 2:4) and was responsible for the vicious persecution and oppression of God's faithful people. It also brings destruction upon the wicked—"those who do not know God and to those who do not obey the gospel of our Lord Jesus" (2 Thess. 1:8). The wicked, unable to stand in the presence of the Lord, seek to hide themselves (cf. Rev. 6:15–17). The brightness of Christ's coming eventually destroys them (2 Thess. 2:8; cf. 2 Thess. 1:8–10). It is logical to assume that at that moment, as Paul explains, "the dead in Christ shall rise first. Then we who are alive and remain shall be caught up together with them in the clouds to meet the Lord in the air, and thus we shall always be with the Lord" (1 Thess. 4:16–17). The destruction of the forces of darkness provide deliverance for God's faithful people.

Revelation 19 provides to God's faithful people experiencing hardship and suffering in a hostile world an assurance that the cosmic drama is drawing to its conclusion. It is the wedding supper of the Lamb—rather than the final battle—that is the focus of the entire book of Revelation. The wedding is approaching and preparations must be made. Heaven is in the process of preparing for the long awaited and complete union between Christ and the church, while the church is preparing herself to be ready for that long-anticipated day. Herman Hoeksema states: "Longing to be with the Bridegroom, through grace she keeps herself unspotted from the corruptions of Babylon, in order that in the day of Christ she may appear in the pure and white linen of the righteousness of the saints, prepared as the bride adorned for the Bridegroom."[49] Hence, bearing in mind the blessedness of that hope, we will be moved "to live sensibly, righteously and godly in the present age, looking for the blessed hope and the appearing of the glory of our great God and Savior, Christ Jesus" (Titus 2:12–13). The blessed hope will prompt us to earnestly long for a soon coming of the wedding day and to get ready to meet him who is the focus of the entire content of

Revelation as well as the entire Bible itself. "Everyone who has this hope fixed on Him purifies himself, just as He is pure" (1 John 3:3). "Therefore, having these promises," Paul insists, "let us cleanse ourselves from all defilement of flesh and spirit, perfecting holiness in the fear of God" (2 Cor. 7:1).

The church is longing for the day when Christ will come "to be glorified in His saints on that day, and to be marveled at among all who have believed" (2 Thess. 1:10). When "He appears, we shall be like Him, because we shall see Him just as He is" (1 John 3:2). At this point, Richard Lehmann's appeal with regard to Revelation 19 seems very appropriate: "On seeing such a dazzling victory and the establishment of Christ in His dignity as King of kings, on hearing the announcement of the end of infernal powers and the proclamation of the victory of the redeemed, the reader is prompted to join John and the heavenly beings in bowing down and worshiping. Uniting his weak voice with that of the powerful thunders, he echoes the heavenly invitation by proclaiming, Hallelujah!"[50]

ENDNOTES

1. Barclay, *The Revelation of John*, 2:168–169.

2. See Mounce, 340.

3. Bauer, 249.

4. Ladd, 249.

5. See General Conference of Seventh-day Adventists, Committee on Problems in Bible Translation, *Problems in Bible Translation*, 252–253.

6. Barclay, *The Revelation of John*, 2:177.

7. Erdman, 148; Harrington, 226; Mounce, 342; Morris, 222; Beasley-Murray, 276.

8. See LaRondelle, *How to Understand the End-Time Prophecies*, 287–290 (who clearly follows Beasley-Murray, 182); the space does not allow any more extensive treatment of his view. I do not find his entire approach convincing because it seems to be more theological and philosophical than exegetical and contextual.

9. Pfandl, 320.

10. Bauckham, *The Climax of Prophecy*, 162; Beckwith, 729–730.

11. Aune, *Revelation 17–22*, 1039; also Caird, 238; Thomas, *Revelation 8–22*, 377.

12. For a further discussion, see *The Seventh-day Adventist Bible Commentary*, 7:876–877; Committee on Problems in Bible Translation, *Problems in Bible Translation*, 244–256; see also Pfandl, 315–322.

13. Fiorenza, *Revelation*, 102.

14. Krodel, 306; Beale, 916.

15. Barclay, *The Revelation of John*, 2:170.

16. Mounce, 338.

17. Ladd, 246.

18. Johnson, 571.

19. As pointed to by Barclay, *The Revelation of John*, 2:172.

20. Mounce, 340.

21. See Richard Lehmann, "The Two Suppers," in *Symposium on Revelation—Book 2*, Daniel and Revelation Committee Series 7 (Silver Spring, MD: Biblical Research Institute, 1992), 215, 221.

22. Ladd, 248–249.

23. Johnson, 571.

24. *The Seventh-day Adventist Bible Commentary*, 7:872.

25. Ladd, 249; LaRondelle, *How to Understand the End-Time Prophecies*, 435.

26. Beasley-Murray, 315.

27. See Hughes, 200; Hoeksema, 618.

28. Neall, *The Concept of Character in the Apocalypse*, 122.

29. Morris, 221.

30. Ladd, 250.

31. Hoeksema, 618.

32. Bauckham, *The Climax of Prophecy*, 160.

33. Paulien, The Bible Explorer, 2.1.

34. Bauckham, *The Climax of Prophecy*, 160.

35. Barclay, *The Revelation of John*, 2:179.

36. *The Seventh-day Adventist Bible Commentary*, 7:875.

37. Barclay, *The Revelation of John*, 2:178; Mounce, 345.

38. *The Seventh-day Adventist Bible Commentary*, 7:873.

39. Barclay, *The Revelation of John*, 2:183.

40. Lehmann, 217.

41. Caird, 243.

42. Neall, *The Concept of Character in the Apocalypse*, 132.

43. Lehmann, 221.

44. Ibid., 221.

45. Mounce, 338.

46. Lehmann, 217.

47. White, *Testimonies for the Church*, 6:406. On Ellen White's view of Armageddon, see LaRondelle, "Armageddon: History of Adventist Interpretations," in *Symposium on Revelation—Book 2*, Daniel and Revelation Committee Series 7 (Silver Spring, MD: Biblical Research Institute, 1992), 444–449.

48. It was Beatrice Neall who called my attention to this pattern in a personal letter.

49. Hoeksema, 623.

50. Lehmann, 223.

In Revelation 19, the cosmic conflict and the history of rebellion against God is about to be concluded. The beast and the false prophet are destroyed in the lake of fire, and the wicked are slain to await the final judgment. What about the fate of Satan? The first part of Revelation 20 provides the answer to that question (20:1–10), and the last part portrays the final judgment of the wicked (20:11–15).

THE FATE OF SATAN (20:1–10)

John turns to the fate of Satan himself, describing the confinement of Satan for a thousand years and his ultimate destruction in the lake of fire.

> *¹And I saw an angel coming down from heaven, having in his hand the key of the abyss and a great chain in his hand. ²And he seized the dragon, the serpent of old, the one who is the devil and Satan, and bound him for a thousand years, ³and he threw him into the abyss and locked it and sealed it over him, in order that he might not deceive the nations any longer until the thousand years were completed; after these things it is necessary for him to be loosed for a little time.*
>
> *⁴And I saw the thrones, and they sat upon them, and judgment was given to them. And [I saw] the souls of those beheaded because of the testimony of Jesus and because of the Word of God, and those who did not worship the beast nor his image and did not receive the mark upon their foreheads and upon their hands; and they came to life and reigned with Christ for a thousand years. ⁵(The rest of the dead did not come to life until the thousand years were completed.)*

This is the first resurrection. [6]Blessed and holy is the one who has a part in the first resurrection; over these the second death does not have authority, but they will be priests of God and of Christ, and they will reign with him for the thousand years. [7]And when the thousand years are completed, Satan will be loosed from his prison, [8]and he will go out to deceive the nations who are in the four corners of the earth, Gog and Magog, to gather them for the battle, whose number is as the sand of the sea. [9]And they went up to the breadth of the earth and surrounded the camp of the saints, namely, the beloved city, and fire came down from heaven and devoured them. [10]And the devil who deceived them was thrown into the lake of fire and sulphur where both the beast and the false prophet were, and they will be tormented day and night for ever and ever.

NOTES

20:1 *An angel.* The identity of this angel is not specified. Some think that he is the star fallen from heaven in Revelation 9:1 ("the angel of the abyss") who was given the key to the pit of the abyss.[1] Despite the similarity in wording of the two texts, differences exist. The star fallen from heaven appears to be Satan himself rather than an angel from heaven (see *Notes* on Rev. 9:1). In Revelation 20:1 the angel was seen with the key to lock and seal the abyss, while in 9:1 the fallen star was given the key to open the abyss.

Abyss. On the meaning of the concept, see *Notes* on Revelation 9:1.

20:2 *The dragon.* See *Notes* on Revelation 12:3.

Thousand years. In view of the symbolic character of Revelation, it is difficult to determine whether the "thousand years" of Satan's imprisonment is a literal or figurative time period. Although the figurative meaning fits into the context of the symbolism of the book, the literal meaning is equally possible. What is apparent, however, is that the thousand years refers to "a real period of time."[2] Three basic views have developed for understanding the millennium.

(1) **Postmillennialism.** According to the postmillennial view, the Second Coming occurs after a literal thousand years. It is generally considered a period of peace and prosperity brought about by means of social and educational reforms, national progress, and personal perfection. This view was particularly popular among Protestants in the nineteenth century, and essentially died out with World War I and its accompanying horrible events. This view stands in opposition to the New Testament teaching of the time of the end, which states that the situation of the world will get worse as the end approaches. Today, postmillennialism is essentially abandoned.

(2) **Amillennialism.** The amillennial view has been widely held throughout the Christian era since Augustine (354–430). Today it is the official view of the Roman Catholic Church, the

Eastern Orthodox Church, and some reformed Protestant groups. Amillennialists understand the millennium to represent the period between the first and the second coming of Christ. The binding of Satan is something that took place on the cross when Satan was defeated by Christ (cf. Matt. 12:29; Luke 10:17–18; John 12:31–32); his activity is greatly (although not entirely) reduced, and, therefore, he cannot prevent the preaching of the gospel. The millennium is thus a symbolic period of the reign of the church on the earth. The amillennialists understand the first resurrection in one of two different ways. Some see it as a symbol of those who accept new birth in Christ (John 5:25; Eph. 2:5–6) and then reign as the saints with Christ through the church during the Christian era. Others believe that the first resurrection refers to the resurrection of the souls of deceased believers who now live and reign with Christ in heaven.

(3) **Premillennialism.** The premillennial view holds that the Second Coming occurs before the millennium. The Christians of the first three centuries were premillennialists; under the influence of Augustine, premillennialism was gradually replaced by amillennialism. Today, the three varieties of premillennialism are the dispensational, the historic, and the Seventh-day Adventist understanding. The main point of disagreement between the three views is whether Revelation 20 refers to recapitulation, which traces the whole course of the Christian era. The context does not indicate that recapitulation is in view with regard to chapter 20, but rather a chronological sequence of events: Revelation 15–16 refer to the close of intercession; chapters 17–18 to the destruction of Babylon; chapter 19 to the destruction of the beast and the false prophet; and, finally, chapter 20 completes the judgment circle with the destruction of the wicked and Satan himself.

As Revelation indicates, the Second Coming brings about the destruction of the living wicked and the first resurrection of the saints who will join Christ in his reign and judgment. Their reign with Christ will be in heaven rather than on the earth (Rev. 20:4–6). Leon Morris observes that the word "throne" occurs in Revelation "forty-seven times in all, and except for Satan's throne (2:13) and that of the beast (13:2; 16:10) all appear to be in heaven. That would fit the present passage [Rev. 20:4]."[3] The binding of Satan occurs at the Second Coming and is followed by a period of one thousand years during which no human being is found alive on the earth.[4]

20:4 *The testimony of Jesus* and *the Word of God.* See *Notes* on Revelation 1:2.

They came to life. The Greek *ezēsan* (from *zaō*, "to live") is here the ingressive aorist which means "came to life," the same as in verse 5 (cf. Rev. 2:8).

20:6 *Blessed.* See *Notes* on Revelation 1:3.

20:8 *Gog and Magog.* The Gog and Magog concept is drawn from Ezekiel 38–39 where Gog from the land of Magog, the prince of Rosh, Meshech, and Tubal (38:2), is the enemy of God invading Israel from the north, and was to be utterly defeated by God. In Jewish tradition, Gog and Magog became equated with the rebellious nations of Psalm 2 who revolted against God and his Messiah.[5] In Revelation, both words represent the eschatological enemy nations that would wage war against God and his people at the end of the millennium.

20:10 *For ever and ever.* On the meaning of this phrase, see *Notes* on Revelation 14:11.

EXPOSITION

20:1–3 In the next phase of the vision, John sees *an angel coming down from heaven* with *the key of the abyss and a great chain.* The keys and chain here must be understood figuratively. The angel comes in all the power of God, for he seizes *the dragon, the serpent of old, the one who is the devil and Satan.* Satan is identified here in the same terms as in Revelation 12:9 which depicts him as being thrown down from heaven to the earth. This time, however, he is confined to the abyss. With the figurative chain in his hand, the angel binds Satan *for a thousand years.* Then he throws the chained Satan *into the abyss and locked it and sealed it over him.* Again, the language is figurative, recalling the text from Isaiah:

> So it will happen in that day,
> That the Lord will punish the host of heaven, on high,
> And the kings of the earth, on earth.
> And they will be gathered together
> Like prisoners in the dungeon,
> And will be confined in prison;
> And after many days they will be punished. (Isa. 24:21–22)

It is especially significant that this prophecy of Isaiah specifies an interval between the imprisonment of "the host of heaven" and their punishment (24:22). As we noted earlier with regard to Revelation 9:1, the abyss is the dark prison where the demonic forces are confined (cf. Luke 8:31; 2 Pet. 2:4). In the context of Revelation 20, the abyss denotes the earth in a chaotic condition, utterly desolated and uninhabited. The devastating seven last plagues have turned the earth into a condition much like that before the creation (Gen. 1:2) and like Palestine during the exile as described by the prophet Jeremiah:

> I looked on the earth, and behold, it was formless and void;
> And to the heavens, and they had no light....
> I looked, and behold, there was no man,
> And all the birds of the heavens had fled.
> I looked, and behold, the fruitful land was a wilderness,
> And all its cities were pulled down
> Before the LORD, before His fierce anger. (Jer. 4:23–26)

The desolated earth becomes a great abyss, an exclusive place for Satan's imprisonment during the millennium until he receives his final punishment in the lake of fire (Rev. 20:10).

Revelation 9:1–2 shows clearly that to unlock and open the abyss is to allow the demonic forces to wreak their wrath. The purpose of the sealing is obviously to ensure the confinement of the prisoner, just as the tomb of Jesus was sealed to prevent an escape (Matt. 27:66).[6] In Rev. 20:7, the locked and sealed abyss is called a prison for Satan. The purpose of Satan's imprisonment is clearly stated: *that he might not deceive the nations any longer.* Satan is bound by a chain of circumstances. Revelation 12:9 identifies him as the deceiver of the whole world, and he is restlessly active on the earth (cf. Rev. 12:12, 17; 16:13). The second half of Revelation stresses that Satan stands behind all deception carried out by the religious and secular powers of this world (Rev. 13:11–17; 18:2–3; 19:20). The wicked are destroyed by the Second Coming (2 Thess. 1:6–10), and all the righteous are taken to heaven with Christ (1 Thess. 4:15–17). Since no person remains alive on the ruined earth (cf. Rev. 19:21), Satan, together with his evil angels, is restrained in his harmful, deceptive influence and activities during the millennium. As Richard Rice says, "He is left to contemplate the bleak consequences of his rebellion against God."[7] However, this period of restraint is terminated. After the thousand years, Satan will *be loosed* to resume his deception of the nations (cf. Rev. 20:7–8), but only *for a little time.* His deception will be of a very short duration that will end with the final judgment.

20:4–5 In the meantime, John sees the redeemed sitting on *the thrones.* To them *judgment was given.* Included in this group of the glorified redeemed are *the souls of those beheaded because of the testimony of Jesus and because of the Word of God.* This is a strong allusion to Revelation 6:9, where "the souls of those who had been slain because of the word of God and because of the testimony that they had" are seen under the altar crying for vindication and acquittal in the heavenly court. They were told to rest a little longer until their fellow servants are brought to fullness (Rev. 6:11). They rested "from their labors" (Rev. 14:13); now they have come back to life. To this group also belong *those who did not worship the beast nor his image and did not receive the mark upon their foreheads and upon their hands.* The ones mentioned in the text are God's end-time people who went through the experience of the great persecution portrayed in Revelation 12:17–13:18. Now they come *to life,* and together with the living saints are taken to heaven (1 Thess. 4:15–17) where they together reign *with Christ for a thousand years.*

John stresses that this is *the first resurrection*, evidently occurring at the Second Coming (1 Thess. 4:16), and, thus, at the start of the millennium. At this same time, Satan is chained and imprisoned; thus the period of their reign corresponds to the period of Satan's confinement. *The rest of the dead did not come to life until the thousand years were completed.* The wicked are the rest of the dead mentioned here. The millennium begins with the first resurrection, which is exclusively for the redeemed (cf. 2 Thess. 4:16b). The wicked are destroyed at the Second Coming by the glory of Christ's appearance (cf. 2 Thess. 1:9). Their resurrection follows the millennium, and might rightly be called the second resurrection.

20:6 Those who have a part in the first resurrection are pronounced *blessed and holy.* They are blessed because they are not subjected to *the second death.* As George E. Ladd states, "the second death is the eternal death"[8] which the wicked experience in the lake of fire (Rev. 20:14–15). This recalls the promise given to the overcomers in Smyrna that they "shall not be harmed by the second death" (Rev. 2:11). Those having a part in the first resurrection are blessed and holy because they are *priests of God and of Christ, and they will reign with him for the thousand years.* This recalls the inscription that the priests in the Old Testament bore: "Holy to the Lord" (cf. Exod. 28:36). Individually, God's people were made kings and priests through salvation (cf. Rev. 1:6; 5:10). During the millennium, they serve as kings and priests collectively for the purpose of judging. Here is the fulfillment of Christ's promise to the overcomers that they would share his throne (Rev. 3:21). The text here does not specify exactly whether the resurrected saints are in heaven or on earth during the millennium. On the basis of Revelation 7:9–17 and 19:1–10, however, we might conclude that they are in heaven, rather than on the earth, reigning with Christ.

We know little from the text of the activities of the saved during the millennium. According to Revelation 20:4, they are given judgment. Jesus promised his disciples that when he sits on the throne of his glory in the kingdom, they would also "sit upon twelve thrones, judging the twelve tribes of Israel" (Matt. 19:28). Paul wrote to the Christians in Corinth that one day "the saints will judge the world" (1 Cor. 6:2). Here is the fulfillment of what was foretold. The saints are now seen serving as judges and priests during the millennium. That they serve as priests means that they are in the immediate presence of God. It has been suggested that the saved will examine God's dealings with those who are lost and will have an opportunity to find answers to all questions about the fairness of God's decisions.[9] The same understanding was expressed by C. Mervyn Maxwell:

> Functioning in their dual capacity they will fill a crucial role in the great-controversy process. They will confirm to their eternal satisfaction how earnestly and patiently God cared for lost sinners. They will perceive how heedlessly and stubbornly sinners spurned and rejected His love. They will discover that even seemingly mild sinners secretly cherished ugly selfishness rather than accept the value system of their Lord and Savior.[10]

20:7–8 The attention turns now to the close of the millennium. **When the thousand years are completed, Satan will be loosed from his prison.** The "loosing" signifies a reversal of the binding of Satan at the beginning of the thousand years.[11] It is like the opening of the pit of the abyss in Revelation 9:1 which releases the demonic forces to harm the people. The releasing of Satan from his prison here is related to the resurrection of the wicked (Rev. 20:5). *The Seventh-day Adventist Bible Commentary* explains: "It was the depopulation of the earth that terminated his deceptive work. His loosing will therefore be accomplished by a repopulation of the earth, an event brought about by the resurrection of the wicked at the close of the thousand years."[12]

The second resurrection provides a new opportunity for Satan to deceive the nations. Filled with hate, he goes out **to deceive the nations** of **the four corners of the earth.** The text identifies them as **Gog and Magog.** This brings to mind the above-mentioned prophecy from Isaiah about the judgment on the earth (Isa. 24:21–22).

Gog and Magog stand figuratively for the nations that are rebellious against God and hostile to his people. The idea is drawn from Ezekiel 38–39. Satan gathers the nations of Gog and Magog one last time **for the battle** against God. The **number** of the gathered multitude under the leadership of Satan is **as the sand of the sea.** The wicked here stand as a parody to the seed of promise to Abraham that was to be "as the sand which is on the seashore" (Gen. 22:17).

20:9 The assembled nations go **to the breadth of the earth** and surround **the camp of the saints, namely, the beloved city,** ready to attack it. At the close of the millennium, the wicked demonstrate once more that they were rightly delegated for destruction. Their rebellious hearts are filled with hatred against God and his faithful people. New Jerusalem has descended from heaven to the earth (cf. Rev. 21:2) and is described in detail in Revelation 21:9–22:5. It comes now under a strong attack by the wicked under the leadership of Satan. This is clearly Satan's last attempt to dethrone God and take dominion over the world. However, no actual battle occurs. At that moment, God intervenes, and *fire came down from heaven and devoured them.* This is a clear allusion to the destruction of Gog as prophesied by Ezekiel: "I shall rain on him, and on his troops, and on the many peoples who are with him, a torrential rain, with hailstones, fire, and brimstone. And I shall magnify Myself, sanctify Myself, and make Myself known in the sight of many nations; and they will know that I am the Lord" (Ezek. 38:22–23; 39:6). This consuming fire is God's holy indignation against sin (cf. Deut. 4:24; Heb. 12:29). Those who have not placed their faith in Christ will realize the delusion of Satan's deception, but it will be too late. Their final and ultimate destruction is only mentioned here briefly. A more detailed description is given in verses 11–15.

20:10 Satan *who deceived* the nations is defeated and *thrown into the lake of fire and sulphur* to share the fate of *the beast and the false prophet* (cf. Rev. 19:20). After the cross and the subsequent ascension to heaven, Satan was quelled by Christ (Rev. 12:7–9). Although defeated in heaven, however, Satan still has reigned on earth. After the millennium, his defeat is certain.[13] It may be noted that God "does not destroy Satan and the fallen angels at the Second Coming, but gives them one thousand years to think about the results of their war against Him, their rebellion against His law, their sin."[14] Now, there is the ultimate destruction of the originator of all evil in "the eternal fire which has been prepared for the devil and his angels" (Matt. 25:41). There, in the lake of fire, Satan and his associates *will be tormented day and night for ever and ever.* This language reiterates Revelation 14:10–11. As we learned earlier with reference to those verses, the phrase "forever and ever" in the Bible is not an indefinite eternity; it rather denotes that the action continues until it completes God's purpose. The punishment of Satan is irreversible; all those who follow him must share his destiny.

THE FINAL JUDGMENT (20:11–15)

After viewing the destruction of Satan, John is positioned to witness in rapid succession the scenes of the final judgment that marks the end of the history of all rebellion against God and the inauguration of God's eternal kingdom.

¹¹*And I saw a great white throne and One sitting upon it from whose face the earth and the heaven fled, and no place was found for them. ¹²And I saw the dead, the great and the small, standing before the throne; and books were opened, and another book was opened, which is the book of life; and the dead were judged by what has been written in the books according to their works. ¹³And the sea gave up the dead who were in it, and Death and Hades gave up their dead who were in them, and each of them was judged according to his works. ¹⁴And Death and Hades were thrown into the lake of fire; this is the second death, the lake of fire. ¹⁵And if anyone was not found written in the book of life, he was thrown into the lake of fire.*

NOTES

20:11 *Throne.* See *Notes* on Revelation 4:2.

20:12 *The book of life.* See *Notes* on Revelation 3:5.

20:14 *Death and Hades.* The word "death" in Greek is used with the definite article. Death here is personified; it is the enemy of the human race. See further *Notes* on Revelation 1:18.

20:15 *The book of life.* See *Notes* on Revelation 3:5.

EXPOSITION

20:11 Having described the destruction of Satan, John goes on to describe the final judgment upon the wicked. John sees a *great white throne.* On the throne he sees *One sitting upon it from whose face the earth and the heaven fled, and no place was found for them.* The One sitting on the throne is God himself, the Judge. John refers to him here in the way he does repeatedly in Revelation. The throne of grace to which humans could come to present their prayers and obtain deliverance from God (cf. Heb. 4:16) now becomes a terror to the wicked. In the face of the grand glory of God's presence, the universe convulses in cataclysmic terror. This evokes the prophecy of Isaiah: "The sky will vanish like smoke, and the earth will wear out like a garment, and its inhabitants will die in like manner" (Isa. 51:6). The time has come for the old order to find its full and ultimate destruction (cf. 2 Pet. 3:10–12).

20:12 Now comes the final judgment. John sees the resurrected *dead, the great and the small, standing before the throne.* People from every socioeconomic level are there. There are no exceptions; nobody is so great or too unimportant "as to escape the judgment of God."[15] In this final reckoning "there will be no evasion of full justice."[16] Here is fulfilled what Revelation 11:18 calls "the time to judge the dead." At this point **books were opened.** These are apparently the books of records of human deeds which reveal whether a person has been loyal to God or to Satan.

In addition to the record books, there is also **the book of life**, an eschatological register containing the names of those who have believed in Christ. Only those whose names are found in the book of life shall live in God's kingdom on the new earth (Rev. 21:27); those whose names are not in the book of life will be cast into the lake of fire (20:15). They are **judged by what has been written in the books according to their works.** The time has now come for God to "judge the world in righteousness, and the peoples in His faithfulness" (Pss. 96:13; 98:9). No sentence executed on "any wicked will be arbitrary, biased, or unfair."[17] While salvation is on the basis of grace, the judgment is according to the works as recorded in the books. Paul states that God would "render to every man according to his deeds" (Rom. 2:6; cf. 1 Pet. 1:17). As Alan Johnson observes, "works are unmistakable evidence of the loyalty of the heart; they express either belief or unbelief, faithfulness or unfaithfulness."[18]

20:13–15 The judgment is universal. It is said that **the sea gave up the dead who were in it, and Death and Hades gave up their dead who were in them.** This statement reminds us of the anticipation of the author of 4 Ezra:

> And the earth shall give up those who are asleep in it; and the chambers shall give up the souls which have been committed to them. And the Most High shall be revealed upon the seat of judgment, and compassion shall pass away, and patience shall be withdrawn; but judgment alone shall remain, truth shall stand, and faithfulness shall grow strong. And recompense shall follow.[19]

What John states here is that all dead, however they died, "are raised and brought to the judgment."[20] None of the wicked is exempt from the second resurrection. Everybody is **judged according to his works.**

The lake of fire is not a literal everlasting burning hell, but rather a metaphorical expression describing complete destruction (cf. Matt. 10:28). It is the place of the full and ultimate end of all rebellion against God. Even **Death and Hades were thrown into the lake of fire.** This indicates that the concept of the lake of fire must be understood figuratively. As we saw in Revelation 1:18, Death and Hades are personified as the two enemies of the human race. These two are now judged. **This is** *the second death, the lake of fire.* The second death also means the end of death. Here is what Paul anticipated: "The last enemy that will be abolished is death" (1 Cor. 15:26). The redeemed cannot experience eternal life "until death itself is banished from the universe."[21]

In concluding his description of the final judgment scene, John states that all those who are *not found written in the book of life* are condemned and *thrown into the lake of fire*. Those who have lived in rebellion against God find their end with Satan, their master. The tormenting flames of the lake of fire destroy them completely, "so that it will leave them neither root nor branch" (Mal. 4:1)—"Satan the root, his followers the branches."[22] An eternity without sin is now ready to begin.

A RETROSPECT ON REVELATION 20

With the destruction of Satan and the unrepentant, Revelation 20 concludes the judgment circle that began in chapter 17. The main subject of the chapter is the millennium or "one thousand years." The author of Revelation does not indicate whether the millennium is a literal or figurative time period; however, he does refer to it as a real period of time for Satan's imprisonment on the desolate and unpopulated earth. Satan will have this time to analyze and review the effect of his rebellion against God and the result and consequence of the course he has pursued.

The millennium is also an opportunity for the redeemed to get answers pertaining to the mystery of sin and God's way of dealing with it. Here what Paul foresaw is fulfilled: "For now we see in a mirror dimly, but then face to face; now I know in part, but then I will know fully just as I also have been fully known" (1 Cor. 13:12). The conclusion of the millennium (Rev. 20:11–15) provides the full revelation of "the mystery of God" that has been hidden for ages, though being partially revealed through the preaching of the gospel (Rom. 16:25–26; 1 Cor. 2:6–10; Eph. 3:1–20; 1 Tim. 3:16). God will then "bring to light the things hidden in the darkness and disclose the motives of men's hearts; and then each man's praise will come to him from God" (1 Cor. 4:5). With the final judgment is fulfilled the announcement of the mighty angel in Revelation 10:7—"in the days of the sound of the seventh angel, when he is about to sound, then the mystery of God will be completed, as he proclaimed to his servants the prophets" (cf. Rev. 11:15–18). The sealed scroll of "the mystery of God" of Revelation 5, containing the record of the cosmic controversy and the sum and substance of

God's plan and purpose for the human race and the entire universe, is finally unsealed and its contents disclosed (see further *Notes* on Rev. 10:7). Now the cosmic conflict is over and the earth is purged of sin and evil. The restored earth is ready to receive its inhabitants and to offer them life free of pain.

ENDNOTES

1. E.g., Mounce, 351; Hughes, 209.

2. Ladd, 262.

3. Morris, 230.

4. For further discussion on the millennial issue, see Joel Badina, "The Millennium," in *Symposium on Revelation—Book 2*, Daniel and Revelation Committee Series 7 (Silver Spring, MD: Biblical Research Institute, 1992), 225–242.

5. Cf. Babylonian Talmud *Berakoth* 7b, 10a, 13a (Epstein, 1/1:37, 52, 73); *Shabbath* 118a (Epstein, 2/2:580); *Sanhedrin* 17a (Epstein, 4/5:85).

6. Barclay, *The Revelation of John*, 2:191.

7. Richard Rice, *Reign of God*, 2d ed. (Berrien Springs, MI: Andrews University Press, 1997), 345.

8. Ladd, 268.

9. Badina, 242.

10. Maxwell, 500.

11. *The Seventh-day Adventist Bible Commentary*, 7:880.

12. Ibid.

13. Collins, *The Apocalypse*, 141.

14. Badina, 242.

15. Barclay, *The Revelation of John*, 2:196.

16. *The Seventh-day Adventist Bible Commentary*, 7:883.

17. Ibid.

18. Johnson, 589.

19. 4 Ezra 7:32–35a (Charlesworth, 1:538).

20. Hughes, 219.

21. Ladd, 274.

22. White, *The Great Controversy*, 673.

With the destruction of Satan and the unrepentant in the lake of fire, Revelation 20 concludes the judgment circle that began with chapter 17. The scene suddenly changes from the execution of judgment to a vision of the new heaven and earth and its capital, the new Jerusalem, coming down out of heaven. The section has two parts: Revelation 21:1–8 is a general overview of the new earth, and 21:9–22:5 provides a description of the new Jerusalem. In portraying the restored earth and its capital, John uses language drawn almost entirely from the Old Testament prophets, particularly from Isaiah and Ezekiel.

THE NEW HEAVEN AND EARTH (21:1–8)

John has witnessed the judgment on the wicked and the destruction of Satan, the originator of every evil. The earth is purged of both sin and sinners. The seer's attention now turns to the reward of the redeemed on the restored earth as their dwelling place.

> *¹And I saw a new heaven and a new earth; for the first heaven and the first earth have passed away, and the sea is no longer. ²And I saw the holy city, the new Jerusalem, descending out of heaven from God, prepared as a bride adorned for her husband. ³And I heard a loud voice from the throne saying: "Behold, the tabernacle of God is among men, and he will tabernacle with them, and they will be his peoples, and God himself will be among them, ⁴and he will wipe away every tear from their eyes, and no longer shall there be death, neither sorrow, nor crying, nor pain, for the first things have passed away." ⁵And the One sitting on the throne said:*

"Behold, I am making all things new." And he said: "Write, because these words are faithful and true." [6] And he said to me: "It is done. I am the Alpha and the Omega, the beginning and the end. I will give freely to the thirsty from the fountain of the water of life. [7] The overcomer will inherit these things, and I will be God to him, and he will be to me a son. [8] But to the cowardly and unfaithful and abominable and murderers and fornicators and sorcerers and idolaters and all liars, their part will be in the lake which burns with fire and sulphur, which is the second death."

NOTES

21:1 *New* (also in vs. 2 and 5). The Greek word *kainos* can be used in different ways: "unused" (e.g., "new wineskins" in Matt. 9:17), "something not previously present" (e.g., "new name" in Rev. 2:17), "in contrast to something old," or in the "sense that what is old has become obsolete, and should be replaced by what is new."[1] It appears that the latter meaning is to be applied in Revelation 21:1. The word is used four times in Revelation 21:1–5 and denotes something fundamentally new. The new creation is not "a simple improvement";[2] the old heaven and earth have become obsolete and are replaced with new ones. Peter speaks of a great conflagration "in which the heavens will pass away with a roar and the elements will be destroyed with intense heat, and the earth and its works will be burned up," to be succeeded by "new heavens and a new earth, in which righteousness dwells" (2 Pet. 3:10, 13). *Kainos* denotes something new in form or quality rather than new in time (the former). The latter is expressed in Greek with *neos* (cf. Matt. 9:17; 1 Cor. 5:7; Col. 3:10), though the two words sometimes appear to be synonymous. By using the word *kainos* rather than *neos* in Revelation 21:1, John is probably stressing that the new creation is a re-creation "of existing elements" rather than "a creation *ex nihilo*" (cf. 2 Pet. 3:10).[3]

The sea. On the negative aspect of sea imagery, see *Notes* on Revelation 13:1.

21:2 *The holy city, the new Jerusalem.* Here the designation as "the *new* [Gr. *kainos*] Jerusalem" suggests a replacement of the *old* Jerusalem. The ancient Jerusalem where the temple was located was called the holy city (Isa. 52:1; Dan. 9:24; Matt. 27:53). The city became filled with sin and disobedience, however; in it the blood of prophets and apostles was shed. Therefore, Jerusalem was condemned and destroyed (cf. Matt. 23:37). In the Old Testament, hope then switched to a new Jerusalem transformed into a glorious dwelling place of God and his people.[4] Jerusalem was expected to become the capital and center of the world (Isa. 45:14). Isaiah described the restored Jerusalem as the center of the new heavens and earth, where there will not be "the sun for light by day, nor for brightness will the moon give you light; but you will have the Lord for an everlasting light, and your God for your glory" (Isa. 60:19–20). Ezekiel envisioned the rebuilt and restored Jerusalem with the twelve gates (Ezek. 48:31–35), where God's throne would be located and where God would dwell with his people (Ezek. 43:7).

The hope and dream for the new Jerusalem never died among the Jewish people; it became particularly strong during the Intertestamental Period in relation to the Messianic Age.[5] For instance, the apocryphal book of Tobit describes the future glory of Jerusalem in language which resembles that of Revelation.[6] In 2 Baruch, the new Jerusalem is referred to as being "renewed in glory, and that it will be perfected into eternity."[7] The New Testament describes God's people since Abraham with their longing and dream for the heavenly city (Heb. 11:10, 16; 12:22; 13:14). Revelation presents the new Jerusalem—the center of the new earth—as the fulfillment of all dreams, hopes, and longings of God's people throughout history. It appears that the portrayal of the new Jerusalem appealed not only to the Jewish dream but also to Greco-Roman hopes for "the ideal city."[8]

21:4 *Death.* The word in Greek is used with the definite article. See *Notes* on Revelation 20:14.

21:6 *The Alpha and the Omega.* See *Notes* on Revelation 1:8.

The beginning and the end. The Greek word *archē* can be used in a variety of ways: it can mean "beginning" (in point of time), "ruler," "origin," "source," or "the first cause."[9] The last two appear to be the meaning here: God is the source of all things (see *Notes* on Rev. 3:14). The Greek word *telos* can also mean several things: "end" (in the sense of termination or cessation), "conclusion," "goal," and "rest" or "remainder."[10] The meaning of the word here seems to be the "goal" rather than the "end" point of time. John is probably saying that "all life begins in God and ends in God."[11] The same thought is expressed by Paul: "For from him and through him and to him are all things" (Rom. 11:36).

EXPOSITION

21:1–John sees *a new heaven and a new earth*, replacing *the first heaven and the first earth* which *have passed away.* Here is a new beginning. God first created the heavens and the earth (Gen. 1:1) to be the home of human beings. However, sin has altered the earth, making it a place of rebellion against God; the whole creation has become subjected to corruption and decay (cf. Rom. 8:19–22). Even in the Old Testament, God promised to liberate the earth from the bondage of sin and corruption.[12] For instance, Isaiah prophesied: "Behold, I create new heavens and a new earth; and the former things shall not be remembered or come to mind" (Isa. 65:17).

Peter anticipated the fulfillment of God's promise: "According to His promise we are looking for new heavens and a new earth, in which righteousness dwells" (2 Pet. 3:13). John stresses that the old earth with its atmospheric heaven is now replaced by a new creation and restored to its original state.

The first thing that John observes on the new earth is that *the sea is no longer*. Although no great water masses will be on the new earth, the statement can also be understood metaphorically. In the Jewish mind, no more sea means the end of forces hostile to God and humanity.[13] John affirms here that all fears and threats are removed—even "the seas will no longer exist as we know them now."[14] It appears that the statement reflects John's own experience on Patmos. Exiled on that barren island, John suffered tribulation while surrounded by the boundless sea (cf. 1:9). The sea had become for him a symbol of evil that threatens and destroys. His own suffering due to his faithful witness to the gospel becomes the precursor of the experience of God's people throughout history. The sea becomes the metaphoric place of "disturbed and stormy social and political conditions out of which tyrannies commonly arise."[15] It is from the metaphoric sea that the beast oppressing God's people comes in Revelation 13:1. No wonder that in his last vision he observes first of all that "the sea is no longer" on the new earth. Whatever the sea may be, its absence on the new earth means the absence of evil that causes suffering and pain.

21:2 The center and seat of the eternal kingdom on the new earth is *the holy city, the new Jerusalem, descending out of heaven from God.* John builds his description of this new reality on Isaiah 65:17–19 where Jerusalem is the center of the new heavens and earth. As the old earth is replaced with the new one, so the new Jerusalem, "the holy city" (also in 21:10), replaces the center of the Old Testament hope, that was called the holy city (Isa. 52:1; Dan. 9:24). As Roberto Badenas observes, the new Jerusalem becomes "to the new heaven and the new earth what the old Jerusalem never succeeded to be to Israel and the world."[16] The fact that John sees the city "descending out of heaven from God" indicates that this is not the rebuilt old Jerusalem in Palestine, but the city prepared by Christ in the heavenly places (John 14:1–3) and actualized on the earth at the end of the millennium (cf. Rev. 20:9). According to the author of Hebrews, the architect and builder of this city is God himself (Heb. 11:10; cf. 12:22). The new Jerusalem in all its glory signifies the final realization of God's promises and the fulfillment of all human dreams for safety and protection.

The new Jerusalem coming down out of heaven to the earth appears *as a bride adorned for her husband.* This echoes Isaiah 52:1: "Clothe yourself in your strength, O Zion, clothe yourself in your beautiful garments, O Jerusalem, the holy city. For the uncircumcised and the unclean will no more come into you." In Revelation 21:9, the new Jerusalem is referred to as "the bride, the wife of the Lamb." The same identification is used earlier with reference to the church (Rev. 19:7–8). The saints and the city together are the bride of Christ. They are closely connected. Both are arrayed as the bride beautifully dressed. The church is dressed in fine linen (Rev. 19:8), and the new Jerusalem is said to be adorned with the glory of God radiating as gold, pearls, and precious stones (Rev. 21:18–21). This stands in sharp contrast to the self-glorification of Babylon lavishly adorned with gold, pearls, and precious stones (Rev. 17:4). The new Jerusalem belongs to Christ. It is populated by God's faithful people who are finally at home.

21:3–4 John hears a ***loud voice*** from the very proximity of God announcing that ***the tabernacle of God is among men, and he will tabernacle with them.*** In the Old Testament, the tabernacle, and later the temple, symbolized God's abiding presence among Israel (Exod. 25:8). It was in the tabernacle that the people could observe the glory of God (cf. Exod. 40:34–35; Lev. 9:23). It is because of Israel's unfaithfulness to God that his presence was removed from them. According to John 1:14, in Christ, the incarnate Word, God tabernacled temporarily among humans, and they beheld his glory. Now, at the consummation, the new Jerusalem is where God tabernacles with his people in "ultimate unity," and where his glory is manifested throughout eternity, as "prefigured through the centuries by the tabernacle."[17] (In Revelation 21:16–27, the new Jerusalem has all the characteristics of the Old Testament temple.) God and humanity are no more separated; the redeemed now live in the very presence of God forever, and without barriers.[18] There is no longer "any need for the ordinary heavenly sanctuary or temple to exist."[19]

The redeemed on the new earth ***will be his peoples.*** This is the promise that was originally given to the people of Israel: "I will make My dwelling among them...I will also walk among you and be your God, and you shall be My people" (Lev. 26:11–12; cf. Exod. 29:45; Jer. 30:22). "My dwelling place also will be with them; and I will be their God, and they will be My people" (Ezek. 37:27). John switches the singular "people" to the plural "peoples." The plural form indicates the inclusion of all God's children from all ages—"from every nation and tribe and people and tongue" (Rev. 7:9)—in the population of the new earth.

It is in the new Jerusalem that ***God himself will be among them*** always. Centuries earlier Ezekiel prophesied that the name of the restored Jerusalem would be "The LORD is there" (Ezek. 48:35). The new Jerusalem becomes the perfect place for the gathering of the redeemed, a symbol of the long-awaited union of God and his faithful people. God's presence in the city will banish the things of the former order.

God will wipe away *every tear from their eyes.* Here is repeated what was announced earlier in Revelation 7:15–17, which states that God will spread his tabernacle over the redeemed and wipe away all tears from their eyes. Tears, normally caused by sorrow, pain, and death, are the result of the fall. Now every cause for tears is banished. In the restored paradise, *no longer shall there be death, neither sorrow, nor crying, nor pain.* This echoes God's promise given centuries earlier through Isaiah: "He will swallow up death for all time, and the Lord GOD will wipe tears away from all faces, and He will remove the reproach of His people from all the earth; for the LORD has spoken" (Isa. 25:8; cf. 35:10; 65:19). Revelation describes the ultimate fulfillment of this promise. God has dealt with the causes of the tears of his people. *The first things have passed away,* for they are "swallowed up in victory" (1 Cor. 15:54, RSV).

——— John uses the definite article with reference to death. He speaks of death as the enemy of the human race. The conclusion of the cosmic conflict and the establishment of God's ultimate rule on the earth marks the end to sin and death. Paul stresses that "the last enemy that will be abolished is the death" (1 Cor. 15:26; lit. trans.). John saw in Revelation 20:14 that "Death and Hades were thrown into the lake of fire." God's presence among his people on the new earth guarantees ultimate freedom from death. When Jesus dwelled in the flesh (John 1:14), his presence removed all pain, tears, and death. This was well understood by Mary and Martha after their brother had died: "Lord, if You had been here, my brother would not have died" (John 11:21, 32). The sisters knew well that in the presence of Jesus tears and death had no place. In the same way, the presence of Jesus among his people on the new earth means freedom from pain, tears, death, or any other trial of life (cf. Rev. 21:4).

21:5–6 At this point, God's voice is heard for the first time pronouncing the conclusion of the earth's restoration: *Behold, I am making all things new.* God pledges that he will do all these things, a fulfillment of what was announced earlier through Isaiah: "Remember not the former things, nor consider things of old. Behold, I am doing a new thing" (Isa. 43:18–19, RSV). According to Paul, all of creation groans and suffers pain in travail, eagerly longing for liberation from corruption. On the new earth, "the creation itself also will be set free from its slavery to corruption into the freedom of the glory of the children of God" (Rom. 8:21). Thus the new earth will be "completely different from the earth of suffering and death which we know and experience."[20]

In order that his people keep these words fresh in their memory, God commissions John to write them down because *these words are faithful and true.* The same statement concludes the invitation to the wedding supper of Christ and his bride (Rev. 19:9). It is repeated to introduce the new Jerusalem, the Lamb's bride, and is reiterated once again in Revelation 22:6. In Revelation, Christ is "faithful and true" (19:11; cf. 3:14), and so is his promise. He is the One who guarantees the trustworthiness of the prophetic words; they are reliable as he himself is reliable. He is *the Alpha and the Omega, the beginning and the end.* This claim opens and concludes the book of Revelation (Rev. 1:8; 22:13). The promise of the coming end is given by the One who is the eternal and omnipresent God. All things begin with him and end in him. He is the beginning and the conclusion of everything that is found in the book of Revelation. His promise is in accordance with his eternal nature and plans. He is in control of the course of history, and he will bring the history of the rebellious world to its ultimate conclusion and make a new beginning.

The restoration of the earth to its original state includes "the satisfaction of man's deepest need."[21] *I will give freely to the thirsty from the fountain of the water of life.* This statement anticipates Revelation 22:1. John alludes here to God's promise spoken centuries earlier through Isaiah:

> The afflicted and needy are seeking water, but there is none,
>> And their tongue is parched with thirst;
> I, the LORD, will answer them Myself,
>> As the God of Israel I will not forsake them.
> I will open rivers on the bare heights
>> And springs in the midst of the valleys;
> I will make the wilderness a pool of water
>> And the dry land fountains of water. (Isa. 41:17–18)

This thirst symbolizes a longing for God. "My soul thirsts for God," the Psalmist states, "for the living God" (Ps. 42:2). "My soul thirsts for You, my flesh yearns for You, in a dry and weary land where there is no water" (Ps. 63:1). Drinking from "the fountain of the water of life" in Revelation 21:6 stands in contrast to drinking from Babylon's wine of fornication (Rev. 17:2). It is in God, and him only, that all human thirst for salvation will be completely quenched (cf. Matt. 5:6).

21:7 The conclusion of this section is given in terms of the Old Testament blessings and curses. *The overcomer will inherit these things.* Which things?

All things that God makes new. The new Jerusalem is for everyone who is willing to fulfill the conditions for entrance. The promise given here recalls the repeated promises given to the overcomers in the messages to the seven churches (Rev. 2–3). The overcomers will receive all things promised: access to the tree of life (2:7); an escape from the second death (2:11); the hidden manna, a white stone, and a new name (2:17); authority to rule over the nations and the morning star (2:26–28); a walk with Jesus; and garments of white. Their names will not be blotted out of the book of life, but acknowledged before the Father and the angels (3:4–5). They will be pillars in the temple who never leave it, they will have the name of God written on them (3:12), and they will sit with Jesus on his throne (3:21). The overcomers will inherit all these things as well as many other things promised in the New Testament. One promise is above every other, however: *I will be God to him, and he will be to me a son.* The overcomers shall be children of God, with all the rights of heirs.

21:8 In contrast to the overcomers, those who followed the satanic trinity are excluded from the family of God and from the inheritance.[22] They stand in obvious contrast to the saints "who keep the commandments of God and the faith of Jesus" (Rev. 14:12). The first ones mentioned are *the cowardly,* evidently contrasting with "the endurance of the saints." This cowardliness does not refer to "a natural timidity" or fearfulness, but to "a lack of genuine commitment."[23] They are those who, for the sake of escaping inconvenience or persecution in the day of trial, deny Christ and choose their personal safety and comfort in place of faithfulness to God (cf. Matt. 13:21; John 12:42–43). "The cowardly" refers in particular to the final crisis when many will give up their loyalty and obedience to God and side with the satanic trinity in obeying and worshiping Satan.

The *unfaithful* are those who slipped away from their faith in Christ in the final crisis. They stand in contrast to the saints in Revelation 14:12 who keep their faith in Jesus. The last ones mentioned are the commandment breakers: *murderers and fornicators and…idolaters and all liars,* all in contrast to those keeping "the commandments of God." To this group also belong *sorcerers*, those having a special relationship with Satan. In the scene of the sixth trumpet which describes the preparation for the final crisis, the wicked refuse to repent of their sorceries, murders, fornication, and thefts, and continue to worship demons (Rev. 9:20–21). It is because of their sin-hardened hearts that they are excluded from the heavenly city and God's family. While God's people have "a part in the first resurrection" (Rev. 20:6), the wicked find their end in *the second death,* in *the lake which burns with fire and sulphur* (cf. Rev. 20:14–15).

THE NEW JERUSALEM (21:9–22:5)

The new Jerusalem was introduced in Revelation 21:2 in terms of "a bride adorned for her husband." Before its detailed description is given, John stresses the certainty of God's acts of re-creation; God's presence with redeemed humanity; and the ultimate banishment of tears, pain, and death. He also describes those who are included and excluded from the heavenly city. Now he turns to the approaching heavenly city itself, describing Jerusalem as shining with radiant glory (21:10–11). As it comes closer, he moves into a description of the city's wall (21:12–20), and finally the city gates (21:21). Having described the exterior of the city, John moves inside (21:22–22:5).

> *9And one of the seven angels who had seven bowls full of the seven last plagues came and spoke with me saying: "Come, I will show you the bride, the wife of the Lamb." 10And he carried me away in the Spirit to a great and high mount, and showed me the holy city, Jerusalem, descending out of heaven from God, 11having the glory of God. Her radiance was like a precious stone, like a jasper stone sparkling like crystal. 12She had a great and high wall with twelve gates, and at the gates twelve angels, and names inscribed which are the names of the twelve tribes of Israel; 13on the east were three gates, and on the north three gates, and on the south three gates, and on the west three gates. 14And the wall of the city had twelve foundations and upon them the names of the twelve apostles of the Lamb.*
>
> *15And the one who spoke with me had a golden measuring rod to measure the city and its gates and its wall. 16And the city lies foursquare, and its length is the same as its width. And he measured the city with the rod to 12,000 stadia: its length and width and height are equal. 17And he measured its wall, 144 cubits, according to a human measurement, which is an angelic measurement. 18And the material of its wall was jasper, and the city was pure gold, like clear glass. 19The foundations of the wall of the city were adorned with every precious stone. The first foundation was jasper, the second sapphire, the third chalcedony, the fourth emerald, 20the*

fifth sardonix, the sixth sardius, the seventh chrysolite, the eighth beryl, the ninth topaz, the tenth chrysoprase, the eleventh jacinth, the twelfth amethyst. [21]And the twelve gates were twelve pearls, each of the gates was of one pearl. And the street of the city was pure gold, like transparent glass.

[22]And I did not see a temple in it, for the Lord God the Almighty and the Lamb are its temple. [23]And the city has no need of the sun or of the moon to shine in it, for the glory of God illuminates it, and the Lamb is its lamp. [24]And the nations will walk by its light, and the kings of the earth will bring their glory into it. [25]And its gates will not be closed during the daytime, for there will not be night there, [26]and they will bring the glory and the honor of the nations into it. [27]And nothing unclean will enter into it, no one who practices the abomination and the lie, but only those who are written in the book of life of the Lamb.

[1]And he showed me a river of the water of life, bright as crystal, coming from the throne of God and of the Lamb [2]in the middle of its street. And on both sides of the river there was the tree of life producing twelve fruits, yielding its fruit each month, and the leaves of the tree were for the healing of the nations. [3]And there will be no curse any longer. And the throne of God and of the Lamb will be in it, and his servants will serve him in worship. [4]And they will behold his face, and his name will be on their foreheads. [5]And there will not be night any longer, and they will have no need of the light of a lamp nor the light of the sun, because the Lord God shall illumine them; and they will reign forever and ever.

NOTES

21:9 *The bride, the wife of the Lamb.* In the Old Testament, the restoration of Jerusalem is described in terms of a wedding. Isaiah portrays the restored Jerusalem as being adorned with ornaments as a bride (Isa. 49:18). He also prophesied that "as the bridegroom rejoices over the bride, so your God will rejoice over you" (Isa. 62:5; cf. 61:10).

21:10 *A great and high mount.* The Greek *oros* can mean "mountain," "mount," or "hill"; the word also may designate a desert place (cf. Matt. 18:12).[24] In the New Testament, a city is consistently located on a mount rather than on a mountain (cf. Matt. 5:14; Luke 4:29; Heb. 12:22). The context suggests that John most likely had in mind a large and high artificial mound formed of the ruins and debris of the destroyed end-time Babylon, the great city (today referred to by archaeologists as a "tell"). This view is supported by the fact that John's vision relates to a similar visionary experience of Ezekiel when God brought him into the land of Israel and set him on a very high mount to show him a restored city of Jerusalem that was rebuilt on the ruins of the destroyed city (Ezek. 4:1–2). To build a city on a mound made up of the ruins of a previous city was a well-known ancient practice. Such artificial mounds are mentioned in the book of Joshua: "Israel did not burn any cities that stood on their mounds [tells], except Hazor alone, which Joshua burned" (Josh. 11:13). Jeremiah speaks of the city to be "rebuilt on its ruin [tell]" (Jer. 30:18). It is likely that it was the same angel who led John to witness both the destruction of end-time Babylon in the wilderness (Rev. 17:3) and the establishment of new Jerusalem on the mount. This would suggest that this mountain is located in the wilderness as the place of Babylon's destruction (Babylon itself is referred to in Revelation 17:9 as the city sitting on seven hills [Gr. *oroi*]).

21:11 *Radiance.* The Greek word *phōstēr* means "luminary" or "radiance."[25] The word denotes something from which light is radiated.[26]

21:12 *Twelve.* See *Notes* on Revelation 7:4.

21:16 *12,000 stadia.* A stadion (furlong) was about 606 feet or 185 meters in length. Twelve thousand stadia would be roughly 1,400 miles or 2,200 kilometers. According to the Greek historiographer Herodotus, the ancient city of Babylon stood "on a broad plain, and is an exact square, a hundred and twenty furlongs in length each way."[27] E. Schüssler Fiorenza suggests that John modeled his depiction of the new Jerusalem after the historical Babylon as known to us from Herodotus, "insofar as he says that the city stands 'foursquare' and gives its size in furlongs, measurements that are found in Herodotus's text. It is therefore possible that Revelation's audience may have recognized that John's visionary description of the New Jerusalem alludes to that of the historic Babylon and thereby pictures God's city as the anti-image of Babylon."[28]

21:17 *144 cubits.* A cubit was about one-half of a yard or 44.5 centimeters; 144 cubits would be roughly 72 yards or 64 meters (on the symbolism of the number of "one hundred and forty-four," see *Notes* on Rev. 7:4).

According to a human measurement, which is an angelic measurement. The meaning of this statement is quite obscure. It may point to the enormous dimensions of the city wall according to both human and angelic standards.

21:19 *Every precious stone.* The twelve stones that make up the foundation of the city wall appear to be the same as those decorating the breastplate of the high priest in the Old Testament upon which the names of the twelve tribes of Israel were inscribed (Exod. 28:17–20; 39:10–19). The problem is that only eight of the twelve stones are repeated in Revelation 21:19–20. Some scholars suggest that this difference may indicate that John made his own translation of the names of the stones from Hebrew.[29]

21:22 *Almighty.* See *Notes* on Revelation 1:8.

22:1 *A river of the water of life, bright as crystal, coming from the throne of God.* "The water of life" here means "the water, which is life." The image of the living water proceeding from the city is drawn from several Old Testament texts. Revelation 22:1 reminds one of the river flowing from the garden of Eden, watering the garden and making it fruitful, with the tree of life on its bank (Gen. 2:9–10). The Psalmist speaks of "a river whose streams make glad the city of God, the holy dwelling places of the Most High" (Ps. 46:4). Ezekiel observed in vision a river flowing out from the temple, producing life wherever it flowed. On the river's two banks "will grow all kinds of trees for food. Their leaves will not wither, and their fruit will not fail. They will bear every month because their water flows from the sanctuary, and their fruit will be for food and their leaves for healing" (Ezek. 47:12). Joel spoke of a fountain flowing out from the house of the Lord (Joel 3:18). Zechariah prophesied of the living waters flowing out of the restored Jerusalem (Zech. 14:8).

Some have identified the river of life with the Holy Spirit.[30] Isaiah may be making this parallel in speaking of the future restoration of Israel: "For I will pour out water on the thirsty land and streams on the dry ground; I will pour out My Spirit on your offspring, and My blessing on your descendants; and they will spring up among the grass, like poplars by streams of water" (Isa. 44:3–4). Jesus stated: "He who believes in Me...from his innermost being shall flow rivers of living water." John understood him to be referring to "the Spirit whom those who believed in Him were to receive" (John 7:38–39). The allusion to the Holy Spirit is also affirmed in Revelation 22:17 where the call of the Spirit to come is followed by an invitation for everyone to come and take freely the water of life. The river flowing from the new Jerusalem symbolizes the abundant life that God provides for his people on the new earth for all eternity. John may be contrasting it with the river Euphrates flowing through ancient Babylon, on the banks of which God's exiled people were longing for Jerusalem while their enemies looked upon them with contempt and scorn (Ps. 137:1–6).

The throne. On the significance and meaning of the heavenly throne in Revelation, see *Notes on Revelation 4:2.*

22:2 *In the middle of its street.* As the original Greek was written without punctuation, the text here can be punctuated in two different ways. The end of verse 1 may have a period after "Lamb," followed by a new sentence beginning with, "In the middle of its street and..." (as in the KJV, UBS, and NE Greek New Testaments). Also, "in the middle of its street" may be the completion of the sentence in verse 1 (as found in NASB, RSV, TEV, NEB, NIV, and NRSV). If one takes the first reading to be correct, then the river and street run side by side, with the tree of life between them. Most scholars, including David E. Aune, favor the second reading because John often begins new sentences with "and" (Gr. *kai*) or sometimes with a prepositional phrase (such as "after these things" in 4:1; 7:9; 18:1; 19:1).[31] In this case, the river appears to flow down the wide street through the city, supplying its inhabitants' needs.

The leaves of the tree were for the healing of the nations. The text is a direct allusion to Ezekiel 47:12 which mentions "all kinds of trees for food" on the banks of the river flowing from the temple; the leaves of the trees are for healing. Ezekiel also stresses that the leaves will not wither. The "healing" referred to by Ezekiel must be understood in the context of the Old Testament idea of "sitting" under the tree. Dwelling "under his vine and his fig tree" refers to the ideal period of peace and safety such as the people enjoyed under Solomon (1 Kings 4:24–25). The Exile deprived the people of such a blessing; Jeremiah announced the withering of the trees in the apostate land (Jer. 8:13). The expression was employed by the later prophets with regard to the peace and safety of the future messianic age. Micah prophesied that everyone will "sit under his vine and under his fig tree, with no one to make them afraid" (Mic. 4:4). "In that day," Zechariah prophesied, "every one of you will invite his neighbor to sit under his vine and under his fig tree" (Zech. 3:10). In the light of the foregoing, the "healing" in Ezekiel refers most likely to the emotional wounds of the Exile; the people's wounds were being healed under the green leaves of the trees of their restored homeland. In Revelation 22:2, the phrase stating that "the leaves of the tree were for the healing of the nations" must be understood against the above-mentioned Old Testament concept. However, while in Ezekiel there are avenues of trees (47:7, 12), John mentions only one—the tree of life; for "their leaves for healing" in Ezekiel, John substitutes "for the healing of the nations."

EXPOSITION

21:9–10 John has earlier witnessed the descent of the new Jerusalem out of heaven to the earth (cf. 21:2). Now, one of the seven angels who executed the seven last plagues summons John in order to show him *the bride, the wife of the Lamb*. The fact that this angel is referred to here in the same terms as the one who earlier summoned John to witness "the judgment of the great prostitute" (Rev. 17:1) suggests that it is the same heavenly being.[32] This time the angel is commissioned to show John the wife of the Lamb in all her glory. In the case of the judgment of Babylon, John was carried away in the Spirit into the wilderness (Rev. 17:3). Now, he is again carried away *in the Spirit*, this time *to a great and high mount* to be shown *the holy city, Jerusalem, descending out of heaven from God*. It can hardly be accidental that both visions use the same language. John is drawing a contrast between the two cities, the traditional enemies, and their fates. The site of the great mount on which the new Jerusalem is located could be the wilderness where the end-time prostitute Babylon— the adversary of Jerusalem and God's people—was judged. This *great* mountain is made, so to speak, from the ruins and debris of the destroyed Babylon, the *great* city. The message John tries to convey in figurative language is that it is over the ruins of "the proud, evil, and corrupted Babylon" that New Jerusalem rises "pure and radiant with the glory of God."[33]

In Revelation 21:3, a heavenly voice identifies the holy city as "the tabernacle of God" in which God dwells with his people. In the new Jerusalem there is no temple (Rev. 21:22); because of the abiding presence of God, the city functions as the temple itself. Therefore, in the rest of the text, John describes the new Jerusalem in terms of the Old Testament temple. The entire description is based on the vision of the restored temple from Ezekiel 40–48. What Ezekiel saw earlier is now being fulfilled. Although the new Jerusalem is portrayed as a city (the place where the people of God live) because of God's abiding presence, it has all the characteristics of a temple.

21:11 The first thing that John notices is ***the glory of God*** radiating from the city. The manifestation of God's glory was the main feature of the Old Testament temple which designated God's presence (cf. Exod. 40:34–35; Lev. 9:23; Ezek. 43:1–5). The radiant glory of God decorates the new Jerusalem (Rev. 21:2). This glory denotes the abiding presence of God with his people. Human words are inadequate to express the ***radiance*** of God's glory in the city. For John it looks like the glow of ***a precious stone, like a jasper stone sparkling like crystal*** (cf. Rev. 4:3). The radiant glory of God's presence is brighter than the heavenly bodies, making their light unnecessary (cf. Rev. 21:23; 22:5).

21:12–14 The further description of the city is patterned after the ancient cities that John was familiar with. These were surrounded by walls with gates for protection against enemies. The new Jerusalem has ***a great and high wall.*** The restored temple in Ezekiel is surrounded by a high wall (Ezek. 40:5); this further affirms the temple characteristics of the new Jerusalem. The wall around the new Jerusalem is not for the purpose of defense, for the evil forces have been destroyed. The wall here stands as a symbol of security and safety. God spoke earlier through the prophet Zechariah with regard to the restored Jerusalem: "'For I,' declares the Lord, 'will be a wall of fire around her, and I will be the glory in her midst'" (Zech. 2:5).

The wall of the capital of the new earth has ***twelve gates.*** Three gates are on each of its sides: ***on the east were three gates, and on the north were three gates, and on the south were three gates, and on the west were three gates.*** The new Jerusalem here is seen in the same way as the restored Jerusalem in Ezekiel's vision with twelve gates (Ezek. 48:31–35). The twelve gates here stand for universality; Jesus foresaw that many will "come from east and west, and from north and south, and will recline at the table in the kingdom of God" (Luke 13:29). Here, this prediction comes to its fulfillment. The new Jerusalem is a universal city; everyone has unlimited access to the presence of God.

On the city's gates are inscribed ***the names*** of ***the twelve tribes of Israel.*** This picture is built on the vision of the prophet Ezekiel (48:31–35). In addition, the wall of the city lies on **twelve foundations** upon which are inscribed **the names of the twelve apostles.** The twelve apostles represent the church. According to Paul, the church of God as a whole is built on the foundation of the apostles and prophets (Eph. 2:20). The juxtaposition of the twelve tribes of Israel and the twelve apostles is already expressed in the number of the twenty-four elders as the symbolic representatives of all the redeemed and faithful people of God (Rev. 4:4). Those represented here come from both the Old and New Testament church as well as in the symbolic number of the sealed 144,000 (Rev. 7:4–8). Through the symbolism of the twelve gates with the names of the twelve tribes of Israel, and the twelve foundations bearing the names of the twelve apostles, John portrays the new Jerusalem as the place of God's people of both the Old and New Testaments in their totality.

At the gate towers are **twelve angels** standing as watchers. By this, John is reminding his readers that the new Jerusalem is well protected; nothing unclean or abominable will enter there (cf. Rev. 21:27). This evokes the prophecy of Isaiah: "On your walls, O Jerusalem, I have appointed watchmen; all day and all night they will never keep silent. You who remind the Lord, take no rest for yourselves; and give Him no rest until He establishes and makes Jerusalem a praise in the earth" (Isa. 62:6–7). The new Jerusalem in Revelation is the fulfillment of the ancient dream and hope for an ideal city—a place of safety. In it, as G. K. Beale observes, "the entire people of God redeemed throughout the ages will experience consummate security in the inviolable new creation because of God's permanent and consummate presence there."[34]

21:15–17 John notices in the hands of the angel **a golden measuring rod to measure the city and its gates and its wall.** This is similar to Ezekiel's vision of the man with the measuring rod measuring the temple (Ezek. 40–42). It also brings to mind Revelation 11:1–2 where John was invited to measure the temple. These elements affirm the description of the new Jerusalem as the temple where God dwells among his people. On the other hand, the act of measuring here "and the stating of measurements are doubtless to give assurance of the adequacy and sufficiency of the heavenly home."[35]

The new Jerusalem appears to John as lying **foursquare.** Each side is **12,000 stadia** in length. The measurements of the new Jerusalem reflect the description of ancient Babylon by Herodotus; according to this ancient historian, Babylon was built in the form of a square.[36] However, the measurements reveal that the actual shape of the new Jerusalem is a perfect cube; its **length and width and height are equal.** It may be noted that a cube consists of twelve edges. Each edge of the new Jerusalem is 12,000 stadia long, equaling 144,000 stadia for the entire city.[37] One hundred and forty-four thousand is the number of totality of God's people (Rev. 7:4). This points to the universality of the city; the new Jerusalem is the ideal home of both the Old and New Testament redeemed people of God (see *Notes* on Rev. 7:4).

The most important symbolism of the shape of this colossal city lies in the fact that it is a perfect cube, as was the Holy of Holies in the Old Testament temple (1 Kings 6:20).[38] The new Jerusalem is indeed the place of God's presence with his people, the temple of God on the new earth. In the ancient temple, the high priest was the only person who had the privilege of entering the Holy of Holies and meeting God there face to face. In the new Jerusalem, "the privilege of being in the immediate presence of God...is now granted to all of God's people" (cf. Rev. 22:3–4).[39]

The measurements of the city's wall also reveal a numerical symbolism. The text does not indicate whether it is the height or the thickness of the wall that is *144 cubits*. However, John has already mentioned that the city wall was "great and high" (v. 12). In addition, he specifies the height of the city as being 12,000 stadia. It is natural, therefore, to understand the 144 cubits to refer to the wall's thickness. The new Jerusalem certainly does not need walls to protect it against enemies. This figuratively thick wall of the city affirms the security of the new Jerusalem. "'For I,' declares the Lord, 'will be a wall of fire around her, and I will be the glory in her midst'" (Zech. 2:5). Whatever the purpose of describing the measurements of the city might be, John provides his readers with an assurance that the capital of the new earth, according to both *human* and *angelic* standards of *measurement*, is an ideal place, protected and safe to inhabit.

21:18–21 John now returns to the subject of the radiance of the new Jerusalem mentioned in Revelation 21:11. Even the city wall radiates the glory of God, being made of *jasper*. The buildings of the city are made of *pure gold,* pure *like clear glass.* This mirrors Josephus' description of Herod's temple: "Now the outward face of the temple in its front wanted nothing that was likely to surprise either men's minds or their eyes, for it was covered all over the plates of gold of great weight, and, at the first rising of the sun, reflected back a very fiery splendor, and made those who forced themselves to look upon it to turn their eyes away, just as they would have done at the sun's own rays."[40] John explains further that *the foundations* supporting the city's wall contain *every precious stone* upon which are engraved the names of the twelve apostles (Rev. 21:14). These stones correspond to the twelve precious stones found on the breastplate of the Old Testament high priest upon which the names of the twelve tribes of Israel were engraved (Exod. 28:17–20). The city also features *the twelve gates* that are *twelve pearls*; each gate is one huge pearl.

Finally, the city street is made of *pure gold, like transparent glass.* The floor of Solomon's temple also was overlaid with gold (1 Kings 6:30). This street is an evident contrast to "the street of the great city" where the bodies of the two witnesses—symbolizing God's oppressed and persecuted people bearing their witness to God in the world—were exposed to public ridicule and mockery (Rev. 11:8–10). In the heavenly city, God's oppressed people have been vindicated. They are now walking the streets of the new Jerusalem; the street of oppression and suffering that they trod has been replaced by the street of victory and glory.[41]

These descriptions of the new Jerusalem reflect Isaiah's prophecy of the future restoration of Jerusalem: "Behold, I will set your stones in antimony, and your foundations I will lay in sapphires. Moreover, I will make your battlements of rubies, and your gates of crystal, and your entire wall of precious stones" (Isa. 54:11–12). Similar language is used in the apocryphal book of Tobit describing the future glory of Jerusalem:

> For Jerusalem will be built with sapphires and emeralds,
>   her walls with precious stones,
>   and her towers and battlements with pure gold.
> The streets of Jerusalem will be paved with beryl and ruby
>   and stones of Ophir;
>   all her lanes will cry "Hallelujah!" and will give praise,
>   saying, "Blessed is God, who has exalted you for ever."[42]

The new Jerusalem fulfills all dreams with regard to the restored Jerusalem of the Jewish people of John's day. The city radiates with the glory of God which is impossible to describe adequately with human language.

21:22 In concluding the description of the adornment of the new Jerusalem, John states that he does *not see a temple in it, for the Lord God the Almighty and the Lamb are its temple.*

21:23–26 All of the precious stones and the buildings and the streets of gold that stand for the glory of God make the light of the sun and moon unnecessary. The new

Jerusalem *has no need of the sun or of the moon to shine in it, for the glory of God illuminates it, and the Lamb is its lamp.* This vision reflects the prophecy of Isaiah:

> No longer will you have the sun for light by day,
> Nor for brightness will the moon give you light;
> But you will have the Lord for an everlasting light,
> And your God for your glory.
> Your sun will set no more,
> Neither will your moon wane;
> For you will have the Lord for an everlasting light,
> And the days of your mourning will be finished. (Isa. 60:19–20)

John states further that *the nations will walk by its light, and the kings of the earth will bring their glory into it.* The nations and kings mentioned here are most likely the redeemed of the entire world (the ones referred to in Rev. 1:6; 5:9; 7:9).[43] Here is fulfilled what Isaiah prophesied regarding ancient Israel: "Nations will come to your light, and kings to the brightness of your rising" (Isa. 60:3). The Old Testament prophets repeatedly speak of nations and their kings coming to worship God in Jerusalem (Isa. 2:2–4; 56:6–7; Jer. 3:17; Zech. 8:21–23). The apocryphal book of Tobit expresses the same hope of the Jewish people: "Many nations will come from afar to the name of the Lord God, bearing gifts in their hands, gifts for the King of heaven."[44] The new Jerusalem is the fulfillment of all Old Testament dreams with regard to the earthly Jerusalem.

The city's gates are never *closed during the daytime, for there will not be night there.* This is another allusion to the prophecy of Isaiah: "Your gates will be open continually, they will not be closed day or night" (Isa. 60:11). The gates of the city need not be shut, not only because there are no enemies there, but because of God's abiding presence in the city. The open gates will make possible for all people immediate and unhindered "access to the presence of God."[45] Once again John picks up on Isaiah 60 and states that the nations and the kings *will bring the glory and the honor of the nations into it.* Isaiah envisioned the day when the gates of Jerusalem would be opened continually "so that men may bring to you the wealth of the nations, with their kings led in procession....To beautify the place of My sanctuary; and I shall make the place of My feet glorious" (Isa. 60:11b–13).

21:27 At this point another list of exclusions from the new Jerusalem is given: *nothing unclean will enter into it, no one who practices the abomination and* *the lie.* Uncleanness and unfaithfulness characterized ancient Jerusalem. Isaiah prophesied that the uncleanness and unfaithfulness will be excluded from the new Jerusalem: "Clothe yourself in your beautiful garments, O Jerusalem, the holy city. For the uncircumcised and the unclean will no more come into you" (Isa. 52:1). Nothing unclean was to enter the Old Testament temple. Since the new Jerusalem is the temple of God, nobody and nothing unclean and abominable has a place in it.

The unclean and those who practice abomination mentioned here are those who drank from Babylon's "golden cup filled with abominations and the unclean things of her fornication" (Rev. 17:4), that is, those who succumbed to the end-time deception. Only *those who are written in the book of life of the Lamb* will dwell in the new Jerusalem, as opposed to those "whose names are not written in the book of life of the Lamb" who sided with the satanic trinity and worshiped the beast (cf. Rev. 13:8; 17:8). They all have found their end in the lake of fire (Rev. 20:15). The only way to live in the new Jerusalem is through total surrender and loyalty to Christ here and now (cf. Rev. 21:7). This is a strong allusion to Isaiah's prophecy: "And it will come about that he who is left in Zion and remains in Jerusalem will be called holy—everyone who is recorded for life in Jerusalem" (Isa. 4:3).

22:1 Now the angel shows John *a river of the water of life* that looks *bright as crystal.* The river comes *from the throne of God and of the Lamb in the middle of its street.* John takes this picture from several Old Testament texts. First of all, the picture shows the river flowing from Eden which watered the garden and made it fruitful (Gen. 2:10). A stronger allusion to the river flowing out from the temple and giving life to all appears in Ezekiel's vision (Ezek. 47:1–12). It also reminds us of other Old Testament texts that speak of the river of living waters flowing out from the restored Jerusalem and making the land fruitful (cf. Joel 3:18; Zech. 14:8). Everything foreshadowed in the prophets, John sees fulfilled.[46] The river of the water of life in New Jerusalem stands here in contrast to Babylon dwelling on many waters (cf. Rev. 17:1, 15). The river Euphrates was an integral part of ancient Babylon; it flowed through the city. According to Psalm 137:1–6, it was at the river Euphrates in Babylon that God's people were sitting as captives longing for Jerusalem. Now, Babylon is a matter of the past, and the captivity of God's people is over. It is beside the living streams of the river of life flowing through New Jerusalem that the redeemed shall finally find their rest.

It is especially significant that this is the first time in the book that the throne is referred to as "the throne of the Lamb." Up to this point, it has functioned as the prerogative of God the Father as a symbol of his rulership. Revelation 3:21 makes clear, however, that Christ took his seat on the Father's throne as the co-ruler. It is not until the ultimate destruction of evil and the establishment of the kingdom after the millennium that Christ takes full control of the throne. The throne is now referred to as the ruling seat of both the Father and the Lamb (Rev. 22:1, 3; cf. 7:17). "And when all things are subjected to Him, then the Son Himself will also be subjected to the One who subjected all things to Him, that God may be all in all" (1 Cor. 15:28).

22:2 *On both sides of the river* is *the tree of life.* Clearly one tree is on both sides of the river. This is an allusion to the Garden of Eden with the tree of life on the bank of the river flowing from the garden (Gen. 2:9). To eat from the tree of life in Eden meant "to live forever" (Gen. 3:22). It was after Adam and Eve were banished from the garden that they were forbidden to approach the tree of life and eat from it (Gen. 3:23–24). The tree of life in the new Jerusalem symbolizes eternal life free of death and suffering. On the new earth—the restored garden of Eden—the tree of life is no longer forbidden; it is located in the midst of the new Jerusalem, and all the redeemed have access to it. Once again human beings will share in the gift of eternal life that Adam enjoyed before sin entered the world. All that was lost through Adam is now regained through Christ.

The tree of life bears *twelve fruits, yielding its fruit each month, and the leaves of the tree were for the healing of the nations*. The life-giving fruit of the tree is perpetually available to the redeemed on the new earth. John draws this description from Ezekiel's vision of the river flowing from the temple: "By the river on its bank, on one side and on the other, will grow all kinds of trees for food. Their leaves will not wither and their fruit will not fail. They will bear every month because their water flows from the sanctuary, and their fruit will be for food and their leaves for healing" (Ezek. 47:12). Unlike Ezekiel, however, John specifies that the leaves are for the healing *of the nations* (or Gentiles). It does not mean, as some expositors assert, that the leaves of the tree of life have a healing power to prevent diseases.[47] With the annihilation of evil, sickness and death have been forever removed from the restored earth. "The healing of the nations" refers figuratively to the removal of all national and linguistic barriers and separation. God's kingdom is not confined to the

Jews or any other nation. New Jerusalem is inhabited by people of all nations, tribes, and tongues (Rev. 5:9; 7:9), including Egyptians, Assyrians, Babylonians, Romans, and Jews. The leaves of the tree of life heal the breaches between nations. The nations are no longer "gentiles" but are united into one family as the true people of God (cf. 21:24–26). What Micah anticipated centuries earlier is now being fulfilled: "Nation will not lift up sword against nation, and never again will they train for war. Each of them will sit under his vine and under his fig tree, with no one to make them afraid" (Mic. 4:3–4; cf. Isa. 2:4). There on the banks of the river of life the redeemed will "invite his neighbor to sit" (Zech. 3:10) with him under the tree of life. The curing quality of the leaves of the tree will heal all wounds—racial, ethnic, tribal, or linguistic—that have torn and divided humanity for ages.

22:3–4 The next statement is problematic because of punctuation: *and there will be no curse any longer.* The statement functioning as the conclusion of the previous sentence makes more sense. Sin has brought a curse on the earth (Gen. 3:17–19; 5:29). The most painful aspect of the curse was the banishment from Eden and the tree of life (Gen. 3:22–24). With the eradication of sin, all curse is removed. The redeemed return to the restored Eden with full access to the tree of life. The prophecy of Zechariah will finally come to its fulfillment: "And people will live in it, and there will be no more curse, for Jerusalem will dwell in security" (Zech. 14:11).

The central object of the new earth is *the throne of God and of the Lamb.* The significance of the reference to the throne of God in the new Jerusalem is found in light of the fact that John wrote to Christians suffering under the persecution initiated by the imperial throne of Rome. The throne as the symbol of Roman authority and power was often used by Satan for destroying and corrupting the earth. In the new Jerusalem, the throne—as the symbol of God's power—signifies the ultimate subjection of the powers of Satan and the abiding presence of God among the saved (cf. Ezek. 43:7). The place in Revelation "from which all judgments are issued" now becomes "the source of eternal life and happiness."[48]

The redeemed can now freely approach God to *serve him in worship.* They *behold his face.* They have the privilege which even Moses was denied: "You cannot see My face, for no man can see My face and live" (Exod. 33:20). The day is coming, however, when "we will see Him just as He is" (1 John 3:2). Not only will they see him, but also *his name will be on their foreheads.* (Here is another fulfillment of the promise given to the overcomers; cf. 3:12.) This repeats what was said earlier with regard to the 144,000 standing on Mount Zion in Revelation 14:1 with the name of God written on their foreheads. Because the redeemed refused to accept the mark with the name of the beast on their foreheads (Rev. 15:2), they are rewarded with bearing the name of God. A name in the Bible stands for character. The redeemed will reflect the character of God in their lives throughout eternity.

22:5 In concluding his description of the home of the redeemed, John repeats what he has said before. The abiding presence of God's glory on the new earth outshines the light of the heavenly bodies, making their light unnecessary. *There will not be night any longer, and they will have no need of the light of a lamp nor the light of the sun, because the Lord God shall illumine them* (cf. Rev. 21:23, 25). In the radiance of the glory of God, the redeemed *will reign forever and ever.* In the book of Revelation, it is repeatedly stated that God is the One who lives and reigns forever and ever (4:9–10; 10:6; 11:15; 15:7). By virtue of Christ's death on the cross, the redeemed are made kings and priests (Rev. 1:6; 5:10). Paul stated: "If we endure, we shall also reign with Him" (2 Tim. 2:12). Now, at the end of the great cosmic drama, the redeemed dwell in God's abiding presence, enjoying intimate relationship with him and reigning with him throughout eternity.

A RETROSPECT ON REVELATION 21–22:5

The description of the new earth in Revelation 21–22:5 with its capital city concludes the full circle of the great cosmic drama. Evil is permanently destroyed, and peace, joy, and safety are restored on the earth as in the beginning. Just as God originally gave human beings a garden for their dwelling place, so on the new earth he gives to the redeemed a city, New Jerusalem, for their dwelling place. The new Jerusalem is the city that God's people—since Adam's banishment from the garden of Eden—have been anticipating. Abraham himself longed for that city (Heb. 11:16). It appears that the new Jerusalem is portrayed in Revelation as the fulfillment of all the dreams and hopes of human beings throughout the history of this world.

A natural question arises: Is the new Jerusalem as portrayed in Revelation 21–22:5 a literal city or is it to be understood as a symbol of higher reality that is beyond human comprehension? Revelation seems to portray the new Jerusalem as a real place inhabited by real people. Yet it is important to keep in mind the symbolic character of the book of Revelation as a whole. At this point, *The Seventh-day Adventist Bible Commentary* suggests caution: "In pictorial prophecy the degree of identity between the picture and the actual calls for careful interpretation."[49] Although a future reality, the new Jerusalem is described in terms of ancient cities familiar to the original readers of Revelation. Badenas reminds us: "At the time of John the city was the human and social unifier of civilization. Everyone belonged to a city. Ancients identified their people with their capital city. The glory of the kings were the cities that they had built or conquered. A city that could be identified as God's city was probably the best symbol to represent the glory of God's kingdom."[50]

It is not always clear to us, however, exactly where the line of demarcation is drawn between the literal and the symbolic with regards to the new Jerusalem. The pictorial language used to describe the city is derived from several sources. It is, thus, impossible to understand the description of the new Jerusalem without understanding some of its background.

First of all, the new Jerusalem functions as the replacement for the garden of Eden, the lost paradise (cf. Gen. 2–3). As there was a river and the tree of life in the very center of the garden (cf. Gen. 2:9–10), so there is a river flowing from the throne of God and the tree of life in the middle of the city (Rev. 22:1). As human beings reflected the image of God in the beginning (Gen. 1:27), so the redeemed reflect God's character (Rev. 22:4). Genesis gives the original curse, the most painful aspect of which was the banishment from the garden and exclusion from the tree of life (Gen. 3:22–24). In the new Jerusalem, "there will be no curse any longer" (Rev. 22:3). The redeemed are brought back to the restored paradise and have unhindered access to the tree of life. Revelation 21–22:5 provides answers to some of the basic questions regarding the appearance of the new earth. The new Jerusalem denotes the fulfillment of God's promises with regard to the lost paradise; everything that was lost in Adam is to be ultimately regained through Christ.[51] It is on the banks of the river of the waters of life and under the tree of life that "God's people, so long pilgrims and wanderers, shall find a home."[52] The promises given to the overcomers in the messages to the seven churches (Rev. 2–3) will all find their ultimate fulfillment in that garden-city.

John continues his description by combining the garden-of-Eden motif with the detailed description of the restored earthly temple from the vision of the prophet Ezekiel (Ezek. 40–48). Both Ezekiel and John were carried away to a high mount from which they saw the city of Jerusalem (Ezek. 40:2; Rev. 21:9–10). As in Ezekiel's vision the temple was filled with the glory of God, so in Revelation 21:11 the new Jerusalem has the glory of God. In both visions, the city is seen as having a high wall with twelve gates—three gates on each side of the city—with the names of the twelve tribes of Israel inscribed on them (Ezek. 48:31–35; Rev. 21:12–13). Both Ezekiel and John saw a heavenly figure with a rod for measuring the city, the gates, and the wall (Ezek. 40:3–42:20). Both saw the city laid square (Ezek. 48:20; Rev. 21:16). In both visions, the city contains the throne of God, who dwells among his people (Ezek. 43:7; Rev. 21:3, 5; 22:1). Finally, both of the texts state certain restrictions concerning potential inhabitants of the city (Ezek. 44:6–14; Rev. 21:8, 27). These features indicate, as Badenas states, that "the promised restoration of Jerusalem, given to Israel through the prophet Ezekiel, has reached its [ultimate] fulfillment in the heavenly city."[53] Revelation thus presents the new Jerusalem as the fulfillment of the prophetic dream and hope of the ideal city, the dream that had never been realized with the old Jerusalem.

The description of New Jerusalem in Revelation 21–22 also has many parallels with the description of Babylon in Revelation 17–18. The two cities are set against each other. The parallels and contrasts between their descriptions are given in the "Overview: Revelation 12–22:5."[54] Both visions were introduced by the same angel of the seven-bowl plagues (17:1; 21:9). In both cases, John is carried away in the Spirit to witness the scene (17:3; 21:10). Babylon is referred to as the great prostitute (17:1), and New Jerusalem as the bride of the Lamb (21:9). Both are decorated with precious stones (17:4; 21:11). Prostitute Babylon offers the cup of abominations (17:4; 18:3), and New Jerusalem offers the water of life (22:1). Babylon is the dwelling place of demons (18:2), and New Jerusalem is the dwelling place of God (21:3). While Babylon is full of unclean things, abomination, and sin (18:2, 4–5), nothing unclean and abominable is found in the new Jerusalem (21:27). The nations and the kings in Babylon (17:15) give their power and authority to the beast (17:12–13); likewise, the nations and the kings bring their glory into the new Jerusalem (21:24). While New Jerusalem has the river of life flowing in its midst (22:1), Babylon is situated on "many waters," namely, the Euphrates (17:1). Finally, while Babylon is characterized by its rebellion against God, the new Jerusalem is characterized by its faithfulness to him.

A sharp contrast exists between the inhabitants of the two cities, however. Those excluded from New Jerusalem are described in the same terms as the inhabitants of Babylon. For instance, the citizens of Babylon are the ones whose names are not written in the book of life (17:8), while the inhabitants of New Jerusalem are those whose names are written in the book of life (21:27). While murderers, fornicators, and sorcerers are excluded from the heavenly city (21:8), Babylon is full of murderers (17:6; 18:24), fornicators (17:2; 18:3, 9), and sorcerers (18:23). Jerusalem symbolizes God's people, while Babylon symbolizes the enemies of God and his people.

In a real sense, Babylon represents the earthly false hopes and dreams. It is the best that human beings are able to create and offer. Babylon offers prosperity, money, power, success, and sensual gratification, all of which sinners desire. No wonder that Babylon's destruction shatters all human delusions, hopes, and dreams, as the series of mournful lamentations in Revelation 18 indicates. On the other hand, the new Jerusalem is God's response to shattered dreams and futile hope. The heavenly city is his offer of the best things that human beings dream about and long for. The city is a place of the gathering of God's faithful people throughout history. Its gates are open wide in all directions, accepting people of every ethnic, tribal, or linguistic group. Barriers of every kind are removed. Everyone who is willing to enter the city and fulfill the conditions is welcome.

Above all, the new Jerusalem functions as the ideal temple of God's dwelling among the faithful. The city was presented in the shape of a perfect cube, like that of the Holy of Holies in the Old Testament temple (1 Kings 6:20). It is the place of the long-awaited union between God and his people. Since banishment from the garden of Eden, humanity has been separated from God. In temple services, only the priests had immediate access to God; the common people could encounter God only through a mediator. In the new Jerusalem, no temple is needed, because the city is the temple itself. God himself will dwell there, and the people will be unhindered in approaching his presence. The privilege of being in the immediate presence of God, formerly reserved only for the high priest in the earthly sanctuary, is now granted to all of God's people (cf. Rev. 22:3–4). In addition, as nothing unclean and abominable had a place in the ancient temple, so "nothing unclean will enter into" the new Jerusalem—"no one who practices the abomination and the lie," but only "those who are written in the book of life of the Lamb" (Rev. 21:27).

Thus, Revelation 21–22:5 presents the new Jerusalem as a real place inhabited by the redeemed and characterized by God's presence. The description of the city, however, is presented in language that human beings can understand; it is drawn from different sources. The description of the capital of the new earth in Revelation 21–22:5 is suggestive. The city itself and the life therein are beyond any human imagination. Paul stated: "Things which eye has not seen and ear has not heard, and which have not entered the heart of man, all that God has prepared for those who love him" (1 Cor. 2:9). All imaginative language used to describe the heavenly reality is inadequate and insufficient. When John portrays New Jerusalem in terms of gold and precious stones, he is not really concerned about gold. Gold and precious stones "only serve as pale illustrations" of the glory and splendor that the redeemed will enjoy on the new earth—"the riches of this age cannot compare to the riches to come."[55]

It is sufficient to say that the new Jerusalem is God's answer to all human longings and dreams of the ideal city which are permeated with hopes and anticipation for a better life. What the prophets prophesied and anticipated will be finally realized. The new Jerusalem is the ideal city because God's presence will banish any fear, pain, and uncertainty. Life in the new Jerusalem is God's final word to futile hopes and utopian dreams of prosperity based on human strategy and effort. The new Jerusalem offers life without end and happiness without limit. Christ lets readers of the book of Revelation know that it is important to be there (Rev. 22:17).

ENDNOTES

1. Bauer, 496–497.
2. Badenas, 250.
3. *The Seventh-day Adventist Bible Commentary*, 7:889.
4. Johnson, 593.
5. Cf. *Testament of Dan* 5:12 (Charlesworth, 1:810); 1 Enoch 90:28–29 (Charlesworth, 1:71); 4 Ezra 7:26; 10:25–55 (Charlesworth, 1:537, 547–548); *The Sibylline Oracles* 5:420–427 (Charlesworth, 1:403).
6. Tobit 13:16–18 (*The Oxford Annotated Apocrypha*,74).
7. 2 Baruch 32:2–4 (Charlesworth, 1:631).
8. Fiorenza, *Revelation*, 113; on the ancient Greco-Roman dreams of the ideal city, see Aune, *Revelation 17–22*, 1191–1194.
9. Bauer, 137–138.
10. Ibid., 998–999.
11. Barclay, *The Revelation of John*, 2:205.
12. Johnson, 592.
13. Barclay, *The Revelation of John*, 2:199.

14. *The Seventh-day Adventist Bible Commentary*, 7:889.

15. Erdman, 105; cf. also 155.

16. Badenas, 252.

17. Neall, *The Concept of Character in the Apocalypse*, 138.

18. Badenas, 260–261.

19. Maxwell, 534.

20. Fiorenza, *The Apocalypse*, 57.

21. Ladd, 278.

22. Mounce, 374.

23. Ibid., 375.

24. Bauer, 724–725.

25. Ibid., 1073.

26. Swete, 284.

27. Herodotus *History* 1.178 (Rawlinson, 40).

28. Fiorenza, *Revelation*, 111.

29. See Caird, 274–275; Sweet, 306.

30. Cf. Swete, 298; Beale, 1104–1105.

31. Aune, *Revelation 17–22*, 1139.

32. Morris, 241.

33. Badenas, 255.

34. Beale, 1079. (Original quotation was italicized.)

35. *The Seventh-day Adventist Bible Commentary*, 7:892.

36. See Herodotus *History* 1.178–179 (Rawlinson, 40).

37. Sweet, 305; Beale, 1076.

38. Fiorenza, *Revelation*, 112.

39. Beale, 1081; also Mounce, 383.

40. Josephus *The Wars of the Jews*, 5.5.6 (Whiston, 707–708).

41. Robert W. Wall, *Revelation,* New International Biblical Commentary (Peabody, MA: Hendrickson, 1991), 254–255.

42. Tobit 13:16–18 (*The Oxford Annotated Apocrypha*, 74).

43. Cf. Beale, 1097–1098.

44. Tobit 13:11 (*The Oxford Annotated Apocrypha*, 74).

45. Ladd, 285.

46. Morris, 248.

47. As Maxwell (p. 534) asserts; so also Mounce, 387; Beale, 1107–1108. Ladd (p. 288) struggles with such an interpretation. On the symbolic understanding of the statement, see Barclay (*The Revelation of John*, 2:222) and Johnson (p. 599).

48. Fiorenza, *Revelation*, 113.

49. *The Seventh-day Adventist Bible Commentary*, 7:892.

50. Badenas, 251.

51. Hughes, 231.

52. White, *The Great Controversy*, 675.

53. Badenas, 252.

54. See also the list of parallels in Aune, *Revelation 17–22*, 1144–1145.

55. Ezell, 101–102.

THE EPILOGUE

*"And behold, I am coming soon. Blessed is the one
who keeps the words of the prophecy of this book."*

THE EPILOGUE
REVELATION 22:6–21

The vision of the new Jerusalem completes the prophecies of Revelation. With Revelation 22:6–21, John concludes his book. Like the prologue (Rev. 1:1–8), the epilogue provides a general summary of the entire book. Much of the prologue is repeated here. Themes introduced in the prologue which run through the book are drawn to their conclusion in the epilogue. The epilogue of Revelation thus functions as the confirmation and reliability of everything that the book contains.

⁶And he said to me: "These words are faithful and true, and the Lord God of the spirits of the prophets sent his angel to show his servants the things which must soon take place. ⁷And behold, I am coming soon. Blessed is the one who keeps the words of the prophecy of this book."

⁸And I, John, am the one who has heard and seen these things. And when I heard and saw them, I fell down to worship at the feet of the angel who showed me these things. ⁹And he said to me: "See, do not do this; I am your fellow servant and of your brothers the prophets and of those who keep the words of this book; worship God." ¹⁰And he said to me: "Do not seal the words of the prophecy of this book, for the time is near. ¹¹Let the unrighteous still do unrighteousness, and let the filthy still be filthy, and let the righteous still do righteousness, and let the holy still be holy.

¹²Behold, I am coming soon, and my reward is with me, to give to each as his work is. ¹³I am the Alpha and the Omega, the first and the last, the beginning and the end.

¹⁴Blessed are those who wash their robes, that their authority may be over the tree of life and they may enter the gates into the city. ¹⁵Outside are the dogs and the sorcerers and the fornicators and the murderers and the idolaters and everyone who loves and practices the lie.

¹⁶I, Jesus, have sent my angel to testify to you these things for the churches; I am the Sprout and the offspring of David, the bright morning star." ¹⁷And the Spirit and the bride say: "Come!" And let the one who hears say: "Come!" And let the one who thirsts come. Let the one who desires take the water of life freely.

¹⁸I myself testify to everyone who hears the words of the prophecy of this book: if anyone adds to them, God will add to him the plagues written in this book. ¹⁹And if anyone takes away from the words of the book of this prophecy, God will take away his part from the tree of life and from the holy city, which are written in this book.

²⁰The One who testifies to these things says, "Yes, I am coming soon." Amen. Come, Lord Jesus.

²¹The grace of the Lord Jesus be with all.

NOTES

22:6 *The things which must soon take place.* See *Notes* on Revelation 1:1.

22:7 *Blessed.* This is the sixth of the beatitudes of Revelation; see further *Notes* on Revelation 1:3.

22:7, 12 *I am coming.* The futuristic present tense suggests an action to take place in the future as it is already occurring in the present. The use of the futuristic present tense stresses the certainty as well as the imminence of an event, in this case the Second Coming (cf. Rev. 1:7; 22:20).

22:13 *The Alpha and the Omega.* See *Notes* on Revelation 1:8.

The beginning and the end. See *Notes* on Revelation 21:6.

22:14 *Blessed.* This is the seventh of the beatitudes of Revelation; see further *Notes* on Revelation 1:3.

Those who wash their robes. The verb "to wash" is the present participle indicating an ongoing and continuing action. The text in the King James Version reads "they that do his commandments." This textual difference is most likely due to a scribal error. In Greek, the two statements resemble each other and sound similar. "Those who wash their robes" is *hoi plunontes tas stolas* in Greek, and "they that do his commandments" is *hoi poiountes tas ēntolas*. In the original Greek New Testament manuscripts, the words were written in capital letters and without spaces between them. In English capital letters, the similarity between the two phrases is obvious:

HOIPLUNONTESTASSTOLAS
HOIPOIOUNTESTASĒNTOLAS

Whether a scribe was reading the phrase or listening to somebody reading it to him, he could easily substitute "those who wash their robes" with "those who do his commandments." The earliest and best manuscripts have "those who wash their robes." The reading "those who do his commandments" could be a scribal error resulting either from a mistaken reading or hearing.

Internal evidence supports such a conclusion. The reading "those who *do* his commandments" would be very unusual, because elsewhere in Revelation John refers to the *keeping* of the commandments (cf. Rev. 12:17; 14:12) or the keeping of the words of the book (cf. 1:3; 2:26; 3:8, 10; 22:7, 9). Furthermore, while the keeping of the commandments is one of the characteristics of God's end-time people in Revelation, the washing of robes provides the ground for their salvation (Rev. 7:14; cf. 5:9–10; 12:11). It is the blood of Christ that provides the victory for God's people. This certainly does not undermine the importance of the commandments, for their keeping is strongly emphasized in Revelation. The importance of the commandments is not based on one text, and in this case nothing is lost with regard to them.

22:15 *The dogs.* Dogs functioned as a negative symbol in antiquity. In the Old Testament a dog is used, for instance, with reference to a male prostitute (Deut. 23:17–18) and evil people (2 Sam. 16:9; 2 Kings 8:13; Pss. 22:16, 20; 59:6; Isa. 56:11). In the New Testament it symbolizes an unholy person (Matt. 7:6), the heathen (Matt. 15:26–27), and evil people (Phil. 3:2; 2 Pet. 2:22).

22:16 *The Sprout…of David.* See *Notes* on Revelation 5:5.

22:20 *I am coming.* See *Notes* on Revelation 22:7.

EXPOSITION

22:6–7 In concluding the description of the new Jerusalem, the angel assures John that ***these words***—namely, everything John has seen and heard and recorded— ***are faithful and true.*** This assurance was already given early in the vision of the new Jerusalem (Rev. 21:5); now, it concludes the vision. Christ in Revelation is "faithful and true" (19:11; cf. 3:14); he promises: "Heaven and earth will pass away, but My words shall not pass away" (Matt. 24:35). The angel stresses once again that the prophecies of Revelation are reliable as Christ himself is reliable. Everything that is predicted in the book will certainly take place because ***the Lord God of the spirits of the prophets sent his angel to show his servants the things which must soon take place.*** "The Lord God of the spirits of the prophets" is a direct allusion to Revelation 19:10, meaning "the God who inspired the minds of the prophets."[1] The statement serves as a confirmation that the things shown to John in the vision were given by the same God who inspired the Old Testament prophets; therefore, they "must be treated with equal seriousness."[2]

Once again Christ reiterates the nearness of his coming: **Behold, I am coming soon** (cf. Rev. 3:11; 22:12, 20). Because he is coming soon, the words of Revelation must be taken seriously. Every generation of God's people is to live in constant expectancy of Christ's imminent coming. The prophecies of the book of Revelation were not given to satisfy one's curiosity about the future, but to admonish God's people to steadfast and unswerving loyalty to Christ in the face of oppression and persecution as they await Christ's soon coming. To all those who heed the prophetic word, a special blessing is promised: **Blessed is the one who keeps the words of the prophecy of this book.** This is the sixth beatitude of the book of Revelation, and it reiterates Revelation 1:3. It is not enough to be acquainted with the contents of Revelation. We must also bear them in mind. Prior to the return of Christ, there will be a great deception, and those who heed the warning message of Revelation will be preserved from that deception.

22:8–9 These verses also contain repetitions. John identifies himself again as **I, John, am the one who has heard and seen these things**, just as he did in the opening of the book (cf. Rev. 1:9). Everything that he has seen is faithfully recorded. The most recent revelation granted to him was with regard to the spectacular glory of the new Jerusalem. Moved by the splendor of everything that he has **heard and seen,** John once again falls down **to worship at the feet of the angel who showed me these things** (cf. Rev. 19:10). Again the angel warns him not to do so: **I am your fellow servant and of your brothers the prophets and of those who keep the words of this book; worship God.** This twofold experience of John and the exhortation to worship God alone is particularly relevant to the end-time generation. The central issue in the final crisis is worship. At the time of the end, when the whole world will turn to worship the beast and the satanic trinity (Rev. 13:12), God sends his end-time gospel—the proclamation of which is portrayed in terms of the three angels—urging the inhabitants of the earth to take him seriously as the Creator and the only one worthy of worship (Rev. 14:7).

22:10–11 In contrast to the instruction given to Daniel to seal up the vision given to him concerning the time of the end (Dan. 8:26; 12:4), the angel commands that John **not seal the words of the prophecy of this book.** The reason for this prohibition is clear: **the time is near**. The visions of the book of Daniel were not relevant to the people of Daniel's time, as they concerned the future end-time. Hence the injunction to Daniel to seal them. In Revelation 5 John saw the seven-sealed scroll which Christ was worthy to unseal. A part of the scroll was revealed through John to the church, and it is recorded in Revelation 12–22:5. It concerns the things that are essential and profitable for God's people as they apply to the earth's final events. Now Christ instructs John not to seal "the words of the prophecy of this book" so that they may be read.

Between the statement that the end is near and the announcement of Christ's speedy coming is sandwiched a solemn pronouncement: *Let the unrighteous still do unrighteousness, and let the filthy still be filthy, and let the righteous still do righteousness, and let the holy still be holy.* Daniel was told that the unsealing of the word of prophecy at the time of the end will result in the polarization of those who will heed the prophetic word and those who will reject it. Those who take the prophetic word seriously "will be purged, purified and refined, but the wicked will act wickedly; and none of the wicked will understand, but those who have insight will understand" (Dan. 12:10). People can resist the gospel for a time. Eventually a verdict will be pronounced, however, and it will be too late to change. The close of probation will mean the cessation of any opportunity to accept the gospel and establish a relationship with God (cf. Rev. 15:5–8). When Christ comes, he will reward each "as his work is" (Rev. 22:12).

22:12–13 John now evidently disappears from the scene. The conclusion of the book belongs to Christ.[3] Once again Christ reminds both John and the readers of Revelation of his speedy coming: *I am coming soon.* He is bringing his *reward* with him, and he will *give to each as his work is.* The statement reiterates what was said in Revelation 1:7–8. This also is almost a repetition of what Jesus told his disciples in Matthew 16:27—that when he comes in the glory of his Father, he will recompense "every man according to his works" (KJV). This statement is repeated often by Paul (Rom. 2:6; 14:12; 2 Cor. 5:10). This does not indicate that a person is saved by works. Elsewhere in the book, John agrees with the plain teaching of the New Testament that salvation is God's gift (cf. Rev. 7:10, 14). While salvation is by grace, however, the judgment is according to works. The works are the strongest evidence of one's salvation and relationship with Christ. Our longing to meet Christ will prompt us to right living. Ellen G. White expresses it in the following way:

> Belief in the near coming of the Son of Man in the clouds of heaven will not cause the true Christian to become neglectful and careless of the ordinary business of life. The waiting ones who look for the soon appearing of Christ will not be idle, but diligent in business. Their work will not be done carelessly and dishonestly, but with fidelity, promptness, and thoroughness. Those who flatter themselves that careless inattention to the things of this life is an evidence of their spirituality and of their

separation from the world are under a great deception. Their veracity, faithfulness, and integrity are tested and proved in temporal things. If they are faithful in that which is least they will be faithful in much.[4]

The one who promises to come again and reward each according to his work is *the Alpha and Omega, the first and the last, the beginning and the end* (cf. Rev. 1:8; 21:6). He is the A to Z of human history. He is the One who knows what the future brings and ultimately controls the course of history. History from the biblical perspective has a meaningful beginning because of Christ; and through him it will have a meaningful conclusion. "I am confident of this very thing," Paul wrote to the Philippians, "that He who began a good work in you will perfect it until the day of Christ Jesus" (Phil. 1:6). It is because of him and through him that the future is marked with hope.

22:14–15 The text speaks of those who have the right to enter the city and those who will be excluded from it. *Blessed are those who wash their robes.* This is the seventh and last of the beatitudes of the book of Revelation. The robe washed in the blood of Christ is the condition for living in the new Jerusalem. This concept fits neatly into the context of the teaching of Revelation as well as the entire New Testament. The bright and clean robes are "the righteous deeds of the saints" (Rev. 19:8). "He has clothed me with garments of salvation," Isaiah exclaimed: "He has wrapped me with a robe of righteousness" (Isa. 61:10). The washing of the robes and making them white is accomplished only by the blood of Christ (Rev. 7:14). Only those washed in the blood of the Lamb have access to *the tree of life* and may *enter the gates into the city.* The salvation of God's people and their access to the new Jerusalem is the result of what Christ has done for them rather than what they have done for themselves.

Now Christ lists those who are excluded from the new Jerusalem. Two similar lists are already mentioned earlier in the last portion of the book (Rev. 21:8, 27). Those excluded are identified as *the dogs* [unholy ones] *and the sorcerers and the fornicators and the murderers and the idolaters and everyone who loves and practices the lie.* All who love and practice things that are contrary to the gospel are excluded from the heavenly city.

22:16 Once again Christ affirms what was made clear in the prologue of the book—that he is the source of the visions of Revelation (Rev. 1:1). *I, Jesus, have sent my angel to testify to you these things for the churches.* The angel who provided the descriptions of the things that John saw in the vision was commissioned by Christ.

As may be seen in Revelation 22:6–16, he functions in the role of Christ and articulates Christ's words. It is often hard to distinguish his sayings from the words of Christ. As was underscored in Revelation 1:11, the things revealed to John through the angel were intended to be Christ's testimony for the seven churches in Asia Minor of John's day.

In order to leave no one in doubt concerning the speaker, Christ identifies himself in the language of Revelation 5 as *the Sprout and the offspring of David, the bright morning star.* Christ, the Messiah, is the fulfillment of the prophecy. All authority and dominion have been given to him (Matt. 28:18; Rev. 5). The overcomers in the church of Thyatira were promised "the morning star" (Rev. 2:28), namely, Christ himself. He is the dawning of the long-awaited new age inaugurating the kingdom of God on the earth.

22:17 Attention now focuses on the witness of the Spirit through the churches. Both *the Spirit and the bride say: "Come!"* Everyone who both hears the call from the Spirit through the church and responds will begin to call others to come to Christ and receive salvation. The conclusion of the book is a strong appeal to God's people to take the book of Revelation seriously and come to Christ. *Let the one who thirsts come. Let the one who desires take the water of life freely.* This evokes Jesus' call at the Feast of Booths: "If any man is thirsty, let him come to Me and drink" (John 7:37). In Revelation 21:6 Christ promised: "I will give freely to the thirsty from the fountain of the water of life." The gospel message is about salvation as a free gift. It is in God that all human spiritual thirst will be ultimately quenched.

22:18–19 At this point, John adds a postscript containing Christ's solemn warning to readers. Revelation is the word of God carefully designed to meet the needs of the "thirsty." Therefore, it is dangerous to tamper with the contents and distort and misinterpret the teachings of the book. Everyone confronted with Revelation in some way is warned that if he *adds to them, God will add to him the plagues written in this book.* If he *takes away from the words of the book of this prophecy,* however, he is just as guilty as the one who adds to the words: *God will take away his part from the tree of life and from the holy city, which are written in this book.* The punishment clearly fits the crime. This warning reflects Deuteronomy 4:2 where Moses admonishes Israel: "You shall not add to the word which I am commanding you, nor take away from it, that you may keep the commandments of the Lord your God which I command you." Christ's warning is not about tampering with the actual words of Revelation, as some concept of verbal inspiration is at stake; rather, it is about misinterpreting the teaching of the book by forcing personal ideas and views upon the text to suit one's own purposes.

22:20-21 For the last time, Christ reminds the readers of Revelation of his speedy coming: ***Yes, I am coming soon.*** All those who come to the realization of the importance of the central message of Revelation will respond with a longing sigh: ***Amen. Come, Lord Jesus.***

In his last statement to those waiting for his return, Christ offers his grace: ***The grace of the Lord Jesus be with all.*** John closes his book by reminding God's people that in the midst of all the confusion and fears regarding the things that are about to come upon the world, their only hope is in the grace of Christ. His grace is sufficient for them. The final events announced in the book may look frightful and the future gloomy, but God's people have the assurance of Christ's presence with them (Matt. 28:20). It is through Christ's grace that the messages of the book of Revelation have been given to the church. This grace is promised to all those who take the message of the book seriously. And it is through Christ's grace that the promises of the book will become reality when God's faithful people reach the heavenly city. There they will reign with Christ throughout eternity.

A RETROSPECT ON REVELATION 22:6–21

The book reaches its conclusion. The epilogue finishes with the same theme as began the book. Thus the prologue and epilogue "stand in close relationship to each other and provide the overall framework for the central section of Revelation."[5] The epilogue affirms what was made clear in the prologue that Revelation was not written for the purpose of informing the reader about the final events in order to satisfy one's curiosity about the future. The book begins and ends with the assurance of the presence of Jesus Christ with his people throughout the course of history until the very time of the end.

M. Eugene Boring remarks that Revelation, "from first word to last, is about the end, but not in a speculative sense. He [John] writes for the encouragement of his hearers/readers who find themselves in a desperate situation some without any awareness of the crucial time in which they live. John's revelation pictures the end of the story that began in Genesis 1 and continues through his Bible, but will not go on forever. It has already had its denouement, and will have its final chapter."[6] Yet, as David L. Barr points out, the ultimate end never seems to be reached in the book of Revelation.[7] This literary strategy can be traced throughout the book. The end has been repeatedly offered and anticipated in the conclusion of all major visions, only to be withdrawn and introduced again in a new vision (e.g., the opening of the seven seals [Rev. 6:17–8:1], the seven trumpets [11:15–18], or the vision of chapters 12–14 [14:14–20]). There is no closure. The ending always "takes us back to the beginning."[8]

The same is the case with regard to the "it is done" of the last vision (21:6). This vision portrays an end: the battle is over, the evil forces defeated, and sin exterminated. The letter is finished. However, John wants the reader to understand that the long-awaited end has not yet come. Jesus is still coming soon and there is still the real battle to be fought. Readers still have "the basic task to keep the words of the book" and to bear witness to the gospel of Christ.[9]

The book refuses to let readers rest. It does not want to put them in a state of some illusory vision or utopian dream. Jesus is coming soon. This is but a first reality. The second one is that we are still here. While waiting for the end to come, the reader must have a clear understanding of the message of the book by reading it again and again until the end of all things comes.

In conclusion, the purpose of Revelation is above all to constantly remind God's people as they face oppression and hardship not to look to the things of the world but to fix their eyes on him who is their only hope. The book is not just a revelation about the course of history or final events, but rather about the presence of Jesus Christ with his faithful people during the course of history and the final events. The Christ of the book of Revelation is the answer to all human hopes and longings amidst the enigmas and uncertainties of life. He is the One who holds the future. Rather, he is our future.

An old missionary couple had been working in Africa for many years and were returning to New York City to retire. They had no pension. Their health was broken. They were defeated, discouraged, and afraid. They discovered that they were booked on the same ship as President Teddy Roosevelt, who was returning from one of his big-game hunting expeditions. No one paid any attention to them. They watched the fanfare that accompanied the president's entourage, with passengers trying to catch a glimpse of the great man.

As the ship moved across the ocean, the old missionary said to his wife: "Something is wrong. Why should we have given our lives in faithful service to God in Africa all these many years and have no one care a thing about us? Here this man comes from a hunting trip and everybody makes much over him, but nobody gives two hoots about us."

"Dear, you shouldn't feel that way," his wife said.

"I can't help it; it does not seem right."

When the ship docked in New York, a band was waiting to greet the president. The mayor and other dignitaries were there. The papers were full of news about the president's arrival, but no one noticed this missionary couple. They slipped off the ship and found a cheap flat on the East Side, hoping the next day to see what they could do to make a living in the city.

That night the man's spirit broke. He said to his wife, "I can't take this. God is not treating us fairly."

His wife replied, "Why don't you go in the bedroom and tell that to the Lord?"

A short time later he came out from the bedroom, but now his face was completely different. His wife asked, "Dear, what happened?"

"The Lord settled it with me," he said. "I told him how bitter I was that the president should receive this tremendous homecoming, when no one met us as we returned home. And when I finished, it seemed as though the Lord put his hand on my shoulder and simply said, 'But, my son, you are not home yet!'"[10]

This is evidently what the book of Revelation is all about. It is intended to remind God's people throughout history that this world is not their home. As Christians go through the hardships of life, experiencing oppression and fierce opposition because of their loyalty to Christ and to the gospel, they must keep in mind that they are not home yet. The day is coming, however, when they will be welcomed home. The whole of heaven will be there to greet them.

Yes, indeed, come, Lord Jesus!

ENDNOTES

1. Barclay, *The Revelation of John*, 2:223–224.

2. Ibid., 224.

3. Marshall, 156.

4. White, *Testimonies for the Church*, 4:309.

5. Fiorenza, *Revelation*, 46.

6. Eugene M. Boring, "Revelation 19–21: End without Closure," *The Princeton Seminary Bulletin*, suppl. 3 (1994): 60.

7. See David L. Barr, "Waiting for the End that Never Comes: John's Apocalypse as Story," paper presented at the annual meeting of the Society of Biblical Literature, New Orleans, Louisiana, November, 1996; Boring has a slightly different view (see "Revelation 19–21: End without Closure," 65–66).

8. Barr, 14, 16–17.

9. Ibid., 13–14.

10. By an unknown author.

BIBLIOGRAPHY

Alford, Henry. *The Greek Testament*. 3d ed. Cambridge: Deighton, Bell, 1866. Reprint, Chicago: Moody Press, 1958.

The Ante-Nicene Fathers: Translations of the Writings of the Fathers Down to A.D. 325. 10 vols. Ed. Alexander Roberts and James Donaldson. Grand Rapids, MI: Eerdmans, 1989–1990.

The Apocrypha of the Old Testament: Revised Standard Version. Ed. Bruce M. Metzger. New York: Oxford University Press, 1965.

Aune, David E. "The Form and Function of the Proclamations to the Seven Churches (Revelation 2–3)." *New Testament Studies* 36 (1990): 182–204.

____. "The Influence of Roman Imperial Court Ceremonial on the Apocalypse of John." *Biblical Research* 28 (1983): 5–26.

____. *Revelation 1–5*. Word Biblical Commentary, vol. 52a. Waco, TX: Word Books, 1997.

____. *Revelation 6–16*. Word Biblical Commentary, vol. 52b. Waco, TX: Thomas Nelson, 1998.

____. *Revelation 17–22*. Word Biblical Commentary, vol. 52c. Waco, TX: Thomas Nelson, 1998.

The Babylonian Talmud. Trans. I. Epstein. London: Soncino Press, 1936.

Bacchiocchi, Samuele. *From Sabbath to Sunday*. Rome: The Pontifical Gregorian University Press, 1977.

Badenas, Roberto. "New Jerusalem—The Holy City." In *Symposium on Revelation—Book 2*, 243–271. Daniel and Revelation Committee Series 7. Silver Spring, MD: Biblical Research Institute, 1992.

Badina, Joel. "The Millennium." In *Symposium on Revelation—Book 2*, 225–242. Daniel and Revelation Committee Series 7. Silver Spring, MD: Biblical Research Institute, 1992.

Barclay, William. "Great Themes of the New Testament: V. Revelation xiii." *Expository Times* 70 (1958–1959): 260–264, 292–296.

____. *Letters to the Seven Churches*. New York: Abingdon Press, 1957.

____. *The Mind of Jesus*. New York: Harper & Row, 1961.

____. *The Revelation of John*. 2d ed. 2 vols. The Daily Study Bible Series. Philadelphia: Westminster Press, 1960.

Barr, David L. "Waiting for the End that Never Comes: John's Apocalypse as Story." Paper presented at the annual meeting of the Society of Biblical Literature, New Orleans, LA, November, 1996.

Battistone, Joseph J. *God's Church in a Hostile World.* Hagerstown, MD: Review and Herald, 1989.

Bauckham, Richard. *The Climax of Prophecy.* Edinburgh: T. & T. Clark, 1993.

____. "The List of the Tribes in Revelation 7 Again." *Journal for the Study of the New Testament* 42 (1991): 99–115.

____. "The Lord's Day." In *From Sabbath to Lord's Day,* edited by D. A. Carson, 221–250. Grand Rapids, MI: Zondervan, 1982.

Bauer, Walter. *A Greek-English Lexicon of the New Testament and Other Early Christian Literature.* 3d ed. Revised by Frederick W. Danker. Chicago: University of Chicago Press, 2000.

Beale, Gregory K. *The Book of Revelation.* The New International Greek Testament Commentary. Grand Rapids, MI: Eerdmans, 1999.

Beasley-Murray, George R. *The Book of Revelation.* 2d ed. New Century Bible Commentary. Grand Rapids, MI: Eerdmans, 1981.

Beckwith, Isbon T. *The Apocalypse of John.* 1919. Reprint, Grand Rapids, MI: Baker, 1967.

Bietenhard, H. "Name." In *The New International Dictionary of New Testament Theology,* 2:648–656. Ed. Colin Brown. Grand Rapids, MI: Zondervan, 1986.

Boring, M. Eugene. *Revelation.* Interpretation: A Bible Commentary for Teaching and Preaching. Louisville, KY: John Knox Press, 1989.

____. "Revelation 19–21: End without Closure." *The Princeton Seminary Bulletin.* Suppl. 3 (1994): 57–84.

Bornkamm, Günther. "*Musterion,* et al." In *Theological Dictionary of the New Testament,* 4:802–828. Ed. G. Kittel and G. Friedrich. Grand Rapids, MI: Eerdmans, 1964–1976.

____. "*Presbus,* et al." In *Theological Dictionary of the New Testament,* 6:651–683. Ed. G. Kittel and G. Friedrich. Grand Rapids, MI: Eerdmans, 1964–1976.

Bowman, J. W. "Revelation, Book of." In *The Interpreter's Dictionary of the Bible,* 4:58–71. Nashville, TN: Abingdon Press, 1962.

Brenton, Lancelot C. L. *The Septuagint with Apocrypha: Greek and English.* Peabody, MA: Hendrickson, 1986.

Bruce, Frederick F. "The Revelation to John." In *A New Testament Commentary,* 629–666. Ed. G. C. D. Howley. Grand Rapids, MI: Zondervan, 1969.

Büchsel, Herntrich. "*Krinō,* et al." In *Theological Dictionary of the New Testament,* 3:921–954. Ed. G. Kittel and G. Friedrich. Grand Rapids, MI: Eerdmans, 1964–1976.

Bullinger, E. W. *The Apocalypse: or, "The Day of the Lord."* 3d ed. London: Eyre and Spottiswoode, 1935.

Caird, George B. *The Revelation of St. John the Divine.* Harper's New Testament Commentaries. New York: Harper and Row, 1966.

Carrington, Phillip. *The Meaning of the Revelation.* London: Society for Promoting Christian Knowledge, 1931.

Cassius, Dio. *Dio's Roman History.* Trans. E. Cary. The Loeb Classical Library. 9 vols. New York: Macmillan, 1914–1927.

Charles, Robert H. *A Critical and Exegetical Commentary on the Revelation of St. John.* 2 vols. International Critical Commentary. Edinburgh: T. & T. Clark, 1956–1959.

Charlesworth, James H. *The Old Testament Pseudepigrapha.* 2 vols. Garden City, NY: Doubleday & Company, 1983.

Collins, A. Yarbro. *The Apocalypse.* New Testament Message, vol. 22. Wilmington, DE: Michael Glazier, 1979.

____. *The Combat Myth in the Book of Revelation.* Harvard Dissertations in Religion, no. 9. Missoula, MT: Scholars Press, 1976.

Committee on Problems in Bible Translation. *Problems in Bible Translation.* General Conference of Seventh-day Adventists. Washington, DC: Review and Herald, 1954.

Corsini, Eugenio. *The Apocalypse: The Perennial Revelation of Jesus Christ.* Good News Studies 5. Trans. and ed. Francis J. Moloney. Wilmington, DE: Michael Glazier, 1983.

Craddock, Fred B. "Preaching the Book of Revelation." *Interpretation* 40 (1986): 270–282.

Cullmann, Oscar. *Christ and Time.* Philadelphia: Westminster Press, 1964.

Davidson, Richard M. "Sanctuary Typology." In *Symposium on Revelation—Book 1*, 99–130. Daniel and Revelation Committee Series 6. Silver Spring, MD: Biblical Research Institute, 1992.

Davis, Dean. *The Heavenly Court Judgment of Revelation 4–5.* New York: University Press of America, 1992.

Davis, John J. *Biblical Numerology.* Grand Rapids, MI: Baker, 1968.

The Dead Sea Scrolls. Trans. Michael Wise, Martin Abegg, Jr., and Edward Cook. New York: HarperCollins, 1999.

Deissman, Adolf. *Light from the Ancient East.* 1927. Reprint, Peabody, MA: Hendricksen, 1995.

Deissner, Kurt. *"Metron."* In *Theological Dictionary of the New Testament*, 4:632–634. Ed. G. Kittel and G. Friedrich. Grand Rapids, MI: Eerdmans, 1964–1976.

Doukhan, Jacques B. *Secrets of Daniel: Wisdom and Dreams of a Jewish Prince in Exile.* Hagerstown, MD: Review and Herald, 2000.

Edersheim, Alfred. *The Temple: Its Ministry and Services.* Updated ed. Peabody, MA: Hendrickson, 1994.

Ellul, Jacques. *Apocalypse.* New York: Seabury Press, 1977.

Erdman, Charles R. *The Revelation of John.* Philadelphia: Westminster Press, 1936.

Ezell, Douglas. *Revelations on Revelation.* Waco, TX: Word Books, 1977.

Farrer, Austin M. *A Rebirth of Images.* Glasgow: University Press, 1949. Reprint, Albany, NY: State University of New York Press, 1986.

Feuillet, André. *Johannine Studies.* Staten Island, NY: Alba House, 1964.

Fiorenza, Elisabeth Schüssler. *The Apocalypse.* Chicago, IL: Franciscan Herald Press, 1976.

____. "Composition and Structure of the Apocalypse." *The Catholic Biblical Quarterly* 30 (1968): 344–356.

____. *Revelation: Vision of a Just World.* Proclamation Commentaries. Minneapolis, MN: Fortress

Press, 1991.

Foerster, Werner. "*Kurios,* et al." In *Theological Dictionary of the New Testament*, 4:1039–1098. Ed. G. Kittel and G. Friedrich. Grand Rapids, MI: Eerdmans, 1964–1976.

Ford, Desmond. *Crisis! A Commentary on the Book of Revelation.* 2 vols. Newcastle, CA: Desmond Ford Publications, 1982.

Ford, J. Massynberde. *Revelation.* Anchor Bible, vol. 38. New York: Doubleday, 1975.

Froom, LeRoy E. *The Prophetic Faith of Our Fathers.* 4 vols. Washington, DC: Review and Herald, 1948.

Giblin, Charles H. *The Book of Revelation: The Open Book of Prophecy.* Collegeville, MN: Liturgical Press, 1991.

Glasson, T. F. *The Revelation of John.* The Cambridge Bible Commentary. Cambridge: University Press, 1965.

Goulder, M. D. "The Apocalypse as an Annual Cycle of Prophecies." *New Testament Studies* 27 (1981): 342–367.

Gulley, Norman R. "Revelation 4 and 5: Judgment or Inauguration?" *Journal of the Adventist Theological Society* 8.1–2 (1997): 59–81.

Guthrie, Donald. *The Relevance of John's Apocalypse.* Grand Rapids, MI: Eerdmans, 1987.

Hagner, Donald A. *Matthew 1–13.* Word Biblical Commentary, vol. 33a. Dallas, TX: Word Books, 1993.

Halver, Rudolf. *Der Mythos im Letzten Buch der Bibel.* Theologische Forschung, no. 32. Hamburg–Bergstedt: Herbert Reich Evangelischer Verlag, 1964.

Harrington, Wilfrid J. *Understanding the Apocalypse.* Washington, DC: Corpus Books, 1969.

Hasel, Gerhard F. "Remnant." *The International Standard Bible Encyclopedia.* 2d ed. Grand Rapids, MI: Eerdmans, 1988, 4:130–134.

Heil, J. P. "The Fifth Seal (Rev 6:9–11) as a Key to the Book of Revelation." *Biblica* 74 (1993): 220–243.

Hendriksen, William. *More than Conquerors: An Interpretation of the Book of Revelation.* 1940. Reprint, Grand Rapids, MI: Baker, 1982.

Heppenstall, Edward. "Sin, Salvation, and the Sanctuary." *Ministry* (March 1977): 13–16.

Herodotus. *History.* Trans. George Rawlinson. Great Books of the Western World. Chicago: Encyclopaedia Britannica, 1952.

Hoekema, Anthony A. "Time, (Two) Times, and Half a Time." In *The International Standard Bible Encyclopedia*, 854–855. 2d ed. Grand Rapids, MI: Eerdmans, 1988.

Hoeksema, Herman. *Behold, He Cometh.* Grand Rapids, MI: Reformed Free Publishing Association, 1969.

Holmes, Michael W., ed. *The Apostolic Fathers: Greek Text and English Translations of Their Writings.* Trans. J. B. Lightfoot and J. R. Harmer. 2d ed. Grand Rapids, MI: Baker, 1992.

Hort, F. J. A. *The Apocalypse of St. John.* London: Macmillan, 1908.

Hughes, Philip E. *The Book of Revelation.* Grand Rapids, MI: Eerdmans, 1990.

The Isaiah Targum. The Aramaic Bible: The Targums 11. Ed. Bruce D. Chilton. Wilmington, DE: Michael Glazier, 1987.

Jamieson, Robert, A. R Fausset, and David Brown. *A Commentary, Critical, Experimental, and Practical, on the Old and New Testaments.* Rev. ed. Grand Rapids, MI: Eerdmans, 1961.

Johnson, Alan."Revelation." In *The Expositor's Bible Commentary*, 12:397–603. Grand Rapids, MI: Zondervan, 1982.

Johnsson, William G. "The Saints' End-Time Victory over the Forces of Evil." In *Symposium on Revelation—Book 2*, 3–40. Daniel and Revelation Committee Series 7. Silver Spring, MD: Biblical Research Institute, 1992.

Kline, Meredith G. "Double Trouble." *Journal of the Evangelical Theological Society* 32 (1989): 171–179.

____. *The Structure of Biblical Authority.* 2d ed. Grand Rapids, MI: Eerdmans, 1975.

Krodel, Gerhard A. *Revelation.* Augsburg Commentary on the New Testament. Minneapolis, MN: Augsburg Fortress, 1989.

Ladd, George E. *A Commentary on the Revelation of John.* Grand Rapids, MI: Eerdmans, 1972.

LaRondelle, Hans K. "Armageddon: History of Adventist Interpretations." In *Symposium on Revelation—Book 2*, 435–449. Daniel and Revelation Committee Series 7. Silver Spring, MD: Biblical Research Institute, 1992.

____. "Armageddon: Sixth and Seventh Plagues." In *Symposium on Revelation—Book 2*, 373–390. Daniel and Revelation Committee Series 7. Silver Spring, MD: Biblical Research Institute, 1992.

____. "Babylon: Anti-Christian Empire." In *Symposium on Revelation—Book 2*, 151–176. Daniel and Revelation Committee Series 7. Silver Spring, MD: Biblical Research Institute, 1992.

____. *Chariots of Salvation: The Biblical Drama of Armageddon.* Washington, DC: Review and Herald, 1987.

____. "Contextual Approach to the Seven Last Plagues." In *Symposium on Revelation—Book 2*, 133–149. Daniel and Revelation Committee Series 7. Silver Spring, MD: Biblical Research Institute, 1992.

____. *Good News about Armageddon.* Hagerstown, MD: Review and Herald, 1990.

____. *How to Understand the End-Time Prophecies of the Bible.* Sarasota, FL: First Impressions, 1997.

LaSor, William S. *The Truth about Armageddon.* New York: Harper & Row, 1982.

Lehmann, Richard. "The Two Suppers." In *Symposium on Revelation—Book 2*, 207–223. Daniel and Revelation Committee Series 7. Silver Spring, MD: Biblical Research Institute, 1992.

Lilje, Hanns. *The Last Book of the Bible.* Philadelphia: Muhlenberg Press, 1957.

Lohmeyer, Ernst. *Die Offenbarung des Johannes.* Handbuch zum Neuen Testament, no. 16. Tübingen: J. C. B. Mohr, 1926.

Marshall, David. *Apocalypse! Has the Countdown Begun?* Lincolnshire, England: Autumn House, 2000.

Martínez, Florentino G. *Dead Sea Scrolls Translated: The Qumran Texts in English.* Trans. Wilfred G. E. Watson. Leiden, NY: E. J. Brill, 1994.

Mauro, Philip. *The Patmos Visions.* Boston, MA: Hamilton Brothers, 1925.

Maxwell, C. Mervyn. *The Message of Revelation.* God Cares 2. Boise, ID: Pacific Press, 1985.

____. "Roman Catholicism and the United States." *Symposium on Revelation—Book 2*, 67–121. Daniel and Revelation Committee Series 7. Silver Spring, MD: Biblical Research Institute, 1992.

____. "Some Questions Answered—Dates: Their Historical Setting." *Symposium on Revelation—Book 2*, 121–132. Daniel and Revelation Committee Series 7. Silver Spring, MD: Biblical Research Institute, 1992.

Mazzaferri, Frederick D. *The Genre of the Book of Revelation.* New York: Walter de Gruyter, 1989.

McNamara, Martin. *The New Testament and the Palestinian Targum to the Pentateuch.* Rome: Pontifical Biblical Institute, 1966.

Metzger, Bruce M. *Breaking the Code: Understanding the Book of Revelation.* Nashville, TN: Abingdon Press, 1993.

____. *The Text of the New Testament.* 2d ed. Oxford: Clarendon Press, 1964.

Midrash Rabbah. Trans. H. Freedman and Maurice Simon. 10 vols. London: Soncino Press, 1939.

Miller, Patrick D. *Deuteronomy.* Interpretation: A Bible Commentary for Teaching and Preaching. Louisville, KY: John Knox Press, 1990.

Milligan, William. *The Book of Revelation.* The Expositor's Bible. Cincinnati: Jennings & Graham, 1889.

____. *Lectures on the Apocalypse.* London: Macmillan, 1892.

Minear, Paul S. "The Wounded Beast." *Journal of Biblical Literature* 72 (1953): 93–101.

The Mishnah. Trans. Herbert Danby. London: Oxford University Press, 1933.

Moffatt, James. "The Revelation of St. John the Divine." In *The Expositor's Greek Testament*, 5:279–494. 1942. Reprint, Grand Rapids, MI: Eerdmans, 1961.

Mollat, Donatien. *Une Lecture pour aujourd'hui: L'Apocalypse.* 2d ed. Paris: Les Editions du Cerf, 1984.

Morris, Leon. *The Book of Revelation.* 2d ed. Tyndale New Testament Commentaries, vol. 20. Grand Rapids, MI: Eerdmans, 1987.

Mounce, Robert H. *The Book of Revelation.* New International Commentary on the New Testament, vol. 17. Grand Rapids, MI: Eerdmans, 1977.

Musvosvi, Joel N. *Vengeance in the Apocalypse.* Andrews University Seminary Doctoral Dissertation Series, vol. 17. Berrien Springs, MI: Andrews University Press, 1993.

Naden, Roy C. *The Lamb among the Beasts.* Hagerstown, MD: Review and Herald, 1966.

Nam, Daegeuk. "The 'Throne of God' Motif in the Hebrew Bible." ThD dissertation, Andrews University, 1989.

Neall, Beatrice S. *The Concept of Character in the Apocalypse with Implications for Character Education.* Washington, DC: University Press of America, 1983.

____. "Sealed Saints and the Tribulation." In *Symposium on Revelation—Book 1*, 245–278. Daniel and Revelation Committee Series 6. Silver Spring, MD: Biblical Research Institute, 1992.

The Nicene and Post-Nicene Fathers of the Christian Church. 2d series. 14 vols. Ed. Philip Schaff and Henry Wace. Grand Rapids, MI: Eerdmans: 1986–1988.

The Nicene and Post-Nicene Fathers of the Christian Church. 14 vols. Ed. Philip Schaff. Grand Rapids, MI: Eerdmans: 1988–1989.

Niles, Daniel T. *As Seeing the Invisible.* New York: Harper & Brothers, 1961.

Oates, Joan. *Babylon.* 2d ed. London: Thames and Hudson, 1986.

Origen. *Commentary on the Gospel According to John.* Fathers of the Church, vol. 80. Trans. Ronald E. Heine. Washington, DC: Catholic University of America Press, 1989.

The Oxford Annotated Apocrypha: Revised Standard Version. Ed. Bruce M. Metzger. New York: Oxford University Press, 1965.

Pala, Alfred. "The Council of Cosmic Rulers," *Perspective Digest* 3.2 (1998): 18–25.

Paulien, Jon. The Bible Explorer. Audiocassette Series. 5 vols. Harrisburg, PA: TAG, 1996.

____. *Decoding Revelation's Trumpets.* Andrews University Seminary Doctoral Dissertation Series 11. Berrien Springs, MI: Andrews University Press, 1987.

____. "Interpreting Revelation's Symbolism." In *Symposium on Revelation—Book 1,* 73–97. Daniel and Revelation Committee Series 6. Silver Spring, MD: Biblical Research Institute, 1992.

____. "The Role of the Hebrew Cultus, Sanctuary, and Temple in the Plot and Structure of the Book of Revelation." *Andrews University Seminary Studies* 33.2 (1995): 247–264.

____. "Seals and Trumpets: Some Current Discussions." In *Symposium on Revelation—Book 1,* 183–198. Daniel and Revelation Committee Series 6. Silver Spring, MD: Biblical Research Institute, 1992.

____. "The Seven Seals." In *Symposium on Revelation—Book 1,* 199–243. Daniel and Revelation Committee Series 6. Silver Spring, MD: Biblical Research Institute, 1992.

____. *What the Bible Says about the End-time.* Hagerstown, MD: Review and Herald, 1994.

Pfandl, Gerhard. "The Remnant Church and the Spirit of Prophecy." In *Symposium on Revelation—Book 2,* 295–333. Daniel and Revelation Committee Series 7. Silver Spring, MD: Biblical Research Institute, 1992.

Pinnock, C. H. "Time." In *The International Standard Bible Encyclopedia,* 4:852–853. 2d ed. Grand Rapids, MI: Eerdmans, 1988.

Plummer, Alfred. "Revelation." In *The Pulpit Commentary,* 22:1–585. 2d ed. London: Funk & Wagnalls, 1913.

Porter, Stanley E. "Why the Laodiceans Received Lukewarm Water (Revelation 3:15–18)." *Tyndale Bulletin* 38 (1987): 143–149.

Pritchard, J. B., ed. *Ancient Near Eastern Texts Relating to the Old Testament.* 3d ed. Princeton, NJ: Princeton University Press, 1969.

Ramsay, W. M. *The Letters to the Seven Churches.* 2d ed. Ed. Mark W. Wilson. Peabody, MA: Hendricksen, 1994.

Rengstorf, Karl H. "*Apostellō,* et al." In *Theological Dictionary of the New Testament,* 1:398–447. Ed. G. Kittel and G. Friedrich. Grand Rapids, MI: Eerdmans, 1964–1976.

____. "*Epta* et al." In *Theological Dictionary of the New Testament,* 2:627–635. Ed. G. Kittel and G. Friedrich. Grand Rapids, MI: Eerdmans, 1964–1976.

Rice, Richard. *Reign of God: An Introduction to Christian Theology from a Seventh-day Adventist Perspective.* 2d ed. Berrien Springs, MI: Andrews University Press, 1997.

Rienecker, Fritz. *A Linguistic Key to the Greek New Testament.* Grand Rapids, MI: Zondervan, 1976.

Rissi, Mathias. "*Krima.*" In *Exegetical Dictionary of the New Testament*, 2:317–318. Ed. Horst Balz and Gerhard Schneider. Grand Rapids, MI: Eerdmans, 1990–1993.

____. "*Krinō, krisis.*" In *Exegetical Dictionary of the New Testament*, 2:318–321. Ed. Horst Balz and Gerhard Schneider. Grand Rapids, MI: Eerdmans, 1990–1993.

Rist, Martin. "The Revelation of St. John the Divine." In *The Interpreter's Bible*, 12:345–613. Nashville, TN: Abingdon Press, 1957.

Robertson, Archibald T. *Word Pictures in the New Testament*. 6 vols. Grand Rapids, MI: Baker, 1960.

Rogers Jr., Cleon L., and Cleon L. Rogers III. *The New Linguistic and Exegetical Key to the Greek New Testament*. Grand Rapids, MI: Zondervan, 1998.

Roloff, Jürgen. *The Revelation of John*. The Continental Commentary. Minneapolis, MN: Fortress, 1993.

Schaff, Philip. *History of the Christian Church*. 8 vols. 3d ed. Grand Rapids, MI: Eerdmans, 1910.

Schaidinger, Heinz. "History Behind the Prophecy of the 1260 days: The Beginning of the Time Period in 538 AD." Unpublished paper, Bogenhofen Seminary, March 2008.

Schmitz, Ernst D. "*Dōdeka.*" In *The New International Dictionary of New Testament Theology*, 2:694–696. Ed. Colin Brown. Grand Rapids, MI: Zondervan, 1978.

Schneemelcher, Wilhelm, ed. *New Testament Apocrypha*. 2 vols. 2d ed. Louisville, KY: Westminster, 1991.

Schurer, Emil. *The History of the Jewish People in the Age of Jesus Christ*. Rev. ed. Edinburgh: T. & T. Clark, 1979.

Scott, Walter. *Exposition of the Revelation of Jesus Christ*. London: Pickering and Inglis, 1948.

Seiss, J. A. *The Apocalypse*. New York: Charles C. Cook, 1909.

Seneca, Lucius Annaeus. *Controversiae*. Trans. M. Winterbotton. The Loeb Classical Library. 2 vols. Cambridge, MA: Harvard University Press, 1950.

The Seventh-day Adventist Bible Commentary. Ed. F. D. Nichol. 2d ed. 7 vols. Washington, DC: Review and Herald, 1980.

Shea, William H. "The Covenantal Form of the Letters to the Seven Churches." *Andrews University Seminary Studies* 21.1 (1983): 71–84.

____. "The Identification of the Seven Heads of the Beast in Revelation 17." Unpublished paper, n.d.

____. "The Location and Significance of Armageddon in Rev 16:16." *Andrews University Seminary Studies* 18.2 (1980): 157–162.

____. "The Mighty Angel and His Message." In *Symposium on Revelation—Book 1*, 279–325. Daniel and Revelation Committee Series 6. Silver Spring, MD: Biblical Research Institute, 1992.

____. "Revelation 5 and 19 as Literary Reciprocals." *Andrews University Seminary Studies* 22.2 (1984): 249–257.

Smith, Uriah. *The Prophecies of Daniel and the Revelation*. Rev. ed. Nashville, TN: Southern Publishing Association, 1944.

Specht, Walter F. "Sunday in the New Testament." In *The Sabbath in Scripture and History*, 114–129. Washington, DC: Review and Herald, 1982.

Stefanovic, Ranko. "The Angel at the Altar (Revelation 8:3–5): A Case Study on Intercalations in Revelation." *Andrews University Seminary Studies* 44/1 (2006): 79–94.

____. *The Background and Meaning of the Sealed Book of Revelation 5*. Andrews University Seminary Doctoral Dissertation Series, vol. 22. Berrien Springs, MI: Andrews University Press, 1996.

____. "The Meaning and Significance of the *epi tēn dexian* for the Location of the Sealed Scroll (Revelation 5:1) and Understanding the Scene of Revelation 5. *Biblical Research* 46 (2001): 42–54.

Strand, Kenneth A. "Another Look at 'Lord's Day' in the Early Church and in Rev 1:10." *New Testament Studies* 13 (1966/1967): 174–181.

____. "The Eight Basic Visions in the Book of Revelation." *Andrews University Seminary Studies* 25.1 (1987): 107–121. Reprinted in *Symposium on Revelation—Book 1*, 35–49. Daniel and Revelation Committee Series 6. Silver Spring, MD: Biblical Research Institute, 1992.

____. "Foundational Principles of Interpretation." In *Symposium on Revelation—Book 1*, 3–34. Daniel and Revelation Committee Series 6. Silver Spring, MD: Biblical Research Institute, 1992.

____. *Interpreting the Book of Revelation*. Worthington, OH: Ann Arbor Publishers, 1976.

____. "The 'Lord's Day' in the Second Century." In *The Sabbath in Scripture and History*, 346–351. Washington, DC: Review and Herald, 1982.

____. "'Overcomer': A Study in the Macrodynamic of Theme Development in the Book of Revelation." *Andrews University Seminary Studies* 28.3 (1990): 237–254.

____. "An Overlooked Old Testament Background to Revelation 11:1." *Andrews University Seminary Studies* 22 (1984): 317–325.

____. "The Seven Heads: Do They Represent Roman Emperors?" In *Symposium on Revelation—Book 2*, 177–206. Daniel and Revelation Committee Series 7. Silver Spring, MD: Biblical Research Institute, 1992.

____. "The Two Witnesses of Rev 11:3–12." *Andrews University Seminary Studies* 19.2 (1981): 127–135.

____. "The 'Victorious–Introduction Scenes' in the Visions in the Book of Revelation." *Andrews University Seminary Studies* 25.3 (1987): 267–288. Reprinted in *Symposium on Revelation—Book 1*, 51–72. Daniel and Revelation Committee Series 6. Silver Spring, MD: Biblical Research Institute, 1992.

Strathmann, H. "*Martus*, et al." In *Theological Dictionary of the New Testament*, 4:474–514. Ed. G. Kittel and G. Friedrich. Grand Rapids, MI: Eerdmans, 1964–1976.

Summers, Ray. *Worthy Is the Lamb*. Nashville, TN: Broadman, 1951.

Sweet, John P. M. *Revelation*. TPI New Testament Commentaries. Philadelphia: Trinity Press International, 1990.

Swete, Henry B. *The Apocalypse of St. John*. New York: Macmillan Company, 1906. Reprint, Grand Rapids, MI: Eerdmans, 1951.

Tenney, Merrill C. *Interpreting Revelation*. Grand Rapids, MI: Eerdmans, 1957.

Terry, Milton S. *Biblical Hermeneutics*. Reprint, Grand Rapids, MI: Zondervan, 1978.

Thiele, Edwin R. *Outline Studies in Revelation*. Class Syllabus. Berrien Springs, MI: Emmanuel Missionary College, 1949.

Thomas, Robert L. *Revelation 1–7: An Exegetical Commentary*. Chicago: Moody Press, 1992.

____. *Revelation 8–22: An Exegetical Commentary*. Chicago: Moody Press, 1992.

Timm, Alberto. "A Short Historical Background to A.D. 508 and 538 as Related to the Establishment of Papal Supremacy." In *Prophetic Principles: Crucial Exegetical, Theological, Historical and Practical Insights,* Scripture Symposium 1, 207–231. Ed. Ron du Preez. Lansing, MI: Michigan Conference of Seventh-day Adventists, 2007.

____. "Miniature Symbolization and the Year-day Principle of Prophetic Interpretation." *Andrews University Seminary Studies* 42.1 (2004): 149–167.

____. *The Sanctuary and the Three Angels' Messages: Integrating Factors in the Development of Seventh-day Adventist Doctrines*. Adventist Theological Society Dissertation Series, vol. 5. Berrien Springs, MI: Adventist Theological Society Publications, 1995.

Treiyer, Alberto R. *The Day of Atonement and the Heavenly Judgment*. Siloam Springs, AR: Creation Enterprises International, 1992.

van Unnik, W. C. "'Worthy Is the Lamb': The Background of Apoc 5." In *Mélanges bibliques en hommage au R.P. Béda Rigaux*, 445–461. Ed. A. Descamps and A. Halleux. [Gembloux]: Duculot, 1970.

Vermes, Geza. *The Dead Sea Scrolls in English*. 3d ed. London: Penguin Books, 1987.

Wall, Robert W. *Revelation*. New International Biblical Commentary. Peabody, MA: Hendrickson, 1991.

Whiston, William, trans. *The Works of Josephus*. Peabody, MA: Hendrickson, 1987.

White, Ellen G. *The Acts of the Apostles*. Nampa, ID: Pacific Press, 1911.

____. *The Great Controversy*. Mountain View, CA: Pacific Press, 1950.

____. *Manuscript Releases* 9. Letter 65, 1898. Silver Spring, MD: Ellen White Estate, 1990.

____. *Selected Messages*. 3 vols. Washington, DC: Review and Herald, 1958.

____. *Testimonies for the Church*. 9 vols. Mountain View, CA: Pacific Press, 1948.

____. *Testimonies to Ministers and Gospel Workers*. Boise, ID: Pacific Press, 1962.

Wilckens, Ulrich. "Charagma." In *Theological Dictionary of the New Testament*, 9:416–417. Ed. G. Kittel and G. Friedrich. Grand Rapids, MI: Eerdmans, 1964–1976.

INDEX OF MODERN AUTHORS

INDEX OF SCRIPTURE REFERENCES

PROVERBS

ECCLESIASTES

SONG OF SOLOMON

ISAIAH

INDEX OF EXTRABIBLICAL REFERENCES